D0152557

LOLLARD
SERMONS

———————

EARLY ENGLISH TEXT SOCIETY

No. 294

1989

British Library MS Additional 41321, ff. 52ᵛ–53 (repro-

LOLLARD SERMONS

EDITED BY

GLORIA CIGMAN

British Library MS Additional 41321
Bodleian Library MS Rawlinson C 751
John Rylands Library MS Eng 412

Description of the Manuscripts
by JEREMY GRIFFITHS

Analysis of the Language
by JEREMY SMITH

THE EARLY ENGLISH TEXT SOCIETY
1989

Oxford University Press, Walton Street, Oxford OX2 6DP

Oxford New York Toronto
Delhi Bombay Calcutta Madras Karachi
Petaling Jaya Singapore Hong Kong Tokyo
Nairobi Dar es Salaam Cape Town
Melbourne Auckland

Associated companies in Beirut Berlin Ibadan Nicosia

Oxford is a trade mark of Oxford University Press

© Early English Text Society 1989

All rights reserved. No part of this publication may be reproduced,
stored in a retrieval system, or transmitted, in any form or by any means,
electronic, mechanical, photocopying, recording, or otherwise, without
the prior permission of Oxford University Press

British Library Cataloguing in Publication Data

Lollard sermons.—Early English Text Society; 294).
1. Lollards—Sermons
I. Cigman, Gloria   II. Series
252   BX4900
ISBN 0-19-722296-X

PR1119
A2
no. 294

Typeset at Oxford University Computing Service

Printed in Great Britain at the
University Printing House
by David Stanford
Printer to the University

for
Rachel and Simon

DE 20 '89

PREFACE

The introduction to this edition includes two sections not written by the editor: Section I, The Manuscripts, by Jeremy Griffiths, and Section II, The Language, by Jeremy Smith. I am grateful to them both for their willing collaboration in bringing to this edition the benefit of their respective skills.

I like to think that G.R. Owst would have welcomed the appearance of the texts edited here; it was his work and enthusiasm that led me to them in the first place. At various stages in the preparation of this edition I have sought and received guidance and advice from Norman Blake, Pamela Gradon, Anne Hudson and Nigel Palmer; and I have been patiently and unstintingly helped throughout by Father Osmund Lewry, O.P. I greatly appreciate the generosity of these colleagues. While discussion with others has always been a valuable way of clarifying my thinking, I have not accepted every suggestion offered. Features of this edition that may be regarded as defects must be attributed to my own somewhat idiosyncratic view of what we are trying to do when we set out to rescue medieval texts from obscurity. The preparation of a hitherto unedited text is a daunting task. Everything is yet to be said. Wherever one turns, there is an apparently endless trail of demands for attention, comment and exploration. Eventually, the publishing of the text must assume priority over enquiry which could, it seems, go on for ever and which will undoubtedly continue once the text becomes widely accessible common property. I offer this, and the relentless passage of time, as justification for ground not covered here.

No separate Bibliography has been included. Published work of immediate relevance has been cited in the Notes to Section III of the introduction. A full literary, historical and theological Bibliography would be very lengthy indeed; it would reduplicate information to be found elsewhere and, in the present welcome state of medieval sermon studies, it would be far from up to date by the time this edition is published.

The task of preparing the Glossary was immeasurably aided by the existence of a full Concordance to the text. I am indebted to the Oxford University Computing Service for

access to their facilities, and to the Data Preparation staff of the
University of Warwick Computing Centre.

Gloria Cigman
University of Warwick
1984

CONTENTS

PLATES

INTRODUCTION

THE MANUSCRIPTS

The texts edited here have been found to date in three manuscripts:

London, British Library, Additional MS 41321 (A)
Manchester, John Rylands Library, MS Eng 412 (M)
Oxford, Bodleian Library, MS Rawlinson C.751 (R)

None contains all eighteen texts: the Additional manuscript contains Sermons 1–12 (including the expansion to Sermon 11, numbered 11a in this edition, but ending imperfectly in Sermon 12); the Rawlinson manuscript contains Sermons 8–16 (including 11a) and the *Sermon of Dead Men* (DM), which is the only one of these texts contained in the Rylands manuscript. The Rawlinson and Rylands manuscripts also contain other material.

London, British Library, Additional MS 41321 (A)[1]

116 parchment leaves, approximately 155 × 115mm, written space approximately 115 × 80mm. Single column, varying between 26–31 lines; column ruling in lead (none evident from fol.53r, the start of the second stint of Hand 1), with corner pricking. Collation: iii paper flyleaves, 1^{12}, 2^{10} lacks 3 (after fol.14) and 6–10 (four guard stubs follow fol.16), $3–5^{12}$, 6^{12} lacks 9–12 (four guard stubs follow fol.56; sewn as two quires, following fols.56 and 58), $7–10^{12}$, 11^{10} lacks 9–10 (two stubs follow fol.110; sewn as two quires, following fols.110 and 113),

1. *British Museum Catalogue of Additions to the Manuscripts 1926–1930* (London, 1959), pp.8–9. See also the note by J.P.G[ilson] on the acquisition of the manuscript, *British Museum Quarterly*, 1 (1926), 49–51. The manuscript was described by Gloria Cigman in 'Four Middle English Sermons', Unpublished B. Litt. thesis (University of Oxford, 1968), pp.243–258 and is referred to repeatedly by G.R. Owst, *Literature and Pulpit in Medieval England* (Oxford, 1961), pp.36ff.

iv paper flyleaves. There are two distinct styles of surviving leaf signatures: in quire 2 there are three signatures ('b.1.' fol.13r, 'b.2.' fol.14r, 'b.4.' fol.15r); in contrast the leaf signatures in quires 3–5 and 8–11 consist of arabic numerals alone, numbering leaves to the centre of each gathering (there is also the trace of a signature, possibly a letter and numeral, on fol.53r, the first leaf of quire 6, but it is not clearly visible under ultra-violet light). Catchwords remain in quires 1, 3–4, 7–10. Foliated in pencil 1–116 (added in July 1926 by 'P.E.J.E.' when the manuscript reached the British Museum, where it was examined by 'E.J.D.', see note on flyleaf).

fols.1r–8v	Sermon 1	fols.61r–70v	Sermon 8
fols.8v–23v	Sermon 2	fols.70v–79r	Sermon 9
fols.23v–34r	Sermon 3	fols.79r–89v	Sermon 10
fols.34r–40v	Sermon 4	fols.89v–96r	Sermon 11
fols.40v–50v	Sermon 5	fols.96r–107r	Sermon 11a
fols.50v–56v	Sermon 6	fols.107r–116v	Sermon 12
fols.56v–60v	Sermon 7		

The manuscript was written by two scribes in closely related, informal, secretary-influenced hands, which appear to date from the middle of the first half of the fifteenth century.[1] In both hands there is marked use of abbreviations, not restricted to the copying of Latin. To the extent that either has a consistent system of punctuation, both use the *punctus elevatus* for a major and the *punctus* for a minor medial pause; the *punctus*, accompanied by an oblique stroke (which is occasionally found alone in the stint of the second hand), is used to indicate a final stop. Both hands use dark brown ink (generally lighter in the stint of the second hand), with some variation from page to page and at points within the text (for instance, on fol.68v in Sermon 8) with no apparent textual significance.

Hand 1 wrote quires 1–2 (fols.1r–16v) and 6–11 (fols.53r–116v). Hand 2 wrote quires 3–5 (fols.17r–52v) (referred to below in the textual apparatus as H1 and H2 respectively).

Despite provision for the inclusion of decorated initials in the stints of both hands, none was provided and the manuscript

---

1. I am most grateful to Dr. M.B. Parkes of Keble College, Oxford for his advice about the handwriting and punctuation of the Additional and Rawlinson manuscripts.

is unrubricated, giving the impression that the manuscript was left unfinished. There is only a limited amount of marginal apparatus (in contrast to the Rawlinson manuscript), no running-titles and little correction of the text by the original scribes. An untidy fifteenth-century hand (not apparently that of either of the original scribes and referred to below in the textual apparatus as H3) provided some corrections, numbering of structural divisions of the text, Latin headings and summaries of contents, and crude paraph marks in the margins. The survival of leaf signatures and pricking for ruling suggests that the manuscript has not been drastically cropped and its relatively small margins may indicate that extensive marginal apparatus was never envisaged. To facilitate access to the text all pages on which new sermons begin (apart from Sermon 1 on fol.1r and the expansion of Sermon 11, beginning on fol.96r) were at some stage provided with 'index' tags, consisting of a thin strip of parchment cut from the outer margin, tucked through a slit in the leaf and left to project from the fore-edge or bottom edge of the manuscript (some have been unfolded and pasted back into the original shape of the leaf).

The manuscript was rebound in 1927 (the date stamped on the lower board), after it reached the British Museum, in dark blue leather with gold- and blind-stamped fillets. There are two printed paper labels on the spine, '680' and 'A', which is gold-stamped in small capitals with a title and the shelfmark. A note on the first flyleaf, initialled J.P.G[ilson], dated 25 January 1927, states that the original parchment wrapper and fragments from the binding are now in Additional MS 41340 (item H, fols.97–103).[1] These items are: a) two parchment leaves from a thirteenth-century English breviary, containing parts of the offices for the 1st and 2nd Sundays in Advent (fols.97–98), the condition of fol.98v suggesting that this was the outer wrapper of Additional MS 41321; b) three strips of parchment with musical notation from a fourteenth-century French book of songs, now barely visible without ultra-violet light (fols.99–101); c) a contemporary draft on paper of the will of Jane Ankurs of Ightfield (Shropshire), dated 12 April 1538 (fol.102r); d) a sixteenth-century letter in Latin on paper, dated

1. The following description of items from the binding is based upon that in the *British Museum Catalogue of Additions... 1926–1930*, p.19.

27 January (no year), from John Tenche, curate of Wrenbury (Cheshire) to the curate of Ightfield, informing him that he has read the banns for the marriage of William Acson of Wrenbury and Elen Hayr of Ightfield.[1] Several names in the manuscript can also be associated with Ightfeld and neighbouring villages on the Shropshire/Cheshire border. The John Maynwaringe, whose name appears in a sixteenth-century hand on fol.116v (now barely visible without ultra-violet light), is identified by the British Museum catalogue with Sir John Mainwaring, knighted at Tournay in 1513, d. 1515, who is said to have been from Ightfield, though it seems certain that he, in fact, belonged to a branch of the family from Over Peover in Cheshire, which however also had an estate at Baddiley, a village in Shropshire, close to Ightfield and Wrenbury.[2] A different, though contemporaneous candidate, the son of Thomas Mainwaring of Ightfield, has also been put forward.[3] The British Museum catalogue suggests that the John Leche

1.   John Tenche is named as perpetual curate of Wrenbury in May 1563; a new name appears in 1593: see George Ormerod, *The History of the County Palatine and City of Chester*, edited by Thomas Helsby, 3 vols. (London, 1882), iii.396. The rector of Ightfield is not named in the letter, but see below and note 9. At the Dissolution, the property of the Cistercian abbey of Combermere included a chapel at Wrenbury and a pension from the church at Ightfield: see *A History of the County of Chester, VCH Cheshire: III*, edited by B.E. Harris (London, 1980), pp.151 and 155.
2.   *British Museum Catalogue of Additions... 1926–1930*, p.9, with reference to *Letters and Papers of Henry VIII*, i.2301, a list of those knighted at Tournay on 25 September 1513. Mainwaring is listed amongst those who crossed with the king of Calais in 1513, with a retinue of 100 men (i.2053) and his dismissal from the army at the end of the campaign is recorded in November of the same year (i.2480). However in a list of captains in the king's army in 1513 (i.2392), Mainwaring is said to have been knighted at Lille; here also he is said to be from 'Eghtfeld'. Sir John Mainwaring was from Over Peover (see Cigman, 'Four Middle English Sermons', pp.255–256), where there is a monument to him and his wife in the church (Ormerod, i.482 and iii.456–458 on Baddiley; see also R. Richards, *Old Cheshire Churches* (London, 1947), pp.269, who also mentions a portrait of Sir John Mainwaring in the stained glass).
3.   Cigman, 'Four Middle English Sermons', p.256. See also the simplified family tree of Mainwaring of Over Peover, Mainwaring of Ightfield and Leche of Carden below, compiled from: Ormerod, i.477–486, ii.702–704; *The Visitation of Cheshire in the Year 1580*, edited by J.P. Rylands, Harleian Society 18 (London, 1882), pp.136–137, 164–167; *Pedigrees Made at the Visitation of Cheshire 1613*, edited by G.J. Armytage and J.P. Rylands, Harleian Society 59 (London, 1909), p.139; *The Visitation of Shropshire 1623*, edited by G. Grazebrook and J.P. Rylands, part ii, Harleian Society 29 (London, 1889), pp.347–349; and from monumental inscriptions in the churches at Ightfield, Over Peover, and Wrenbury.

whose name appears on fols.33v, 72v and 116v was probably from the family of Carden, Cheshire and it has been suggested that he is to be identified with the John Leche who married Margaret Mainwaring in 1478; she was the niece of the Thomas Mainwaring mentioned above.[1] These names may indeed have been written in the manuscript early in the sixteenth century, though a slightly later date would be equally possible palaeographically. There was a John Leche in every generation of the descendants of John Leche and Margaret Mainwaring throughout the sixteenth century, and one source states that their great-grandson, John Leche, married back into the family of Mainwaring of Ightfield.[2] Another relative of Margaret Mainwaring, John Mainwaring, was rector of Ightfield in the second half of the sixteenth century and it may be

1. Cigman, 'Four Middle English Sermons', p.256; *British Museum Catalogue of Additions... 1926–1930*, p.9. The name in the Additional manuscript does not appear to be in the same hand as the ownership inscriptions of a John Leche, Fellow of Exeter College and All Souls (d. by 1521) in Oxford, Trinity College MSS D16a (*Prick of Conscience*), D49 (*Canterbury Tales*), E14 (Nicholas Munshull, *Nominale*) and F13 (prayers, Psalms etc. in Latin). I am indebted to Miss P.R. Robinson of Queen's University, Belfast for bringing these manuscripts (and San Marino, Huntington Library, MS HM 136, also owned by a John Leche) to my attention. Though this John Leche ended his life as vicar of Walden in Essex (Emden, *BRUO*, ii.1120), he appears to have been from the family of Leche of Nantwich, themselves related to Leche of Carden and, by marriage, to Mainwaring of Nantwich, a branch of the family of Over Peover (see *Visitation of Cheshire 1613*, pp.140, 159 and J.M. Manly and E. Rickert, *The Text of the Canterbury Tales*, vol.i (Chicago, 1940), pp.540–544). A number of the names written in Trinity College MS D49 appear to be connected with Nantwich families (Manly and Rickert, i.541–542). Nicholas Munshull, the author of the *Nominale* and *Verbale* in MS E14, is possibly also to be linked with the Nantwich family of Minshull (see *Visitation of Cheshire 1613*, pp.183–184), though his identity remains obscure (see Thomas Tanner, *Bibliotheca Britannico-Hibernica* (London, 1748), p.537). Manchester, John Rylands Library, MS Eng 202 (Robert Hassall, *Commonplace Book*) was owned by a John Leche and subsequently by J.H. Leche of Carden Park, Chester; it contains a pedigree of Leche of Carden 1584–1711.
2. The family tree of Leche of Cardin in the *Visitation of Cheshire 1613* (p.139) has John Leche 'now living 1596', the son of John Leche and Jane Fitton, married to Ursula, daughter of Sir Arthur Mainwaring of Ightfield (the 1580 Visitation, pp.136–137), also shows the marriage, but omits her father's christian name). However in John Burke, *A Genealogical and Heraldic History of the Commoners of Great Britain*, vol.ii (London, 1835), pp.365–368, John Leche (baptised 1558, will proved 1591) is said to have married the daughter of John Mainwaring of Drayton. Ursula does not appear amongst the children of Sir Arthur Mainwaring of Ightfield listed in the *Visitation of Cheshire* in 1580 or 1613.

SIMPLIFIED PEDIGREE OF THE FAMILIES OF MAINWARING OF OVER PEOVER, MAINWARING OF IGHTFIELD AND LECHE OF CARDEN

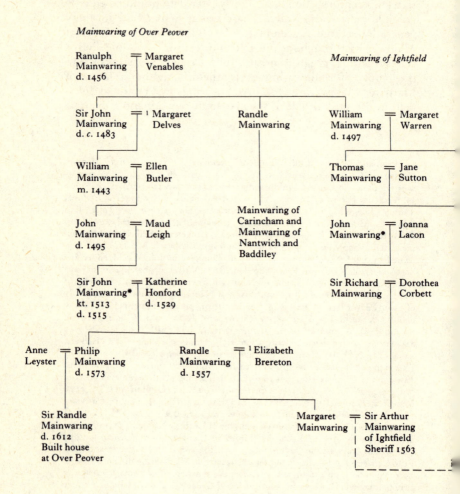

Mainwaring of Over Peover

Ranulph Mainwaring d. 1456 = Margaret Venables

Mainwaring of Ightfield

Sir John Mainwaring d. c. 1483 = ¹ Margaret Delves

Randle Mainwaring

William Mainwaring d. 1497 = Margaret Warren

William Mainwaring m. 1443 = Ellen Butler

Thomas Mainwaring = Jane Sutton

John Mainwaring d. 1495 = Maud Leigh

Mainwaring of Carincham and Mainwaring of Nantwich and Baddiley

John Mainwaring* = Joanna Lacon

Sir John Mainwaring* kt. 1513 d. 1515 = Katherine Honford d. 1529

Sir Richard Mainwaring = Dorothea Corbett

Anne Leyster = Philip Mainwaring d. 1573

Randle Mainwaring d. 1557 = ¹ Elizabeth Brereton

Sir Randle Mainwaring d. 1612 Built house at Over Peover

Margaret Mainwaring = Sir Arthur Mainwaring of Ightfield Sheriff 1563

* Denotes principal candidates
for the ownership of British
Library, Additional MS 41321

Leche of Carden

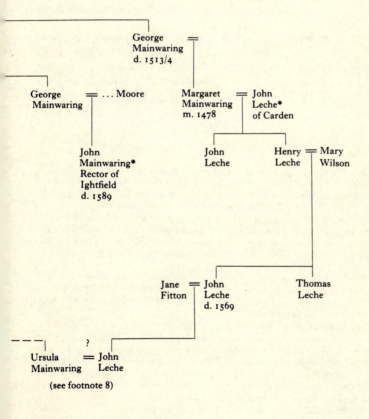

George
Mainwaring
d. 1513/4

George
Mainwaring = ... Moore

Margaret = John
Mainwaring   Leche*
m. 1478   of Carden

John
Mainwaring*
Rector of
Ightfield
d. 1589

John
Leche

Henry = Mary
Leche   Wilson

Jane = John
Fitton   Leche
         d. 1569

Thomas
Leche

Ursula = John
Mainwaring   Leche

(see footnote 8)

that he would have been in a position to have collected the material once contained in the binding of the manuscript and he may even have been the recipient of the letter from John Tenche, curate of Wrenbury; he might also be judged to have had the most obvious interest in the texts contained in the manuscript.[1] In any event it seems clear enough that the manuscript is to be connected with these families and with this part of the country, especially with a group of Shropshire villages around Ightfield. Other names in the manuscript, also apparently in sixteenth-century hands, are John Jackson (fols.16v and 60v), Parker (fol.71v) and Arthur Hussey (fols.60v and 116v). The latter is probably to be associated with the Shropshire family from Albright Hussey, about 15 miles from Ightfield.[2] It has been suggested that the manuscript remained in the possession of the Leche family until it was sold at Sotheby's 20 May 1926, lot 855, where it was bought for the British Museum.

The scribal stints in the Additional manuscript conform to divisions between quires; the second hand's stint begins on the first page of a new quire. The first stint of Hand 1 had ended on line 3 of fol.16v (the last remaining leaf of quire 2) with the words '...3he shullen multiplie'. The rest of the page is entirely blank; there is no catchword.[3] The stint of the second hand

---

1. John Mainwaring, rector of Ightfield, was buried on 2 February 1589 (Shropshire County Record Office, SRO 975/1/1: Ightfield Parish Register). I am grateful to Mrs. Janette Shepherd of the Shropshire Record Office for this information and for searching the Ightfield parish records in vain for any occurrence of the surnames Ankurs and Hayr. A Robert Mainwaring was rector in 1534/5: see R.W. Eyton, *Antiquities of Shropshire*, vol.ix (London, 1859), p.212. I am grateful to Miss Mary Ellison of Ightfield and to Miss Sheila Armstrong of Whitchurch for their help in connection with the history of the church at Ightfield.

2. See *A History of Shropshire, VCH Shropshire: III*, edited by A.T. Gaydon (London, 1973), pp.177–260 and Eyton, *Antiquities of Shropshire*, x London, 1860), pp.80–86, where it is pointed out that the family had much earlier rented land at Ightfield.

3. The pattern of the occurrence of catchwords may, itself, be significant (though, of course, some may have been lost). Only quires 2, 5 and 6 lack catchwords. At the end of quire 2 the catchword of the exemplar seems to have been included in the text copied, possibly in the expectation that the next quire of the exemplar would be copied onto the same page of the manuscript (as seems also to have been the expectation in the final quire). However the next portion of exemplar was in fact copied by another scribe, who also fails to provide a manuscript catchword at the end of his stint in quire 5. There may have been no need for a scribal catchword at the end of quire 6 if, as is

begins on fol.17r (the first leaf of a new quire) with the words 'multiplie your preieres...', continuing on in the middle of Sermon 2. In all probability the one word overlap between the two scribal stints at this point arose from the inclusion at the end of Hand 1's stint of a catchword that originally stood at the end of a quire in the exemplar. This can be seen to have happened also at the end of Hand 1's second stint, on fol.116v. This page is blank but for two words 'onelie for' at the top of the page and an erased catchword 'onelie for' at the foot of the page (visible under ultra-violet light).

It seems probable that the exemplar was divided by quires between the two scribes. However, for whatever reason, the first hand was unable in either of his two stints to copy the exemplar to fit exactly into complete quires of the manuscript; by contrast the second hand's stint fills exactly quires 3–5 of the manuscript. However, the situation here may be more complicated than it appears. Sermon 7 ends half-way down the last page of quire 6 (fol.6ov). Quire 6 has been bound as two separate quires: the first of 4 leaves (fol.53–56) followed by 4 guard stubs, the second also of 4 leaves (fols.57–60), sewn between the conjoint leaves fols.58 and 59. In effect, the second quire should be placed 'inside' the first. If fols.58 and 59 were originally the centre bifolium of a regular 12-leaf quire, 4 leaves would have been left blank following the end of Sermon 7 on fol.6ov. I suspect that the 4 guard stubs which now follow fol.56 represent these 4 cancelled leaves, originally from the end of the quire. Sermon 8 begins on the first page of the new quire 7 and though Hand 1 copied both quires, there is clearly a marked break between quires 6 and 7. Whilst there may have been any number of reasons for this pattern of scribal activity, one explanation in particular suggests itself. If the second hand was to have copied up to the end of Sermon 7, Hand 1 would have begun to copy his allocation of exemplar in a new quire, beginning as it does at the start of Sermon 8. If subsequently the second hand ended his stint with the material that had been copied to the end of quire 5, Hand 1 would have had to go back to copy that part of Hand 2's allocation of exemplar left uncopied at the end of his stint. This would serve to explain

suggested below, the scribe had already copied the material in quires 7 onwards. In these three cases the provision of catchwords by the scribes would appear to have as much to do with the organization of copying and the extent of scribal stints as with the ordering of quires in the manuscript as a whole.

the dislocation between quires 6 and 7, within the stint of Hand 1. It would also explain the apparent contrast between the ability of each hand to accommodate his allocation of exemplar exactly in complete quires of the manuscript, Hand 2's stint conforming, in effect, to the physical make-up of the copy and not to a portion of the examplar.

Whatever explanation is chosen for these features of the manuscript, it would appear that a distinct portion (and probably a new quire) of the exemplar began with Sermon 8; it is the only point within the Additional manuscript at which the beginning of a sermon coincides with a marked division of scribal activity. In the light of the fact that the Rawlinson manuscript's text begins with Sermon 8, it may be that both manuscripts attest to an exemplar tradition in which there was a distinct break between Sermons 7 and 8, though the manuscripts themselves offer no clues to the possible significance of such a division of contents.

Manchester, John Rylands Library, MS Eng 412 (M)

This manuscript has been described very recently in N.R. Ker's *Medieval Manuscripts in British Libraries III* (pp.425–6) and there seems little point in repeating a full description here.[1] The *Sermon of Dead Men*, also contained in the Rawlinson manuscript, appears on fols.50r–72r, with no apparent distinction from surrounding material or significant correlation between the contents and the physical make-up of the manuscript.

There are some signs that the manuscript was corrected by the original scribe, but there are other indications that the manuscript was not completed. There are no running-titles (though these may not, anyway, have been envisaged). Despite provision for decorative initials (as at the beginning of the *Sermon of Dead Men*), none was originally included (though some were added later). The pattern of inclusion of paraph marks and other rubrication (underlining of Latin quotations

---

1. *Medieval Manuscripts in British Libraries III: Lampeter-Oxford* (Oxford, 1983), pp.452–426; see also M. Tyson, *Handlist of the Collection of English Manuscripts in the John Rylands Library* (Manchester, 1929; reprinted from the *Bulletin of the John Rylands Library* 13), p.49; and G.A. Lester, *The Index of Middle English Prose: Handlist II: John Rylands University Library and Chetham's Library, Manchester* (Cambridge, 1985), pp.58–63.

and references in the text) follows the quiring of the manuscript and whilst there is no rubrication in the early part of the
Sermon of Dead Men, paraph marks and other rubrication
appear from fol.57 (the first leaf of quire 8). The *Sermon of
Dead Men* is provided with a marginal apparatus of biblical
references in the hand of the original scribe, though such
references also appear at times in the text. A different, though
probably contemporary, hand added further biblical references
in the margins (for instance on fols.56v–57r). The note 'of
prelates' in the margin on fol.59v is in the hand of the
Elizabethan antiquary John Stow, who also annotated other
works in the manuscript.[1] A later hand, possibly that of the
notes on fol.1r (said to be by Thomas Percy, Bishop of
Dromore, 1729–1811), added annotations in the margins
throughout the manuscript.[2] A pencil note in the margin on
fol.69r, glossing a word from the text, may be in the hand of
J.J. Green, who owned the manuscript in the nineteenth
century and collected the miscellaneous material now included
on the flyleaves.[3]

Oxford, Bodleian Library, MS Rawlinson C.751 (R)[4]

161 parchment leaves, approximately 150 × 100mm, written
space approximately 105 × 70mm. Single column of between
26 and 30 lines (generally 29); column ruling in brown crayon,
line ruling in quires 1–5 only, after which the pattern of
column ruling also changes slightly, with pricking for column
and line ruling throughout the manuscript. Collation:[5] ii
paper flyleaves, 1^8 lacks 1 (before fol.1; stub from fol.7 follows
fol.16), 2^{10} lacks 1; 10 (fol.16) is single (stub before fol.8),

1. The lost portions of the manuscript do not appear to be amongst the list
of books owned or annotated by Stow, given in *A Survey of London*, edited by
C.L. Kingsford, rev. edn., 2 vols. (Oxford, 1971), i.lxxxvi–xciii.
2. The manuscript is not recognizable amongst Bishop Percy's books
catalogued in Oxford, Bodleian Library, MS Percy c.9, but was sold with with
his collection at Sotheby, Wilkinson and Hodge 29 April 1884 lot 285.
3. Green also owned John Rylands Library, MS Eng 413, a copy of
Nicholas Love's *Myrrour of the Blessed Lyf* (Ker, *Medieval Manuscripts*,
p.426).
4. W.D. Macray, *Catalogi Codicum Manuscriptorum Bibliothecae Bodleianae
V, Fasciculus Secundus* (Oxford, 1878), col.388.
5. The collation of the manuscript is discussed below and see also the
diagram on pp.xxvi–xxvii.

3–6¹⁰, 7⁸, 8⁸ lacks 1; 8 (fol.71) is single (stub before fol.65),
9¹⁰, 10¹⁰ lacks 1 and 4; 7 (fol.86) and 10 (fol.89) are single
(stubs before fols.82 and 84), 11⁸, 12¹⁰ lacks 2; 9 (fol.105) is
single (stub before fol.99), 13⁸, 14¹⁰ lacks 4 and 10; 1 (fol.115)
and 7 (fol.120) are single (stubs before fol.118 and after
fol.122), 15⁸ lacks 4; 5 (fol.126) is single (stub before fol.126),
16–17⁸, 18¹⁰ lacks 4 and 10; 1 (fol.146) and 7 (fol.151) are
single (stubs before fol.149 and after fol.153), 19⁸, i paper
flyleaf. No signatures survive. Catchwords remain in quires
1–18 and indicate that quires 4 and 5 have been reversed in the
present binding. Foliated in pencil 1–161 (though not in series
due to misbinding; this foliation is followed here); deleted
pencil foliation and earlier ink foliation place the final quires in
the order 15, 18, 17, 16, 19, presumably reflecting an earlier
misbinding (see also notes at the end of quires 15–18); the ink
foliation jumps from '60' on fol.6or to '70' on fol.61r, the
centre bifolium of the present quire 7.

| fol.1r | begins imperfectly '…brymston and the spirit of tempest, that is the fende of helle, shullen be a party of her peyne, as it is writen in the sauter. When these dampnid wrecchis ben in this wo, thei shullen synge this ruful songe, that is writen in the boke of mournyng. The ioy of oure herte is ago…'¹ |
| | ends '…Ioy for thei ben ascapid the peyne of helle, and ioy for the endles blisse that thei han in the sight of god, to whom be worship and honoure, worlde withouten ende amen.' |

fols.1r–25v	*Sermon of Dead Men*	fols.6ov–71v	Sermon 11a
		fols.71v–8ov	Sermon 12
fols.26r–34v	Sermon 8	fols.81r–89r	Sermon 13
fols.34v–43r	Sermon 9	fols.89r–94v	Sermon 14
fols.43v–54r	Sermon 10	fols.94v–102v	Sermon 15
fols.54r–6ov	Sermon 11	fols.102v–11ov	Sermon 16
fols.111r–161v	Five tracts from *Pore Caitif*²		

1. In the transcriptions from the Rawlinson manuscript all abbreviations
have been silently expanded; 'thorn' is printed as 'th' and 'yogh' as 'gh'; the use
of u/v has been regularized and punctuation modernized.
2. See P.S. Jolliffe, *A Check-List of Middle English Prose Writings of
Spiritual Guidance* (Toronto, 1974), item 'B' (pp.65–66), which lists the
Rawlinson manuscript. I have checked the completeness of the Rawlinson text

fols.111r–119v The Creed
begins 'The grounde of al goodnes is stedfast
feith eyther byleue, for there thorow grace and
mercy is purchasid of god. Feithe wes the
principale grounde that made the womman of
chanane to purchase helthe of soule and of
body to hir doughter of crist that wes yuel
traveilid with a devel...'
ends '...In that everlasting liif of ioy and blisse
good men and wymmen that eendiden wel [s]
shullen dwelle in body and soule worlde with
outen eende. That liif he to us graunt that
bought us with his hert blode. Amen.'

fols.119v–143r The Ten Commandments
Prologue begins 'A man askid crist what he
shuld do for to have the liif that everlastith and
crist seide to hym ageyn, If thou wolt entre in
to everlasting liif, kepe thou the comaundementis. By this witty answere of crist iche man
may understond that there is none other wey to
heven with oute keping of these heestis...'
Prologue ends fol.120r '...for he that lovith not
his neighbore that he may se with his ighe, hou
may he love god whom he seith not as seint Ion
seithe. Primum mandatum.'
Text begins fol.120r 'The first comaundement
god hotith in these [w] wordis, seying him self.
I am thi lorde god that lad the oute of Egipt out
of the hous of thraldome. Thou shalt not have
bifore me straunge goddis. Thou shalt not
make to thee a graven ymage, neither ony
lickenes whiche is in heven above...'
ends '...the chast conversacion of women thus
sum tyme good wymmen and holy bileuing in
god ourneden hem as seint Peter seithe. Pe.3.'

fols.143r–147v The Charge of the Heestis
begins '⟨T⟩hese ten heestis of god after the
whiche it bihouith alle men and women to rule

against Oxford, Bodleian Library, MS Douce 288, which is cited as complete
by M.T. Brady, 'The *Pore Caitif*, Edited from MS Harley 2336', Unpublished
Ph.D thesis (Fordham University, 1954). I am most grateful to Dr. Anne
Hudson of Lady Margaret Hall for telling me of the Douce manuscript.

her liif if thei wolen be saved. And therfore crist seithe to iche man, that if he wole enter in to the liif that ever shal last kepe he these heestis...'

ends '...And that we moun lyve and eend in this love and to come to everlasting blisse graunte us Ihesu that lyueth and regnith with out eend merciful god amen amen.'

fols.147v–151v **The Charter of Heavenly Bliss**

begins '⟨E⟩very wyse man that cleymith his heritage either askith greet pardoun, kepith bisily and hathe oft mynde up on the chartre of his calenge. Therfore iche man lerne to lyue vertuously and kepe and have mynde up on the chartre of heuen blis and studie stedfastly ⌈in⌉ the witt of this bulle, for the pardoun therof shal dure with outen eend...'

ends '...gyve me grace to kepe the feithe un-wemmed with outen ony errour and my werkis to be worthi up feithe. Al this sentens seithe seint Austyn in his boke to the Erle.'

fols.151v–161v **Exposition of the Lord's Prayer**

Prologue begins '⟨C⟩rist seithe who that louith him shal kepe his comaundementis and thei that kepen hem ben his frendis as he here seithe in another place, and he wole heere his frendis and graunt hem al resonable thing that thei asken of him nedful to help of soule and body, and al thing nedful to man goostly either bodile is conteynid in the pater noster...'

Prologue ends fol.153r '...he that abidith knoc-king that is worching wel shal underfong, and seint Ion Crisostom seithe: If thou seching shalt continu thou shalt take.'

Text begins fol.153r '⟨T⟩he first asking of these seuen that answerith to the fader of heuen, thus seide in this maner: Oure fader that art in heuenis halowid be thi name. In that that thou clepist him fader, thou knoulechist that he is maker and lorde of heuen and erthe and helle, and gouernour of alle creaturis...'

ends '...And he shal be made worthi to be herde of god in his preyer and to be delyuered

> fro al yuel and to come to everlasting ioy and
> blis. Thider he us bring that bought man with
> his hert blode. Amen.'

The manuscript was written by one hand in an anglicana script
influenced by secretary forms, which appears to date from the
beginning of the fifteenth century.[1] The *punctus elevatus* is
used for a major and the *punctus* for a minor medial pause; the
punctus is also used for a final stop (at times with an oblique
stroke, also found alone). Marginal notes in red in a fifteenth-
century hand (on fols.6v, 9r and 152r) may be by a separate
rubricator or possibly in the scribe's informal hand. Another
fifteenth-century hand added corrections in the margin (on
fols.88v and 152v). The manuscript was heavily corrected in
certain places, with subpuncted or deleted material (for the
most part duplicated words and phrases) generally later
erased.[2]

Despite provision for the inclusion of decorated initials,
these were not always included (though a number were filled-in
later). Where initials were added originally they are in red,
unflourished. A new sentence is frequently marked by a red
highlight of the initial letter or an introductory red paraph
mark. Latin quotations in the text are generally underlined in
red. Marginal annotations in the original hand (generally
highlighted and underlined in red) include corrections, headings, biblical references and notes of other sources quoted or
referred to in the text and Latin quotations supporting references in the text. There are some running-titles. Though the
manuscript appears to be an informal production, the apparatus (in contrast to that of the Additional manuscript) is full and
detailed, which may suggest a particular interest in the texts
and their sources. The careful correction of the manuscript
indicates a corresponding concern for the accuracy of the copy.

The manuscript is in a binding of brown calf on strawboard,
possibly of the eighteenth century, with blind-stamped fillets

1. I am indebted to Professor Angus McIntosh of the Middle English
Dialect Survey, University of Edinburgh, for telling me that the scribe of
London, British Library, MS Cotton Titus D.XIX has a linguistic profile
strikingly similar to that of the scribe of the Rawlinson manuscript. However,
the two hands in the two manuscripts do not appear to be at all similar, though
this might be accounted for by differences between the script used in each case.
2. The corrections on fols. 89r and 95v are not simply corrections of scribal
dittography, but substantive corrections of the text; similarly the correction on
fol. 152v, though dittography is also corrected on this page. See Sermon 14/7
and 13 (marginal insertions), and Notes to the Text Sermon 15/61.

OXFORD, BODLEIAN LIBRARY, MS RAWLINSON C.751: COLLATION DIAGRAM

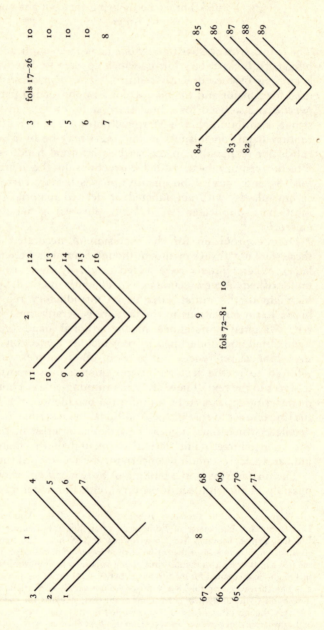

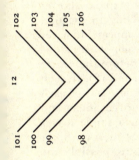

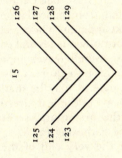

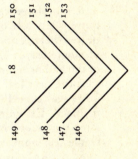

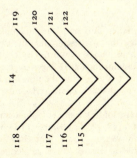

and on the spine, a title and the shelfmark, gold-stamped. A fragment of paper pasted to a flyleaf, possibly once a label on the spine, has the number '557'.

The name of Thomas Ailesbury 'cleric', with the date 1621, appears on fol.110v; the same hand may have been responsible for the running-titles added in quires 7 and 8, which contain Sermon 11 and the expansion 11a. Other names in the manuscript, also apparently of the seventeenth century, are John Donston (fol.2r), Jhon Cobb (fol.7r), Richard Jones (fols.17r and 64v; also 'Richard' fols.122v and 123r), and Francis Lucas of London (fol.22r with various other christian names, and fol.64v). On the flyleaf, facing fol.1r, is a list of contents and other notes by Edward Umfreville, made in the eighteenth century.[1]

The collation of the manuscript is complicated by the presence of a number of single leaves, as shown on the accompanying diagram. Eight of the nineteen quires contain single leaves, which may have been added to expand shorter quires or have resulted from cancellations. Only in the first quire is any loss of text apparent where a stub appears; in other quires there is no loss or obvious textual confusion where stubs or single leaves appear. Single leaves appear before the centre of the gathering in two of these quires only (14 and 18). In each case the first leaf is single; it may be that the last leaf of each quire was cancelled, leaving the leaf already written intact and in place. Excluding the first quire, seven have single leaves after the centre of the gathering (2, 8, 10, 12, 14, 15, 18). A single leaf appears at the very end of the quire, possibly the most natural position if a leaf were being added to accommodate a unit of text, in only three of these quires (2, 8, 10). There

---

1. These notes are initialled only and I am indebted to Dr. A.C. de la Mare of the Bodleian Library for suggesting the identification. I have found a number of items owned, annotated or written by Umfreville, including a series of letters to Richard Rawlinson, dated between 1744 and 1754. From comparison with these items it is clear that the notes in Rawlinson MS C.751 are by Umfreville, with his particularly characteristic use of double full stops after his initials.

Umfreville's books were sold by Samuel Paterson at the Feather's Tavern in the Strand 13 February 1758, by T. Osborne of Gray's Inn in 1764/5 and by Leigh and Sotheby 28 March 1792. The Rawlinson manuscript is not immediately recognizable in any of these catalogues. I intend to publish a complete account of books and manuscripts owned by Umfreville.

is no obvious division of contents at the end of quire 2; by
contrast the addition to Sermon 11 (numbered 11a in this
edition) ends on the last leaf of quire 8 and Sermon 13 on the
last leaf of quire 10. Other explanations than that the single
leaves were included at the ends of these quires to accommodate these sermons may be more attractive and these cases may
be less significant than they appear. In particular, since the
regular quires in the manuscript are all of 8 or 10 leaves, one
might be reluctant to assume that quire 8 was not also
originally an 8-leaf quire with one leaf cancelled, rather than an
irregular 6-leaf quire with one leaf added. Similarly, if all the
quires were originally of at least 8 leaves, some, if not all of the
single leaves in quires 10, 14, 15 and 18 must also have resulted
from cancellation. In the absence of other evidence it has
seemed simplest to assume for the collation given above that all
single leaves resulted from cancellation, though this should not
be taken to preclude other explanations. It is, of course,
possible that the scribe was constrained to use whatever
parchment was available and that this accounts for the inclusion of so many single leaves (and, indeed, on a few leaves, such
as fol.102, the text has been carefully written around major
defects in the parchment). However, the majority of quires in
the manuscript are regular and the occurrence of so many
single leaves may reflect some feature of the exemplar. The
cancellation of a number of leaves might have been occasioned
by serious and extensive scribal error, though once again the
concentration in a minority of quires might suggest some
confusion in the exemplar, rather than phases of scribal
incompetence. Confusion in the exemplar or in the supply of
the exemplar to the scribe might, equally, have had to be
accommodated by the addition of single leaves. In all probability the single leaves in the manuscript reflect both additions
and cancellations in the original quires (though it may be
impossible for us to distinguish which now), and should be
taken as an indication of confusion in the exemplar or in its
supply.

Jeremy Griffiths
Birkbeck College
University of London

THE LANGUAGE

Abbreviations used

CMS	Central Midlands Standard
EME	Early Middle English
ME	Middle English
MED	*Middle English Dictionary*
MS(S)	manuscript(s)
NE	New (i.e. Modern) English
OA	Old Anglian
OE	Old English
OED	*Oxford English Dictionary*
OF	Old French
OKt	Old Kentish
ON	Old Norse
WS	West Saxon
adj.	adjective
adv.	adverb
n.	noun
part.	participle
pl.	plural
pres.	present
pret.	preterite
sg.	singular
subj.	subjunctive
v.	verb

In the following description of the language of the manuscripts, the line-references are to the first occurrence of a given form within each scribe's stint. When a form occurs only rarely, more references may be given.

---

* I am indebted to Professors N. Davis and, especially, M.L. Samuels for helpful comments and criticism, and to Professors A. McIntosh and M. Benskin for discussion and information. The text of this discussion was completed in 1983, and I was therefore unable to make direct reference to *A Linguistic Atlas of Late Medieval English*, Aberdeen, 1987.

Additional MS, first hand (H1)

The principal points of interest in accidence and in the reflection of Old English sounds in spelling are as follows:

A.   In reflexes of OE stressed vowels:

(1)   OE ȳ̆ appears as *i, y* in *firste* 1/2, *hil* 1/121, *kynde* (n.) 1/15, *myri* 2/148 and 11/101 only, *synne* (n.) 1/98, *wirche* (inf.) 1/148; OE *y*, however, is reflected in *e* in *cherche* 1/2 beside, less commonly, *chirche* 1/145. A few forms in *u, uy* appear: *gulti* 9/316 and 10/92, *fuyre* (n.) 8/405 (once; cf. also *fire* 9/226, *fier* 9/231). *euele* 1/59 indicates the lowering associated with lengthening in open syllables in EME. (For NE 'much', OE *miċel*, *myċel*, see A(2) below. For NE 'stead', OE *stede*, *styde*, and NE 'yet', WS *ġīet*, late WS *ġȳt*, OA and OKt *ġēt*, see A(3) below.)

(2)   OE *i* appears commonly as *i, y* as in *bile* 11A/118, *þys* 1/2. NE 'if' appears as *if* 1/76 beside, less commonly, *ȝif* 1/97 and *ȝef* 1/84 (OE *ġif*, *ġef*). OE *miċel*, *myċel* appears commonly as *miche* 1/4, but more commonly as *myche* 1/3. OE *ī* is reflected generally as *i, y*, as in *ride* (3rd pres. subj. sg.) 1/28, *rydinge* (pres. part.) 1/32, but also as *yi* in *lyif* 1/137, *iȝ* in *liȝf* 7/7, *liȝfe* 8/219 and 9/174, and as *iy* in *liyf* 1/250 (beside *life* 1/196, 1/232 and 11A/157 only). Forms such as *spiriȝt* 9/151, beside *spirite* 11/12, suggest that these *iȝ-* forms have no significance other than as, perhaps, sporadic indicators of a long vowel. (See A(7) below for similar back spellings with OE *ū*, and B(3) below for a discussion as to the status of *ȝ, ȝt*.)

(3)   OE *e* generally appears as *e*, as in *lette* (inf.) 10/435. NE 'stead' (OE *stede*, *styde*) appears as *stede* once 8/334, beside the usual form for this item in this scribe's repertoire of spellings, *stide* 7/118. OE *ē* frequently appears as *ee*, as in *feet* 2/201, *heere* 1/8, beside *e*, as in *kepeþ* (3rd pres. sg.) 1/50. OA *ēġ* by smoothing appears as *iȝ* in *iȝen* 6/201. NE 'yet' appears as *ȝet* 1/211 beside, rarely, *ȝit* 11/183 and 11/272 only.

(4)   OE *æ* appears as *a* in *was* 1/10 and, as the first component of the digraph *ai* (OE *æġ*), in *dai* 1/40, *mai* (v.) 1/154. OE *ǣ* appears as *e* in *weren* 1/419, but as *a* when shortened in *lad* (past part.) 10/460, *rad* 1/7 and *yrad* 1/2 (both past part.), and in *any* 1/321, *ani* 1/97 (*eny* appears twice only, 7/200 and 8/341). For NE 'where' (WS *hwǣr*), *where* 1/23 is usual (once, however, *whar* appears 11/64).

(5)   OE *a* followed by a nasal appears as *a* in *mani* 8/189, *many* 1/212, but once as *o* in *mony* 8/138. *name* (n.) 1/37 has EME

lengthening. OE *ā* appears as *o, oo* in *holi* 1/2, *hooli* 1/4, *knowen* (pres. pl.) 1/180, *sore* (adv.) 1/27, *stonde* (with late OE *ā*) (1st pres. sg.) 1/52. Retracted OA *a* + lengthening group appears as *o* in *olde* 1/63.

(6) OE *o* appears as *o* in *bolle* (n.) 11A/123, and in *world* 1/26 (OE *woruld*, but cf. the OE by-form *weoruld*). OE *ō* appears as *o, oo* in *blod* 1/13, *blood* 8/117, *dom* 1/64, *doom* 1/63.

(7) OE *u* usually appears as *u*, *ful* 1/33. Forms in *o*, such as *dore* 1/52, *woke* (OE *wucu*) 1/402, *wokes* 1/14 display lowering associated with EME lengthening in open syllables. OE *ū* appears as *ow(ʒ), ou(ʒ)* in *now* 1/4 (beside, rarely, *nou* 1/448, *nouʒ* 10/213), *how* 1/387 (beside *houʒ* 8/146, *howʒ* 10/62, *hou* (rarely) 9/62), and *cowʒ* 11A/400.

(8) OE *eo* (OA *e* by smoothing) appears as *e* in *werk(e)* (n.) 1/255 etc. (cf. OE by-forms *worc, wurc*). OE *ēo* appears as *e, ee* in *erþe* 1/251, *been* 1/357, *beþ* 1/34, *freendes* 1/357; but as *eo* in *beo* (sg. subj.) 1/300.

B. In reflexes of certain OE consonants:

(1) OE *hw-* appears almost always as *wh-*, as in *whiche* 1/34; however, there is a single occurrence of *wiche* 1/201.

(2) OE initial *sc-* appears as *sch-*: *schal* (sg.) 1/49, *schullen* (pl.) 1/88.

(3) OE *ht*, both medially and finally, appears usually as *ʒt*: *miʒti* 1/200, *riʒt* 1/192, *riʒte* 8/318. But there are some forms, occurring only rarely, which suggest that the pronunciation of the spirant to be presumed in OE had been, or was in the process of being, lost: *almyti* 1/77, *rith* 1/154, *syth* 1/86. Back spellings such as *asauʒt* 11/332, *prouʒt* 9/18, *prouʒte* 8/369, *spiriʒt* 9/151 are further evidence of this loss.

(4) OE *āxian* appears as *axen* (pres. pl.) 1/99. NE 'burn', 'third' appear as *brenne* 8/405, *þridde* 1/47. Of interest is the form for NE 'worldly': *word(e)li* 1/151 beside *worldeli* 1/436.

(5) OE initial palatal *ġ* appears as *ʒ* in *ʒet* 1/211, *ʒouen* (past part.) 9/40; rarely, it appears as *ʒh*, as in *ʒhif* 9/61.

C. In unstressed vowels, final *-e* does not appear in the possessive *his* (pl.) 1/24, but it does appear in *þese* 1/136 (beside, rarely, *þes* 1/308—although this occurs here before a vowel, and might be considered to have been liable to elision). Final *-e* is extended to forms which would not historically have employed it: *life* 1/196, for instance. However, there are residual indications of a distinction between forms with and without -*e* in some adjectives. I note, for instance, *good* (strong sg.) 1/250, *gode* (pl.) 1/294, *firste* (weak sg.) 1/67. These appear, however, beside mistaken uses: *first* (weak sg.) 8/212, *first* (pl.) 2/209. For -*er* in NE 'after', -*er* appears: *after* 1/59 (there is one example of *aftir* 1/14. It should be noted,however, that the ending frequently appears in contracted form; see p.lxix, Editorial Procedures).

D.   Other points of accidence include:

(1)   In nouns, the plural endings vary between -*es* and -*is*, with fewer, but still fairly widespread, -*us* forms (if we interpret 9 as -*us* and   as -*is*): *maneres* 1/9, *placis* 1/9, *prelatus* 1/27, *sides* 1/14 etc. The same is the case with the possessive forms of the noun: *disciplis* 1/24, *mannes* 1/46, *mennus* 1/294. There are still a few plurals in -*en*: *breþeren* 1/94, *iȝen* 6/201.

(2)   The pronoun system is very regular. Of interest are *I* 1/17 (*y* in the first sermon only, 1/202), *his* (sg.) 1/21, *his* (pl.) 1/24, *sche* 7/154, *hit* 1/31 beside more common *it* 1/97 (the persistent, if unequal, variation between these two forms does not appear to be stress-conditioned), *þey* 1/28 beside rather more common *þei* 1/37, *her* 1/25 beside *here* 1/227, *hem* 1/85.

(3)   In verbs, 3rd pres. sg. endings are regularly in -*eþ*: *comeþ* 1/41, *makeþ* 1/5, *spekeþ* 1/6. Pres. pl. endings are most commonly in -*en*: *axen* 1/99, *knowen* 1/180, *maken* 1/93. However, there are endingless forms of the pres. pl., *repente* 1/98, and persistent -*eþ* forms, *biholdeþ* 1/89. In the verb 'to be', *is* is the 3rd pres. sg. form, as at 1/2, and *be(e)n* 1/157 is rather more common for the pres. pl. than *beþ* 1/34, although there are many examples of both; *arn* appears once in this scribe's stint, in his (unprinted) text of sermon 12. The present participle ending of the verbs is -*ynge*, less commonly -*inge*: *comynge* 1/21, *folewinge* 1/25, *goynge* 1/33, *ridynge* 1/23, *rydinge* 1/32. In weak past participles, the endings are generally -*id* or -*ed*: *clepid* 1/3, *lyued* 1/19; but occasional forms in -*ud*, -*ide* or -*it* occur: *arerud* 1/38, *groundit* 1/330, *passide* 1/68. In strong past participles, forms in -*(e)n* appear: *born* 1/14, *bonden* 1/71. Prefixed forms of the past participle, strong and weak, are common: *ibounde* 1/37, *yfalle* 1/37, *yrad* 1/2. We might note, too, that the strong forms in this case are lacking final -*n*.

Additional MS, second hand (H2)

The main points of interest in sounds and forms are as follows:

A. In reflexes of OE stressed vowels:

(1) OE ȳ appears as *i, y* in *first* 3/121, *firste* 2/540, *fyrste* 3/51, *hillis* 2/463, *kynde* (n.) 2/712, *synne* (n.) 2/414, *wirche* (inf.) 3/177 (beside *worche* (inf.) 4/268); as *e* in *cherche* 2/442 (beside, once, *chirche* 3/124). NE 'evil' appears as *euele* 2/521. (For NE 'yet', 'stead' see A(3) below.)

(2) OE *i* generally appears as *i, y* as in *riȝt* 2/514, *hym* 3/8. NE 'if' appears with *i* in *if* 3/299 (beside *ȝef* 2/518, *ȝif* 2/589, *ȝyf* 3/95). NE 'much' (OE *miċel, myċel*) appears as *miche* 2/412, *myche* 5/26. A lowered form of the short vowel is indicated by *cheldern* 2/574, *þredde* 2/444 (beside *þridde* 6/12), *wheche* 2/464 (beside *whiche* 2/430, *whyche* 3/88). OE ī appears generally as *i, y* as in *biden* (pres. pl.) 3/4, *lyf* 2/616, *lyfe* 4/330; but cf. *yi* in *lyif* 2/467, *wyif* 3/8.

(3) OE *e* appears as *e* in *selleris* (n.) 2/453 etc. NE 'stead' (OE *stede, styde*) usually appears as *stide* 5/261, beside single occurrences of *stede* 4/302 and *stude* 5/260. OE ē frequently appears as *ee*, as in *heere* 2/451 beside *e* in *here* 2/430. *ȝet* 3/78 appears for NE 'yet'; OA ēġ by smoothing appears as *iȝ* in *iȝen* 6/201.

(4) OE *æ* appears as *a* in *was* 2/574 and, as the first component of the digraph *ay* (OE *æġ*), in *day* 2/426. OE ǣ appears as *e* in *were* 2/430, but as *a* when shortened, as in *lad* (past part.) 3/507, *rad* (past part.) 6/2, and in *ani* 2/518, *any* 2/425 (beside, rarely, *eny* 3/209 only, and *eni* 3/220 and 4/23 only). For 'where', *where* 3/462 appears throughout.

(5) OE *a* followed by a nasal appears as *a* in *manye* 2/429, *manie* 2/495, *mani* 2/697, *many* 3/61, but once as *o* in *mony* 3/38. *name* 4/17 has had EME lengthening. Retracted OA *a* + lengthening group appears as *o* in *olde* 3/276. OE ā in general appears as *o, oo* in *holi* 3/11, *hooli* 2/605, *hooly* 4/55, *knowen* (pres. pl.) 2/684, *sore* (adv.) 3/44; with late OE lengthening, *hond* (n.) 3/368, *honde* 6/230.

(6) OE *o* appears as *o*, as in *cockel* (n.) 2/704; also in *world* 2/587 (OE *woruld*; cf. the OE by-form, *weoruld*). OE ō appears as *o, oo* in *blod* 2/413, *blood* 6/142.

(7)   OE *u* appears as *u*, as in *ful* 2/492. OE *ū* appears as *ou* in *hous* 2/454; as *ow* in *how* 2/436, *now* 2/567; as *ouȝ* in *houȝ* 3/297; and, once, as *owe* in *howe* 3/205.

(8)   OE *eo* (OA *e* by smoothing) appears as *e* in *werkes* 2/414 (cf. OE by-forms *worc*, *wurc*). OE *ēo* appears as *e* in *erþe* 2/627, *frendes* 2/625 but as *eo* in *seon* (pres. pl.) 2/674.

B.   In reflexes of certain OE consonants:

(1)   OE *hw-* appears as *wh-* in *whiche* 2/430, *whanne* 2/534, *who* 2/481, *whom* 3/52, *whoom* 3/38 (once only); but it also appears as *w-* in *wanne* 2/452, *woom* 2/475 and, once, *wo* 2/480. The back spelling *whise* 2/655 appears only once, but it suggests the disappearance of a distinction between forms with OE *hw-* and OE *w-*.

(2)   OE initial *sc-* appears as *sch-*: *schal* (sg.) 2/412, *schul* (pl.) 2/429.

(3)   OE *ht* appears regularly as *ȝt* in *liȝt* 2/490, but loss of the spirant is suggested by spellings such as *boute* (3rd pret. sg.) 2/677.

(4)   OE *āxian* is reflected in *axiden* (pret. pl.) 2/542. NE 'worldly' appears as *worldeli* 3/299, *worldely* 4/249, and *worldly* 3/322, but also as *worely* 3/503. NE 'third' appears as *þridde* 6/12, *þredde* 2/444.

(5)   OE initial palatal *ġ-* generally appears as *ȝ*: *ȝe* 2/454, *ȝet* 3/78, *ȝouen* (past part.) 3/467; but also as *ȝh-* in *ȝhe* 2/411.

C.   The status of final *-e* in this scribe's stint corresponds to that in the first hand of the MS. I note *his* (pl.) 2/624; unetymological *-e* in *where* 3/462 etc.; and correct use of weak and plural adjectival *-e* in *goode* (pl.) 3/28, *good* (strong sg.) 4/220, *firste* (weak sg.) 3/170 (but *good* (weak sg.) 2/705). The main form for NE 'after' is *aftur* 2/441 (with occasional *afftur* 2/650), but *after* 5/129 is also quite common.

D.   Other points of accidence include:

(1)   In nouns, the plural endings vary between *-es* and *-is*, with sporadic *-us* forms: *castellis* 2/419, *halles* 2/420, *hondes* 2/413, *miraculus* 3/101, *preieres* 2/411, *prelatis* 2/417, *synnes* 2/416, *þyngis* 2/418. There are forms in *-(e)n*: *cheldern* 2/574, *iȝen* 3/138. The possessives are also in *-is*, *-es*: *kyngis* 2/438, *lordes* 2/418; there are occasional *-us* forms: *mannus* 3/200.

(2) As in the main hand in this MS, the pronoun system is very regular. *I* 2/412 appears throughout. Other forms include: *sche* 5/60; *his* (sg.) 2/451, *his* (pl.) 2/624; *it* 2/440, beside a few examples of *hit* 2/453 (as in the main hand, these *h-* forms do not appear to be stress-conditioned); *þey* 2/428, but more commonly *þei* 2/489; for 'their', *here* 2/421, *her* 2/427, less commonly *hir* 2/417, *hire* 3/200, *hure* 3/174; for NE 'them', *hem* appears throughout 2/489.

(3) In verbs, the 3rd pres. sg. is regularly in *-(e)þ*: *seiþ* 2/412, *sueþ* 2/413. The pres. pl. is regularly in *-en*: *swymmen* 2/515, for example; but *-eþ* forms do appear: *bereþ* 2/523. In the verb 'to be', the 3rd pres. sg. is regularly *is* 2/414, while the pres. pl. is most commonly *ben* 2/413, although *beþ* forms are quite frequent, as at 2/414; there are two examples of *buþ* 5/283 and 5/472, and one of *arn* 3/409. The present participle is regularly in *-ynge*, as in *sittynge* 2/426, while the weak past participle usually appears in *-ed*, *-id*, as in *disgysid* 2/425, *turned* 2/415 (I do note, however, an example in *-it*: *aparaylit* 2/420). Strong past participles appear in *-n*: *forbodoun* 2/447, *geten* 2/557. I can find no prefixed past participles.

Rawlinson MS

The following are the main points of interest in sounds and forms:

A. In reflexes of OE stressed vowels:

(1) OE *ȳ* appears as *i*, *y* in *birþe* 12/252, *bisile* 12/4, *chirche* 12/51, *fire* (n.) 12/61, *first* 12/49, *gylty* 16/266, *hil* 13/20, *kynde* (n.) 12/12, *synne* (n.) 12/48. NE 'yet' appears as *ȝit* 12/162, *ȝitt* 14/149. An unlowered—and, therefore, presumably unlengthened—form for NE 'evil' occurs, *yuel* 12/175.

(2) OE *i* appears as *i* in *þis* 12/2, *wille* (n.) 12/5, and as *y* in *nyȝt* 12/42 etc. NE 'if' appears as *if* throughout, as at 12/56. OE *mycel*, *micel* appears as *myche* 12/17 (beside, rarely, *miche*, found only in this scribe's texts of sermons 9 and 10, not printed here). OE *lif* regularly appears as *lijf* 12/281, beside usual *i*, *y* for OE *ī*, as in *liking* 12/64 (although this form may be derived from ON *i*). Lowered forms of the short vowel appear in *wheche* 14/256, beside more frequent *whiche* 12/19.

(3) OE *e* appears as *e* in *sett* (inf.) 12/142 etc. OE *stede*, *styde* does not appear in the sermons printed here from Rawlinson, other than in the compound adjective *stedfast* 12/3; but it

appears as *stid* in sermons 10 (twice) and 8 (once), as *sted* in sermon 10 (once), and as *stude* in sermon 11 (once). OE *ē* appears as *e, ee*: *eend* (presumably with late OE *ē*, as yet unshortened) 12/18, *spedile* (adv.) 12/44 etc. OA *ēġ* by smoothing appears as *iʒ* in *iʒen* 12/94.

(4) OE *æ* appears as *a* in the first component of the digraph *ay* (OE *æġ*) in *day* 12/21, *may* (v.) 12/11 etc., but as *e* in *wes* 12/15. OE *ǣ²* + dental with shortening appears as *a* in *lad* (past part.) 13/155, but as *e* in *led* (past part.) 12/166. NE 'where' appears as *wher* 16/106, *where* 12/239. NE 'any' appears as *ony* 12/6.

(5) OE *a* followed by a nasal appears as *a* in *many* 12/75, but once as *mony* (in sermon 11, not printed from the Rawlinson text here). *name* (n.) 12/536 has EME lengthening. OE *ā* appears as *o, oo* in *holy* 12/50, *hooly* 12/37, *knowen* (pres. pl.) 12/302, *sore* (adj.) 12/92, *stonden* (pres. pl.) (with late OE *ā*) 13/257. Retracted OA *a* + lengthening group appears as *o* in *olde* 13/221.

(6) OE *o* appears as *o* in *folke* 12/95, *worlde* (OE *woruld*, but cf. OE *weoruld*) 12/12. OE *ō* appears as *o, oo* in *blode* 13/380 and 15/371 only, *blood* 13/275.

(7) OE *u* appears as *u* in *luste* (adj.) 12/86, but as *o* in *dore* 15/173 (with EME lengthening and lowering). OE *ū* appears as *ou(ʒ), ow* in *hou* 12/44, *houʒ* 13/8, *how* 13/6, *now* 12/39.

(8) NE 'work' (n.) appears with *e* in *werkis* 12/283. OE *ēo* appears as *e, ee* in *erþe* 12/158, *freendis* 15/40.

B. In reflexes of certain OE consonants:

(1) OE *hw-* appears as *wh-* throughout: *whiche* 12/19.

(2) OE *sc-* appears as *sh-*: *shal* (sg.) 12/27.

(3) OE *ht* appears as *ʒt*: *brouʒte* (3rd pret. sg.) 12/20, *myʒt* (3rd pret. sg.) 12/119.

(4) OE *āxian* is reflected in *aske* (inf.) 12/263, *asken* (pres. pl.) 12/8. The regular spelling for NE 'worldly' is *worldly* 12/468, while NE 'third' appears as *þrid* 12/68.

(5) OE initial palatal *ġ-* generally appears as *ʒ-*: *ʒit* 12/162, *ʒouen* (past part.) 12/333.

C. No attempt is made by the scribe to distinguish between *his* (sg.) 12/22 and *his* (pl.) 12/27. Unetymological -*e* appears in *seiþe* (3rd pres. sg.) 12/8, *haþe* (3rd pres. sg.) 12/40 etc. There seem to be few remnants of weak and plural adjectival *-e* in correct use: *good* (pl.) 13/216, *first* (weak sg.) 13/252, but *olde* (weak sg.) 13/221. NE 'after' generally appears as *after* 12/193, although there are a few examples of *aftur* 13/298.

D.   Other points of accidence include:

(1)   In nouns, the plural endings are usually in *-is*: *bowis* 12/45, *confessouris* 12/37, *cuntreis* 12/2, *houndis* 12/45, *soulis* 12/42, *þingis* 12/25; but there are also forms in *-s*, *-es* and *-ys*: *martirs* 12/37, *armes* 12/28, *synnys* 12/332. Possessives are either in *-is* or *-es*, but also sometimes in *-ys*: *douȝtris* 12/520, *mannys* 12/35, *neiȝboris* 12/331, *wormys* 12/171. There are a few examples of possessives in *-us*: *mannus* 12/360. There are a few forms of the plural in *-en*: *iȝen* 12/94.

(2)   In pronouns, as in the hands of the Additional MS, there is a great degree of regularity: *I* 12/79, *she* 12/4, almost always *it* 12/35 (*hit* occurs only once in the printed sermons, 13/8), *his* (sg.) 12/22, *his* (pl.) 12/27, *þei* 12/21, *her* for 'their' 12/83 (generally carefully distinguished from the form for NE 'her', *hir* 12/4), *hem* 12/61.

(3)   In verbs, 3rd pres. sg. endings are regularly in *-þ*: *kepiþ* 12/25, *spekiþ* 12/24, *weldiþ* 12/26. NE 'says' often appears as *seiþe* 12/8, NE 'has' as *haþe* 12/40. Pres. pl. endings in the sermons printed here from Rawlinson are regularly in *-en*: *ȝeelden* 12/115, *rennen* 12/132, *seruen* 12/112; but there are one or two forms in *-þ* in the unprinted sermons, e.g. *springiþ* (sermon 8). In the verb 'to be', the 3rd pres. sg. is regularly *is* 12/14, while the pres. pl. is almost invariably *ben* 12/84. However, *arne* appears once 12/87. The pres. part. is regularly in *-yng*: *rennyng* 12/45. Most weak past participles end in *-id*, as *huntid* 12/19, but there are a number in *-ed*: *conteyned* 12/277. Strong past participles appear with *-n*: *bounden* 12/33, *ouercomen* 12/32. There are no prefixed past participles.

Dialect and vocabulary

Traditional methods of dialect analysis[1] suggest that the three hands involved in the production of these two MSS are from the South Central Midlands with a South-West Midlands

---

1.   The traditional methods of dialect analysis most commonly employed for ME are conveniently outlined in H. Kurath, S.M. Kuhn *et al.*, *Middle English Dictionary: Plan and Bibliography*, Ann Arbor, 1954.

'colouring'. The Midlands is suggested by a combination of features, such as the reflection of OE *ā* in *o*, *oo* (ruling out the North), the regular endings of the 3rd pres. sg. in -*þ* and the pres. pl. in -*en* (ruling out the South), and by the particular combinations of *þ*- and *h*- forms in the 3rd plur. pronouns. The Southern part of the Midland area is suggested by, among other things, the shortening of OE *ǣ*² + dental in *a*, as in *lad* (past part.) 10/460, the occasional pres. pl. in -*eþ*, and the occasional prefixed forms of the past participle found in the main hand of the Additional MS. Sporadic forms, such as *beo* (sg. subj.) 1/300, *buþ* 5/283, *fuyre* 8/405, *mony* 3/38 (and in the Rawlinson text of sermon 11), and the plurals and possessives in -*us*, such as *mannus* 12/360, *mennus* 1/294, *miraculus* 3/101, *prelatus* 1/27 suggest an area bordering on the West.

The vocabulary of these sermons does not add anything to this localisation. As we might expect at this date, the influence of French has been considerable; for instance, no fewer than seven loans from French appear in the first ten lines of sermon 1: *special* 1/5, *pertynentli* 1/7, *diuerse* 1/9, *placis* 1/9, *maneres* 1/9, *seconde* 1/10 (although this is possibly from medieval Latin), *persone* 1/10 (again, possibly from medieval Latin). Most of the Scandinavian loan-words in the sermons are those adopted ultimately throughout the country, such as *toke* (3rd pret. sg.) 'took' 12/12. However, there are a few words, Scandinavian, French and native in origin, which may have had a restricted currency in the dialects of ME.

(1) *greiþe* (v.) 'prepare' 9/400. This is from ON *greiða*, and indicates an area subjected to influence from Norse. In modern dialects, it is restricted to Scotland, Ireland and the North of England. Kaiser[1] includes it in his list of ME Northern words. However, OED has quotations for this verb from Laȝamon's *Brut* (Caligula MS) and from 'Robert of Gloucester's' *Chronicle*, both of which are South-West Midland texts.

(2) *gresis* (n.) 'stairs', 'steps' 11/185. From OF *gré*, this word is now restricted to Northern dialects. However, references in the OED and MED show it to have had a wide currency in ME; see OED *Grece*.

---

1. R. Kaiser, *Zur Geographie des mittelenglischen Wortschatzes* (Palaestra 205), Leipzig, 1937. For information as to modern English dialect vocabulary, see J. Wright, *The English Dialect Dictionary*, London, 1898–1905.

(3) *ripe* (v.) 'dig' (OE *rypan* 'to spoil', 'plunder'; Kaiser notes a sense 'to search', 'examine strictly') 9/203. Kaiser includes this in his list of Northern words in ME. The OED (*Ripe*, v.[2]), says of this form: 'After OE, only in northern and Sc. use.'

These three words, therefore, have connections with the North, and thus could be separated from the set of South Midland/South-West Midland features which characterises the three hands in the MSS. They may be traces of some earlier stage in the copying of the text, and this stage might be supported by the presence of sporadic *arn(e)* 'are' in both MSS and in all three hands and, possibly, by *whar* 'where' 11/64 (?ON *hvar*). However, without further evidence, this suggestion must remain speculation.

A closer dialect localisation than that obtained by traditional criteria, however, can now be made by applying the techniques of linguistic analysis evolved by Professors McIntosh and Samuels for the *Survey of Middle English Dialects*.[1] According to the evidence of the *Survey*, the combination of, among other features, *chirche* 12/51, *wes* 12/15 with OE *æ* in *e* (the marked persistence of this form suggests something more regular in influence than stress-conditioning, the usual explanation for occurrence of this form when beside other words with OE *æ* in *a*), *ony* 12/6, *led* (past part.) 12/16 beside *lad* 13/155, *-en* in pres. pl. endings beside very sporadic *-eþ*, *þorow* 12/58 and *eche* 15/179 beside equally common *yche* (the *y*-form is restricted to the unprinted sermons of this scribe) suggests a Warwickshire provenance for the Rawlinson scribe. The main hand of the Additional MS seems rather more Southerly, with *cherche* 1/2 beside *chirche* 1/145, *euele* 1/59, *was* 1/10, *rad* (past part.) 1/7, *been* 1/357 beside *beþ* 1/34 and *beo* (subj. sg.) 1/300, *ani* 1/97 and *any* 1/321. This combination suggests a Worcestershire provenance for the hand. More certainly to be placed in Worcestershire is the second hand in the Additional MS, with *cherche* 2/442, the sporadic *stude* 5/260, the mixture of *whanne* 2/534 and *wanne* 2/452, the combination of *ben* 2/413 with *beþ* 2/414 and sporadic *buþ* 5/283. In both hands in the Additional MS, the mixture of forms for the neuter singular pronoun 'it',

---

1. The *Survey* is described in A. McIntosh, 'A new approach to Middle English dialectology', *English Studies* 44, 1963, 1–11, and in M. Benskin, 'Local archives and Middle English dialects', *Journal of the Society of Archivists* 5, 1977, 500–514.

hit and *it*, and the confusions over the spelling of 'worldly'
point to the Southern part of the West Midlands.[1]

All three hands show some of the features distinguished by
Professor Samuels as characteristic of so-called 'Central Midlands Standard' (CMS), a form of written English found in
many religious texts from the middle of the fourteenth century
to the middle of the fifteenth.[2] In Rawlinson, these features
include: *myche* 12/17, *ony* 12/6, *stid* (in the unprinted Rawlinson versions of sermons 8 and 10), possibly *ʒouen* 12/333 (CMS
ʒouun). In the Additional MS (main hand), we find: *myche* 1/4,
stide 7/118, *ʒouen* 9/40. In the second hand of the Additional
MS appear: *miche* 2/412 beside *myche* 5/26, *stide* 5/261, *ʒouen*
3/467.

If we conceive of CMS as a standard written language in the
modern sense—that is, as a fixed variety of the written medium
which all writers in the language, whatever their spoken
dialect, make a conscious attempt to achieve in every respect—
then it would appear that not one of these three scribes engaged
on these MSS is employing it correctly. However, it is now
known that CMS was not such a written standard, but rather a
lingua franca in the written medium, admitting of a fair degree
of variation but based on Central Midlands English, and
tending to exclude forms peripheral to that central region. By
definition, Central Midlands English could have been understood in surrounding districts, even though it may not have

---

1. For the method used in localisation, see the articles referred to in note 3
above. Full information must await the publication of the *Survey*, but localised
Worcestershire texts of approximately this date include: B.L. Additional 37787
(E. Worcs.), Bodl. Rawlinson C.81 (mixed in dialect, but includes a S. Worcs.
layer), and *olim* Phillipps MS 12056 (Heraldic MS including an *Art of
Hunting*; microfilm in Edinburgh University Library). Localised Warwickshire
texts include: PRO C1/9/189 (Coventry), PRO C1/17/45A (Coventry), PRO
C1/26/109 (Knoll), Göttingen U.L. MS jurid. 822 I. I am grateful to Professor
Samuels for this information and for his help with localisation. It may be of
interest to record here, for future study, the close similarity between the
spelling system of the Rawlinson MS and that of B.L. Cotton Titus D.xix
(with the important exception of the form for the item 'any'; Titus has *any* as
opposed to Rawlinson's *ony*). I am indebted to Professor McIntosh for this
reference.

2. See M.L. Samuels, 'Some applications of Middle English dialectology',
English Studies 44, 1963, 81–94. See further A.O. Sandved, 'Prolegomena to a
renewed study of the rise of Standard English', in M. Benskin and M.L.
Samuels eds., *So meny people longages and tonges: philological essays in Scots
and medieval English presented to Angus McIntosh*, Edinburgh, 1981, 31–42.

shared the distinctive dialect features of those districts. The Rawlinson and Additional MSS, although not providing us with especially good examples of CMS (given their use of forms which might be regarded as peripheral), can nevertheless be seen as part of the linguistic complex within which CMS was situated. Further study of these and of similar texts will doubtless provide us with more information as to the exact nature of CMS within the wider picture of the dialects of ME.

Jeremy J. Smith
University of Glasgow
1983

THE TEXTS: NATURE AND CONTENT

The texts in this edition are in the three manuscripts described and discussed above, pp.xi–xxix: BL Additional 41321 (A), Bodleian Rawlinson C. 751 (R), and John Rylands English 412 (M). There are eighteen texts in all: Sermons 1 to 16, an optional expansion to Sermon 11, called 11A, and the Sermon of Dead Men (called DM). With the exception of Sermon 12 and DM, each of the texts occurring in two of the manuscripts is of equal legibility; such differences as there are between these substantially similar texts are discussed below, pp.lii–lxi.

Summary:

Sermons 1, 2, 3, 4, 5, 6, and 7 are in A only.

Sermons 8, 9, 10, 11, and expansion 11A are in A and R; in the absence of any reliable criteria to distinguish one of these as a 'better' text, A has been selected as the base text, giving the advantage of consistency throughout some two-thirds of the sermons in the group 1–16.

Sermon 12 is in A and R, but it is badly rubbed in A and the text stops abruptly in mid-sentence some twenty lines short of the R reading. R has therefore been selected as the base text.

Sermons 13, 14, 15, and 16 are in R only.

The Sermon of Dead Men (DM) is in R and M. R has been selected as the base text, despite the fact that several passages are missing where the manuscript is damaged, because so many of the other texts in this edition are in this manuscript. The missing material has been supplied from M, with the orthography emended to that of R. Folio numbers of both manuscripts are indicated in the margins accordingly. Because DM is unlike Sermons 1–16 in many important respects, it is discussed separately here.

(a) Sermons 1–16

These sermons are all on gospel lections corresponding to those in the Sarum Missal for fifteen days in the liturgical calendar. Details are listed on the Contents page above, from which it will be seen that Sermons 14 and 15 are alternatives for the same day.

The question arises of whether the sermons that we have here are part of a cycle, or of a collection: i.e. whether they were originally compiled as a unified whole or simply brought together later as a physical entity.

Both manuscripts contain sequences of consecutive sermons with portions of the liturgical calendar omitted between the groups thus formed. The period beyond Lent and before Advent is represented in neither. While A contains only sermon texts, R contains both sermons and devotional prose treatises. Nothing can be deduced from this, however, since A is incomplete, stopping suddenly near the top of the final page. (See above p.xix.)

Evidence of an overall design, or organisation, comprising a cycle is strongly suggested by cross-references within the texts. Sermon 2 (296–7) refers to a passage in Sermon 1 (280–2 and 283–5), and Sermon 3 (49–51) refers to a passage in Sermon 1 (134–7). All of these sermons are in A only. But Sermon 2 (663–4, and see Note), also refer to DM, which is in R and M but not in A. DM is also cited in Sermon 15 (416), which is in R only. And Sermon 15 (254–5, and see Note) directs the preacher to Sermon 7, which is in A only. There are internal references to some texts that are in neither manuscript. Sermon 12 (396–7), which is in both A and R, directs the preacher to a sermon for Easter Day. Sermon 15 (387–8), which is in R only, refers to a sermon for 'Corpus Þirsday' (i.e. Corpus Christi day). Sermon 3 (340–2), which is in A only, directs the preacher to a sermon for the twenty-third Sunday after Trinity and, later (477–9), to another for the first Sunday after Trinity:

i.e. two points in the liturgical calendar well beyond the time span of the sermons in R. Another suggestion of a missing text is in Sermon 6 (309–10), which is in A only, where the preacher is directed to the 'sermoun of Myd Lente Sundai', i.e. the fourth in Lent; but neither Sermon 14 nor any of the other Lenten sermons, which are in R only, contains the subject matter referred to. There may have been an alternative sermon for this day, as there is for the fifth Sunday in Lent (Sermons 14 and 15).

In contrast with the clear directive cross-references mentioned here are two asides in Sermon 1 (329–37) and (377–9) indicating to the preacher that he might expand on the subjects of begging and obedience, but with no reference to Sermon 10 (371–409) and Sermon 5 (72–120) where there is substantial material on each of these topics. It may be that Sermons 10 and 5 had not yet been composed, or added to the collection, when the passages in Sermon 1 were inserted.

All of this suggests a lost original collection of gospel sermons, which may or may not have fully covered the entire year, but which was certainly larger than the combined total in A and R and may well have been compiled over an extended period.

When we turn to the content of these sermons, certain features give them a consistent 'personality', despite many differences of style and method. Throughout, the voice of the preacher is evident as separate from the 'þou' or 'ȝou' who is being addressed.[1] From time to time, this presence makes explicit the nature of its relationship to the hearers: a two-fold relationship, sometimes sharing with them a common spiritual and moral identity ('we'), sometimes as an authority set apart from them ('I'):

> Lift we vp oure hertis þen togedir, and make we þankingis to oure Fader of heuen for alle þe grete goodnessis þat he haþe done to vs, his vnkynd children, fro þe bigynning of þe worlde into þis day! And prey we him herafter of his co[n]tynaunce, and specialy at þis tyme þat he wole vouchesafe of his grace þat he wole multiplie so þat litel

---

1. N.B. The singular form of the pronoun occurs six times as often as the plural.

goostly mete þat I haue in þe scrip of my soule, whiche I
purpose wiþ his help to make ȝou a goostly feest, þat we
moun alle, þorow þe taking þerof, be fulfillid of grace...
Cristen freendis, now we han made þankingis to þe
Fader as I seide tofore, now it is tyme to me, þat shulde be
oon of Goddis panteris, to sett forþe a boord to his
peple...[1]

In every text except Sermons 9 and 14, the voice of the
preacher often interpolates phrases such as 'as I seide (bifore)'
or '(at þe bigynning'); or 'þat I spake of', or 'þat I shewid'; or 'I
purpose to speke' or 'make' or 'sett forþ'. By far the most
frequent of these is 'I seide' which seems to assert not only an
authorial identity but, by strong inference, the speaking presence of a preacher. This device is, however, open to somewhat
different interpretation in DM (see pp.xlix–l).

In eleven of the seventeen texts, complex moral and spiritual
argument and instruction culminate in a formal prayer, ending
in nine instances with 'Amen'. The rhetorical style and the
relationship of these prayers to the preceding text suggest that
each was intended as the dramatic crescendo of an oral
performance.

Evidence that these texts were not, in their entirety, intended
for oral delivery to a formal gathering of people can be adduced
from several passages in which the sermon-writer is addressing
the preacher only: talking about and not to the audience, giving
advice about possible expansions on specified topics, and
offering information as to where suitable additional matter can
be found (see pp.xliii–xliv above). Four such passages refer
explicitly to the 'auditorie', some emphasise the need to gauge
their mood before embarking on any extended demands on
their attention and concentration, and many defer to the
judgment and the inclinations of the preacher himself, by
means of the insertion of a 'whoso wol(e)' or a similar phrase.
Each of these features is exemplified in the following passage
from text 11A, the optional expansion of Sermon 11:

For as myche as þis gospel spekeþ principalli of þre
synnes (þat is: gloteyne, veynglorie, and couetise) þerfore,
whose wole, after þe tyme þat he seeþ þat he haþ
disposicion of his auditorie, he mai dilate his matere,

---

spekynge scharpeli bi þe ground of Scripture aȝens þese
þre synnes.[1]

A certain duality of intention is thus apparent in these
sermons, suggesting that they were conceived partly as preaching material suitable for oral delivery, and partly for the
guidance of the preacher himself. This latter 'reference-book'
element includes the cross-references to other sermons and
topics for expansion in the asides already discussed, as well as
amplifications in the form of exposition and interpretation for
the preacher's own edification, or for use in preaching, or both.

The interpolated asides can be lifted out of the text in every
instance without disrupting the continuity of the discourse.
This is also true of some of the amplifications which at times
have the completeness and internal structure of treatise prose:
e.g. Sermon 6/217–50 and Sermon 10/136–62. All of these
elements are held together by their relevance to the gospel
lection. It seems probable that the sermon as preached was the
outcome of the preacher's selection and adaptation from what
the sermon-writer had assembled for him. This is perhaps
particularly well illustrated in Sermon 8/131–51, where the
preacher is offered three different interpretations of a single
phrase in the vineyard parable (Matthew 20:1–16). That the
three are alternatives is made quite clear by the mode of
introducing each:

> Þat he bigynneþ at þe laste to rewarde first mai be
> vnderstonde... Or ellis hit mai be vnderstonde þus... Oþer
> þus it mai be vnderstonde...

It is possible that a preacher might want to offer a lay audience
the clarity of one interpretation, rather than the uncertainty
implicit in participation in a debate, and therefore that such
multiplicity of exegesis is intended for the theological educ-
ation of the preacher alone.

All of these features—asides, suggestions for expansions, and
passages which seem to be alternative components and not
essential to the sequential structuring of the material—are

---

1. Sermon 11A/1–5. Cf. also Sermon 1/377–9, Sermon 3/340–2, Sermon
6/309–10, Sermon 12/289–90, 512ff, 538–40; Sermon 14/275–8, Sermon
15/387–8, 415–6. See the discussion of cross-references above, pp.xliii–xliv.

consistent with what Lechler[1] observed as being characteristics of Wycliffite writings composed for itinerants 'in order that unlearned and simple preachers, who are burning with zeal for their souls, may have material for preaching.' Some of Lechler's notions about Wycliffite preachers may be in need of modification in the light of more recent research, but he does observe certain features of their preaching material that are consistent with what is now known. Of particular interest are some passages which closely resemble several found in these texts, and which he sees as evidence of composition by a writer producing 'sketches intended for the use of others rather than himself.'

One important source of insight into the uses of this material may well lie in the manuscript marginalia,[2] more copious in R than in A, but present in both and all of obvious practical value to someone wanting to know what is in the text and to locate specific passages with some ease.

It is evident that the mind behind these sermons is educated, with access to commentaries and compilations, skill in comprehending, selecting and assembling both primary (Scriptural) and secondary (exegetical) material, and the ability to grasp and transmit the relationship between the two. The method varies considerably from sermon to sermon, from simple exposition *secundum ordinem textus* (e.g. Sermon 7) to elaborate structuring and subdivision superimposed upon the gospel text (e.g. Sermon 15), corresponding to what is generally known as the homiletic or ancient tradition and the university or modern method of sermon construction. Whichever mode is used, each sermon incorporates a complex interweaving of relevant Scriptural cross-references and passages from commentaries by selected authorities, some named, others likely to be identified in future research.[3]

The most frequently used named authorities are Augustine, Gregory, and the *Opus Imperfectum* on Matthew, wrongly attributed to Chrysostom.[4] Quotations from the Scriptures and

---

1. G.V. Lecher, *John Wycliffe and his English Precursors* (London, 1904), p.220.
2. All recorded in the Apparatus, with the exception of various 'nota' markes that are neither verbal nor numerical.
3. E.g. Sermon 8/226ff.; cf. St Bernard (*P.L.* 184, col.490).
4. See Notes to the Text, Abbreviations: *Op. Imp.*, below p.242.

other sources are almost invariably given in Latin, then translated into English. The English passage is usually longer than the Latin that precedes it and, with only a few exceptions (see Sermon 15/237–8 and Note, and the discussion at pp.lv–lvi below), the English is of impeccable fluency and considerable stylistic merit.[1]

A glance at the Scriptural Index (I),[2] and the Notes to the Text[3] reveals the extent of the variation in the distribution of selected authorities from sermon to sermon. Sermon 7 is alone in including no Scriptural locations, although it does have Scriptural quotations. It is also much shorter than the other sermons. Sermon 13 is alone in giving no attribution to any secondary authorities. Sermon 2 is very much longer than any of the others. Sermon 6 opens with a distinction between 'þe comune peple' and 'lettrid men' which is reflected in the two levels of content throughout the sermon.

In addition to the dense and earnest use of authorities, and despite the total absence of the kind of narrative *exempla* found in Mirc's *Festial*, there are many lively passages of what might be called 'dramatic *exempla*': segments of realistic detail from everyday life, representing all ranks of society and depicting aspects of social and private behaviour that it is the preacher's business to admonish. In 11A/66–70, such exemplification is introduced to rebuke the sin of Gluttony (as in *Piers Plowman*, B, V, 345–65). The same sin is rebuked again at 11A/117–129, by means of a simile *exemplum*. The pride of the clergy is exposed in closely-observed detail in Sermon 1/26–33 and in Sermon 2/417–30. Further manifestations of pride, this time among the common people, are shown in 11A/286–300.

(b)   The Sermon of Dead Men (DM)
Although DM is not in A, which contains only gospel sermons, the references to it within that manuscript show that, like the missing texts mentioned there,[4] it was once part of a larger collection. It is linked to Sermons 1–16 less by resemblance than by its presence in R and by the cross-references to it in Sermon 2, which is in A only, and Sermon 15, which is in R

---

1.   E.g. Sermon 8/401–6.
2.   Below, pp.270–87.
3.   Below, pp.241–69.
4.   See Sermon 3/341–2, 478–9; Sermon 12/397.

only. There are some thematic correspondences between DM and the sermon texts,[1] but these may be no more than coincidence, reflecting preoccupations that were commonplace in the religious instruction of the time. One feature may be significant, however, in any consideration of the relationship and perhaps the authorship of these texts: it is that the gospel lections for Sermons 2 and 15 are single verses, as is the Old Testament lection for DM. In all three texts, this generates a far more concentrated and less diffuse theme than is the case where the lection comprises a sequence of verses.[2]

In form and content, DM is unlike Sermons 1–16 in most particulars. As has been pointed out, it is not based on a gospel lection, not is it a sermon for a specific day in the liturgical calendar. It is considerably longer than any of the other texts in this edition: some six times the length of the shortest of them (Sermon 7), and almost twice the length of the uniquely long Sermon 2. The contention that DM is to be regarded as a sermon-treatise is, however, based on more than mere quantifying of this sort; it is based on the method and structure of the text, on the seemingly hybrid nature of the material it contains, and on its presence in R and M which are unlike A, as we know it, in containing devotional treatises. In R, we see DM in company with both sermons and treatises; in M with treatises only.

The first part of DM is very clearly and explicitly a funeral sermon. It addresses an audience (lines 11, 79–80, and 134), and it establishes the separate identities and presence of the preacher and those gathered together to hear him (lines 104–9). Unlike Sermons 1–16, the second person singular pronoun is not used at all as a mode of address. The preaching voice does, however, use the plural form with this function until line 157, after which these pronouns are found only within Scriptural quotations.

The reminder devices (e.g. 'as I seide' etc.) which were discussed earlier as possible evidence that the presence of a preacher is to be assumed, are quite frequently used in the second part of DM (from line 162); but, with only three

---

1. E.g. DM/374–5, cf. Sermon 1/208–9; DM/987–94, cf. Sermon 8 *passim*, and Sermon 1/148 and 317–8; DM/1071–90, cf. Sermon 10/176–80.
2. The only other text based on a single Scriptural verse is Sermon 6, where a similar sharpness of thematic focus is evident.

exceptions (lines 484–5, 820 and 822), they refer to matter in the second and not the first part of the text. In the conspicuous absence of any other indications of intended oral delivery, we cannot be sure here whether these colloquial interpolations are anything more than reminders of what has gone before, inserted as much with a private reader in mind as for members of an audience.

Sermons 1, 3, 4, 5, 6, 7, 8, 9, 11, 13, and 15 culminate in a formal prayer which, each time, fulfils a marked crescendo function in the structure. The use of formal prayer in DM is somewhat different. The text opens with a prayer that is both longer and more formulaic than any in the sermon texts listed here.[1] An abbreviated version of this opening prayer is repeated at lines 131–3 as a culmination of this segment of the text. The matter at lines 134–61 serves as a link between what has gone before and the second part of the text: it sets out the theme, and introduces the discourse on the Four Last Things which is to constitute the rest of the text and which culminates in a crescendo prayer of the kind seen in the eleven sermons indicated.

Uncertainty about the status of this lengthy text as sermon, or treatise, or both, stems from the change of mode of address from line 162 onward, and from the patchwork nature of the material assembled within the many subdivisions of each of the four headings. Everything in this Four Last Things section of DM is entirely consistent with the introduction (to line 161). The four topics, Death, Judgment, the Pains of Hell, and the Joys of Heaven, are an appropriate expansion of the preaching theme of a funeral sermon. But some of the parts contributing to this whole have a completeness of form and interior structure that may be said to characterise treatise prose for private reading. As with some of the passages in Sermons 1–16, they could be removed without impairing the continuity of the section that contains them:

e.g. *exempla* 328–52, and 462–75;

allegory 353–90;

Seven Deadly Sins 704–53.

Particularly striking is the section on the Seven Unrequited Prayers of the Damned at 754–815, an extended cumulative

---

1. But cf. Sermon 15/1–2 and Note, also 15/38–9.

structure on the model of our more familiar House that Jack Built.

The observations here are more in the nature of clues than of conclusions. This is deliberate. Before the certainty implicit in Jolliffe's exclusion of DM from his *Checklist*[1] is allowed to ossify, more thought must be given to its curious duality of construction and style, and to its context. What was the intention behind the compilation of texts in R and M? Who was the user/reader of these manuscripts, which surely bring together the kind of instructive prose that Owst had in mind when he wrote that 'as lay reading increased, the simpler message declaimed in church passed eventually into the religious handbook of the home'?[2]

Any attempt to categorise DM firmly as 'sermon' *or* 'treatise' may well be misguided. Serious consideration should be given to the possibility that it evolved, via the pulpit, in response to the demands of 'independent domestic piety.'[3]

Analysis of some of the differences between A and R versions of Sermons 8–12 may eventually contribute to the evaluation of them, or serve to determine which is the earlier, two tasks which are quite distinct. Sermon texts such as these may have been written by one man, or by several. An original version of a text could have been revised (not merely corrected) by its author, or by someone who shared his convictions. It therefore becomes possible that a later text, whether or not it was the result of revisions by an original author, could be seen as a 'better' text. It is far from clear what 'better' means when used by textual critics. Authors of purely literary texts make mistakes, or change their minds later. This is even more likely to occur with material which has so pronounced a didactic and polemical purpose as these sermons, particularly if it can be shown that there was some organised collaboration and supervision in their composition and production.

---

1. P.S. Jolliffe, *A Checklist of Middle English Prose Writings of Spiritual Guidance* (P.I.M.S. Toronto, 1974).
2. G.R. Owst, *Preaching in Medieval England* (Cambridge, 1926: reissued New York, 1965), p.280.
3. *Ibid.*

THE RELATIONSHIP OF THE MANUSCRIPTS

Discussion of this question must, of course, be confined to material to be found in both R and A, or R and M, and must take into account the fact that, with no more than two manuscripts, there can be only a limited number of possible relationships. Given the nature of these texts, the likelihood of multiple authorship should be kept in mind. This means that the term 'scribe' may often be less useful and relevant than the terms 'corrector' and 'reviser', which carry an assumption of involvement in the text akin to that of an author or, at least, an editor. The hypotheses set out here cite many readings that reinforce the assumption of interventions in an 'original' text, and show that in texts of this kind, 'correct' and 'better' are by no means always the same as 'original'. In discussing these texts, the term 'error' is used throughout for inadvertent occurrences of defective sense; all other divergent readings, where no judgement of correctness can be made, are referred to as 'variants'.

(I) *Sermons 8–12: in both R and A*

Hypothesis 1: that R was the exemplar for A

The initial argument against this rests on errors in R that are not found in A:

e.g: (a) the omission of the object noun at 9/59 and 367, and a lengthy omission at 12/158–60, clearly attributable to 'eye-skip' between two occurrences of the same word;

(b) a curious clustering in Sermon 8 of errors perhaps attributable to the defective memory of a scribe with auditory rather than visual habits of working:
135 A good deedis R goodis; 314, 422 A god R good

(c) puzzling lexical aberrations:
10/148 A lyne R lijf; 11/96 A porere R wroþere
Sermon 9 contains a lexical divergence at 60 and 62 which could be an error in R arising from a misreading of the exemplar[1]
A deserue, deseruest R discerne, discernyst

---

1. See Notes to the Text, 9/60, 62.

There are, however, several instances in Sermon 10 and 12 of variant loan words that are similar in form but not in satisfactory sense, suggesting intervention in R on the part of a copyist or reviser who is not comfortable with such words:

10/137	A substaunce	R sustenaunce
10/514	A conuercion	R conuersacion
12/149	A coniectide	R coueitid
12/343	A contempte	R competent

Elsewhere, isolated variants in R at some points where A uses loan words reinforce the impression that the transmission of R has been coloured by an underlying unease in the presence of such words and a preference for avoiding them:

8/133	A enteerli	R hertily
9/9	A auditorie	R hearers
10/498	A perpetueli	R for euer
11A/16	A commaundement	R heest
12/52	A serpent	R addre

Hypothesis 2 : that A was the exemplar for R

The argument against this rests on errors in A that are not found in R:

e.g. the omission of single words at 10/32, 11/42, 11A/201 and 234, and lengthy omissions at 8/60–1, 10/36–7, and 11/189–90, clearly attributable to 'eye-skip' between two occurrences of the same word.

However, very few of the other divergencies between A and R are clearly erroneous. Of those that are, the lengthier omissions suggest the existence of an exemplar from which each was able to supply the passages missing from the other. More often by far, the divergent readings are valid variants where emendation is neither called for nor justifiable. Some reflect differences of style or idiom:

8/352	A	gret and horrible oþes
	R	his gret oþis and orrible[1]
12/188	A	as sone as he is turned þe bac[2]
	R	as sone as his backe is turned

---

1. Cf. *Piers Plowman*, Prologue B.55 **Grete lobyes and longe** (also A Text, 52, and C Text, 53).
2. Cf. OED 'Back' *sb.* VI.24.g.

Other lexical variants can be seen as reflecting a different understanding of the text, or different linguistic usage:

10/86	R	defouleþ his name (cf. lines 86, 92)
	A	defouliþ his face (cf. lines 83, 88, 95)
9/110	A	children
	R	sonys
9/400	A	greiþe
	R	diȝt

In the first of these, both readings are consistent with the context; in the second, each translation of *filios* conforms to medieval Latin usage; in the third, R echoes the collocation used at 9/201–2 so that, despite the weakening of the alliteration, this reading appears to be a deliberate lexical choice and not an error.

Overall, instances of 'fuller' readings in R may indicate that this text has more intervention and revision than the other. Some such readings are simply corrective:

9/118   A persecucyon   R persecucyon and
tribulacion[1].

Others offer more smoothly intelligible and explicit renderings of passages that are by no means unclear in A:

8/165–6	A	after hire loue was here
		more or less proportional þerafter
	R	as her loue is here
		so shal her blis þer
		be more or lasse proportional
9/79–80	A	þat is whan þei heren þe word of god
		comeþ þe fend and
	R	þese it ben seiþe crist
		þat when þei heren þe word of god
		comeþ þe fend and

There are, however, exceptions to this expansive tendency of R which, at some points in the text, lacks redundancies of phrasing that occur in A:

| 10/480 | A | also as wel |
| | R | also |

1. Mark 4:17.

11A/117–8 A   lickned to a foul þat is clepid a bitore
           R   likened to a bytore

A picture emerges of two texts equally concerned with accuracy of transmission and coinciding in substance far more than they diverge, but each with a number of errors not found in the other. A diligent scribe could well correct some mechanical defects that he finds in his exemplar, as well as inevitably introducing new ones in the course of copying. A copyist-reviser would be bound to introduce variant readings and might even be capable of rectifying long omissions, particularly if these involved quotation from well-known sources such as the Bible, as at 9/118 (cited above). Hypotheses 1 and 2 are therefore not impossible, but a more likely view of the transmission of A and R takes shape if we look beyond each for the source of the other.

Hypothesis 3: that O, the authorial original, was the exemplar for A and R

If we accept the belief in the notion of an idealised original text, representing the author's intentions and containing no errors, the argument against this hypothesis must rest on shared errors in A and R, discussed below in Hypothesis 4. However, since human beings are fallible and, for the most part, incapable of sustaining any piece of verbal composition without making mistakes, this traditional view is not altogether convincing, but it does lead on to the next stage of the argument without influencing its conclusions one way or another.

Hypothesis 4: that X was the exemplar for A and R

The argument for this rests on errors shared by A and R which X is assumed to have generated in the course of its descent from authorial original O. The number of such shared errors is very small. About half of them are incorrect scriptural locations, which could have generated from the defective memory of the author. These occur in Sermon 9/267, 10/27 and 12/104 (wrong chapter); also 11A/535 (wrong book).

     Of the five shared errors that remain, three render the syntax defective, but each is small enough to be missed even by a habitually diligent scribe:

10/328 þat ben *for* ben
10/406 we *for* ȝe
11A/561 bileueþ(-yþ) *for* bileue

Two other shared errors are, by contrast, significantly incompatible with the context and difficult to explain in texts of such a high level of clarity of argument. In the first instance, the error arises from omission.[1] There is one variation in each reading, and a further (different) flaw in the A and R renderings of the rest of the same sentence. The uncharacteristic degree of instability here may indicate confusion in the face of a corrupt reading transmitted by X, a reading which each version partly, but only partly, rectifies:

8/92–3 A Ȝef þou enuiest not þou art not idel
        R If þou enuyoust not þou art ydel

emended to Ȝef þou enuiest not,
           [and naþeles þou ioiest not, þan] þou art idel[2]

NB also

8/94–5 A þe vyne of goodwille or of charitee
        R þe vyne of goodwille of charitee

The second of the two major errors is like the preceding example in that it too contains no disruption of syntax and could similarly go undetected by a scribe who was an intelligent and impeccable copyist but who was not following the intricacies of the subject matter:

10/454–5 A þat clepen oonli wiþ mouþ and no þynge wiþ herte
         R þat clepen oonly wiþ mouþe and no þing wiþ hert

emended to þat clepen wiþ mouþ and no[t oonli] wiþ herte[3]

Although the manuscript readings are identical, emendation has been dictated by the exposition set out at 474ff. If the manuscript readings are left, *no þynge* contradicts *as wel as*, at 478; and *oonli* contradicts *also as wel*, at 480.

---

1. See Notes to the Text, 8/66–94.
2. Interlinear insertion of **þou**.
3. See Notes to the Text, 10/454–5.

Neither of the errors discussed here is easily accounted for. The first could be a mechanical slip, or an accurate copy of a faulty original translation from Chrysostom; the second remains baffling. Both of them do, of course, support the case for a shared exemplar at some stage of the transmission of the texts.

The argument against Hypothesis 4 rests on the number and nature of the variant readings in the two manuscripts, which seem too diverse to have arisen from a shared exemplar, unless we assume a degree of intervention great enough to revive Hypothesis 2: i.e. to make the possibility of A as an exemplar energetically revised by R as feasible as the possibility of A and R descending from X. Further readings from the texts, added to those already cited, lead to a hypothesis more convincing than any of these.

Hypothesis 5: that X was the exemplar for A and Y; and that Y was the exemplar for R

The argument for this rests on close correspondences between A and R which demonstrate that neither is very far from a shared source X, and on the nature of the many variant readings which, although they do not at any point introduce substantial modifications to the content of these texts, often suggest that R is further from that source than A. All the variants chosen to illustrate this contention seem to have arisen from deliberate intervention rather than miscopying.

In the following example, the punctuation of each manuscript indicates how precise and deliberate the variant readings are:

11/254–5 A alle þoo þyngis þat þe deuele delite .
 crist he despisede hem
 R alle þingis þat þe deuel leyde to crist .
 he despisid hem

Some of the divergencies seem to endorse the traditional view that readings of greater and lesser complexity correspond to earlier and later versions of a text, the argument being that the direction of intervention is always likely to be towards making a text more clear. Other divergences call into question the assumptions underlying this approach. In the variant readings cited next, there is a discernible tendency towards conciseness in R, although it might be argued that the lengthier A versions are more explicit and therefore more clear. Since complexity and clarity coincide in A, we cannot be certain whether intervention has given rise to the amplified or the compressed readings:

9/311–16 A For ri3t as þou wolt not abide if þou see þat þy plouh goo amys to hi3e or to lowe to amende it til þou haue al eerid vp þi lond but anon þou gost and rennist a wegge and stentist not til þou haue temprid him and sett him in his kynde ri3t so in þe same wise as tyme as þou fyndest...

R For ri3t as þou woldist not abyde if þat þou saw þi plow 3ede amys to hi3e or to lowe til þou haddist amendid it or þou 3edist ony ferþer til he were temperid in his kynde ri3t so in þe same wyse as þou felist...

11A/154–5 A impossible to haue þe gras and þe seed to springe boþe at ones

R impossible to haue ony of þe grasse and þe seed boþe

It should be noted that the A reading in 11A is in part (*gras... boþe*) a later addition, written over an erasure in the hand of a corrector.[1] This same later hand has inserted the words *at ones* in the margin. To judge by the length of the erasure, the corrector of A could have had before him an exemplar with a reading closer to R, which he subsequently revised.

A motivation towards easier readings is consistent with the tendency observed[2] in R to modify loan words; but that this tendency is that of an exemplar from which R has descended rather than that of the R scribe may perhaps be inferred from the fact that A and R contain the variant readings *artificers/men of craft*, at 11A/406, while M and R both have *artificer(es)(is)*, at DM/549.

Many of the numerous lexical variants in these manuscripts testify to the activity of one reviser or more, keenly concerned with nuances of content. In each sermon, examples can be

1. Hand 3, see Introduction, p.xiii.
2. See above, p.liii.

found of substitutions apparently by a considered personal understanding of the text, and/or individual usage and preferences:

8/200	A bodili	R erþeli
9/208	A smaller	R feyrer
10/69	A pursute	R purpose
11/43	A plese	R serue
11A/376	A hold	R gold
12/488	A deserte	R deseruing

It is arguable that in some of these instances the R reading is 'easier' because less abstract (as 8/200 and 12/488), or more explicit (as 10/69 and 11/43).

A more ambiguous example than any of these occurs at 11/296–8 where carefully deliberated intervention rather than error seems evident in the variant readings purporting to translate the Vulgate text:

A   oþer þat one... þou schalt hate
and þat oþer þou schalt loue
or ellis to þat one he schal cleue
and þat oþer he schal despise

R   eiþer þe ton... þou shalt hate
and þe toþer þou shalt loue
or ellis þe ton þou shalt plese
and þe toþer þou shalt despise

The variant readings *cleue/plese* may be explicable in terms of A 'remembering' *adherebit* from Luke (16:13), while R is rendering and glossing *sustinebit* from the parallel passage in Matthew (6:24). The presence of the preposition 'to' in A further authenticates the reading found there.

The shift from the Vulgate 3rd person singular reading into 2nd person singular in all of R but only part of A is more puzzling, but not self-evidently erroneous. The consistency of R could be attributable to a preference for the rhetorical force of 'þou', particularly in view of the presence of this pronoun throughout the invented direct address to the devil at 11/285–6 and 299–308. Similarly the pronoun change in A at 297 and 298 only could be seen as giving the '*aut*/or' of the Vulgate text the function of introducing a gloss on the preceding two causes. Given the degree of uncertainty arising from these possible indications of authorial intention, editorial emendation at this point was rejected as unjustifiable interference with the text.

Finally, the view that R is further from the original than A, and that they do not share an immediate exemplar is strongly supported by the curiously divergent readings at 10/14–16:

A in gloriam suam... into his blisse
R in regnum celorum... into þe kyngdom of heuen

Both A and R attribute this quotation to the last chapter of Luke's gospel, but A has the correct reading, while R conflates Luke 24:26 and Matthew 18:3, replacing a phrase rarely found in the gospels (*in gloriam suam*) with one frequently found in Matthew (*in regnum celorum*). It can be seen that in each version the vernacular translation renders the Latin correctly, which supports the assumption, demonstrated elsewhere, of revisions of an authorial nature (that is, rewriting, as distinct from mere correction) at different stages in the transmission of these texts. If this were indeed so, how might the variant readings cited here have come about? Perhaps relevant to the intrusive 'Matthean' phraseology in R is the fact that the lection for the day is in both manuscripts wrongly attributed to Matthew: 10/1 A Mt 18, R Mt 28. The following reconstruction thus becomes feasible:

X has Mt 18, which A copies without detecting the error;

Y is a more active reviser: he sees Mt 18, is uneasy about the unfamiliar *in gloriam suam*, and replaces it with the phrase so often occurring in Matthew, *in regnum celorum*; he also alters the translation to correspond with this;

R copies what is in Y but, in the course of so doing, inadvertently miscopies the already erroneous Scriptural attribution, giving the reading Mt 28.

Conclusions

The evidence set out in Hypotheses 4 and 5 has been largely drawn from variant readings in A and R. That there is a shared exemplar at some stage of transmission recent to the two closely similar versions on which this edition is based is beyond doubt. The differences between A and R can be 'explained' in at least two ways. Hypothesis 4 argues for A as predominantly a copyist and R as a more active reviser of X; while Hypothesis 5 could be seen as showing that both were copyists, but that R was working from a manuscript Y further away from the exemplar used by A. Neither can be proved. The editor's preference, on the basis of the nature of the variant readings, and on the far less tangible basis of hunches arising from long and close involvement with these texts, is for Hypothesis 5.

(II)   *The Sermon of Dead Men: in both R and M*

Scrutiny of the R and M versions of this text reveals differences that are more limited in kind than those observed in the R and A versions of Sermons 8–12. The few divergent readings that occur are, for the most part, simple omissions or substitutions of one or two words. By no means all of these can be categorised as 'errors'. The argument generated here is therefore simpler than that put forward for the other group of texts.

Hypothesis 1: that R was the exemplar for M

The argument against this rests on errors in R that are not found in M. There are only a few instances of defective sense in R, the most significant of which, for the purpose of this discussion, are omissions clearly attributable to 'eye-skip' between two occurrences of the same word (e.g. at 861 and, more substantially, at 436–7, 459–60, and 989), and omissions arising from momentary inattentiveness on the part of the scribe, such as the clustering of errors at 571, 572, and 580, and the deviation from a formulaic phrase at 787–8.[1]

As has been argued earlier, not all errors can be seen as conclusive evidence that a given manuscript was not the exemplar for a manuscript without them. A diligent corrector-reviser might well spot and rectify defective sense arising from omissions and substitutions—particularly when the context furnishes a clear indication of what the sense should be. A possible instance of this is the mechanical error *he* for *we* at 354 R, which is not difficult to explain, coming as it does after eight lines in which the pronoun *he* has been used no fewer than seven times before a sudden switch to the first person plural construction. An alert scribe, like an alert modern editor, could be in no doubt about what the reading should here, and the alert scribe is certainly as feasible a phenomenon as the careless scribe. It is therefore the presence in M of the longer passages missing from R that makes an examplar without these omissions likely.

---

1. Cf. 1/448–9, 3/524–5, 6/302–3, 13/412.

Hypothesis 2 : that M was the exemplar for R

The argument against this takes into account errors in M that
are not found in R, but ultimately rests on other features of the
two versions. M has even fewer instances of defective sense
than R. One apparent omission (cf.457–8) could instead be a
flawed revision of the text: i.e. the M reading *þis dredeful
bataile and perelous whiche* would 'work if *þis* were inserted
before *is* at 458. Another omission, at 529, is similarly far from
straightforward and is discussed in Hypothesis 4 below.

Of the small number of divergent readings arising from
lexical substitutions, the only certain instances of error are:

572	ful M *for* foule R
804	araying M *for* tarying R

The first is probably attributable to faulty auditory memory in
the course of copying; the second to an unintentional echoing
of *arayed* from the previous line.

Two other divergent readings are only revealed as possible
errors when seen alongside each other:

192–3	R	if it be loste he shal be vndone
		and lefte into perpetual peyne of helle
	M	if it be loste he shal be vndon
		and loste into perpetuel peyne of helle
580–1	R	wiþ costious metis and delicious drinkis
	M	wiþ deliciouse metis and deliciouse drinkis

We cannot know whether the repetition of *loste* in M is a
scribal error. The reading makes reasonable sense in the
context and could be a faithful copy of an examplar. On the
other hand, the similarity of letter forms does not preclude the
possibility of a misreading of *lefte*. Similarly, the repetition of
deliciouse M could be an error, but could equally well be taken
as a valid reading, with the notion of 'expense' intentionally
confined to the following clause.

A probable, but again by no means certain, error occurs in
the passage on the 'armour of God' (360–85):

375	R	þe gospel of crist
	M	þe gospel of god

Unusual though the M collocation is, the possibility that it is
deliberate cannot be ruled out, given the context: cf. *þe armure
of God* (362), *þe comaundementis of God* (370–1), and *þe mercy of*

God (381–2), *þe sweerde of þe word of God* (383), *þe worde of God* (389).

A less ambiguous instance of an inferior M reading than any so far discussed here occurs in the allegorical passage at 134–50,[1] where imagery and word-play sustained effectively in R are lost. The variant readings indicate interventions motivated by unease about the comprehensibility of the passage or, perhaps more likely, dislike of the extended metaphor. At 136, the use of *techinge* where R has *tilying* flattens the metaphor, but retains some sense; at 137 and 139, however, the readings *tyme* where R has *teme* eliminates both metaphor and word-play, and does so at the expense of sense.

The divergent readings at 136, 137 and 139, seen alongside some of the other variants, lead the argument closer to the likelihood of an exemplar shared by R and M.

Hypothesis 3: that O, the authorial original, was the exemplar for R and M

As was argued at this stage of the scrutinising of the A and R versions of Sermons 8–12, the traditional view of an authorial text as being free of errors precludes O as the exemplar for R and M which have some shared errors.

Hypothesis 4: that X was the exemplar for R and M

The argument for this rests on two shared errors in R and M which X is assumed to have generated in the course of its descent from an authorial original O. These errors, however, are unlike those observed in A and R which were, it will be remembered, discernible only to a reader closely aware of the argument within the text. In contrast, the shared errors in R/M are such as one would expect to be evident to scribes of the level of competence sustained throughout these texts.

The first shared error is a simple omission:

805 þei wolden not be her by [vb. answerid *omitted*]

Possibly a shared exemplar omitted this word at the end or the beginning of a line, a position vulnerable to defective memory or wandering attention on the part of a copyist.

---

1. See Notes to the Text, DM/134–50.

The second is a coincidental, but not identical, error. It occurs at 156, where editorial emendation has been necessary because both R and M are defective, R more radically so:

>R haue in mynde þat last þingis
>
>M haue in mynde þe laste þingis

These readings seem to support the assumption of a shared exemplar with an omission or an unclear reading, again perhaps at the beginning of a line.

Two shared errors that should be mentioned but that cannot reliably be taken into account in this discussion are the incorrect Scriptural locations that occur at 91 (wrong gospel) and 873 (wrong chapter), errors which, as was observed of similar instances in Sermons 8–12, could have emanated from the author.

We thus reach a convincing point of convergence of the two version of DM. The other variant readings to be cited here do not conflict with the hypothesis of a shared exemplar. They do, however, indicate interventions, the motivations of which often seem quite clear and offer insights into distinctive characteristics of each version. For example, the Latin quotations in M are usually longer than those in R, sometimes considerably so:

>e.g. 92, 123, 200, 314, 477, 508, 520, 680, 842, 860, 865, 983, 1054, 1134.

At 47–8 and 709–10, R has only the English translation of a Scriptural source of which M also includes a part in Latin.

Variants of this kind are consistent with a shared exemplar, with R abridging or omitting Latin quotations in the course of transmission. This being so, other instances where R is more concise than M may be similarly attributable to a tendency towards economy on the part of R, rather than expansiveness on the part of M. On the other hand, give that expansions within a text are often motivated by a desire to aid intelligibility, it may be more proper to see the longer variant as a later modification of an original text:

204	R	siþen þat
	M	seþen it is so þat
679	R	is hope and mercy
	M	is coumfort and hope of mercy
740–1	R	þe foule filþe of leccherie
	M	filþe of þe foule synne of lecherie

810	R disese	M gret disese
840	R a faget	M a knycche oþer a faget
899	R synnes	M foule synnes

Sometimes stylistic preference as well as a desire for clarity seem to lie behind variant readings which are not open to objective evaluation on either count:

423–5	R	þe synne þat þou didest . þou didest it of þin owne malice and þe synne þat I did . I did it at þe stiring of þee
	M	þe synne þat þou didest is of þin owne malice wiþouten ani oþere stirynge . and þe synne þat I dide . was at þe stiryng of þee
216	R	in h3e and orrible cursid pride
	M	in cursid lyif and orrible pride

Several instances of variant readings suggest no more than lexical preference, presumably determined by personal usage:

507	R a3eynstonde	M wiþstonde
569	R specialy	M principali
854	R seiþe	telleþ

There are no lexical variants in DM of the kind isolated in our earlier discussion of Sermons 8–12, where a preference for non-loan words seemed evident here and there in R, although there are some that are not easily explicable. The occurrence at 650 of *axinge* M where R has *approuyng* may represent a substitution for reasons of intelligibility on the part of M, but no such explanation adequately accounts for the readings at 949: *fermeþ*[1] M where R has *preueþ*, given that both have *preueþ* nearby at 988. And what of the variant *lijf* R and *blisse* M at 972, where the contrast with *peynis* (970) makes M the 'better' reading?

Further evidence of intervention or self-correction can be detected at 907–16 and 1113–16, where what at first appear to be radically different readings turn out to be no more than rearrangements of words and/or clauses that in no way alter the sense of either version.

---

1. **fermeþ** = 'confirms'.

Another divergence in the two versions of DM that warrants careful consideration is the repeated variant reading ȝet M / if R sustained throughout the entire passage from 568–96.[1] We have to decide here whether one reading is erroneous or whether, as is more often the case with variants within these texts, each is valid. This edition, which has taken R as the base text, punctuates this passage as a series of 'if' clauses, culminating in a long-delayed main clause at 595–6. A viable alternative can be constructed, however, based on the M reading and introducing the following glosses and repunctuation:

a) *but if* (at 577) = 'unless'
b) *ȝet* (at 568, 575, 580, 586, 592) = 'in addition, moreover'[2]
c) the semicolons in the edited text (at 567, 579, 585, 591) to be replaced by full stops
d) a new paragraph to begin at 595 with *Harde veniaunce*

This interpretation of M has been undertaken in such detail because it is of fundamental relevance to our speculations about the two texts. If, as has been argued here, M is indeed a valid alternative version, the view that the two are different but each of a high level of meticulous fidelity to an original version remains unimpaired. Our interest is thus demonstrated to lie in the variants and not in 'errors'. Different readings in R and M may represent separate revisions of a shared exemplar such that sometimes one and sometimes the other is closer to an original reading. In the case of the elaborate *ȝet/if* reconstruction, the intervention is assumed to be on the part of M is consistent with the observed tendency in M towards clarification and easier intelligibility. The interpretation of the M reading set out here offers an alternative to a syntactic structure that some might regard as too lengthy and unwieldy for oral delivery. Instead, it comprises a series of parallel passages: a simple inventory of manifestations of the seven deadly sins among the clergy, culminating in the punishment to be meted out to those who are culpable: *harde veniaunce wole come... hard doom shal be...* (595, 598).

1. See Notes to the Text, DM/557–96.
2. Cf. OED 'Yet' I.1.

The foregoing discussion has considered the relationship between the A and R versions of Sermons 8–12, and the R and M
versions of the Sermon of Dead Men. The argument set out in
each case has been that which seemed the most simple and the
least contentious. Given the nature of these texts, however, we
must remain alert to the scope for continuing speculation about
their transmission on the basis of far more extensive analysis
than has yet been attempted. One illustration of this is the M
reading at DM/529–30, already mentioned in the discussion of
Hypothesis 2, which gives rise to several interesting though
unverifiable interpretations of the possible relationship of these
versions to an 'original' version:

R by þe dore as a true heerde . or by þe rofe as a false þefe
M bi þe dore as   oþer bi þe roof as a þeef

The space that follows *as* (1) in M approximates in length to
the words *a heerde*, giving a reading perfectly consistent with
the correlative *as a þeef*, which similarly lacks the adjective
found in the R reading. It is surely significant that the space
here is just that, it is not an erasure. A possible explanation is
that the exemplar used by M was damaged and illegible at the
point where M has a space. This does not necessarily invalidate
Hypothesis 4: i.e. X could have been damaged after version R
was made, but before the making of M.

Ultimately, the transmission of these texts may only be
explicable in terms of several stemmata: perhaps one for each
sermon, or for groups within the collection. As was suggested
earlier, there may have been more than one author. This
possibility is reinforced by the many differences of style and
method across the texts, perhaps most notably the presence of
densely alliterative passages in some sermons and not others.

If other manuscripts of some or all of these texts come to
light, further permutations of the author-scribe-manuscript
relationship may bring more certainty than is possible at
present.

EDITORIAL PROCEDURES

The policy and procedures throughout this edition have been determined by a desire to make the text accessible to the widest possible interested readership at the same time as preserving for the specialist reader evidence of the original manuscript readings. Conjectural readings necessitated by wear, damage, or defective writing are placed within ⟨ ⟩. Other departures from the base text are placed within [ ] to alert the reader to editorial interventions, including the insertion of Scriptural locations, readings supplied from the non-base manuscript or, where there are reasonable grounds for assuming error, by the editor. Such readings where there is only one manuscript may have no corresponding entry in the Apparatus if the change is simply one of editorial addition: e.g. 1/371 and 2/85. Readings 'borrowed' from the non-base manuscript are recorded in the Apparatus and, where necessary, discussed in the Notes to the Text. All such borrowings are converted to the dialect and/or orthography of the base manuscript. In particular, it should be noted that, because some passages in R are damaged or missing, DM readings from M have been inserted within [ ], witb the use of ⟨ ⟩ confined to conjectural readings of partly visible words or characters. Each of these passages is indicated in the margin by the M folio number and is recorded in the Apparatus. In the Apparatus as elsewhere, the hands of the two main scribes of A are called H1 and H2. The hand of the later annotator of A is called H3. No similar procedure is required for R, which has only one scribal hand. Other conventions adopted in the Apparatus include the following abbreviations:

(*int.*)	Interlinear insertion, usually with a caret mark in the text.
(*mar.*)	Marginal insertion, corresponding to a caret mark in the text.
(*mar:*)	Marginalia alongside the text at the point indicated by the line number(s) given. The reference is to the base manuscript, unless otherwise indicated.
(*m. for r.*)	Marked for reversal: i.e. the manuscript indicates that these words should be transposed.
(*n.*)	Refers the reader to an entry in the Notes to the Text.

In accordance with the policy of the Early English Text Society, the only exceptions to the practice of recording all information about the manuscripts readings have been:

(a) the silent expansion of all scribal abbreviations (with the exception of Scriptural proper names—see below). Throughout the edition, *Ihu* and *Ihc* are expanded as **Jesus**; *dd* is expanded as **Dauid**; suprascript **t** in verbs is expanded as **-eþ**; ambiguous **I/J** in the initial position in proper names is transcribed as **J**. The contraction *cō-* and *coū-* has been expanded as **co(u)n-** (e.g. **co(u)nfort-**) throughout, with the exception of the entire Dead Men text, where one occurrence of uncontracted **discoumfortid** (R.f.lv.) has determined the use of the form **-co(u)m-**.

(b) the addition of modern capitalisation and punctuation. Punctuation of these texts presents the modern editor with some difficulties. Scribal punctuation lacks any evident systematic relationship to syntax. The prose is often highly complex and convoluted, characterised by a persistent tendency to interrupt itself, to explain, to inform, or to prod the hearer's attention. Clauses are interpolated into discernible sentence structures, in apposition or as digressions; at times the effect seems disjointed, but close reading shows firm control of the grammatical organisation throughout. The editorial intention has been to keep the punctuation as unobtrusive as possible, but to intervene where lengthy interpolations might confuse the modern silent reader: e.g. Sermon 9/271–6 and Sermon 16/70–81.

Scriptural Locations

In the context of continuous English prose, both manuscripts frequently use fully expanded English forms of Scriptural proper names. Accordingly, any abbreviations encountered in such contexts have been expanded, with [ ] to alert the reader to the editorial intervention. The forms used in these expansions correspond to those found elsewhere in the text or, if there are no such occurrences, to forms found in the Earlier Wycliffe Bible (*WEV*). However, proper names superimposed on the text as location references, as distinct from elements integral to the syntax, are abbreviated throughout the manuscripts. This distinctive feature suggests that they should be regarded as Latin, an assumption supported by the occasional presence of a Latin preposition [e.g. *ad*, Sermon 4/80, Sermon 12/104], also the single occurrence of an expanded form [*psalmi*, Sermon

4/167] and the recognisable abbreviation Thi*motheum* [Sermon 16/127]. In the absence of certainty about the inflexions of the expanded Latin forms, all occurrences of this kind have simply been italicised but otherwise left as in the manuscript. The only exception is the editorial addition of *i* to distinguish *Ecci* (Ecclesiasticus) from *Ecc* (Ecclesiastes). Wherever Scriptural locations are given in the text, information omitted (usually only verse numbers) has been supplied by the editor, within [ ]. Indices of Scriptural locations have been compiled for ease of reference, both (I) by sequence within each sermon, and (II) by alphabetical listing according to Scriptural Books. This has been done in response to the valuable suggestion, made by the late J.A.W. Bennett, that all vernacular translations of the Bible occurring in other texts should be recorded.

MS Rawlinson C 751, ff. 23ᵛ–24 (reproduced by permis-

I
FIRST SUNDAY
IN ADVENT

Cum appropinquasset Jesus Jerosolimis, et cetera (*Mt.*21.[1]). Þys f. 1ʳ
Sunday in whiche þys gospel is firste yrad in holi cherche is
clepid þe Firste Sunday of Aduent. Aduent is as myche for to
seye as 'comynge'; and, for as miche as þys hooli tyme now fro
5 þys Sunday into Cristenmasse Day makeþ special mynde of
Crist, and þis gospel spekeþ of þe comynge of Crist, þerfore þis
gospel pertynentli is rad þys day.

But heere men musten vnderstonde þat Hooli Scripture in
diuerse placis spekeþ of foure maneres of comyngis of Crist.

10 Þe firste comynge was whan ⟨þ⟩e seconde persone of þe
Trinite cam doun out of þe ⟨fa⟩d⟨ir⟩is bosum into þis
wrecchide world, and of þe clan⟨nest partis⟩ of a maidenes
flesch and blod he made to hym a bodi, and restede wiþinne
hire sides fourti wokes, and aftir was born, and þus bicam oure
15 broþer of oure kynde. Of þis comynge spekeþ Crist in Jones
gospel, seynge þus (*Jo.*16.[28]): *Exiui a Patre et veni in*
mundum. Þat is: 'I went out fro þe fadur and cam into þe
world.'

Þe secunde comynge was whan ⟨he⟩ hadde lyued in þis
20 world heere þre and þri⟨tti⟩ wyn⟨ter and⟩ m⟨o⟩re and, þorou
þe knowinge of his godhede, he saw þe t⟨y⟩me comynge nyȝh
of his passion. He cam mekeli and wilfulli toward Jerusalem,
where he wiste wel he schulde suffre deþ, ridynge poreli vpon
an asse, trussid wiþ a fardel of his disciplis cloþes, and a fole
25 folewynge, and xij pore men folewinge sempeli on her feet.

And heere auȝten proude men of þis world, but principalli
prelatus ⟨and pres⟩tis, be sore aschamed to see her Lord and
her Mayster, whom þey schulden principalli ⟨s⟩uen, ride in
þus pore a⟨r⟩ay, as is seide bifore, and þey to ride so proudeli
30 in gai gult sadeles wiþ gingelinge brideles and v score or vi

---

1 *Cum*] (*Text indented for three lines; capital* C *written into the space; no*
rubrication).   10 was] whas.   11 fadiris] (*hole*).

score hors of prout arayid men, as þou3 hit were a / kynge   f. 1ᵛ
rydinge toward a reuel, and her chariottis wiþ her jeweles
goynge tofore ful of grete fatte hors fed for þe nones. But fer
beþ þe true disciplis of Crist from þis arai, of whiche boþe
35 spekeþ þe Psalm Maker þere he seiþ þus: *Hij in curribus, et hij
in equis, et cetera.* 'Þese in charis, and þese in hors; but we schul
inclepe þe name of oure God. Þei beþ ibounde, and han yfalle;
but we haue arise, and beþ arerud up.'

Of þis seconde comynge spekeþ þe lettre of þe gospel of þis
40 dai, and þe prophete Zacharie, seynge þus: *Ecce rex tuus venit,
et cetera.* Þat is: 'Loo! Þi kyng comeþ to þe myldeli, sittynge on
an asse,' *et cetera.*

Þe þridde comynge is goostli and is doun eueri day whanne
God, of his endeles merci and grete grace, þorou inspiracion of
45 þe Hooli Goost in bap⟨tem⟩, or in prechinge, or in gret sorwe
of synnes, comeþ into synful mannes soules as into his owne
temple. Of þis þridde comynge spekeþ Crist in Jones gospel in
þis wise (*Jo.*14.[23]): *Ad eum veniemus, et mansionem, et cetera.*
Þat is: 'My Fadir and I schal come to him þat loueþ me and
50 kepeþ my word, and we schal make dwellyng wiþ him.' And
God seyþ also in þe Apoc[alips](3.[20]): *Ecce sto ad hostium et
pulso, et cetera.* Þat is: 'I stonde at þe dore' (þat is, of mannes
soule) 'and knocke. Whoso heereþ my voice and openeþ to me
þe 3ate, I schal entre to him, and soupe wiþ him, and he wiþ
55 me.'

Þe fourþe comynge and þe laste schal be at general Dai of
Jugemente, whan he schal come rialli in gret power and
mageste to deme alle men 'wiþouten acceptynge of persones'
after þei han deserued: þe goode to ioie, þe euele to peyne. Of
60 þis fourþe comynge spekeþ þe prophete Ysaie, in þe þridde
chapitre [14], seyinge þus: *Deus ad iudicium veniet cum senibus
populi sui, et cum principibus eius.* Þat is: 'Þe Lord schal come to
þe doom wiþ þe olde men of his peple, and wiþ his princis.' Þe
tokenynge of þe comynge of þis Lord to þe Dom, as Seynt
65 Jerom seyþ vpon Mathew, schal be⟨o⟩ 'whan his gospel schal /
be prechid into al þe world, þat no man be excusable,' *et cetera.*   f. 2

Þe firste comynge and þe seconde of þis blessid Lord (þat is,
firste into þis world, and after to his passion) beþ now passide,
as þe lettre of þe firste gospel of Cristemasse Dai and þe lettre
70 of þe gospel of þis dai openli makeþ mencion, for whiche alle

31 (*Foot of* f. 1r: þey to ride he⟨r⟩ ? *indistinct*).
45 baptem] (*hole*).
51 in] in a.

men beþ bonden wiþ herte, mouþ, and dede to ȝheue him grete
þankyngis wiþoute any cesynge.

But for þe þridde comynge (þat is, þoroȝ grace into mannes
soule) is euermore necessarie and nedeful to vs, seþþen wiþoute
75 him we moun noo þyng doo to profite of oure soule, of whiche
spekeþ þis gospel if it be gostli vnderstonde, þerfore, wiþ þe
help of almyti God, I purpose at þis tyme to speke of þis
comynge.

Þis gospel bigynneþ þus: 'Whanne Jesus hadde neyhed ny to
80 Jerusalem, and hadde come to Bethfage, at þe Mount of
Olyuete, he sente two of his desciples, seyinge to hem: "Gooþ
⟨i⟩nto þe castel þat is aȝens ȝou, and þere ȝhe schullen fynde an
asse ibounde, and a fole wiþ here. Vnbyndeþ, and ledeþ to me,
and ȝef any man sey any þing to ȝou, say ȝe þat þe Lord haþ
85 werke to þese, and anon he schal leue hem to ȝou".'

Jerusalem is as miche for to seye as 'þe syth of pees', bi
whiche may wel be vndurstonde al holi cherche: þat is, þe
g[e]neral congregacion of alle þat schullen be saued, for þey
biholdeþ euur God in her soule, whiche is oure pees, as Seynt
90 Poule seiþ: *Ipse est pax nostra.* Of whiche 'biholdinge' spekeþ
Dauid, seyinge: *Prouidebam Dominum in conspectu meo semper.*
Þat is: 'I haue ordeined þe Lord euere in my siȝte.'

And þorou pees þat suche men maken bitwixe God and hem,
and bitwixe hem and her breþeren, and bitwixe her bodi and
95 her soule, þei beþ clepid of Crist 'þe sones of God' and þus
euere in þis world beþ goynge toward euerelastynge pees. And
ȝif it be soo þat ani tyme ani of hem, þorou frelte, necligence,
oþur ignoraunce, falle into ani synne, as tyme as þey repente
hem / and axen of God wiþ deuoute preiere of merci and of   f. 2ᵛ
100 grace, anon God neyheþ to suche a soule and forȝeueþ him his
synnes. And þerfore seiþ þe Psalm Maker: *Prope est Dominus
inuocantibus eum in ueritate, et cetera.* Þat is: 'Þe Lord is niȝ to
alle men inclepinge him, inclepinge him in truþe.' And also bi
Ezechiel þe prophete: *In quacumque hora peccator ingemuerit,*
105 *saluus erit, et cetera (Eze.*18). Þat is: 'In whateuer hour þe
synful [man] repenteþ him, he schal be saf.'

But for as myche as þis neiȝhinge of God þus þorouȝ grace
comeþ ofte in þorouȝ þe word of God trueli prechid of þe mouþ
of his prestis, and also þorou true confession maad of mannes
110 mouþ þorou deuout preier, þerfore it is wel seid þat Jesus cam
bi Bethphage (þat is as myche for to sey as 'hous of mouþ')
toward þis gostly Jerusalem (þat is, hooli cherche). Þat þis

91 *in*] (*followed by* s).

Bethphage was sette at þe Mount of Oliuete bitokeneþ þat
deuoute and effectual preier muste be knitted to mercy, whiche
115 is bitokened bi þe Mount of Oliuete, as Crist haþ taut vs in
oure *Pater Noster*, seyinge: *Dimitte nobis, et cetera.* Þat is:
'Forȝeue to vs oure trespaces, as we don to oure trespasouris.'
Also, confessioun of mouþ muste be ioyned to tristi hope of
mercy, oþer ellis it is like to þe vnfruteful confessioun of Judas.
120   Also, true prechinge of þe word of God must be ioined to þis
Hil of Olyuete (þat is, oure Lord Jesus Crist), firste for to lyue
holili, and after to preche trueli. Þat Jesus sente his disciplis
bitokeneþ þat no man schulde take vpon him þe office of
prechinge but if he hopede þat he be sente boþe of God and of
125 man.
     Whanne schal he suppose oþer hope þat he is þus sente?
Whanne he is dueli ordeyned eþer orderid of a prelate, and
after bisili studieþ in Goddis lawe, and þerwiþ lyueþ poreli,
mekeli, and vertuousli, and is in ful wille to preche Goddis
130 word oute to þe peple bisili, trueli, and freli, þanne may he
verili suppose and hope þat he is sente boþe of God and of man
/ to þis office. And herto nedeþ him non oþur lettre, but oneli   f. 3ʳ
þe lettres of his orderes and true practisynge in þis werke.
     Þat Jesus sente two disciplis, raþer þan þre or foure, or ellis
135 oon bi himself, bitokeneþ þat þoo þat schulde be prechoures of
þe word of God schulden haue þese two þyngis: þat is, vertuous
lyif and truþe of prechinge. Also, þat þey schulde be fulfillid of
þe two membris of charite: þat is, of þe loue of God and after of
loue of her breþeren. Also, þat alle true prechoures, as Crist
140 seiþ in Mat[hewes] gospel, schulden be 'like to þe housholdere
þat bryngeþ forþ of his tresoure boþe oolde þyngis and
newe,'—þat is, þat he schulde haue kunnynge boþe of þe Oolde
Lawe and of þe Newe.
     Þat Jesus bad hem goo bitokeneþ þat prelatis and prestis of
145 Cristis chirche schulden not reste and be idel in worschipes and
honouris of þis world, and lustis and likyngis of her flesch, and
cese fro prechinge of Goddes word to wraþþe God and dampne
her soule, but hertli wirche in his vyne, and spare for no wordli
hate.
150   Þis castel þat he bad hem goo intoo, whiche he seiþ is euere
aȝens hem, bitokeneþ þe falce wordeli men of whiche John
spekeþ in his gospel, seyinge þus: *Et mundus eum non cognouit*
(*Jo*.1.[10]). Þat is: 'And þe wor[l]d knew him noȝt.' Þis world

---

mai wel be likenyd to a castel, for rith as a castel is a stronge
hoold maad of stones ioyned wiþ lym to kepe oute men wiþoute
forþ, so wickide men confederid togidre wiþ falce loue and
euele wille ben strengþid in her malice, and kepeþ euere
Goddes word oute of hire soules, and hateþ þe true prechoures
þerof.

Þe depe diche of stondyng watir þat cumpaceþ aboute þis
castel mai wel be þe foule vnordynat loue þat þei han in her
euele, of whiche spekeþ þe Wyse Man in his Prouerbis and /
seiþ þus: *Letantur cum malefecerint, et cetera* (*Prouer.*2.[14]). f. 3ᵛ
Þat is: 'Þey gladen whan þei haue doon euele, and ioyen in
worst þyngis.' And þis ioie makeþ hem falle deepe out of oo
synne into anoþer, and þerfore seiþ Dauid þus: *Abissus abissum
inuocat.* 'Depnesse inclepeþ depnesse.'

Þe enbatelynge aboute aboue þe walles þat makeþ hit fair to
mannes siʒte mai wel be her feyned holynesse wherbi þei
colouren al her euele.

Þis castel is euermore aʒens Criste and þe true prechoures of
his word, and þerfore seiþ Crist in Jones gospel,
(*Jo.*15.[18–19]): *Si mundus uos odit, et cetera.* 'Ʒif þe world
hateþ ʒou, wite ʒe and knoweþ þat þe world hadde me in hate
tofore ʒou. If ʒe hadde be of þe world, þe world wolde haue
louede þat hadde be his; but, for ʒhe beþ noʒt of þe world, I
haue chosen ʒou fro þe world, þerfore þe world hateþ ʒou.' And
Seynt Johun seiþ in his pistil: *Nolite mirari si odit uos mundus,
et cetera* ([1] *Jo.*3.[13–14]). Þat is: 'Merueileþ noʒt, breþeren,
þou þe world hate ʒou, for we knowen þat we ben translatid fro
deþ to lyif for we loueþ (þat is, God and oure breþeren), and
þei þat loueþ noʒt (þat is, noþer God, neþer breþeren, as þese
loueris of þis world dooþ), þei dwellen in deeþ,' as Seynt Johun
seiþ. And lyif and deþ ben contrarious directli, þerfore moun
þei neuer acorde.

Þis femele asse þat is þus bounden is an old synful mannes
fleisch, þorou consent of his soule þat is bounden wiþ longe
contynuaunce in his olde rotid synne. And wel it is clepid a
femele asse, for his frelte and vnstablenesse; and wel mai synful
mannes flesch rotid in synne be licned to an asse, for an asse is
a dul beste, and alwey gooþ oo pas, and for no prikynge ne
betynge he wole not change his olde gate. Riʒt so, an old rotid
man in synne alwey holdeþ hym þerynne and, for no prikynge
of scharpe sentencis / of Hooli Writ, ne for no betynge wiþ þe f. 4ʳ

---

171 euermore] euerimore.

195 ȝerde of God þorȝ tribulacion and disese, he chaungeþ neuere
his olde life.

Also, an asse is leþi and feble tofore in his ferþer partis, and
strong and myti in his hyndere partis. Riȝt so, suche fleschli
synful men ben febel to do any good to gete wiþ þe kyngdom of
200 heuene, but þei ben miȝti and strong ynow to alle þyngis bi
wiche þei mai gete goodes of þis world.

Þis asse is bounden, as Y saide, wiþ long continuaunce in
olde rotid synnes. Þerfore seiþ Dauid in þe Psauter þus: *Funes
peccatorum circumplexi sunt me, et cetera*. Þat is: 'Þe coordes of
205 synnes han al aboute bounden me.' And þe Wyse Man seiþ also
in his Prouerb[is], *Prouer.*5.[22]: *Vnusquisque vinculo peccatorum constringitur.* Þat is: 'Eueri man is constreyned wiþ þe
bounde of his synnes.' Wiþ þese bondes þei beþ bounden þe
feet (þat is, hire affecciones), þat þei moun not desire to do wel;
210 and also here necke, þat þei mai not speke wel.

Þis ȝonge fole þat goþe biside al loos and noȝt ȝet bounden
bitokeneþ here childeren þat ben ȝonge, þat fallen into many
synnes bi ensample of here eldres. But her synnes ben not
rootid wiþ longe contynuaunce in synne, þerfore þei mai more
215 liȝtliere and sonnere be rerid of hire synne; for þou ȝonge men
ben cumbrid wiþ synne for frelnesse of her owne flesch, ȝet if
þei be prikid wiþ scharpe sentencis of Holi Writ, or be bete wiþ
þe ȝerde of God, anon þei leue her cursid synne, and ben sori
þat þei haue don amys.

220 Þe blessid Lord, seeynge many asses þus harde bounden in
þe castel of þis world and many folis suynge hem, of his endeles
merci haþ ruþe and pitee of hem and, also desirynge to haue
hem to his roode, comaundeþ to his disciplis, seyinge: 'Vnbyndeþ and bryngeþ to me.' Þat is, wiþ true prechinge of þe
225 word of God, and heleful conceil in / holi schrift, vnbyndeþ   f. 4ᵛ
synful men of synnes, for þis longeþ to ȝoure office.

Þat prechinge of þe word of God vnbyndeþ men of here
synnes mai be be proued verili bi Holi Scripture and ground of
resoun. Crist seiþ in Jones gospel (*Jo.*[5.24]): *Qui verbum meum
230 audit, et cetera.* Þat is: 'He þat hereþ my word, and bileueþ to
him þat sente me, he comeþ noȝt into dom, but schal passe fro
deþ to life.' And he þat schal passe fro deþ to lyif is vnbonden
of alle his synnes and so maad free and Goddes childe. Also, if
prechyng of Goddes word miȝte not vnbynde men of here
235 synne, þanne hadde þis word 'vnbyndeþ' in veyn be seid to þe
apostlis, for in here tyme ne longe after was þis maner schrift
no þyng vsed, but þorou true prechynge of Goddes word þei
maden many þousendes come to feiþ, and leue here erroures,

and be baptised; and many [were] martirid for loue of Crist,
240 and alle suche were vnbounden of alle þe synnes þat þei haue
doon.

But ȝet seiþ Crist forþermore: 'Bryngeþ to me þat he
vnbyndeþ,' for it sufficeþ noȝt to be vnbounden, but if þei be
brout to Criste. And þerfore seiþe þe Psalme Maker: 'Bowe
245 awei from euele, and doo good.' For, if a man schulde lede a
beeste from oo place into anoþer, þe leder bihoueþ to go tofore
and drawe þe best þe same wei after; so it sufficeþ noȝt ynow to
prestis to preche trueli þe word of God, but also wiþ ensaumple
of god lyfe to go tofore and drawe þe peple after hym. And þus,
250 for þese two officis (truþe of prechinge and good liyf), clepeþ
Crist his true prechoures 'salt of þe erþe' and 'lyȝte of þe
world'.

After Crist seide to his desciplis þe wordes þat suen after in
þis gospel: 'and if ani man seie ani þyng to ȝou, seieþ þat þe
255 Lord haþ werk to þese' (oþer ellis, as Lu[ke] seiþ: 'Þe Lord
desireþ þe werk of hem') and 'anon he / schal leue hem to ȝou', f. 5ʳ
þis Lord Jesus Crist, souereynst of alle oþere, vnderstood in
þese wordis it semeþ þe tyme þat now is, in whiche he knew
wel men wolden axe questyons like to þese wordes of prestis
260 whiche traueloun faste in prechinge for to vnbynde synful
peple, seyinge: 'Wherto preche ȝe so faste now, more þan men
weren wonte to doo, seþþe as holi men as ȝe haue beo
heretofore of longe tyme, as Thomas of Canter[bury] and oþer
moo whiche prechide seelde, as we reden, and ȝet þei ben holi
265 seyntis and hiȝe sitteþ wiþ God in blisse? It semeþ it is but a
proude presumpcion to be seen aboue alle oþere. Also, tofore
so myche prechynge was, men lyueden wel and eche louede
oþere; but now, seþþe prechynge haþ so myche be vsed, þe
peple haþ be euermore enpeired.'

270 Heereto men musten answere in þis matere to þese obiectis
þat ben maad: We schal suppose and tristili hoope þat þese
seyntis ben glorious and hiȝli rewardid in blisse of God for þe
goodes þat þei diden. So schal we suppose þat þei repentiden of
alle synnes þat þei diden, and specialli in necligence of
275 prechynge, if þei diden so as men seyn, for þat was principal of
here office, whiche Crist enioynede to alle prestis whan he
schulde departe fro hem as þyng þat lai most on his herte,
seyinge: *Predicate euangelium omni creature* (*Mr.*[16.15]). Þat
is: 'Preche þe gospel to eueri creature.' And Seynt Gregorius

255 Luke] luc'.
278 16.15] vltimo.

280 seiþ þus: *Officium preconis suscipit quisquis ad sacerdotium accedit.* Þat is: 'Þe office of crier he takeþ, hosoeuere to presthode goþ.' And also, in anoþer place, seiþ þe same doctour þus: *Sacerdos ingrediens | vel egrediens moritur, si de eo sonitus* f. 5ᵛ *predicacionis non audiatur.* Þat is: 'A preest goynge in and 285 goynge out dieþ, if þe soun of prechyng be not herd of him.'

Also to þis obiect þat is maad of weyward men in þis matere (þat þe world is now worse þanne tofore þer was so miche prechynge), men mai answere and sei þus: þat it is not longe on þe word of God, but vpon þe schrewede hertis þat ben 290 vndisposid to receiue it; for þe sunne melteþ wex on whiche it schyneþ, and hardeþ clei, as men knowen wel, and þat is not longe on þe sunne, but on þe materis dyuerseli disposid. So þe word of God, þat is prechid among miche peple of diuerse willes, melteþ gode mennus hertis to repentaunce and vertuous 295 dedis, and hardeþ synful and weiward hertis to more malice in her synne.

Crisostom also, to þis matere, makeþ anoþer symilitude of a piler þat is sett for to bere vp a werk: if it be croked (he seiþ) of himself, þe more þat is leid aboue, þe sonnere it wole ȝelde hym 300 and falle doun vnder his charge; but and it beo riȝt euene of hymself, þe more þat is leid aboue, þe stiflier it wole stonde and beere his birdoun mytili. Riȝt so, a crokid weiward herte: þe more hit bereþ of Goddis word, þe more sonnere hit boweþ and falleþ doun into grettere synnes; but a soule þat is riȝt sett 305 and euene to fulfulle Goddis wille, þe more hit beereþ of Goddes word, þe stiflier it stondeþ in bileue and bereþ þe charge of Goddis hestus, which is liȝt to alle suche.

And þus, to considere þes answeres in þis matere, and many oþer þat myȝten bee maad, it scheweþ it is no presumpcion 310 prestis to ȝeue hem bisili to preche trueli þe word / of God, but f. 6ʳ a fulfullynge of þe Lordes heeste, þat sendeþ hem for þis ende.

Or ellis men mai answere as Crist techeþ bi þe wordes of þe texte, seiynge þus: 'Þe Lord haþ werk to þese,' or ellis: 'Þe Lord desireþ her werke.' God hateþ alle ydel men, and clepeþ 315 werkmen into his vine; and suche and non oþere he wole rewarde at þe grete Dai of Acountee. In þis vineȝerd, God haþ werk ynow to alle men þat euere were. Þis wirchyng in þis vyne is holi liyf in þis world, whiche God desireþ of alle men, as Seynt Poule seiþ in his pistel: *Hec est voluntas Dei, sanctificatio* 320 *vestra.* Þat is: 'Þis is þe wille of God, ȝoure holynesse,' for no nede þat he haþ to any part of oure seruice, but for we schulde haue þe grete reward of heuene blisse for oure trauele. And, to brynge men to þis werk, euery man shulde bisie him in his part

and, most specialli, alle prestis þat schulde be procuratouris of
325 þis vyne.

And þus, euery man herying þese answeres, if he be
groundid in any resoun, wo⟨le⟩ cese and suffre þe asse beo
loosed and be brou3t to Goddi⟨s⟩ werk.

Here men moun touche, 3if þei wole, of wilful beggynge þat
330 is myche vsed, where hit mai be groundit schilfulli in þese
lordli wordes of Crist: 'Þe Lord haþ werk to þese beestis', or
ellis: 'Þe Lord desireþ her werk'. For þis word 'lord', taken bi
hymself wiþoute any oþer puttynge too, signifieþ þe most
famous Lord: þat is, Lord of Lordis, whiche bi titele of boþe
335 his kyndis was verrei Lord of alle wordeli godes; and so it
semeþ raþer an hie commaundement þan wilful beggyng
wiþoute nede.

And þat proueþ also þe sentence þat sueþ after of Cristis
wordis: þat as sone as þei heere þe Lord nemp/ned, þei schul   f. 6ᵛ
340 lete þe beestus goo. Þis was doun ones, after þe lettre, to fulle
Zacharies prophecie, and eueri dai is doon gostli in dyuerse
mennes soules, after þei haue receyued grace. Þe blessid Kyng
of oure kynd comeþ myldeli to suche soules þat haue be dullid
wiþ synne (as assis) and after repentid, and left hire synnes, as
345 he dide to Maud[elyn], Petre, and many oþere, as Hooli
Scripture makiþ mynde.

'Þe disciplis wenton forþ', as seiþ þe texte, 'and diden as
Crist comaundide to hem; and þei brow3ten to hym þe asse,
and þe foole also wiþ hire' and sparide no3t for strengþe of þe
350 castel, ne for no peple þat was þerinne, ne for no grucchyng ne
denyinge þat þei mi3ten haue for her dede. So schulden alle
true prestis boldeli doo þe Loordes heeste, and spare, noþer for
worde ne deede of weiward men of þis world, to preche bisili
Goddes word and brynge soules þicke to Crist. And suche
355 prestis schulden be Cristis frendes, as he himself seiþ in þe
gospel: *Vos amici mei estis, si feceritis que precipio vobis*
(*Jo.*[15.14]). Þat is: '3e been my freendes, 3if 3e doo þat I bidde
3ou.'

Þe gospel seiþ after þat þe apostles puttede here cloþes vpon
360 þese beestis and made þe Lorde sitte aboue to ride forþ in his
iorne. Bi þese cloþes of þese hooli apostles þat weren leide þus
on þese beestis mai be vnderstonde doctrine of vertues of oure
prelatis þat been aboue vs; for ri3t as cloþes enorneþ þe bodi
and kepeþ hit also fro þe coolde, ri3t so vertues ennorneþ þe
365 soule and kepeþ hit in hete of charite. And so we muste to hem
applie oure backes boþe of bodi and of soule, and be sadelid
wiþ here hooli techynge (þat is, groun/did in Goddis lawe) or   f. 7ʳ

ellis, forsoþe, we ben not able þat Jesus Crist sitte in oure
soule. And þis confirmeþ Crist himself in his gospel and seiþ
370   þus: *Qui vos audit, me audit; et qui uos spernit, me spernit.* Þat is:
'He þat hereþ ȝou, heereþ me; and he [þat] dispiseþ ȝou,
dispiseþ me.' And Poule seiþ also to þe Hebreus: *Obedite*
prepositis vestris, et subiacete illis; ipsi enim pervigilant, quasi
rationem reddituri pro animabis vestris (*Hebr.*[13.17]). Þat is:
375   'Obeieþ to ȝoure prelatis, and beþ suget to hem; for þei,
forsoþe, wakeþ, as þei þat schul answere for ȝoure soules.'

And heere men moun touche more largeli of good obedience
and of euele, after þat men mai haue tyme and spedeþ also to þe
auditorie.

380   Þis gospel seiþ forþermore, as þe storie telleþ after, þat
myche peple strawyde heere cloþes of here bodies in þe weie,
and summe hewiden branches of trees, and strawiden hem also
in þe weie. Þe peple also þat wentoun bifore, and þo þat
sueden, crieden and seiden, 'Osanna!' (Þat is: We biseche þe,
385   saue vs!) 'þou þat art þe sone of Dauid. Blessid is hee þat
comeþ in þe name of þe Lord!'

Þis sentence telleþ openli, after þe lettre þat is rad, how þre
maner of pepl⟨e⟩ diuerseli worschipeden God in here manere,
summe wiþ cloþes, and summe wiþ bowes, and summe wiþ cri
390   of here mouþes, and þe nexte Fridai suynge after þei diden
hym vileny in alle þese þree. Aȝens þe worschipe of here cloþes,
þei robbeden him of alle his cloþes, and bounden him nakid to
a piler, and beeten him sore `vp´on his bodi. Aȝenst þe
secounde worschi/pe þat þei diden wiþ branches þat þei   f. 7ᵛ
395   hewiden of trees, þei maden after a cros of tree to hange vpon
his blessid bodi. Aȝens þe þridde worschipe of hire mouþ, wiþ
whiche þei knoulechiden hym boþe God and man, þei crieden
after wiþ þe same mouþ: 'Doo hym on cros! Do him on cros!'

Þus vnstable is þe peple ȝet, ȝef men take hede to here dedis,
400   for summe þat wenen to worschipe God wiþ here bodies in
fastyng Fridai oþer Satirdai doþ him as myche vileny on þe
toþer side wiþ gloteny vpon þe Sundai and alle þe woke, and
summe þat worschipen him wiþ almesdede to pore men þat ben
bisidis don him more vileny wiþ extorcions [and] r⟨o⟩bberie of
405   hire breþeren, and summe þat þe Sundai tofore noon, wiþ
multitude of preiers in here cherche, wenen to worschipe God
ful hie and to be rewardid of him in heuene þei dooþ him
myche more vileny after noon wiþ þe same mouþ, in lyinge,

374 13.17] vltimo.

sweryng, and cursynge, and fals disclaundrynge of hire
410 breþeren.

Þe gostly vnderstondynge of þis texte mai be þis, as me
þynkeþ: þat of þe conuersyon of a synful man al holi chirche
makeþ ioie, whiche mai schilfulli be vnderstonde bi þese þre
maner of peple. Bi þe firste moun skilfulli be vnderstonde hooli
415 martiris þat þrewen forþ hire bodies here to suffre peynus and
deþ for Crist. Þe secounde beþ confessourus and doctouris þat
hewen out of Holi Scripture many faire and grene truþes, as
out of þe tre of lyfe, and precheden hem tofore synful peple
when þei / weren here in þe weie. Þe þridde beþ alle oþer hooli f. 8ʳ
420 men of alle þre partis of Cristus chirche, þat wiþ opene louynge
of herte and mouþ worschipeþ God for synful men þat been
conuertid and ablid to grace. And noȝt oneli þese but, as Crist
seiþ, alle þe angels þat been in heuen makeþ ioie and looueþ
God for þe repentaunt synful man. Also, me þynkeþ, it mai be
425 vn⟨d⟩erstonde ȝet in anoþer manere: þat euery synful man
repentaunt, in whom God sitteþ þoru his grace, schulde haue
euere in his mynde þe þre partis of satisfaccion, for to amende
him of his eerdon synnes and for to geten him more grace, þat
is: penaunce in his bodi, large almesdede, and preier, whiche
430 moun wel be vnderstonde bi þese þre werkis of þis peple.

Bi þe firste mai beo vnderstonde penance þat men doon in
her bodies, as fastynges, wakyngis and longe knelyngis, hairis
in schertis and eke in schetis, goynge bare wiþ hire feet, and
also scharpe disciplinis. Suche setten litel bi her bodies, as men
435 þat þrowen þyngis into þe weie.

Bi þe secounde mai be vnderstonde al mesdedes of worldeli
godes; for riȝt as a grene branche of a tree cleueþ and groweþ to
þe bodi, riȝt so þe godes of þis world cleueþ to a couetous
mannes herte. But whan he, þoru drede of acountee þat he
440 schal make þe last dai, ȝeueþ of hem faste aboute to nedi men
while he is heere, þenne heweþ he doun þe bowes fro trees and
þrowe[þ] hem forþ in þe weye.

Bi þe þridde mai be vnderstonde deuoute preieer of mannes
mouþ, to whiche þe herte mo/te acorde, and also þe dede riȝtli f. 8ᵛ
445 sue. And suchon crieþ þries 'Lord!' and he mut nedes be herd
of God and entre into þe kyngdom of heuene, as Crist himself
seiþ in þe gospel.

Nou God for his endeles mercy, þat diede on a cros for al
mankynde, ȝeue vs grace, þat been bounden as assis wiþ longe

---

437 tree] tree þat.   442 þroweþ] þrowet.
443–4 mannes mouþ] mouþ mannes (*m. for r.*).

450 liynge in oure synnes, to be loosid þoru þe word of God and
true confession of oure mouþ, and faire sadelid wiþ hooli
vertues trueli taut of oure prelatis, so þat oure soulis moun be
likynge hors þe Kyng of heuen to ride onne toward þis gostli
Jerusalem (þat is, þe glorious blisse of heuene in whiche is þe
455 siȝt of pees þat euere schal laste wiþouten end), and þat it mai
be seid þanne to vs: 'Blessid is he þat comeþ in þe name of þe
Lord.' Amen.

455 of] of of.

2

SECOND SUNDAY
IN ADVENT

Erunt signa in sole, luna, et stellis, et cetera (*Lu.*21.[25]). 'Þer
schulle be tokenes in sunne, mone, and sterris,' *et cetera* and so
forþ.

Þis gospel makeþ mencion of þe fourþe comynge of oure
5 Lord, Jesus Crist, þat schal be whanne he schal come in þe
glorie of his mageste, in þe laste dai, to deme iustli 'wiþoute
acceptynge of persones' euery man after he haþ deserued. But
of þat dredful dai and hour whan it schal be, in certeyn, Crist
seiþ þat no man wot, but oneli þe Fader of heuene. For þre
10 þyngis been vnknowen to euery man: þat is, þe predestinacion
of man, and þe dai of his deþ, and þe Last Jugement. But, for
as myche as we schulden not bee necligent and slepe in synne,
but wake in vertuous life / and make vs redi to þat grete   f. 9ʳ
acountee whiche may not faile but nedes mut come, þerfore þat
15 blessid Lord cam into þis world to seche and make saaf þat was
perisched, and wilneþ and desireþ þe sauacion of mankynde
and, in as myche as in him is, þat no man bee dampned but if
he wole himself.

Þerfore he haþ told vs many dyuerse signes or tokenes
20 whiche schullen come tofore þat day, bi whiche we schal fulli
knowe þat þe dai is nyȝ and not fer. Among whiche signes or
tokenes he procedeþ in þe gospel of þis dai, and seiþ þus: 'Þer
schullen be signes in þe sunne, moone, and sterris.'

Ȝhe schullen vnderstonde þat þe signes þat Crist spekeþ of in
25 sunne, mone, and sterris, moun not oneli be vnderstonde of
wondres þat han be⟨n⟩ seen in þese visibile planetis whiche
beþ sette in oure syȝte in þe firmament aboue vs. For, as
cronicles telleþ, and also as hit haþ be schewed in oure tyme,

---

1 *Erunt*] (*Text indented for two lines; small* e *written into the space; no
rubrication*).   15 Lord] lord þat.

and many dyuerse cuntrees, many merueile⟨s⟩ han be schewid
30 in hem, and ȝet is not come þat dai. And þerfore many men
þynken þat þei mai bettere be vnderstonde of goostli tokenes,
whiche ben more sotil to vnderstonde, for sodeyn comyng of
þat doom.

Joel þe propet spekeþ of þese tokenys and scheweþ what
35 maner tokenes þei schul be þere he seiþ þus: 'Þe sunne schal be
turn⟨e⟩d into derkenessis, and þe moone into blod, tofore þe
grete and horribile dai of þe Lord is come.'

Bi þis sunne, men moun vnderstonde Crist and his / lawe,   f. 9ᵛ
whiche is þe sunne of riȝtwisnesse. And pertynen[t]li he mai be
40 likned to þe sunne for many diuerse propurtees þat acorden in
hem. For riȝt as þe sunne is aboue alle oþer planetus most
excellent and most worþi, and alle oþer han hire liȝte of him, so
Crist [is] most excellent aboue alle oþer creatures, and alle
oþere creatures han of him boþe liȝt of kynde and liȝt of grace,
45 and þer is noo þyng þat mai lyue goostli, ne growe, ne encrese
in vertues, but þoru grace of þe sunne of riȝtwisnesse, for Crist
seiþ (*Jo.*[15.5]): *Sine me nihil potestis facere*, and Seynt Poule
acordeþ þerwiþ (2 *Cor.*3.[5]).

Also, þe sunne schyneþ vniuerselli to alle creatures boþe
50 faire and foule, as myche as þei beþ able to receyue, but if þer
bee any obstacle bitwene; so Crist ȝeueþ out [h]is grace to alle
(as Seynt Jame seiþ: *Qui dat omnibus affluenter Ja.*1.[5]), as
myche as þei beþ able to, but þei putte any obstacle of synne
bytwene hem and þis grace. Goddes lawe is aboue alle oþer
55 lawes as þe sunne is aboue alle oþer planetes, and so God haþ
maad also his lawe to schyne to alle men þat wolen able hem to
receyue it, and no men mai lyue goostli but þoru rule of þat
lawe.

Þis sunne is turned into derknesse whan þe lyf of Crist and
60 knowyng of his lawe beþ hid or maad derk to þe peple. Wiþ þre
þyngis þe material sunne is maad derk fro men: þat is, wiþ þe
nyȝt, and wiþ cloudes, and wiþ þe eclipce. Riȝt so, bi þese þre
goostli vnderstonden is þe sunne of riȝtwisnesse derked fro þe
peple.

65 Bi þis nyȝt mai be vnderstonde derknesse of synne, of whiche
spekeþ / Seynt Poule (*Ro.*13.[12]): *Abiciamus opera tenebrarum,*   f. 1‹
et cetera. Þat is: 'Caste we awei' (he seiþ) 'þe werkis of
derknesse, and be we cloþid wiþ þe armuris of liȝt,' þat is, of
vertues. Þis nyȝt of synnes letteþ men, þat þei moun not take þe
70 liȝt of Cristus liȝf and of his lawe.

---

45 and] and as.   47 15.5] 5.

Þre mescheues makeþ þe wantyng of þe sunne and comynge
of ny3te. First, it makiþ þat men moun not knowe wel hire wei.
Þe secounde is þat it makeþ men worche vnperfite werk. Þe
þridde is þat it engendreþ a mannes sikenesse. Ri3t so, þese
75 same mescheues goostli han þei þat been in ny3t of dedli
synnes, and wanteþ þe sonne of Cristus li3fe and of his lawe.
First, þei moun not knowe wel þe wei to heuene wiþoute li3te
of þes sunne, for þer is non oþer wei to þe li3fe of heuene but bi
þe commaundementis of God, as Crist seiþ (*Mt.*19[17]): *Si vis*
80 *ad vitam ingredi, serva mandata.* 'Þat is: 3ef þou wolt entre into
li3fe, kepe þe commaundementis.' And Dauid seiþ: *Viam*
mandatorum tuorum cucurri. 'Þe weie of þi commandementis I
haue ironne.' And into þis weie mai no man come after þe
sunne is downe and ni3t is come, and þerfore alle suche been
85 led al ny3t wiþ gobelyn, and erreþ hider and þider, and faileþ
euere of þe ri3t weie til þe sunne bee risen a3en.

Summe beþ lad bi þe wey of synguler fastyngis; summe bi
multiplying of many preieres; summe bi heryng of many
messes; summe bi feyned religioun; summe bi lewide vowus of
90 hire feyned pilgrymagis; summe bi makynge of abbeies, and
summe of freris housis; summe bi collegis; and summe bi
chauntries; and bi many oþer weies wiþoute nombre, moo þan
my wytt wil suffice to reherce. And þus þei erren euer mo/re   f. 10ᵛ
and comen neuere to þe wey of truþe, for alle suche setteþ litel
95 or no3t bi alle þe commaundementis of God, but [wenen] þat in
her owne fyndyngis stondeþ alle perfeccion. And al þis makeþ
þe derkenesse of þe ny3te of here synnes, and wantynge of þe
sunne of Goddis lawe. But whanne þe sunne of ri3twisnesse
schal rise vp in hire soules a3en heere in þis world þoru grace,
100 or at þe last Dai of Dom whan þe sunne schal schyne wiþoute
lette and euery man see clerli his defautis, þanne schul þei
knowe verrili þat þei erriden al here li3fe.

Þe secounde mescheef þat is causid of þe derknesse of þe
ny3t is þat þerinne men moun not wirche perfite werk, as in li3t
105 of þe dai. So, in ny3t of synful liyf, men moun wirche not
merytorie deedis to encrecynge of hire blisse, as þey mai whan
þei stonden in þe dai of grace and beþ rulid by Goddis lawe.
And þerfore seiþ Seynt Poule: 'While dai is, wirche we,' þat is,
while we been in grace, and rulid by Goddis lawe, wirche we
110 goode werkis in kynde, for þanne þei encrecen oure blisse in
heuene. For 'ny3t comeþ' (he seiþ) 'whan [no] man may

78 (*mar: de via ad celum*, H3).
93 (*Foot of* f.10r: *de negocio perambulante in tenebris*, H3).   95 wenen] *om.*

wirche,' þat is, whan þe ny3t of synne comeþ, and ignoraunce
of Goddis lawe, þanne noo suche werkes profiten vs to
encrecyng of oure blisse.

115   But, naþeles, þou3 werkes doon in dedli synne profiteþ no3t
to encrecyng of blisse, 3eet þei profiten to þre þyngis. Oon is
þat þe wor`d´li goodes of suche men schul encrece þe more.
Anoþer is þat þei / schullen þe sunnere haue grace to arise ou3t   f. 11ʳ
of here synne. Anoþer is, if þei schul be dampned, hire peyne
120   schal be þe lesse. And þerfore it is good euere to wirche wel.

Þe þridde þat comeþ of þe wantyng of þe sunne and comyng
of þe ny3t is þat þe disese of a sike man is engreggid þe more.
For al þe while þat suche a man haþ þe conforte of þe sunne, it
is a greet releuyng to him of his disese; but whan þe sunne is
125   goo doun, and þe derknesse of ny3t is come, he is greetli
disconfortid, and his peyne is engreggid. Ri3t so, 3ef a man be
gostli sike in synne, al þe while þat he haþ li3t of þis goostli
sunne (þat is, clere cnowyng of Cristus liyf and his lawe), he is
3et myche confortid and releued of his sikenesse þoru hope þat
130   he haþ of mercy, whiche he fyndeþ ensamplid ofte tyme to
synful men in Cristus li3f and his lawe; but whan þe ny3t of
ignorance of Goddis lawe is come to any suche goostli sike
man, þanne he is greteli disconfortid for defaute of goode
ensamplis, and ful ofte engreggid to dispeir. But it semeþ to me
135   þat many men faren in goostli sikenessis as mani men doun in
bodili sikenesses. A sike man in bodi þat li3t in ni3t gretli
tormentid in his disese, and he desire gretli his helþe, he
herkeneþ and desireþ euer more after þe crowynge of þe cok
and, as tyme as he hereþ hym, he is gretli confortid, for þanne
140   he hopeþ þe dai be nyh. So a gostli sike man in dedli synne þat
desireþ gretli helþe of his soule, desireþ gretli after / crowyng   f. 1
of þe cok (þat is, after true prechynge of þe word of God) and,
whanne he heereþ þe prechour, he is gretli reioised for he
hopeþ þat grace be ni3.

145   And wel þe prechour mai be likned to þe cok; for ri3t as þe
cok is sente as a messanger tofore þe dai, so is þe true prechour
sente tofore Crist þat is sunne of ri3twisnesse and of grace, to
[c]rowe þe myri notes of þe word of God to conforte synful
mennes soules, for Crist sente his desciplis two and two tofore
150   his face in euery place þere he was for to come (*Lu.* 10.[1]). And
Malachie þe prophet seiþ: *Ecce, mitto angelum meum ante
faciem, et cetera* (*Mal.* [3.1]). Þat is: 'Loo! I sende myn angel
(or, my messenger) tofore þi face þat schal araie þi weie tofore

þe.' And Seynt Gregorius seiþ: *Officium preconis suscipit quis-*
155 *quis ad sacerdotium accedit, vt ante aduentum iudicis qui ter-*
ribiliter sequitur ipse scilicet clamando gradiatur. Þat is: 'Þe
charge of a crier he receyueþ, whosoeuere goþ to presthode, þat
he go cryinge þe comynge of þe iuge þat dredfulli sueþ.'

But þer been summe sike men þat been so enfebelid and
160 browt so lowe þoru wantynge of brayn wiþ her longe lyinge þat
her wit is al aweie; and suche takeþ non hede, neþer of þe coc
crowynge, ne of þe dai suynge, but is euer iangelyng and
talkynge of þyng þat is litel worþ. So men þat han leyen longe
in custom of synne wantoun brayn of discrecion to cnowe good
165 fro euele, for þat þat hem þynkeþ good for hem, ofte tyme it is
ful euele for hem, and þat / þat is good for hem, hem þynkeþ is   f. 12ʳ
ful euele. And suche takeþ non hede, neþer of true prechynge
of Goddis word, ne of grace þat sueþ after, for þei hauen no
desir after gostli helþe, but han myche leuere to heere oþer to
170 speke vanites, þat lite⟨l⟩ profiten, or nouȝt, þan prechyng of þe
word of God. And of suche spekeþ Dauid, þere he seiþ: *Noluit*
⟨*inte*⟩*lligere vt bene ageret.* 'He wolde not vnderstonde þat he
myȝte do wel.'

But ȝet þer been oþer þat ben in worse plite þat haten þe
175 crowyng of þe cok, as þeues whiche, whan þei heren þe cok
crowe, beþ aferd lest þe liȝt of dai schulde come sodeynli vpon
hem and þei be take[n] in here euele and knowen for suche as
þei been. Þese nyȝt þeues moun bee vnderstonde þoo þat Crist
seiþ in Jones gospel 'comeþ noȝt in bi dore, but stieþ vp by
180 anoþer wei': þat is, proude symonient prelatis, and curatis, and
prestis, þat al hire lyif, whiche is derke nyȝt, þoru synne and
ignorance of Goddis lawe, spoyleþ Goddes peple þoru her
priuei ypocrisie and her feyned lawes.

Alle suche haten þe crowyng of þe cok, if he crowe trueli and
185 in tyme (þat is, hateþ þe true prechynge of Goddes lawe, for
dred of comyng of liȝt of truþe), for þei wite wel, and it be
knowen, hire malice schal be maad open and þei knowen suche
as þei ben. And such, but if þei haue þe more special grace, ben
now demed, for Crist seiþ in Jones gospel: *Hoc est iudicium:*
190 *quia lux venit in mundum, et dilexerunt homines magis tenebras*
quam lucem; erant enim illorum mala opera (*Jo.*[3.19–20]). 'Þat
is þe doom: for liȝt came into þe world, and men louedon more
derknesses þan liȝt; for soþe, þe werkis of hem we/ren euele.   f. 12ᵛ
Euery man þat doþ euele hateþ liȝt, and comeþ noȝt to liȝt, þat
195 his werkis be not reproued.'

And þus alle suche þeues, for fere of knowyng of here liyf,
ben aboute as myche as þei mai to stoppe þe true cokkis

crowyng; but þou þe cokkis mouþes ben stoppid, [þe dai]
comeþ neuer þe lattere. So, þou such prechours ben stoppid for
200 a tyme, ʒet at þe last God wole haue his lawe knowen and þeues
taken wiþ þe feet.

Þe secounde þynge þat letteþ þe syʒt of þe sonne is cloudes;
for riʒt as cloudes in þe eire þat ben bitwene þe sonne and men
bineþe letteþ þat þe sonne mai not schyne vpon hem, so goostli
205 cloudes letten þe sonne of Cristus liyf, and his lawe mai not
schyne to his peple. But ʒe schullen vnderstonde þat þer ben
two maner of cloudes: oon is þat bereþ in him watir; anoþer þat
is clene wiþoute watir.

Bi þese first cloudes, I vnderstonde alle þoo þat han take to
210 þe office of presthode among þe peple. Of such spekeþ Ysa[ie],
þere he seiþ þus: *Qui sunt isti qui vt nubes volant?* 'Who beþ
þese þat flien as cloudes?' Þei moun wel be clepid cloudes, for
þe office þat cloudes han: þat is, þat þei bere watir in hem and,
whan tyme is, heelde it oute doun into þe erþe, to moiste wiþ
215 þe erþe where þoru þat it mai þe bettere brynge forþ his frute.
So schulde prestis bere in her herte þe watir of doct[ri]ne of
Hooli Writ and, bi hire discrecion, whan þei see þat it is nede,
preche it oute to þe peple and moiste hire erþely / hertes þoru   f. 13
grace of his blessid reyn, so þat þei moun springe in goode wille
220 and brynge forþ leeues of edificatorie wordes, and floures of
mylde and honeste conuersacion, and after frute of goode
werkes.

Of þis reyn of þe word of God, whyche scholde come oute of
goostli cloudes (þat is, of hooli prestis), spekeþ God bi Ysaie þe
225 prophet, þere he seiþ þus (*Ysa.*55.[10–11]): 'Riʒt as reyn and
snow comeþ doun fro þe eir, and þider turneþ not aʒen, but
watereþ þe erþe, and moisteþ hit, and makeþ to burione, and
ʒeueþ seed to þe so[we]r, and breed to þe eter, so schal my
word bee, þat schal goo oute of my mouþe.' And prestis
230 schulden be þe mouþ of God, for God seiþ by Jeremie þe
prophet (*Jere.*[15.19]): *Si separaueris preciosum a vili, quasi os
meum eris.* Þat is: 'ʒef þou departe precious þyng from vile, þou
schalt be as my mouþ.' But þese cloudes letteþ nouʒt þe siʒt of
þe sunne, but anon after þat þei haue ʒeue hire reyn þe sunne
235 bersteþ vp ful cleer, and ofte þei faren as men seen al dai: how
it reyneþ and schyneþ boþe atones.

But þer been oþer cloudes, as I seide, þat ben clene wiþoute
watir; and suche letten þe liʒt of þe sunne, for þei been lenger

---

198 þe dai] dai þe (*m. for r.*).   218 (*Foot of* f.12v. *catchword*: hertis).
228 sower] souer (*with defectively-formed* e).   231 15.19] 7.

endurynge, and euere semeþ to regne and regneþ noȝt. And
240 suche, for defaute þat þe sunne mai not come doun, gendreþ
corrupte eir, and so pestilence sueþ, as clerkis seyn. Bi þese, I
vnderstonde þoo prestis þat han take vpon hem þe office of a
crier of Goddis lawe, as Gregorius seiþ, and eþer kunne not
preche Goddis lawe, eþer ellis ben necligent and wolen not
245 preche. Þese it ben þat Jude þe apostle in his pisteel clepeþ
'cloudes wiþoute watir' and 'heruest trees wiþoute frute'. Þese
it ben also þat Salamon spekeþ of (*Prouer.*25.[14]): *Nubes et*
uentus, et pluuie non sequentes; | vir gloriosus, et promissa non   f. 13ᵛ
complens. Þat is: 'Cloude and wynd, and reynes noȝt folewyng;
250 a glorious man, and biheestus noȝt performyng.' So suche
prelatis and prestes ben most glorious men in hire astatis, and
al hire aparaile; but þei fulfullen noȝt or perfoorme noȝt here
biheestes. For in þe takyng or acceptynge of suche astates, þei
professiden to performe alle þoo þynges þat perteynen to þoo
255 astatis, to whiche most principalli longeþ to preche þe word of
God, and þis performe þei noȝt.

Suche cloudes gendren gostli pestilence and deþ of mannes
soule for ignorance or necligence of suche prechynge. Þe deuel
spredeþ aboute corupte eire of his temptacions of synnes and,
260 whanne men receyuen hem, þan bi processe þei gendren
togydere manie foule corupcions of lustus and likyngis þat þei
han to þoo synnes. And so, at þe last, of hem groweþ in mannes
herte a ful consente, whiche is a foule pestilence boche in þe
siȝt of God almyti, and þis is gret tokene of gostli deþ. But
265 whanne þe blake spottis ben borsten oute (of foule horribile
synnes, as pride, wraþ, and enuye, couetise, gloterie) into dede,
þanne a man mai haue ful knowyng þat suche a man is at þe
deþ. And, in suche pestilence, þe grete hete of þe ague þat þei
han smyteþ vp into her heed, and so it makeþ hem raue and
270 speke þanne as wode men.

So suche men han so gret luste in hire synne þat þe luste
smyteþ vp and ouercomeþ her resoun, þat is þe heed of her
soule, and so þanne speken þei as wode men, cursynge hem þat
letten hem of her purpoos, lyinge on hem, and bacbitynge, and
275 sweryng grete and horibile oþes. And þese ben wode men and
oute of her wytte, for and þei weren in hire wytte, and biþouȝte
hem what goodnesse God haþ don for hem, and in what perel
þei stonden, hem / were ful loþ to do so.   f. 14ʳ

---

249 folewyng] folewyng sueynge (*n.*).   271 men] men þat.

And þe ground and cause of al þis goostli pestilence þat I
280　haue schewid, ben þese cloudes wiþoute watir—þat is, prestis
wiþoute prechyng. But, allas! whi taken suche waterles cloudes
(þat is, doumbe prestis) non hede of þe scharpe sentencis of
Holi Scripture and hooli doctouris, þat so dredfulli speken aȝen
suche men? For Crist seiþ in þe gospel (*Mt*.25.[30]): *Inutilem*
285　*seruum proicite in tenebras exteriores, et cetera.* Þat is: 'Þe
vnprofitable seruant þroweþ into þe vttermer derknessis, þere
schal be wepyng and gnaastyng of teeþ.' Also, Crist likneþ his
prechoures to 'liȝt of þe world' and 'salt of þe erþe'
(*Mt*.5.[13–14]). Of þe liȝt, he seiþ: *Nemo accendit lucernam, et*
290　*ponit eam sub, et cetera.* Þat is: 'No man tendeþ a lanterne, and
putteþ it vnder a buschel; but on a candel stike, þat it schyne to
alle þat ben in þe house.' And of þe salt, Crist seiþ: *Si sal*
euanuerit, in quo salietur? Ad nihilum, et cetera. (*Mt*.5.[13]). Þat
is: 'Ȝef þe salt vanische awei, in whom shal he be salted? It is no
295　þyng ouer worþ, but þat it beo þrowen oute and defoulid of
men.' Also, Seynt Gregorius spekeþ scharpli, as it was seide in
þe laste Sundai bifore. And Crisostom seiþ: *Nisi sacerdotes*
manifestauerunt omnem veritatem in populos, dabunt rationem in
Dei Judicij. Þat is: 'But if prestis make opene alle truþe in þe
300　peple, þei schullen ȝeue acountee in þe Dai of Doom.' And
Aust[eyn] seiþ in *Prologo sermonum suorum* : *Pauci, inquit, sunt*
sacerdotes qui verbum Dei iuste predicant; sed multi sunt qui
dampnabiliter tacent, et cetera. Þat is: 'Fewe þer ben prestis þat
iustli prechen þe word of God, but manye þer ben þat
305　dampnabli holden hire pees: summe of vnkunnynge, þat re-
fusen to be tauȝte, and oþer of necligence, þat dispisen þe word
of God. But neþer þo ne þese moun be excusid of þe blame of
silence, seþþe þat neþer þoo schulden be sette in gouernance
þat kunne noȝt preche; neþer þese schulden be stille þat kunne
310　/ preche, þouȝ þei haue no gouernance.' Al þis seiþ Austeyn.　　f. 14

Þe þridde þyng þat letteþ þe schynynge of þe sunne is þe
eclipce. Ȝe schulleþ vnderstounde þat þe derknesse of þe eclipse
is of no defaute in þe sunne, as it semeþ in mennus siȝt; but, as
clerkys seyn, whan þe moone is direttli bitwixe þe erþe in
315　whiche we dwellen and þe sunne, þanne is causid þe eclipse.
Riȝt soo, whan men of holi cherche (þat is, prelatus and
prestus, whiche principalli schulden take liȝt of kunnynge of þe
sunne of Cristis lawe, as þe moone of þe sunne) beþ direttli
bitwixe it and þe comen peple, wiþ al hire power stoppynge
320　and hidynge fro hem þe verrei knowyng þerof, þan is causid a
greet goostli eclipse of þe sunne of Cristus liȝf and his lawe in
cristen mennes soules.

For manie of hem seyn þat it is noȝt lefful lewide men to
knowe þe blesside lawe of þe gospel of oure Lord Jesus Crist,
325 but oneli prestus and clerkus, but it sufficeþ too hem to kunne
her *Pater Noster*, and to bileeue wel. And þus, wiþ þis fals
opynyon, þei stoppen þe liȝt of Cristus lawe þat it may not
schyne in þe soules of þe comune peple and so, for defaute of
knowyng þerof, þei ben in manie derknesses of synnes.

330   But alas! ȝet many of hem fallen in grettere defaute, for þei
diffa⟨men⟩ þe sunne, and seyn þat þe derknesse of þ`is´ eclipse
is in þe defaute of þe sunne (þat is, of Goddis lawe), and not in
hire defaute. For þei seyn þat Goddis lawe is fals, and þis is þe
foulest eclipse þat myȝte be put on þis sunne, for a fouler
335 blasfemye myȝte no man putte to God þan þis, to seye þat he is
fals. For ȝif Goddes word be fals, God mut nede be fals þat seiþ
it; / [and if God]des lawe, as þei seyn, be fals, þanne haue þei   f. 15ʳ
professid hem for to kepe a fals lawe; and if þei kepen þis lawe,
as þei wolen presume and graunte, þenne kepen þei a fals lawe,
340 and þer mai no man kepe a fals lawe but ȝef he be fals himself.
And so, fro þe firste to þe laste, þei beþ false euerichon; and so,
ȝef men be wel auysid, þei schullen ȝeue no credence to her
wordes.

     And þus þis gostli eclipce þat I haue schewid is þe þridde
345 þyng þat causeþ derkenesse to þe peple of þe sunne of
riȝtwisnesse (þat is, of Crist and his lawe) whiche is þe firste
signe þat Crist seid in his gospel þat schal come tofore þe
Doom.

     Þe seconde signe þat Crist seid in þis gospel þat schal come
350 tofore Doom schal beo in þe mone. And þat schal beo whan þe
moone, as Joel seid, 'schal turne into blood.' Bi þis moone mai
be vnderstonde prelates, curatus, and alle þoo þat han taken þe
order of presthode. For, riȝt as þe Book of Genesis telleþ
(*Ge*.1.[16]) þat at þe makyng of þe world God ordeynede þe
355 more liȝt (þat is, þe sunne) to schyne to men bi dai, and a lasse
nyȝt liȝt to schyne to men bi niȝte, so it is gostli. Þis 'more liȝt'
is þe lomb, Jesus Crist, whiche, as þe Apoc[alips] seiþ, ȝyueþ
sufficient liȝt inowȝ to alle seyntes þat been in þe blisse of
heuene, whiche is euerlastyng daie, 'but þe cl⟨e⟩erte of God
360 liȝteneþ hem.' But here in þis world, whiche is as nyȝt in
compar/ison ⟨o⟩f þat blessid `day´, and also for temptacions of   f. 15ᵛ
wikked spiritus þat wandren in þis world as in nyȝte, and for
derknesse of ignoraunce and of synne whiche is among þe
peple, þe 'lesse liȝt' (þat is, þe moone, whiche ben prestus)

---

331 þis] þᴀᴇ (*int. is*).   337 and if God] (*n.*).   361 day] (*int.* H3?).

365 schulden take þe liȝt of liȝf, and of þe techyng of Crist, as þe
moone doþ of þe sunne, and schyne bi hire vertuus lyuynge
and hire techynge to hem þat sitten in derknesse, and in
schadeue of deþ (þat is, in dedli synne), to dresse hire feet (þat
is, hire affeccions) into þe weie of pees (þat is, into kepynges of
370 þe commaundementis of God), which leeden to euerlastyng
pees. And for þis office Crist clepeþ hem 'þe liȝt of þe world.'

But it schal þan fare bi þis goostli moone (þat is, prestis) as it
fareþ bi þe moone þat is a visibile planete. In þe bigynnyng,
whan þe moone is first changid, þe moone schyneþ a litel in þe
375 bigynnyng of þe nyȝt. And after, as þe moone wexeþ, hee
schyneþ more and more til he be at þe fulle, and þan he
schyneþ al 'þe' nyȝt. But a litel tofore þat þe moone schal
change aȝen, þe moone schineþ but a litel tofore þe dai. Riȝt so
fareþ it bi þis goostli moone: for anon after þe ascencion of oure
380 Lord Jesus Crist, whanne þe sunne of riȝtwisnesse wiþdraweþ
bodili out of þis world and goon to reste, þanne was þe moone
first changid, for þere newe presthode after Cristus order was
browȝt in.

Of þis changyng spekeþ Seynt Poule, þere he seiþ: *Translato*
385 *sacerdotio.* Þat is: 'Whan presthode was translatid or / chaun-   f. 16ʳ
gid.' Þanne, in þe bigynnynge of þis niȝt, þis presthode
schynede in fewe persones: þat was in þe xij apostelis, and a
fewe disciplis. But afterward, þis presthode encrecid in gret
noumbre. And þanne þe liȝt of her werkes, and of here
390 techynge and wilful suffryng, þerfore gret martirdoom, schynede longe tyme þoo into al þis world and so brouȝten manie
men out of derknesses of her synnes into þe liȝt of grace and
gode vertues, in so myche þat many wynter duryng togidere
þer was greet plente of popes, bischopis, and prestis martired
395 for here holi liȝf and here true prechynge.

But, as I seide, whan þe moone schal chaunge aȝen, it
schyneþ but a litel tofore þe dai. So tofore þe eende of þe
world, after whiche presthode schal be changed aȝen for it
schal be chaunged more briȝtere and perfitere foorme, þanne þe
400 presthode schal schyne but in a fewe chosen persones tofore þe
dai come—þat is, þe Dai of Doom, whiche schal bigynne þenne
and be euerlastyng in ioie to hem þat schullen be saued. And þe
cause whi þat it schal schyne þan so litel, þat is, in so fewe
persones, is þis: for þe moore part þanne of þe moone schal be
405 turned into blood. Þat is: þe more part of þe presthode þanne
schal be turned into synful liȝf, whiche is vnderstonde bi
'blood' in mani placis of Hooli Scripture. And to hem it schal
be pertinentli seid þe wordes þat God seiþ bi his / prophete   f. 16

([*Ysa*.1.15]): *Cum multiplicaueritis orationes vestras, non*
410 *exaudiam uos, quia manus uestre sanguine plene sunt.* Þat is:
'When ȝhe schullen multiplie / ȝoure preieres (as þey schulle   f. 17ʳ
doo ful miche in þat tyme), I schal not heere ȝou,' he seiþ, and
þe cause sueþ: 'for your hondes,' he seiþ, 'ben ful of blod,' þat
is, ȝoure werkes beþ ful of synne.
415   Principally þanne þe presthode schal be turned into þre
synnes: þat is, into pride, couetise, and symonie.
    Pride þanne schal be ful hiȝ in prelatis, for hir pride schal
passe alle temperalle lordes in alle þyngis þat longe[þ] to lordes
astaat, as in stronge castellis and ryalle maneris, proudeli
420 aparaylit wiþinne, in halles, chaumbres, and alle oþure houses
of office. Also, in proude araye of here owne personnes, boþe in
costlew cloþ and pelure, as fyn as emperoure, kyng, or quene.
Also, in gret multitude of fatte horses and proude, wiþ gai gult
sadeles and schynynge brideles, wiþ miche wast and proude
425 meynye, more niseli disgysid þanne any temperal lordes meynye, sittynge atte mete eche day schynyngeli, wiþ precious
vessel and rial cuppebord boþe of seluer and of gold, and her
meynye fallynge doun, as to a god, at euery drauȝte þat þey
schul drynke, and many oþure poyntes of pride schulle folowe
430 hem, whiche / were to longe to reherce here.   f. 17ᵛ
    Þe secunde synne (þat is, couetise) schal be ful plenteus in
prestes in þo dayes, for þanne schal þe prophecie of Jeremie be
fulfillid (*Jere*.[6.13]): *A minore ad maiorem omnes student auari-*
cie, [*et cetera*] 'Fro þe prophete to þe prest, alle þey doun gyle.'
435 Þanne þey schulle[n] studie and ȝeue al here bisinesse nyȝt and
day how þey may gedere manye temperal lordschepes into her
hondes and do litele good for hem, oþure to þe kyngis, oþure to
þe rewme. Þanne þei schullen drawe into kyngis seruices, as
into chauncerie, or into checker, or into kyngis houses, for to
440 gedere togedere gold and leye it vpon an heep to marchaunde
þerwhit aftur dignitees, or prelacies, or ben[e]fices of þe
cherche. And oþure lowere men also, in her degre, in þe same
manere.
    Whiche is þe þredde foul synne (þat is, symonie) þat schal be
445 plenteuous þanne in prestes, boþe in byinge and in sellynge þe
sacramentes of holy cherche, as ordres, weddynges, and confes-

---

409 *Ysa*.1.15] Jere.1
411 multiplie] H1 *stops here,* f.16v. *line* 3; H2 *starts at the top of* f.17r.
repeating the word multiplie).   418 longeþ] longet.
431 schal] þat schal.   433 *Jere*.] þat jere.   435 schullen] schullem.

sioun, and oþure sacrament[is] also, whiche ben forbodoun bi
þe Scripture and bi þe Popes lawe boþe. Þis is þe hiest synne
þat God hateþ, and princepalli in þe prestis. And þat semeþ
450 wel, for we reden neuere þat Crist euere tok so real veniaunce
heere in his meke manhede as he dede in figure of destruccion
of þis synne, wanne he made a scourge of cordis, and þreew out
of þe temple boþe / bieris and selleris of dowues, and seide 'It   f. 18ʳ
is writen: Myn hous schal be cleped an hous of preieres, and ȝe
455 han mad hit a denn of þeues'—for wanne so euere suche doinge
schal befalle, þanne schal þe cherche be a foul den of þ`e´ues.

And wanne prestes schul be cumbrid wiþ þese þre foule
synnes (þat is, wiþ pride, couetice, and symonie), þanne schal
þis gostli moone foule be turned into blod, whiche is a gret
460 signe þat þe Day of Doom is niȝh. Hereto acordeþ þe doctour
Crisostom in his Omelie þere he seyþ: 'Wanne derkenesse is in
þe valeyes, it is tokene þat it is `ny´ nyht; but wanne it is derk
on hillis, þan noo dowte it is fulli niȝt.' So, wanne þe com[un]e
peple, wheche ben valeies in regard of prestes, ben ful of
465 derknesse of synne, þanne it is tokene þat þe Doom is niȝh; but
wanne þe derknesse of synne haþ taken þe hilles (þat is, prestes,
whiche schulden ⟨be⟩ hie in lyif aboue þe com[un]e peple as
mounteyns ⟨abo⟩ue þe valleyis), þanne it is token of þe Day of
Doom ⟨is⟩ come to þe ȝates.

470 Þe þredde sygne þat Crist telle[þ] in his gospel þat `schal´
come tofore þe Doom schal be in þe sterres whiche, as Matheu
seiþ, 'schul falle þanne fro heuene.' Bi þese sterres moun be
vndurstonde þe comyn peple, whiche, bi here sad bileue and
here good lyuynge, schulde schine in stedefast keepinge of þe
475 comaundementis of God, in woom hangeþ al. 'Godes lauwe
schulde be þe fyrmament' (as Dauid seiþ: *Firmamentum est
Deus timentibus eum*; *et testamentum ipsius vt manifestetur illis*) /
in whiche alle criste[n] men schulden ben as stabelli festened as   f. 18
sterres in þe firmament. Þerfore seiþ Seint Paule: *Quis nos
480 separabit a caritate Christi? et cetera*. Þat is: 'Wo schal departe
vs fro þe charite of Crist?'—as who seiþ 'no þynge'. Þese sterres
(þat is, þe comyn peple) tofore þe Doom schullen falle fro þis
firmament (þat is, fro þe kepinge of Godes comaundementis),
for þanne sum of Goddes lawe schal be derkid fro hem for
485 defaute of prechinge of þe prestis. And þe prestis þat schulden
ȝeue hem ensaumple schul lyue so synfulli tofore hem þat þey

---

447 sacramentis] sacramentalis.   448 Popes] (*erased but still legible*) (*n*).
463 commune] ? (*The fourth minim is dotted*; *cf. also* 467 *where the fourth
and seventh minims are dotted*).   470 telleþ] tellet;   schal] (*int.*).

schulle not sette bi alle þe comaundementis of God, and so falle
awey fro þe kepinge of hem, holdinge it no synne syþþe here
lederes diden so bifore hem. And þanne þei may seie: *Justicie*
490 *lumen non luxit nobis* (*Sap.*5.[6]). Þat is: 'Þe liȝt of riȝtwisnesse
haþ non lyȝtened to vs.' And þanne þe loue þat þey schulden
haue to God and to her breþeren schal be ful cold, for Crist
seiþ: *Habundabit iniquitas, refrigescet caritas multorum*
(*Mt.*[24.12]). 'Wickednesse þanne schal be plenteuous ⟨and⟩
495 þe charite of manie schal wexe cold.' For in þat time men schul
ȝeue al her loue to fulfylle here owne synguler auantage and
lytil take hede of oþure mennes.

Of þis tyme spekeþ Seint Paule to Timoþe, his disciple ([2]
Thimo.[3.1–4]): *In nouissimis diebus instabunt tempora, et cetera.*
500 / Þat is: 'In þe laste dayes schul be perelous tymes: men   f. 19ʳ
schullen be louynge hemself, couetous, hiȝe, proude, blasfemes
(as grete swereris and men falsinge Goddes lawe, as it is seid
byfore), not obeiynge to her faderis and moderis, vnkynde,
wickide, wiþoute affeccioun, wiþoute pes, synful liueris,
505 vncontynent, vnmylde, wiþoute benygnite, froward, swellynge,
blynde, loueris of lustes more þan of God, hauynge þe spice of
petee but denyinge þe vertu. And þese,' seiþ Seint Paule, 'flee
þou.'

Þe fourþe signe þat schal come tofore þe Doom, as Crist
510 telleþ in þis gospel, schal be 'in erþes pressure of puttynge
doun of folkys for confusioun of þe soun of þe see, and of
flodes.'

Bi þe see mai skylfully be vndurstonde temperal lordes or
knyȝthode. For riȝt as þe see bereþ vp þe fisches, and in hit þey
515 swymmen hedur and þedur, and in hit þey beþ norisched and
han her refute, riȝt so, lordes and knyȝtis schulden bere vp þe
comyn peple þat no man dide hem wrongis, þat þei myȝtte frely
do her laboure, and ȝef ani man wrongwisly disesed hem þei
shulde eueremore haue her refute / of hem. And so þei   f. 19ᵛ
520 schulden cherische and norische goode men in here goode-
nesse, and chastise euele men for her wickednesse. And for þis
seiþ Seint Paule (*R.*[13.4]): *Non sine causa gladium portat.* 'Not
wiþoute cause þei bereþ þe swerd' but, as Seint Petre seiþ, *ad
vindictam malefactorum, laudem vero bonorum.* Þat is: 'to þe
525 veniaunce of euele doeres and preisinge of goode men.'

And riȝt as þe see bereþ vp schippes, so schulde also lordes
and knyȝtis bere vp hooly cherche, and stifly maynteyne trewe
techeres of þe gospel, and helpe to chastise false prechoures or

499 *tempora*] tempera.

errouris and eresie, and hem þat prechon in þat entent to
530 spoyle þe peple of her temperal godes.

Þe see also haþ hiȝe bankes on þe lond side for to keepe it in
his kyndeli cours þat God haþ set hit inne, but oþure wile þer
comen vnkyndeli flodes and bresteþ þe see bankes, and so gooþ
it vp into þe lond and dryncheþ þe contree, and whanne hit
535 bresteþ vp hit makeþ so gret a noyse þat men may here it a fer
cuntree þennes. Riȝt in þ[i]s manere fareþ it bi temporal lordes
and knyȝttis: þei han grete flodes of large londes and rentes, as
þe see bankes, wheche þei holden of God bi þis seruice and for
þis ende, to holde hem in þe cours and order for whiche God
540 ordeynde hem firste, as I seyde toforre. Of þese / ban[k]es   f. 20ᵛ
spekeþ Seint Lu[ke] in his gospel þere he telleþ how þat
knyȝttis comen to John Bapt[ist] and axiden of hym what
þei schulden doo, and he answerede and seide: *Neminem
percutiatis, neque calumpniam faciatis, sed contenti estote*
545 *stipendijs vestris.* Þat is to seie: 'Smyteþ no man tog[e]dere,
neþur makeþ any false chalenge, but holdeþ ȝou apayid wiþ
ȝoure sondes'—þat is, wiþ ȝoure londes and rentes wiþ whiche
God haþ sondi[d] ȝou wiþ hym for þis ende.

But oþure while þer comeþ vnkyndely flodes of foul lust and
550 desir þat suche men han to passe in aray here astat; eueri lord
biholdeþ oþur: how he is arayed, how he is horsid, how he is
manned, and so eueri man enuyeþ oþur. And, for to parforme
þis, her owne lyflodes wolen not suffice, and þerfore þei bersten
ouer and drynchen þe cuntree—þat is, þei pilen and opressen
555 here pore tenauntis and þe comyn peple, til þei haue not
wherewiþ for to liue, and so ben cause of here deþ. For
Salomon seiþ: 'He þat takeþ awei bred þat is geten wiþ swot is
as he þat scleiþ his neihebure.' Of suche wickede tyraunte
lordes seyþ Ysa[ie] ([57.20]): *Impij autem quasi mare feruens*
560 *quod quiescere non potest, et redundant fluctus eius in con-*
culcacionem. Þat is: 'Wickede men ben as þe feruent see þat mai
not reste in his herte til he be gretter þan his neihebure, whos
flodes turnen into defoulynge'—þat is, of þe comyn peple,
þorou here cursid / extorciouns. And þis brestynge vp of   f. 2
565 vnkyndeli flodes (þat is, þis wickede pride amonge lordes and
kny[ȝ]ttis, þat causeþ þis opressinge of þe pore peple) makeþ
now so gret a noyse and soun þat it is a gret clamour in al þis
rewme, in eueri schire þ⟨er⟩of, of þe extorcioneris þat dwellen

---

529 prechen] prechon.   536 þis] þ (*and suprascript* s).
540 bankes] banbes.   541 Luke] luc'.   545 togedere] to godere.
548 sondid] sondis.   559 57] 56.

þerinne, whiche beþ as tiraunt[e] kyngis, ouerledynge þe peple
570 as Pharao ladde þe childern of Israel. Or ellis þus þe tirauntrie
and wrongful ouerledynge on þe pore peple (þat ben þe
chelderen of Israel) of [þese] tirauntis is so gret and peineful to
bere þat þe noyse and þe cri of here preyeris is herd into þe
heres of God in heuene, as it was of þe cheldern of Israel for þe
575 wrongful oppressinge of Kyng Pharao in Egipte, as it telle[þ] in
þe ii and iij chapetur of *Exodi.*

Of þis see and of þese flodes mai wel be vndurstonde þat
Abacuch þe prophet seiþ in his chapetre: *Numquid in flumin-
ibus iratus es, Domine? et cetera.* 'Wheþer in floodes þou art
580 wroþ, Lord? Oþur in þe flodis is þy wood[n]esse? Or in þe see
is þin indignacion?'—as who seiþ 'ȝe'; for hard doom and
streyte veniance schal be to suche. For *Sap.* seiþ (vi chapitre
[6]): *Judicium durissimum hijs qui presunt.* Þat is: 'Hard doom
schal be to hem þat ben set in gouernaunce and miȝtti men
585 schullen miȝttily suffre tormentis.' ⟨And⟩ for þis cause, / as þe f. 21ʳ
gospel seiþ aftur, 'men schul wexe drye for dreede and
abidyng[e] þat schal come to al þe world'—þat is, men schullen
wexe drye in auarice from almesdede, abidinge for fere of such
tyrauntrie þat schal regne in al þe world, leste ȝif þei departede
590 here goodis awey and þis tirauntrie endure þei schulden not
haue wherewiþ to lyue.

Or ellis it may be vndurstonde þus: þat resenable ʼmenʼ
þanne, for drede of þese tokenes and abidinge hem whiche
schulle come to al þe world, schul þanne do make hem redy
595 aȝen þe comynge of þe Lord. And þanne 'þe vertues of heuene
schul be meued.' Þat is, aungelis schullen þanne, as þe glose
seiþ, be meued wiþ a kyndely horroure or hidownesse seyinge
þe dredful doom and gret veniaunce þat is ordeyned of God for
sinful men, þouȝ þei ben sikir hemself, riȝt as a man stoundinge
600 on þe sikir brynke and seynge oþur men vndur hym in þe see
beynge in poynte to perische haþ a kyndeli horroure.

And herfore þe glose allege[þ] for hym Job, þat seiþ: 'Þe
pelers of heuene schul quake togederis, and drede at þe
mouynge of hem.'

605 Or þus: bi 'heuenes' in Hooli Scripture ben vnderstounde
hooli mennes soules. For Salomon seiþ: *Anima iusti sedes est
sapientie.* 'Þe soule of a riȝtwis man is þe seete of wisdoom.' For
riȝt as God sittiþ realli in heuene in his trone, so þe wisdoom of

---

572 þese] þis.   575 telleþ] tellet.
580 woodnesse] woodmesse.   585 cause] (*Repeated at the top of* f.21r.).
592 men] (*mar.* H3).   602 allegeþ] alleget.

þe Fadir, þat is God þe Sone, sitteþ realli in iuste / mennes f. 21ᵛ
610 saules þorou grace. Þe vertues of þese heuenes ben hardi, and
miȝtti knyȝtes of God, þat ben true prechouris of his lawe,
seynge suche wrecchednesse of synnes regninge in alle astatis,
knowynge þerbi in her soules þat þe Doom is nyȝhur, schullen
þanne be meued to preche scharpli aȝens hem, and boldeli, wiþ
615 Baptist and Heli, reproue boþe grete and smale of here synful
lyf. For whiche þei schullen be pursued, and prisoned, and
summe þerfore lese here lyf.

And soone aftur þis tyme, as þe gospel seiþ, 'þei schullen see
þe Sone of Man comynge in a cloude wiþ gret power and
620 maieste'—þat is, oure Lord Jesus Crist. As he wente vp in a
cloude, so schal he come aȝen to þe dredful Doom, as þe
aungelis tolden þe apostlis at his assencion. And he schal come
wiþ 'grete powere' of legeounes of aungelis, as a lord comeþ
aȝens his enemies wiþ his ooste. And 'in maieste': þat is, in gret
625 bryȝtnesse, ful confortable to his frendes and his derlingis. Also
þanne he schal appere in his 'mageste' for, as Seint Paule seiþ
to þe Philipensis, 'eueri creature of heuene, erþe, and helle
schullen þanne bowe to his heestis'; and þanne, as Matheu seiþ,
'alle kynredes of erþe schullen weyle'—þat is, of alle manere of
630 sectis summe, for Crisostom seiþ vpon þis text (Om[elie 49])
þat Crist haþ kept his woundis in his bodi til þat day to þis
ende: in wytnesse of his passioun aȝens þe Jewes and alle þat
denyen þe Sone of God to be cru[ci]fied in bodi. And at þat
siȝte alle kynredes schullen weyle / —þat is, Jewes, heþen men, f. 22
635 false cristen men, heretikes, and so alle kynredes, and so
Crisostom telleþ þere þe cause whi.

Of þis dredful day spekeþ Sophonie þe prophete, þere he
seiþ: 'Þat dai schal be a dai of wraþþe, þe dai of tribulacion and
of anguische, þe dai of chalenge and of wrecchidenesse, þe dai
640 of derknesse and of myiste, þe dai of hye cloude and of
whirlewynd, þe dai of trumpe and of noise, vpon wardid citees
and hie corneris.'

Þis dai schal also be dredful in þre þingis: in þe apperynge of
þe iuge; in þe siȝte of hem þat schullen be aboute; and in
645 sentence of þe Doom.

For þe firste, þe iuge schal appere miȝtili, for 'in gret powere
and maieste,' as I seide tofore. Also, he schal appere iustli, for
he schal be iust þat day to alle men. For þat day riȝtwisnesse
schal appere and merci schal in parte be hid, for he schal deme
650 eueri man afftur he haþ deserued 'wiþoute acceptinge of

610 heuenes] heuenesse.   630 49] 56.

persones' boþe popes and kyngis, as þe knaues of þe kechene.
Herto acordeþ Scripture ([2] *Paralip*.19.[7]): *Apud Dominum
nostrum non est iniquitas, nec acceptio personarum.* Þat is: 'Anens
oure God is no wickedenesse, ne accepting[e] of persones.'
655 Also, he schal spare to no man, for þe Whise Man seiþ
(*Prouer*.6.[34]): *Zelus et furor viri non parcet in die vindicte.* Ne
he schal not be bowed for þe preieris of ani man, ne for no
ȝeftes preuente his doom, for þe Scripture seiþ: 'Gold and
siluer schal not profite in þat day.' Also, he schal appere oponli,
660 for Dauid seiþ: *Deus noster manifeste veniet.* Þat is: / 'Oure God   f. 22ᵛ
schal come openli.'
   Of þe siȝt of hem þat schal appere wiþ him in þat dai, and of
his dredful sentence, it is largili tretid in þe sermoun of Dede
Men þat biginneþ þus: *Memorare nouissima, et cetera.*
665 Riȝt as Crist wiþ þese dredful tokenes goinge tofore þe
Doom haþ ferid synful men þat lyuen in lystes and wolen not
rise out of here synne, so he conforteþ his derlingis þat
wiþstondeþ synne and lyuen here peinfulli bi þe wordes þat
suen, in hope of hasti deliueraunce and rewarde for here
670 trauayle, seyinge þus: 'Wanne þese þyngis bigynnen for to be
doon, biholdeþ, and lifteþ vp ȝoure hedes, for whi ȝoure
redempcion neiheþ niȝ.' Þat is, ȝe þat han lyued here in þis
world in tribulacions and desesis for my loue and for to
wiþstonde synne, whanne ȝe seon þese dredful tokenes biginne
675 to come, beþ not agast as sinful wrecches, but biholdeþ wiþ sad
bileeue and lifteþ vp ȝoure hertis in gostli ioye. For þanne is
ȝoure Lord faste bi, wheche boute ȝou wiþ his blod, þat schal
deliuere ȝou of al desesis, and fulli rewarde ȝou for ȝoure
trauayle.
680 And, for to sadde men more in þis hope, Crist `putteþ´ heere
a bodili ensaumple of conforte aftur wynteris stormes, in hope
of somur þat comeþ soone aftur: 'Biholdeþ,' he seiþ, 'þe figge
tree, and alle trees. Whanne þei brynge forþ frute of hemself, ȝe
knowen þat somer is niȝh.' For þe more certeynte of þis
685 biheeste, Crist / putteþ þis ensaumple principalli bi þe figge   f. 23ʳ
tree, as Crisostom seiþ, þat 'aftur þat oþur trees han boriouned
out, ofte it falleþ þat colde comeþ aftur, and letteþ þe somer,
and so þe tres harden aȝen; but þe figge tree, for he boriouneþ
aftur alle oþur trees, þerfore of hard, oþur ful selden, comeþ
690 coold aftur.'
   But for as men miȝten wene þat for þe grete persecucion þat
Crist spekeþ of in his chapetur biforre þat trewe cristen men

673 tribulacions] (*An otiose* i *above the* t).   680 putteþ] (*mar.* H3?).

schulde be destried and haue an ende longe tofore þe Dai of
Doom, Crist answereþ þerto be þe wordus þat suen, seiynge:
695 'For soþe I seie to ȝou, þis generacion schal not passe til alle
þynges ben doon.' Crisostom seiþ þat 'anentis men þer ben
mani generacion[s], but anentis God but two,' whiche han her
bigynnyngis in Caym and Abel.

Alle þoo þat haue be, and beþ, and schul be into þe Day of
700 Doom, pursueris of true cristen peple, ben of þe generacioun of
Caym; and alle þoo þat han `be´ pursued for þe loue of God,
and ben now, and schul be into þe Day of Doom, beþ of þe
generacioun of Abel. And, as Crisostom seiþ, neuer neiþer of
þese schul faile into þe ende. For, as Crist seiþ, þe cockel schal
705 growe amonge þe good whete, into þe dai of ripe.

And, for as miche as men schulden ȝeue ful credaunce to
þese wordes þat he haþ seid, þerfore he seiþ þat þe eyr and erþe
schullen / passe, but his wordes schullen not passe. He putteþ   f. 2
þe stabelte euerelastynge of his wordes aboue þe firmamente,
710 and þe erþe, whiche ben þyngis most durable semynge to oure
seyȝte. But þei schullen passe and be chaungid fro þe occupacion þat þei haue now into a betur kynde aftur þe Dai of
Doom; but Cristes wordes ben so stable þat þei schullen neuere
be chaunged in ani manere, *et cetera*.

3

THIRD SUNDAY
IN ADVENT

Cum audisset Johannes in vinculis opera Christi, et cetera
(*Mt.*11.[2–3]). 'Whanne John þat was in boundes hadde herd
þe werkes of Crist, he sente two of his disciples, and seide to
h[i]m: "Art þou he þat art to come, or ellis we biden anoþur?"'
5   For þe litteral witt of þis gospel, 3e schulleþ vndurstounde
firste þe cause whi þat Johun was in boundes of prisoun.
Mar[k] telleþ in his vj chapitre [17–18] þat 'Heroude sent and
hil⟨d⟩ Johun and boun hym in prison for Herodeas, þe wyif of
Philip his broþur, for he hadde wedded here. For John seid to
10 Heroude: "It is not lefful to þee to haue þe wyif of þy broþur".'
    Heere mai prestes lerne of þe glorius baptist of Crist and holi
martir scharpeli to repreue open synneris of her synnes, and
spare for no schame, maugre ne violence, þat men mai do to
hem in þis world, hauynge in mynde þe wordes of oure Lord
15 Jesus Crist, in þe gospel þere he seiþ þus: *Nolite timere eos, et*
cetera (*Mt.*[10.28]). Þat is: 'Dredeþ not hem þat, aftur þat þey
han sclawe þe body, þei han no more what þei moowe doo; but
dredeþ him / þat, aftur he haþ sclayne þe body, he haþ power to   f. 24ʳ
putte body and soule to helle.' And þis is a glorius cause to die
20 inne, for in þis Baptiste was mad martir.
    But whanne Baptist was in prisoun, for þis cause þat is seid
bifore, he was not bisi aboute hi⟨s o⟩wne perel of deþ, ne for
no drede of de⟨þ which⟩ he knew in spirite was ny3 comynge
⟨set he no⟩ wey aboute to make frendes to voide ⟨him þerfro⟩,
25 but he þou3te more and was more bisi aboute oþur mennes
helþe—þat is, his disciples. He desirede lyuynge to see ful feiþ
of his disciples and wiþoute ani doute to see hem fulli leeue in
Crist. Ri3t as a fadire dyinge, 3if he see his chyldren of goode
maneris and parfite in al wysdoom, sikerli dieþ, dredynge no

---

1 *Cum*] (*First line of text indented; small* c *written into the space; no rubrication*).
4 him] hem.   7 Mark] Marc'.
22–4 (*Badly rubbed*).

30 þynge afturward, so John wolde see his disciples parfite in
Crist, þat he myȝte þe more ioyefulli die.

Heere miȝtten alle men þat han ani gouernaunce of peple, as
lordes of tenauntis, faderes of childeres, householderis of here
maynee, but speciali gostly curatis of here peple, lerne at þis
35 glorius seynt to desire þat here sugetis weren fully enformed in
Godes lauwe ar þei die fro hem.

Here also moun þei be sorre aschamed þat han peple vndur
here gouernaunce, but moost prestis, of whoom mony men
schulde axe þe lawe of [God], þat oþur þei haue no kunnynge to
40 teche here peple, or ellis þouȝ þei haue kunnynge beþ necligent
þerof. And ȝif þei gon to oþur men, þat ben more kunnynge, or
ellis wollen gladly teche / þat kunnynge þat God haþ sente   f. 2
hem, þei wollen be wroþ, and blame hem, and pvnysche hem
þerfore. Alle suche moun be sore adrad of þe curs of God, þat
45 he ȝeueþ to hem in þe gospel þere he seiþ þus: *Ve vobis qui
tulistis clauem sciencie, et cetera* ([*Lu.*11.52]). Þat is: 'Woo to
ȝou, or cursid be ȝe, þat haue take þe keyes of kunnynge and ȝe
entreþ not; and þoo þat entreþ, ȝe han forbode.'

Þe cause whi John sente on his message two disciples raþur
50 þan moo or lasse is tretid, whoso lokeþ wel, in þe gospel of þe
fyrste Sunday of Aduent.

We schullen truli bileue þat John whom Crist comendide so
hiȝli, as þe gospel makeþ mynde aftur, was stidefast in his
bileue. But he couetede aboue al þyngis þat þe feiþ and þe loue
55 of Crist growed and wexede tofore he diede, for true men
coueiten more honour of God þan here owne, for ellis þei were
vnresonable. And þerfor caste John þis wey to þe honoure of
Crist, to sende þus his disciples on þis message to Crist,
seiynge: 'Art þou he þat art to come to saue mannes kynde, þat
60 þe lawe spekeþ of, or we abideþ anoþur?'

Þis wolde seme to many men a meruelous doynge of John þat
he þat was prophete and more þan prophete, as Crist witnessede of him (of whos also worþinesse and dignitee þe aungel
witnessede tofore his concepcion, whiche also gladede at his
65 Lordes comynge in his mo/deris wombe and made his moder a   f.
prophete, and aftur, wanne his Lord cam to be baptis[ide] of
hym, seide: 'I owe to be baptiside of þe, and þou comest to me
to be baptisid?' and seide forþermore of hym: 'Loo! þys is þe
lomb of God, þat dooþ awei þe synnes of þe world'), þat he

---

38 moost] (t *added at end of line*, H3?).   39 God] good (*n*.).
46 *Lu.*11.52] Mt.   66 baptiside] baptist.

70 schulde sende his disciples to him wiþ suche a doutful
question.

But þe doctoure Crisostom seiþ þat þerfore he axede þis
question bi his disciples: not for he wolde take answere aȝen of
Crist, but þat þe disciples þat weren send, þorou here gracius
75 comunicacioun wiþ Crist, schulden see wiþ here yȝen his
werkes and so bileue to his witnessynge of him þat he was
verrei Messie bihiȝte in þe lawe, to whom þei beleeuede noȝt
ȝet, but hilde her mayster more þan hym. Crist answerede, it
semeþ, noȝt directli to þis questioun; for he miȝte haue seide
80 ful trueli anon to here axynge: 'I it am, þat is come to sauacioun
of þe peple', but he answerede noȝte so, as þe gospel seiþ, but:
'Goþ and scheweþ aȝen to John þoo þynges þat ȝe han herd and
seien.' For, as miche as dedis prouen more spedili þan nakede
wordes wiþoute dede, þerforre Crist wolde þei were sped of
85 here axynge most spedili to here profite; for as Lu[ke] seiþ (vij
chapitre [21]): þat 'in þat houre þat in þe whyche þe messingeris comen for John he helide manye of here siknesses, and
woondes, and wickede spiritis; and to many blynde he ȝaf siȝt.'
And þus he dide in her siȝt meruelous werkis, whiche weren
90 prophesied of Messie longe tofore bi Ysaie þe prophet
(Ysa.35.), þat non oþur man dide but onli he, whiche / werkis f. 25ᵛ
schulden fulli stabulliche hem in bileeue of hym þat he was
Crist.

And for þis cause seide Crist to þe Jewes in þe gospel: Si mihi
95 non vultis credere, operibus credite. Þat is: 'Ȝyf ȝe wole not leue
to me, naþeles bileeueþ to þe werkes.' And also in anoþur place
he seiþ: Opera que ego facio ipsa testimonium perhibent de me .
Þat is: 'Þe werkes þat I doo beren wytnesse of me.' Neþur Crist
seide ȝet of his dedes: 'Gooþ and seieþ to John þat I make
100 blinde men see, and crokede men to goo' and so forþ [of] alle þe
seuene miraculus, but he seide in þe þridde persoun: 'blinde
men seen, crokede men goon' and so forþ `of´ alle, noȝt
wiþstondynge þat þei sawen wiþ here yȝen þat he dide þoo
deedes. But in þis doinge he tauȝte men þat schulden come
105 aftur, and specialli prestis, to flee pompe and boste of hire gode
dedis, and specialli of her gostli werkes, but stonde euere in
drede and arette hem al to God.

Crist dide alle þese bo[di]li miraculus and manie oþure, as þe
cours of þe gospel telleþ in diuerse places, to conforme wiþ his
10 doctrine of þe feiþ. And so diden þe postles and manie oþure

85 Luke] luc'.
108 bodili] boli (defectively-formed b; but cf. line 133).

hooli seintes in þe bigynnynge of þe cherche. Men miȝten axe
þanne here þis question: seþþe Crist bad his apostlis and
disciples, and in hem alle prestis, to preche his gospel to þe
peple and noȝt cese þerof (as Ysaie seiþ: *C [lam]a ne cesses*) into
115 þe Day of Doom, but euere be bisi (he seide) in þis werk as
principal parte of her office, whi þanne / conferme þei noȝt her   f. 26
wordes wiþ bodili miracles, as þei diden in þat tyme, seþþe þer
ben ȝet men hard of bileeue, as þei weren þoo?

Hereto men moun answere bi diuerse doctoures sentencis,
120 þat speken of þis matere.

First, Seynt Bede seiþ, rehersinge Gregorius in þe [29]
Omelie, in þis manere: *Signa, inquit, miraculorum, et cetera*:
'Signes or tokenes,' he seiþ 'of miracles in þe biginnynge of holi
chirche onli were necess⟨a⟩rie þat it, norsched wiþ miracles,
125 schulde wexe to þe feiþ, riȝt as we, wanne we sette ȝiynge trees,
so longe we helde to hem watur into þe time þat we see hem
wexe or þryue in þe erþe, but wanne þei haue ones fesned her
roote, þanne we cese forto water hem.'

And Seynt Austyn seiþ, in a book þat he made of þe Lordes
130 Wordes, in þe 18 sermoun: *Dominus aliquando fecit corporalia
mi[ra]cula, vt homines inuitaret ad fidem; et nunc maiores
sanitates operatur, propter quas non est dedignatus nunc exhibere
illas minores, et cetera.* Þat is: 'Þe Lord sumtime dide [bodili]
miracles, for to meue men to þe feiþ; and now he worche
135 grettere helþes, for þe whiche he degneþ not now to shewe
forþe þoo lasse. Riȝt as þe soule is better þan þe bodi, riȝt so þe
helþe of þe soule is better þan þe helþe of þe bodi. [N]ow þe
blynde fleysche openeþ noȝt his iȝen þorou miracle of þe Lord,
but þe blynde herte openeþ þe iȝen to þe word of [þe Lord].
140 Now riseþ not vp þe dedli careyne, but þe soule ariseþ þat lay
ded in þe quyke careyne. Now þe deef erys of þe / bodi ben   f. 2
noȝt opened, but how manye haue eris of [þe] herte closid
whiche, naþeles, bigynneþ ofte to wexe open þorouȝ percynge
of þe word of God, þat þei bileeue þat bileeued not, and lyue
145 wel þat euelle lyueden, and obeye þat obeyede not?'

Also, Ysid[or] seiþ in a book þat he made, *De Summo Bono,
libro primo, capitulo 26*: [*Nunc*] *in ecclesia plus est bene viuere,
quam signa facere, et cetera.* Þat is: 'Now in þe cherche it is

114 *Clama*] Cauta.   121 29] 32.
133 bodili] holi (*cf. line* 108).   137 Now] þow.
138 miracle] miralcle.   139 þe Lord] lord þe (*m. for r.*).
141 (*Foot of* f.26v: *De cessacione miraculorum corporalium*, H3).
147 *Nunc*] Nemo.

more to lyue wel, þan for to do miracles. Þat now þe cherche of
150 God doþ not miracles, wheche [it] dide vndir þe apostles for it
bihouede þe world to beleeue þorou3 miracles. But now þe
world þat bileeueþ bihoueþ to schyne þorou3 goode werkes.
Þanne wiþ outeward signes þe feiþ was strengþed; now beynge
in feiþ sechynge miracles, it secheþ veyneglorie þat it be
155 preisid.'

Seint Gregorius seiþ in a Omelie þat ri3t as in time of þe
apostles miracles confermede her prechynge, so now vertues lyf
of holi prestis schal conferme her prechynge.

And þus it semeþ, bi alle þese doctouris sentencis and manye
160 moo þat men mi3te alegge in þis matere 3yf time wolde suffice,
þat in þis time bodili miracles ben not necessarie, but vertuous
lyf of holi prestis and trewe prechynge of þe word of God, for
þei doon gostli miraculus, whiche ben more worþ þan worchynge of bodili miracles. And so þe word of God truely preched
165 doþ alle þese miracles gostly which ben rehersid here in þis
gospel þat Crist dide bodily here.

First, þe prechour, þorou3 vertu / of þe word `of´ God,   f. 27ʳ
makeþ blynde men for to see. A man haþ two gostli i3en as he
haþ two bodili i3en, bi whiche I vndurstonde at þis tyme:
170 resoun and vnderstoundynge. Þe firste i3e is blended bi
vnclannes and malice of synne, for þe malice of grete synnes
þat a man is inne stoppen and blenden his resoun for he wole
here no resoun þanne contrarie to his lust. And þe[r]forre seiþ
þe Wyse Man: *Malicia eorum excecau[i]t eos.* Þat is: 'Hure
175 malice haþ blended hem.' Þe toþur i3e (þat is, vnderstondynge)
is blended wiþ euele wylle, for an euele willed man wole not
vnderstonde no trueþe by þe whiche he schulde wirche wel.
And þerfor seiþ Dauid in þe Psauter: *Noluit intelligere vt bene*
ageret. Þat is: 'He wolde not vnderstonde þat he mi3te do wel.'
180 Þese two i3en ben so necessarie eche to oþure þat woos haþ þe
toon, he haþ þe toþur; and woos wanteþ þe toon, he wanteþ þe
toþer. For woos haþ resoun, he haþ vnderstondynge; and woos
haþ good vnderstondynge, he haþ reson.

Þe blyndenesse of þese two i3en ben helid bi vertu of þe
185 word of God. For þe ly3tenynge of þe firste i3e (þat is, resoun)
wheche is blynded bi malice of filþis of synne, Godes lauwe
seiþ: *Deponentes omnem immundiciam et habundantiam malicie,*
et cetera. Þat is: 'Doþ awey al vnclannesse and habundaunce of
malice; in myldenesse or tretablenesse takeþ þe word of God
190 whiche, 3yf it be sette in [3]oure hertis, may br[i]nge in resoun

187 *et*] diciam et.   190 3oure] houre;   bringe] brñge.

and so saue 3oure soules.' For þe ly3tnynge of þe secunde
blyndenesse (þat is, of euele wille) whiche blyndeþ þe i3e of
vnderstoundynge, Dauid seiþ in Goddes lawe: *Declaratio ser-*
monum / tuorum illuminat, et intellectum dat parvulis. Þat is: 'Þe   f. 27ᵛ
195 declarynge of þi wordes ly3teneþ, and 3eueþ vnderstoundynge
to meke men.'

Þe word of God trueli prechid makeþ also gostli croked oþur
halte men to goo. A man comuneli halteþ whanne his oo leg is
schortere þan his oþure. Bi þe feet of men ben vnderstounde
200 hire affeccions or here loue. Whanne a mannus affeccioun is
sette to miche to erþeli þynges and to litil vpon heuenli þyngis,
þanne suche a man halteþ; and þerfore Helye þe prophet,
seynge þe peple of Israel to miche settynge here loue vpon þe
erþeli ydole Baal and litel vpon God, seide to hem þus:
205 *Vsquequo claudicatis in duas partes?* Þat is: 'Howe longe halte 3e
into twey parties?' Þis gostli haltynge þe word of God heleþ,
þere he seiþ þus (*Hebr.*12.[13]): *Egressus directos facite pedibus*
vestris, vt non claudicans quis erret, magis autem sanetur. Þat is:
'Euene passis makeþ wiþ 3oure feet, þat not haltynge eny man
210 erre, but more þat he be helid.' Whiche ben þese ry3t pasis,
Seynt Paule sheweþ, seiynge þus: *Que sursum sunt querite, non*
que super terram. Þat is: 'Secheþ þoo þynges þat ben aboue and
þeron setteþ 3oure affeccion, and not on þoo þyngis þat ben
vpon þe erþe.'

215 Also, þe prechoure, þorou3 vertu of þe word of God, heliþ
gostli meselis. Doctours vnderstonden þe gostly meselrie is
herisie, and specialli herisie of symonie. For Seynt Ambros[e]
seiþ: *Qui non canonice sed symoniace ali/quem in sacrum ordinat*   f. 2?
ordinem, non officium sed lepram confert (*I'.'.q.1'*; *Si'*). Þat is: 'He
220 þat no3t lawfulli but bi symonye ordeyneþ eni man into holi
ordre, he 3eueþ hym not office but lepre.' Also, þe same
doctoure seiþ (*I'q.1'*): *Cum ordinaretur sicut Geesi propter*
pecuniam lepram incurrit, sicut pecunia male quesita corpus et
animam con[macul]at. Þat is: 'Ri3t as Geesi ran into a lepre for
225 moneie, so moneie euele geten defouleþ togeder bodi and
soule.'

Þis gostli lepre is helid wiþ þe word of God, þere it seiþ þus
(*Mt.*[10.8]): *Gratis accepistis, gratis date.* Þat is: 'Freli 3e haue
take, freli 3eueþ to oþere.'

---

217 Ambrose] Ambros'.
218 *aliquem* (ali *end of* f.27v; *repeated at start of* f.28r.).
219 Si'] siᵗᵒ.   220 þat] (*Followed by* ani *deleted*).
224 conmaculat] conculcat.   228 10.8] 18.

230   Heere may men touche, whoso wole dilate þe matere, of
symonient prestis and curatis þat fallen into þis gostli lepre
þorou doynge of þe seuene sacramentis for couetise of temperal
lucre.

Also, þe prechour, þorouȝ þe vertu of þe word of God,
235 makeþ deue men to here. Þe gostli ere of mannes soule is a bisi
tendynge of herte to þe word of God, of whiche spekeþ þe
Psalm [Maker] þere he seiþ: *Attendite, populle meus, legem
meam, et cetera.* Þat is: 'My peple, bisili takeþ entent to my
lawe, and boweþ ȝoure ere to þe wordes of my mouþ.' And of
240 þese double heeringe, boþe of bodi and of soule, spekeþ Crist
in þe gospel þer he seiþ þus: *Qui habet aures audiendi, audia[t].*
Þat is: 'He þat haþ eres of heringe, heere he.'

Þei beþ deef of þis heeringe gostli þat ben of froward wille to
heere þe word of God, and euere contrarius aȝens hit and aȝen
245 þe true precheres þerof, of whiche spekeþ / Seint Stephene in   f. 28ᵛ
þe Deedis of þe Apostelis, *Act.*7.[51] seiynge: 'ȝe of hard nolle
and vncircumcisid hertis and eris han alwey wiþstounde þe
Holi Gost.' Þis [is] a perelous deefnesse, for hire preier is
acursid, as þe Wyse Man seiþ (*Prouer.*): *Qui obturat aurem
250 (scilicet) ne audiat legem, oratio eius erit execrabilis.* Þat is: 'He
þat turneþ awey his [ere] þat he heere noȝt þe lawe, his preier is
cursid.' And heere may religious ypocritis and prestis be sore
aferd, þat ȝeuen hem so miche to multitud[es] of preieris
vndeuoutli momelid wiþ her mouþ, and haten communi-
255 cacioun of Goddes lawe and alle true prechoures þerof, leste
her preieris ben cursid and so stere God to more veniaunce, as
Seynt Gregorius seiþ, and harmen hem þat þei preien fore.

Also, a true prechoure, þorouȝ þe vertu of þe word of God,
reised deede men gostli to þe lyif of grace; for riȝt as þe soule is
260 þe lyif of bodi, so charite (þat is, God) is lyif of þe soule. And
so, whanne a man wanteþ charite and lyueþ in hate, [he] is deed
gostli, and þerfor seiþ Seynt John: *Qui non diligit, mane[t] in
morte.* Þat is: 'He þat loueþ noȝt, dwelleþ in deþ.' Suche a ded
man is reised fro deþ to lyif wanne he heereþ effectuelli þe
265 word of God þat seiþ þus: *Diliges Dominum Deum tuum ex toto
corde tuo, et ex tota anima tua, et ex tota mente tua, et ex omnibus
viribus tuis, et proximum tuum sicut teipsum.* Þat is: 'Þou schalt
loue þy Lord þy God of al þyn herte, of al þy soule, and wiþ al

---

249 *Prouer*] prouer.8 (*n.*).   253 multitudes] multitudo.
262 manet] maneþ.

þi mynde, and of alle þ⟨i⟩ / strengþis, and þy neihebure as f. 29ʳ
270 þyself.'

And of þis gostli reisinge spekeþ Seint John in his pistle,
seyinge þus: *Nos scimus quoniam translati sumus de morte ad
uitam, quoniam diligimus fratres.* Þat is: 'we knowen þat we ben
translated fro dee[þ] to lyif, for we louen breþeren.'

275 Þe sixte miracule þat Crist spak to Jones disciples is þat pore
men ben preised of þe gospel. Richesses in þe Olde Lawe
weren noȝt miche lacked, and pouerte noȝt miche preised. For
Abraham, Ysaac, and Jacob, and manie oþere patriarches
weren ful riche, and þerwiþ ful goode and true seruauntes to
280 God, to whom in þat tyme he bihiȝte a lond in wheche weren
manie richesses, wheche weren figures of þe sacramentis of þe
Newe Lawe þat makeþ vs riche in soule and ableþ vs to euere
lastynge richesses in heuene.

But now, syþe þe secunde persoun in Trinite ha[þ] lowed
285 him so miche to take oure pore kynde, and lyuede a pore lyif
heere al his lyif tyme, it is no wonder þouȝ pouerte be preised
of Crist in þe gospel, seyinge: 'Blessed be pore men'—as
Lu[ke] seiþ. But for pouerte of temporal goodes in hitself is no
vertu, but raþer mysese or mischef, but for it is a mene to a
290 blessed pouerte (þat is, pouerte in spirite), þerfore Matheu
seiþ: 'Blessed be pore men in spirite, for heren is þe kyngdom
of heuenes.' And Seint [James] seiþ: *Nonne pauperes elegit Deus
in hoc mundo?* Þat is: 'Wheþer God chees not pore men in þis
world?'—as who seiþ 'ȝes'.

295 Heere men may touche þ[at] seþþe to sue Crist in wylful
pouerte, / as his moder dide and his apostles, is moste and f. 29
hieste perfeccioun, houȝ it is þanne þat prelatis and prestis, þat
stonden heere in erþe in staat of his apostles and disciples, for
þe more partie lyuen so lustly in plente of worldeli rechesses? If
300 þei ˋwolenˊ vnderstonde þis pouerte oneli pouerte in spirite, me
þynkeþ þe best exposicioun o⟨r⟩ vnderstondynge of Cristes
wordes was þe ensaumple of his lyif.

Þe last of [þe] seuen was þat Crist seide: 'Blessid is he þat
schal not be sclaundred in me.' Þouȝ 'sclaundere' mow be take
305 for defamynge of a man anentis þe world, naþeles, more
pertinentli aftur þe vnderstoundynge of Crist 'sclaunder' may
be take for spiritual hurtynge, bi whiche a man hirteþ hymself
aȝen Crist bi synne. Aftur whiche vn[der]stoundynge of

---

269 (*Foot of* f.28v. *catchword:* strengþis).
274 deeþ] deet.   276 of þe] of þe of.   284 haþ] hat'.
288 Luke] luc'.   292 James] Poule.   295 þat] þe.

'sclaunder' þese wordes moun be vndurstounde ⟨þ⟩us: þouȝ it
310 be so þat I do grete miracles whiche no man may do but God,
as Nicodemus seide, naþeles, I schal suffere bodili deeþ as
anoþur [man]; but blessid is he þat seeþ me dye and bileeueþ
me noȝt oneli a pure man, but God and man togedere, noȝt
wiþstoundynge þat foule deeþ þat I suffere onli in my man-
315 hede. Riȝt so, gostli blessed is he þat schal not be sclaundred in
þe word of God. For summe men þat ben vnstable of beleeue,
noȝt wiþstoundynge þat þei see þe word of God þat is trueli
preched, do alle þese gostli miracles þat ben rehersid tofore, as
þe lyf of men conuerti⟨d⟩ proueþ openli, bi whiche, as
320 Crisostom seiþ (O[melie] 21), a man / mai knowe þe quyk word   f. 30ʳ
of God fro ded lesinge; naþeles, whanne þei see þis inpugned of
false worldly clerikes, to whos lyif Goddes word is aduersarie
and wiþ her feyned disputacions and false exposicions scleen it
in hemself and in oþere as miche as þei may, as þouȝ it were
325 gret herisie or elles but as anoþur pure seculer word, and
pursuen men þat speken it and holden þerwiþ, as Crisostom
seiþ in þe same Omelie, þanne suche vnstable men ben
disclaunderid in it and fallen awey þerfro, as Crist seiþ in þe
gospel.
330   But he þat fulli bileeueþ to þe true word of God and styfli
stondeþ þerbi to his lyues ende, noȝt wiþstoundynge alle suche
false defamynge and scharp persecusioun, he is blessed of God
heere in þis sentence.
   And, aftur þese miracules þat Crist hadde told to Jones
335 disciples, þei wenten aȝen fro Crist; and Crist in hire absence
preisede Johun to þe peple, and not in here presence, to teche
vs for to enchewe flaterynge tofore mennes face, or elles tofore
hir maynie, or hem þat þei suppose wolen telle hem þ⟨at⟩ þei
preisen.
340   Houȝ perelous þis synne of flaterynge is and whi it schulde
be enchewid þou mayst fynde more pleynli treted in þe xxiij
Sundaies gospel aftur þe Trinite.
   Cristus preisinge of John was þis: 'What wente [ȝe] into
deserte for to see? A rud wagged wiþ þe wynd?'—as who seiþ
345 'nay'. / Or: 'Wat wente [ȝe] into deserte for to see? A man   f. 30ᵛ
cloþed wiþynne softe cloþynge?'—as who seiþ 'nay'—'for loo!
þoo þat ben cloþed in softe cloþynge ben in kynges houses.'
Jones disciples and manye oþere weren in þis erroure: þat þei
supposiden þat John was more þan Jesus, for his wounderful

350 berþe and his holi lyif; but for men schulden not suppose þat
John were so vnstabele to synne in þis misbileeue so sodeynely,
seþþe he hadde preised him so hiȝli tofore, þerfor Crist
preisede hym to þe peple.

And first he affermeþ þe stablenesse of John, syþþe bi non of
355 foure affecciouns (þat `is´, joye and hope, drede and sorwe) he
was not meued as a rud to bowe wiþinne forþ fro þe truþe. Þe
secounde tyme Crist preiseþ þe sternesse of Jones penaunce,
whiche schewe[d] þe deuocioun of his loue, for he was not
cloþid in softe cloþes but in cloþynge of camelis heer, as Mar[k]
360 seiþ in þe firste [chapitre, 6]. And to suche penaunce he chees a
couenable place þat was deserte, and not houses of kynges, as
mynstralles wiþ her iapynge, and flater[is] wiþ her liynge, and
folled religius men wiþ her feynynge.

But Crist seide he was a prop[h]ete, for he hadde a cleer
365 knowynge of vnderstoundynge of Crist of woom he spak of.
And he was more þan a prophet, for he hadde more þan þis
anentis effectuel worchynge: for he saw wiþ his yȝe, and
schewide wiþ his fynger, and handelid wiþ / his hond, þat þat　f. 31ʳ
he propheciede of, whiche þat passeþ þe office of a prophete.

370 Also, Crist seiþ þat þe Fadire preisede Jon to him bi
Malachie þe prophet, seiynge: 'Loo! I sende my messynger,
ledynge an aungel lyif tofore þy face (þat is, tofore Crist,
whiche is þe schynynge of þe Fader and þe figure of his
substaunce aftur his manheede, whiche is þe face by whiche þe
375 word of God, þat is: Goddes sone, is knowen of vs), whiche
schal araie þe wey tofore þee.' Þat is, John araied þe wey
spiritual of Crist bi ensaumple of penaunce, prechynge, and of
baptem, et cetera.

Þis questioun þat Crist axide of þe peple ('Wat wenten ȝe
380 into deserte to se?') may now pertinentli be axid of alle men
dwellynge heere in þis world, meruelynge of þe wonderful syȝt
þat men may nowadayes see in þe deserte of þis world. Þis
world may wel be clepid a desert, for a desert is a place in
whiche ben fewe profitable frutes, and in whiche also ben fewe
385 men wandringe; but it is gladli ful of rauenous and venemous
beestes. Riȝt so, in þis world ben fewe profitable gostli frutes of
goode werkes, þerfore seiþ Osee þe prophet: Non est veritas,
non est misericordia, non est scientia Dei in terra. Þat is: 'Þer is

---

358 schewed] schewet.
360 chapitre 6] oº.
364 prophete] proplete.
385 rauenous] rauenōūs (and at line 401).

359 Mark] Marc'.
362 flateris] flaterynge.

no truþe, ne þer non merci, ne þer is no knowynge of God in
390 erþe.'
Also in þe desert of þis world beþ fewe men walkynge—þat
is, fewe ruli[d] bi resoun, as men schulde be aboue beestes.
And þerfore / seiþ Dauid: *Omnes declinauerunt, simul inutiles* f. 31ᵛ
facti sunt. Þat is: 'Alle han bowed awey (þat is, fro resoun), and
395 þei ben maad vnprofitable togedere.' For wanne man is not
rulid bi resoun, al þat he dooþ is vnprofitable and he is but a
fool. But þis world is ful of suche foolis, lyuynge aftur her
flesche a beestli lyi[f], of whiche spekeþ þe Wyse Man and seiþ:
Stultorum est numerus infinitus. Þat is: 'Þe noumber of foolis is
400 wiþoutte ende.' And noȝt onely þei lyuen þe lyif of tame
beestis, but of rauenous beestis þat þorouȝ false extorciouns
and w[ro]nges destryeþ her breþern as lyouns and wolues doon
scheep. And summe lyuen as venemous beestis, styngynge her
breþeren wiþ venemous chydynges, cursinges, bacbitynges,
405 lyinges, and sclaundringis.
In þis deserte, men moun see gret plente of reodes growynge
instide of trees þat schulden bere profitable frute. A rud haþ
þre condiciouns. First, it groweþ in moori or miri placis. So,
miche peple of þis world, þe more harm is, arn geten of her
410 eldres, noȝt in þe drede of God desiringe to haue vertues
cheldren to þe seruice of God, but in ful mirþ of lusti desir to
fulfulle her lust; and manye of hem in fornicacioun, auoutrie,
stup[r]e, and incest, and suche oþere orribule synnes, and
þerfore þei hauen of þe lasse grace to lyue in vertues, but
415 drawen aftur þe condicions and maners of hem þat engen-
driden hem. And of suche ben seide þe wordes of þe Wyse
Man, þat seien: *Spuria vitulamina non dabunt radices altas.* Þat
is: 'Bastarde si/ouns schullen not ȝeue depe rotes.'   f. 32ʳ
Þe seconde properte of þe rud is þis: þat wiþoute it is feire
420 and wiþinne voide. Riȝt so, þe more partie of þe peple now ben
fayre wiþoutte forþ anentis þe flesche, for þei be⟨þ⟩ norisched
now so tenderli and delicatli fro her birþe, al her ȝouþe, al oþur
wyse, þan weren her eldres tofore hem. And þat makeþ fayre in
face and in forme, whyche is but a veyn þyng, for it is a þyng
425 þat wol soone be lost and ofte tyme is cause to drawe men to þe
more synne. And þerforre seyþ þe Wyse Man: *Fallax gratia et
vana est pulchritudo.* Þat is: 'A deceyuynge grace and a veyn is
beute of bodi.'

---

392 rulid] rulit.   398 lyif] lyil.
402 wronges] wornges.   413 stupre] stupⁱe.
418 (*Foot of* f.31v: *De spurijs vitulaminibus,* H3).

Also, þey ben fayre to mennes siȝte anentis þe soule bi
430 ypocrisie, for more ypocrisie was þer neuere in þis world þan is
nowadayes, as in makynge of grete costi and curious cherches
and manye diuerse and rialle ournementis þerinne, wiþ gret
multitude of syngeris and gay chaunteris, in heerynge of manye
masses, and manie suche oþure signes of hoolinesse. But lasse
435 charite amonge breþeren was þer neuere þan is now, but eueri
man aboute wiþ al manere of soteltees to deceyue his broþer.
And þerfor it semeþ wel þat it neyheþ þe Day of Doom, for
now wyckednesse is ple[n]teous and charite wexeþ colde,
whiche is tokene of þe Doom.

440 I sei noȝt þat þese deedes þat I haue reherced heere tofore
ben reprouable in hemselue; but for to ȝeue entent al to suche
outward signes and leue charite, þat God loueþ / so miche and   f. 32ᵛ
wiþoute whiche no man may be saued, is but feyned ypocrisie
of þe fader of lesynges. Herto acordeþ þe doctoure Crisostom
445 (O[melie 45]), seynge of hem þat maken suche bildynges: ȝef
alle her oþure deedes acorden vertuousli herto, þanne it semeþ
þat her byldyngys ben maad to þe worschepe of God; and ȝyf
her oþure deedes ben vicious, and acorden noȝt herto, þanne it
semeþ þat her bildynges ben oneli maad to 'þe' syȝte of men.

450 And þus þe peple nowadayes is faire wiþoute, as I haue
schewed, as a rud, bi beute of bodi and ypocrisie [of] wordes;
and voyde wiþinne fro grace and vertues of soule.

Þe þrydde properte of a rud is þat at þe blast of a lytyl wynd
he is schaken to euery syde. So faren men of þis world: for as
455 miche as þei ben sette in so fals a grounde (þat is, in þe mirþe of
lustis of flesche and welþe of þe world, and noȝt in þe stoon,
Jesus Crist), þerfore at þe leste puf of þe fendes blast þei ben
dreuen lyȝtly into what synne þe feend lykeþ. And þus in
deserte of þis world, as I haue schewid, þer ben moo rudes
460 growynge þan fruteful trees.

Ȝet forþermore men moun axe: what wente he into deserte of
þis worlde for to see? Where men 'weren' doynge penaunce, as
þe place axeþ, and as Baptist dide and prechede, and Crist
tauȝte þe same, and in scharpe werynge of cloþus, and semple
465 mete and drynke? To þis question men may seye nay, as þe
dede proueþ. But what may men see? For soþe, men cloþid in
softe cloþes and al ȝouen / to ese for, as þei weren norisched in   f. 3

442 (*Foot of* f.32r: *De ypocrisi*, H3);   loueþ] (*Repeated at the start of* f.32v.).
445 45] 42.   451 of] *om.*
461 he] (*int:* y *above* e).   462 weren] (*mar.* H3).

her ȝouþe, so þei moosten contynue, and þerfore þei ȝeuen
`hem´ to þe kynges houses, oþur lordes; to craft, oþer to
470 religioun; to lyue eseli and ydel, wiþoute any trauayle. And
`not´ onli men desiren now to be softe cloþed, but costiousli,
proutli, and niseli, alwey newe contryued. And herwhyt þei
terren God to venyance aȝens his peple, as Dauid seiþ in þe
Psauter þer he seiþ þus: *Irritauerunt eum in ad[in]uentionibus*
475 *suis.* Þat is: 'Þei haue terrid him to wroþþe in her newe
fyndingis.'

Houȝ perelous is pride of cloþynge, and what harm comeþ
þerof, þou mayst see more plentili in þe fyrst Sunday aftur þe
Trinite.

480 But he þat schulde preche aȝens þese synnes and reproue
hem scharpli as Baptist dide in his tyme boþe kyng and
comunes, schulde be he þat is prophete and more þan a
prophete: þat schulde be prelatis and prestis, for suche is her
dyngnite. First, þei schulden be prophetis, schewynge þynges
485 to comynge, boþe of ioyes of heuenes and of þe peynes of helle;
and houȝ Crist schal come at þe Day of Doom and rewarde
men alle atones, summe to ioye and summe to peyne, aftur þei
haue deserued. Also, her astaat axeþ in sum maner to be more
þan prophetes, whanne þei ben at her masse, and handeleþ
490 bitwexe her handes þe sacrament of his bodi þat þei precheden
bifore; and whanne þei sey afturward, to þe same Lord: 'Þou
lomb of God, þou dooste away þe synnes of world, haue merci
on vs / and ȝeue vs þi pees.'   f. 33ᵛ

Of hem also schulde be verefied þe prophecie of Malachie,
495 þat was not oneli seid of John but `of´ alle goode prestis.

First, houȝ þei schulde be sente boþe of God and man is
schewid sumwhat bifore in þe firste Sunday of Aduente.

Þe secounde of þis prophecie seiþ þei schulden be aungelis.
Þre þynges þat longen to aungelis schulden longe to prestes: þei
500 ben spiritus, and her dwellynge is in heuene and, þow þei be
sent of God in any message, euere þei seen his face. Riȝt so,
preestis schulde be spiritual in her werkes, as þe principal sones
of God; not in pleynynge hem in seculer nedes and wor[ld]ely
ocupacions, but studyinge and prechynge and preyinge for þe
505 peple. And þerfore seiþ Seint Poule in oon of his pistles
(*R*.8.[14]): *Qui spiritu Dei aguntur, hij filij Dei sunt, [et]cetera.*
Þat is: 'Þat ben lad bi spirite of God, þei ben Goddes sones.'
And also he seiþ: *Nemo militans Deo implicat se negocijs*

---

493 vs] (*Repeated at the start of* f.33v.).
503 worldely] wordldely.

secularibus. Þat is: 'No man þat is Goddis kny3t schulde wynde
510 him in seculer nedes.'

And 3yf þei doon in þis manere, her conuersacion is in
heuenes and euere þei seen þe face of God bi verrey contemplacion, as Dauid seiþ: *Sicut oculi ancille in manibus domine
sue, ita oculi nostri ad Dominum Deum nostrum.* Þat is: 'Ri3t as
515 þe i3en of þe hanmayden ben euere on here lady, so beþ oure
i3en on oure Lord.'

Also, God seiþ bi þe prophete þat þei schulde be his aungelis
for difference of ypocritis, þat ben þe deueles aungeles, whiche
þat ben transfigured into aungelis of li3te. Also, / þei schulden   f. 34ʳ
520 be sente tofore þe face of Crist for to araie his goostly wey into
mannes soule þorou3 bisi prechynge, to leue her synnes and
keepe Goddes heestes, whiche is þe wey and non oþure by
whiche God comeþ to man.

Now God, for þe wey þat he cam to die for al mankynde,
525 3eue vs grace in þis wor-[ld] so to araye his wey þat he may
dwelle in oure soules and we wiþ hym for euere. Amen.

520 for to] forto (*Repeated at the start of the next line*).
525 world] wordl.

4

FOURTH SUNDAY
IN ADVENT

[*M*]*iserunt Judei ab Jerosolimis sacerdotes et leuitas, et cetera*
(*Jo*.1.[19]). Þis gospel telleþ aftur þe lettere a playn storie: how
þat Jewes senten fro Jerusalem prestes and dekenes to John, for
to axe of him what he was.

5   Jewes supposiden þat Crist was niȝli comen for þe fulfill-
ynge of þe prophecie of Jacob (*Gen*.49.[10]) and Daniel (þe
nynt chapetre [25–27]), and for þe miracles at Jones berþe, and
þe hoolinesse of his lyif, and for his opene prechynge and his
baptiȝinge. Also, þei weren in doute wheþer he were Crist þat
10 bigan suche newe þynges. But for þei wyste not þe soþe,
þerfore þei senten solempne messygeris (þat is, prestes and
dekenes þat bi wey of resoun schulde kunne mooste of þe lawe
and of þe prophecies) fro Jeresolem, where was þe mooste
principal studie of þe lawe and of þe prophecies, to wyte who
15 he was. But for as miche as Johun knew (by þe Hooli Goost) þe
opinion of þe peple, and wyste wel for t[o] take vpon him þe
staat and name of Crist was moost perelous synne, for hit
hadde be a gret pride and blasfeme in God, þerfore at þe
bigynnynge he putte awey þes estimacions and worschepe, and
20 knelechede þat he was not Crist.

Heere moun prelatis and preestes lerne at þis hooli prophete,
fro / þe hieste degree doun to þe lowest, þat ȝyf þe peple   f. 34ᵛ
suppose of hem þat þei haue bi her dignite eni power whiche
þei haue not, or more þan þei haue, or in oþure wyse in
25 baptiȝinge, or sacringe, or asoylynge of synnes, or in any oþer
sacrament whiche þat þei doon, þei schulden not take þis vpon
hem bi no similacion for enhauncynge of her pride and leue þe
peple in þis erroure, but voide it sone fro hem for fere of hyȝe
blasfemie. And so dide Seint Poule, as he telleþ in his pistel,

---

1 Miserunt] (*Text indented for two lines*; M *om*.).
16 for to] forte.

30 þat wanne þe peple of Corenthis weren brou3t in þis erroure
þat þei wende þat her baptem hadde vertu of her ministres,
þerfore summe seiden þei weren of Poule, and summe seiden
þei weren of Petre, and summe of Apollo, and so of oþure
disciples. Þere as Poule mi3te haue take þis worschepe vpon
35 him, he voidide hit, for he wolde not leue þe peple in erroure
and, for fe⟨r⟩e of blasphemie, to receyue ⟨d⟩yuyne worschepe
and lassene in ani þyng þe honoure þat longede to God aboue.

And for as miche as þe peple of Jewes hadde in her prophecie
(Malachie, þe laste chapetre) þat Helye schulde come, but þei
40 wyste neuere what tyme, ne how longe tofore þe Doom, and þei
herden þat he hadde denyed þat he was not Crist, and saw þat
here lyues acordiden in many þynges, as in deserte dwellynge,
and in semple foode, in scharpnesse of cloþynge, and reprou-
ynge of a kyng; for alle þese causis þei weren in doute where he
45 was Helye. Þei aske⟨d⟩en him þat question, and he seide nay.

Heere / it wol`de´ seme to many men þat John contrariede f. 35ʳ
Crist seþþe Crist, as þe gospel seiþ, seide þat he was Helye, and
þis seemeþ two contraries. But heere we musten vndurstonde
for þe declaringe of þis mater þat Crist and [þese] messyngeris
50 vnderstoden in diuerse maneres. Crist vn⟨d⟩erstood of John
þat he was Helye in figure, for in manie þinges þei weren like,
as it is seyd bifore, but specially for John was þe foregoer of
Cristis firste comynge, as Helye schal be tofore his comynge to
þe Doom. And þe messingeris vnderstooden þat `he´ was Helye
55 in persone þat was translatyd in a firi chare as Hooly Wryt
telleþ. And þus John seide þat he was no3t Helie in persone, as
messingeris vnderstooden; but he denied not þat he was Helye
in figure aftur Cristis menynge, and so Baptist was in no wey
contrarious to Crist.

60 John mi3te haue answered heere, 3yf þat he wolde, to þese
messingeris þat weren sente, þat he hadde be Helye aftur þe
vnderstondynge of Crist and not aftur her menynge, and so
deseyuede hem, for þei mente no3t so. But John wolde not do
þus, but answerde hem to her menynge, for Johnes answere
65 was a doctrine to vs þat comen aftur þat bi no sutel answere we
schulden not deceyue oure breþerne (þou3 þe wordes of oure
answere to oure menynge be true, and we knowe þat it is
contrarious to oure breþeren menynge), but answere hem to

49 þese] þis.
63 (*Dashes and flourishes in long space between* hem *and* for; *perhaps covering erasures?*).

her menynge as ferforþ / as we knowe or, ȝyf it be not f. 35ᵛ
70 prophetable, for t[o] holde oure pees.

And heere marchaundes in gret defaute wiþ her sutel wordes
to deceyue her breþeren in biynge and sellynge. For, ȝyf a man
chepe a ȝerde cloþ of a draper þat vseþ þe craft, he wole seie it
schal coste hym þus, and sette a gret price—as miche, perauen-
75 ture, as two ȝerdes ben worþ. Ȝyf þe bier seiþ it is to dere and
be looþ to bie so, þe draper seiþ it coste hym so and swereþ gret
oþe and meneþ bi al þe cloþ to deceyue þe biere. And þus, seli
semple bieris beþ ofte tyme deceyued bi suche sutel wordes
and her grete oþes.

80 Aȝenst þis synne, Poul spekeþ ful scharpli in his pistil (1 ad
Thess.4.[6]) þere he seiþ þus: Nemo supergrediatur, neque cir-
cumueniat in negocio fratrem suum, et cetera. Þat is: 'No man go
aboute, ne in marchaundie bigyle his broþer, for vpon alle þese
synnes God himselfe is venioure.' And Seint Austyn seiþ in a
85 bok þat he made (De Conflictu Viciorum et Virtutum 22.q.2):
Nec artificioso mendacio, nec symplici verbo, oportet quemquam
decipere; quia quomodolibet mentitur, quis occidit animam. Þat is:
'Neþer bi crafti lesynge, neþer bi semple word, it byhoueþ to
deceyue any man; for what manere wyse þat any man lyueþ, he
90 scleeþ his soule.

And whanne þe messingeris weren certefied of Johun of her
secounde doute (þat he was not Helye, to her vnderstondynge),
þanne for as miche as þei hadde in prophecie in þe Book of
Deutronomye þat a gret prophete of here seed schulde God
95 arere, þei douteden wheþer it were he, and axeden hym þis
questioun: wher he were a prophete? And he sei/de nay. Heere f. 36ʳ
it wolde seeme þat John made a gabbynge seþþe Crist, þat is
truþe, seide he was a prophete, for he wolde not be holde of þe
peple so gret as he was.

100 And vpon þis men myȝten axe a questioun: wher it were
lefful, for any mekenesse, for to make a lye? To þe firste doute,
men may answere and seie hardely þat John liede noȝt. For
Seint Austyn seiþ, and þe Maister of Stories reherceþ it, þat 'a
lesinge is a false significacion' of voice 'wiþ intencioun of
105 deceyuynge', and þis hadde not John in þe answerynge to þe
messingeris, for he was not þe gret prophet bihiȝt in þe lawe,
and þerfor he seide he was not a prophet (for þei menede soo),
and so he deceyuede hem not, for boþe hadde oon intencioun.

To 'þe' secounde doute, men may answere bi þe senten[ce] of
110 Seint Austyn in a book þat he made of þe Wordes of þe

70 for to] forte.   109 sentence] senten'.

Apostel. Þere he seiþ þus: *Cum humilitatis causa mentiris, si non eras peccator antequam mentireris, menciendo efficeris quod euitares, et cetera, et sequitur: quomodo est humilitas vbi regnat falsitas?* Þat is: 'Whanne þou lyest bicause of ani mekenesse, ʒif
115 þou were no synner bifore þat þou lyedest, þou art maad þat þat þou escheuedest' for, as þe same doctoure seiþ afturward, 'houʒ may þer be mekenesse where þat regneþ falsenesse?' Also, þe same doctoure seiþ, vpon John: *Non ita caueatur arrogancia, vt veritas reliquatur.* Þat is: 'Noʒt so be escheued
120 pride, þat truþe be lefte.'

Ʒet men miʒten axe forþermore in þis matere a que[s]tioun: wheþer / men miʒten wiþoute synne in any cause, lye? Summe f. 36ᵛ men seyn in þis matere þat þer is no lesinge forboden, but onely þoo þat harmen and prophiton to no man, and alle oþer
125 ben venial or ellis no manere of synne. And on þis part hangen alle prechouris þat prechon for wynnynge; pardeneris also, þat wiþ here false wordes deceyuyn þe peple; prestes also, þat syngen principalli for seluer; and chapmen þat, for wynnynge, wiþ lyes sellen her ware. For alle suche wynnyn more wiþ her
130 lyes þan wiþ her soþsawes, and it semeþ bi her dedis þat þe more part of þis world is of þis opinioun: þat lyinge is lytel synne.

Herto mai be answered bi Seint Austynes sentence in a book þat he made (*De Mendacio*), and also it is sette in Comune
135 Lawe of þe cherche, 22.q.2 *primum: Quisquis, inquit, esse aliquod genus mendacij quod peccatum non sit putauerit, decipiet seipsum turpiter.* Þat is: 'Whosoeuere,' he seiþ, 'supposeþ ani kynde of lesinge for to be no synne, he deceyueþ hymself foule.'

Also, þe same doctoure seiþ in anoþer book þat he made, þat
140 is *Enche[ridion]*, in þe [18] chapetre: *Michi autem videtur peccatum esse omne mendacium, et rationes assignat multiplicem, et cetera.* 'To me,' seyþ þis doctoure, 'it seemeþ alle lesinge to be synne'—and assigneþ manifold resoun. Þe first: 'for eueri lyere, eþer in dede oþer in word, d[e]nieþ þe feiþ, for he denieþ
145 þe truþe, and eche suche is a synnere, þan eche lyere is a synnere.' Also, he seiþ: 'Eche lyere misvsuþ þe signes of God, in as miche as alle signes ben ordeyned of / God for to schewe f. 3 þe truþe'—and þis resoun he scheweþ in *Enche[ridion]*, in þe 14 chapetre. 'Also, eche lyer wole explicite or inplicite deceyue his
150 nehebur; but eueri suche intencion is wyckede seþþe it is aʒens þe grete rule of God.' (*Mt.7.[12]*): *Omnia quecumque vultis vt*

faciant vobis homines, et facite illis. Þat is: 'Alle þyngis
whateuere ȝe wolen þat men do to ȝou, þese þyngis do ȝe to
hem.' Þanne eche lier haþ a wyckede intencioun.

155   Also, Seint Austyn seiþ (*primo De Doctrina Christiana,
capitulo* [36]): 'Manie men we han founde þat wylnen to lye;
but þat wylnen to be deceyued we han founde noon.' And,
seþþe it is better to be deceyued þan for to lye, it semeþ þat þer
schulde no man resonabli wilne for to lye in any caas. Þerfor
160 eche doublenesse of lyeris is synne.

And to þis Seint Austyn in a book þat he makeþ allegeþ
fyfefold Scripture. First, *Exod*.20.[16]: *Falsum testimonium non
dicas.* Þat is to seie: 'Þou schalt not seie fals wytnesse.'
'Whosoeuere,' he seiþ, 'scheweþ oute any þyngis, he bereþ
165 wytnesse to his soule.' Þe secounde is *Sap*.1.[11]: *Os quod
mentitur occidit animam.* Þat is: 'Þe mouþ þat lyeþ scleeþ þe
soule.' Þe þridde is in þe 5 *Psalmi* [7]: *Perdes omnes qui
loquuntur mendacium.* Þat is: 'Þou schalt lese alle þat speken
lesinge.' Þe fourþ is *Mt*.5.[37]: *Sit sermo vester: est, est; non,
170 non.* Þat is: 'Be ȝoure wordes: ȝey,ȝey; nay, nay.' Þe fyfþe is
Ephe.4.[25]: *Deponentes mendacium, loquimini veritatem.* Þat is:
'Dooþ awey lesinge, and spekeþ truþe.'

And þus, bi þese autoritees of Scripture þat ben heere
alegged, and of Seint Austyn in manie diuerse / places, and   f. 37^v
175 manie oþere hooli doctoures þat men miȝte alegge in þis matere
if tyme wolde suffice, it seemeþ þat in no caas men mai lye
wiþoute synne. Seþþe eueri lesinge is contrarie to truþe and
God is truþe, þan eueri lesinge is contrarie to God, and þat mut
nedes be synne.

180   And whane þese messingeris hadden answere of John to alle
her þre doutis, and for to go hoom aȝen wiþoute knowynge
what it were, þei weren sore aschamed to be holden suche
fooles. Þerfore þei axeden forþermore, as þe gospel telleþ:
'What art þou? þat we ȝeue answere to hem þat senten vs. What
185 seist þou of þyself?' And John answerede mekeli, and seide þus
to þe messingeris: 'I am a voice of a criere in deserte. Dresseþ
þe wey of þe Lord, as Ysaye þe prophet seide.'

Aftur þat John hadde denied þ⟨ri⟩es þat he was not, he
knolechide aftur þat þat he was. John miȝte haue seid truli 'I
190 am a criar in deserte' for his open prechenge, but he wolde not
so, but answerede in meker manere: 'I am but a voice,' he seiþ,
'of a criere.' Þe voice gooþ tofore and þe word comeþ aftur; but
a voice is a feble þyng and goþ awey wiþ þe wynt, but þe word

þat comeþ aftur dwelleþ in mennes hertes. So John wente
195 tofore and prechede Cristis comynge, þat aftur vanischede
awey bi kynde of flesche, as wynd doþ or schadue, as Joob seiþ
in his book (chapitre [14.2]): *Fugit velut vmbra, et numquam in
eodem statu permanet.* Þat is: 'Man flieþ as þe schadue, and in
oo staat he abideþ neuere longe.' /

200 And Crist com⟨e⟩ aftur, þat was þe word of þe Fadere, f. 38ʳ
wheche dwelleþ wiþoute ende boþe heere and in heuen. Þat
Crist was þe Faderis word, Seint John seiþ in his gospel (1
chapitre [1]): *In principio erat verbum, et verbum erat apud
[Deum], et Deus erat verbum.* Þat is: 'In þe gynnynge was þe
205 word, and þe word was anentis God, and God was þe word.'

In deserte also Seint Gregorius seiþ John schewede to þe
Jewes þat weren destitute and forsake, redempcioun general,
whoso wolde it take. Þat is, whoso wolde do as Ysaye baad:
make redi his wey bi penaunce in his soule tofore.

210 Þis answere ȝet sufficide not to þe messingeris þat weren
sente, for þei weren of þe Pharisees, as þe gospel seiþ, noȝt
wiþstoundynge þat he aleggede hem þe Scripture of þe
prophet. Þe Pharisees weren religious men of a secte bi
hemself, and weren holde ful hooli of comune peple. And
215 þerfore þei weren afert to lese þis worschipe bi ani newe
religioun þat schulde be brouȝt yn. And þerfore [þei] seiden to
John in þis manere: 'Seþþe þou art n⟨o⟩t Crist, ne Helye þe
grete prophete, wherto þanne baptiȝest þou and bryngest yn þis
rule?'

220 Riȝt so it fareþ nowadayes, whoso takeþ good heed. Þer ben
semple prestes þat prechen now Goddes lawe faste aboute,
þorouȝ grace of God, to plese hym w[iþ] and profite of his
peple, and to maken `him´ knowen among his peple þer he haþ
be longe hid þorouȝ necligence of curatis and worldeli
225 ocupacion. But now erchedekenes, and officiallis / and oþur f. 38
ministres, and þerwiþ begger prechouris (as Pharisees, diuidid
þorouȝ byddynge of oure bischopes þat rulen oure Jerusalem)
axen þis question of þese pore prestis:

'Seþþe þe Pope precheþ noȝt þat is Goddes viker, ne none
230 bischopes but selden, ne oþer grete prelatis for fere þei miȝte
lyȝ[t]ly brynge men into herisie, and oþer curatus moun lyue
ful wel þouȝ þei prechen noȝt, but þis office is oneli committid
to þe ordres of freris, whiche ben clerkis apreued and kunne

---

222 wiþ] whᵗ.
223 him] (*Added at the end of the line; i.e. immediately following* maken, H3).
225 (*Foot of* f.38r: *De obiectione facta simplicibus sacerdotibus*).

wel Goddes lawe, and bi her prechynge as foure postis beren
235 vp Cristis cherche, and ȝe ben neþer popes, ne bischopes, ne
oþure grete prelatis, ne curatus of cherches, ne of þe foure
ordres, but ydiotes and fooles þat vnneþe kunne ȝoure gramer
or þe litteral sense of Scripture, þat liȝtly makeþ men erre,
wharto preche ȝe þanne so faste and bigynnyn a newe manere
240 þat haþ not be vsed a long tyme but of þe hooli freres?'

Þouȝ þese pore prestis allegge hem Hooli Scripture of
diuerse prophetes of þe Olde Lawe, and Cristes own word in þe
gospel, and his hooly apostlis, and manie hooly auctoritees of
þe foure doctoures, how eche prest is bounde to þe office of
245 prechynge, þei leien to þe deef ere, and setten þerbi riȝt noȝt,
and seien þei wyten not what þei menen for þei vnderstounden
noȝt þe Scripture. But þe cheef cause herof is for þe drede þat
þei haue þat, ȝef þe truþe of Goddes lawe were knowen to þe
peple, þei schulden lacke miche of her worldely worschepe and
250 of her lucre boþe. And / alle feyned religious I sette ful lytyl bi. f. 39ʳ

Þe Pharisees hilden a gret presumpcioun of John þe bapt-
isinge þat he bigan, as þouȝ he wolde be a patron of a newe
ordre. But þei miȝten haue seie, bi þe meke answere of John,
þat John `was´ but a seruaunt of þe verrey patron, Crist, for
255 John seide: 'I baptise aloneli in watur, but oon stoundeþ in
middis of ȝou woom ȝe knowe noȝt, and þat is þe grete prophet
þat ȝe seche aftur, for he is boþe God and man to saue al
mankynde.' In þat þat he is God, he is eueriwhere middel, as
he is þe middel persone in þe Holy Trinite. And in þat þat he
260 is man and heed of hooly cherche, he is middel of alle men
gederid in his name. And in vertu of þis man þat was verrey
patron, John came as a seruaunt, to make redy byfore, as a rude
werk gooþ bifore a sutel. And so he baptisede only in watur,
and Crist in þe Hooly Goost. And for þis cause came John
265 bifore: to doo Crist al þis worschepe.

Heere schulden preestis lerne, ȝyf þei token goode heede, þat
of þe sacramentis þat þei doon þei ben not prinsepal doeres but
as instrumentis to worche in a werkmannes hond. God is þe
principal werkman, and Crist is his hond, and þe preest is þe
270 tool þat God worche wiþ. Or elles, þei worchen þe rude werk of
þe nakede sacrament, and God is þe sutel wercher þorouȝ þe
Hooly Goost. And þis oon þat stoundeþ in middes, bi his
manhede is 'he þat is to come aftur me, þat tofore me was /
maad.' Crist came aftur John bi his berþe into þis world, and f. 39ᵛ
275 also to prechynge, and `to´ baptem boþe; but he was maad

274 into þis] (*Repeated*).

tofore John (ȝea! bi his manhede) in grace and in worþinesse,
and alle manere vertues. And herfor seide John þat he was 'not
worþi for to vnbinde þe þonge þat was of Cristes scho.'

280 Þe foot of Jesus Crist is his godhede þat bereþ vp al þe world
as þe foot dooþ þe bodi. Þe scho is his manhede þat keuereþ his
godhede; for riȝt as a scho is of deed beestis skynnes, so he took
þis manhede of oure deedly kynde. Þe þonge of þes schoo is þe
kniȝttynge togedere of þe manhede to þe godhede in þat oo
persone. Þanne doctoures vnderstonden, bi þis formere texte,
285 þat John seide he was not worþi ne kunnynge ynow to dec[l]are
þe incarnacioun, þe we[che] is so hyȝ.

Here moun clerkes lerne at þis hooly prophete þat þorouȝ
vertu of þe Holy Goost hadde so hiȝ kunnynge and ȝet he
knowelechide in summe þyngis mekely his ignoraunce; so,
290 wanne ani meuynge of pride wole rise in her hertis of her hiȝ
clergie of science þat þei can, biþenkeþ hem on þe toþur side of
þe manie þyngis þat þei can not, and sone schal þat herte falle
adoun bi mekenesse—riȝt as two boketes þat goon in a welle:
wanne þe toon comeþ vp wiþ water, þe toþer goþ voide adoun.

295 Also, here may preestis be ful sore adrad to heere þese meke
wordes of þis hooly prophet, seþþe he (þat was halewed in his
moder woombe, and also was / prophete and more þan   f. 40ʳ
prophete, and amonge þe chylderne of wymmen þer roos noon
more þan he, as truþe bar wytnesse of hym in þe gospel) seide
300 he was not worþi to vnlase Cristis schoo, whiche is þe lowest
office þat ani man may doo; and þat þei presume not onely to
vnbynden his schoo, but stounden in his owne stede, and
specialli at þe auter, and handele wiþ her hondes þe blesside
sacrament of his bodi.

305 And moost þei moun be sore aferd þat comyn to þat order by
symonie of seluer, or for any euele entente to lyue in ese and in
lustis, and to gedere worldeli goodes and leue her duwe office
þat God haþ enioyned hem. Alas! what schul suche seie in þat
dredful day whane God schal seie vnto hem as þe gospel makeþ
310 mynde: *Reddite racionem villicationis tue.* Þat is: 'Ȝelde þou
acountees of þi grete bailie.'

And to hem þat haue lyued and endid as I haue seid bifore,
schal be seid þese dredful wordes þat Crist spekeþ of hymselue:
Invtilem seruum proicite in tenebras exteriores, vbi erit fletus et
315 *stridor dentium.* Þat is: 'Þe vnprofitable seruant þroweþ into þe
vttermere derkenesse, where schal be wepynge and gnastynge
of teþ.'

285 declare] dechare.   286 weche] wek.

Alle þese þynges þat þis gospel reherceþ heeretofore weren
doon in Betanie, biȝonde Jordan, where John was baptiȝynge.
320 Men musten conceyue þat þer ben two Betanies: oon biside
Jerusalem, where Lazar was rerid; and anoþer biȝonde Jordan,
/ where water was nyȝh to baptise, and alle þese þynges weren   f. 40ᵛ
doon in þat place. Bethanie haþ þre interpretacions, as clerkes
knowen wel: oon is 'hous of penaunce' and 'hous of hobediens'
325 and 'hous of þe ȝefte of God'. Jordan is as miche to seie as 'þe
ryuer of Doom'.

Now preye we þanne to God þat we moun be John þorouȝ
grace, for John is as miche to seie 'in woom is grace', þat we
moun dwelle in Bethanie heere in þis world (þat is, in
330 penaunce, as þis John dide), and be obedient al oure lyfe to
oure Lordis biddynge, and spende wel þe ȝeftis þat he haþ vs
lent, so þat we moun wynde þe liȝtlier þe grete ryuer of þis
Doom, and be seid to vs aftur of his blesside mouþ: *Euge, serue*
bone et fidelis, quia super pauca fuisti fidelis, super multa te
335 *constituam; intra in gaudium domini tui.* Þat is: 'Wel be to þe,
goodde seruant and true, for þou hast be true vpon fewe þingis;
entre into þe ioye of þy lord,' to whiche ioye God vs brynge,
þere to wone wiþoute endynge. Amen.

5
CHRISTMAS
DAY

[*E*]*xijt edictum a Cesare Augusto vt describeretur vniuersus orbis*
(*Luc.*2.[1]). Þis gospel telleþ aftur litteral wyt þe byrþe of oure
Lord Jesus Crist, and comprehendeþ principalli fyfe þynges:
first, þe tyme of his birþe; and secounde afturward, þe place of
5 his birþe; and þe þrydde, þe / manere of aray at his berþe; þe   f. 41ʳ
fourþe, to woom cam first typynge of his berþe; and þe fyfeþe,
of þe ioye þat was maad at his berþe.

    First, it makeþ mencioun of þe tyme of his berþe for, as
cronicalers sein, þat it was in þe two and fourti зer of Octouian,
10 þat was þe emperoure of Rome, whyche also was cleped August
Cesar, as þis gospel makeþ mencioun. First 'August', þat is:
echinge, for he echede in his tyme moost þe emperrie of Rome.
And 'Cesar' he was clepid, aftur Julius Cesar, a gret con-
queroure whiche was emperoure tofore hym. Þis Octouian,
15 what bi rial power, what bi gret wit, sugetide þe more part of
þe world in his tyme to hym, so þat þer was in þat tyme a gret
vniuersal pees in þe world to alle peple þat were suget to þe
emperrie of Rome.

    And in þis tyme Crist was boren. And þus Crist was boren in
20 tyme of gret pees, as Dauid seide bi hym tofore, seiynge in þis
manere: *Orietur in diebus eius iusticia et habundancia pacis*
(*P.*71.[7]). Þat is: 'In his dayes riзtwisnesse schal sprynge, and
plente of pees.' And resonable it was, and hiзly ordeyned of þe
wyt of God, þat þer schulde be gret pees in tyme of þe birþe of
25 'þe Prince of Pees', as Ysaye seide.

    Þis emperour, Octouian, wanne he saw þat myche peple was
suget to his emperrie, he comaundede alle rewmes to be
noumbrid, þat he miзte knowe þe quantite of peple in eueri
lond and how miche tribute eueri lond miзt зeue to þe emperrie
30 of Rome. And eueri persone schulde paye a maner / of moneye   f. 41

---

1 Exijt] (*Text indented for two lines; small e written into the space; no
rubrication*).   5 (*Foot of* f.40v. *catchword*: manere).

þat þei vseden, þis manere of noumbrynge moneye, whyche
conteynede in hit ten pens of suche moneye as þei vseden. Þis
maner of noumbrynge oþur discreyuynge of þe peple, as þe
gospel seiþ forþermor, was fyrst maad of þe gouernoure of þe
35 contree of Sirie, whos name was Sirine. Þis cunt[r]`e´e of Syrie
was niȝh þe middel, as þe nauele of þe world, and þerfor it was
bigunne þere, and also to ȝeue oþer reumes aboute ensaumple
þat þe prophecie of Dauid were fulfilled, seiynge: *Operatus*
salutem in medio terre. Þat is: 'He wrouȝte helþe in middel of þe
40 erþe.' And þus sumwhat bi þis processe it is schewid what tyme
Crist was boron.

But for to knowe forþermore þe secounde þynge þat þis
gospel spekeþ of (þat is, þe place of Cristis berþe), ȝe schulleþ
vnderstounde þat þe gospel seiþ afftur þat 'alle men ȝeden to
45 make her professioun, eueri man into his owne cytee'. Þe wylle
of þe emperoure was þis: þat euery man, whersoeuere he
dwelled, schulde drawe hym to þe contree of his birþe and, in
þe chyif citee of þat cuntree, he schulde make his profession or
his knowelechynge, paiynge þat money to him þat I seide of
50 bifore and so be writen into þe emperoures bookis, whiche was
cleped a 'discreyuynge'. And þus, as þe gospel seiþ in þe
bigynnynge, þis emperoure sente oute for to discreue þus al þe
world.

Joseph þanne, þat dwelled in þe cuntree of Galilee in a citee
55 þat was cleped Nazareth, wente vp into þe cuntree of Jude into
þe citee of Dauid whiche was / cleped Bethleem, for as miche as   f. 42ʳ
he was of þe lond and of meynie of Dauid (þat is, of his
kynrede) to make þere his profession or his knowelechynge wiþ
Marie, his weddide wyif þat was wiþ chylde. And it bifel þat,
60 wanne þei were þere, þe dayes weren fulfillid þat sche schulde
chyilde and sche brouȝte fourþ her firste bigeten sone. And al
þis processe was ordeyned tofore of þe priue doom of God to
þat entente þat, þouȝ Cristis moder and her housbonde dwel-
leden in Galilee, naþeles, bi þis enchesoun, þei schullen come
65 at þat tyme into Bethleem, þat Crist miȝte be bore as it was
prophecied of him tofore bi þe prophete (*Michie.*5.[2]), þer he
seiþ þus: *Et tu, Bethleem, terra Juda, nequaquam minima es in*
principibus Juda; ex te enim exiet dux regat populum meum
Israel. Þat is: 'And þou, Bethleem, in þe lond of Juda, art not
70 þou þe leeste among þe principal citees of Juda; of þee, forsoþe,
schal goo out a duke þat schal gouerne my peple Israel.'

35 cuntree] (*int.* e; *no caret mark*).

Heere men may lerne [of] Oure Lady, Seint Marie, and of
þat worþi persone, Joseph her housbounde, gret ensaumple of
mekenesse and of obediens to temperal lordes, and for to pay to
75 hem wylfulli tributes of oure worldli goodes, seþþe þei boþe
were come of kyngis kynde. For Oure Lady was nexte eyr bi
lyne to Kyng Dauid, and also sche was chosen to be Goddes
moder, and naþ`e´les þei weren obedient to þis emperoure and
mekeli wenten wiþ gret trauayle fer out of oo cuntre into
80 anoþur to paye / þis tribute.   f. 42ᵛ
And hymself also approuide þis obedience. First, in þat he
my3te haue lette his moder 3yf he hadde wolde to goo to paye
þis tribute, naþeles he sufferde his moder to do so. Also, in as
miche as he was Lord of al tyme and so þe tyme of his birþe
85 was in his owne disposicioun, and naþeles he chees to be born
in tyme of þis jornee. Also, Crist approuede þis obedience, for
afftur, whanne he was at mannes estaat and þis tribute was
axid, he payide hit wilfully for hym and for Petre. And þus, bi
þis deede and also bi his word, he tou3te þe peple to do þe same
90 wanne he seinge þe moneye whiche þei vseden to paye, and saw
þeronne þe emperoures ymage and his name, þanne he seide
þese wordes: *Reddite que sunt Cesaris Cesari.* Þat is: '3eldeþ to
þe emperour þoo þynges þat ben þe emperoures.'
And þus, bi ensaumple of Jesus Cristis dedes and also bi his
95 lawes, it seemeþ þat þer nys no man, neþer clerk, neþer seculer,
except from obedience to temperal lordes. Heereto acordeþ
Seint Paule, and seiþ þus: *Omnis anima potestatibus sublimioribus subdita sit (Ro.*13.[1]). Þat is: 'Euery soule' (and heere
is non except) 'be it suget to hiere poweris.' And in þis texte þe
100 soule is take for al þe man; and, for to schewe þat þe apostle
meneþ of temperal power as wel as of spiritual, / Seint Petre   f. 43
seiþ in his pistel: *Subiecti estote omni humane creature propter
Deum; siue regi quasi precellenti; siue ducibus ta[m]quam ab eo
missis* (1 *Pe.*2.[13–14]). Þat is: 'Be 3e suget to eche creature of
105 man for God; first to þe kyng, as he þat is most worþi; oþer ellis
to dukes, as [þ]ey þat ben send from hem.' And soone aftur, he
seiþ þese wordes: þat 'no3t oneli men schulden be suget to
goode and manerli lordes, but also to truauntis'—þat is, to
euele men, in as miche as þei comaunden lefful þyng. And þe
110 hooly doctoure Seint Ambrose seiþ in his sentence [þat] is
writen in þe Lawe, 11.*q.*I.*c.*[28]: *Magnum quidem est document-
um et speciale quo Christiani viri sublimioribus potestatibus
docentur debere esse subiecti, ne quis ter[r]eni regis constitutionem*

72 of] þat.   103 *tamquam*] tanquam.   106 þey] hey.

putet esse so[l]uendam. Si enim censum Filius Dei soluit, quis tu
115 *tantus es, qui non putas soluendum?* Þat is: 'A gret, forsoþe, and a
special techynge is by þe whyche cristen men ben tauȝte to be
suget to hiere poweres, þat no man schulde suppose þe
ordinaunce of an erþely kyng to be vnbounden or broken. Ȝef,
þanne, þe Sone of God payede tribute, who art þou so gret þat
120 supposest not to be payed?'
    Also, in þese wordes of þe laste texte of þe gospel þat is seid
bifore (þere it seiþ þat Joseph cam to Bethleem wiþ Marie, his
weddide wyif þat was so wiþ chyilde), men may haue autorite
aȝenst hem þat seiyn þat fleschli couplynge of man and
125 womman makeþ matrymonie, for a blessider matrimo/nie or   f. 43ᵛ
wedlok was þer neuere þan was þis, vnder whiche was born þat
blesside chyld þat was boþe God and man.
    Also, þe aungel þat was send fro þe Fader of heuene to
Joseph whane, after þat he wiste þat sche was [wiþ] chylde and
130 he wolde haue lefte her, he clepede Oure Lady hys wyif, and
ȝet þei hadden neuere couplid togedere, for sche was mayden
boþe tofore and aftur.
    Also, þe gospel hadde neuere clepid Marie and Joseph þe
parentes of Crist but if þer hadde be perfite matrimonie
135 bitwexe hem; neþer Oure Lady hadde clepid Joseph Cristis
fader to hymself but ȝif þer hadde be perfite matrimonie
bitwexe hem. Of þis þou mayst fynde in M[atheu], þe [1]
chapitre [18–25]. Þerfor þe Mayster of Sentence in his fourþe
book seiþ þat þis was a perfite wedlok, þere he seiþ þus:
140 *Perfectum igitur coniugium Marie et Joseph in sanctitate; per-*
fectum etiam fuit `secundum´ triplex bonum coniugij: fidem,
scilicet prolem et sacramentum, omne enim bonum nupciarum; vt
ait Augustinus: Impletum est in istis parentibus Christi fides,
proles, sacramentum. Prolem cognoscimus ipsum Dominum; fidem,
145 *quia nullum adulterium; sacramentum, quia nullum diuorcium. Et*
sequitur postea: Licet non intercessisset coniugalis concubitus,
coniuges tamen vere fuerunt. Þat is: 'Perfite was þe wedlok
bitwexe Marie and Joseph in holynesse; it was also perfiȝt after
þe þrefold good of matrimonie: þat is, feiþ, chyld, and sacra-
150 ment;' and, as Austyn seiþ, 'þer was fulfillid in þoo parentis of
Crist feiþ, chyld, and sacrament. Þe chyild we han known to be
þe Lord; feiþ, for þer was non avoutrie; sacrament, for þer was
no diuorce.' And after it sueþ / in þe same texte of Seint   f. 44ʳ

---

125 matrimonie] matrimo | monie.   129 wiþ] was.
137 1] 2.   141 *secundum*] (*mar.*).

Austyn: 'Þou3 þer was non fleschli couplinge bitwexe hem,
155 naþeles þei weren verrey housbonde and wyif,' *et cetera.*

And þus it is preued þat hooli wylles of man and womman,
faste knytted wiþ þe sacrament of matrimonie in þat entente to
dwelle togedere in maydenhood to her lyues ende, is perfite
matrimonie and pleseþ God as wel, oþer bettere, as þat þat is
160 ioyned in fleschly couplinge.

In þis texte also a man may see and lerne what worschepe
God haþ do to þe hooly order of matrim[o]nie, syþþe he wolde
not be born but vnder þis hooly ordere.

Also, a man may lerne in þese wordes þere þe tex[t]e seiþ þat
165 'þe dayes of Oure Lady weren fulfillid' þat God wolde þat sche
had þe fulle procese of tyme of berynge of her chyld in her
wombe after kynde and custum of oþur wemmen, for to schewe
þat þynge þat sche bar in here wombe was no þyng of fantasie,
but a verry child of þe kynde of man.

170 Þat þe text seiþ after þat 'sche brou3te forþ her firste
engendrid sone' schal not be vnderstounde þat aftur him of her
was engendrid oþer born ani oþer, but þus: þat he was þe first
engendrid, for he was born tofore whom, ne aftur whom, non
oþer, and mene no man to þe contrarie.

175 Þe gospel makeþ mynde of his moder and of his breþeren
whanne Crist stood and prechede to þe peple, and oon cam to
hym and seide: 'Loo! þy moder and þy breþeren stounden
þeroute, sechynge þee.' For heere his aunte sones weren clepid
his breþeren, for þe manere of Scripture is in manie places to
180 clepe cosyns breþeren; and in / þis manere weren Abraham and   f. 4
Loth callid breþeren, as þe firste book of Hooly Writ makeþ
mencioun (13 chapitre [8]). And þus, as ys bifore heere
schewid, is sumwhat declarid þe secounde þyng þat þis gospel
makeþ mencioun of: þat is, of þe place of Cristis berþe.

185 Þe þrydde, as I seide bifore, þat þis gospel makeþ mencioun
of is þe manere of aray at Cristis birþe. Wherefor 3e schullen
vnderstounde þat þe texte of þis gospel forþermore seiþ þat
whanne þis blesside chyld was born his moder 'wonde hym in
cloþes and leyde hym in a cracche, for þer was no place to hym
190 in þe hosterie.'

In þat þat þis texte seiþ (þat his moder woond hym in
cloþes), may men marke þat þis blessed chylde þat was þe Sone
of God took vpon hym, for oure loue, þe passions and
mescheues þat longen to oure kynde, as colde and hete, hunger

---

162 matrimonie] matrimanie.   193 for] for for.

195 and first, and suche oþere. And þerfor, for mescheef of colde of
his lymes, aftur þat kynde of þe tyme of þe ȝer axide, sche
woond hym in cloþes.

He was also þus leyd in cloþes in tokene þat whoso wole
heere in þis world vncloþe himself of þe olde man (as Seint
200 Paule seiþ: þat is, do awey olde custum of synne), and cloþe
hym wiþ þe newe man þat is formed aftur God (þat is, wiþ
newe vertues lyuynge), and also of his temperal goodes cloþe
his nakede breþeren, þanne þis blesside chyld wole cloþe alle
suche in þe blysse of heuene wiþ ouerpassynge clerete, / boþe f. 45ʳ
205 in bodi and soule. Of whyche spekeþ Dauid in þe Psauter
Book, þere he seiþ þus: *Amictus lumine sicut vestimento.* Þat is:
'Þei schullen be cloþed wiþ liȝt, as wiþ cloþynge.'

Þat þis blesside Ladi dide þis werk wiþ here owne hondes
and after leide hym in cracche, scheweþ wel þat sche chyldide
210 not wiþ sorwe and peyne, as oþer wemmen doon, but wiþ gret
ioye, wiþoute peyne, sche brouȝte forþ þis chyld. For riȝt as þe
sunne comeþ þorouȝ glas, ryȝt so þe Hooli Gost wrouȝte boþe
þe conceyuynge and þe birþe of þis blesside chylde, wiþoute
wem of bodi or any desese of þe worþi maydenes bodi, his
215 moder. And þis proueþ also wel þat her nedide at þat tyme no
midwyues, ne non helpe to þat birþe, as oþere wymmen neden.
And so þei dremen þat seien þat Anastase, wiþ [c]reuen
hoondes, was Oure Ladi midewyif, and at þat tyme sche was
helid of her hondes. And þis blynde euidence moueþ hem, it
220 seemeþ, þat on Cristemasse Day at þe secounde masse þe
cherche seiþ a memorie of here. But þis euidence is to lewede;
for many a ȝeer aftur Crist suffride passioun, Anastase, on þe
same day þat Crist was born, sche diede, and þerfore þe
cherche makeþ memorie of hire at þat tyme.

Þat þis blesside Ladi, aftur þis chyld was born and whoun-
den in cloþes, sche leyde hym in a cracche, þat was for
streytenesse of place for, as þe texte seiþ, 'þer was no place to
hym in þe hosterie.' For whanne þe peple drowȝ hem to
Bethleem for to be noumbrid and paye þe emperouris tribute, /
230 riche men weren preferrid and receyued into hosteries til þei f. 45ᵛ
weren fulle of peple. And Joseph and Marie, þouȝ þei weren of
hyȝe kyn, þey weren pore of worldli godes, and of suche
worldly men tooken but lytil heede. And þerfor, as doctouris
seyn, þei miȝten gete hem non oþere herboru but an hous
235 stoundynge in þe strete, keuerid aboue and opene on euery
syde, and seruede for þe citesens to stounde vnder and haue her

217 creuen] treuen (*n.*).

commitacions togedere in reynes and oþere scharp wederis.
And into þat hous þei wenten, and ladden wiþ hem an oxe and
an asse, as þe dottoure Lire seiþ, þe asse for þe blesside mayden
240 to riden on for to ese her for sche was grete wiþ chylde, and þe
oxe for to selle for to paye wiþ her tribute and her dispensis.

And in þe cracche, bitwixe þese beestes, þis blesside mayde
leyde her child whanne he was born. Heere men may see,
whoso biholdeþ wel, gret pouerte in þe aray at þis lordes birþe.
245 And boþe pore and riche moun lerne heere a lessoun. Þe pore
to be glad in her pouerte and bere mekely hire astaat, seynge
hire Lord and hire Makere wylfully to ȝeue hem suche
ensaumple. Þe riche also, to be adrad of misvsynge of her
richesse in lustis and lykyngis out of mesure, and lyttil or noȝt
250 to departe of hem to Cristis pore breþeren.

Wher weren þe grete castellis and hye toures, wiþ large halles
and longe chaumbres realli diȝt wiþ doseris, coste/ris, and   f. 46
costious beddes, and corteynes of gold and selk, able to þe birþ
of so hiȝ an emperoure? Where weren þoo rial ladies and worþi
255 gentel wymmen, to be entendaunt to þis worþi emperise, and
bere hire cumpenie at þat tyme? Wher weren þoo knyȝtis and
squieris to brynge seruice to þis Ladi, of noble metes, costeli
arayes, wiþ hoote spices and denteuous drynkes of diuerse
swete wynes?

260 In stude of þe real castel arayed wiþ riche cloþes, þei hadden
a stinkynge stable in þe hyȝe wey. In stide of real beddes and
corteynes, þe[i] hadden non oþer cloþes but suche as longede to
a pore carpenteris wyif in pilcrimage. In stide of cumpenie of
knyȝtis and ladies, þei hadden but pore Joseph, her hous-
265 bounde, and two doumbe beestes. Heere moun feynide ypoc-
rites be sore aschamed, þat seyn þat þei folewen Crist in
pouerte next of alle men heere in erþe, þat seyn þat Crist was
born in so pore a place and þei dwellen in so rial placis of
halles, chaumbris, panteries, boteries, kechenes, and stables,
270 and alle oþere housses of office real ynow for kyng, prince, or
duke to holde hire housholdes inne.

Þat þis blesside chylde was born in a hous open oon euery
side bitokeneþ þat God wole be closed fro no man þat wole
come to his merci, but is euere redi to alle men þat wolen clepe
275 to hym of mercy and of grace. Þerfore seyþ Dauid: *Prope est
Dominus, (id est) invocantibus eum, omnibus inuocantibus eum in
ver[itate], et cetera.* Þat is: þat he was born / in þe hyȝe wey   f.
bitokeneþ þat þer is non oþere wey to þe blysse of heuene, but

262 þei] þen.   277 *veritate*] verum.

only þe ensaumple of his lyif and his techynge. And þerfore he
280 seiþ: *Ego sum via, [veritas], et vita.* Þat is: 'I am wey, truþe, and
lyif.'

Also, he was born in þe wey to ȝeue vs ensaumple to haue
euere in mynde þat al our lyif we buþ heere but in exile and in
pilgrimage, hauynge heere no dwellynge citee, but abidynge þe
285 blysse of heuene for oure owne cuntree and kynde heritage.

Þat þis blessid chyld, aftur þat he was born, was leid in stide
of his cradel in a cracche among þe mete of þe beestes,
bitokeneþ not onely þat he came to saue hiȝe wyttede men and
grete clerkis, but also semple, bustis, beestliche men, ȝef þei
290 wolden loue hym aftur kunnynge, and keepe his heestis. And
þerfore seiþ Dauid in þis wyse: *Homines et iumenta saluabis,
Domine.* Þat is: 'Men and beestes þou schalt saue, Lord.'

And þus, whoso takeþ goode heede of þis þat is seid bifore,
he may see sumwhat þe maner of aray at Cristis birþe, whiche
295 is þe þrydde þyng þat þis gospel spekeþ of.

Þe fourþe þyng þat þis gospel spekeþ of is to wham come first
typynges of þis birþe. Ȝe schullen vnderstounde þat God sente
noȝt his messengeris to schewe þis blesside birþe to þe grete
emperour of Rome, which was þe grettest temperal lord of þis /
300 world, neþer to Kyng Heroudes, þat was kyng of Galilee, in   f. 47ʳ
whiche cuntree dwellede Oure Ladi, þe moder of þis blesside
chyld, and in whiche he was also conceyued, neþer to `þe´ hyȝe
bischop of Jerusalem, þat was in þoo dayes hiest in spiritual
dignitee, but as þe gospel seyþ:
305 'Þer weren scheperdes in þat same cuntree, wakynge and
kepynge þe wacches of þe niȝt vpon her flok. And loo! þe
aungel of þe Lord stood bisides hem, and þe cleernesse of God
schynede hem aboute, and þey dradden wiþ gret drede. And þe
aungel seyde to hem: "Dredeþ ȝe noȝt. Loo! I preche to ȝou a
310 gret ioye, þat schal be to al þe peple. For þis day is born to vs a
Saueour, whiche is Crist, Lord, in þe citee of Dauid. And þis
schal do to ȝou a tokene: ȝe schul fynde a chyld wounden in
cloþes, and putte in þe cracche".'

Heere it semeþ openly bi þis text þat God sente first message
15 and ioyful typynges of his Sonus birþe to semple, pore
sch[e]perdes, to schewe þat he was not born in to þis world to
regne on mennus bi worldely excellence and temperal power,
but in pore estaat and semple to lede his lyif, and so to regne
þorouȝ grace vertuously in mennes soules. And þerfore he
20 schewede first his birþe to pore men of semple craft.

Þe tokene also þat þe aungel ȝaf to þe scheperdes to knowe bi
þis chyld proueþ þe same, for it was not a tokene of gret
excellence and dignite, but a tokene of greet semplenesse and
pouertee, whanne / he seyde: 'ȝe schul fynde a chyld wounden f. 4ᵛ
325 in cloþes, and putt in a cracche.' He seide þis also to schewe þat
he is not acceptor of persones, but þat acceptable may be a pore
scheperde, eþer anoþer poore man of any lefful craft eþer
ocupacioun, ȝef he loue God and keepe his heestes, as þe hieste
man of degree in þis world, temperal eþer spiritual.

330 And so no riche man schulde despice ani pore man for his
pouertee, eþer for his semple craft, ȝef he be vertueus in his
lyuynge, ȝef þei biholde wel houȝ he chees raþer poore men to
his knowlechynge þan riche. And þerfore seiþ Seint [James]:
Nonne pauperes elegit, et cetera. 'Wheþer God chees not pore
335 men in þis world?' Also to þat: þat God ofte tymes scheweþ his
priuetees of Scripture to semple men and of esi lettere whiche
beþ meke, and hideþ it fro grete clerkis and hiȝe litterid men
þat beþ proude of her kunnynge. Þerforre Crist seiþ to his
Fader, as þe gospel makeþ mynde: *Confiteor tibi, Pater celi et*
340 *terre, et cetera.* Þat is: 'I knowleche to þe, Fadir of heuene and
of erþe, þat þou hast hid þese þynges fro wyse and prudent
men, and þou hast maad hem open to meke men.'

But to what maner of scheperdes aperide þis blesside messenger wiþ þese ioyeful tyþynges? Not to necligent and slewful
345 scheperde[s] lyinge in her beddes, and suffrynge þeues to stele
her schep, eþer wilde beestes to deuoure / hem, oþer elles to f.
breke ouer þe folde and renne into mennes corn; but to diligent
and wakynge scheperdes þat kepten þe wacche of þe niȝt vpon
her flokkes from alle þese forseide mescheues, in tokene þat
350 God ministreþ þe lyȝt of sad bileue and true knowynge of his
blesside Sone (ȝea! boþe of his lyif and of his lawe) to hem þat
beþ diligent and wel ocupeed in her degree, weþer it be
spiritual eþer temperal, and specialli to hem þat beþ wakeris in
keepinge of her cure whiche þei han vpon Cristis scheep. Also,
355 wheþer it be temperal oþer spiritual, and not to sleuful, hurid
hynes, þat beþ recheles and takeþ non heede of Cristes scheep,
but onely of muk, and wolle, and oþer temperal lucre þat
comeþ of hem.

Þat þis aungel þat brouȝt þis message aperide so gloriously
360 wiþ lyȝt, bitokeneþ þat he was come to schewe þe day of grace
aftur þe niȝt of veniaunce, for þe sunne of riȝtwisnesse was
sprongen vp. And þerfore seiþ Ysaie þe prophet: *Habitantibus*

---

333 James] Paule.

in regione v[m]bre mortis, lux orta est eis, et cetera. Þat is: 'Lyȝt
is sprongen to men dwellynge in þe regioun of schadewe of
365 deeþ.' And for þis cause, þouȝ it were þat tyme about midniȝt,
þe aungel clepede it day wanne he seide 'þis day is born to vs a
Saueoure.'

Þat þe aungel cam wiþ lyȝt may also bitokene þat wanne
prestes (þat beþ þe aungelis of God, as Malache þe prophet
370 seiþ) bryngeþ confortable messages to þe peple of truwe
doctrine of Goddes lawe, þei schulde apere / wiþ lyȝt of goode   f. 48ᵛ
werkes, of whiche Crist spekeþ in þe gospel, þer he seiþ þus:
Sic luceat lux vestra, et cetera. Þat is: 'So schyne ȝoure liȝt
tofore men þat men se ȝoure goode werkes and glorifie ȝoure
375 Fadir þat is in heuen.' And bi þis liȝt men moun knowe þe
aungel of God fro þe aungel of Lucifer.

Þe fyfþe þynge þat þis gospel makeþ of mencion is of þe ioye
þat was maad at þis birþe. Ȝe schulleþ vnderstounde þat at þis
birþe was maad gret ioye not onely in heuene among aungeles,
380 but also in erþe among men, and in helle among priseneris þat
weren þere. And þus þis birþe was not onely ioye to manie, as
was þe birþe of John Baptist, but to alle [þ]e peple, as þe aungel
seide þat was send to þe scheperdes at þat tyme in message.

First, to hem þat weren in heuenes, as to aungelis, þis birþe
385 was gret ioye, for þei sawe wel þat, bi þe kynde of man þat God
hadde taken, þat þe falling[e] awey of her noumbre schulde be
restored, helid, and saued. And þerfor `gret´ ioye þat þei hadde
of þis restorynge, helynge, and sauynge, onehede maad; and of
þe knyttynge togedere and, bitwixe hem and man, of gret loue,
390 oon of hem was sente into erþe to brynge to man þis ioyful
typynges, seiynge: 'þis day is born to vs a Saueoure.' /

To man also, heere in erþe, þis birþe was gret ioye, and no   f. 49ʳ
wounder! For if it were so þat þer weren men whiche hadden
lost her heritage bi a fals tiraunte and so bi hym holden out
395 þerof, ȝef ani tyme þei myȝten heere of þe birþe of þe eyr bi
whiche þei hopiden to be restored aȝen to her rewme, alle
suche wolden make ful gret ioye. Ryȝt so, mankynde hadde
`lost´ þe rewme of heuene bi þe fals tyraunte, þe fynde, and þis
blesside chylde as riȝt eyr was born to restore hem aȝen to here
400 rewme. For oneli to [him] it perteynede, in as miche as he was
man, clene and wiþoute synne; and oneli he miȝte, in as miche
as he was God. And in tokene of þis, þe aungel seide þat þis
Saueoure was Crist and Lord. Bi þis word 'Crist' was vnderstounde his manhede; and bi þis word 'Lord', his general

405 lordschepe, and so his godhede. And þerfor þei hadden grete matere to ioye at þis birþe; and, for þis cause, men heere in erþe, boþe tofore, and in þat tyme, and afturward also.

Tofore: as hooli Abraham, and Johun Baptist in his moder woumbe. In þat tyme: as his moder wiþouten peyne berynge or 410 chyldynge, þe scheperdes him seinge, and Symeon him biclip-pynge. Also aftur: men maden ioye, as Poule seinge in þis wyse: *Gaudete in Domino semper; iterum dico: gaudete!* Þat is: 'Ioyeþ in þe Lord alwey; and efte I sei: ioyeþ!' And not oneli / ȝe, but f. 4c alle oþere þat schullen be saued, into þe worldes ende, schullen 415 ioye of þis birþe.

Also, þe prisoneris þat weren in helle hadden ioye of þis blesside birþe. And no wounder þouȝ þei hadden gret ioye of þis birþe! For ȝef it were so þat a man wer[e] taken and þrowen in prisoun bi a grete tyraunte, out of whiche prisoun he miȝtte 420 neuere be deliuered vnto þe tyme þat þer were a chyld born, whiche chyld aftur wanne he cam to ful age schulde fiȝte wiþ þis tiraunte, and ouercome hym, and deliuere him out of prisoun, ȝef suche a man miȝte heere of þe birþe of þis chyld, gretly he wolde ioye in hope of nyȝ delyueraunce. Riȝt so, 425 mankynde, lyinge in þe prisoun of helle, beynge in þe same caas.

And not onely þe aungelis in þe blysse of heuene, as I seide bifore, maden ioye of þis blesside birþe, ne sengulerli þis oon was sente into erþe on þis message, but for þis special miracle 430 allone aboue þat þat euere was schewyd tofore þere aperide wiþ him grete multitude of aungelis (whyche beþ knyȝtes of heuene to fiȝte euere aȝen fendis vnder þe baner of God) whiche maden ioye heere in erþe amonge men, declaringe his spiritual ex-cellence and lordschepe in his godhede, as tofore was declared 435 his temperal pouerte in his manhede, seiynge: 'Glorie be in hiȝnesse' (þat is, in heuene) 'to God, and in erþe pees to men of good wylle.'

In þese wordes, riȝt as þis spiritual knyȝthode declarede þe goostly lordschipe of þis pore chyld in / hiȝe glorie of heuene, f.
440 riȝt so acordeþ to þis lordschipe: þei preferreden heere in erþe good wylle of men tofore alle maner of temperal rechesses. For þis bryngeþ in pees of soule, whiche is principalli in þe wylle, þat is souerenst power of mannes soule, and þis is more worþ þan alle þe lordschepes of þis world, for it makeþ him to be 445 Goddes sone, as Crist seiþ in þe gospel: *Beati pacifici: quoniam filii Dei vocabuntur.* Þat is: 'Blessid beþ pesible men: for þei

418 were] wer*ee*.

schullen `be´ cleped Goddes sones', and so eyres of his goostly
lordschepe, þat is: þe blysse of heuene.

Þereas ofte tyme temperal richesses norischeþ miche vnreste
450 and trobel in herte and ofte stryif and debate wiþ neyheburs,
and þis pees in soule moun neuere wyckede men haue, for hem
wanteþ good wille, þerfor seiþ þe prophete Ysaie: *Non est pax
impijs.* Þat is: 'Þer is no pees [to] wyckede men.'

And heere men moun touche, ȝef hem þynkeþ it be to done,
455 more largeli of good pees and euelle pees, also of good wille and
euele wylle.

Heere men moun also touche a goostli sense of þis laste
processe of þe gospel: þat riȝt aftur þe firste aungel hadde
schewed his message to þe s[ch]eperdes, anon stood wiþ him a
460 gret multitude of oþer aungelis confermynge þat þat he hadde
seid; riȝt so, whan þat a preest, þat is þe aungel of God, haþ
seid þe message of þe truwe word of God to þe peple, þanne
alle oþer truwe preestes, as truwe gostli knyȝtes of þe host of
God þat beþ ordeyned / to fyȝt wiþ scweerd of þe word of God, f. 50ᵛ
465 schulde stoonde forþ boldeliche to conferme and maynteyne þe
truþe of his message, and not contrarie eche oþer, as þei dooþ
nowadayes. And ȝef þei diden þus, þanne þis schulde turne into
gret glorie of God, þat his knyȝtes halden þus togedere in
truþe, and also norischinge of vertues and destryinge of vices
470 amonge þe peple, whiche comeþ neuere but of good wille; and
so, forþermore, reste and pees, vnite and charite, þorouȝ
whiche aftur þis temperal lyif alle suche buþ b⟨r⟩ouȝte to euere
lastynge pees in þe blysse of þe Kyng of Pees. To þe whiche
blysse he vs brynge þat þis tyme cam to make pees wiþ
475 mankynde. Amen.

459 scheperdes] speperdes.

6

CIRCUMCISION
(NEW YEAR'S) DAY

`Postquam consummati sunt dies, et cetera´ [Lu.2.21]. [T]his day
in whiche þis gospel is rad is clepid among þe comune peple
'Newe ȝeres Day' for as miche as, aftur þe cours þat cristen
men vsen, þe ȝer bigynneþ þe firste day of Geneuer, in whiche
5 alwey þis gospel is rad.

But letterid men clepen þis day 'Circumsicioun Day' for as
miche as oure Lord Jesus Crist was circumsicid þat day. But,
for to haue more cleer vnderstoundynge in þis matere of
circumsicioun, vs bihoueþ for to knowe þre þynges. Þe firste is
10 þis: what is circumsicioun, and what tyme it was first ordeyned.
Þe secounde is: wharto circumsicioun was ordeyned, and
whereof it seruede. Þe þridde is: whi þat Crist was
circum/cided.   f. 5

For þe firste: ȝe schulleþ vnderstounde þat circumsicioun
15 was a ryte and a religioun in Olde Lawe, comaundid to þe
chyldren of Israel, þat in þe eyteþe `dai´ aftur þat a chyld were
born þei schulden kutte away a lytel garland round aboute of þe
vttermure part of þe skyn of his ȝerde. And what tyme þis rite
oþer ordynaunce first bigan, þe firste book of Hooly Writ (þe
20 x[ii] chapitre) telleþ pleynly, where it seiþ þat God seide to
Abraham: 'Goo out of þi lond, and of þi kynr[e]de, and of þe
hous of þi fadir, and come into þe lond whiche I schewe to þee.'
And Abraham obeyede, and wente forþ, and cam into þe lond
of Chanaan. After þat, whanne þat God hadde seyin his holy
25 lyif and his obedience, he bihiȝte to ȝeue him þat lond into
eritage, and his seed aftur him. And forþermore, God, seynge
þat Abraham encresede in goode werkes and hooli lyif fro day
to day, he comaundide him þat he schulde circumcide þe
vttermere parte of his ȝerde, seyinge þus: 'Eueri male be he

---

1 Postquam...et cetera] (Written into blank half line at end of preceding
sermon, H3);   This] (Text indented for two lines; T om.).
20 xii] xvij (n.).   21 kynrede] kynrsde.

30 circumcidid, þat it be a couenaunt of my bound bitwixe me and
3ou.' And anon, Abraham, at þe biddinge of God, he circum-
cidide hymself, and Ismael [h]is sone, and alle `þe´ males of his
hous. And þus in þat tyme, as it is now schewid, þe sacurment
of circumsicioun first took his bigynnynge of þe blesside
35 patriark, Abra/[ham].   f. 51ᵛ

Þe secounde þyng þat vs bihoueþ to knowe in þis matere is
þis: wherto circumsicioun was ordeyned, and whereof it
seruede. Herto may be answered þus: þat circumcision was
ordeyned þat bi þe obedience of þe comaun`de´ment of circum-
40 cisioun Abraham schulde plese to God, to woom Adam
displeside bi brekynge of his comaundement.

It was ordeyned also in tokene of þe fey of Abraham þat, in
þe olde age of him and of his wyif boþe, bileeuede to haue a
sone in whom schulde be maad þe blessynge of alle men.

45 Anoþer cause of þis ordinaunce was þis: for as miche as
Abraham was þe first to whom expressly was maad biheeste of
þe `in´carnacioun of Crist, þerfor it was reson[a]ble þat þe
feyful peple þat schulde come of him (of whom Crist schulde
be born, to whom þe lawe schulde be 3ouen after) weren
50 knowen bi a certeyn signe fro vnfeyful peple; and so, bi þe
same signe, whane any of hem were ded in batayle, mi3te be
knowe and so taken and biried wiþ her breþeren.

And circumcisioun was comaundid to be maad in þat part of
þe bodi oneli for þis cause: for it was ordeyned in remedie a3en
55 original synne þat we token of oure formere faderis bi luste,
whiche haþ most lordschipe in þat parte. For in þat partie þe
firste man / felide synne of vnobedience, þerfore it was   f. 52ʳ
cordynge þat þere he schulde take þe sygne of obedience.

Whereof þis circumcisioun seruede, þe Maister of þe
60 Sentence telleþ openly in his fourþe book, and alleggeþ for him
boþe Augus[tine] and Bede, þat circumsicioun seþþe þe tyme
þat it was ordeyned in þe peple of God it seruede boþe `to´ olde
and 3enge of þe same seruice þat now dooþ baptem seþþe it was
ordeyned (þat is, to do awey origynal synne) except þat it mi3te
65 not opene þe 3ates of heuene to hem þat token oneli circumcisioun, whiche now dooþ baptem. Naþeles, þei þat weren
circumcidid aftur her deþ weren confortid þorou3 a blesside
reste in þe bosum of Abraham, and biden þe entree of
heue[n]ly pees in blesside hope.

70 Þe þrydde þyng þat vs nedeþ to knowe in þe mater of
circumcisioun is þis: whi þat Crist was circumcidid. Heereto

35 Abraham] Abra (*Foot of* f.51r.) braham (*Top of* f.51v.).

men moun answere þat for seuene resonable causis Crist was circumcidid.

Þe firste cause: for to schewe in him þe truþe of flesche aȝen
75 þe erroure of Manicheijs, þat seiden þat he hadde a fantastik bodi; and also aȝen Valentyne, heretik, þat seide þat he hadde an heuenli bodi.

Þe secounde cause was for to approue circumcisioun, whiche God ordeyned tofore.

80 Þe þridde cause was for to schewe þat he was of þe kynde of Abraham, þat was þe firste prince of circumcisioun, takynge þe biheeste of Crist.

Þe fourþe cause was þat he were not put abak out of þe cumpenie of Jewes for his prepucie, þat is þe custum of hem
85 þat ben not / circumcidid.   f. 52ᵛ

Þe fiyfþe cause was for to comende to vs obedience, wile he þat was not suget fulfillide þe lawe.

Þe sixte cause was þat, as he cam in liknesse of flesche of synne, so he schulde take remedie for synne.

90 Þe seuenþe cause was þat he þat bar þe birþen of þe lawe in himself schulde deliuere oþere men fro þe charge of þe lawe.

And þus, for þese seuen causes rehersid bifore, Crist Jesus, þis ȝenge child, was circumcidid in his tender flesche, for it was doon in þe eyteþe day suynge aftur þat he was born of his
95 moder into þis world.

Miche ben we holden to þis blesside Lord þat was and is so gret, as John seiþ in þe Apoc[alips], þat he is 'Kyng of Kynges, and Lord of Lordes'; and as Dauid seiþ in þe Psauter: *Magnus Dominus et laudabilis, et cetera*. Þat is: 'He is a gret Lord' þat of
100 his gretnesse is non ende, and ȝet he wolde fouchesaf to brynge himself so lowe in staat of a litel child to 'take þe forme of a seruaunt', as Poule seiþ to *Philip*.[2.7]. Of þis blesside child spekeþ Ysaie þe prophet, seyinge: *Puer natus est nobis, et filius datus est nobis, et cetera*. Þat is: 'A child is born to vs, and a sone
105 is ȝouen to vs.'

And þus, in þis eyteþe day, þat was þe day of circumcisioun as þis gospel seiþ, þe name of þe child was clepid 'Jesus', whiche was clepid of þe aungel tofore he was conceyued in his moderis woombe. But heere men musten vn[der]stonden þat
110 þis name 'Jesus' / þat þilke dai was putt to þis blesside childe   f. 5:
was not first clepid and assigned of þe angel, as it semeþ þat þe gospel meneþ, but it was nempned of þe Holi Trinite wiþoute

85 (*Foot of f.52r: quod 7 de causis Christus fuerat circumcisus*, H3).
110 (H2 *stops at foot of* f.52v; H1 *resumes at top of* f.53r.).

ani bigynnnge, as þe prophete Ysa[ie] seide: *Vocabitur tibi nomen nouum, quod os Domini nominauit.* Þat is: 'To þe schal be
115 clepid a newe name, þat þe mouþ of God haþ nempned.' But þe clepynge of þis angel and of his parentis boþe was not ellis but a pronuncynge, declarynge, eþer openynge þe clepynge of God tofore. Riȝt so, þe asoylyng eþer byndyng of prestis heere in Cristis cherche is noȝt ellis but a schewyng bi certeyn euidencis
120 þat suchon is eþer bounden eþer assoiled of God tofore.

After þis litel declarynge of þis schorte gospel of þis dai, me þynkeþ it were necessarie for to k[nowe] whi þat cristen men halewen þis dai so hiȝli eueri ȝer, as it comeþ aboute. For þe declaracion of þis matere, men musten vnderstonde þat neþer
125 for it is þe firste dai of þe newe ȝer, neþer for it was riȝt eþer custom of þe Olde Lawe is cause whi þat cristen men halewen þis dai. Þe firste cause were ouer lewid; þe seconde is also now no cause. For, as Seint Poule proueþ in his pistole to þe Galatheis, after Cristus deþ and general publicacion of þe
130 Newe Lawe, þe riȝtes of þe Olde Lawe weren dede, and specialli circumcision voide bi þe comynge in [of] baptem, for baptem ȝeueþ al þat circumcision ȝaf and miche more, for it ȝeueþ more plenteuosli grace and entree anon into þe blisse of heuene.

135 But ȝhe sc[h]ulde vnderstonde þat for twei causes more / resonable þis dai is halewid amonge criste[n] men: f. 53ᵛ

Oon is for þis dai is þe vtaues of þe birþe of oure Lord Jesus Crist, and ȝef men make solempne þe vtaues of oþer seyntis eþer halewes, miche more resonable it is to make solempne and
140 holi his vtaues þat haleweþ or makeþ holi al oþer halewes.

Anoþer cause is þis: for þis dai oure blesside Lord Jesus schedde oute þe firste blood of his tendir bodi to paie ernest of þe raunsum for mankynde, whiche he paied after fulli on þe Goode Fridai in his passion. And þis is a blessid cause þis dai
145 eueri cristen man is hoolde to make solempne and holde hooli in ȝildyng þankyngis to [h]is blessid Lord for his grete kyndenesse and loue.

But heere ȝe schulleþ vnderstonde þat fyue tymes, and in fiue placis of his boodi, we reden þat þis blessid Lord schedde
150 oute his blod fro þis dai into þe laste ende of his liȝf, and þe sixte tyme after þat he was ded. And so he paiede þis raunsum at sixe payementis. Noȝt for he was not sufficiente to paie hit al

---

122 knowe] knwone.
131 voide] (*Preceded by a space about five characters in length; no erasure*);
of] *om.*   140 his] in his.

atones, eþer for o dayes payment was not sufficient but ȝef he
had paid so myche, for þe leeste drope of his blod was sufficient
155 raunsum for al mankynde—ȝea! þou þei hadden bee a þousand
fold moo. But it was don for to ȝeue vs oute of musure grete
cause and matere to loue hym for euere.

Þe first payment was, as I seide bifore, þis dai / whan he at þe   f. 54ʳ
eyte dayes of age schedde his blood in his tendere lyme. In
160 þis dede he ȝaf vs gret matere of loue and also gret ensaumple
of clannesse and chastite, and for to refreyne vs fro al maner of
lecherie in þouȝt, word, and dede; seþþe he þat schulde neuere
haue luste to any synne, ȝet he suffride so gret peyne in þat
membre in whiche men fynden most stirynge to þat synne.
165 And hereto acordeþ his owne biddyng in þe gospel, seyinge
þus: *Sint lumbi vestri precincti, et cetera.* Þat is: 'Be ȝoure
reynus gurd eþer refreyned' fro alle maner lecherie, boþe of
bodi and soule.

Þe secounde paiment whas whanne he knelyng preyede to
170 his Fader in wakynge, þe nyȝt tofore he suffride deþ. And, at
þat tyme, as Lu[ke] makeþ mynde, he preiede so hertili þat his
swot was maad as dropes of blood rennynge doun into þe erþe.
In þis also he ȝaf vs gret matere of loue, and also gret ensample
to traueile bisili, wiþ deuocion in preier, for oure owne synnes,
175 and for oure breþeren, and for special grace to gete vertues, and
also þat we be not ouercomen þorouȝ temptacions of oure
enemies, seþþe he þat was clene wiþouten synne, and so hadde
no nede to preie for his owne synne, trauailede so sore to preie
for vs, his seruantes. And þerfore he conceileþ vs in þe gospel,
180 seyinge in þis wise: *Vigilate / et orate, et cetera.* Þat is: 'Wakeþ   f. 54ᵛ
and preieþ, þat ȝe entre not into temptacion.

Þe þridde payment of þis blessid raunsum was þat tyme
whanne his cloþes weren strept of his blessid bodi, and he so al
nakid was bounden to a piler, and wiþ scharpe schorges so
185 beten his tender bodi þat þe blood barst ouȝt at euery strook, so
þat 'fro þe toppe of þe hed', as [Isaiah] þe prophet seiþ, 'non
hool place was founden in him doun to þe sole of þe foot.' In
þis dede ȝet he schewide to vs more largere matere of loue, and
also gret conforte and lernynge to suffre wilfulli gret penance in
190 oure bodies for oure synne, and for to gete þerwiþ þe rewme of
heuene, seþþe he [þat] was clene wiþouten synne so wilfulli
suffride for oþer mennes synnes. And þerfore he conceileþ vs
himself in þe gospel to penance, seyinge þus: *Penitentiam agite;*

appropinquabit enim regnum celorum. Þat is: 'Doþ penance; þe
195 kyngdom of heuene schal neiȝhe.'

Þe fourþe payment of þis blesside raunsum was maad at þat
tyme whanne þe cursede mynistres of Pilate token a coronne of
scharpe þornes wriþen togidere and, in scorn of his kyngdom
and in stide of a corowne of golde, presten doun on his hed,
200 þoru whiche þe blood barst oute at þe veynes, and guschede out
into his iȝen, and so doun into al his face. And so, what þoru
þis blood and þoru þe cursede spittynge of here mouþes into
his blessid face, he þat was tofore þe fairest in schap tofore al þe
children of men / he was maad after so horrible in siȝt þat, as   f. 55ʳ
205 Ysa[ie] seiþ, he was like to a mesel.

In þis dede also, oure Lord Jesus Crist schewide to vs a gret
matere of loue, and also gret ensaumple of mekenesse, þat we
schulden noȝt be prouȝte, for no bieute of bodi, ne faire fetures
of face, for a litel sikenesse eþer disese mai sone make it fade
210 and foule to mannes siȝte. Þerfore seiþ þe Wise Man
(*Prouer.*[31.30]): *Fallax gratia et vana est pulcritudo.* Þat is:
'Deceyuynge grace and a veyn is fairenesse.'

Also, in þis blessid dede God techeþ vs þat for no spiritual
neþer temperal dignite, estaate, ne power, we schulden not lifte
215 vp oure hedes into pride aboue oure breþeren, to holde vs self
þe bettere eþer þe worþiere þerfore doynge wronges to oure
sugetis bineþe vs; but mekeli knowleche vs self as oon of hem,
þouȝ God eþer Fortune haþ sette vs in suche estaat. And
þerfore seiþ þe Wise Man: *Rectorem te posuerunt? noli extolli,*
220 *sed esto in illis quasi vnus ex ipsis.* Þat is: 'Þei han put þe a
gouernour? Be þou noȝt enhauncid, be þou in hem as oon of
hem.'

Þe fifþe payment of þis blessid raunsum was maad whanne
þe blesside hondes and armes of oure Lord Jesus Crist weren
225 streytli streyned vpon þe cros and grete bustus nailes dryuen
þoru oute hem into þe tree, and oute of þe woundes, as oute of
grete goteris, largeli þe blood ran oute on eueri side.

In þis blesside dede oure Lord Jesus Crist ȝet also schewide
to vs alle a gret matere of loue, to sprede þus abrod his riȝt
230 honde and his lifte hond boþe, in tokenynge of loueli biclippyngis boþe of his frendes and also of his enemies. And in þis
he ȝaf to vs ensample to naile fast oure hondes wiþ þe drede of
God fro al maner of sleynge and wrongful smytynge, extorcions, robberie, and lecherous handelynge, / falce deceytes   f. 55ᵛ
235 in wiȝtes and mesures, and alle oþer wrongful doynges in

displesynge of God and harmynge of oure breþeren; but to
strecche out eþer to loose oure hondes into large almesdedes to
oure pore breþeren, and euere redi to wirche wiþ hem sum
good and profitable werk and so doyng to ablen vs self to ete of
240 Goddes godes, and haue þe blessyng þat he haþ hiȝte to alle
suche, witnessynge Dauid in þe Psauter, seyinge þus: *Labores
manuum tuarum quia manducabis, beatus es, et bene tibi erit.* Þat
is: 'For þou schalt ete þe traueiles of þyne hondes, þou schalt be
blessid, and it schal be wel to þe.'

245 Þe sexte payment of þis blessid raunsum, as I seide tofore,
was after his deþ, whan oon þat was left of þe knyȝtis wiþ a
scharpe spere openede his side and cleef his herte atwo, out of
whiche wounde cam oute þe laste blood and watir also þerwiþ.

In þis blesside payment and ouerpassynge kyndeli dede, he
250 schewide to vs þe moost and þe hiest cause of loue. For in þis
dede he schewide to vs þat for al his benefetis þat euer he dide
to man, and for his grete trauaile and peyne in his blesside
passion, he desireþ non oþer reward but þe hool loue of oure
herte, and þerfore he seiþ þus: *Fili, prebe mihi cor tuum.* Þat is:
255 'My sone, ȝeue to me þyn herte.'

Also, in þis blesside dede he ȝaf vs ensample þat we schulden
haue an open herte and noȝt closid, þoru verrei pite and merci,
forȝeuyng to oure breþeren þat haue trespacid to vs, as he let
opene his herte to haue mercy vpon vs. And þerfore he
260 seiþ hymself in þe gospel: *Estote misericordes, sicut Pater | vester*   f. 56ʳ
misericors est. Þat is: 'Beþ merciful, as ȝoure Fadir is merciful.'

And þus, as it is sumwhat schewide in þis schorte processe,
in þese sixe maneris and in þese sixe tymes Crist schedde out
his blesside blood to paie þe ful raunsum for mankynde, of
265 whiche þe firste payment, as I seid, was maad þis dai in his
hooli circumcision in ernest of þis worþi price, for whiche
trewe cristen men haleweþ [þis dai] euery ȝere as it comeþ
aboute.

And riȝt as þe Jewes weren bounden to bodili circumcision
270 in þe Olde Lawe (þat is, a peyneful kuttynge awei of here
flesch, as þe texte seiþ (*Ge*.17.[14]): *Masculus, cuius caro
prepucij circumcisa non fuerit, delebitur anima illa de populo suo.*
Þat is: 'A knaue childe, whos flesch of his ȝerde schal not be
circumcidid, þat soule schal persche from his peple), so cristen
275 men [beþ bounde] to gostli circumsision in þe Newe Lawe (þat
is, a peyneful kuttynge awei of al maner of synne þoru verrei

---

245 (*mar:* vjᵗʰ, H3?).   267 þis dai] dai þis (*m. for r.*).
275 beþ bounde] bounde beþ.

penance doynge, er þei passen ouȝt of þis world), seyinge Crist
hymself, ȝeuer of þat lawe, in þis manere: *Nisi penitentiam
egeritis, omnes peribitis.* Þat is: 'But ȝef ȝe do penance, ȝe
280 schullen perische.' And riȝt as bodili circumcision myȝte noȝt
be don bi lawe til after fulfullynge of þe vij daies in þe eiteþ dai,
riȝt so þis gostli circumcision (þat is, clensynge of synne þoru
verrei penance) mai neuer be wel don til after vij gostli daies
ben fulfillid, and so in þe eiteþ gostli dai.
285   Þe firste gostli dai is contynuel sorwe for synnes. Þe seconde
is abhominacion of synne. Þe / þridde is ful wille neuer to turne   f. 56ᵛ
aȝen to synne. Þe fourþe is trewe schrift of synne. Þe fiȝfþe is
hooli fastynge. Þe vj is deuoute preyynge. Þe seueneþe is
charitable almesdede doynge. Þe 8 dai is good perseuerance in
290 alle þese.
     And whan a man haþ fulfilled alle þese 7 gostli daies, and is
comen into þe eiteþe dai (þat is, into perseuerance), þanne he is
able to be circumcidid gostli—þat is, to be clansed of alle
maner of synne, and so to be euerlastyngeli saued in heuene,
295 whiche is gostli clepyng of his name. For euery man þus
doynge mai be clepid Jesus, þat is as myche for to seie as
'saueour', for in þis manere he is cause of his owne sauacion.
And for to schewe verili þat þis sentence is true, Crist seiþ
himself, þat mai not lie: *Qui perseuerauerit in finem, hic saluus
300 erit.* Þat is: 'He þat lasteþ in verreie penance to þe ende, þis
schal be saaf.'
     God, for his endeles mercy, as he was þis dai circumcidid for
vs bodili, ȝeue vs grace in þis manere to be circumcidid gostli,
þat he mai clepe vs alle bi name, seynge in þis wise: 'Comeþ, þe
305 blesside children of my Fader, and weldeþ þe kyngdom þat is
to ȝou araied fro þe bigynnyng of þe world.' To whiche
kyngdom he brynge vs at þe endynge, þat ordeynede it for vs
tofore þe bigynynge. Amen.
     Whoso wole trete lenger of þis matere of eyte dayes, he mai
310 see more herof in þe sermoun of Myd Lente Sundai.

7
EPIPHANY

[C]vm natus esset *Jesus, et cetera*. Þis gospel gostli men moun
vnderstonde þus: þat oure Lord Jesus Crist is euery dai born
gostli in Bedleem / (þat is, in hooli cherche whiche is 'þe house f. 57ʳ
of bred') boþe þoru true techinge of þe word of God and
5 admynistracion of [þ]e holi sacramentes whanne, after priuei
wirchyng of þe Hooli Gost enspirynge mennes soules, þoru
grace þei bersten oute into meritorie dedes acordynge to þe liȝf
and techyng of oure Lord Jesus Crist.
'In þe daies of Heroude'. Þat is, in þese daies specialli, in þe
10 ende of þe world, whan þe deuel þat is prince of þe world is
vnbounden and most power haþ among þe peple, in whiche
tyme Heroudes, þe fend intruser and not trewe eire, regneþ in
þe lond of biheste—þat is, in cristen mennes soules, to whom is
bihote þe kyngdom of heuene, whiche ben coldid þoru enuie
15 fro þe heete of charite. And 'þese daies ben euele', as Seint
Poule seiþ.
Þese þre kynges þat camen fro þe eeste to Jerusalem þoru
ledynge of a sterre (whiche aperide to hem and ladde hem in
hire pilgrimage to seche Jesus, boþe God and man, Kyng of
20 Jewes and of oþere) moun beo gostli euery cristen man here in
þis world whiche, þoru sad bileue as `in´ þe Hooli Trinite,
Fader, and Sone, and Holi Goost, and true wirchynge in word
and dede, schulde be kyng, gouernyng his owne soule wiþinne
forþ to þe wirschipe of God, and eueri oþer cure bodili eþer
25 gostli whiche he haþ take vpon hym wiþoute forþ.
Þe sterre þat ledeþ hem toward Jesus fro þe eeste mai be hire
bileue whiche þei take first at baptem, whiche mai wel be clepid
þe eest, where þe sunne first ariseþ, for þere springeþ first to
hem þe dai of grace after þe niȝt of original synne and actual
30 boþe. And þis sterre of bileeue ledeþ a man euene þe riȝt wei to
see Jesus, boþe in his godhede and in his manhede. And, riȝt as
þe kynges hadden neuer come to þe presence of þ[e] blessid

---

1 Cum] (*Text indented for two lines; small* c *written into the space; no
rubrication*).   5 þe] þhe (þ *in margin*).   21 in] (*mar: no caret mark*).

child ne but bi ledyng of þe sterre, so 'it is impossible wiþouten
bileeue', as Seint Poule / seiþ, 'to plese God' wiþ any werkes.   f. 57ᵛ

35   But whanne þei camen to Jerusalem where Kyng Heroud[e]
regnede, þe sterre no lenger aperide to hem. Jerusalem is as
myche to seie as 'siȝt of pees'. Riȝt so, whan [a] man haþ siȝt
and reward to þat pees in whiche Heroudes þe deuele regneþ
and norischeþ (þat is: pees in synne, meytenynge hem þerinne,
40 flaterynge and glosynge, and not repreuynge), þan þe sterre of
foormed bileue is awei fro hym, for eueri such pees is synne
dedli, and 'þer is bileeue ded', as Seint Jame seiþ.

Þat þese kynges axedon in Jerusalem of þe birþe of þis child
whan þe sterre failede hem, bitokeneþ whan þe bileue of a man
45 is any þyng aslepe þoru ani doute, or ded þoru ani synne, þat
þei schulden axe bisili in hooli cherche (þat is, of suche men of
hooli chirche þat han knowynge of þe Scripture of God) and
enquere til þei hadden þe certeyn truþe, wiþoute s[l]ombrynge
or slepyng of sleuþe in synne.

50   Þat Kyng Heroud[e], whan he hadde herd of þe childes
berþe, he was distorbelid, and al Jerusalem wiþ hym, bitokeneþ
þat whan þe feend hereþ þat Crist is born þoru feiþful
wirchynge of a true soule whiche was conceyued tofore þoru
grace, whiche Crist is, Kyng of Jewes (þat is, regneþ in hem
55 [þat] trueli knoulecheþ him), þenne þe fend is distorblid greteli,
and al þo also þat beþ in reste and pees and delite in synne in
whiche beþ principalli cite in whiche hertis is his restynge
palice, for þe fend is aferd to lese his lordschipe in suche þoru
conquest of swerd of þe word of God whiche Crist
60 bryngeþ wiþ hym / to destrie such fals pees.   f. 58ʳ

Þat Heroudes made þe prestis and kunnynge men of lawe to
telle þe prophecie of Cristus birþe, whiche drowen not afterward þerto but þe seculer kynges, bitokeneþ þat þe deuele
stireþ oþerwhile prestis and kunnynge clerkis to seie þe truþe of
65 Goddes lawe to hire owne dampnacion whan þei folewen not
þerafter in hire lyuinge, and oþer seculer mennes sauacion þat
leeueþ and doþ þeraftir.

Þat Heroudes cleped priueli þe kynges, and lernede of hem
þe tyme of þe sterre, and after sende hem into Bedleem to aspie
70 of þis child vnder colour and fals feynynge, bitokeneþ þat þe
deuele wiþ his priue and sutel wirchynge aspieþ, þoru contynance in word eþer dede, þe disposicion of mannes soule
wheþer he be saddid eþer vnstable. And ȝef he be vnstable, he

35 Heroude] heroud'.   37 a] ha.
48 slombrynge] l *written over an* e.   50 Heroude] heroud'.

moueþ him to stiȝe into sum hiȝ liuyng to þat ende þat he make
75 him after falle into deppere confusion.

Þat þe kynges, after þei hadden herd þe kyng, wenten fro
hym, and þe sterre, whiche aperid to hem in þe eeste, wente
tofore heere and ladde hem riȝtli to þe siȝt of þe child,
bitokeneþ þat whan a man haþ herd þe entisynges of þe fend
80 and boweþ noȝt to hem and, þouȝh he haue bowed to hem,
after forsakeþ hym and al his werkes, þe riȝt bileeue þat he first
took in baptim wole go tofore him and redili lede him to þe
grace of oure Lord God, which makeþ him to haue wiþ gostli
siȝt of þe manhede of oure Lord Jesus Crist, and of al his
85 werkes and tech/ynges, and suen þerafter.   f. 58ᵛ

Þat þe kynges entriden into þe hous honoureden him,
bitokeneþ þat whanne a man haþ grace and gostli siȝt of al þis
of þe birþe of oure Lord Jesus, boþe God and man, þat he goo
into his owne conscience and priue þouȝt, and worschipe God
90 wiþ al his soule, þat wolde fouchesaaf so mekeli to become a
litel child of oure kynde to restore vs to oure heritage of
heuene.

Þat þei opende hire tresoures tofore þis child, and not tofore
Kyng Heroudes, bitokeneþ þat þou schuldest neuere schewe þi
95 gode dedes tofore wordeli men, for noo pompe, ne pride, ne
wordeli wynnynge which pleseþ þe fend, but oneli to þe
worschipe of God and edificacion of þi breþeren.

Þat eueriche of þese kynges offriden þus to þe child þre
maner of ȝeftes (þat was gold, encense, and myrre) bitokeneþ
100 þat euery cristen man schulde b⟨eo⟩ a gostli kynge, as I seide
at þe bigynnyng, [and] schulde offre gostli þese þre gostli ȝeftes
to þis blessid Lord, whiche is as a child in þis world, þoru
mek⟨e⟩nesse, pacience, and longe abidynge, and dissimyleþ
105 wronges þat ben don to him. But at þe Dai of Dom he wole be
seie a perfite man: lordli, strong, and myȝti to venge all manere
of wronges þat han be don to him here, and no man schal mow
seie nay.

Þe firste ȝefte (þat is, gold) bitokeneþ wisdom of Goddes
lawe, whiche is 'more / worþ', as þe prophete Dauid seiþ, 'þan f. 5⟨
110 material gold', or topazion (þat is, precyous ston), and elles so
wise a prophete wolde not haue loued þe ton bifore þe toþer.
Alle þo þat principalli louen þe wisdom of Goddes lawe tofore
al oþer wor[de]li þyng offereþ to God þis gold þat is þe first
ȝefte.

115 But alle þoo þat loueþ more þe wisdom of wordeli and
seculer lawe, or ellis þe wisdom of wordeli worschipe, or of
catel, beþ aboute to bigile þis blessid child as men doþ oþer

children wiþ a counter of stynkynge bras in stide of a nobel of
clere gold. For þe wisdom of þis world is not so myche in
120 comparisoun to þe wisdom of Goddes lawe as is bitwene
stynkyng bras and most fynest gold; for þe comparison bitwene
hem two is as bitwene folie and wisdom, as Seint Poule seiþ.
But be þ[e]i wel war, þou3 he be a child in persone of his
manhede, he is þe wisdom of þe Fadir in his godhede, and
125 'God wol not be bigyled ne scorned', as Seynt Poule seiþ.

Þe seconde presaunt þat þou schuldest offre is encense. And
þis offryng, if it schulde be pleasaunt to God, it bihoueþ to
haue þre condicions:

Þe firste is þat it be for gostli þyng, whiche is worschipe to
130 God and profite to þi soule. For Seint Poule, whan he preiede
to God for þyng whiche was not worschipe to God ne pro[f]ite
to his soule, it was not graun[t]id him of God, alþou þat he
hadde tofore grantid to his disciplis: 'whateuer þyng 3e schullen / axe my Fader in my name, he schal 3eue to 3ou.' Euery   f. 59ᵛ
135 þyng þat is not gostli ne profite to mannes soule is not axede in
Jesus name, whiche bitokeneþ 'saueour'. But Salamon, whan
God put in his chois þre þyngis, summe bodili and summe
goostli, for as miche as he chees wisdom and discrecion to rule
his peple, was gostli þing to worschipe of God, helþe of his
140 soule, and prophite of his breþeren, þerfore God granted him
alle. So, axe þou first gostli þyng, and God wole grante to þe al
bodili þyng þat is nedeful to þe: *Primum querite regnum Dei, et
cetera.*

Þe secounde condicion is þat it be do lastyngli, as Seint Jame
145 seiþ: *Multum valet, et cetera.* No3t 3ef þou bigynne to preie
and, so beo not granted to þe, þat þou cese of þi preier, but þat
þou continue þerynne til þou gete. Not for þis ende God
desireþ þis continuance, but bi manie curiouse and piteouse
wordes he wole be þe raþer bowid to graunt[e]n; for,
150 as he seiþ, 'er we axe, he wot what vs nedeþ'—and what he
wole grante. But he desireþ to see þe encrecynge of oure good
wille, whiche was wel schewid bi þe womman of Chanan þat
preiede lastyngli for þe helþe of hire dou3tere, and sparid no3t
for no schame ne reprof, and þerfore at þe laste sche hadde fulli
155 hire wille.

Þe þridde condicion is þis: þat preier be maad in charite, for
wiþouten þat is no þyng worþ þat we don here in erþe, as Seint
Poule seiþ: *Si linguis hominum, et cetera.* Hit fareþ bi preier þat

is maad in charite, as Crisostom seiþ, as doþ bi encense þat is
160 þrowen on quik colis: þe fume ascendeþ an hiȝ, and sauereþ
swete to alle men þat beþ aboute. Riȝt so, preier maked in
charite: þe vertu þerof is born vp bi angels into þe siȝt of God,
as it is seid in Thobie, / and sauereþ swete to God and to his   f. 60ᵛ
seyntis. But riȝt as encence put on dede colis liȝþ ful hool and
165 stondeþ in no stide ne is noȝt plesante to God, and þerefore
oure blesside Fader, Jesus, whanne he tauȝte vs to preie, for he
wolde oure preiere were effectuel, he sette in oure preiere a
clause of charite whanne he seiþ 'forȝeue vs, as we forȝeuen to
oþere.'

170   Þe þridde offrynge þat we schulden offre to þis blesside
childe is mirre, þat is 'mynde of þe deþ.' Mirre is a bitter þyng
whos kynde is to kepe a ded bodi fro rotyng. So, mynde of
mannes deþ is ful bittere, as þe Wise Man seiþ: *O mors, et
cetera*, and kepeþ hool þe goostli body of þi gode werkes þat it
175 falle noȝt into corrupcion þorou synne. Þerfore seiþ þe Wise
Man: *Fili, memorare nouissima, et cetera*. Biþenke þe þat þou
must nedis die. Biþenke þe þat þou wost not whanne þou schalt
die. Biþenke þe þat þou wost not what deþ þou shalt die.
Biþenke þe þat þou wost neuer after þi deþ whider þou schalt
180 go. And ȝif þou haue al þis in þi mynde, þou offrist blessideli þi
þridde offryng t[o] God—þat is, mirre.

Þat after þe offryng of þese kynges þe angel of God warnede
hem in her slepe þat þei schulden not turne aȝen to Heroudes,
but bi anoþer wei þei schulden turne aȝen into her cuntre,
185 bitokeneþ þat eueri cristen man þat offreþ þese þre gostly
offrynges, as I haue bifore schewid, his gode angel þat is
bitaken to hym fro his birþe wole enspire him and warne him
graciously whanne he resteþ him in vertues lyuynge fro werkis
of vices, as men doþ in sleep fro werkes of bodi, þat he turne
190 not aȝen to þe fend, whiche he haþ forsake in / baptem and   f. 6
seþþe bi sorwe of herte and schrifte of mouþe, but bi anoþer
wei turne into his cuntre. Þat is: ȝef he came bi Heroudes (þat
is, þe fend) bi pride, turne anoþer wei bi mekenesse. Ȝef bi
wraþþe, turne awei bi pacience. Ȝef bi enuye, turne awei bi
195 charite. Ȝef bi couetise, turne awei bi discrete almesdede. Ȝef bi
glotenie, turne awei bi abstinence. Ȝef bi ydelnesse, turne
aw⟨e⟩y bi good and prophitable ocupacion. Ȝef bi lecherie,
turne aȝen into þe cuntre bi anoþer wei, þat is: chastite. And ȝef
þou go þese weyes, þou schalt neuer drede þis curside tiraunte,
200 Heroudes, þe foule fend of helle; but riȝtli wiþouten eny

181 to] t⟨o⟩o.

errynge drawe into þyn owne cuntree (þat is, þe blisse of
heuene), of whiche, ȝef þou þus doo, þou schalt be eire to þe
hiȝe emperour, þe Fader of heuene, and so a gostli kyng and
euene eire, as Seint Poule seiþ, wiþ oure Lord Jesus Crist, his
205 blesside Sone. To þat cuntre bryng us he, þat diede for vs on þe
rode tree. Amen.

8
SEPTUAGESIMA
SUNDAY

[S]imile est regnum celorum homini patrifamilias qui exijt primo
mane conducere operarios in vineam suam (Mt.20.[1]). 'Þe kyngdom of heuene is like to an housholdere þat wente oute firste in
þe morewetide to hure werkmen into his vyneȝard', *et cetera.*

5   Þis gospel techeþ vs to wirche faste and be not idel while we
been here wandrynge in þis wei, for þe hure of þe hiȝe blisse of
heuene þat God haþ bihiȝte to alle suche; and also to haue a
tristi hope: þouȝ we haue misspendid oure tyme, ȝet naþeles,
and we ben founde his trewe seruantes in oure laste age, we
10 schullen haue þe same reward of euerlastyng blisse.

    Þis housholder þat þis gospel spekeþ of is oure Lord God,
whiche haþ an housold of þre stagis—þat is, heuene, erþe, and
helle. And his meynee beþ heueneli and ⟨er⟩þeli resonable
creaturis þat, as Seynt Poule seiþ *(Phil.2.[10])*, schullen bowe
15 hire knees to þis worschipeful Lord.

    In heuene beþ ouercomeris, as angels and hooli soulis. In
helle beþ þei þat ben ouercome, as fendes and soules þat ben
ouercome bi hem. And we beþ ordeyned heere in erþe, in þe
middel, to fiȝte wiþ oure enemies, and stryue to ascende to hem
20 þat ben in heuene aboue and not descende to hem þat ben in
helle bineþe.

    Alþouȝ Seynt Gregor/ius vnderstonde here bi þis vyneȝerd   f. 6
hooli cherche, and [bi] þese houres þe diuerse ages of þe world
fro þe firste man into þe laste: as from Adam into Noe, fro Noe
25 into Abraham, from Abraham into Moyses, fro Moyses into
Dauid, fro Dauid into Transmigracion, fro Transmigracion
into Crist; fro Crist into Dai of Dome, and in alle þese ages
God clepede wircheris into his vineȝerd (patriarkis, and proph-

---

1 *Simile] (Text indented for three lines;* S *om.).*   2 mane] *om.* R.
6 hiȝe] *om.* R.   22 (R *mar: De vinea et etatibus mundi).*
23 þese...þe(1)] þe oures of R.   24 into(1)] vnto R.   26 into] into þe R;
fro(2)] fro þe R.   27 into (2)] into þe R.   28 his] þe R.

etis, and prechoures of his lawe); naþeles, after þe sentence of
30 Crisostom, þis vineȝerd here mai [not be wel] vnderstonde
men: 'for þe wircheris þerinne ben men, and þerfore [þis
vyneȝerd ˈisˊ riȝtwisnesse], in whiche ben sette diuerse spicis of
riȝtwisnesse as vines: þat is, mekenesse, charitee, and pacience,
and oþer goodes wiþoute noumbre, whiche alle ben generalli
35 clepid riȝtwisnesse.'

Þis vineȝerd God haþ maad in mannes soule whan he made
him like to þe Trinite, whiche is verrei riȝtwisnesse, þorouȝ
resoun, mynde and wille, bi whiche he haþe [knowynge boþe]
of good and euele.

40 And to wirche in þis vineȝerd God haþ clepid men in diuerse
agis of hire liȝf, as in diuerse houres of þe dai, stondynge in þe
market or chepyng of þis world, in whiche is miche byinge and
sellynge and deceite of hire breþeren as custummabli falleþ in
such place, as Seynt Jon seiþ: *Totus mundus in maligno positus*
45 *est.*

Summe he haþ clepid / in childhode, as Jon Bapt[ist], Seynt   f. 62ʳ
Nicholas, and oþer diuerse, and summe in ȝonge wexynge age,
and summe in mannes age, and summe in eelde, and summe in
þe laste ende of hire liȝf, into þis vineȝerd of riȝtwisnesse, to
50 wirche þerinne þorou trewe kepynge of þe comandementis of
God.

Þe hure þat þis Lord haþ bihiȝte hem for hire daies iorne (þat
is, for þe trewe trauaile of þis liȝf) is a peny, þat is: þe
euerlastynge blisse of heuene, whiche mai wel be likened to a
55 peny for þe roundenesse þat bitokeneþ euerlastyngnesse, and
for þe blessid siȝt of þe kyngis face þat is in þat peni, and also
for þe Scripture þat is þerinne, þat is: þe Booke of Liȝf, in
whiche al þo þat schullen see þat siȝte beþ euerlastyngli writen.

Þat in þe elleueþe houre þis housolder fonde summe stond-
60 yng in þe markeþ idel, [to whiche he seide: 'Wherto stonde ȝee

---

30 not be well] R, wel be A.
31–2 þis...riȝtwisnesse] he vnderstondeþ bi þis vineȝerd A.
33 as vines] (*Preceded by* spices *deleted*), as R;
charitee] myldenes . chastite R.   34 ben generalli] generally ben R.
38 mynde, and wille] wil and mynde R (*m. for r.*);
knowynge boþe] R, boþe knowynge A.   41 hire] þis R.
43 and] in R.   46 as] as seint R.
47 wexynge age] age waxing R.   48 eelde] olde age R.
52 (R *marg*: De denario).   53 þis] her R.
54 of] in R;   wel] *om.* R.
59 (R *mar*: hora ij).   60–61 to...idel] *om.* A.

here al dai idel?] to wham þei answeriden: 'For no man haþ
hurid vs', bi þese in þe elleuenþe hour þat God fyndeþ
stondyng idel moun vnderstonde olde men in hire laste age,
whiche han stonde idel al hire liȝftyme and neuer wrowten in
65 þe vineȝerd of God.

'Synful men,' seiþ Crisostom, 'beþ not idel, but ded; but he
is idel þat wircheþ not þe werk of God. Ȝef þou take [a]wei oþer
mennes godes, þere þou art not idel, but ded; but ȝef þou take
not awei oþer mennes goodes, and naþeles / þou ȝeuest not of þi   f. 62ᵛ
70 godes to vnmiȝti men, þan þou art idel. Wole þou not be idel?
Take þou not awei oþer mennes godes, and of þyne owne ȝeue
to pore men, and þenne þou worchest in þe vineȝerd of God þe
vine of mercy.

'Ȝef þou art drunke and art in delicis, þou art not idel, but
75 þou art ded, as þe apostle seiþ; but ȝef þou mesurabli ⟨etist⟩
and drynkist, þou synnest not, for þou etist not euele; naþeles,
þou art idel, for þou worchest not þe vertu of fastynge (þat is,
almes). Wolt þou not þerfore be idel? Faste, and þat þou
schuldest ete on þe dai, ȝeue it to [þe] vnmyȝti man, and þou
80 hast itiled þe vine of fastynge.

'Also, ȝif þou dost lecherie, þou art ded and not idel. Ȝif þou
haue þi owne wife, þou synnest not; naþeles, þou wirchest not
þe vertu of chastite. Wole þou not be idel? If þou be wiþoute
wife, seche þou not a wife; ȝif þou be a widue, seche þou not þe
85 seconde weddyngis, and þou wirchest þe vine of chastite. Or
ellis, ȝef þou haue a wife, I schal shewe þe how þou schalt
wirche þe vine of chastite: kepe þe fro þi wife in hire priue
sikenesse, and whan she is grete wiþ childe, whanne also it is
hiȝ feste dai, and in bedenfastynge dai, after þe commaunde-
90 mentis of þe apos/tele.   f. 6ᵣ

'Also, ȝef þou art enuious to þi bettere, þou art not idel, but
ded. Ȝef `þou´ enuiest not, [and naþeles þou ioiest not, þan] þou
art idel; þerfore, not oneli enuie þou not, but haue þou ioie of þi
bettere, and þan hast þou tiled þe vyne of goodwille,' or of
95 charitee.

---

64 han stonde] stonden R.   67 awei] a *om.* A.
68 ȝef] þowȝ R.   74 art(1)] be R.
78 Faste] *om.* R.   79 þe(2)] *om.* A.
89 bedenfastynge] boden fasting R.
89–90 commaundementis] comaundement R.
92 and...þan] *om.* A, R.   93 idel] not idel A.
94 or] *om.* R.

Þe cause whi þat suche maner men haue stonde ofte tyme in þe market of þis world idel is for no man haþ hured hem (þat is, hire prelatis and hire curates, whiche schulden be þe bailifes of God to hure his werkemen into his vyneȝerd), neþer wiþ good
100 ensample of lyuinge, whiche was ofte more worse þan þe commyn peple, neþer wiþ trewe techyng of Goddis lawe of whiche þei hadden no knowynge, or ellis ful litel, and of þat litel þei weren ofte stoppid bi þe gobet of talwe (þat is, worldeli muk) þat was þrowen in hire mouþ so þat þei weren as houndes
105 þat myȝten not ne wolden not berk þe lawe of oure Lord to hire sugestis, bi whiche þei schulden be confortid to wirche in þe vyneȝerd of riȝtwisnesse for hope of reward of þe blisse of heuene.

But þat þe housholdere seide to hem: 'Gooþ into my
110 vineȝard' mai be vnderstonde þat þouȝ þe prelatis and curatis, for vnkunnynge [and] necligence / oþer euele wille, faile to do f. 63ᵛ hire office, naþeles God, of his grete curtesie and merciful grace, faileþ not to his peple wiþ priuei inspiracion to bidde, or þei passe oute of þis world, at alþerleest in þe last houre, to
115 wirche in his vine and so to haue þe peni.

O, þou merciful Lord, þat so tenderli louest þi peple þat þou bouȝtist wiþ þi blood þat, þouȝ alle men hem faile, þou failest hem not at nede!

'Whan þe euentide cam, þe housholdere seide to þe pro-
120 curatur of his vyneȝerd: "Clepe þe werkmen, and ȝelde to hem hire mede, bigynnynge at þe last vnto þe first".'

Þe euentide mai be vnderstonde þe g[e]neral Day of Dome, for þat schal be þe last dai, as þe eue of þis world.

Þe procuratour of þis vyne mai wel be vnderstonde [he] þat
125 clepeþ werkemen togidere and ȝeldeþ hem her hure, oure Lord Jesus Crist, Goddes Son of heuene, þat euermore procureþ oure profite tofore his Fadres face. To him þe Fadir haþ grantid fulli þe dome in þat dai (*Omne iudicium dedit Filio, Jo.5.*[22]) and to rewarde his werkmen þat wircheþ in his
130 vineȝard.

96 maner] maner of R;
(R *mar:* ⟨caus⟩*a quare homines* ⟨st⟩*eterunt otiosi*).
100 was] is R.
109 But þat] Ferþermore R.
111 and] *om.* A, (*int.* R);
114 alþerleest] þe leest R.
116 so] *om.* R.　　　　122 Þe] þis R;
123 eue] euen R;　　　　þis] þe R.
125 (R *mar:* Procurator).
129 Jo.5] *vnde* jo.5 (*Precedes the Latin*) R;

ofte tyme] *om.* R;
97 world] wolrld A.
107 blisse] hyȝe blis R.
110 mai] By þis may R.
oþer] or ellis for R.
115 vine] vyneȝerd R.
general] e(1) *om.* A.
124 he] *om.* A.
128 grantid fulli] fully grauntid R.
to] also to R.

Þat he bigyneþ at þe laste to rewarde first mai be vnderstonde þat summe of þoo þat bigynnen to trauaile in þe
vineȝard first in hire laste age morneþ and wepeþ so enteerli for
þei han dispendid in idel so her / tyme, and bieþ aȝen þe tyme   f. 64ʳ
135 wiþ good dedis as Seynt Poule biddeþ, þei encrecen so greteli
in loue in þat litel tyme þat þei ouerpassen many oþere þat
bigunne in her childehoode, as Marie Magd[elyn], Seynt
Poule, Mautheu, and mony oþere. And of suche Seynt Gregorius vnderstondeþ þis texte of þe gospel þat seiþ: *Maius*
140 *gaudium erit in celo, et cetera.* Into suche God rewardeþ blisse
as sone or sonnere as summe oþer þat traueliden fro ȝouþe.

Or ellis hit mai be vnderstonde þus: þat God seiþ þese
wordes to conforte hem þat first bigynnen to serue God in her
laste daies, þat þei dispeire not to be rewardid for her schort
145 trauaile, for þei schullen haue þe peny paied as wel as þe first.

Oþer þus it mai be vnderstonde: to schewe houȝ grete þe
merci of God is aboue alle his werkis; for it is oneli of þe grete
grace and mercy of God to rewarde so fulli so schort and litel
traueile, and so no man haþ cause of dispeire, but matere of
150 gret hope seþþe, in what hour þat he comeþ, God him wole
receyue.

Þis grucchynge of þese [first] werkmen aȝen þe laste mai not
be vnderstonde here an enuyous wille or indignacion þat men
schul haue in þe Dai of Doom for þe gracious reward of hire
155 breþeren. For no suche wille mai be amonge hem þat schullen
be saued, for þanne þei weren out of charite, whiche is þe bride
cloþ þat eueri man muste haue þat schal come to þat feeste, but
eche of hem schal be ioieful and / glad of oþeres goode.   f. 64ᵛ

Seynt Gregorius seiþ þat þis grucchynge is not ellis but a
160 wonderful merueilynge in mannes soule or mannes þouȝt of þe
grete mercy, bounte, and grace of oure Lord, þat rewardeþ
eche man iliche, boþe firste and laste, þe peni of euerlastynge
blisse.

131 (R *mar*: ⟨*N*⟩*ota de remuneracione*).   133 enteerli] hertily R.
135 good dedis] goodis R.   137 bigunne] bygynnen R;
Magdelyn] Magd' A, Maudlen R.   140 Into] and to R.
141 þat] oþat A.   142 vnderstonde] vnderstoden R.
148 so(2)] for so R.   149 dispeire] þis dispeyre R.
150–51 God...receyue] god wole receyue hym R.
152–5 (R *mar*: *De murmuracione operariorum primorum*);   first] *om.* A;
not] *om.* R.   153 an] *om.* R;   men] þei R.
157 þat(3)] þis R.   160 wonderful] wonder R.   162 þe] wiþ þe R.

But here þou schalt vnderstonde þat not eche man haþ iliche
165 myche blisse, but after hire loue was here, [so schal her blisse
þere be] more or less proportioned þerafter.

But as to þe euerlastyngnesse of blisse, whiche is vnderstonde bi þis peny for þe roundenesse whiche haþ non eende,
eche man schal be iliche ry[u]e, boþe he þat comeþ in age and
170 he þat comeþ in ȝouþe. And al þis oþer disputynge þat is told
heere in þis gospel bitwene þe lord and his werkemen is not
ellis but þe priue spekynge of God in mennes soules.

Or ellis it mai be vnderstonde þus, as anoþer glose seiþ:
suppose þat þei wolden grucche or myȝten grucchen, whiche
175 þei myȝten not, þei ne hadde no cause, for in no þyng þe
housholdere dide vniustli wiþ hem. For to him þat cam first,
hee quytt him his couenaunt, and more myȝte he not axe, bi
lawe ne bi resoun; and him þat came laste, he rewardide him of
his grace. And þat þat is gracyousli grauntid, no man ouȝte
180 bigrucche, ne take no matere of euele of anoþer man/nes f. 65ʳ
godnesse, for it is lefful of a mannes owne to do what him likeþ.
And þus oþerwhile: þei þat ben lattere clepid to grace schul be
raþer rewarded in blisse, for ofte þei þat ben clepid in þe last
houre departeþ sonnere hennes þan þei þat comen in ȝouþe,
185 and so sonnere rewardid.

But heere miȝten summe seyn: 'I here bi þis parable þat,
boþe first and laste, alle þei hadden þe peny; and so it wolde
seeme þat alle men schulden be saued'. But þe last worde of þis
gospel answereþ herto: 'Mani men ben clepid, and fewe ben
190 chose.' For many men in childhode, mani in ȝonge waxynge
age, many in mannes estaat, and mani in olde age, and mani in
þe last eende, 'beþ clepid', summe bi prechyng, summe bi
reedynge, summe bi good conseilynge, summe bi priue enspirynge, summe bi prosperitee, summe bi aduersite, to blisse

164 not] *om.* R; iliche] not yliche R.
165 myche] *om.* R; after] as R; was] is R.
165-6 so...be] *om.* A. 166 þerafter] *om.* R. 169 ryue] R, ryne A (*n.*).
170 oþer] *om.* R; told] *om.* R. 174 wolden] wil R.
175 ne] *om.* R. 178 bi] *om.* R; him(1)] he R.
179 ouȝte] owe R. 180 bigrucche] grucche R.
183 þei] þo R. 185 rewardid] ben rewardid R.
186 summe seyn] sum man seie R. 187 first] þe first R;
laste] þe laste R; þei] *om.* R.
190-91 waxynge age] age waxing R. 191 estaat] state R.
193 summe(2)] and summe R. 194 prosperitee] prosperiteis R;
summe(2)] and summe R; aduersite] aduersiteis R; to] to þe R.

195 of heuene; but 'fewe beþ chose', þat is: fewe wirchen þeraftir to
make þat þei moun be chose. And so defaute is not in God in
whom is alle goode, for and he wolde not þat þei come, he
wolde hem neuer clepe, for þat were but a deceite, and so dide
he neuere.

200   Vpon þis gospel a man miȝte touche þat riȝt as in a bodili
vineȝard ben þre maner of werkfolk wiþ diuerse occupacions,
so in þis gosteli vineȝerd beþ also þe same:
    Þe first beþ þo þat remouen / þe olde erþe, and openeþ þe   f. 65ᵛ
rotis, and after leien to dunge and newe erþe, to make it þe
205 bettere to growe, and þe plenteuousere bere his frute. And þese
moun be vnderstonde bi þe lowist estaat of holi chirche, þat is:
þe comyne peple, whos occupacions stondeþ in grobbyng
aboute þe erþe, as in erynge, and dungynge, and sowynge, and
harwynge, and oþer ocupacions þat longeþ to þe erþe. And þis
210 schulde be do iustli and for a good ende, wiþoute feyntise, or
falsede, or grucchynge of hire estaat. And þis mai be þe roote,
for þis was þe first degree þat longeþ to alle men; and þus wiþ
hire trwe labour þei schul bere vp and susteyne þe oþere tweie
parties of þe chirche, þat is: knyȝtes and clerkis.

215   Or ellis þus þis openynge of þe rote wiþ puttynge awei of þe
olde erþe mai wel be vnderstonde openynge of þyn herte, in
whiche schulde stonde þe rote of riȝtwis dedis, wiþ trewe
confession of þi synnes and doynge awei þe olde conuersacion
of þi erþeli and synful liȝfe, and leie þerto dunge of scharpe
220 penaunce, as fastynge, wolward goynge, hard liggynge, sore
disciplynes, and oþer dedes of penaunce.

    Or ellis leie þerto anoþer maner of dungynge, þat is: an
entiere remembraunce of þi mescheues and wrecchid / estaat.   f. 66ʳ
Anentis þi bodi: how viliche, houȝ vnmiȝti, how careful þou
225 come into þis world, wepynge, and weilynge, and wiþ non oþer
murþe. Afterward, what þou art, and what þou schalt beo at þe
ende: þou art but a sac ful of dritte, keuered vndir cloþes; and if

196 so] so þe R.   197 goode] goodnes R.
200-204 (R mar: De vinea spirituali et eius bonis operar⟨i⟩is).
200 miȝte] may R;   bodili] erþely R.
205 þe] om. R;   bere] to bere R;   þese] bi þese R.
206 bi] om. R;   estaat] state R.   207 ocupacions] occupacion R.
211 estaat] state R.   212 longeþ] longid R.
216-19 (R mar: Iustitia est radix spiritualis vinee).
217 riȝtwis dedis] riȝtwisnes R.
222-3 an entiere] haue a R;   219 dunge] þe dunge R.
224 Anentis] of R.   estaat] state R.
                                              226 þe] þin R.

it were turned outweis þat þat is wiþinne, he þat most makiþ of
himself, þe world wolde sette [him] at nouȝt. Afterward,
230 biholde al þi bodi aboute: what felþe comeþ oute of eche issu of
it, what at þe ien, what at þe nese, what at þe mouþe, also what
at þe eren, and what bineþe in oþer priue places. Þis is no
poynt of pride, if it be wel ipreued!

And þenke also on þin eende: how peineful it schal be,
235 grunnynge, and gronynge, and grisbatynge of teþ, and sauer-
ynge vnsoteli to hem þat sitteþ aboute. Whan þou art deed, þus
delfeli doluen þou schalt be, and iwastid wiþ wormes, be þou
neuer so worþi!

Wiþ þe mynde of þis matere, þou mai make good dunge to
240 make þe rote of riȝtwis werkis þe raþlier to growe, so þat þou
leie to newe erþe þat nedeþ also, þat is: goodwille to wirche wel,
for þat mai not wante.

Þe seconde maner of werkfolk in þis vyner ben þese þat taken
vp þe vyne fro þe ground, þat breres and wedes / ouergo hem   f. 66ᵛ
245 noȝt and lette hem to growe and bere her frute, but wiþ grete
stiffe trees forkid [aboue], and wiþ oþer longe trees leide on
hem, miȝtili bere hem vp so þat þei moun wiþoute l⟨e⟩tte
growe and bere her grapes. Þese moun be vnderstonde þe
seconde partie of þe chirche, þat is, þe cheualrie whiche, bi þe
250 miȝti power þat þei han take of God (as Seynt Poule seiþ,
Ro.13.[1]: Omnis potestas a Domino Deo est; þat is, þe grete and
forkid stif [trees] þat I spak of, whiche þat oo suyche is þe loue
of God, þe toþer of her breþeren) and bi helpe of þe longe tree
þat is leid aboue, (þat is, for hope of þe blisse of heuene),
255 schulde bere vp þe vine of riȝtwisnesse þat it were not ouergon
and oppressid wiþ breris and wedis of weiward and worldeli

228 outweis] outwarde R.   229 himself...him] þee wolde sett þee R;
him] þe A.   230 felþe] foule filþe R.
231 þe(1)(2)] om. R;   also] om. R.
232 in] and at R.   235 grunnynge] wiþ grunching R.
236 vnsoteli] vnswetly R.   237 and] om. R.   239 Wiþ] by R.
240 riȝtwis werkis] riȝtwisnes R.   241 goodwille] of goodwille A.
243 (R mar: ij);   vyner] vyneȝerd R.   245 her] om. R.
246 aboue] aboute A;   longe] om. R.   247 lette] lettyng R.
248 Þese] þese men R.   249 þe(2)(3)] om. R.
251 Ro.13] Ro' xiij c⁰ (Follows the Latin) R.
251–2 þat is...stif] þese ben þe grete stif forkid R.   252 trees] tre A.
252–3 of, whiche...breþeren] þe whiche þe ton forkid tre is þe loue of God . þe
toþer of her euencristen R.   253 bi] bi þe R.
254 for] for þe R.

tirauntis. For so vnderstondeþ Crisostom bi 'busches of breris'.
For riȝt, he seiþ, as vnder busches of breris is no refreschyng of
schadue, beestes for to reste hem vnder, as vnder oþer trees,
260 but oneli to snakis and to addris and suche oþer wormes, 'so
biside a good man, boþe good men and euele moun take reste',
but biside suche tirauntes, none moun reste but if it be suche
venemous bestes as þei ben, oþer ellis 'addres (þat is: fendes)
whiche han her couches in hire hertis'. And if a seeli good man
265 / þat is likned to a scheep for his simmplenesse dwelle bisides f. 67ʳ
hem, þei faren bi him as þe busche of breris dooþ bi a scheep,
[for] if he reste him bi [it], [it] pulleþ him and pileþ him while
he ouȝt haþ.

To þe office of þe þridde werkmen þat wirchen in þis
270 vineȝerd longeþ to kutte þis vine in tyme, þat it wexe not ouȝt
into wilde branches and bere his frute þe worse. And bi þese
moun be vnderstonde þe þridde degree of þe chirche, whiche
beþ: prelates and prestes, to wham it longeþ, if any wantunnesse or wildenesse of synne þat groweþ of mennes herte
275 sprede to fer into dede whiche letteþ riȝtwisnesse to beere his
frute, in himself or ellis in his breþeren bi euele ensample
ȝeuen, wiþ scharpe bitynge sentencis of Holi Writt or, if nede
axiþ, wiþ censures of holi chirche (þat is: wiþ scharpe punisch-
yngis), to kutte hem aweie, and seþþe after to lede hem forþ
280 þe vine of riȝtwis werkes in hire sugetis bi ensaumple of
hemselfe, and seþþe bynde hem togedere to hope of blisse wiþ
þe bond of pees in charitee.

Þese þanne beþ [þe] þre manere of officers þat longeþ to
kepynge and meyntenaunce of þis vyneȝard, if it schulde be wel
285 kepte to þe worschipe of God and / profite of his peple. But as f. 67ᵛ
faste as þese þre ben aboute to kepe þis vine, þer ben oþer þree
whiche ben aboute niȝt and dai to destrue þis vine, whiche ben
þe world, þe flesch, and þe fende, of whiche þre spekeþ Dauid,
in þe Psauter, þere he þus spekeþ of þe vine and seiþ:
290 *Vindemiant eam omnes qui pretergrediuntur viam. Exterminauit*

257 of] and R. 258 of(1)] and R. 259 beestes] of beestis R.
260 to(2)] *om.* R; suche] to suche R. 261 biside] bisidis R.
263 oþer] or R. 267 for] *om.* A; it(1)] him A; it(2)] *om.* A.
269 (R *mar:* iiij). 274 of(2)] oute of R; herte] hertis R.
278 axiþ] happiþ R. 279 to(2)] *om.* R; hem(2)] *om.* R.
283 þe] *om.* A; longeþ] logen R. 284 schulde] shal R.
285-7 (R *mar: De malis operarijs in ista vinea*).
286 faste as] *om.* R; ben aboute] nyȝt and day R.
289 þus] *om.* R.

eam, et cetera. Þat is: 'Alle þat gon bisides þe wei han plokkid aweie þe grapes. Þe wilde boor of þe wode haþ wrotid it vp, or cast [it] out of hire place, and þe singuleer wilde beest haþ eten it vp.'

295 Bi þo þat gon bisides þe wei moun be vnderstonde worldeli couetus men, for þe weie toward þe blisse of heuene is þe commaundementis of God, and alle suche goon bisides þe weie, for þei maken hire goodes hir God, and so doþ maumetrie, as Seynt Poule seiþ: *Auarus, quod est idolorum seruitus, et*

300 *cetera*, whiche is fulli contararie to þe first maundement, and so suyngeli to alle þe oþer. And alle suche plocken aweie þe grapes of hire goode werkes of kynde, whiche þei wirchen ar þei ben ripe; for wiþoute good bileue, whiche þei wanten, þei schul neuer ripe to any profite to hem, as Seynt Poule seiþ to

305 Hebr[eus]: *Sine fide | impossibile est placere Deo* (*Hebr.*11.[6]).   f. 68ʳ [Þat is: 'Wiþouten feiþ it is impossible to plese God.']

Also, suche wordli couetouse men plockeþ aweie þe grapes in hire breþeren as if faderles children, or any oþer widues, or any oþer persones, ben put awei fro hire due eritage, hire lond, or

310 hire goodes. Þe grapes of þis vyne of riȝtwisnesse were þat þei weren restored truely þerto. Þenne, if any true man of concience bisie him here aboute, þenne þese grapes bigynneþ to put oute a litil. But þese wordeli men, as I seide, þat gon bisides þe wei wiþ hire bodeli muk (whiche is hire God, þat

315 helpeþ hem, and spekeþ so for hem to iusticis, to men of lawe, to meyntenouris in cuntre, to cisouris), for seluer selleþ hire soule þat þei plocken of þe grape or it be ripe, þat þei moun neuer keuere, ne come to hire riȝte [ripyng].

Þe same it is als⟨o⟩ of oþer þat ben put wrongfulli in prisoun

320 for þefte, or manslauȝtere, or any oþer trespace: þe true tiliers of þis vyne wolde þat suche weren delyuered; but þei þat goþ bisides þe weie plocken of þe grapes, and sleeþ suche wiþ hire sotel craft, and seyn þat it is riȝte.

291 þat(2)] þo þat R.   293 it] her A;   hire] his R.
298 goodes] god R;   God] good R.
299–300 *et cetera*] *om.* R.   300 maundement] comaundement R.
302 hire] *om.* R;   þei(1)] þe R.
305 Hebreus] hebr' A, to þe hebreis.xi.cᵒ R;   *Hebr.*11] *om.* R.
306 Þat is...God] *om.* A.   308 any oþer] *om.* R.
309 hire(2)] or R.   310 were] wolde R.
311 restored truely] truly restorid R;   man] men R.
314 God] good R.   316 for] þat for A *and* R.   318 ripyng] *om.* A, (*mar.* R).
319 wrongfulli] wrongly R.   323 seyn] seint R.

In þe chirche also is þe same caas, if men loken wel. If a
325 prelacie or a personage be voide of a pastour, or any oþer cure
þat nedide of an hed, Goddis / wille were, and þe lawe also it f. 68ᵛ
seiþ, þat whos were most mekid and lest settid bi þe world, bi
fre eleccion of þe cherche or patrons presentacion, schulde
haue such cure to saue mannes soules. Þanne, if any suche be
330 chosen freli bi þe cherche, or þe patron wolde presente suche a
perfiȝt persone, þenne bigynneþ þis grape first for to growe.
But þei þat goþ bisides þe weie, as I seide bifore, plocken awey
þe grape of riȝt þat it may neuere be ripe (wiþ symonie of
seluer, or wiþ lordis ceelis) and, in stede of a good man, sette a
335 schrewe on benche. And þus, as I haue sumwhat schewid, þe
worlde is þe firste enemy þat is aboute to destrie þis vyneȝerd.

Þe seconde enemy is þe boor of þe wode, þat is: mannes
flesch. Þe boor of a wode is more wylde þan þe boor of þe feld;
so mannes flesch, but if it be rulid vndur resoun of Goddes
340 lawe, he is more wylde þan eny oþer vnresonable beest.

To þis boor may mannes flesch wel be likened, for þre
propurtees þat longen to þe boor whiche moun be likned to þre
synnes þat comen of þe flesch: first, a boor smyteþ sore wiþ his
tusckis þat stonden in his mouþe; þe seconde is þat he wole
345 gladli reeste him in foule slowis, or mury placis; þe 3 is þat he
haþ a foule stynkynge sauur where he goþ. And bi þese moun
be vndirstonde glotenye, sleuþe, and stynkynge lecherie.

First I / seie þe boor smyteþ wiþ his tusckis þat stondeþ in f. 6
his mouþe. So þe glotoun, whan he is drunke, is þanne hardy to
350 smyte ful sore wiþ his curside wordis boþe God and man. First
God, wiþ grete and horrible oþes whiche þanne ben [rife] ynow
in his mouþ; and seþþe his breþeren, wiþ foule sc[h]rewide and
slaundri wordis, lying and cursynge, he smyteþ and spareþ
noȝt. And þus wiþ þe wrot of his mouþe he turneþ vp þe vine,
355 boþe in himself and eke in his breþeren.

Þe seconde condicion of þis boor is þat he wol gladli reste
him in slowis. And bi þis mai be vndurstonde þe seconde synne
þat comeþ of þe flesche, þat is: sleuþe. For whose wol not

328 (R mar: symony).   329 cure] a cure R;   soules] soule R.
331 for] om. R.   335 on] on þe R.
337 (R mar: secundus inimicus vinee).   338 a] þe R.
341-2 (R mar: Tres proprietates apri).
348 (R mar: I).   350 ful] om. R.
351 grete...oþes] his grete oþis and orrible R;   rife] R, rynede A (n. 8/169).
352 breþeren] broþer R.   353 slaundri] sclaundrous R.
354 þe(1)] his R.   356 (R mar: ij).

laboure his office þat longeþ to him in þis vyneȝerd, þe breris
360 and þornes wolen ouergo þe vyne þat neuer wyn schal come
þerof but wexe al awyldid. Þerfore seiþ þe Wise Man
(*Prouer*.24.[30–31]): 'I wente bi þe slowe mannes feld and I
fond it ful of breris and of þornus'—þat is, of schrewde þouȝtis
þat destrieþ al þe vyne.

365   Þe þridde propurte of þis boor is his stynkynge sauour. And
bi þis mai be vnderstonde þe þridde synne þat comeþ of þe
flesch, þat is: lecherie, þat stynkiþ ful foule in þe siȝt of God;
and wiþ þis [þe] wilde boor (þat is, mannes flesch) turneþ vp þe
vyne of alle riȝtwis werkis. For suchon is boþe prouȝte and
370 vnpacient to alle þat repreuen him of his synne; and envious to
venge him, whan he seeþ his tyme; and he is couetous also, to
mayntene wiþ his lustis; and slouful and glotenous to kepe his
complex/ion. And þere as suche synnes ben, vertues ben turned
vp þat þer mai no gret profite come þerof while þei lyen soo.   f. 69ᵛ
375 And þus þis boor of mannes flesch is þe seconde enemy þat is
aboute to destruye þis vyneȝard.

    Þe þridde enemy of þis vineȝard is þe singuler wilde best, þat
is: þe fend. Synguler he is, for þer is no power vppon erþe þat
mai bee likned to his, as Job seiþ in 41 chapitre: *Non est potestas*
380 *super terram que comparetur ei*. And also he is a wylde beest, for
Seynt Petre likneþ him to a rorynge lyon.

    And þis singuler wilde beeste gnaweþ vp alle þe grapis or
grene þat groweþ on þis vyne wiþ his þre synnes þat longen
vnto him, þat is: hiȝ pride, wraþþe, and enuye. For, as þe
385 comune prouer[b] seiþ:
       Si tibi copia, seu sapientia, formaque detur;
       Sola superbia destruit omnia, si comitetur.
    'Þou[ȝ] þou haue plente of wordeli goodes, and wisdom,
       and fair schap of bodi;
390   If pride be partener, it is not worþ a pese.'
And Seynt Gregorius seiþ: 'Whos gadereþ vertues wiþoute
mekenesse', whiche is contrarie to pride, 'he fareþ as he þat
bereþ dust in þe wynd, þat bloweþ al aweie.'

    Also, wiþ veyneglorie he eteþ vp þis vyne. For if þou haue
395 pride of þi dedis, þi mede is here amonge men, for more geetist
þou noȝt.

---

360 þe vyne] þis vyneȝerd R.   365 (R *mar*: iij).
370 þat] þo þat R.   372 glotenous] glotorous R.
374 lyen] ben R.   384 vnto] to R.
385–7 (R *mar*: *Prouer' versus*).   388 Þouȝ] ȝ *om*. A.
394–5 (R *mar*: *De vana gloria*).

Also, wiþ wraþþe and enuye he gnaweþ vp þis vyne of al
riȝtwis werkis / þat wexe moun þei noȝt, while charitee is f. 70ʳ
aweie, þat is chef of vertues. For þis witnesseþ Seynt Poule,
400 and warneþ vs alle: *Si linguis hominum loquar, et cetera* ([1]
*Cor.*13.[1–3]). 'Þouȝ I speke,' he seiþ, 'wiþ angels tungis and
wiþ mennis boþe, and haue prophecies and priuetees and
science proued, and also riȝt bileeue þat I mai remoue hillis,
and þouȝ I parte alle my godis to pore mennes mete, and eke
405 my bare bodi to brenne in þe fuyre, al is lost þat I haue doon al
my liȝftyme, wiþouten charite'—þat is cheef of alle vertues.

Þus þis wickide wilde best wircheþ nyȝt and dai to make þe
vyne of vertues voide of alle grace, and letteþ hit of his licour
þat like schulde oure Lord. And þis is þe 3 enuyous enemy þat
410 eteþ vp þis vyne.

Þus þese 3 enemyes of þis vyneȝard of whiche I haue spoke
bifore, þat is: þe world, þe flesch, and þe fend, han longe
trauelid to destruye þe vyne of riȝtwisnesse; and þe þre forseide
werkmen so idel also in hire labour, eche in his degre, þat it is
415 al awyldid. And þerfore þe Lord of þis vyneȝard mai playne
him now on þis vyne and seie þe wordes of Ysaie, in þe V
chapitre: *Expectaui vt faceret vuas; et fecit labruscas.* Þat is: 'I
haue abide þat it schulde make grapes; forsoþe it made wylde
gra/pes þat beþ not able to man.'   f. 7

420 What þese wylde grapes beþ, Osee þe prophet (4) expowneþ
in þis wise: 'Þer is no truþe, þer is no mercy, þer is no
knowynge of God in erþe, whiche schulde be verreie grapes of
þe vyne of riȝtwisnesse, but cursidenesse, and þefte, and
lesynge, manslauȝter, and spousebreche, han iswollen vp; and
425 blod touchede blod'—þat is, synne vpon synne. Þese ben þe
wilde grapes þat growen on þis vyne. Weileaweie þe while þat
euere weren þei wrouȝte!

God, for his grete godnesse, grante vs þoru his grace to
wirche so wiseli in þis world oure werkis in þis vyne, eche man
430 in his estaat þat he stant inne, þat we moun like þe Lord þerwiþ
and be alowed [þ]e peny.

403 science] sciencis R.   415 awyldid] wyldid R.   422 God] good R.
423–4 þefte, and lesynge] lesing and þefte R.
425 touchede] haþe touchid R;   is] *om.* R.
429 so wiseli in þis world] in þis R;
oure...þis] (R *has this phrase deleted by a fine line*).
431 þe] pe A.

9
SEXAGESIMA
SUNDAY

Exijt qui seminat seminare semen suum, et cetera. (*Luc.*8.[5]). 'He
þat soweþ wente out to sowe his seed; and while he sowiþ, sum
felde bisides þe weie and was defoulid, and þe briddes of
heuene, or of þe eir, eeten hit.'
5   In þis gospel, oure Lord Jesus Crist, bi an ensample of seed
þat was sowen, of whiche þe 4 parte made frute, techeþ prelatis
and prestis of þe cherche to be besy euere and not be idel fro
sowynge of gostli seed of þe word of God, þou3 it profite not
alweie to þe auditorie after hire desire.
10   Oure Lord Jesus Crist (Goddis Sone of heuene, þe seconde
persone of þe Trinite, þe wisdom of þe Fadir) haþ expowned
þis gospel as is schewid in þe lettre, and he seiþ: '3he clepen /
me "Maister" and "Lord", and 3he seyn wel, for so I am'   f. 71ʳ
(*Jo.*13.[13]). And he seiþ in anoþer place, *eodem capitulo*: 'Þe
15 disciples schulden not be aboue þe maister, but it sufficiþ to þe
disciple þat he be as his maister.'
    Seþþe þenne oure Maister þat is þe welle of wisdom haþ
expouned þis gospel, it were a prou3t presumcyon to any erþeli
persone, [were] he neuere so perfite, in any maner wise to
20 weyue fro his witt. Þerfore bileue we fulli to his sentence, and
hoolde we vs apaid.
    But tofore þat oure Lord expounede eþer openede his
parable (þat is, his ensample) to his disciples, he criede as þe
gospel seiþ, and seide þus: 'He þat haþ eris of herynge, here

---

1 *Exijt*] (*Text indented for two lines; small* e *written into the space; no
rubrication*).   4 þe] *om.* R.   5 an] *om.* R.
6 4] fourþe R.   7 besy euere] euer bise R;
fro] of R.   9 auditorie] herers R.   12 as] as it R.
14 *Jo.*13] *om.* R.   16 þat he] to R.
19 were] where A.   20 weyue fro] weyne forþe R (*n.*).
22 tofore þat] bifore or R;   eþer] or R.
23 þat...ensample] *om.* R.

25 he!' For Seynt Jerom seiþ: 'Where so euere þis word is seid, þer
is an excellent goostli vndirstondynge of þe wordes of Crist.'
And þus, bi þis cryinge and þese wordis suynge also is schewid
a greet feruent wille of oure blessid Lord þat he haþ to þe
profite of mannes soule, bi whiche he wolde þat euery man þat
30 hereþ þe word of God wiþ his bodili eris, herde hit also wiþ his
gostli eris, þat is: wiþ þi muynde vndirstonde it, loue it, kepe it,
and wirche þerafter. Þerfore he seiþ: 'He þat haþ eeris of
herynge, here he!' For bestis and wickide men heren þe word of
God wiþ þe bodili eeris, as doon true cristen men, but for þei
35 beeren it not aweie, and kepe it not, and wirche not þerafter,
þerfore þou3 þei haue eeris, þei haue no eeris of heerynge / after f. 7
þe vndirstondynge and menynge of Crist.

But heere my3te a man argue a3en þis sentence bi þe wordis
þat Crist seide after þat his disciplis hadden preied him to
40 expowne hem þe parable, where he seide: 'To 3ou it is 3ouen to
knowe þe priuetees of þe kyngdom of God; to oþer forsoþe in
parablis, or hid ensaumplis.' Bi þis a man my3te seie: 'It is not
my gult þat I knowe not, or vndirstonde not, for God haþ not
3ouen it to me.' But Crisostom seiþ 'suche wolden putte þe
45 synne of hire necligence to God, and þei seie not þis sorwynge
for þei knowen not þoo þyngis þat ben harde, but þei sechen
excusacyon of hire synnes. Of suche seiþ þe prophete: *Non
declines cor meum in verba malitie ad excusationes, et cetera.* "Ne
bowe not myn herte into wordis of malice to excuse ex-
50 cusacions in synnes, wiþ men wirchynge wickidnesse."

'Euery vnderstondynge is of þe Hooli Gost, and is of þe
grace of God. But God 3eueþ oþer maner grace to alle in
g[e]neral in þe firste formynge, and oþer to oþer worþier and
more chosen. To alle men he 3eueþ a general grace, þat is:
55 vndirstondynge of good and euele, but to worþier he 3eueþ a
special grace, þat is: knowyng of priuetees of þe word of God,
whiche is vndirstonde bi þe kyngdom of heuene, for it ledeþ to
þe kyngdom of heuene and openeþ it to man. Þanne, if þou
wolt dispende þe general knowynge of good and euele ri3tfulli,
60 þou / schuldest deserue þe special science of knowynge of f.
priuetees. 3hif þanne þou hast hid in þe erþe þat general
kunnynge, hou deseruest þou þanne þis special kunnynge?'

31 vndirstonde] vnderstonding R.   34 þe] *om.* R.   35 and(2)] ne R.
36 no] not R.   39 þat(1)] of R.   42 Bi] But R.
45 sorwynge] sorowingly R.   46 þat] *om.* R.   47 *Non*] Ne R.
51 of(2)] *om.* R.   53 general] e(1) *om.* A.   59 knowynge] *om.* R.
60 deserue] discerne R (*n.*).   62 deseruest] discernyst R (*n.*).

Also, Crisostom seiþ: 'Truþe is not hid in Scripturis, but
derk. Not þat þei schulden not fynden it þat sechen it, but þat
65 þei see hit not þat wole not seche it. Þ⟨at it⟩ perteyne to her
glorie þat fynden it, for þei desireden it, and souȝten and
founden it; into her dampnacion þat fynden it not, for þei neþer
desireden it, ne souȝten, ne founden. Neþer vnknowynge of þe
truþe mai be to hem excusacion of her dampnacion, for þei
70 myȝten haue founde if þei wolden haue souȝte.'

Turne we þanne now to þe declarynge or openynge of þis
gospel. Þis blessid Lord Jesus, of whom we han spoke, 'wente
oute fro þe Fadir' (*Jo*.[16.28]): *Exiui a Patre*, but he lefte him
neuere, into þis wrecchide world, and took flesch of a maide;
75 and after, from his moderis wombe into comun of þe pepul,
whiche þat was þe erþe in whiche he þreu his seed of þe
gloryous gospel, take it whoso wolde. 'But sum,' he seiþ, 'felde
bisydes þe weie, and was defoulid wiþ tredynge, and turnede to
no profite, but briddes of þe eir camen and eeten it vp.' [Þese it
80 ben, seiþ Crist, þat] whan þei heren þe word of God, 'comeþ þe
fend and takiþ it awey fro hire hertis, leest þei leeuynge be
maad saaf'.

Þe commaundementis of God ben þe wey toward heuene, as
Crist seiþ in þe gospel and Dauid in þe Psauter, and whoso
85 kepeþ not hem / is bisydes þe wey, and suche a soule is troden   f. 72ᵛ
playn wiþ tramplynge of fendes wiþ hire wickide suggestyons
and hire foule þouȝtis wiþ whiche þei traueilon as wiþ tredynge
suche a voide soule. For who þenkeþ not bisili in þe heestis of
þe Lord, he is ydel and voyde in þe siȝt of God, and in suche a
90 soule þe fend haþ alle his wille. Þerfore seiþ Seynt Jerom, þat
spekiþ of þis matere: *Semper aliquid boni operis facito, et cetera.*
'Euer doo þou sum good, þat þe fend fynde þe not vnocupied.'

Þanne, if þe word of God be cast into suche a soule, it haþ
noon erþe of goodwille to keuere wiþ þe seed, but lyiþ aboue al
95 open to þe siȝt of fendis, whiche camen and smartli eeten it vp

66 souȝten] souȝten it R.　　　　　　　　　　68 it] *om*. R;
founden] founden it R;　　　　　Neþer] Ne R;　　　　þe] *om*. R.
71 þanne] *om*. R;　　　　　or] and R.　　　　　73 16.28] 6 A, vj R.
74 þis] his R.　　　　　　　　　　　75 comun] þe comun R.
76 his] þe R.　　　　　　　　　　79–80 Þese...þat] þat is A.
84 whoso] who R.
85 (*Top of f.72v. mar: Ista prosa est edit[a?] instar cadencie*, H3);
is(1)] he is R.　　　　　　　　　　88 who] whoso R.
90 seiþ] *om*. R.　　　　　　　　　91 matere] mater seiþe R.
92 Euer] þᵗ is Euer R.　　　　　　94 noon] no R.

anoon. Not þat fendis moun eete þe hooli word of [God] but,
for as myche as þey wasten þe effect of þe word þat it worche
not in þat soule. And of suche, men seyn in comun prouerbe:
'It gooþ in at þe ton eere and oute at þe toþer.' And þese ben
100 like to þe goos þat goþ to þe water: for be þer neuer so myche
water held on hire bak, sche schakeþ her feþeres and sche is
neuer þe wettere.

Crist clepeþ heere suche fendes 'briddes of heuene' or
'briddes of þe eir' for as myche as þei hauen alwei þer heuenli
105 kynde, þou3 þei ben maad malicyous þoru synne of enuye. Or
þei been 'briddes of þe eir' for þei been dwellynge heere in þe
eyr amonge vs, and alwey sturynge / men to hi3e pride to   f. 7
brynge hem into þe same synne bi whiche he fel fro heuene.
Þerfore seiþ Job (41): *Ipse est rex super omnes filios superbie.* 'He
110 is kyng vpon alle þe children of pride.'

Þe seconde part of þe seed 'fel into stoony lond'. Þat is: hertis
þat han a litil erþe of ioie and good wille whan þei heren þe
word of God, bi whiche it springeþ sumwhat vp; but for þei
haue no moistur of formed bileeue, deuocyon, and loue,
115 þerfore þe word mai not take roote of perseuerance in hire
soule. But at þe tyme of prechynge þei han þerto bileeue, and in
tyme of temptacyon þei goon awei þerfro. Þerfore seiþ Marc of
þis matere: 'Anon as þe heete of persecucyon [and tribulacion]
is maad for þe word, þei beþ foule disclaundrid and feyntli
120 faileþ þerfro.'

Alle suche þynken ioie oþurwhile for to heere þe word of
God, whiche techeþ vertues as mekenesse, paciense, charitee,
chastitee, and suche oþer and, for a tyme of þe heerynge, han a
good wille to wirche hem in dede. But whanne þe proude man
125 comeþ in cumpanie þere he seþ men gayli araied, or take gret
worschipe, or stie to hi3e astaatis; or to þe wraþful man is seid a
word a3ens his wille, 3ea! þou3 it bee of correccion ful helpynge
of his soule; or þe enuyous man seeþ any man fare bettere þan
he or is more worschipid, or holde more wisur; or ellis þe
130 lecherous man comeþ in cumpanye of wymmen þat beþ feire

96 anoon] *om.* R;   word] wordis R;   God] good A.
101 held on] vpon R;   sche(2)] *om.* R.   103–4 or...eir] *om.* R.
104 þer] her R.   107 (*Foot of* f.72v. *catchwords*: men to).
109 He] þᵗ is he R.   110 children] sonys R.   111 into] in R.
114 no] not R.   118 matere] same mater R;
and tribulacion] *om.* A.   121 Alle] Also R.
123 a(1)] þe R;   þe] *om.* R.   124 whanne] *om.* R.
127 þou3 it bee] *om.* R;   helpynge] helplingly R.

fetured and feyneþ hem feire chere, anon as / þis heete of f. 73ᵛ
temptacion towchiþ mannes soule, þe word of God drieþ vp,
for it was not rooted faast for defauȝte of moisture.

Þe þridde part of þis seed 'fel among þornes, and þe þornes
135 groweden vp þerwiþ and baare þe corn adoun.' Þese been suche
þat hereþ þe word of God ypreched, and bisynesse of þe world
and lustis of þis liȝf bereþ hit doun and brekeþ it, and so it
bereþ no frute.

Seynt Gregorius seiþ: And anoþer man þan Crist hadde
140 clepid richesse 'þornes', fewe men wolde haue ȝeue credence to
him, seþþe þat oon prickeþ and þat oþer deliteþ and conforteþ.
But wiseli and wel if men take hede beþ þey lickened to þornes,
for riȝt as þornes prickeþ mannes flesch and bryngiþ oute
blode, so þe trobel and bisynesse þat man haþ aboute richesses,
145 wiþ trauaile in þe getynge, drede in þe kepynge, and sorwe in
þe leesynge, prickeþ and al torendiþ mannes soule, and is cause
of norischynge of many synnes, whiche beþ vndirstonde bi
'blood'.

And riȝt as a man þat is strangelid, þe breþ bi whiche he
150 lyueþ is stopped, so þe lust and likynge þat a man haþ in þe
richesses of þis world stoppeþ þe spiriȝt of liȝf [in] þe word of
God bi whiche he scholde lyue in soule and so sleeþ him gostli.

Many wordeli riche men han ioie and delite to heere þe word
of God, and ben in greet wille to performe myche þerof; but þe
155 loue to þe richesses wole þei not leue, and so springen vp
togidere þe / wille þat þei haue to þe word of God and þe loue f. 74ʳ
þat þei haue to hir richesses. But, for Crist seiþ: *Nemo potest
duobus dominis seruire* 'no man mai serue two loordes at oones'
(þat is: God and false richesses), þerfore richesses ofte tyme
160 han þe rule aboue.

If a riche man hereþ in þe gospel houȝ men schullen rikene at
þe Dai of Dome of þe visitynge of hire breþeren þat lyuen heere
at meschef, sike or in prisoun, he is sore adrad þerof and haþ
wille to performe it, but [þanne] comeþ þe Bisynesse of þis
165 World and biddeþ him abide, and seiþ he schal do it anoþer dai
whanne he mai haue more leiser.

131 heete of] *om.* R.   133 defauȝte] þe defaute R.
136 þe(2)] þis R.   141 oon] þe ton R.
146 al torendiþ] alto rendeþ A.   150 a] *om.* R;
þe(2)] *om.* R.   151 in] and A.
155 to] of R.   158 two] to two R.
164 þanne] *om.* A (R þen).   165 him] *om.* R.
166 haue] better and of R.

If he here in anoþer place Goddis word, houȝ it techeþ: *Facite vobis amicos de mammona iniquitatis,* 'Make ȝe to ȝou frendes of þis wordli muk', [also he seiþ]: *Omni petenti te,*
170 *tribue,* 'To euery man þat axeþ ȝou, ȝeue ȝe, for my sake', þis hym þynkiþ were wel doon, for al it comeþ of him, and for þei `beþ´ oure breþeren and brouȝt forþ of oo Fadir. Þanne comeþ Couetise of Catel and seiþ: 'Care for þiself, for þou knowist noȝt þe lengþe of þi liȝfe, ne what myscheef þou schalt haue.'
175 Whanne he hereþ þe word of God, þat seiþ: *Oportet semper orare [et numquam deficere],* 'It bihoueþ euer to preie, and neuer for to faile', and Seynt Poule also, in anoþer place: *Sine intermissione orate,* 'Wiþouten any cesynge preie ȝe to God', and Seynt Jame seiþ: *Multum valet deprecatio iusti assidua,* þat
180 is: 'Ful myche avayleþ þe bisi preier maad / of a riȝtwis man', f. 74 þanne him þynkeþ it is good to be busi and bidde faste to God, for al hangeþ in his hond, oure hap and oure hele, boþe at mateyns and at messe for þat myche auayleþ, and wiþ þe perfite *Pater Noster* for þat preier pleseþ God. But þanne comeþ his
185 Muk into his muynde and marreþ him amydde, and seiþ: 'Leef þi labour for a litil tyme, and go redresse þat is mysrulid or þou maist rue foreuere, and do þi deuer anoþer dai and double it þerfore.' And þus is þe word of God strangulid and destried wiþ þornes of richessis whan þei han þe rule, þat it fadeþ and
190 falleþ awei and faileþ of his frute.

If þe word of God be prechid, þat of fastynge spekiþ to fiȝte wiþ hire foule flesch þat is so fayn to falle, þat him þynkeþ resonable, and þenkeþ to rule him þerafter. But þenne springeþ vp þornes of Chyncherie, and spredeþ aboue, and seiþ: 'Faste
195 ofte, and spende litil, and þe more maist þou spare.' Þus Auarice ouergoþ Abstynence and vnableþ it to frute.

Þe 4 part of þis seed 'fel in good lond, and sprong vp, and made 100 fold frute.' Þese ben þo þat wiþ good herte hereþ þe word of God, and kepiþ it in hire herte þat it falle neuer awei,
200 and in preued pacience bryngeþ forþ myche frute.

As plouȝmen han preued þat practisen in þe craft, þat lond must beo ful dueli diȝt þat scholde do wel his deuer. First, if it

168 Make] þat is make R.   169 also he seiþ] *om.* A.   170 To] þat is to R.
172 beþ] (*int.* H3).   175 hereþ] heriþ also R.   176 *et numquam deficere*] *om.* A;
It] þat is it R.   177 place] place seiþe R.
178 Wiþouten] þat is wiþouten R;   any] *om.* R.
180 (*Top of* f.74v. *mar: de oratione,* H3);   riȝtwis] iust R.
187 foreuere] þe while R.   191 fiȝte] feynt R.   192 hire] oure R.
195 maist þou] þou maist R.   197 4] fourþe R.   202 ful dueli] riȝt wel R.

be þicke of þornes þat makeþ þe lond to vnþryue, ripe hem vp
bi þe roote lest þei renne to fer. After, it must be tilid / in tyme f. 75ʳ
205 and turned ful ofte, and seþþe þrowe dunge þeron, for þat dooþ
myche good þat no wedes vpwaxen and make þe lond þe worse,
and þenne erli eggid after, ar it be sowe, to make hit falle þe
smallere as many men vsen. Lond þat is þus araied is redi to
receyue his seed, and seþþe springen vp ful spedili and after
210 greyn manyfold. Þus muste mannes soule be serued, if it
scholde be able to sowe þerynne þe word of God þat it myȝte
frute. First, drawe vp þe þornes of richessis bi þe roote, þat is:
sette not harde þyn herte on hem, þouȝ þei happili to þe falle,
[for Dauid seiþ, in þe Psauter]: *Diuitie si affluant* [*nolite cor*], *et*
215 *cetera*.

Þe greet clerk Groosthed, in a sermoun þat he makiþ þat
bigynneþ þus: *Pauper et inops laudabunt nomen tuum*, seiþ þus:
'Man is disposed to loue of temperal richessis in foure degrees,
of whiche þe first degre is sett in helle, þe seconde is sett in
220 purgatorie and fynalli in heuene, þe þridde and þe fourþe
degree ben sett anon in heuen.

'Þe first degre is whan a man loueþ so myche þese rychessis
þat he wole breke a commaundement of God to gete oþer
hoolde þese temperal þyngis. And þanne he loueþ not God, but
225 forsakiþ him for a litil temperal þynge, and if he dieþ oute of
charitee (R[omaynes] 6 chapitre), anon he is dampnyd to þe fire
of helle.

'Þe seconde de/gree is whanne a man loueþ so temperal f. 75ᵛ
þyngis þat þei moun not be lost wiþouten sorwe; neþeles, he
230 haþ leuer leese alle þanne to breke Goddes heeste. But þe droos
of þis loue mut be purgid bi fier, for oþer þe brennynge of
penauncis in þis liȝf schal waste þis ruste, oþer þe flamme of
heete of þe fier of purgatorie.

'Þe þridde degre is whanne a man is so disposid to temperal
235 þyngis þat he mai lese hem alle wiþoute sorwe, and welde
wiþoute gladnesse. And þis man haþ anon þis meede: þat he
mai not be maad soruful bi any aduersitee comynge on him.

---

206 vpwaxen] wexen vp R.   208 smallere] feyrer R;   men] folke R.
209 ful] *om.* R.   210 Þus] And þus R.   212 frute] bere fruyt R.
213 happili] happly R.   214 for...Psauter] *om.* A;   *nolite cor*] *om.* A.
216 Groosthed] Gosthed R;   in...makiþ] *om.* R.
217 *tuum*] *tuum et cetera* R.   219 sett(2)] *om.* R.
222 (R *mar*: I);   rychessis] temporal riches R.
223 he] *om.* R.   226 Romaynes 6 chapitre] R 6 cᵒ, *om.* R.
228 loueþ so] haþe R.   232 oþer] or ellis R.   237 aduersitee] aduersites R.

For Salamon seiþ: *Non contristabit iustum quicquid ei acciderit.*
Þat is: "Whateuer þyng bifalliþ to a iuste man, it schal not
240 make him sori", for non aduersitee takeþ awei fro him any of
þo þyngis þat ben desirid of him. And al heuynesse of herte and
sorwe is felynge of absence of a þyng coueitid; þerfore, if a man
desireþ or loueþ no þyng þat mai be take[n] awei from him
vnwillynge, no þynge is whereof he mai be soruful. And he þat
245 is in þis degre mai vse riȝtfulli temperal goodis, and no man
mai fille þe riȝtful vsynge in þese temperal goodis bifore þat he
come to þis degre.

'Þe fourþe degre is whanne a man despisiþ so temperal
þyngis þat he hadde leuere to welde hem noȝt, and is sori if he
250 be char/gid wiþ hem, and ioieþ whanne he is dischargid', and f. 76'
þis degre is of apostlis and of perfite men þat schal sitte in seetis
biside God and deme al þe world.

Wheresoeuere þanne þat þese þornes growe, þei musten be
drawe vp bi þe roote if it schal be maad able to receyue þe seed
255 of þe word of God. Þerfore þis blessid sowere Jesus Crist, of
whom þis gospel spekiþ of, sawe þat it was 'more esi to a
camele to entre bi a neldul ye' þan a man louynge or tristynge
in richessis to entre into goostli knowynge of Hooli Scripture,
þat is: þe word of God, whiche is vndirstonde bi 'þe kyngdom
260 of heuenes.'

Tofore þanne þat Crist seew þis seed in his apostlis, he ripte
vp þe þornes of wordeli goodis, whanne boþe Petre and
Andreu, John and James, forsoken hire nettis and hire boote
whiche was hire wordeli possession. And it was take vp clene bi
265 þe roote whanne, as Jerom seiþ, þei forsoken wille of hauynge,
whiche is greet in þe siȝt of God, þouȝ þe possession be litil.

Also, as Actis of þe Apostlis telleþ in þe [4] chapitre, in þe
bigynnynge of þe cherche, after þe ascencion of oure Lord, in
tyme of þe apostlis whiche weren principalli sent of him to
270 sowe þis gostli sed, as Mar[ke] seiþ in þe last chapitre, myche of
þe comune peple (hauynge in mynde þe wor/des of oure Lord, f. 7
þat seide: *Vendite que possidetis, et date elemosinam. Facite vobis*

239 Þat is] *om.* R.   243 taken] n *om.* A.   248 so] *om.* R.
253 þanne þat] þat þanne (*m. for r.*), þat *om.* R.
256 sawe...was] seiþe þus . *Facilius est camelum intrare per foramen acus*
quam diuitem et cetera . Mt . þat is it is R.
257 neldul] neldis R;   man] riche man R;   louynge] (*repeated*) A.
261 þat] *om.* R;   seew] shew R.   262 boþe] *om.* R.
265 wille] þe wille R.   267 4] 5 A, fifþe R.   270 as] and R;
Marke] marc' A.   272 seide] seide þus R;   date] datee A.

sacculos, [*qui non veterascunt, thesaurum non deficientem in celo,*
þat is:] 'Selleþ þoo þyngis þat ȝe weelden, and ȝeueþ almes.
275 Make ȝe ȝouȝ baggis þat waxen not oolde, tresour not failynge
in heuene') maden clene hir hertis of alle suche maner þornes,
sellynge hur possessions and þrowynge þe price to þe apostelis
feet. And þus þei maden hire hertis able to þe word of God.
And þerfore it seiþ, in þe nexst chapitur suyinge, þat 'þe word
280 of God waxide, and þe noumbre of disciplis was multiplied ful
myche.'

Þerfore oure Maistur, Jesus Crist, as þe principal sowere,
tauȝte vs þat beþ his seruauntis and schulde sowe þis seed þat
we haue a good yȝe þat no þorne vp arise; and if he do, soone
285 pulle him vp for peirynge of þe lond: *Videte, et cauete, et cetera.*
'Seeþ,' he seiþ, 'and beþ war of al maner of auarice.'

After þis stockynge or pullyng vp of þornes, þis lond
byhoueþ be dungid. What þis dunge is is tauȝte in þe gospel
sermoun of þe nexte Sundai bifore.
290 After þe dungynge, þis lond must be eerid. Bi þis 'eerynge' is
vndirstonde confession, for riȝt as þoru erynge of þe plouȝ þe
cultur and schar kerueþ þe erþe, and turneþ þe grene gras
donward and þe foule erþe vpward, so bi þe schewynge of þy
tunge þou schalt kerue / and departe þi goode dedis fro þyn   f. 77ʳ
295 euele, and turne vp and schewe forþ þe blake erþe of þi olde
erþeli conuersacion of synnes, and hide and turne adowun þe
goode grene deedis fro al maner of bost and pride, but oneli to
God, whiche knoweþ þe priueite of mannes herte, þat wol fulli
rewarde euery good dede, be it neuer so priuei, after þat it is
300 worþi.

And riȝt as a plouhman, þat turneþ not vp al þe lond and
makeþ it al blac, but leeueþ many grene placis whiche men
clepiþ 'balkis', vnableþ þis lond to beere a good crop; riȝt so,
whoso in schrift knoulecheþ noȝt fulli out his synnes wiþ þe
305 publican, but bosteþ his goode dedis wiþ Pharisee, suchon
balkiþ foule his soule and vnableþ hit to grace.

Þe plouh of schrifte bihoueþ to be temprid wiþ þre weggis, if
it schulde go trueli and sikurli:

273 *qui...celo, þat is] et cetera* A.   275 Make ȝe ȝouȝ] makiþ ȝoure R.
283 seed] worde R.   284 vp arise] vprise R;   he] it R.
285 pulle] plucke R.   286 of(2)] *om.* R.   288 is is] is it is R;
gospel] *om.* R.   289 nexte] gospel of þe next R.
291 þe(1)] a R.   292 schar] þe share R.
298 knoweþ] *om.* R.   302 al] not al R;   placis] plottis R.
303 þis] mennys R.   306–7 (R *mar: aratrum confessionis*).

Þe firste is þat it be doo hastili, wiþoute delaynge; not
310 abidynge til þei ligge sike and wene to be deed, neþer til þe
ȝeris eend, þat is: til Lente. For riȝt as þou wolt not abide if þou
see þat þy plouh goo amys, to hiȝe or to lowe, to amende it til
þou haue al eerid vp þi lond, but anon þou gost and rennest a
wegge, and stentist not til þou haue temprid him and sett him
315 in his kynde; riȝt so, in þe same wise, as tyme as þou fyndest
þiself gulti in any dedli synne, tarie þou noȝt, but as sone as
þou mai gete a good discrete preste þat kan bynde and
vnbynde, as Seynt Austeyn seiþ, goo and schryue þe to him,
and take þi penance for þi / synne.   f. 77ᵛ

320 Þe seconde wegg þat tempreþ þi plouȝ and setteþ hit in his
kynde [is þis]: þat it be hool, wiþoute departynge. Not for to
telle a parcel to oo preest and anoþer to anoþer, for perauenture
þi curat scholde not knowe of what condicions þou art. Or ellis,
for he is discrete and wole ȝeue þe resonable penance for þi
325 synnes, þou gost and tellest him a parcel of þe leeste euel, and
after oþer tofore þou gost to [a] stranger and tellest him alle þe
foule bagge, for þou woldest not be aschamed whiche, as Seynt
Aust[eyn] seiþ, is þe principal partie of þi penance. Or ellis
[þou] gost to him þat, for couetise of a peny or two, wol ȝeue þe
330 litil penaunce or non, whiche is verreie symonye, for penance is
oon of þe seuene sacramentis, whiche scholde noþer be bouȝte
ne soolde. If þou in þis maner departist þi schrift, it is noȝt in
þe siȝt of God.

Þe þridde wegge þat tempreþ þi plouh is þat it be nakid,
335 wiþoute excusacyon. Not whanne þou comest to schrifte to
seie: 'I hadde no better grace', and so putte þe defauȝte in God
or ellis in þi neiboure, seyinge: 'He made hit' or 'Sche made
hit' and 'Ne hadde þei been, I ne hadde neuere do so.' But þou
must fulli and uttirli accuse þiself in þe worste maner, þat þou
340 didist hit and no man ellis.

And lete eueri man schryue himself. And if þou wiþ þese 3
weggis tempre wel þi plouh, þou schalt ere in rule redili, and
raie wel þi lond.

---

309 firste] first wegge R.   311–2 if þou see þat] if þat þou saw R.
312 goo] ȝede R.
312–4 to amende...sett him] til þou haddist amendid it or þou ȝedist ony ferþer
til he were temperid R.   315 as tyme...fyndest] as þou felist R.
320 (R. mar: ij);   þi] þis R.   321 is þis] R, þat is A.
323 art] were R.   325 euel] yuelis R.   326 a] anoþer A.
329 þat] þat wil R;   wol] om. R.   334 (R. mar: iij);   þi] þis R.
339 þat] om. R.   342 ere] here R.   343 raie] aray R.

After þis it must be wel harwid, to drawe oute rootes and
345 oþer filþes þat is / laft in þe lond, and to make þe lond þe   f. 78ʳ
smallere and þe more able to receyue his seed. And by þis
eggynge or harwynge, whiche haþ many scharpe tyndes, mai be
vndirstonde werkes of penance as fastynge, wakynge, wolwarde
werynge, barefoot goynge, harde lyinge, scharpe disciplines,
350 and many suche oþer.

And þis harwe, if it be drawe discreteli and þerto þat þese
tyndes ben longe inouȝ (þat is: þat þei ben continued, 'for
whoso contynueþ too þe ende,' seiþ Crist, 'he schal be saaf'; qui
perseuerauerit [vsque in finem, hic saluus erit]), þenne þei
355 bryngen ouȝte after hem al þe rootes of loue of synnes, and
makeþ þe herte falle smale þoru mekenesse, whiche þynge most
ableþ þe soule to þe seed of þe word of God.

And þat Crist scheweþ wel (þat not in hilli lond, þat is,
proude hertis, but in þoo þat ben maad smale þoru mekenesse
360 bi þis harwe of penaunce, þe word of God mai entre) þere he
seiþ: Confitebor tibi, Pater celi et terre, quia abscondisti hec a
sapientibus, et cetera. Þat is: 'I kn⟨o⟩wleche to þe, Fader of
heuene and of erþe, þat þou hast hid þese þyngis' (þat is,
whiche I haue spoke) 'fro wise and prudent men, and hast
365 opened hem to litel men.'

Þerfore Crist, þis principal sowere whiche knowiþ al maner
hosbandrie poynt deuys, tofore þat he seew þis seed he tauȝte
þat mennys hertis musten be þus / araied, bi þese wordis þat   f. 78ᵛ
suen: Penitentiam agite, et cetera. 'Dooþ penaunce, for þe
370 kyngdom of heuene is nyȝ.'

Þat lond þat is þus araied, as is seid bifore, and in whiche is
sowe þe word of God, is able for to brynge forþ plenteuousli
his frute, as Matheu seiþ of þis same matere in þe 13 chapitre:
'sum 30 fold, and sum 60 fold, and sum a 100 fold.'

375 Þese þre degrees of vertues, figurid bi pritti, sixti, and an
hundrid, moun be vndirstonde in euery spice of vertues. But
for euery vice is spiritual fornycacyon and, bi þe same resoun,
euery vertu is chastitee, þerfore comynely bi 'þrittifold frute' is
vndirstonde chastitee of wedloc, echewynge al vnlefful coupl-
380 ynge, holdynge apaid of þe werk of matrimonye. And [in] þe

354 vsque...erit] et cetera A.   355 þe] om. R;   of(1)] om. R.
356 falle] to falle R.   357 séed...word] loue R.
360 bi] om. R;   mai] mai not A.   361 quia] qui R.
364 fro] to R.   367 poynt deuys] om. R;   seed] om. R.
374 30] þritti R;   60] sixti R;   a 100] an hundrid R.
379 al] om. R.   380 in] om. A.

same maner, a stronge man for vertu suffrynge harme in his outeward goodes makeþ þe lowist frute, þat is: 30 fold.

And riȝt as þe chastitee of widuhoode, eschewynge al manere flescli couplynge þat hee mai þe more freliere ȝeue tente to
385 Goddis seruice, answereþ togidere to þe 60 fold frute; riȝt so, in strengþe sufferynge (not oonli in temperal goodis, but also in hire owne bodi, as prisenynge, and betynge, and suche oþer) answereþ to þe same frute.

And riȝt as chastitee of maidenhood (bi whiche foreuere is
390 echeuwid al maner of flescli couplynge [and] bi whiche þe mynde is couplid alweie to God as to þe spouse, as / Seynt   f. 79ʳ Poule seiþ: *Virgo cogitat ea que Domini sunt, vt sit sancta tam corpore quam anima*, þat is: 'A maide þenkeþ þoo þyngis þat beþ of þe Lord, þat sche beo hooli boþe in bodi and soule'),
395 answereþ to þe hundred fold frute, riȝt so in strengþe þe studefastnesse of martirs and, in þe same wise, of alle spicis of vertues. But to maidens, and to martiris, and to prechouris, longiþ a special worschipe in heuene þat is clepid 'laureola'.

Þe souereyne sower þat soweþ þis seed, oure saueour Jesus
400 Crist, graunte vs of his godenesse to greiþe so oure lond þat it be abil and redi to receyue þe word of God, and after þoru his grace to frute manyfold, and seþþe be brouȝte into þe berne of þe blisse of heuene. Amen.

382 30] þritty R.   383 þe] om. R.   385 60] sixti R.
393 corpore quam anima] anima quam corpore R.   395 so] om. R;
þe(2)] of R.   396 of(2)] in R.   400 greiþe] diȝt R.
402 frute manyfold] multiplie manyfolde fruyt R;   be] to be R.

QUINQUAGESIMA
SUNDAY

[*A*]*ssumpsit Jesus discipulos suos et ait illis: Ecce, ascendimus Jerosolimam* ([*Luc*].18.[31–43]). 'Jesus took his xij apostles and seid to hem: "Loo! we stien vp to Jerusalem, and alle þyngis schullen be endid or fulfullid þat ben writen of þe Sone of man.
5 He schal be taken to heþen men, and he schal be scornid, and scorgid, and spitt vpon. And after þei han scorgid him, þei schullen slee him, and þe þridde daie he schal rise".'

In þe byginnyng of þis gospel, Crist techeþ vs bi his word / and his ensaumple þat þer mai no man stiȝe vp þe redi wei to   f. 79ᵛ
10 heuenli Jerusalem but bi meke pacience, or wilful suffrynge of tribulacyon whanne hit comeþ, or ellis þat he be redi in wille to suffre if God sende it, þouȝ non come. For þis weie wente oure Lord Jesus Crist, as he witnesseþ in Lu[ke] (þe last chapitre [26]): *Nonne `hec´ oportuit Christum* [*sic pati*], *et sic intrare in*
15 *gloriam suam?* 'Ne bihoueþ it not Crist suffre þese þyngis, and so to entre into his blisse?'

Also, þe same weie wente oure Ladi, as Symeon profeciede of hire (*Luc*.2.[35]): *Tuam* [*ipsius*] *animam pertransibit gladius.* Þat is: 'Þe swerd of tribulacion schal passe þoru þi soule.'
20 Þat wei also passide alle þe hooli apostlis, martirs, confessouris, and virgins, and alle true Goddis seruantes, as wit-

---

1 *Assumpsit*] (*Text indented for two lines*; A *om.*).
2 *Luc* 18] Mt.18 A, Mt.28 c⁰ R;   apostles] disciplis R.
5 scornid, and scorgid] scourgid sco`r´nyd R.
9 þe redi wei] *om.* A.   13 Luke] luc' A;
last] *om.* R.   14 *hec*] (*int.*);
sic pati] *om.* A.   15 *gloriam suam*] regnum celorum þat is R;
it] *om.* R;   suffre] to suffre R.
16 his blisse] þe kyngdom of heuen R.
18 2] 2 capitulo A, þe ij chapitre seying þus R;   *ipsius*] inquit A.
20 hooli] *om.* R.

nesseþ Seynt Poule in þe 2 pistle to Thi[mothe] (þe 3 chapitre
[24]): *Omnes qui pie volunt viuere in Christo Jesu, persecutionem
patientur.* 'Alle þat wolen lyue piteousli or holili in Crist schul
25 suffre persecucyon.' And in anoþer place: 'Bi many tribulacyons it bihoueþ [vs] to entre into þe kyngdom of heuene.'
Seynt Johun [seiþ], in þe firste pistle ([2.6]): *Qui dicit se in
Christo manere, debet sicut ipse ambulauit et ipse ambulare.* Þat
is: 'Whoso seiþ þat he dwelleþ in Crist, he muste goo as he
30 wente.'

Þanne, riȝt as þis gospel seiþ Crist suffride scornynge,
[scourgynge], and spittynge vpon, and seþþe deeþ vpon a cros,
riȝt so [it] bihoueþ treue Cristen men to suffre and bi þat wei to
foloue oure blessid Duke and oure Maister, Jesus Crist, to þe
35 blisse of heuenli Jerusalem. For in þese foure maneris of
tribulacyons [rehercid tofore moun be vnderstonden alle maner
of tribulacions] whiche stondeþ oþer in scornful dedis or
wordis, or in tribulacyon of bodili persecucyon, as of catel or of
frendes, or ellis of fals diffamacion, oþer of bodili / deeþ.   f. 80ᵛ

40 First, þe bihoueþ to suffre scornynge if it comeþ, boþe in
word and dede, and take ensample of oure Maister, Jesus Crist,
and suffre mekeli for his loue as he suffride for þi loue. For ȝif
þou beo a iust lyuer amonge lyueris of þe worlde, þou schalt be
scorned of hem as a fool, as Salamon rehercid of dampnid men
45 how þei schullen seie in helle of iuste men: *Ecce, hij sunt quos
aliquando habuimus in derisum.* Þat is: 'Loo!' he seiþ, 'þese it
been þat we hadde sum tyme in scorn.'

But þenke þanne on Cristes scorn: houȝ his þralles and his
handiwerk scorneden her Lord, whanne þei cloþede him in an
50 oolde mantel of purpur, in stide of a kyngis clooþ; and setten
on his heed a crowne of þornes, in stide of a crowne of gold;
and in his hande a rude, in stide of a septre; and, knelynge in
scorn, seiden: 'Heil, Kynge of Jewis!' And if þou þenke on þis

22 2] secound R;   3] þrid R.   23 *Jesu*] *om.* R.
24 Alle] þat is . Alle R;   lyue] *om.* R;   holili] holily lyue R.
26 vs] *om.* A.   27 seiþ] *om.* A;   þe] his R;
2.6] 1 A, þe first R.   28 *ipse*(2)] ille R.   32 scourgynge] *om.* A (*n.*).
33 it] *om.* A.   35 foure] 4.foure.
36–7 rehercid...tribulacions] *om.* A.
38 bodili persecucyon] persecucion bodile R.
40 (R *mar: derisio*).   43 lyueris] þe lyuers R;   þe] þis R.
45 helle] hellis R;   *Ecce*] *om.* R.
46 *aliquando*] alibi R;   Þat is] *om.* R;   Þese] þesse A.
47 been] werne R.   48 But...scorn] *om.* R.

entierli in þyn herte, it schal make þe more mekeli and pacientli
55 to suffre al maner of scorn þat is doon or seid to þe, and so
þanne þou folouiste him in þe first tribulacyon, þat is:
scornynge.

Þe bihoueþ also to folowe Crist in his scorginge. Þat is: if any
bodili harm beo doon to þe, of bodili persecucion, or los of
60 catel or of frendes (for alle þese been scorgyngis to mannes
bodi), suffre þanne mekeli and pacien[t]li, and biþenke þee
how3 oure Lord Jesus Criste was scorgid in his nakid bodi wiþ
scharpe knottede scorges þat, as [Ysay, 1.6] seiþ: *A planta /
pedis vsque ad verticem capitis, non est in eo sanitas.* Þat is: 'Fro   f. 80ᵛ
65 þe sole of þe foot to þe top of þe heed, þer was non hool place in
him.' Biþenke also hou3 he hadde also a scharp buffet vnder þe
eere, of an harlot stondynge tofore þe iuge. Biþenke þe also
hou3 þe bischopis, scribes, and Pharisees cesiden neuere of hire
fals pursute, and procureden also þe comyne peple to crie after
70 his deeþ. Biþenke also hou3 pore he was maad for oure loue þat
at his deþ was laft him not so myche as a cloþ to hile wiþ his
priue lymes. Biþenke 3et hou3 he suffride los of frendes, for þe
Jewes, þat scholden haue be his frendes bi resoun for þei weren
his kyn, stoden a3ens him and weren his moste enemyes, as
75 Dauid seiþ in þe Psauter: *Amici mei et proximi mei, et cetera.*
'Mi frendes and my next kyn nei3heden and stoden a3ens me.'
And if þou hast þis in þi mynde continueli, ne doute it schal
make þe suffre ful pacyentli alle þese scorgyngis, or whiche
euere of þese þat þou art scorgid wiþ, and þanne þou folewist
80 Crist in þe seconde tribulacyon, þat is: scorgynge.

Þe bihoueþ also to folewe Crist in þe 3 tribulacion, þat is:
spittynge vpon. Bi þis mai be vndirstonde falce diffamynge.
For ri3t as a man is knowen bi his face whiche he beo anentis
his bodi, ri3t so he is knowe bi his fame whiche he is anentis his
85 soule. Þanne, whoso falsli sclaundreþ his broþer and so apeireþ
his name, he spitteþ and defouleþ his [face]; but a kynde and a
louynge broþer, 3if he perceyuede any de/foulynge in a mannes   f. 81ʳ

54 more] *om.* R.   58 (R *mar:* flagellatio).
59 of(1)] or R.   61 pacientli] t *om.* A.
63 Ysay 1.6] Jeremye A, ysay primo R.   65 þer] *om.* R.
66 also(1)] þe also R;   hou3] *om.* R;   also(2)] *om.* R.
68 Pharisees] his phariseis R.   69 pursute] purpose R.
72 lymes] membris R.   76 Mi] þat is . My R;   me] *om.* R.
78 þese] *om.* R.   79 þat] *om.* R.
82 (R *mar:* spitting).   81 3] þrid R.
85 sclaundreþ] disclaundriþ R.   83 beo] is R.
                                            86 face] name A.

face, schulde wipe it aweie, oþer warne him þerof if he myȝte.
So schulde any true cristen man, ȝif he herde any defame his
90 broþer, be redi to answere þerfore, and excuse it, and stopp[e]
hit, and helpe hit what he myȝte; or ellis, if he supposide he
were gulti þerynne so þat his name bigunne for to apeire, þanne
broþerli, and priueli, and curtesli, warne him þerof, þat he
myȝte amende him and so wipe it aweie and make fair aȝens his
95 fame, þat is: his gostli face.

But, þe more harme is, þer been moo now redi to spitte in
mennes facis þan for to wipe hem. If þanne þat any man spitte
in þi face bodili, or in þi gostli face, apeirynge falseli þi goode
name, suffre mekeli for his loue þat seide: *Exemplum dedi uobis,*
100 *vt quemadmodum ego feci, ita et vos faciatis.* Þat is: 'I haue ȝeue
ȝou ensaumple' (þat is, of meke sufferynge) 'þat riȝt as I haue
doo, so doo ȝe.'

Þenke houȝ he suffride mekeli for þi loue þe foule, horrible
spotil of hire curside mouþus in his blesside face, whiche was
105 þe fairest of alle children þat euer were bore, as Dauid
witnesseþ in his Psalme: *Speciosus forma, et cetera,* and þei
maden hit so foule þat it seemede like to a mesel to alle mennis
siȝte.

Haue þou mynde also houȝ þei bispatten his gostli face (þat
110 is: his worschipeful name and his fame) whanne þei seiden he
was not on Goddis half for he kepte not þe Sabot. Þei seiden
also þat he hadde a deuele wiþinne him; and also þat in
Belsebul, þe Prince of Fendes, he caste ouȝte fendes; and wiþ
many moo / oþer suche dispitouse wordes apeirede his name as   f. 81
115 myche as was in hem.

And al he suffride mekeli, to ȝeue vs ensaumple to suffre also
for his loue and for oure owne synne. And merueile þou noȝt
þouȝ men doon þus to þe, þou[ȝ] þou deserue hit noȝt to hem,
for Crist seiþ: *Si patremfamilias Bel[z]ebub vocauerunt, quanto*
120 *magis domesticos eius?* Þat is: 'If þei han clepid þe fadir of þe
householde "Belsebul", hou myche more þei wolen his homeli

---

88 if] if þat R.   89 any(1)] euery R;   any(2)] any man R.
90 it] ιιym R;   stoppe] stoppid A.   91 what] in þat R.
94 his] hīs A.   98 face bodili] bodile face R.
99 *Exemplum...uobis*] Dedi vobis exemplum R.
106 *forma*] forma pre filijs homini R.
109 bispatten] bispatelid R.   107 to(1)] *om.* R.
114 apeirede] apeyring R.   111 on] of R.
to(2)] of R.   118 þouȝ(2)] þou A, þowȝ R;
120 þe(1)] þee A.   119 Belzebub] Belbebub A.

meyne?' For þou3 þou haue not deserued hit a3ens þoo
persones, þou hast deserued hit a3en God wiþ oþer synnes þat
þou hast doon, for whiche God punyschiþ þe and so wole
125 purge þe, or ellis proue þe as gold in þe fier, and encrece þi
mede in þe blisse of heuene. And if þou suffre þus mekeli, as I
haue seid, þanne folewiste þou oure Lord Jesus Crist in his
þridde tribulacyon, þat is: in spittynge vpon.

After þanne þat þou hast denied þus þiself bi wilful and meke
130 suffrynge of tribulacions, þou moste take þi cros and suen him,
as Crist seiþ. An esier cros mai no man take þanne þe cros of
loue, of whiche cros spekeþ þe doctur Lyncoln, expownynge
þis text of þe apostle (ad Gal.5.[24]): *Qui Christi sunt, carnem
suam crucifixerunt cum vitijs et concupiscencijs.* Þat is: 'Þei þat
135 ben of Crist, or Cristis childeren, han crucified hire flesch wiþ
vicis and desiris':

'Þe flesch here mai be vndirstonde þe bodili substaunce of a
man, wiþ þe dedis / of his membris. Vicis ben euele customs,   f. 82ʳ
wiþ hire dedis. Desiris ben lustis, whiche mouen hem
140 a3en resoun.

'Þese þre it bihoueþ after þe apostle to fastene to þe cros, for
þei þat ben Cristis araieþ to hem first a cros in hire mynde
whanne, fro þe myddul of hire soule (þat is, loue or wille), þei
drawen his lyne into God aboue al þyngis to be loued; and
145 anoþer, on þe ri3t side, þei dressen to hire frendes as hemself to
be loued; and þe þridde, on þe lifte side, to hire enemyes as
hemself to be loued, for God haþ ordeyned hem of þe same
kynde; ⟨and⟩ þe fourþe lyne of loue, donward, for to loue
dueliche hire flesch and oþer bodili creatures, in as myche as
150 þei ben matere of knowynge, and of loue, and of preisynge of
God.

'In þis cros of loue, þe flesch is crucified whanne al þe werkis
whiche þat ben don bi þe membris of þe bodi ben dresside after
summe of þese foure forseid loues. And if þe werk of þe flesch
155 passe forþ bi none of þese foure weies, þe crucifyynge of þe
flesch is left. And bi no weie mai not þe lyne of loue be dressid
bi any of þese four weies, but in so myche he strecche him to
alle; and so þanne it foloweþ þat þe vicis of vnordynat lust þat
moun not stonde wiþ þese louys been slayn, forsoþe, for þer

128 vpon] on hym R.   129 þus] *om.* R.   133 þis] þe R.
137 substaunce] sustenanunce R;   a] *om.* R.   139 hem] men R.
142 Cristis] of crist R.   148 lyne] lijf R.   150 þei] *om.* R.
154 foure forseid] forseide foure R.   159 forsoþe, for þer] (*Repeated in
mar:* for þere for soþe, H1 A), For þere forsoþe R.

160 leueþ not euele wille where þat þese foure ben streiȝt oute. Þe
desiris also of þe flesch in þis cros contynuli / beþ maad lasse, f. 82ᵛ
and so þei beþ alweie in dyinge, til to goynge oute of þe liȝf.'

Þis cros of loue made Crist to stie vp into þe cros of treo, in
whiche he suffride his deþ for mankynde. Whanne þou hast
165 don þiself vpon þis cros of loue, þanne schalt þou rise after þe
þridde daie, as Crist dide:

Þe first dai, Crist suffride passioun and deeþ; þe secounde
dai, he restide in þe sepulcre; and þe þridde dai, he roos wiþ a
bodi glorified, whiche myȝte no more suffre deþ.

170 So schalt þou also þe firste daie (þat is: daie of þi lyuynge)
suffre mekeli tribulacions, as is bifore seid, and deeþ on þe cros
of loue; þe seconde dai (þat is: after þou art passid oute of þis
world, into þee Daie of Doom) reste in þe ioie of Paradise, or in
Purgatorie for a litil tyme, if þer leue any þyng to be purgid at
175 þi diynge; þe þridde dai (þat is: þe Dai of Doom, whiche daie
schal neuer haue ende) þou schalt rise aȝen, and þi soule schal
be knyttid to þi bodi, whiche schal be glorified wiþ foure
`þyngus´: þat is, clerete, agilite, sutilte, and immortalite (þat is:
vndedlynesse), for it schal not mowe die aȝen, but endelesli
180 lyue wiþ God in his blisse, world wiþouten ende.

After Crist hadde tolde his disciples of his wilful suffrynge,
passyoun, and deeþ, þe text seiþ þat þe apostles vndirsto[n]den
no þynge of þese þyngis, for þis word was hid fro hem. Mar[ke]
seiþ in þe 8 chapitre þat whanne Crist tolde to his disciples of
185 his passioun, Petre, takynge Crist, bigan for to blame him, and
seide: 'Lord, be þou merciful to þiself, for þis schal / not beo.'   f. 8

Vpon þis text seiþ Crisostom: we seyn it is no wondir þouȝ
Petre knew not þis whiche took reuelacion of Cristis passyoun.
Petre lernede bi reuelacyon þat Crist was þe Sone of God, but
190 soþeli þe mysterie of þe cros and of þe riȝsynge aȝen of Crist
was not schewid to him in þis place.

Also, men moun vndirstonde þat seþþe þe disciples, þat
weren chose of God bifore al oþer, for þei weren ȝet þat tyme
sumwhat flescli and not fulli enspired wiþ þe Hooli Gost as þei
195 weren after, vndirsto[n]den not þe speche of wilful suffrynge,

162 to] to þe R.   165 þiself] þiself wilfully R;   þis] þe R.
168 a] om. R.   170 þi] om. R.   178 þyngus] (mar. H3), dowereis R.
179 mowe] om. R.   183 Marke] Marc' A.
184–5 to...passioun] his passioun to his disciplis R.
189 þe Sone of God] goddis son R.
193 bifore] tofore R.   195 vndirstonden] n(2) om. A;
speche] (Malformed c in A, clear in R).

myche more men þat been al flesch and ȝouen to wordli lustis
moun not vndirstonde þe techynge of meke and wilful
pacyence and tribulacioun, but in al maner tribulacions and
aduersitees grucchen aȝen þe curteis visitacion of God.

200 But for as myche as blyndenesse in soule letteþ man ofte þat
he mai not knowe þe weie, ne see to goo þerynne to heuenli
Jerusalem, þerfore as þe gospel telleþ suyngli oure Lord Jesus
helide a man of his bodili blyndenesse þat criede bisili after his
siȝt, and made him for to see, to teche vs to desire fulli in herte,
205 and to crie bisili to God wiþ mouþe after goostli siȝt, whiche is
þe grettist helpe þat mai beo to knowe þis weie and redili
wiþoute errynge to goo þerynne.

Þe gospel seiþ þat whanne Crist neiȝhede, or cam nyȝ, to
Jericho, a blynde man saat bisides þe weie beggynge. Jericho is
210 as myche for `to seie´ as 'þe mone', bi whiche is vndirstonde /
oure fleschli kynde whiche is vnstabul and neuer dwelleþ any
while in þe same state, as Job seiþ, but wexeþ and wanyeþ as þe
moone dooþ: nouȝ sike, nouȝ hol; now hoot, now cold; now
hungri, now ful; now pore, now riche, and so forþ of many oþer
215 passions of kynde to whiche kynde oure Lord Jesus is nyȝ, for
of his gracyous and endeles godnes he haþ so knyttid his
godhede þertoo þat þei moun neuer fro hennis forward be
departid. And so, bi takynge of oure kynde, and bi experience,
he haþ þe more compassion of oure freelte, and þerfore he
220 scheweþ his manhede tofore his Fadir contynueli, and (as
Seynt John seiþ: *Aduocatum habemus apud Patrem*) he is oure
aduoket euermore, to preie for vs for mercy and for grace.

Bi þis blynde man þat saat bisides þe weie beggynge mai be
vndirstonde euery cristen man whiche haþ take bileue of oure
225 Lord Jesus Crist and is maad after blynd þoru synne þat he haþ
doon, whiche is sori for his synne and in wille for to amend[e]
his liȝfe. Such a man, in as myche as he haþ not werkes of
charitee, he is not in þe weie; but, in as myche as he haþ ful
bileue and is in wille to arise of his synne, he is nyȝ bisides þe
230 weie.

And riȝt as þer is many maner bodili blyndenesse, riȝt so, þer
ben many manere goostli blyndenesse: þer is blyndenesse in

198 and] in R.   201 see] so R.   205 wiþ mouþe] *om.* R;   after] after oure R.
210 for to seie] (*mar.* to seie, H3, *after* as myche for A), to mene R;
(*Foot of* f.83r: *hic de ceco mendicante*, H3).
214 ful; now] *om.* R.   215 Jesus] Jesu Crist R.   218 of] *om.* R.
222 euermore] euer R.   224 bileue] þe bileue R.   226 amende] amendis A.
227 werkes] þe werkis R.   229 arise] rise R.

bileue; þer is blyndenesse in wirchynge; [and] blyndenesse in demynge.

235   First þer is blyndenesse in bileue, of whiche spekeþ Seynt Poule / (þe seconde pistle to Cor[inthis], þe 4 chapitre [4]),   f. 84 seyinge þus: *deus huius seculi excecauit mentes infidelium, vt non fulgeat illuminatio euangelij glorie Christi.* Þat is: '[þe] god of þis world haþ blynded þe myndes of vnfeiþful, þat þe liȝtenynge of

240   þe euangelie of þe glorie of Crist schyne not to hem.' And þis makeþ þat manye men, for þei hauen no ful bileue to þe truþe of þe euangelie of Cristis wordis, þerfore in peyne of þat synne, God suffreþ hem to falle into erroure of mysbileue of many false þyngis.

245   And in þis caas ben all wicches and telisteris, and alle þat bileueþ in charmes and writtes maad wiþ wordes vngroundid in Scripture. And þouh it be wiþ wordis groundid in Scripture, Crisostom spekeþ ful scharpli aȝen hem in þe 4[3] Omelie, seyinge þus: 'Sey,' he seiþ, 'þou vnwise preest' (þat makest

250   suche writtes), 'ne is not þe euangelie euery dai rad in þe chirche and herd of men? How moun þei profite to hem aboute whos neckis þei ben hangid, to whom þei moun not profite þat euery dai hereþ hem rad wiþ hire eris? Wheþer,' he seiþ, 'is þe vertu of þe euangelie? In þe figuris of þe letteris, or in

255   vndirstondynge of þe writyng⟨i⟩s? If it be in þe letteris, þanne þou hangest hem wel aboute hire neckis. If it be in þe vndirstondynge, þanne it profiteþ more putte in mennis hertis þanne hangid aboute hi/re neckis.'   f. 8

Also in þis blyndenesse beþ alle þoo þat bileueþ in destenyes

260   of sterris of mennys birþis, aȝen whiche also spekeþ streiteli Crisostom in þe 2 Omelie; also, þat bileueþ in rauenes gredynge, pies chiterynge, oules whulynge, and manye suche oþere fante⟨si⟩es vngroundid whiche þe leude peple han amongis hem, and eke many lew[id]e clerkis, for blyndenesse of vnkun-

265   nynge, consenteþ to þis blyndenesse of old misbileue.

Also in þis blyndenesse of mysbileue beþ alle þoo þat bileuen þat þei schullen no part haue of gode dedis þat been don in

233 blyndenesse(1)] *om.* R;   and] *om.* A.
236 4(1)] iij R;   (*Foot of* f.83v: *quod* ⟨3?⟩ *est cecitas*, H3).
238 *glorie*] gracie R.   241 *þat*] *om.* R.   248 43] 40 A, xl R.
249 (*mar*: Cris' *om.* 40, H3; R *mar*: aȝeyns writtis).
251 to hem] *om.* R.   253 euery] yche R;   hire] his R.
258 (*Foot of* f.84r: *De breuibus et carminibus*, H3).   260 whiche] hem R;
streiteli] sharply R.   262 pies chiterynge] chetering of pyes R.
264 lewide] lewdie A;   for...of] *om.* R.

housis of religion but if þei ben receyued of hem a broþer bi
lettre and bi seel, and euery ȝer ȝeue hem a certeyn of rente.
270 For þis is aȝen þe article of þe Crede Commynynge of Seyntis,
þat is: þat alle þoo þat schullen be saued schullen be parteners
of alle þe goode dedis þat han be doon and schul be doon, fro
þe firste Adam into þe Dai of Doom, more or lesse as God wole
departe hem, after þei han deserued, and þoru his grete mercy.
275 Þei schullen stidefastli bileue þat alle we beþ breþeren of oo
Fadir in heuene, and breþeren to oure Lord Jesus Crist, and
into his broþerhede we beþ receyued bi þe worschipeful chartre
of þe hooli Trinyte: Fadir, and Sone, and Hooli Goost.
    Þe chartre of þis breþerhede is þe blessid bodi þat hynge on a
280 cros; writen wiþ þe worþi blood þat ran doun fro his herte,
seelid wiþ þe precyous sacramente of þe auter in perpetuel
mynde þerof. And þis blesside breþerhede schal abiden foreuere in blisse (whanne alle false faitouris schullen fare) wiþ
hire Fadir.
285 Also in þis blyndenesse beþ alle þoo þat bileuen / þat for a   f. 85ʳ
bulle purchasid of a fals pardener, þoru a fals suggestion and
symonye of seluer, and þei paie him þanne a peny and leie hit
on hire heuedes, þei beþ asoiled of alle hire synnes, as þei
witterli wene. But þe Holi Goost seiþ, in þe Book of Priueites:
290 *Quantum glorificauit se, et in deliciis fuit, tantum date ei*
tormentum et luctum. Þat is: 'How myche a man haþ ioied in
delitis of synne, so myche ȝeue him tormente [and] sorwe or
weilynge.' Þat is, þe riȝtwisnesse of God wole þat as myche lust
and likynge as a man haþ had in synne, so myche peyne euene
295 weied þerwiþ him bihoueþ to haue þerfore oþer, in þis world,
of sorwe of herte, oþer of penance wilfulli taken, or enioyned of
here souereyne in schrifte, or of meke suffrynge of tribulacioun, or ellis, at þe laste, in þe peyne of Purgatorie. And ȝet
God wircheþ wiþ suche mercifulli of his grace, for ne were
300 schrifte of mouþe and sorwe of herte, euery dedli synne
schulde be punyschid wiþ þe endeles peyne of helle.
    Alle suche ben maad blynde or blyndefeld for a tyme, as men
pleyen abobbid, for þei beþ bobbid in hire bileue and in hire

272 þe] *om.* R;   and] or R.   275 of] to R.
277 broþerhede] breþeren R.   279 a] þe R.
285 (*Foot of* f.84v: *de indulgencijs?*, H3);   (*catchwords:* þat for a).
287 (R *mar: contra indulgentias precum emptas, Red ink, a different hand*);
of] and R.   288 alle] *om.* R.   289 witterli wene] wenen witterly R.
290 et] *om.* R;   fuit] *om.* R.   292 or] of R.   296 of(1)] *om.* R.
298 peyne] peynis R.   301 peyne] peynes R.   303 abobbid] at þe bobet R.

catel boþe bi suche lepers ouer londe þat libbeþ bi hire
305 lesyngis.

Also in þis blyndenesse of bileue ben alle þoo þat for any
siknesse or sorwe þat hem eileþ bihoteþ and renneþ fro cuntre
to cuntre, to ymage[s] ȝoten or grauen wiþ mannes hondes, of
gold or of seluer, of tree or of ston, wenynge and tristynge þat
310 þer be any dyuyne vertu in hem, or þat þei moun any þyng
helpen, or oon more þan anoþer for any maner / affeccion, or f. 85ᵛ
fairenesse, or costis. For alle suche (as þe Hooli Goost seiþ bi
Dauid, þe prophete) þat tristeþ in hem ben maad like to hem;
for þei han iȝen and seeþ noȝt, as þese ymagis han, for þei seen
315 wel wiþ hire bodili iȝen of wham þei ben maad, and of what
metal, and ȝet þei beþ blyndid in hire gostli iȝen, wenynge þer
be vertu in þat grauen þynge.

If þei seyen þat þei bileeuen not þat þer is any vertu þerynne,
but oneli in God (þat loueþ more and [worschipeþ more] in oo
320 place þan anoþer), it wole seme, if it be prouyd, þat þei lien
falseli; for if men stele aweie þat ymage þat þei seche, þei wolen
cese of hire pilgrymage in a schort tyme, and ȝet is God as
myȝti as he was, and þe place þere stille. And þus þei prouen bi
hire deedis hire trist was in þat ymag[e].

325 And þis firste blyndenesse (of mysbileue) is cause of þe
seconde blyndenesse: of wickid wirchynge of synful dedis. For,
as Seynt Poule (to þe Romaynes, þe 1 chapitre [23–31])
reherseþ, many foule synnes ben brouȝt in bi þe synne of
mawmetrie, as manslauȝter, spousebrekynge, fornicacion,
330 auarice, couetise, debatis, and stryues, and many moo synnes
whiche he nemeneþ þere, and speciali þe foule and horrible
synne of Sodom, of boþe men and wymmen. And so, þoru gret
lust in hire synnes and long contynuaunce is gaderid corup-
cion, and gendereþ a web in hire goostli iȝen and so makiþ hem
335 blynd. Of þis blyndenesse spekeþ þe prophete Sophonye (þe 1
chapitre [17]): *Ambulabunt [vt] ceci, quia Domino peccauerunt.*
Þat is: 'Þei schullen wandre as blynde men, for þei haue /
synned to þe Lord.' And in anoþer place is seid: *Excecauit eos* f. 86
malicia eorum. Þat is: 'Hire malice' (þat is, of synne) 'haþ

308 ymages] s *om.* A.   309 or(1)] *om.* R.   311 (*Foot of* f.85r: *see n.*).
319 worschipeþ more] worcheþ A.   320 place] place more R.
322 tyme] tyme aftur R.   325 of mysbileue] *om.* R.   327 þe(1)] *om.* R.
328 ben] þat ben A, R.   331 nemeneþ] meuiþ R.   332 of boþe] boþe of R.
333 in] of R.   335 1] first R.   336 vt] *om.* A.
337 þat is] *om.* R;   Þei] Thi R;   wandre] wandre he seiþe R.
338 is seid] *om.* R.   339 Þat is(1)] *om.* R.

340 blendid hem.' In þis blyndenesse ben preestis and lettrid men
þat lyuen in dedli synne and ȝet seeþ wel bi Scripture houȝ
perelous it is, for þe lust of hire synne (þat is: þe web in hire
goostli iȝen) stoppeþ so hire siȝte þat þei moun not see what
perele þei stondeþ inne. Judas þe traitour sai as wel þe blessid
345 conuersacion and þe myracles of oure Lord Jesus Crist as Petre
and John and alle his felawis, and ȝet naþeles his couetise was
so greet to wynne wordeli muk þat it made him goostli blynde
to bitraie his Lord, and þat he solde him for seluer and his
owne soule to helle.

350   And of þis blyndenesse comeþ þe þridde blyndnesse: þat is,
of demynge. And þis boþe in seculer iugis and in chirchis
whanne þei, for any presauntis or mede, wolen not see to þe
riȝt, but deme after wronge and dredeþ not hi⟨r⟩e God, as it is
seide in olde prouerbe: 'Po⟨re⟩ be hangid bi þe necke; a riche
355 man b⟨i þe⟩ purs.' Of þis blyndnesse spekeþ þe Wise Man
(Ecci.20.[31]) seyinge þus: Exenia et dona excecant oculos iudi-
cum. Þat is: 'Presauntis and ȝiftes blynden þe iȝen of iugis.' In
þis blyndnesse ben prelatis and curatis of þe chirche þat demeþ
a gretter synne and more scharpeli chastiseþ hire peple for
360 failynge of hire tiþes þanne for leuynge of greuousere þyngis of
þe lawe, þat is: meercy, feiþ, and doom. And suche, seiþ
[Crisostom], techeþ þe peple by hire ensaumple / to 'siȝe þe   f. 86ᵛ
gnatte and swolewe þe camele.'

In þis also (blyndenesse of demynge) beþ alle oþere ypocritis
365 þat kunne see a mote in anoþer mannes iȝe, but þei kunne not
see a beem in hire owne, þat is: þei kunneþ see a defaute in hire
breþeren deedis, but setteþ at noȝt wel grettere in hire owne.

Euery cristen man þenne, as I seide first, þat haþ take þe
bileue of oure Lord Jesus Crist and is blyndid wiþ þese forseid
370 blyndnessis, or wiþ any of hem, and is in wille to arise ouȝte of
hem, sitteþ bisiȝdes þe hiȝe weie and is a beggare. For, as Seynt
Aust[eyn] seiþ, euery man is 'þe beggare of God', seþþen we
ben nedid to axe of God euery daie oure eche daies brede in
oure Pater Noster.

340 blyndenesse] blynd (Followed, overleaf in mar: dyngis R).
343 stoppeþ] stopping R;   so] om. R.   345 and] om. R;
myracles] myraclis & þe teching R;   oure] his maister & oure R.
351 of] om. R;   þis] is R;   chirchis] holy chirche R.
354 Pore] a pore man shal R.   356 seyinge þus] om. R.   357 Þat is] om. R.
362 Crisostom] R, Crist A.   366 beem] grete beme R;   defaute] litel defaute R.
367 wel] a wel R.   370 blyndnessis] blendingis R.
371 hiȝe] om. R;   is] he is R.   372 þe] a R;   (mar: see n.).

375   But we schal vndirstonde þat beggynge is take dyuerseli in
Scripture. Oon is speciali maad to God, as is seid tofore.
Anoþer beggynge is schewynge maad to man, for himself or for
anoþer, bi þe maner þat sum men schewen hire owne nede or
ellis oþer mennys bi priuee wordis, as oure Ladi schewid to
380 hire Sone þe nede of m[e]n þat w⟨ere⟩n togidere at þe feeste in
þe Cane of Gali⟨lee⟩, whanne sche seid: 'Þei haue no wyn.'
       Anoþer beggynge þer is: þat is, of menynge. And so Crist
beggide ofte of men while in dede he seide his nede ofte to þe
peple, to be releued bi almes. And þus wise men seyn Crist was
385 ofte clepid 'beggare' in Psalmis, not only in his membris, but in
his owne personne.
       Anoþer þer is ȝet: a cryous beggynge maad to man for
himself. And þis [is] clepid an axynge bi voice, maad to man,
for temperal helpe to re/leeue þat þat clepeþ his nede in þe   f. 87ʳ
390 maner þat men beggen of oþer fro dore to dore. And þis mai
not be groundid on þe gospel þat Crist euere beggide þus while
he was Lord of alle þyngis, hauynge no resoun whi he schulde
begge þus. And so, for þis laste beggyn[g]e is euermore synne,
oþer of him þat beggiþ if he begge wiþoute nede þerto, or ellis,
395 if [he] be nedid þerto, þanne it is synne of þe peple þat schulde
see to his nede er he were constreyned to axe, and þerfore of
suche seiþ Dauid in þe Psauter: *Beatus qui intellegit super
egenum et pauperem, et cetera.* Þat is: 'Blessid is he þat
vndirstondeþ vpon þe nedi and þe pore', þat is: to see his nede
400 and releue him ar þat he axe. In þe Oolde Lawe, Jewes hadde a
commaundement to suffre no nedi man ne beggare to be
amongis hem, for he schulde be releued tofore þat he schulde
not nede þerto. Miche more perfite schulde we beo bi lawe of
þe gospel (þat is: þe lawe of loue), for Crist seiþ 'þat but ȝif
405 ȝoure riȝtwisnesse be more perfite þanne scribes and Pharisees',
whiche weren techers of þe Olde Lawe, '[ȝe] schul not entre
into þe kyngdom of heuene.' Þanne, if we kepten trueli þe lawe

375 (R *mar*: *mendicacio*).   377 beggynge is] is beggyng R.
378 sum men] summe n A, summe R.
379 ellis oþer menys] ellys oþer ellis oþeris R.
380 men] m⟨a⟩n.   382 of menynge] a bymenyng R (*n*.).
384 þus] in þis R.   389 þat(2)] þat he R.
392 no] þe R.   393 beggynge] beggynne A.
395 he] *om*. A;   of] to R.   397 seiþ] spekiþ R.
398 *et pauperem*] *om*. R;   Þat is] *om*. R.   þat(2)] þat þat R.
402 amongis] among R.   403 lawe] þe lawe R.
405 ȝoure] oure R;   more] þe more R.   406 ȝe] we A, R (*n*.).

of loue and `of´ charitee, myche raþer schulde we suffre noo
nedi man ne beggare to be among vs.

410   Þanne þe gospel seiþ forþermore: 'whanne þis blynd beggare
herde men passe forþ, he axide what þis were; and þei seiden
þat Jesus of Nazareþ passid bi.' Þis mai bymene þat whanne
suche a blynde man in synne, as I seide bifore, hereþ hou
Dauid, / (spousebreker and mansleer), Magdelyn (defoulid in   f. 87ᵛ
415   alle þe dedli synnes), Mathew (þat gat his liȝflode bi an vnlefful
craft), Petre (þat denyede and forsok his Maister, for fere of a
womman), þe þeef þat hynge bisides Crist in þe oure of his deþ,
Poule (þat ful crueli pursuede Cristis peple), þat alle þese been
passid to heuene and beþ ful glorious seyntis, þenne if suchon
420   axide hou þis may be þat þus synful peple as þese weren ben
passid þus to heuen, Hooli Writt and treue prechouris
answeren to þis question þat bi þe gracyous mercy of oure Lord
Jesus Crist, þat seiþ himself bi þe prophete Eze[chiel]: *Nolo
mortem peccatoris, sed magis vt conuertatur et viuat.* Þat is: 'I
425   wol not þe synful mannes deeþ, but þat he be conuertid and
lyue'; and, as Poule seiþ: *Deus vult omnes homines saluos fieri.*
'God wole þat alle men weren sauyd', and no man were
perisched.

Whanne þis synful man hereþ of þis grete mercy, he is scired
430   þanne gretli in herte, and þe bolder to crie to God for grace and
seie: 'Jesus, þe Sone of Dauid, haue mercy on me!'

Þe peple þat wente tofore þat vndirnam him to holde his pees
mai be vndirstonde wickide þouȝtis and veyn, whiche þe fend
putteþ in mannes herte and renne þerynne euermore tofore to
435   lette mannes preier; or ellis it mai be vndirstonde wickid concel
of þe louers of þe world, and of þe fendis seruan/tes þat goþ   f. 88ʳ
tofore Crist and sueþ not his techynge, neþer his lifynge, for
þei wolen haue hire wille doon aȝen þe wille of Crist. Suche
ofte tyme letteþ men to repente hem of hire synne and crie to
440   Crist for mercy. Þei seyn it nediþ not to morne to myche for
synne, for God wole neuer lese þat he bouȝte so dere, and þus
ofte tyme þei letten men of hire good wille. But þe best concel
in þis mater is to do as þe blynde man dide: þe more þei lettide
him, þe fastere he criede. So, for no such lettyngis cese þou
445   noȝt to crie and þou schalt not faile to be herde atte laste.

408 of(2)] (*int.*).   416 fere] þe fere R.   417 bisides] by þe side of R.
423 himself] by himself R.   426 as Poule] Seynt Poule R.
429 is] *om.* R.   431 on] vpon R.   437 tofore] by fore R.
439 hem] *om.* R;   crie] to crie R.
441 he] he haþe R.   445 atte laste] at þe last R.

Þat þe Lord stod stille mai bymene þat while a man resteþ him in his synne, þe grace of helþe of oure Lord Jesus passeþ forþ afeer fro him, and abideþ no þynge wiþ him, as Dauid seiþ: *Longe* [*a peccatoribus salus*], *et cetera*. 'Helþe is fer fro
450 synful men.' But whanne a man is in wille to rise of his synne, and repenteþ him þerof, and crieþ after mercy, þe grace of þe blessid Lord is ny3 to alle suche þenne, as Dauid seiþ: *Prope est Dominus, et cetera*. 'Ni3,' he seiþ, 'is þe Lord to alle men þat clepeþ him in truþe'—þat is, for hem þat clepen wiþ mouþ, and
455 no[t oonli] wiþ herte.

Þat þe Lord commaundid him to be brou3te to him mai bitokene þat God commaundide to prestis to brynge synful men to Crist bi prechyng and techynge, bi conceilynge in schrifte, and most principali bi hire good ensaumple of lyu-
460 ynge. / For ri3t as [a] blynd man þat schulde be lad, men   f. 88ᵛ musten go bifore and take him bi þe hond and make him suen, and if þer be any þyng in þe weie at whiche he my3te li3tli stomble and hirte himself, his leder schulde warne hem þerof to make him eschewe it and go biside hit, ri3t so schulde prestis
465 ensaumple of good li3fe schewe to semple peple þat my3te folewe hem in hire goode dedis. And if it so beo þat þer ben oþer synnes of whiche þei haue no knowleche of whiche þei my3te li3tli falle ynne, þei schulden bi Holi Scripture warne hem þerof. But what if þe preestis ben as blynde hemself, boþe
470 in Scripture, and eke in hire li3f? Þanne, as Crist seiþ in þe gospel: *Si cecus cecum duxerit*, [*ambo in foueam cadunt. Þat is:*] 'If þe blynde lede þe blynde, þei fallen boþe in þe diche'—þat is, boþe þe preest and his peple wendeþ boþe to h[e]lle.

And whanne þis blynd man hadde nei3hid, he axide him,
475 seyynge: 'What wolt þou þat I do to þe?' Oure Lord Jesus axide not þis for he wiste not wiþoute his schewynge what he desirede in herte, but for he schulde schewe his nede and his wille wiþ his mouþ as wel as wiþ his herte. So, if a synful man desireþ þe merci and þe grace of God in his herte, God wole
480 þat he axe hit also as wel wiþ his mouþe.

448 and...him] om. R.   449 a...salus] om. A.
454 is] as R;   wiþ mouþ] oonli(y) wiþ mouþ(e) A, (R).
455 not oonli] no þynge (þing) A, (R) (n.).   460 a] om. A.
461–2 suen, and] to sue⟨?⟩ R.   464 eschewe] to eschew R.   465 þat] þat þei R.
467 knowleche] knowing R.   469 if] and R;   as] om. R;
hemself] as þei R.   471 duxerit] ducat R;   ambo...cadunt] R, et cetera A;
Þat is] om. A.   472 in] in to R;   þe(2)] om. R.
473 helle] holle A.   474 hadde nei3hid] ny3ede R.   480 as wel] om. R.

Þo þis blynde man seide: 'Lord, þat I mow see,' þis blynde
man axid not gold, ne seluer, ne worschipe of þis world, ne
venyaunce on his enmyes, ne non oþer wordeli þynge, but onli
he preiede þat he myȝte see. Riȝt so, þe moost necessarie þynge
485 þat we myȝte axe of / God is oure goostli siȝte, þat is: þat iȝen   f. 89ʳ
of discrecion he opened in oure soules to knowe þe goode fro þe
euel, and for to chese þe goode and leue alwei þe euele; for
wiþoute openynge of þese iȝen, we moun not goo ariȝte. Þanne
if we preie bisili, and laste þerynne contynueli, we schulde not
490 faile sikerli to gete hit of oure Lord.

Whanne oure Lord Jesus haþ seid to vs: 'Biholde!' (þat is:
haþ maad vs clerli to see wiþ þese goostli iȝen) þanne schulde
we openli see in what staat we stonden ynne while [we] were
blynde: hou we hadden loste oure blesside spouse, Jesus Crist,
495 and bitake vs to þe spousebreker, þe foule fend of helle; houȝ
also we hadde loste þe swete ioyus of heuene, and þat faire
feloschipe of alle hooli seyntis, and þe siȝt of oure Faderis face,
for a litul lust, and purchased peyne perpetueli in helle.

'Þi feiþ,' seiþ Crist, 'haþ maad þe saue.' Þat is: good feiþ is
500 cause of þi goostli [s]iȝt, for it is grounde and roote of al maner
of vertu; for, as Seynt Poule seiþ: *Sine fide impossible est placere
Deo.* Þat is: 'Wiþoute bileeue mai no man plese God.'

'And anon he sawe, and suede him, and magnyfied.' Þat is:
anon as a man haþ geten þis gostli siȝte of discresioun of
505 knowynge good fro euele, he schal leue þe weies of pride,
wraþþe, and enuye, in whiche þe fend haþ lad him; þe weie also
of couetise, in whiche he haþ sued þe world; and þe weies also
of gloterie, sleuþe, and lecherie, in / whiche he haþ sued þe   f. 89ᵛ
flesch; and suen fro hennes forward Jesus Crist, in mekenes,
510 pacience, and charitee; pouerte, mesure, good bisinesse, and
chastitee; and also, boþe in worde and dede, magnyfie his Lord,
for þe worschipe of a lord is his good mayne.

'And alle þe peple, whanne þei siȝe þis, ȝauen pre[i]synge to
God.' Þat is: þe conuercion of a vicious man fro vices into

---

482 worschipe] worshipis R.   483 on] of R.   485 iȝen] þe yȝen R.
487 for(1)] *om.* R.   490 hit] *om.* R.   492 þese] his R.
493 openli see] se opunly R;   while] when R;
we] *om.* A.   497 alle hooli seyntis] þe swete seyntis of heuen R.
498 peyne...helle] þe peyne of helle for euer R.   500 þi] *om.* R;
siȝt] R, liȝt A.   500–1 maner of] *om.* R.   501 *fide*] fidie A.
503 and(2)] he R;   magnyfied] magnified god R.
507 sued] also sued R;   world] worde R;   also] *om.* R.   509 fro] *om.* R.
513 preisynge] i *om.* A (R *has* y).   514 conuercion] conuersacion R.

515 vertues profiteþ not onli to his owne soule, but to manye oþere
þat seeþ hit, to amendement of hire liȝf and to preise þe blessid
Lord þat is so ful of grace.

FIRST SUNDAY
IN LENT

[D]uctus est Jesus in desertum a spiritu, et cetera (Mt.4.[1]). In
þis gospel, cristen men moun lerne to be hardi aȝens alle
temptacions of þe fend. For riȝt as oure Lord Jesus Crist
ouercam him myȝtili in his þre grete temptacions wiþ meke
5 answerynge of Holi Scripture, so if we wolen arme vs in þe
confortable help of God, and alwei answere bi Holi Scripture,
we moun be tristi þat he schal not mowe harme oure soules wiþ
alle his sotil wiles.

Þis gospel telleþ þat Jesus Crist was lad into desert of a
10 spiriȝt, to be temptid of a fend. Ȝhe schul vndirstonde þat, as
[Matheu and Luke] telliþ boþe, þis ledynge into desert of a
spirite þat was þe Hooli Gost, as alle doctours acorden, was
anon suynge þat Jesus was baptiȝed of John in Jordan, tofore
þat he prechide þe kyngdom of God. Riȝt so, eueri cristen man,
15 after þat he is baptised, muste be lad here in þis world bi þe
Hooli Goost in þe deserte of penaunce tofore / þat he come to   f. 90ʳ
þe kyngdom of heuene. For þis schewide wel Crist in his word,
as in his dede, for þe firste sermoun þat euere he prechide to
brynge men to þe kyngdom of heuene, his theme was þis:
20 Penitentiam agite, et cetera. Þat is: 'Doþ penaunce, for þe
kyngdom of heuene is nyȝ.'

Figure we han herof in þe Olde Testamente, whanne þe
children of Israel (whiche bitokenen Cristis peple, for þei seen
God bi feiþ) weren lad oute of Egipte fro þe þraldom of Kyng
25 Pharao (þat is, oute of þe derknesse of synne fro þe þraldom of
þe fend), and hadden passid þe Rede See (þat is, oure baptym,
whiche haþ his vertu of þe reed blood þat spronge ⟨ou⟩te of

1 *Ductus*] (*Text indented for 2 lines*; D *om*);   4] 5 R.
7 mowe] *om*. R.   9 Jesus] *om*. R.
11 Matheu and Luke] R, Mt and luc' A.   12 þe] of þe R.
13 þat] after þat R.   16 (R *mar*: *desertum penitentie*).
17 wel Crist] crist wel R.

Cristis side). Þanne þei weren in deserte fourti ȝeer ar þei
myȝte come into þe lond of biheeste (þat is, here in þis world in
30 deserte of penaunce, kepynge þe Ten Commaundementis and
þe doctrine of þe 4 euange[listis]), whiche is bitokened bi þis
fourti ȝeer ar þei mai come to þe blisse of heuene, whiche is þe
lond of biheste to alle suche.

But sum men ben lad into þe desert of penance, noȝt bi þe
35 Holi Gost, but bi oþer þyngis: as sum men ben lad of þe flesch,
as þoo þat fasten and forberen metis and drynkis principali for
þe helþe of hire bodies, as men þat ben rulid bi phisike; and
sum men beþ lad bi þe world, as nygardes þat fasten principalli
to spare for to be riche; sum men ben lad bi þe deuel, as
40 ypocritis þat fasten principalli to be holde hooli in þe siȝt / of   f. 90
men.

And summe ben lad bi þe Hooli Goost: as þoo [þat] fasten
principalli to plese God, to folowe him in penaunce for his loue
as he dide for oure loue, to do also satisfaccioun for
45 hire synnes, to make þe flesch suget to þe soule to wiþstonde þe
myȝtliere þe temptacion of þe fend (as Seynt Poule seiþ: *Cum
infirmus sum, et cetera*), to lesse hire peynes in purgatorie to
encrese hire blisse in heuen.

And wel penance mai be clepid to þe flesch a deserte, for
50 deserte is as myche for to seie as 'forsaken', and þe flesch
euermore forsakiþ al maner of penance, as fastynge, labour,
and chastitee, but euere desireþ glotenye, slewþe, and lecherie,
and alle maner of lustis.

And riȝt as þe fend temptide oure firste fleschli fader, Adam,
55 pryncipalli in þre synnes (þat was: glotenye to ete þe forbeden
appel, veynglorie whanne he seide þei schulden be as goddis,
and couetise whanne he bihiȝte hem to haue kunnynge as God
to knowe good and euele, and in alle þese þe fend ouercam
him), riȝt in þe same wise he temptid oure first goostli fadir,
60 Jesus Crist:

First, in glotenye, whanne he hadde fastide and hungride,
and bad him make loues of stones.

After, in veynglorie vpon þe pynnacle of þe temple, whan he
bad him falle doun to loke whar God wolde kepe him.

29 into] to R.
34 desert] londe R.
40 principalli] *om.* R.
43 plese] serue R.
50 for] *om.* R.
53 of] *om.* R.

31 þis] *om.* R.
39 for to] te R.
42 þat] *om.* A, ʻþoˊ þat R.
46 þe temptacion] her þre temptacions R.
52 desireþ] he desiriþ R.
57 kunnynge] þe kunnyng R.

65   And þe þridde tyme, vpon þe hil, schewynge to him alle þe
rewmes of þe world, and seide he wolde ʒeue him al þat if he
wolde falle doun and worschipe him.

And in alle þese temptacions, oure Lord Jesus / mytili   f. 91ʳ
ouercam þe fend, as þis gospel makiþ mynde.

70   Whanne þe fend þanne seeþ þat a man is lad bi þe Hooli
Goost, in þe manere þat I seide, into [þe] deserte of penaunce,
anon he goþ ner to him and bisieþ him for to tempte him, to
brynge him oute of his gode purpos and make him falle to
synne; for þe more hiere purpos þat a man is aboute, þe more
75   enuye þe fend haþ to him and is þe more bisier aboute to lette
him, and principalli in þese same þre synnes.

First, if a man be lad bi þe Holi Gost into þe desert of
penaunce as into fastynge, anon þe fend comeþ ner to him and
tempteþ him into glotenye, and biddeþ him make of stones
80   loues, and seiþ þus: 'For to ʒeue þe to so grete fastynge, I holde
hit a gret folie; for wel þou wost þi bodi mai not lyue and be
stronge to serue God but if it take mete and drynke to strengþe
it wiþ, and ʒif þou wiþdrawe þerfro mete and drynke so þat it
wexe feble to serue God, þou plesist not God. And þou wost
85   wel Seint Poule seiþ: *Corporalis exercitacio ad modicum valet.*
"Bodili excercitacion of werkis of penance is of litil valu, but
pitee auaileþ to alle þyngis." And so haue þou a pitous herte
and ʒeue þou almesdede, and let be þi fastynge, for þat wole bi
processe, if þou vse hit in ʒouþe, make þe lese þi brayn in age
90   and so waxe mad, and þenne plesist þou litel God, for þou
myʒtest abide til þou come to sadnesse of age, and þanne were
tyme inowʒ / f⟨or⟩ þe to faste.   f. 91ᵛ

'Also, alle þe goodes of þe world, as foule⟨s⟩, beestis, and
fisches, weren ordeyned of God for þe loue of man, men to take
95   þerof hire fille whanne hem luste. And þerfore, þouʒ þou take
of hem, God is neuere þe porere; ne, þouʒ þou leue hem,
neuere þe richere, for he haþ no nede to hem. And þerfore I
rede þe leue þis fastynge, and ete and drynke such as God send
of þe beste and make þe mury. For Salamon seiþ: *Animus tristis*
100   *exsiccat ossa; animus gaudens etatem floridam facit.* Þat is: "An

65 þe(ʒ)] *om.* R.   66 he(1)] þat he R.   68 in] *om.* R.
69 (R *mar*: *De temptacione diaboli*);   þis] þe R.
70 þanne seeþ] seeþ þen R.   71 þe(2)] *om.* A.   73 falle] to falle R.
76 same þre] þre same R.   78 into] to R.   79 (R *mar*: *Temptacio gule*).
82 it] þou R.   89 processe] proces of tyme R;   ʒouþe] þi ʒouþe R.
91 were] were it R.   95 hem] þei R.
96 porere] wroþer R.   96–7 ne...nede to hem] *om.* R.

heuy herte dryeþ vp a mannes bones; and a myri herte makeþ a
man to haue faire age".'

And þus alle þese wordes of þe fend is no more to seie þanne
as he seide to Crist: 'Make of þese stones loues'—þat is,
105 changynge þi fast þat is hard as stones into tender loues of
glotenye. But now beþ wel waar of þe fend, þat art þus slili and
vndir coolour temptid to glotenye, and answere to him bi þe
same auctorite of Scripture þat oure Lord Jesus dide in þe
same caas, seyynge: 'Not in onli bred lyueþ man, but also in þe
110 word of God. Fals fend! wel I wot þat wiþoute mete and
drynke my bodi mai not lyue any while; but I wot wel I am
maad of twei kyndes, þat is: of soule and bodi. And riʒt as my
bodi mai not lyue wiþoute bodili fode, riʒt so my soule mai not
lyue wiþoute gostli food, whiche is þe word of God, as Crist
115 seiþ here. And þe more principal parte is my soule, whiche is
like to þe Hooli Trinyte, and schal laste euer more whan my
bodi schal / rote in þe erþe and be wormes mete. Þenne haue I   f. 92ʳ
more nede to ʒeue tente for þe mete of þe soule þanne of þe
bodi; and þe mete of þe soule (þat is, þe word of God) seiþ:
120 *Penitentiam agite, et cetera.* Þat is: "Doþ penaunce, for þe
kyngdom of heuene is nyʒ."

'Þanne, fals fende, þouʒ I do bodili penaunce, I fede þerwiþ
my soule; for þe word of God þat is my goostli fode biddeþ so,
and I destrie not my bodi ne displese not þe Lord so I do hit in
125 mesure.'

And þus, in þis manere answerynge þoru þe help of God,
þou maist answere þe fend and disconfite him in his firste
temptacion—þat is, in þe synne of glotenye.

Þe seconde temptacion þat þe fend temptide wiþ oure Lord
130 Jesus was to þe synne of veyneglorie, vpon þe pynnacle of þe
temple, as I seide bifore. Riʒt in þe same wise, ofte tyme he
enforceþ him to make hooli men to falle into þe same synne. Ʒe
schullen vndirstonde þat, as Seint Poule seiþ, þat hooli mennes
soules beþ 'þe holi temple of God'. *Templum Dei sanctum est, et*
135 *cetera.* 'Þe temple of God,' he seiþ, 'is hooli, whiche ben ʒe';
and riʒt as pynnaclis of a material temple oþer chirche makeþ
hit feir to þe siʒt of men, riʒt so vertues makeþ mennes soules

102 age] chere or age R.   104 þese] þe R.
105 changynge] chaunge R;   fast] fasting R;   into] into þe R.
106 beþ] be þou R.   107 (R *mar: Responsio*).   111 wel] *om.* R.
118 þe(2)] þee A.   119 seiþ] þat seiþe R.   128 in] *om.* R.   129 (*mar: 2*);
temptide...Jesus] temptid oure lorde Jesus wiþ R;
(R *mar:* ij *Secunda temptacio vane glorie*).   133 as] *om.* R.

feir in þe siȝt of God. And whanne a man ȝeueþ him to any
vertu, as mekenesse, paciense, charite, chastite, fastyng, preier,
140 oþer almesdede, þanne he stondeþ vpon þe pynnacle of þe
temple. But ofte þe deuel ledeþ a man and setteþ him vpon þis
[pynnacle], whanne he / meueþ him to drawe him to cumpanye f. 92ᵛ
of hooli men and ȝeue him to vertues for an euele ende. For
whanne he haþ sette him þere, þenne anon he meueþ him to
145 falle doun (þat is, into veyneglorie) and seiþ þus:
      'Be prouȝt now of þin holynesse, and sette myche bi þi liyf,
for þou plesist now God and maist do wiþ him what þou wolt.
And sette lasse bi oþer men þat doþ not suche dedes, for whos
most doþ, most he is worþ!' And þus he meueþ man to falle
150 doun, and al tosquatte his soule and alle his gode dedis, and
brynge hem to noȝt.
      And if a man in his herte dredeþ of þis veynglorie, for fere of
þis falle leste he neuere rise, þenne þe deuel conforteþ him bi
Scripture as he dide Crist:
155   'Knowist [þou] not wel þat Hooli Scripture seiþ: *Nouit Deus
qui sunt eius*, "God knowiþ whiche ben his" tofore þe world
bigan, and suche moun not fare amys whatsoeuer þei don.
Omnia cooperantur in bonum, et cetera, "Alle þyngis worcheþ
into good" to hem þat schullen be saued. For Seint Poule
160 boostide of his hiȝe liyf, as his pistles witnesseþ, whanne he
seide he hadde more trauailid þanne alle þe oþer apostles; but
for he was ordeynyd to blisse, þerfore he synned noȝt. So, if
þou be Goddis sone, bi grace ordeynyd to blisse, al schal turne
þe to goode, drede þe riȝt noȝt, whatsoeuer þou þenkest,
65 spekest, or dost; for God haþ ordeynyd his angels to kepe alle
suche, þat þei synne noȝt dedli whatsoeuer þei doþ.'
      And þus þe deuel ofte tyme, as I haue schewid, stireþ a man
to hooli lyif to make him after falle into veynglorie,/ for þat is f. 93ʳ
þe worste fal, for þe hiere þat a man falliþ, þe worse is his fal.
70   Now be war, þou þat sittest vpon þe pynnacle of þe temple
(þat is, in hiȝe vertuous liyf, what degre euer þou be), of þis
sotil sleiþe of þe fend þat is so ful of wilis, for he wolde make þe
falle into veyneglorie to lese al þi myȝt. And answere him bi
Hooli Writ, as oure Lord Jesus dide, seyynge: 'It is writen, þou

---

141 ofte] ofte tyme R.   142 pynnacle] temple A.   143 him] hem R.
144–5 to falle] *om.* R.   148 whos] who so R.   149 most he is] he is moost R.
150 al tosquatte] al to swatt R.   152 þis] his R.
153 rise] arise R.   155 þou] *om.* A.   164 þe to] to þe R.
168 falle] to falle R.   170 (R *mar*: Responsio).   173 (*mar*: Responsio).

175 schalt not tempte þi God.' He tempteþ his Lord God þat
secheþ experyment oþer asaie of þe vertu of God wiþoute nede
þat mai not be eschewid. And þerfore seie to him:

'Þou fals fend! Þouȝ it be so þat I lyue a vertuous liyf,
semynge to alle mennus siȝte, ȝet wot I neuere, as Salamon
180 seiþ, wheþer I be worþi hate or loue. And so it is vnknowen too
me wheþer I be oon of þoo þat schal be saued or dampned. And
þouȝ I schul be saued, and alle my gode dedis in kynde ben
appreued of God, ȝit it is an hiȝe folie to falle doun into
veyneglorie, and putte me into so gret perele in þe hondes of
185 God, and leue þe riȝt gresis þat ben ordeyned to come doun bi
wiþoute any `pride´, þat is: by verreie mekenesse knowlechynge
þat I haue no good but oonli of God, as Seint Poule seiþ: *Quid
habes quod non accepisti? et cetera.* "What hast þou þat þou hast
not take? [If þou take, wherto joyist þou as þou hadist nouȝt
190 taken?]." And if I haue no good but borwid of God, þanne it is
an hiȝe folie to be proute of þat þat is not myn owne.

'And þere as þou seist þat Seint Poule cam doun bi þat weie,
and synnede noȝt whanne he boostide of his trauaile aboue alle
his felawis for he was or/deyned to blisse whiche þat myȝte not   f. 9?
195 faile, I seie þou farest in þis as þou didest whanne þou aleidest
Hooli Scripture to Crist. Þou dockedist þe Scripture whanne
þou took þat þat þe þouȝte was for þe, and leftest bihinde þat
þat was þi vilenye, whanne þou seidest þat þe angelis schulden
kepe him þat he schulde not hir`te´ his foot, and leftest bihynde
200 þat þat sueþ after—þat is: "Vpon þe addir and basilisk þou
schalt goo; and þou schalt defoule þe lyon and þe dragoun",
whiche is vndirstonde of Crist, and of þee. Riȝt so þou farest in
þis same place in þe texte þat þou allegest for Poule boostynge,
for þou hidest þe eende whiche is aȝens þe, þat seiþ not: "I
205 traueilede þus but [bi] þe grace of God in me", where hit
semeþ þat he fel not doun bi pride, as þou falseli feinest, but
"bi þe grace of mekenus", as þe eende preueþ.

'Now seþþe þanne þat þis hooli apostle, þe chosen vessel of
God þat was lad alyue into þe þridde heuen and schewide his
210 sauacion, durste not falle into veyneglorie, but bi mekenesse
cam doun, what wisdom were hit to me, synful wrecche þat
knowe not howȝ I schal ende ne where I schal bicome, to putte
me in perel and leue þe certeyn?'

---

176 oþer] or to R.   186 pride] (*mar.*).   189–90 If...taken] *om.* A.
192 þat(2)] þe R.   196 Hooli] *om.* R.   197 þat(2)] *om.* R.
199 schulde not hirte] (*int.* te), hirte not R.
205 bi] *om.* R.

And þus in þis maner, answerynge þoru þe helpe of God,
215 þou maist answere þe fend, and discunfite þe fend in his
seconde temptacion—þat is, veyneglorie.

Þe þridde temptacion þat þe fend temptide oure Lord Jesus
Crist was to þe synne of couetise vpon þe hiȝe hil, as I seide
bifore. Riȝt in þe same wise he bisieþ him euere to make men to
220 falle into þe same synne.

First, þe processe of þe gospel telleþ þat he ladde Crist into a
ful hiȝ hil and schewide him alle þe kyngdoms of þe world, and
al þe glorie of hem, and seid / to him: 'Alle þese þyngis I schal   f. 94ʳ
ȝeue to þe, if þou wolt falle doun and worschipe me.' Þis same
225 processe he haþ ȝet al dai to men þat he seþ disposid to
couetise, and desireþ to be hiȝe and gret in þis world. First, þe
fend ledeþ him vpon þe hil. After, þe glorious þyngis of þe
world ben schewid to him. Þe þridde tyme, þer is putte to him
a condicion: þat is, if he worschipe þe deuel alle þingis schul be
230 maad hise.

Þis is þus myche to mene: whan a man desireþ to be maad
grete and hiȝ in the world, þanne he stieþ into þe hil att þe
deuelis ledynge. And whanne he bigynneþ nyȝt and dai to
þenke into richessis and worschipis, and putteþ alle suche
235 þyngis tofore þe iȝen of his mynde, þanne þe prince of þis
world scheweþ to him þe glorious þyngis of his kyngedom. And
whan h⟨e⟩ feleþ þat þi þouȝtis ben longe tyme sette afire in þe
desiris of þe same godes, þanne þe þridde tyme he putteþ to þe
such causes: þat if þou wolt gete hem, þou must worschipe þe
240 fend, leuynge þe feiþ of God, and serue to him, forsakynge þe
riȝtwisnesse of God, and do þefte, and raueyne, and deceite,
and suche oþer. If þou chese to worschipe God in his feiþ, and
serue him after his commaundementis, þou schalt not gete al þo
þyngis.

245 Þerfore þe apostle techeþ: 'I biseche ȝou, breþeren, to haue
studie of reste, and of ȝoure owne nedes, and of wirchynge wiþ
ȝoure hondis, and þat ȝe desire no mannes good of hem þat beþ
wiþoute forþ.' And efte he seiþ: 'Hauynge / foodes and þoo   f. 94ᵛ
þyngis wiþ whiche we schul be helid, wiþ þese þyngis be we
250 apaied. For þei þat wolen be maad riche fallen into dampnacion, temptacion, and into snare of þe deuele, and manye

---

216 is] is in R.   217 (*mar: 3 temptacio*, H3), (R *mar: 3 temp⟨tacio⟩ auaricie*).
219 wise] *om.* R.   220 into...synne] *om.* R.   221 (*mar: I*).
221–2 a ful hiȝe] an hiȝe R.   227 (*mar: 2*).   228 (*mar. 3*).
234 into] in þo R.   238 (*mar. 4*).   241 and(2)] *om.* R.
250–1 dampnacion] *om.* R.

vnprofitable and noyus desiris, whiche drenchen men into deþ
and losse. But forsoþe, of alle euelis þe bigynnynge is couetise.'
Þerfore alle þoo þyngis þat þe deuele [leyde to] Crist, he
255 despisede hem bicause þat he schulde not ȝeue þe glorie of God
to þe deuele. And to teche man þouȝ al þe world schulde be
ȝeue to him oneli to leue God, he scholde not do it, not to loue
more richesses þan þe glorie of God, for it is not riȝtwis ne
resonable for to despise þe creatour for þe creature, but þe
260 creature for þe creatour; for God mai ȝeue þe richesses, but
richesses moun not ȝeue þe God.

And þerfore, be wel war of þese þre sotil nettis of þe fende:
þat is, glotenye, veynglorie, and couetise. For Crisostom seiþ
þat þe deuele, whan he temptide Crist, seide 'þese þre nettis I
265 haue streiȝte oute ouer al þe world: þat whatsoeuere scape oute
of þe nettis of glotenye, renne into þe nettis of veyneglorie, and
whatsoeuere schape oute of þe nettis of veynglorie, renne into
þe nettis of auarice. For þese þre no man perfiteli ascapeþ. And
if any man ascapeþ, he ascapeþ not hool, but broken.' And
270 þerfore, þouȝ a man ascape þe nett of glotenye and ȝeue him to
abstynence, and also þe nette of / veyneglorie for his abstyn-   f. 9:
ence, ȝit it is good þat he be war of þe þridde sotil nette of
couetise þat so many men beþ deceyued wiþ, as Seint Poule
seiþ, bi þe textus rehersid tofore. And þe prophete Jere[mie]
275 seiþ: *A maiore usque ad minimum, et cetera.* 'Fro þe meste to þe
leeste', fro þe prophete to þe preste, 'alle studien to auarice.'
And Salamon seiþ: 'Alle þyngis obeien to moneie.'

Þerfore, if þou wolt wiseli ouercome þe fend in þis temptacion and ascape his nette of couetise, answere to him as
280 Crist answeride in þe same caas, for he is þe beste maister, and
whoso doþ after him he mai not faile, for he seiþ: 'I haue ȝeue
ȝow ensaumple, þat riȝt as I haue doo, so do ȝe.' And Seint
Gregorius seiþ: *Omnis Christi actio, et cetera.* 'Euery dede of
Crist is oure informacion.' And sei þus to him:
285 'Goo, Sathanas! It is writen: "Þou schalt worschipe þi Lord
God, and to him alone þou schalt serue." Wherbi I vndir-

253 of...bigynnynge] byginnyng of al yuelis R.
254 þoo] *om.* R;   leyde to] delite A.
258 more richesses] riches more R.
265 streiȝte] streyned R;   whatsoeuere] who so euer R.
268 no man] may no man R;   ascapeþ] scape R.
270 þouȝ] if R;   ascape] scape R.   272 þat he] to R.
274 tofore] bi fore R.   279 (A, R *mar: Responsio*).
284 informacion] confirmacion R.

stonde, if I consente to þi suggestion of couetise of worldeli
godes, or of worschipe whiche I mai not com to but if I do þe
worschipe wiþ fraude and euele conscience, þanne worschipe I
290 an alyen God (as Seint Poule seiþ: "Auarice is seruise of ydolis
or mawmetis") and so I breke þe firste commaundement of
God.

'Also, if I consente to þe in þis temptacion, þanne make I
myself seruant to þe deuel þat is Lord of alle couetous men, or
295 ellis to þoo ryches/sis, and Crist seiþ in þe gospel þat "no man   f. 95ᵛ
mai serue two lordes at ones: for oþer þat one," he seiþ, "þou
schalt hate, and þat oþer þou schalt loue; or ellis to þat one he
schal cleue, and þat oþer he schal despise."

'And þus I can not see but þat þe ende of alle þat þou art
300 aboute is not ellis but to make me to hate and despise my Lord
God of heuen and helle and of al þe world, and chese þe to my
Lord God, fals þeef, whiche, for þi stynkynge pride and foule
couetise þat wilned to haue be euen and like to God, my
worschipeful Lord and þyn þrew þe doun into þe depe putt of
305 helle, þere to wone, world wiþouten ende. And I haue þe
suspecte, seþþe I conceyue þi malice. And þerfore goo, Sathanas, into þyn owne propre place þat God haþ ordeyned for þe
and for þi curside cumpanie!'

And whosoeuere stifli wiþstondeþ to þe fend, as Crist haþ
310 ȝouen vs ensample in þis gospel and as I haue expowned tofore,
wiþoute any doute he schal anon cowardli flee aweie fro him;
for Seint [Jame] seiþ: *Resistite diabolo, et cetera.* 'Strongeli
wiþstondeþ þe fend and he schal fle aweie fro ȝow', and þenne
Goddes hooli angels schul come ner to suche a man, and
315 mynystre to him.

Þou schalt vndirstonde, as þe doctour Crisostom seiþ vpon
þis same gospel, þat 'þer ben alweie twei angels duellynge wiþ
men: a good, and an euele. And as longe as þe goode angele is
wiþ vs, þe wickid angel mai neuere brynge vs into temptacion.

290 seruise of] seruaunt to R.
295 þoo] *om.* R.
oþer þat one] eiþer þe ton R.
297–8 to...cleue] þe ton þou shalt plese R.
298 þat oþer he] þe toþer þou R.
301 of al] *om.* R.
depe putt] deppist pit R.
311 wiþoute] wiþ a oute.
316 (R *mar: De bono angelo et malo*);
318 men] a man R.

294 is] arte R.
296 at ones] atones A;
297 þat oþer] þe toþer R.

300 to(2)] *om.* R.
304 þyn] þerfore he R;
309 to] and answeriþ to R.
312 Jame] R, Petre A.
as] þat as R.

320 But oþerwhile, after þe dispos[ic]ion of God, he hideþ himself
     (þat is, makeþ himself ynuysible tofore þe fend); for, but þe
     goode angele wole, he is not seie of þe / fend. Þerfore he f.
     wiþd⟨ra⟩weþ himself þat he ȝeue leue to þe fend to tempte, and
     stondeþ and bideþ þe comynge of þe temptacion. Þerfo⟨r⟩e
325 whanne any desire of euele stieþ vpon þyn hert⟨e⟩ and meueþ
     þe to any kinde of synne, þenne þe goode angele is not aboute
     þe, but þe deuel spekynge in þyn herte tempteþ þe and
     compelleþ þe. But whanne þou brekest þe deuelis temptacion
     in þyn herte and he seeþ þat he mai not ouercome þe, he goþ
330 aweie fro þe. And whanne þat þe desire goþ aweie, and þyn
     herte bigynneþ for to ioie þat þou hast ascapid þat wickid
     asauȝt and, as a manere of a spiriȝt of lyif, gladeþ and doþ
     þonkynges to God, knowe þou þanne þat þe fend goþ aweie fro
     þe and, after þe victorie of þe temptacion, þe angel comeþ ner
335 and mynystreþ to þe, and he spekeþ in þe and worcheþ ioie.'
     And not oneli þis seruice he doþ to þe, but also mynystreþ to þe
     fro God grace more plenteuousli for þi grete bataile and
     glorious victorie, and also offreþ vp tofore þe trone of God
     þyne almesdedes and þi preiers, as he did of Thobie and
340 Centurio. And in þi laste houre, in þat perelous bataile bitwixe
     þe fend and þe, he schal myȝtili helpe þe to haue of him
     gloriousli þe victorie, and after be þi leder þoru þe peynes of
     purgatorie to euerlastynge blisse. Amen.

320 disposicion] disposion A.   321 but] but if R.
322 wole] whil R;   seie] seyne R;   of] wiþ R.
325 vpon] vp in R.   329 he(ȝ)] þen he R.   330 þat þe] om. R.
331 ascapid] scapid R.   335 he] om. R.   341 and þe] þe and A.
342 gloriousli þe victorie] glorious victory R.
343 Amen] om. R.

AN OPTIONAL
EXPANSION TO
SERMON 11

[F]or as myche as þis gospel spekeþ principalli of þre synnes
(þat is: glotenye, veynglorie, and couetise) þerfore, whoso wole,
after þe tyme þat he seeþ þat he haþ disposicion of his
auditorie, he mai dilate his matere, spekynge scharpeli bi þe
5 ground of Scripture aȝens þese þre synnes.

First aȝens glotenye, for glotenye is a gret synne, hiȝli
forbo/den of God, and harmeþ mannes bodi, and mannes f. 96ᵛ
so⟨u⟩le, and his temperal goodes, and his neiȝbour boþe.

First, it is forboden of God (*Luc.*[21.34]) where he seiþ þus:
10 'Takeþ hede to ȝou[re]self, lest perauenture ȝoure hertes be
greued wiþ glotenye, and drunkschipe, and bisinesse of þis
liyf.'

Also, it is a maner of despite don to God; for he leueþ him
and cheseþ him a newe god, for suchon makeþ his beli his god,
15 as Seint Poule seiþ (*Phil.*3.[19]): *Quorum deus venter est, et
cetera*. And so he brekeþ þe firste commaundement, makynge
him a fals god.

Also, it makiþ a man grucche aȝens God; for, as Goddes lawe
seiþ: 'Mi loue was maad fatt, and he kikede.'
20 Also, glotenye harmeþ mannes soule; for a gloton pleseþ þe
deuele, for þe gospel seiþ þat a legyon of fendis preieden Crist
þat þei scholden goo into swyn, bi whom ben vndirstonde
glotenos men.

---

1 For] (*Text indented for two lines*; F *om.*). 2 (*mar*: Glotony, H3).
4 spekynge] *om.* R.
6 (*Foot of f.96r: Nota bene*, H3?) (R *mar: Nota bene de Gula*).
7 mannes(2)] *om.* R. 9 21.34] c⁰ A, 21 c⁰ R.
10 ȝoure] R, ȝouȝ A, 3(2) *added later*. 16 commaundement] heest R.
23 glotenos men] glotouns R.

Also, þei ben cursid of God; for þe prophete Ysa[y] seiþ (5
25 chapitre [11]): 'Cursid be ȝe þat ariseþ erli for to suen
drunkschipe, and for to drynken til to euentide.'

Also, glotenye harmeþ mannes bodi; for hit bryngeþ in
sikenesse and is ofte cause of destruccion, boþe of bodi and of
soule. Þerfore seiþ þe Wise Man (*Ecci*.37.[33–34]): 'In many
30 metis wanteþ not sikenesse, and for glotenye many men han
perischid', and 'he þat is abstinent schal eche his liyf.' And
Seint Poule seiþ: 'Þe mete to þe wombe, and þe wombe to þe
mete; and God schal destrie þat oon and þat oþer.'

Also, glotenye deformeþ in man þe ymage of þe Trynite; for
35 bi þis ymage he excelleþ oþer passeþ alle oþer beestis—þat is: in
resoun, mynde, and good wille. Þanne his resoun is aweie, for
he discernyþ not bitwixe good and euele, for þat þat is euele, he
weneþ be good; and / þat þat is good, he weneþ be euele. And   f. 97
þus, whanne he is in þis plite, what is he but mad? Þerfore
40 Senec[a] seiþ: 'What is drunkenesse but wilful wodnesse?' And
þe doctour Lync[oln] seiþ: 'Drunkeschipe is wodnesse, for
"fornycacion, wyn, and drunkenesse taken aweie þe herte".'
And þus, in þis madschipe, he is redi as a wod man to al maner
of synnes:

45   Firste to pride, settynge myche bi himselfe and litil bi al
oþere, grete oþes swerynge, and lyynge, and bostynge of his
witt [and] of his strengþe, whanne he haþ neuer neiþer, and of
hise goodes, myche more þanne euere he hadde.

Þenne is he also redi to wraþþe; for if any man displese him,
50 ȝe! þouȝ it were for his goode, þanne anon he is wroþ, and
swelleþ as a tode, chideþ, þreteþ, and curseþ, as he be wood;
and redi to debate wiþ alle oþer men; and ofte tyme sleþ his
neiȝbur, or his neiȝbur him.

And but he mai be avengid anon at his wille, þanne comeþ in
55 enuye to destruye him wiþ his tunge; and if he knowe any
concel bi him þat was doon many wynter bifore, bi whiche he
myȝte be hynderid in his bodi, or in his name, or in his catel,

33 mete] metis R;   þat oon and þat oþer] boþe þe ton and þe toþer R.
35 oþer passeþ] or ouerpassiþ R.   36 for] for þen R.
38 and] & (*End of* f.96v.) and (*Start of* f.97r.);
(*Foot of* f.96v. *catchwords:* and þat).
41 Lyncoln] Lync' A;   for] *om.* R.   40 Seneca] Senec' A.
48 goodes] (*Followed by* dedes *deleted*, A).   45 (*mar*: I).
is he] he is R.   50 were] be R.   49 (*mar*: 2).
ofte] often R.   54 (*mar*: 3);   52 debate] bate R;
                                                    but] but if R.

þenne it goþ alle forþ, for þe flood3ates ben vppe. And if he non
suche knoweþ, þanne he wol lie on him, and disclandre him,
60 and falseli swere þerto.

Þanne also he is redi to coue⟨i⟩te oþer mennes godes bi þefte
or bi sotil bargaynes, if his witt wol serue þerto; and if he mai
not ellis, he wischeþ faste after hem.

Slouful also þanne he is of alle manere of goode, boþe to
65 seruise of holi chirche and preiers of his mouþ, but raþer to
slumbur and sle/pe and do non oþer god. And ofte, as þei goþ   f. 97ᵛ
homward toward hire beddes, þei drencheþ hemself in dichis bi
þe weie. And, þou3 þei comen hoom into hire chambre, þei
leteþ þe candel falle, and brenne hire bed, hemself, and hir
70 wyfe, hire children, and alle hire godes.

And ofte men fallen þoru drunkenesse into lecherie, þei
recken not wiþ what persones, frende or sibbi, maidenes or
wyues, or of holi ordre, as Loth in his drunkeschipe lay bi his
two doutres and gat on hem two children, of wham cam myche
75 peple þat euere weren contrarie to þe peple of God.

And þus, as I haue schewid, a gloton, whanne he wanteþ
resoun, is redi to alle manere of synnes. And 3if men take hede
of alle maner of synnes, drunkenesse is [þe] most perelous
synne. For þou3 a man be proude, wraþful, or enuyous,
80 couetous, slewful or lecherous, if he haue resoun, he mai do
penaunce and be saued; but if he be drunke, he lesiþ þe rule of
his resoun. And þerfore, if he di3e in þat estaat, he repenteþ
him neuere and so dieþ in alle his synnes.

I seide also bifore þat a drunken man leseþ also þe seconde
85 symilitude of þe Trynite—þat is, mynde. For þanne haþ he no
mynde of þe benefetis þat God haþ do to him, ne of his
bihotynge of blisse, ne þretynge of peyne, ne how perelous caas
he stondeþ ynne, ne hou3 he wraþþid God, ne vnneþe knoweþ
any of his dedis whiche he dide todai, so clene is his mynde
90 waschen aweie wiþ a litil drynke.

Hijs good wille is also agoo, for to plese God wiþ; but for to
serue þe deuele, þerto he haþ wille; and for to / hyndere   f. 98ʳ
himself, boþe in bodi and soule and in his temperal godes, as I
seide tofore, for Salamon seiþ: 'He þat loueþ metis schal be in
95 nede, and he þat loueþ wyn and fatte þyngis schal not be maad

---

58 vppe] open R.   61 (mar: 4).   62 serue] serue hym R.
64 (mar: 5);   he is] is he R;   of(2)] om. R.   66 do] to do R.
73 drunkeschipe] drunkenes R.   75 weren] was R.
78 þe] om. A, (mar. R).   79 proude] proroude A.
85 of þe] of þe of þe A;   haþ he] he haþ R.   88–9 knoweþ any] om. R.

riche.' For suche glotouns waasten cursideli hire goodis in
goode morsellis and d⟨e⟩licious drynkis til þei come to beg-
garis estaat, and þenne lyueþ vpon þe pore peple and ben
chargeus to hem aȝen þe wille of God and ensample of þe
100 apostle. And so þei harmen, as I seide at þe bigynnynge, to hire
neiȝeboris, ȝhe! boþe to pore and to riche:

To þe pore, for al þe superflu of mennys resonable sus-
tynaunce is due to pore mennes almes, for Crist seiþ: *Quod
superest, et cetera.* 'Þat þat is ouerplus, ȝeueþ to almes.' And so,
105 in as myche as þe glotoun eteþ and drynkeþ ouer mesure, in so
myche he wiþdraweþ of pore mennes liyflode and so he is cause
of hire deþ, in as myche as in him is. For Salamon seiþ: 'Þe
bred of n⟨e⟩di men is þe liyf of pore men' and 'He þat
defraudeþ him is as a man of blood'—þat is, a mansleer.

110 Þey harmen also to riche men, for þei robbeþ hem, and
steleþ of her goodes, borweþ also and neuer quyteþ, to
meyntene wiþ hire glotenye. And ofte in hire drunkeschipe, if
þei dwellen nyȝ hem, brenneþ vp al hire godis.

And þus, as I haue schewid, many harmes comeþ of þis
115 synne of glotenye, boþe bodili and goostli. And þerfore seiþ þe
Wise Man: 'Many men for glotenye han perisched.'

Þese glotenos moun wel be lickned to a foul þat is clepid a
bitore, þe whiche wol sitte bi þe / watir and pu⟨t⟩te his bile in a   f. 98
rude, and þerwiþ makeþ an huge soun so þat men may here
120 him afer cuntre. But whanne he sitteþ on drie grounde, fer fro
þe watir, þenne he lifteþ vp his bile into heuen, and sitteþ stille
and no noyse makeþ. Riȝt so, glotons sittynge in þe tauerne,
puttynge hire mouþes into þe bolle til þei ben drunke; þenne
þei crien wiþ grete voice, boostynge, swerynge, lyynge, and
125 slaunderynge, and al hire euele dedes whiche þei haue doun of
many ȝeres afore freschli rehercynge and reioisynge. But suche
men sittynge in þe drie cherche bi hire confessour, fer fro þe
tauerne, for to schryue her synnes, sitten as dombe and wolen
speke no word. Þerfore to suche seiþ þe Wise Man: 'To whom
130 woo? to whos fadir woo? to whom striues? to whom diches? to
whom puttenynge oute of yen? but to hem þat duellen in wyn
and studien in swyngynge vp of bolles.'

99 ensample] þe ensaumple R.   104 þat(2)] *om.* R.   109 as] *om.* R.
110 to] *om.* R.   117 (R *mar: Exemplum de gula*);   a...clepid] *om.* R.
118 þe(1)] *om.* R;   bi þe] in a R.
121 into heuen] vnto heuenwarde R;   sitteþ stil] stil sittiþ R.
124–5 and slaunderynge] swerynge and slaunderynge A.
125 of] *om.* R.   130 striues] strynes R.

Also, glotenye mai be lickned to þe deueles bridel; for riȝt as
a rider, after [þat] he haþ bridelid his hors, ledeþ him whider so
135 he wole, so [þe] deuele, after þat he haþ bridelid a man wiþ þe
bridel of glotenye, ledeþ a man into what vice so him likeþ, as I
seide and rehercid bifore. Þerfore seiþ Dauid, in þe Psauter: *In
chamo et freno, et cetera.* Þat is: 'In halter and bridel constreyne
her cheke bones.'

140 Þe seconde synne of þese þre synnes þat I spake of is
veynglorie, whiche is a foule wille to be preisid of any good þat
man haþ of God, of whiche he scholde preise God oneli and
ȝeue þe worschipe / to him, for þat falleþ to God as his part,   f. 99ʳ
and to vs þe profite. Veyneglorie is a synne þat doþ myche
145 harme, for it robbeþ boþe God and man.

First it robbeþ God of þat þat is aproprid to him, þat is:
worschipe and glorie, whiche a veyngloryous man desireþ to
himself in as myche as in him is. Þerfore seiþ Seint Poule: 'To
þe kyng of worldis, vndedli, ynuysible, oneli to God, honure
150 and glorie.'

It robbeþ also man of his goostli godis wiþ wiche he myȝte
bie him heuene, for it fordoþ hem, be þer neuer so manie, and
makeþ hem turne to noȝt; and þat þat good schulde be, makeþ
turne to euele. And as it is impossible to haue þe gras and þe
155 seed to springe boþe `at ones´, so it is impossible to desire here
wordeli preisynge for ouȝt þat men doon in þis liyf, and also
after þis life to haue þerfore mede in heuene. For Crist biddeþ
to alle suche: triste to non oþer mede but suche as þei axen
here, for wiþ wronge þei axen mede of God for þat þyng þat is
160 not don for his loue.

Also, veyneglorie not oneli robbeþ man of his goodes, but
also turneþ him to gret harme in oþer sidis. For of hool it
makeþ him sike, and of life it bryngeþ in deeþ. And medicyn
sore woundeþ him. Good he turneþ to euele, and vertu to vice.

165 What wisdom is hit for to ȝeue mennes gode dedis for
fleynge wordes þat passen as þe wynd, and forsake mede þat
euer schal laste? Bet⟨e⟩re were no good to doo, þan to do hit in

133 (R *mar: Exemplum*).   134 þat] *om.* A.
135 þe] *om.* A.   140 (R *mar: De vana gloria*).
141 of] for R.   143 (*Foot of* f.98v: *De vana gloria*, H3).
151 man] a man R.   154 haue] haue ony of R.
154–5 þe gras...boþe] (*Written over erasure in text*, H3) A.
155 to springe] *om.* R;   at ones] (*mar.* H3), *om.* R.
157 (R *mar: Amen dico vobis rece[þerunt] merce[dem] suam*).
159 þei] he R.   161 man] a man R.

ful wille to be preisid. Caste in / þyn herte what [he] þynkeþ bi f. 99ᵛ
[þe] of whom þou þenkest to be preised for þi goode dede.
170 Þerfore he loueþ þe: for he troweþ þat þou dost hit for þe loue
of God oneli. If he wiste þat þou it didest oonli for him, noȝt
ellis wolde he doo but scorne þe for þi dede. Þerfore, wiþ emty
hondes þei gooþ to God þat coueiten mede in þis world of hire
goode dedis.
175   Veynglorie is þe peny þat þe fend haþ euer redi to eche
mannes harme in þe feire of þis world, to bie wiþ al hire dedis.
      Veynglorie is þe grete wynd þat ouercasti[þ] grete toures,
steples, and trees þat weren depe rotefast in þe ground as it
semede, þat is: hiȝe men and hooli in life to mennes semynge
180 þis curside synne casteþ into helle. He þat loueþ veynglorie
makeþ losengeris and liers his domesmen, and setteþ þe
preisynge of hem bifore þe preisynge of God. And þis mai not
be wiþoute grett despite of God, and þus it semeþ a foule
blasfemye, for it draweþ fro God þat þat longeþ to him.
185   A ueynglorious man mai wel be lickned to an hen þat, as
tyme as sche haþ leide an eie, sche makeþ grete noise; so suche
a man, anon as he haþ do any good d⟨e⟩de, he willeþ to be
preisid and grete noise to be maad of him.
      And not oonli þis synne of veynglorie is to be hatid, whiche
190 is a spice of pride, but also al maner of pride. For pride was þe
firste synne and bigynnynge of al euele, as þe Wise Man seiþ
(*Ecci.*10.[15]): *Initium omnis peccati superbia.* Þat is:
'Bigynnynge / of al euele was pride. He þat holdeþ hit schal be f. 10ͨ
fulfillid wiþ cursis, and it schal ouercome him in þe ende.'
195   Pride made þe faire aungel, Lucifer, to be apostata and firste
breke þe swete ordre and feloschipe of angelis whanne he, for
his fairhede and his myche witt, wolde haue aboue alle oþer
angelis and made him pere to God þat, of his godenesse, made
him so faire and so wise. Þerfore he hadde a foule falle fro þe
200 heiþe of heuen into þe deppest pit of helle and bicam a lodli
fend, and alle þat to [him] assentide.

168 he] R, þe A;   þynkeþ] (*An* e *written above the* y) A.
169 þe] þē A, þee R.   170 for(2)] oonly for R.
171 oneli] *om.* R;   it didest] didest it R;   for him] for loue `of´ hym R.
175 euer redi] redi euer (*m. for r.*) A, euer *om.* R.
176 wiþ] þerwiþ R;   dedis] good deedis R.
177 ouercastiþ] ouercastid A.   180 He þat] þat he A.
186 tyme] sone R.   187 a man] on R.   190 but...of pride] *om.* R.
192 (R *mar: Nota de superbia*).   193 hit] hem R.   194 fulfillid] fillid R.
197 oþer] *om.* R.   200 lodli] bodile R.   201 him] *om.* A.

But, alas for sorwe! hou many men nowadaies ben apostatas,
brekynge þoru hire foule and horrible pride þe feire feloschipe
of holi cherche? Þe more harme is, men mai seie wiþ grete
205 mornynge and sorwe þe wordes of Dauid þe prophete, where
he seiþ: 'Þe pride of hem þat hatide þe stieþ alweie vp hiere and
hiere.' So hie it is stied nouȝ þat non astaat of holi cherche (þat
is, neþer presthode, ne knyȝthode, ne comyn peple) holdeþ
hem apaied wiþ hire estaat, but bisieþ hem euer wiþ al hire
210 power, wheþer wiþ riȝt or wiþ wronge, to stie euermore hiere
and hiere. And þey þat next scholden sue Crist in mekenesse
and alle maneres of vertues, to whom principali he seiþ:
'Lerneþ of me, for I am mylde and meke of herte', beþ nouȝ
mooste hie and most proude, passynge hire estaat of alle maner
215 of peple. For, þeras Crist mekeli comynede wiþ his disciplis,
and serued hem and louli wische her feet, and callid hem his
frendes and breþeren, prelatis nowadaies ben as hie aboue
semple curatis and preestis as kyngis aboue þe comen peple,
and takeþ of hem grete taliagis and subsidies, and trauaileþ
220 hem to gret / cost, whider hem likeþ and whanne hem likeþ, for   f. 100ᵛ
þynge þat ofte litil auaileþ to any helpe of soule, as þouȝ þei
hadde non oþer kyng but oneli hem alone.

Þere also, Crist hadde neuer hous of his owne bi title of
worldeli lor[d]schipe to hile in his heued; ne greet multitude of
225 proude araied meyne, but 12 seli pore men wiþoute ȝemen or
pagis to whom we reden he seruede ofter þan euer we rede þei
seruede him; whiche also neuer rood at greet araie, neþer he
neþer his meyne, but ones sempeli on an asse, sadelid wiþ his
disciplis cloþes; prelates þat ben nowadaies han many dyuerse
230 castellis, and maners as rial as þe kynge himselfe, to chaunge
whanne so euere h⟨e⟩m likiþ for to take diuerse eiris wiþynne,
araied as realli wiþ costli cloþes of gold and selk, and in
multitude of oþer iewellis, boþe of seleuer and of gold, in al
maner housis [of] office, as þouȝ it were in Salamons temple.
235 And so grete multitude of meyne of kynȝtis, squyers, ȝemen,
and gromes, myche more nyseli disgisid þan any seculer lordis

206 (R mar: De mala vita prelatorum).   208 ne(1)] om. R;
ne(2)] ne þe R.   211 And þey] om. R.
215 of] om. R;   mekeli comynede] comynede R;
disciplis] disciplis mekely R.   216 louli wische] lowly wesshe R.
220 cost (Added in margin at start of line, A);   and...likeþ] om. R.
224 lordschipe] d om. A.   230 as(1)] om. R.   231 euere] om. R.
232 in] om. R.   233 of oþer iewellis, boþe] om. R;
of seleuer and of gold] of gold and siluer R.   234 of] om. A.

meyne, whan he schal ouwer ride oute, ȝea! þouh it be to visite
his pore scheep, he mut ride wiþ foure or fyue score hors,
proudeli apareilid at alle poyntis, his owne palfrai for his bodi
240 worþ a 20 or 30 pound, al bihangid wiþ gliterynge gold as þouȝ
it were an hooli hors, himself aboue, in fyn scarlet or oþer cloþ
as good as þat, and wiþynne wiþ as good pelure as þe quene haþ
any in hire gowne, hir persons and hir clerkis rydyn/ge aboute f. 101
hem, al in gult harneise, wiþ bastard swerdis ouergild bi hire
245 sides hangynge, as þou it were Centurio and his knyȝtis ridynge
toward Cristis deþ.

Þis mai wel be þe abhomynacion of discunforte þat Daniel
spekiþ of, stondynge in holi place (þat is, here in Cristis
cherche). God, for his endeles merci, make of hem sone an
250 ende, þat alle cristen men þat louen þoo mai seie þe wordis of
Dauid in þe Psauter þere he seiþ þus: 'Þe enemyes forsoþe of þe
Lord anon as þei beþ honoured and enhaunced, riȝt as smoke
þei schullen faile'—þat is, oþer þoru verreie mekenesse
know[ynge] hire defauȝtes, and wilfulli takynge vpon hem þe
255 meke and pore estaat þat longeþ to Cristis prestis, or ellis, if þei
wole not come wilfulliche, þat þei ben compellid for to entre, as
Crist seiþ in þe gospel: *Compelle eos intrare.*

Also, þei þat ben in þe estaat of knyȝthode, þoru þis foule
synne of pride stieþ faste and passeþ hili hir estaat in al maner
260 aparaile þat longeþ vnto hem, aboue hire auncetres þat weren
bifore hem, whiche hadden myche more lifelode þan þei haue
now:

First, in proude araie of houshold. Þere as hir auncetres
weren wond to be seruid in hir houses at mete in pewtre vessel,
265 but if þere weren any peeris of þe reem, now it is noȝt worþe
but if a mene bacheler, ȝea! and dyuerse squyers also, whiche
ben come vp of non olde auncetrie, but bi extorcions crepen so
hiȝe, musten be serued wiþ selueren vessel, and þe leste page in
his house.

270 Hire cloþynge also axeþ so hie cost, boþe in cloþ, peerlis, and
pelure, þat oo garnemente passeþ in coste half moneie of
hire lifelodes / in a ȝeer.   f. 10

---

241 hooli] hobi (?) R.   243 persons] perosones A.
250 seie] *om.* R.   251 þere...þus] *om.* R.
254 knowynge] knowe A;   hire] her owne R;
defauȝtes] defaute R;   wilfulli takynge] wisely take R.
258 (R *mar: De mala vita militum*).   259 estaat] state R.
260 aparaile] paraile R.   264 in...mete] at mete in her housis R.
271 moneie] þe rente R.

Þere also as sum tyme a worþi bacheler of gret estaat hilde
him apaide to ride wiþ 5 or 6 hors, now a pore squyer wole ride
275 wiþ 8 or 10 ȝemen, alle of sute of as gret araie as sum tyme
weren ful worþi squyers.

But what wole falle of þis pride, I am sikir, as it is seid in
comen prouerbe: 'Pride goþ bifore, and schame comeþ after.'
Þat is: oþer þei mut be stronge þefes, to robbe here neiboris in
280 þe cuntre; or wrongful extorcioneris, to meyntene wiþ hire
proude estaat; or falle into so gret dette for borwynge to þat
proude araie þat neþer þei ne hire excecutours moun neuer
quyte haluen del, and hire eiris hauen leuere hire faderis soulis
liȝe in helle þanne selle any parcel of hire heritage to quyte wiþ
285 hir faderis dettes.

Nouȝ also þe comyn peple is hie stied into þe synne of pride,
for now a wrecchid cnaue þat goþ to þe plouȝ and to [þe] carte,
þat haþ no more good but serueþ fro ȝer to ȝer for his liflode,
þereas sum tyme a white curtel and a russet gowne wolde haue
290 serued suchon ful wel, now he muste haue a fresch doublet of
fyue schillyngis or more þe price, and aboue, a costli gowne wiþ
baggis hangynge to his kne, and iridelid vndir his girdil as a
newe ryuen roket, and an hood on his heued, wiþ a þousande
raggis on his tipet, and gaili hosid an[d] schood, as þouȝ it were
295 a squyer of cuntre, a dagger harneisid wiþ seluer bi his gurdel,
or ellis it were not worþ a pese. Þis pride schulle þer maistres
abuye / whanne þat þei schul paie hir wagis for, þereas þei   f. 102ʳ
weren wont to serue for x or xij schillin[g]s in a ȝer, now þei
musten haue xx oor þritti, and his lyuerei also þerto, not for he
300 wol do more werk, but for to meynten wiþ þat pride.

Þus pride stieþ in alle astatis, as ȝe haue herd rehercid bifore,
þat ful greuousli greueþ God and harme[þ] boþe bodi and
soule. Þis synne of pride doþ many harmes, as Holi Writt
witnessiþ in many placis:
305   First, it vsurpeþ to himself þat þat longeþ oneli to God,
aȝens þat þat God seiþ bi Ysaie: *Gloriam meam alteri non dabo.*
Þat is: 'I schal not ȝeue my glorie to anoþer man.'

---

273 as] *om.* R.   275 of(1)] of oon R.
280 wrongful extorcioneris] do wrongful extorcions R.
281 proude estaat] pride R;   or] or ellis R.   283 leuere] leuer lete R.
286 (R *mar: Nota de mala vita vulgi*).   287 þe(2)] *om* A.   291 þe price] *om.* R.
292 kne] kneis R.   295 wiþ seluer] *om.* R.   298 schillings] g *om.* A.
299 lyuerei] leuersun R.
herd rehercid] reher herd rehercid R.   302 harmeþ] harmed A, harmen R.
301 in] into R;
305 (*mar:* I).   307 ȝeue my] my ȝeue (*m. for r.*);   man] *om.* R.

Also, pride is cause ofte of þe los of many men, boþe bodi and soule, as it was of Pharao and of al his hoost (*Ex.*14.[28]), 310 and also of Chore and of his feloschipe ([*Nm.*16.32]).

Also, it deformeþ þe feiþ and þe resonable ymage of men, as it dide of Nabugodonosor, of whiche also spekeþ Dauid in þe Psauter, þere he seiþ þus: *Homo, cum in honore esset, et cetera.* Þat is: 'Man, whan he was in worschipe, vndirstod not. He is 315 comparisond to vnwise beestis, and maad like to hem.'

Also, pride deposeþ a man fro þe worschipeful estat and frendschipe þat he haþ wiþ God, as Oure Ladi seiþ in hire songe (*Luc.*1.[52]): *Deposuit potentes de sede.* Þat is: 'He haþ deposid myȝti men fro þe sete.' And Jere[mie] (50.[32]) seiþ: 320 *Superbus corruet, et non erit qui suscitet eum.* Þat is: 'Þe proude man schal falle, and no man schal arere him.' Also, God seiþ, bi Abdie þe profete (1 chapitre [4]): *Si exaltatus fueris ut aquila, et inter sidera posueris nidum tuum, inde detraham te, dicit Dominus.* Þat is: 'If þou be enhauncid / as þe egle, and putte þi   f. 102 325 nest amonge þe sterris, I schal drawe [þe] fro þennes, seiþ þe Lord.' And God also seiþ ([1] *Mac.*2.[62]): *A verbis viri peccatoris ne timueritis, quia gloria eius stercus et vermis est; hodie extollitur, et cras non invenietur; quia conuersus est in terram suam, et cogitatio eius periet.* Þat is: 'Ne drede ȝou noȝt of þe 330 wordis of þe synful man, for his glorie is tort and wormes; todai he is enhauncid, and tomorwe he is not founde, for he is turned into his erþe, and his þouȝt schal perische.' And Job [20.6–7] seiþ bi þe proud man: *Si ascenderit usque in celum superbia eius, et caput eius nubes tetigerit, quasi sterquilinium in fine perdetur.* 335 Þat is: 'If his pride stieþ vp into heuene, and his heued touche þe cloudes, [in] þe ende as a dunge hil [he] schal be destruyed.'

Also, pride gendereþ stryues, for þe Wise Man seiþ (*Pro.*11.[2]): *Vbi sunt superbia, ibi et contumelia; vbi autem humilitas, ibi et sapientia.* Þat is: 'Þere as pride is, þere is strife; 340 and þere as mekenesse is, þer is wisdom.' And, in anoþer place (13 chapitre [10]): *Inter superbos semper iurgia sunt.* 'Among proude men euer more ben stryues.'

---

308 many men] man R;   bodi] in bodi R.
310 *Nm.*16.32] *om.* A, Nm' 8 R.   311 þe(1)] *om.* R;   men] man R.
316 (R *mar: de superbia*);   estat] state R.
318 *sede*] sede et cetera R.   325 þe(2)] *om.* A.
326 also seiþ] seiþe also R.   329 ȝou] (*Preceded by* þou *deleted*).
330 þe] a R.   332 his(1)] *om.* R;   20] 30 A.
333 *in*] ad R.   336 in] and A.   337 gendereþ] groundiþ R.
338 *sunt*] fuerit R.   342 euer more] *om.* R.

Also, pride schal confounde men in þe Dai of Dom, whanne
þei schul seie: 'What profitede to vs pride, or ȝaf to vs
345 boostynge of richessis? Al þo þyngis ben now passid as
schadue.'

Also, proude men ben hatid boþe of God and men, as þe
Wise Man seiþ (*Ecci.*10.[7]): *Odibilis coram Deo et hominibus est
superbia.* Þat is: 'Pride is hatable to God and men.' And suche
350 men God hiȝli schal punysche, for Dauid seiþ: 'He schal ȝelde
plenteuousli to hem þat doþ pride.' And Seint Jame seiþ (4
chapitre [6]): *Deus superbis resistit; humilibus autem dat gratiam.*
Þat is: 'God wiþstondeþ to proude men; and to meke m⟨e⟩n he
ȝeueþ grace.'

355 Þe proude man mai wel be likened to a beere: for þanne
aboue it is maad gaie, whanne a deed man or a womman is putt
þerynne; so men and wymmen / þanne nameli maken gaie þe   f. 103ʳ
beere of hire soule (þat is, hire bodi) wiþ gaie garnementis,
whanne þe soule wiþynne is deed bi pride.

360 Pride also mai be likened to an vnwar wrasteler: for if in
wrastelynge oon of þe wrastelers mai rere þe foot of þe toþer,
sone after he casteþ him. So, if þe fend mai rere þe affeccion of
a man bi pride, anon he þroweþ him into euerlastynge dampn-
acioun. Þerfore seiþ Dauid: 'Þou hast caste hem doun while þei
365 weren arerid.'

Also, a proude man mai wel be lickned to a tree þat is callid
Yuy, for Iuy haþ þis kynde: as longe as it haþ hous, wal, or tree,
or any þynge to holde hit bi, it stieþ euermore hiere and hiere,
til it come to þe hiest place; but whanne he haþ noȝt to holde
370 him bi, þanne crokeþ [he] doun aȝen, for he is not myȝti to
kepe himself. And þis Iuy is not able to be no timbir in no
mannes hous, but it serueþ most to getis mete. Riȝt so proude
men, al þe while þat þei haue any þyng to lyue on, oþer on
lordschipe, oþer rauayne, extorcion, þefte, oþer borwynge, þei
375 stien euer hier and hier, and kunne make non ende of her pride;
but whanne hir hold bigynneþ to faile, þanne þei ben not
myȝti to bere hemselfe in suche estaat. Þei fallen doun into
schame and vileny and myche repreef of alle men, and suche
proude men ben not able to be no tymber in Goddis hous, but

347 men(2)] man R.
355 (R *mar: Exemplum de superbia*);   þanne] *om.* R.
360 (R *mar: Aliud exemplum*).   362 sone] þen sone R.
364 hem doun] doun hem R.
366 (R *mar: Aliud exemplum de superbia*).
370 he] *om.* A.   373 oþer] eiþer R.   376 hold] golde R.

380 þei ben able to mete of geett—þat is, to þe foule stynkyng fend
of helle.

Þe þridde synne is couetise whiche, as Seint Poule seiþ, is
rote of alle vicis. Couetise is a maister redynge in scole, and so
grete scole he holdeþ þat of alle generacions of folke and of al
385 degrees / comen to his scole for to lerne, as þe prophete f. 103
Jere[mie] seiþ: 'Fro þe leeste to þe meeste, fro þe prest to þe
prophete, alle studien to auarice.' Pryncis, prelates, [prestis],
lerid and lewd, and ȝet religious amonge oþer prestis, gon to þis
scole for to lerne of þis curside lore. Þere gret lordis lernen to
390 oppresse hire peple nedles wiþ grete taxis and talliagis, t⟨o⟩o
make hemself riche and lyue in grete lustis.

Smallere men, as knyȝtes and squyers of þe cuntre,
ouerledeþ hire pore tenauntis and hir semple neiȝheboris
aboute, wiþ wronge amerciamentes and hire proude þretynge
395 wordis, þat þei ben ful fayn for to lyue in pees to fyne at hire
wille. And if he mai haue any color to his neiȝhboris lond, he
myȝte as wel atte firste goo þerfro and seie it is not his as for to
wiþstonde suche a man bi plee.

Þere also lerneþ prelates, þat schulden punysche synne, to
400 selle it for seluer, as an oxe or a cowȝ; [and], but if þei wole paie
wiþ good wille, sumpne hem to dyuerse placis and suffre hem
neuer haue reste.

Þere lernen persons and vikeris to plede for hire tiþis, and
pun[y]sche hem more þerfore þan for alle þe dedli synnes.

405 Þere lerneþ religiouse men, aȝen prophession of her ordre, to
haue godes in propre þere þei non schulden haue, and for to
coueite officis to rake togedere goodes þere [þei] scholde be
pore and dede to þe world.

Þere lernen also in þis cursid scole marchauntis and
410 artificeres to be perfite in þis lore, wiþ wilis and wiþ falsede, for
to gete good.

---

380 mete of geett] getis mete R.
(R mar: Nota de Auaricia).
384 þat] and þat R.
389 (R mar: De Auaricia dominorum);
Þere] The R.
391 lyue] to lyue R.
399 (R mar: De Auaricia prelatorum).
401 hem] hym R.
404 punysche hem] (Malformed y), punche þe peple R.
407 togedere goodes] goodis togedir R;
409 (R mar: De auaricia vulgi).

382 (mar: 3 au');
383 so] a R.
387 prestis] om. A.
for] om. R;
390 grete] om. R.
394 wronge] strong R.
400 and] om. A.
403 plede] plete R.
þei] he⟨e⟩ A.
410 artificeres] men of craft R.

Þere lernen housbondes to tiþe ful euele; to erie into his neihboris lond and ripe into his corn; to mowen into his medewe and tiȝe into his lesewe; to destrie him wiþ his beestis
415 and make neuere amendes.

Þus, from a litil / childe til we haue an hoor beerd, hem   f. 104ʳ þynkeþ of þis science [þ]ei haue neuer lerned inouȝ. And ȝet naþeles þis science ouȝte gr⟨e⟩tli to be despisid, if men token heede what harme it doþ, for auarice bryngeþ in alle maner of
420 synnes:

First: pride, for þe Wise Man seiþ (*Ecci*.21.[5]): *Domus que nimium est locuples adnullabitur superbia.* Þat is: 'Þe hous þat is to riche schal be brouȝt to noȝt wiþ pride.'

Þe seconde: for it is moder of enuy, for þe Wise Man seiþ in
425 his prouerb (*Prouer*.[28.22]): *Vir qui festinat ditari et inuidet alijs, ignorat quod egestas veniet ei.* Þat is: 'A man þat hieþ to be maad riche and haþ enuye to oþere, he wot not þat nede schal come to him.'

Þe þridde hit gendreþ: wraþþe, for it telleþ in þe first booke
430 of Hooli Writt (*Gen*.13.[7]) þat þer was made striȝfe bitwene þe herdes of Habraham and Loth his cosyn for multiplyynge of hire beestes.

Þe fourþe: for it bryngeþ forþ slouþe, for Crist telleþ in þe gospel (*Lu*.12.[19]) howȝ þe riche man seide to himself: 'Mi
435 soule, þou hast many goodes putt into many ȝeris; reste, ete, and drynke, and make þe glaad.'

Þe fifþe: it gendreþ glotenye, as Crist scheweþ in þe gospel of þe riche man þat eete euerei daie schynyngli.

Þe sixte: it is noreschynge of lecherie, for þus it was seide in
440 Hooli Scripture to Salamon: *Collegisti quasi auricalcum aurum; et post: inclinasti femora tua mulieribus.* Þat is: 'Þou hast genderid togeder gold as þouȝ þou haddest a gold oore', and after: 'þou boudest þyne hipes to wymmen.'

ȝet also þis synne ouȝte to be hatid for þe manyfold cursis þat
445 God ȝeueþ in Holi Writte to þes riche men þat geten worldeli godes falseli, or holdeþ hem to streiteli, or loueþ hem to hertili.

414 his(2)] *om.* R.   416 an] and R.   417 þei] hei A.
418 gretli to be] to be greetly R.   421 (*mar*: I).
422 *est locuples*] locuples est R.   424 (*mar*: 2).
425 *Prouer*] *om.* R;   28.22] 24 A, R;   *Vir*] *om.* R.
427 þat] what R.   429 (*mar*: 3).
433 (*mar*: 4;   for] *om.* R;   forþ] in R.
437 (*mar*: 5).   439 (*mar*: 6);   þus] þusus A.
442 gederid] *om.* R;   oore] hoore R.

Firste, God curseþ to suche bi Ysaie þe prophete (5.[8]) þere
/ he seiþ þus: *Ve qui coniungitis domum ad domum, et agrum agro*   f. 104
copulatis. Þat is: 'Wo to ȝou þat ioyneþ hous to hous bi fals
450 couetise, and coupleþ felde to felde.' Also, he seiþ bi þe
prophete Abachuch: *Ve qui multiplicant non sua.* 'Cursid be þei
þat multiplyen þo þyngis þat ben not hiris.' Also, he seiþ bi his
prophete Ysaie [33.1]: *Ve qui predaris; nonne et ipse predaberis?*
Þat is: 'Cursid be þou þat robbest; wheþer þou schalt not be
455 robbid?' Also, Crist seiþ in þe gospel (*Luc.*6.[24]): *Ve vobis*
divitibus, qui habetis hic consolacionem vestram. 'Curside be ȝe
riche men, þat here haueþ ȝoure conforte.' Also, þe apostle
Judis seiþ: *Ve illis, qui in via Caym abierunt.* 'Cursid be þei þat
gon in Caymes weie', þat first couetise bigan. Also, þe Wise
460 Man seiþ (*Ecci.*10.[9]): *Auaro nihil est scelestius.* 'No þyng is
cursider þan þe couetus man.' And þerfore, for þese cursis and
many mo þat God ȝeueþ to couetous men, þis synne of couetise
is to be hatid.

Also, kynde stireþ vs to hate þis synne, seþþe mannes soule
465 þoru his kynde is hiere and clannere þan heuene; for he is maad
like to þe Trinite, whiche ouȝte here to be hied fro erþeli
þyngis as heuene is hiȝe fro erþe. A wonder þynge it were, and
aȝens kynde, þat heuene scholde neiȝhe þe erþe. So it semeþ
aȝen kynde þat couetise schulde brynge a mannes soule doun so
470 lowe to erþeli þyngis to make him loue hem, and on hem sette
his triste. Þerfore God haþ sette þe erþe so lowe, as vilist
element þat men schulden defoule wiþ feet and despise hit.
And, in token herof, hooli fadris in þe bigynnynge of þe
cherche, tauȝte bi þe Hooli Goost, solden erþeli possessiouns
475 and þrewen þe price to þe apostles feet.

Þe couetous man is like to þe see, to deeþ, and to helle. Þe
see / drynkiþ al þe watres of þe world; so þe couetous mannes   f. 1c
wille swoleweþ alle þe richessis of þe world, þerfore he is þus
vnsaciable (þat is, vnable to be fulfillid). He is likened also to
480 deeþ and to helle, for þei beþ neuer fillid, þe toon sleynge and
þe toþer swolewynge. Þerfore þe prophet Abachuc seiþ of þe
couetous man (*Aba.*2.[5]): *Dilatauit quasi infernus animam*

447–8 þere…þus] *om.* R.   449 hous(1)(2)] housis R.
452 his] þe R.   453 33] *om.* A;   *nonne et]* *om.* R.
460 No] þat is no R.   461 þerfore] *om.* R.
461–2 and many mo] *om.* R;   men] men and many mo R.
465 he] it R.   468 neiȝhe] nyȝe to R.   469 a] *om.* R.
471 God] he R.   476 (R *mar: Exemplum de Auaricia*).
478 he is] þat he R.

suam, et ipse quasi mors non adimplebitur. Þat is: 'He haþ
enlargid as helle his soule, and he as deþ schal not be fulfillid.'
485 And, for þe same cause, he is likened to a dropesi man, for þe
more þat h⟨e⟩ drynkiþ, þe more he firstiþ.

Whi þanne þat a couetous mannes herte mai neuer be fillid
mai be schewid bi diuerse resouns. First is þis: if a man were
sore afirst and he hadde bisides him a tunne ful [of] wyne, þou3
490 he drowe oute al þis wyne into anoþer vessel and putte non in
his mouþe, his first scholde neuere þe more be quenchid or
stanchid. So þe couetous mannes herte þat firsteþ after þe
richessis of þis world, þou3 he fille wiþ hem his whicchis vp to
þe brerdes, [h]is herte þerfore is neuer þe more fillid, but more
495 desireþ.

Þe seconde resoun is þis: if a man bisied him faste, for to fille
a gret berne wiþ oo corn of senevi, ri3tfulli of alle men he my3te
be holde a fool. So als is þat man þat weneþ to fille his
soule wiþ failynge richessis of þis world, for mannes soule is
500 wiþouten ende, and so no þynge þat haþ ende mai fille so laarge
a þynge, and no þyng mai fille mannes soule but oneli God,
which is also endeles.

Þe 3 resoun is þis: if a man bisili axide / and sou3te for to fille   f. 105ᵛ
a boket ful of wisdom, wheþer ⟨þis⟩ question of wise men
505 schulde not be holde fol and vnpertynent, for þat vessel is not
apte ne acordaunt to receyue wisdom. So, of men þat ben lad bi
resoun, suche a man schulde be hoolden a fool þat weneþ to
fulfille his soule wiþ richessis, for it is not apte to receyue
goodes of þis world, but wisdam of þe Fadir, comynge fro
510 aboue.

Þe 4 resoun is þis: if þer were a greet fier whiche þou woldest
fayn sleke, and þou leidest þerto mo drie schides, wise men
wolden holde þe for a fool for, after þat, þe more kenliere it
wolde brenne. So a mannes herte, þat hote brenneþ wiþ þe fier

---

487 þanne] *om.* R.   488 (*mar:* I) A, R.   489 of] *om.* A.   490 in] into R.
491 þe more be] be þe more R;   quenchid or] *om.* R.
492 þe(2)] *om.* R.   493 wiþ hem] *om.* R;   whicchis] hucchis R.
494 brerdes] brinkis R;   his] h *om.* A;   þerfore is] is R;
fillid] filde þerfore R.   496 (*mar:* 2) A, (R *mar:* ij);   for] *om.* R.
498 als is] also R.   503 (*mar:* 3) A, (R *mar:* iij).
504–5 wheþer...for] ri3tfully men my3ten holde hym a fool . for whi R.
506–7 of...fool] is þat man R.   508 fulfille] fille R.
511 (*mar:* 4) A, (R *mar:* iiij).   512 leidest þerto] leydist R;
schides] shidis þerto R.   513 after þat] þen R.
514 a] *om.* R.

515 of couetise, þe mo godes þat he rakeþ togedere, þe more it
setteþ his herte afiere. Þerfore seiþ þe Wise Man (*Ecci*.14.[9]):
Insatiabilis est oculus cupidi. Þat is: 'Þe iȝe of þe couetous man is
vnable to beo fillid.' And also he seiþ, in anoþer place: *Avarus
non implebitur pecunia.* 'Þe couetus man schal not be fulfillid
520 wiþ   moneie.'   Also   þe   Wise   Man   seiþ   in   prouerb
(*Prouer*.30.[15]): *Tria sunt insatiabilia, et quartum est quod
numquam dicit: sufficit.* Þat is: 'Þre þyngis þer ben þat ben
vnable to be fulfillid, and þe fourþe þat neuer seiþ "Hoo!"'—
þat is, þe couetous mannes herte, *et cetera.*

525   Also, couetise of worldeli mennes goodes mai wel be likened
to a dunge hil: for as a dunge hil þat is gaderid togidere roteþ
and stynkeþ, and whanne it is sprad abrood it makeþ feeldes for
to bere frute, so þe richessis of a couetous man þat ben gaderid
togedere and leide vp to roten þe soule and makeþ it stynke in
530 þe siȝt of / God, and whanne þei ben sprad abrod to pore men,   f. 10ɾ
þei norischen hem and geten remission to þe soulis of riche
men. Þerfore seiþ Crist, in þe gospel: *Facite vobis amicos, et
cetera.* 'Makeþ ȝouȝ frendes of þe goodes of wickidenesse'—þat
is, whiche for þe more part bryngeþ men to wickidenesse. And
535 of þis dunge hil spekiþ [Ezekiel] þe prophete ([7] chapitre [19]),
þere he seiþ þus: *Aurum eorum in sterquilinium erit.* 'Hire gold,'
he seiþ, 'schal be to hem a dunge hil.'

    Also, couetise mai wel be lickned to a postyn: for a postyn
þanne is perelous whanne it is nyȝe þe herte, so richessis þenne
540 ben perelous and dedli whanne man setteþ on hem herteli loue.
Þerfore seiþ Dauid: *Diuitie si affluant, et cetera.* 'If richesses
flowen to ȝow, setteþ not ȝoure hertes on hem.'

    Also, a riche man is likened to a woute or a moldwarpe: for
he is blac bi wickidnesse and synne, and blynd bi ignorance. As
545 manie possessions as he haþ, so many biriels he haþ, in whiche
he birieþ himselfe bi contynuel bisynesse. And as myche as he

---

516 afiere] on fire R.
couetus] (*Followed by* no *deleted*).
523 fulfillid] fillid R;
525 (R *mar: Exemplum de auaricia*);
529 roten] rote R.
7] 8 A, R.
Hire] þat is her R.
wel] *om.* R;
542 ȝow] *om.* R.
woute or a] *om.* R.
546 contynuel] contynueli A.

519 Þe] þat is þe R;
521 *Prouer*.30.15] *om.* R.
        Hoo] who R.
        mennes] *om.* R.
535 Ezekiel] Osee A, R;
536 þere] where R;
538 (R *mar: Exemplum de A*[*uaricia*]);
        for a postyn] *om.* R.
543 (R *mar: Exemplum aliud*);
        545 so] as R.

delueþ he þroweþ aboue him, for þe goodes þat he loueþ so
passyngli he makeþ his god.

Also, a couetous man mai wel be likned to a somer hors þat
550 bereþ a lordes tresour: whanne he is al tobroke wiþ trauaile þat
he haþ vsid, þenne þe tresour þat he baar is holli fro him take,
and no þyng he leueþ him of þat he baar for his long trauaile,
but bare weri sides, crachi feet, and gallid bac. Riȝt so, þe
couetous man, þat kepeþ togedere worldeli godes þat heuy on
555 him lieþ, and pyneþ him sore wiþ many angris, wiþ sorwe, and
drede, and perel of deþ; at þe laste ende, he schal not ha/ue of   f. 106ᵛ
alle his trauaile but leeste, as a wrecche in pouerte and peyne,
and born to þe erþe wiþ bare sides saue a wrecche schete.

Also, he mai be likned to a scheep þat bereþ wolle: for al þat
560 he al þe ȝer gadereþ atte laste is clene fro him taken, and he
bileue nakid and oþer þerof han cloþes.

Also, he mai be likened to an oxe þat sore is pyned and
fordryuen in þe plouh, oþer eten þe corn þat he traueleþ fore,
and leueþ him noȝt to his part but vnneþe þe chaf.

565 Þerfore seiþ Seint Poule ([1] ad Thi.6.[7]): *Nichil intulimus in
hunc mundum; haut dubium nec aliquid auferre possumus.* Þat is:
'No þyng,' he seiþ, 'we brouȝten into þis world; ne no doute ne
no þyng we moun bere hennes.'

Seþþe þanne couetise is so perelous, as is schewid here
570 bifore, it were þanne grete wisdom wiseli to be war þerof, as
Crist warneþ in þe gospel and seiþ (*Lu.*12.[15]): 'Biholdeþ, and
beþ war of al manere of couetise' and 'makeþ ȝoure tresourie in
heuen', bi large almesdede to hem þat beþ verreie pore, 'where
it mai neuer faile, whe[re] ruste mai not destruye it, ne mouþ
575 mai not waste hit, ne þefes moun not stele it.' If we don so,
þanne schulle we haue þongke of God, help of alle seyntis, and
þe endeles blisse of heuene.

First, þonke of God, for he seiþ in þe gospel: 'Þat ȝe doþ to
þe leeste of myne, ȝe doþ to me.' Also, helpe of hooli seyntis,

549 (R *mar*: *Aliud exemplum*);
550 whanne] but when R.
553 and] and a R.
559 (R *mar*: *Exemplum*);
561 bileue] bileueþ A, bileuyþ R.
562 (R *mar*: *Aliud Exemplum de Auaricia*).
566 *possumus*] possimus R.
572 of(2)] *om*. R.
574 where] re *om*. A;
575 ne þefes...it] *om*. R.

mai wel be] *om*. R.
552 he leueþ him] is left hym R.
555 angris] angris and trauelis R.
þat(2)] þat þat R.

567 he seiþ] *om*. R.
573 hem] pore men R.
mouþ] mouȝt R.

580 whiche weren pore men, for þei moun helpe vs to brynge vs
into euerlastynge tabernaclis, whiche is þe blisse of heuene to
whiche Crist schal clepe alle suche in þe daie of / general   f. 107
reward, to whom he schal seie þese wordes (*Mt.*25.[34]):
'Comeþ, ȝe blessid children of my Fadir, and takeþ þe kyng-
585 dom þat is to ȝou ordeyned fro þe bigynnynge of þe world,' *et
cetera.*

582 whiche] whiche blis R.

SECOND SUNDAY
IN LENT

Egressus Jesus, et cetera (*Mt*.15.[21]). 'Jesus wente oute and
ȝede into þe cuntreis of Tire and Sidon', *et cetera.* In þis
gospel, by þe ensaumple of a deuoute and stedfast womman þat
cried bisile for þe helþe of hir douȝter and cesid not til she had
5 geten graunte of hir wille, we ben tauȝt, when we preyen for
ony þing to God, to contynu in oure preyer wiþ stedfast bileue
fourmed wiþ charite, and we shullen not feile to haue þat we
asken or oþer þing þat God seiþe is more necessarie and
profitable to vs.
10 Þis goyng out of Jesus þat þis gospel telliþ of in þe
bygynnyng may bitoken þe going oute þat he wente fro þe hyest
heuen into þis wrecchid worlde and toke oure pore kynde on
hym to þe saluacion of vs alle. Of þis going oute spekiþ Dauid
in þe P[sauter]: *A summo celo egressio eius, et cetera.* Þat is: 'His
15 going out wes fro þe hiȝest heuen into þe cuntreis of Tire and
Sydon', as þe gospel seiþe.
Tyre is as myche to sey as 'hunting', and Sydon 'anguysshe'.
Þat is, þe comyng of hym wes to þat eend: for to delyuer vs fro
þe ʼhunting of þeʼ deuel, by whiche he had huntid in oure
20 former fadris in paradise and brouȝte hem into anguysshe, in
whiche þei haden ben alwey inʼtoʼ þat day, and euer shulden
haue ben ne had his blessid comyng ben.
Of þe comyng of Crist to þe destruccion of þis cursid /
hunter spekiþ Crist in þe gospel (*Luc*.11.[21–22]), þere he seiþe f. 72ʳ
25 þus: 'When a strong, armed man kepiþ an hous, alle þyngis ben

---

1 Egressus] (*Text indented for four lines; rubricated* E *written into the space,*
R. *Text indented for two lines;* E *om; no rubrication,* A).
8–9 and profitable] *om.* A. 11 hyest] hiest fadir A. 13 vs] *om.* A.
14 Psauter] P' R, Psauter þere he seiþ þus A; *et cetera*] *om.* A.
17 myche] myche for A. 19 hunting of þe] (*mar.*) R.
23 (*Foot of* f.71v. *catchwords:* hunter spekiþ Crist).
24 gospel] gospel of luc' A.

in pees whiche he weldiþ. But when a strenger þen he comeþ
vpon hym and ouercomeþ hym, he shal take awey alle his
armes in whiche he tristid, and departe abrode his robries.'
But here men mosten vnderstonde þat fro þe tyme of þe
30 blessid passion of oure Lorde Jesus Crist and his glorious
resurreccion and wonderful ascencion into heuen aȝeyn, by
whiche þis strong hunter, þe feend, wes ouercomen and
bounden as M[atheu] seiþe, he lay þus bounden forþe for a
þousand ȝere, as Jon witnesiþ in þe Apoc[alips]: þat is, his
35 power wes made lesse to hunte mannys soule þen it wes bifore.
For in þat þousand ȝere wes myche more perfeccion of lyuing
of hooly martirs, confessouris, and virgyns, þen euer wes siþen
into þis day.
And þerfore it semeþ wel now, by þe synful lyuing of þe
40 peple, þat þis cursid hunter is now vnbounden—þat is, he haþe
had fro þat tyme myche more power þen he had þo, and more
bisile nyȝt and day huntiþ now mennys soulis. And, riȝt as
hunteris hunten dyuerse maner of preyes in dyuerse maner to
asay hou þei moun most spedile cacche hem, summe wiþ
45 bowis, summe wiþ houndis rennyng wiþ open mouþe, and
summe wiþ grehoundis, and summe wiþ priue nettis, in þese
maners þe feend huntiþ mannys soule to loke hou he may most
spedile bringe hem into synne.
First, he huntiþ wiþ bowis. Þis bowe is crokid and sotil
50 sleiȝtis, whiche he vsiþ to disceyue wiþ mankynde. Þerfore holy
chirche syngiþ þus of him: O tortuose serpens, et cetera. 'O, þou
crokid serpent, whiche by a þousand wilis and crokid disceitis
traueilist restful hertis.' Þe longe stringe wiþ whiche he bendiþ
his bowe / redy to shete is þe longe enuy þat he haþe had to   f. 72
55 man siþen he fel from heuen and sawe þat man wes made to
fille þat place þat shulde haue ben his for euer if he had not
trespased. Of þis enuy spekiþ þe Wyse Man, þere he seiþe:
'Þorow þe enuy of þe feend, deeþ entrid into þe worlde.' Þe
drawing of þis bowe is þe temptacion or þe suggestion þat he
60 makiþ to synne. In þis bowe þe feend shetiþ þre arowis, or þre
fire dartis, and whomsoeuer he woundiþ wiþ hem, he sleeþ
hym.

27 and ouercomeþ hym] om. A.   28 armes] armuris A.
40 he] om. A.   40–41 haþe...tyme] haþ fro þat ⟨t⟩yme had A.
46 summe] summe also hunteþ A;   in] in alle A;
(mar: De venacione diaboli et eius instrumentis).
49 (mar: De arcu diaboli).   52 serpent] ⟨addre⟩ A.   57 seiþe] seiþ þus A.
58 þe(1)] om. A.   59 þe(2)] om. A.   62 hym] hem A.

Þe first arow þat he drawiþ vp and smytiþ wiþ is delectacion
or liking þat he makiþ him to haue in synne whiche he temptiþ
65 hym to. And if he se þat he hittiþ him þerwiþ, þen is he þe
more bolder to shete þe secound arow, þat is: consente to
synne. And if he may hit him, and falle him þerwiþ, þen he
shetiþ þe þrid arow and sleeþ h[i]m al oute, þat is: wiþ ful dede.
And by euery suche man þat he shetiþ þus, he may sey þe
70 wordis of Dauid in þe P[sauter]: *Sagittas meas complebo in eis.*
Þat is: 'Myn arowis I shal fulfille in hem.'

Þis cursid hunter slepiþ not ne restiþ, nyȝt ne day, but euer
cumpassiþ þe worlde aboute, as he seide to God, as þe Boke of
Job witnessiþ. Wiþ þese þre arowis redy drawen in his bowe,
75 he shetiþ so many wiþ hem þat vnneþe ony may ascape clene
vnbounden fro his hondis.

Hou many men shetiþ he now, wiþ þe arowis of pride? It
semyþ wel ny al þe worlde, for so myche nyce disgising and
new fyndingis of aray wes þer neuer, I trowe, fro þe bigynnyng
80 of þe worlde, in whiche þei hyȝely steren God to veniaunce, as
Dauid þe prophete seiþe: *Irritauerunt eum | in adinuencionibus* f. 73ʳ
suis. And þerfore I am as siker as God is true God þat þis londe
wole be lost for her new fyndingis of cursid pride, but if þei
ben sone amendid.

85 Hou many also [now] shetiþ þe feend wiþ þe fire dartis of
foule glotony, luste leccherie, and horrible spousebreking? Þere
arne so many slayne wiþ þese dartis, þe more harme is, þat no
man knowiþ but oonly God, for of suche foolis, as þe Wise
Man seiþe, 'þe noumbre is wiþouten eend.' Therfore euery
90 true cristen man, and specialy þe Pope, and alle prelatis and
prestis, seing þis grete slauȝter þat þe feend haþe sleyne of
cristen men wiþ þese þre dartis, shulden now sey wiþ sore
hertis þe wordis of Jeremy þe prophete, seying: 'Who shal ȝyue

---

63 (*mar: prima sagitta*).   64 to] *om.* A;   in] in þe A.
66 (*mar: 2*);   consente] to consente R.
68 (*mar: iij*);   arow] *om.* A;   him] hem R;
al oute] ou´t´riȝt A.   70 of Dauid] þat Dauid seiþ A.
72 euer] euer more A.   75 may ascape] man ascapeþ A.
76 vnbounden] vnwoundid A.   78 nyce] *om.* A.
78–9 and new fyndingis] *om.* A.   81 *adinuencionibus*] in *om.* A.
82 þat] *om.* A.   85 now] *om.* R;
dartis] arwes A.   87 dartis] arwis A;
slayne...dartis] (*Preceded, not followed, by* þe more harm is A).
88 as] *om.* A.   90 Pope] (*Erased but still legible* A).
92 dartis] arwis A.

water to my heed, and to myn iȝen þe welle of teeris, þat I may
95 wayle þe sleyne folke of my peple?'

To be war of þis sotil feend, and of þe best remedy aȝeyns his
arowis, techiþ vs Seint Petre in his first pistle (v chapitre [8–9])
þere he seiþe þus: *Vigilate: quia aduersarius vester diabolus, et
cetera.* 'Wakiþ! for ȝoure aduersarie þe feend, as a
100 lyoun rauysshing, cumpassiþ þe worlde, seching whom he may
deuoure; to whom wiþstonde, ȝee strong in feiþe.' Þen it
semyþ, by þis autorite of þe apostle, þat feiþ is best help aȝens
þe arowis of þe deuel.

Herto acordiþ Poule ([*ad*] *Eph.*[6.16]), seying: *In omnibus*
105 *sumentes scutum fidei, et cetera.* 'In alle þingis taking þe sheelde
of feiþe, in whiche ȝee moun alle þe fire dartis quenche of þe
wickid en[m]y'—þat is, þe feend. For þe defaute of þe defence
of þis sheelde þat þe feend fyndiþ men nakid, and not keuerid
þerwiþ, / þerfore it is þat he sleiþ so many wiþ his arowis. Þat   f. 73ᵛ
110 is, al þe synne þat is done in þe worlde is for defaute of feiþe;
for if men bileueden fully þe byheestis of euerlasting joy þat
God bihotiþ to men `þat´ seruen hym truly, and myȝtily
wiþstonden her enemy þe feend, and also þe þretingis of
euerlasting peyne to hem þat ben slayne of þis enmy, I am ful
115 siker þat þere is now many oon þat ȝeelden hem to [þ]is enmy
and is cowardly sleyne, wolde he myȝtily turne aȝeyn wiþ þe
help of God and wiþ þis sheelde tofore hym, and a litel or nouȝt
sette by [þe] cruelte of þe enmye and alle his sotil sleiȝtis, þen
euery suche man in suche case myȝt seie þe wordis of Dinie, þe
120 prophetes, seying: *Arcus fortium superatus est; et infirmi accincti*
sunt robore. Þat is: 'Þe bowe of þe strong (þat is, of þe feend) is
ouercomen; and vnstedfast men (þat is, of her owne power) ben
girde wiþ strengþe', tristing oonly in þe help of God.

Þen, when þe feend seeþ þat he may no þing auayle wiþ his
125 bowe and his arowis aȝeyn a man (þat is, þat he seeþ þat he may

94 þe] *om.* A.   96 (*mar: Remedium contra diabolum*);
his] þese A.   97 first] *om.* A;   v chapitre] *om.* A.
98 þus] þus pe.4. A.   100 þe worlde] *om.* A.   101 ȝee] *om.* A.
104 Poule] þe aplē Poule A;   *ad*] *om.* R;
6.16] 16 A, R;   seying] in his pistle seiynge A.
107 wickid] wickidest A;   enmy] enuy R, ennemy A;   þe(2)(3)] *om.* A.
108 and] *om.* A.   115 þat(1)] *om.* A;   hem] him A;
þis] his A.   116 he] *om.* A.   117 wiþ] of A.
118 þe(1)] *om.* R;   þen] and þenne A.   119 Dinie] Dyne A.
120 prophetes] prophetisse A.
121 of(2)] *om.* A.
                                                                                  125 a] *om.* A.

not bring a man to haue ony liking, or consenting, ne in ful
dede doing none of þese forseide synnis: þat is, pride, glotony,
and leccherie) þen anone he huntiþ in anoþer maner. He
vncoupliþ vpon h[i]m his rennyng houndis, to renne at him
130 wiþ open mouþis; or ellis lett slip his grehoundis to hym, for to
take him.

By þese rennyng houndis þat rennen wiþ open mouþe
mowne wel be vnderstonden chiders, cursers, and sclaundreris.
And þese þe deuel vncoupliþ oft vpon good men þat wolden
135 feyn lyue in pees, to cacche hem in vnpacience, for so he ho/piþ   f. 74ʳ
to sle her soulis, for Crist seiþe by men þat ben pacient, 'in her
pacience þei kepen her soulis'.

And, for to counfort his houndis in þis werke, he blowiþ his
horne wiþ a blast of pride, when he seiþe þus to hem: 'Art not
140 þou of as hyȝe kyn, and as riche, and as good or better þen he in
alle degreis? Suffre hym not. Ȝyue hym a worde for anoþer.
Ouerlede hym, or he wole neuer herafter sett by þee. And if
þou knowe ony þing by him, seye it oute to make hym
ashamed.' And þus he blowiþ to his houndis, to counfort hem
145 in þat cursid werke.

Of þese cursid mouþis þat ben þus open of þe deuelis
houndis spekiþ Dauid, in þe P[sauter]: *Os tuum habundauit
malicia, et cetera.* Þat is: 'Þi mouþe wes ful plenteuous of
malice, and þi tungee [conie⟨c⟩tide] trecheries. Sitting, þou
150 spakist aȝeyns þi broþer, and aȝein þe son of þi moder þou
puttest sclaundre. Þou wendest þat I shal be like to þee, setting
no more þerby þen þou doist; but I shal vndernym þee þerfore'
ful sharply at þe Day of Dome when þou shalt be anectid ful
streitly, 'and I shal sett it aȝeyn þi face' when þou shalt be
155 dampned wiþoute ony mercy.

Lo! in þis maner þe deuel huntiþ wiþ his rennyng houndis to
cacche men in vnpacience. Þe best refute aȝeyns þese rennyng
houndis [is for to fle to erþe, þat is: first for to renne into oure

126-7 liking...doing] likynge consent ne ful dede in A.
128 and] ne A;   þen] *om.* A.
129 (*mar: De canibus diaboli*);   him] hem R.
131 him] in þat manere A.   138 for] *om.* A;
his...werke] in þis werke his houndes A.
139 þus] þis A.   148 Þat is] *om.* A.
149 coniectide] A, coueitid R.   152 but] If A.
153 anectid] areyned A.   156 Lo] *om.* A.
157 (*mar: Remedium contra canes currentes diaboli*).
158-60 is...houndes] *om.* R.

Lord Jesus Crist, þat for þe loue of man took oure erþeli kynde;
160 and biholde hou þese rennynge houndes] were at abay vpon
hym, openly cursing hym, defamyng him, and falsly disclaundring him, and ȝit opened he neuer his mouþe to sey ony
wickid worde aȝeyn. Of þese houndis spekiþ Dauid, in þe
persone of Crist, seying þus: 'Many houndis han gon aboute;
165 þe counsel of wickid han bisegid me.' And of his pacience
spekiþ Ysay þe prophete, seying: 'As a shepe led to þe sleing,
he o/pened neuer his mouþe.' And Seint Petre seiþe þat 'when   f. 74
he wes cursid, he cursid not aȝeyn; and when he suffrid, he
þretid not.'
170 Also, renne into þe erþe in anoþer maner. Byþenke þee þat
[þou] arte comen of erþe, and þat þou art but erþe and wormys
mete, and into erþe þou shalt turne. And wherto þen shuldist
þou be proude, þat arte erþe and eskis, as þe Wise Man seiþe,
to ȝyue ony wickid answere aȝeynwarde? But biþenke [þat] ful
175 yuel þou maist suffre betingis or buffetis for þe loue of þi
Lorde, but if þou may suffre for him a litel breþe of wordis
blowen bi þi chekis.
Also, as I seide, þe deuel huntiþ a man þat is his prey, and
letiþ slip at him his grehoundis þat rennen not wiþ open
180 mouþe, but pursuen ful stilly, and sharply rennen at þe backe,
þat ben bacbiters and priue sowers of discorde. Of þese, þe
deuel haþe many a lees þat rennen fast in þe worlde. For now
vnneþe a man shal fynde two or þre men speke togedir ony
while þat anone þe secound worde or þe þrid shal be of
185 bacbiting of summe of her neiȝboris. Ȝe! and þouȝ þe same
persone in þe mene tyme come bysidis hem, þei shullen salue
hym and make hym as feyre chere as þouȝ þei wolden put h[i]m
in her bosum, and as sone as his backe is turned of hym þei
speken ful shrewidly! Of suche pl[e]yniþ Dauid þe prophete, in
190 þe P[sauter] and seiþe: 'Vpon my backe, as vpon a stiþie, synful
men (þat ben suche bacbiters) forgeden her malicious wille and
drowen alonge her wickidnes þat wes of longe tyme roted in
her hertis.' But þe veniaunce of suche / sueþ sone after, seying   f. 7
þus: 'Þe riȝtwis Lorde shal smyte togedir nollis of suche synful

163 in] þe prophet in A.   165 han] men haþ A.
166 spekiþ] aȝenward spekiþ A.   170 þat] houȝ A.
171 þou] om. R;   þat] om. A.   172 þen] om. A.
174 biþenke] þenke A;   þat] om. R.   175 or] and A;   þe] om. A.
178 (mar: De leporaribus diaboli).
188 her] his A;   187 him] hem R.
188–9 of...speken] speke of him A.   his...turned] he is turned þe bac A.
189 þe prophete] om. A.
                                                                     194 nollis] þe nolles A.

195 men'—þat is, but if þei amenden hem, at þe Day of Dome
dampne togedir boþe body and soule. And herto acordiþ
[Dauid] in anoþer plase, seying: 'Þe priue bacbiter to his
nei3bore, þus I pursued'—þat is, I shal pursue as myn enmy in
þe same day.

200   Þe best refute a3eyn þe rennyng of suche grehoundis is for to
draw to couerte, for when þe prey haþe taken couerte, þe
grehoundis mowne not harme it after. By þis couerte may wel
be vnderstonden charite, for couerte is no more to seie þen
'hilling', for ri3t as in þe þicke wodis or busshis beestis hilen
205 hem fro her enmyes, so vnder þe vertu of charite men mowne
hile hem fro alle her goostly enmyes. And þerfore seiþe Seint
Petre: *Caritas operit, et cetera*, 'Charite hileþ, or kyuereþ'.
Þerfore, and þou se þe deuelis grehoundis renne byhynd þee
(þat is, his bacbiters speke yuel of þee), anone fle to þe couerte
210 of charite. Biþenke [þee] vpon þe bacbiters of Crist: hou þat
summe seyden byhynd hym þat he wes a synner; and summe
þat he wes not on Goddis halfe; and summe seiden þat he
deceyued þe peple; and manye oþer wickid wordis, as þe gospel
rehersiþ in dyuerse placis, and 3it he for3aue to alle his
215 enemyes and preyde for hem to his Fader. So did also Seint
Steuen, þat first wes matrid for Cristis loue. So, if þou be in þe
same caas, renne to þe couert of charite, and alle þe grehoundis
þat þe deuel haþe shullen not hyndre þi soule a dele.
       When þe deuel þen seeþ þat he may not auaile a3eyns þee
220 wiþ his bowe to bring [þee into] / oopen synnys, neiþer wiþ   f. 75ᵛ
[his] rennyng houndis into impacience, ne wiþ his grehoundis
to bring þee oute of charite, þen he settiþ to þi feet wiþ his
pryue nettis, into whiche he driueþ þee wiþ þese flaterers and
glosers. Of þis net may wel be seide þe wordis of Jeremy, in þe
225 Boke of Lamentacions, þere he seiþe þus: *Expandit rethe
pedibus meis*. Þat is: 'He haþe sprad his net to my fete.' And þis

---

196 dampne] dampne hem A;
And...acordiþ] And acordaunt herto seiþ I Dauid A.
197 seying] *om.* A.   198 þus] þis A;   myn] my A.
200 (*mar: Remedium contra leporarios diaboli*).
201 haþe] *om.* A.   204 þe] *om.* A.
207 Petre] (*Followed by* pe.4. þat) A;   *et cetera*] *om.* A.
208 þe] *om.* A.   210 þee] *om.* R;   Crist] oure lord jesu crist A.
215–6 Seint Steuen] Stefne A.   220 þee into] *om.* R;
oopen] (*The first* o *defectively formed; apparently written after the rest of the
word*) R.   221 his] *om.* R, *rubbed* A;   impacience] vnpacience A.
222 (*mar: De retibus diaboli*);   wiþ] *om.* A.   224 of(2)] of his A.

is þe most sotil gyn þat he haþe to deceyue man wiþ, for vnneþe
þer is ony man so holy þat clerly can ascape þis net. Þerfore
God warniþ his derlingis, by Ysay þe prophete, of þis net, and
230 seiþe þus: *Populus meus, qui beatum [te] dicunt, ipsi te decipiunt.*
Þat is: 'My peple, þei þat wiþ flatering wordis seyn þat ȝee ben
blessid, þei deceyue ȝou, for þei ben aboute to bring ȝou into þe
deuelis net of veynglorie.'

Þe best remedie aȝeyn þe net of veynglorie is first to prey
235 God hertily þat þi fote (þat is, þe affeccion of þi soule) be neuer
taken wiþ þis nett of veynglorie, seying þus wiþ Dauid þe
prophete: *Non veniat mihi pes superbie.* Þat is: 'Þe fote of pride
come neuer to me.'

Afterwarde, biholde warly wisele aboute where þe deuel
240 haþe put his nett, and wisely wiþdrawe þi fote þerfro and go
awey by anoþer wey. And sey þen as þe prophete seiþe: *Oleum
autem peccatoris, et cetera.* Þat is: 'Þe oyle of þe synful man (þat
is, þe feyre wordis of þe gloser) shal not make fatt myn heed'—
þat is, delite þe reson of my soule to bring me into veynglorie.
245 For if þou loke wel in þe lawe of God, þou shalt fynde oþer
weies inowe by whiche þou maist scape, if þou wilt:

Loke þe weyes þat Poule spekiþ of, þere he seiþe þus: *Quid
habes quod non accepisti? et cetera.* / [Þat is]: 'What hast þou þat   f. 76
þou hast not taken? And if þen þou hast taken, wherto gloriest
250 þou as þouȝ þou hadist not taken?' Also, he seiþe: *Non enim
sumus sufficientes cogitare aliquid a nobis.* Þat is: 'We ben not
sufficient to þenke ony þing of vs self, as of oure selfe, but oure
sufficience it is of God.' And þerfore Crist seiþe: 'Wiþouten me
ȝe moun not do.' And if þou loke wel alle þese weies, and oþer
255 paþis þat Goddis lawe techiþ, and go not oute on no side, þou
shalt falle neuer in þe deuelis nett. And if þou wilt take wysely
þe menys þat ben seide tofore, þou shalt neuer drede þis cursid
hunter, ne none of his sotil gynnis.

When synful man seeþ þat þe cause of þe comyng of oure
260 Lorde Jesus Crist into þis worlde wes for to delyuer hym oute
of þis cursid hunters honde (þe feend of helle), þen he wexiþ þe

---

228 þer is] is þer A.
229-30 warniþ...þus] bi þe prophet ysaie warneþ his derlyngis of þis nett & seiþ
ysa .3. A.   230 *te*(1)] se R.
234 þe(2)] þis A;   to] for to A;   (*mar: Remedium contra rethe diaboli*).
239 warly wisele] warli A.   240 put] piȝt A.
243 þe(2)] *om.* A;   myn] my A.   248 Þat is] *om.* A.
253 seiþe] seiþ himself A.   256 falle neuer] neuer falle A.
259 (*mar: De muliere chananea*).

more bolde to go oute of his cuntre wiþ þis woman of Chanane,
to aske mercy for his synful soule as she did for hire seke
douȝter. By þis woman of Chanane may be vnderstonden euery
265 synful man repentaunt þat is in wille to leue his synne, and
preyeþ deuoutly to God for mercy, whiche is goostly helþe for
a synful soule. Chanaan is as myche to seye as 'penitens', þat is:
forþinking, or *comutatus*, þat is: 'chaungid', whiche may wel be
vnderstonden by a soule synful repentaunt whiche is chaungid
270 [out of] synful wille [into wille] to lyue vertuously.

But whoso wole able hym to prey to God for his synful soule,
he most go oute wiþ þis woman of Chanane, and folowe Crist,
criyng bisile after hym. In what maner he shulde go oute wes
tolde of God, in figure, to oure fader Abraham (*Gen*[*esis*   f. 76ᵛ
275 12.1]): 'Go oute,' he seide, 'of þi londe, / and of þi kynrede, and
of þe hous of þi fader.' By þese þre goingis oute ben vnderstonden þre maners of synne, in whiche ben conteyned alle
oþer synnis oute of whiche euery man most cast hym to go if he
shulde able hym to aske mercy for his synful soule. Þat ben
280 þese þre whiche Seynt Jon spekiþ of in his pistle: Couetise of
yȝen; couetise of fleishe; and pride of lijf. By '[þi] cuntre', or
'[þin] erþe', is vnderstonden coueityse of erþely goodis. By 'þi
kynrede' is vnderstonden werkis þat ben gendrid of þi fleishe,
as þi kyn ben, þat is: slouþe, glotony, and leccherie. Bi 'þi fadris
285 hous' is vnderstonden: pride, wraþe, and enuy, whiche comen
of þe deuel þat is fader of alle suche þat ben wrappid in þo
synnes, as witnesiþ Crist þere seiþe þus: *Vos ex patre diabolo
estis*. Þat is: 'Ȝe ben of þe fader þe deuel.'

And here may pertinently whoso wole touche of alle þe
290 seuen dedly synnis.

But þouȝ it be so þat a man go oute in þe maner þat is seide,
ȝit neþeles he must open his mouþe and cr`i´e fast after Crist as
þis woman did, þat is: wiþ deuoute preyer and open shrift of
mouþe, seying wiþ þis woman: 'Haue mercy vpon me, Lorde,
295 þe son of Dauid, for my soule is traueilid yuel wiþ a feend.' In

267 a] *om.* A;   Chanaan] for chanaan A;   to] for to A.
269 soule synful] synful soule A.   270 out of] by R;   into wille] *om.* R.
271 to(2)] *om.* A.   274 (*mar: figura*).   275 12] 21 R, A.
278 synnis] maneris of synne A.
280 (*mar: Tria peccata in quibus pendent omnia peccata*).
281 þi] þe R.   282 þin] *om.* R.   283 gendrid] engendrid A.
286 þat(1)] whiche A;   wrappid] wlappid A.
288 Þat is] *om.* A;   þe(2)] ⟨o⟩þe A.
289 may...wole] mai who so wole pertynentli A.   295 wiþ] of A.

þese wordis ben vnderstonden many condicions whiche ben nedful in effectual shrift:

Þe first is þat a man haue sadde bileue, þat is: þat God onely may forȝiue synnis. For 'wiþouten bileue, it is impossible to plese God,' as Seint Poule seiþe, whiche `is´ notid in þis worde 'Lorde', when she seide 'Lorde, haue mercy on me'. For, as clerkis knowen wel, when a worde is seide by þe self, it is taken for þe most famous; and so þis worde 'Lorde', by þe self, bytokeniþ Lorde of alle Lor/dis, þat is: God, to whom oonly longiþ mercy and forȝiuenes of synnes, as þe gospel witnesiþ: *Quis potest dimiterre peccata, nisi solus Deus?* Þat is: 'Who may forȝyue synnis, but oonly God?'

Þe secound is tristi hope of mercy, whiche is notid in þat þat she seiþe 'haue mercy on me'. For, wiþouten tristi hope, sorow of hert, ne shrift of mouþe, ne satisfaccion, auaylen not, for þese þre in a maner had Judas. First sorow of þe hert, as þe gospel seiþe ([*Mt.*27.3]): 'when he saw [þat] Jesus wes dampned, him forþouȝt þat he had done.' And in a maner he made satisfaccion, for he brouȝt hem aȝeyn þe xxx penys þat he toke. And he had shrift of mouþe when he seide: 'I haue synnid.' But him lackid hope of mercy, and þerfore it came to an yuel eend, for he wente and heng himself.

Þe þrid is þat a man haue charite, being sory and preying for oþer mennys synnis as for his owne, whiche is notid in þis worde 'haue mercy on me, for my douȝter is yuel traueilid of a feend'. For in þis preyer she arettid þe sekenes of hir douȝter to be hire owne, and so euery true membre of God knyttid to his breþeren wiþ þe senowis of charite owiþ þus to fele and bere þe sekenes of synne of his broþer in himselfe as his owne, wiþ pite and compassion. And þus did Seint Poule þere he seiþe þus: *Quis infirmatur et ego non infirmor? Quis scandalizatur et ego non vror?* Þat is: 'Who is seke and I am not seke?'—as who seiþe 'none', or 'Who is s`c´laundrid and I am not brent?'—þat is, in my hert, wiþ pite and compassion þat I haue on hym.

300

305

f. 77

310

315

320

325

296 (*mar: De condicionibus confitendi*).   298 (*mar: Prima condicio*); God onely] oneli god A.
299–300 wiþouten...seiþe] wiþ oute bileue as .s. Poule seiþe it is impossible ⟨to⟩ plese god A.   300 is] (*int. red ink*) R.   302 þe] him A.
303 þe(2)] him A.   308 (*mar: ij condicio*).   309 she] hee A.
310 ne(2)] neþer A.   312 Mt.27.3] *om.* A, Mt 28 R;   þat] *om.* R.
314 hem] to hem A.   318 (*mar: iij condicio*).
324 of(1)] or A.   326 *scandalizatur*] scanda A.
328 sc!aundrid] (*mar.* c) R, disclaundrid A.   329 on] of A.

330   Þe iiij condicion is þat a man acuse oonly himself, and not his
nei3bore, as summe men done þat tellen her nei3boris
synnys or shrift, and leuen her owne, 3e! þou3 her nei3/boris   f. 77ᵛ
haue 3ouen hem no lettris of atourne to seie for hem in þat caas!
Þis condicion is noted in þis worde 'my dou3ter', and of þis also
335 spekeþ þe prophete Dauid in þis wise: *Domine, vitam meam
annuncia`ui´ tibi.* 'Lorde,' he seiþe, 'myn owne lijf and none
oþer mannys I haue schewid to þee.'

   Anoþer [condicion] is þat a man in his owne repentaunce
holde euer his owne synne greet; for euery synne is a3eyn
340 summe comaundement of God, and breking of ony comaundement of God is greet and not litel, hauynge rewarde to þe
worþines of þe lordis comaunding, and to þe vnworþines and
[contempte] of þe seruaunt breking. And þerfore seide Dauid:
Iniquitates mee supergresse sunt caput meum, et sicut onus graue
345 *grauate sunt super me, et cetera.* Þat is: 'My wickidnessis ben
gone fer aboue my heed, and as a greuous birþen þei han ben
greued vpon me.' Þis condicion is noted in þat worde *male*—
þat is: 'yuel'.

   Anoþer condicion is þis: þat a man bileue þat euery synne
350 comeþ prinspaly of þe feend, and none of God, as þei þat seyne
in excusacion of hemself: 'it wes my desteny, or þe sterre of my
birþe; it wes shapid to me tofore ony cloþe', turnyng þus þe
feendis temptacion and her owne foly consenting into God.
And þat euery synne deedly prinsepaly comeþ of þe feend
355 preueþ wel þe Wyse Man þat seiþe: *Inuidia diaboli mors*
introiuit in orbem. 'Þorow þe enuy of þe feend, deeþ (þat is,
deedly synne) entred into þe worlde.'

   In þis þat þe woman seide (þat hir dou3ter wes traueiled wiþ
a feend), euery synful man shulde knowe hou þat synne
360 traueileþ mannus soule and puttiþ him oute of pees, and what
harme it doþe to hym, whiche is notid in / þis worde *vexatur*—   f. 78ʳ
þat is: 'trauelid'. Synne traueiliþ mannys soule in whiche `it´
dwelliþ, as fendis done mennys bodies in whiche þei dwellen,
as it preueþ by an ensaumple whiche þat Marke (ix chapitre)
365 rehersiþ in his gospel of a man þat brou3t his childe to þe

330 (*mar:* 4 condicio);   oonly] *om.* A.   334 Þis(1)] þis fourþe A.
336 annunciaui] (*mar.* ui);   *tibi*] tibi et cetera A.
338 (*mar:* v *condicio confitendi*);   condicion] *om.* R;
repentaunce] reputacion A.   342 lordis] lord A.
343 contempte] comp⟨e⟩tent R.   346 gone] ago A.
349 (*mar:* vj *condicio*).   350 seyne] seyne whan þei haue synned A.
355 þat seiþe] þere he ⟨se⟩iþ þus A.   356 Þorow] þat is þo⟨u⟩ A.

disciplis of Crist, whiche had in him a spirit þat made him
doumbe; and whersoeuer he toke him, he þrew hym doune and
made hym froþe at þe mouþe, and gnast wiþ [þe] teeþ, and wex
drie; and oft, as Matheu seiþe, he fel into fire, and oft into
370 water.

By þese condicions whiche [þis] lunatike man hade ben
vnderstonden þe seuen dedly synnis wiþ whiche þe deuel
traueiliþ mannus soule:

By þat þat þe feend þrew hym doun is vnderstonden pride,
375 whiche þrew þe feend doun oute of heuen to helle, and oure
former fader Adam oute of paradise into erþe, and out of erþe
into helle. And þerfore seiþe Crist in þe gospel: *Qui se exaltat
humiliabitur*. Þat is: 'He þat hiȝeþ him by pride, shal be meked
and þrowen doune to helle.'

380 By þat þat he froþid at þe mouþe is vnderstonden glotony.

By gnasting of teeþ, wraþe and enuy ben vnderstonden.

By þat þat he wexe drie is vnderstonden slouþe.

By þat þat he fel into fire is vnderstonden ʿbrennyngʾ
leccherie.

385 By þat þat he fel into water is vnderstonden couetise, whiche
slakiþ neuer mannys þrist.

And þus synne traueiliþ man and it puttiþ him out of pees, as
Ysay seiþe: *Non est pax impiis*. Þat is: 'Þere is no pees to wickid
men.' And Job seiþe: *Quis resistit ei et pacem habuit?* Þat
390 is: 'Who wiþstondiþ God and he had pees?'—as who seiþe
'noon'.

What harme synne doþe to man may be schewid in many
þingis. First, synne makiþ of Goddis Son þe feen/dis childe, as f. 7
Crist witnesiþ himself: *Vos estis de patre diabolo*. Þat is: 'Ȝee
395 ben of þe fader þe deuel.'

Synne also doþe many [mo harmes], whiche þou may se
more pleynourly in þe sermoun of Estre Day.

Firþermore, þe gospel seiþe þat Crist answerid not to þe
woman ony worde. Here þou shalt vnderstonde þat it wes not
400 for no dedignacion þat he had of þis heþen womman, as þe

368 þe(2)] *om*. R.   371 (*mar: De septem peccatis mortalibus*);   þis] *om*. R.
378 by] in A.   380 (*mar*: ij);   at þe] atte A.
381 of] wiþ A;   wraþe] is wraþþe A;   ben] *om*. A.
383 þat(2)] *om*. A.   385 þat(2)] *om*. A.   386 þrist] first A.
388 seiþe] seiþ .57. A.   390 he] *om*. A.
393 makiþ...Son] of goddes sone makeþ A.
394 himself] himself seiynge A.   396 mo harmes] men harme R.
397 pleynourly] playnli A.   399 not] *om*. A.   400 dedignacion] dedeyn A.

eend proueþ wel whil he preysid hir so myche of hir grete
feiþe, but it wes to make hir to contynue in her preier, and to
eche her desire to þe encrece of her merite. And þus here we
may lerne: when we preyen, þou3 oure preyour be not grauntid
405 vs anone, þat we cese not þerfore, but contynu. And if we
contynue in preyer wiþ due circumstaunsis þat longen to
preyoure, it `is´ no doute þat we shul haue þat þat we asken, as
þis woman had, or ellis oþer þing þat is more profitable to vs, as
Poule had when he preyed þries for þe remuyng of þe
410 temptacion of his fleishe and it wes not grauntid hym, but
better þing, þat wes: grace to wiþstonde and so þe victory,
whiche grace is better þen goyng awey of sikenes þat tormentiþ
man. 'For vertu,' he seiþe, 'is mad perfite in sikenes.'

Þen þe disciplis wenten nere to þe Lorde and preyden for þis
415 woman. Here we may lerne þat prelatis and curatis, þat shulden
be Cristis prinspal disciplis, whiche han Cristis shepe to kepe,
when þei seen ony of her peple in disese or tribulacion, bodile
or gostle, shulden go nere to hem (þat is, by vertuous lyuing)
and prey to God hertily for hem, whiche is oon of þe
420 prinsepal þingis þat longiþ to her office.

Here also we mowne lerne þat ri3t as þis womman made no
special preyer [to þe apostles] but oonly to Crist, 3it neþeles
when / þe`i´ sawen hir in disese þei preyden for hir. Ri3t so,   f. 79ʳ
when we maken oure preyouris oonly to God for þing þat is
425 due or able to be preide fore, þou3 we maken no special
preyouris to seintis, 3it neþeles alle þe seintis þat ben in heuen
ben redy to prey for vs to God.

Here also we may lerne þat if a man kepe þe comaundementis of God and lyue vertuously, þen alle preyouris of
430 seintis, boþe of heuen and of erþe, ben ordeynid, and God
acceptiþ hem as meenys to his help, þou3 his preyer be not
dressid immediat to seintis. And for þis seiþe Dauid þus:
Participes ego sum omnium timentium te [*et custodientium man-*
data tua]. Þat is: 'I am partener of alle þat dreden þee and
435 kepen þi comaundementis.'

And in þis place is a foule confusion, if þei loke wel to suche
symonientis þat wolen not prey wiþ her mouþe but if þei haue
Mammon in her honde. But God kepe vs fro suche cursid
preyouris, for it is licly þat her blessingis turnen into cursingis.

407 þat(3)] *om.* A.   408 or ellis] *om.* A;   to] for A.
409 remuying] remouyng A.   411 and so] in A.   413 he] as he A.
416 kepe] kepynge A.   417 þei] *om.* A.   422 to þe apostles] *om.* R.
424 oonly] hertili oneli A.   426 to] to þe A.
433–4 *et...tua*] et c.m.t. A, etc. R.   439 turnen] ben turned A.

440 By þe answere þat Crist seide to his disciplis, þat he wes 'not
sent' (þat is to seie, prinspaly, as þe glose seiþe) 'but to þe shepe
þat perisheden of þe hous of Isr[ae]l', here may men lerne þat it
is more nedful to preche to þe peple þat onys wes conuertid and
made to se God by feiþe, and after fallen to synne, þen to peple
445 þat weren neuer conuerted. And so it is more nedful to preche
to cristen synful men þen to Jewis or heþen men.

Also, we may lerne here to do prinspaly þe dedis of mercy,
gostly or bodily, to oure owne kyn, to oure owne parishenys,
and to oure owne neiȝboris. And þus Crist, when he sent his
450 disciplis to preche, he bade hem þat þei shulden not go into þe
weyes of heþen men, neiþer into þe citeis of Samaritanys,
whiche / weren of mysbileue; but after his resurreccion, he   f. 79
bade hem go forþe ouer al þe worlde. Herto acordiþ Seint
Poule þere he seiþe: *Operemur bonum ad omnes, maxime autem*
455 *ad domesticos fidei.* Þat is: 'Worche we good to alle, but most to
[þe] homely of þe feiþe.'

When þis woman sawe þat she myȝt not spede, neiþer by her
owne pre[y]er ne by þe preyer of þe disciplis, as þe gospel
seiþe, she wente aȝen ȝit, and worshipid him, and preyed hym
460 for to be hir helpe. Riȝt so, þou cristen man þat preyest, when
þou seest þat þi preyer is not anone herde at þi wille, go and
worship þe Lorde wiþ almesdede in his pore membris, and þen
þi preyoure shal be þe raþer herde after þat almesdede. And
þerfore seiþe God in his lawe: 'Þou shalt not apere in my siȝt
465 (þat is, to prey) voyde'—þat is, wiþouten almesdedis.

Þat doing of almesdede is worship to God proueþ þe Wyse
Man, þere he seiþe þus: *Honora Dominum de tua substantia.* Þat
is: 'Worship þou God of þi substaunce of worldly goodis',
doing almesdedes. Þat almesdede shulde go tofore to make þee
470 raþer to be herde, proueþ wel Crisostom in his x⟨v⟩ Omelie,
þere he seiþe þus: 'Whi goþe almes tofore preyer? For almes,'
he seiþe, 'is a marchaunte and araier of lijf tofore þe face of þe
preyoure; þat after a`l´mes, preyer suying fyndiþ tofore God a
place of mercy redy araied.' Þus preyed Centurio, þat wes an

442 here] *om.* A.   443 þe] *om.* A.   444 peple] þe peple A.
445 weren] was A.   446 cristen synful] synful cristen A.
450 to] firste to A.   453 forþe ouer] into A.
456 þe(1)] *om.* R;   þe(2)] *om.* A.   458 ne] neþer A.
459 hym] *om.* A.   466 worship to] worschipynge of A.
468 of(1)] wiþ A.   470 raþer to be] raþeþ A;
xv] (*mar:* crisostomus omelia iij), iij A.
472-3 þe preyoure] preier A;   almes] (*int.* l);   a] *om.* A.

475 heþen man, as þe Dedis of þe Apostlis witnesen (*Act*[*us*]
10.[1–4]), and þerfore þe Scripture seiþe þere þat God sent to
hym his aungel and seide to him: 'Þi preyouris and þin
almesdedis han stied vp into mynde into þe ⟨si3t⟩ of God.'
And þerfore in þis maner he deserued ferþermore ⟨t⟩o ha⟨ue⟩
480 þe visitacion of Petre, and receyued of hym þe wor/shipful   f. 80ʳ
sacrament of baptym to his saluacion.

Þo þe Lorde answerid to þe woman and seide þat it wes not
good to take þe breed of þe children and sende it to houndis,
[and þe womman seide]: '3e, Lorde, for whi? And þe whelpis
485 eten þe crummys þat fallen fro þe boordis of her lordis.' By þis
text a man may lerne þat whoso wole gete grace of God in his
preyouris, him byhoueþ to meke himself, knouleching þat
þorow his owne deseruing, for his houndisshe condicion turnyng so oft a3eyn to þe voment of synne, þat he is not redy, as
490 Goddis children and his true seruauntis, to gete of God suche
grace as þei. But neþeles, he may haue tristi hope þat, if he þus
meke himself and make himself litel in malice, as whelpis,
þorow verrey sorow of herte and knouleching alle Goddis
children and his true seruauntis to be as hy3e aboue him in
495 merite as lordis aboue seruauntis in worship or dignite, þat he
shal gete of God grace, þou3 he be not worþi so myche. For
God seiþe, by his postle Jame, þat he wiþstondiþ to proude
men, and to meke men he 3yueþ grace.

And þus, whoso haþe in his preyoure þis sad feiþe þat is
500 shewid in þis gospel tofore, wiþ tristi hope, and clene charite,
and verrey mekenes, þen God may sey to him þe wordis þat he
seide to þe womman: 'Greet is þi bileue.' For þat bileue is
oonly greet þat bringiþ a man to [þe] blis of heuen; for feendis
and dampned men knowen God and han bileue, but for þei han
505 no charite, her bileue is litel worþe. And to suche men grete in
byleue shal be grauntid al ⟨her⟩ wille, for her wille shal be
confo⟨urmyd holy⟩ / to Goddis wille, and his soule shal be   f. 80ᵛ
helid anone in þat same houre. For þe prophete E3echiel seiþ,

483 þe] *om.* A.   484 and...seide] *om.* R.
485 þe(1)] of þe A.   488 deseruing] deserte A.
489 a3eyn] *om.* A;   redy] worþi A.
490 of God] *om.* A.   491 grace] a grace A.
491–2 þus meke himself] meke þus himselfe A.
492 himself(2)] him A.   496 grace] sum grace A.
497 þat] to þat A.   503 þe] *om.* R.
505 suche men grete] suche grete men A.
507 confourmyd holy] confoormed hoolli A;   to] al to A.

speking wiþ þe mouþe of God: 'In whatsoeuer houre þe synful
510 [man] sorowiþ hertily wiþinne of his synne þat he haþe done,
he shal be saaf.'

In þis woman þat þis gospel makiþ mynde of a man myȝt
shewe, whoso wolde, þe seuen vertuys aȝeyn þe seuen deedly
synnis:

515   First, mekenes aȝeyn pride, in þat she sett so litel by herself
to knowleche hirself of houndis kynde.

Pacience aȝeins wraþþe, 'in' þat þat she wes so oft repreued
and put abacke, and neuer grucchid in worde ne dede.

Charite she had aȝeyn enuy, in þat þat she arett[ide] hir
520 douȝtris sekenes as hir owne in hir asking. Also, [in] þat she
helde þe Jewes, [þat weren Goddis] children, more worþi grace
of God þen she.

Pouerte she had, or litel setting by þe worlde, aȝeyn þe synne
of couetise when, for helþe of hir [douȝter], she wente oute of
525 hir owne cuntre and lefte boþe hous and kyn byhinde, only for
hir douȝtris helþe.

Good mesure she had aȝeyn þe synne of glotony, when she
desirid none oþer deynteis but crummys þat fallen fro þe
boorde to houndis.

530   Good bisines she had aȝeyn þe synne of slouþe, when she
folowid after Crist in traueiling fast wiþ her body, and cesid
neuer wiþ herte and mouþe til she had geten helþe for hir
douȝter.

Chastite she had aȝein leccherie, when she in straunge cuntre
535 drewe hir to þe clene cumpany of Crist and his disciplis, and
laft al þat suspect cumpany by whiche hir name myȝt be
apeyrid.

And þus, in þis place, a man may touche of þese vertuis more
or lasse þat God ȝyue hym grace, and after þat he seeþ þe
540 auditorie is disposid.

509 whatsoeuer] what euere A.   510 man] *om.* R.
512 myȝt] *om.* A.   513 þe(1)] *om.* A;
(*mar: septem virtutes contra septem mortalia peccata*).
515 aȝeyn] aȝen þe synne of A.   519 þat(2)] *om.* A;
arettide] arette R.   520 in(2)] *om.* R.
521 þat weren Goddis] *om.* R;   grace] *om.* A.
524 douȝter] *om.* R.   525 for] (A *breaks off here*).

THIRD SUNDAY
IN LENT

Erat Jesus ei[i]ciens demonium, et illud erat mutum (*Luc.*11.[14]). f. 81ʳ
'Jesus wes þrowing oute a feend, and it wes doumbe', *et cetera*.

The effect of þis gospel stondiþ in þre þingis. First, in a
myracle whiche Crist did in þrowing oute of a feend of a man,
5 whiche made him doumbe, deef, and blynde. The secounde
parte telliþ how perilous it is, after þat a man haþe put oute þe
feend of his soule and left his synne, to turne to his synne
aȝeyne. In þe þrid parte hit telliþ houȝ profitable it is to here
deuoutly þe worde of God, and kepe it, and worche þerafter.
10 As for þe first, ȝee shullen vnderstonde þat God þrew oute þe
feend of heuen, and of þe worlde, and þrew him into helle.

First, he þrew hym oute of heuen for his hiȝe stinking pride,
siþen he þat wes made so feire aboue his felawis helde him `not´
apaied wiþ þat state, but desirid to `stie´ hiȝer and hiȝer and be
15 made like to God hymself, þerfore it wes resonable þat he were
þrowen oute of þat worþi plase and feire felawship. And
þerfore seide God to hym þus in Holy Scripture: *Peccasti, et
ei[i]eci te de monte Dei et perdidi te, O cherub.* Þat is: 'O, þou
feire aungel of þe ordre of cherubym! Þou hast synned and I
20 haue þrowen þee out of þe hil of God' (þat is, heuen), as a
mysproude harlot þat fouliþ al þe felauship.

God also þrew þe feend oute of þe worlde as hym þat had
longe holden a wrongful possession, for þorow his lesing he
deceyuid mankynde of his heritage and helden hym in prison
25 til þe comyng of Crist þat wes riȝtful eyre of Adames in-
nocence. Of þis casting oute spekiþ Crist in þe gospel
(*Jo.*[12.31]), and seiþe þus: *Nunc princeps huius mundi ei[i]cietur
foras.* / Þat is: 'Now þe prince of þis worlde shal be þrowen f. 81ᵛ
oute'—þat is, boþe oute of mennys bodies þat ben traueilid wiþ

---

1 *Erat*] (*Text indented for four lines: rubricated* E *written into the space*).
10 (*mar: Primum principale*).
18 *eiieci*] eiecisti.
27 12] 2.

30 feendis, and oute of mennys soulis þat prinspaly louen þis
worlde, in whom þe deuel regniþ as a prince in his rewme.

And after þis, þe deuel wes þrowen of God into helle. As he
þat takiþ vp wrongfully þe kingis state in his rewme (and þe
kyng lyuing) is worþi to be deed or dampned to perpetual
35 prison, so þe feend wes worþi þe same iugement for þe same
cause. Of þis þrowing oute spekiþ Jeremy þe prophete: *Ei[i]ce*
illos a facie mea, et egrediantur. Quod si dixeri[nt] ad te: Quo
egrediemur? Dices ad eos: Qui ad mortem, [ad mortem]; qui ad
gladium, ad gladium; [et] qui ad famem, [ad famem]; [et] qui ad
40 *captiuitatem, ad captiuitatem.* Þat is: 'Seiþe God, "Cast hem
oute fro my face, and go þei forþe. And if þei seyne to þee:
whider shul we go oute? þou shalt sey to hem: þei þat to deeþ,
[to deeþ]; þei þat to swerde, to swerde; þei þat to hungur, to
hungre; and þei þat to captiuite, [to captiuite]".' In 'deeþ' is
45 vnderstonden departing of lijf (þat is, God); in 'swerde', þe
peyne of helle; in 'hungur', defaute of alle good; in 'captiuite',
euerlasting peyne. For þese fourefolde peyne[s] ben feendis
punysshid.

And riȝt as þat tyme Crist casted oute feendis of mennys
50 bodies and of her soulis boþe, riȝt so ȝit alwei þe worde of God
is so precious þat, if it be truly prechid, it castiþ oute feendis
oute of mennys soulis when it makiþ men to forsake þe seuen
dedly synnys and taken in þe seuen vertuis whiche þat ben her
contraries.

55 Of þis maner of casting oute of feendis spe/kiþ þe gospel of   f. 82
Luke, þere he seiþe þat Crist þrew oute of Madaleyn seuen
feendis—þat is, þe seuen dedly synnis, as diuerse holy doctouris in þis mater acorden. And þus in þis maner is cast oute
of proude men Lucifer, þe deuel; and oute of wraþful men
60 and enuyous þe deuel Belȝebub; and oute of coueitous mennys
hertis Mammona, þe feend; and oute of glotonus soulis þe
deuel Belial; and fro ydel men and lecchouris þe deuel As-
modeus. For comenly ydelnes and leccherie ben two sworne
sustris.

65 And here men may touche largely þe seuen deedly synnis,
and hang al þeron, if þei se it be profitable, or ellis procede in
þis mater as it sueþ after.

And riȝt as þe gospel seiþe þat, when þe feend wes þrowen
oute of þis bodile seke man, he þat wes doumbe tofore spake,

---

37 *dixerint*] dixerim.   46 captiuite] captiuitate.
55 (*Foot of* f.81v. *catchwords:* kiþ þe).
56 (*mar: Nota de eieccione demonum*).

70 riȝt so, when þe feend þat regniþ in a man þorow an heed synne
is þrowen oute of him by þe vertu of þe worde of God, anone
he þat wes tofore goostly doumb byginniþ to speke.

But here myȝt a man seie þat þis is no verrey knouleching
herin, for he spekiþ as myche in whom þe feend is as he in
75 whom þe feend is not, and oft tyme more.

Herto may be answerid þat by þre maner of speche þou maist
know hym oute of whom þe feend is cast fro him in whom þe
feend is abyding: for he spekiþ effectuelly anend himsilf;
and he spe/kiþ truly anentis his broþer; and he spekiþ onestly   f. 82ᵛ
80 anent his God.

First, he spekiþ effectuely for himselfe. Þat is, þo þingis þat
he spekiþ wiþ his mouþe, he doþe þe same in werke. And þus
spake þe apostle to þe Romayns þere he seiþe þus: *Non enim
audeo loqui aliquid eorum que per me non efficit Christus.* Þat is: 'I
85 dar not speke ony þing of þo þingis whiche Crist worchiþ not
by me.' But many men ben like to a cros þat stondiþ in þe
weye, whiche schewiþ to oþer men þe weye and goþe himself
neuer þerinne. So summe men shewen to oþer men þe wey of
penaunce and lyuen hemselfe in glotony; and summe þe weie of
90 mekenes and lyuen hemself in pride; and so forþe of oþer
vertuis, and lyuen hemself in vicis.

Also, he spekiþ truly anentis his breþeren, not deceyuing
hem þorow no sotil wordis, but þat alwey his herte and his
mouþe acorde in oon. And herof spekiþ Zacharie þe prophete,
95 seying: *Loquimini veritatem vnusquisque cum proximo suo.* Þat is:
'Eueryche of ȝow spekiþ þe truþe wiþ ȝoure broþer.' But
summe ben like to þe deuel, of whom Crist seiþe þat he is a lyer
and fader of lesingis, for þei speken in disceite and in lyes to
her breþeren, and oft bringen vp new lesingis contryued of
100 hemself. And alle suche God / shal destrie but if þei amende   f. 83ʳ
hem, for of suche Dauid seiþe: *Perdes omnes qui loquuntur
mendacium.* Þat is: 'Lorde, þou shalt lese alle þat speken
lesyng.'

Also, suche a man of whom þe feend is cast oute spekiþ
105 honestly anentis God and þe worship of God. And of suche
spekiþ Peter in his canoun, seying þus: *Si quis loquitur, quasi
sermones Dei.* Þat is: 'He þat spekiþ, speke he as þe wordis of
God.' But summe men ben like to hoggis, þat raþer rennen to

---

71 anone] þat anone.   73 (*mar: questio*).   76 (*mar: Responsio*).
77 (*mar: Per 3 loquelam cognoscitur de quo eicitur demones*).
81 (*mar: I*).   86 (*mar: Exemplum*).
92 (*mar: ij*).   104 (*mar: iiij*).

toordis þen to flouris. So summe han more liking to speke
110 harlotrie and vnhoneste þen þe wordis of God or wordis þat
sounen to vertuis, wherfore of suche spekiþ þe Psalme maker in
þis wyse: *Sepulcrum patens est guttur eorum.* Þat is: 'An open
graue is her þrote.' For riȝt as oute of a graue þat is opened
goþe oute foule stynke, so oute of þe mouþe of many men goþe
115 no þing oute but stynke of foule and velayns wordis.

And þus, as I haue shewid, whoso spekiþ in þese þre maners
haþe token þat he is vertuously helid of his goostly doumbnes.
And not oonly þerof, but also of his deefnes and blyndnes. For
whoso wole gladly speke þe wordis of God and vertuys and
120 truþe, he wole also gladly here þe same. And whosoeuer leueþ
boþe to here and to speke wickid þingis, and chesiþ to here and
to speke good þingis, þe iȝen of his discrecion ben opened and
so he seþe þe weye to heuen.

Riȝt as þis seke man þat þe gospel spekiþ of, whiche wes
125 helid of Crist, had þre grete bodile myscheuys, þat is: blyndnes, as Matheu seiþe, and doumbnes, / as Luke seiþe here, and   f. 83ᵛ
by kynde, as philosofres seyen, he þat is doumbe is deef also;
riȝt so, euery man þat haþe in hym ony of þese feendis þat ben
rehersid tofore þorow ony deedly synne haþe þese same goostly
130 myscheuys in his soule, þat is: blyndnes, doumbnes, and
deefnes.

First, he þat is in deedly synne is blynde, for he seþe not hou
he is oute of þe weye of heuen and is in þe weye to helle. He
seþe not what grace he haþe lost, and what peyne he haþe
135 purchasid. He seeþ not how he haþe forsaken his Fader, God,
and bytaken him to þe feend. Who is more blynde þen suche
on? as God seiþe by þe prophete Ysay (42.[19]): *Qui cecus sicut
seruus meus?* Þat is: 'Who is so blynde as my seruaunt is?'—þat
þorow his baptem made comenaunt wiþ me, in whom is al
140 goodnes and wolde haue brouȝt him to þe blisse of heuen for
his seruise, and is gone awey fro me wiþouten cause to myn
enmy, in whom is alle shrewidnes and wole bring him for his
seruice to þe peyne of helle.

Euery suche man is doumbe. But here men mosten vnder-
145 stond þat þere is doumbnes boþe vertuous and vicious. Vertuous, as summe men ben doumbe þorow þe vertu of pacience,
as þei þat wolen not answere to wickid wordis and repreuable
þat ben seide to h[e]m. Wherfore in þe persone of suche is seide
in þe Psalme: *Ego autem tamquam surdus non audiebam, et sicut*

---

132 (*mar: spiritualiter cecus*).   144 (*mar: spiritualiter mutus*).
148 hem] hym.

150 *mutus non aperiens os suum.* Þat is: 'I, as deef man, herde not
repreues seide to me, and I, as doumbe man, not openyng my
mouþe to answere ony yuel worde aȝeyn.' Þer/fore suche ben f. 84ʳ
like to Goddis son, of whom it is seyde in Ysaie: *Sicut ouis ad*
occisionem ductus, et quasi agnus coram tondente se obmutescit, et
155 *non aperiet os suum* (*Ys.*53.[7]). Þat is: 'As a shepe lad to sleing,
and as a lombe tofore þe clipper, so he openiþ not his mouþe.'
Also, summe men ben doumbe þorow þe vertu of pr`u´dens, as
holy men þat kepen silence þat þei offende not in her tunge, for
it is impossible a man to speke many wordis wiþoute summe
160 offense. Þerfore seiþe þe Wyse Man (*Prouer.*10.[19]): *In multi-*
loquio non deerit peccatum. Þat is: 'In myche `speche´ wantiþ not
synne.' Þerfore þei ben called `wise´ men in Holy Writt, seying
þus: *Homo sapiens tacebit vsque ad tempus* (*Ecci.*20.[7]). Þat is:
'A wyse man shal be stille til he se tyme'—þat is, for to speke.
165 And Seint Jame seiþe (*Ja.*1.[19]): *Sit autem omnis homo velox*
ad audiend[*um*]*, tardus autem ad loquendum.* Þat is: 'Be euery
man swift to here and slow to speke.'

Þere is also, as I seide, doumbenes þat is vicious, whiche is
vnderstonden by þis man here whiche, as þis gospel makiþ
170 mencion here, þat þe feend made doumbe. And þis doumbnes
comounly is in þre maners, as summe men ben doumbe fro
true confession to God and man of her synnis. And suche,
when þei comen in Lenton to þe prest to confession, þei knelen
stille tofore þe prest and wolen seie no worde, as a doumbe man
175 þat myȝt not speke. And suche ben like to a bytore þat, when
he sittiþ on þe dr`i´e londe, he holdiþ vp his heed and makiþ no
noyce, but when he sittiþ by þe watris syde and puttiþ his bil in
a rede, he makiþ an hoge noyce. So suche, / when þei sitten at f. 84ᵛ
s[h]rift, where is no moysture of wyne ne ale, þen wolen þei
180 speke no worde to knouleche her synnis, but when þei sitten at
tauernis by þe barellis syde and putten her bil in þe bolle ful of
ale or wyne, þen kunne þei make grete boost and noyse of her
shrewid dedis þat þei diden twenti ȝere tofore.

And þe cause of þis doumbnes is for þe deuel þat is wiþinne
185 hem haþe stopped her mouþis wiþ shame, and þen þe deuel
whitiþ hem þat he borowid bifore. For tofore þat a man synniþ,
he haþe shame to synne. And þe deuel seeþ þat, and borowiþ of
him þat shame and so, when shame is gone, þen falliþ he into
synne. And al þe while þat he lyueþ in synne, þe deuel kepiþ
190 þat shame fro hym. But at Lenton, when þe deuel seþe þat he

166 audiendum] (*caret mark indicating omission of* um).
168 (*mar*: ij).

shulde shryue hym of his synne, þen bringiþ he home shame
aȝeyn, and stoppiþ his mouþe þerwiþ and so, at þat tyme,
makiþ him doumb.

195 Aȝens þis shame and þis doumbnes counseliþ þe Wyse Man,
seying þus: *In tempore infirmitatis ostende conuersacionem tuam,
et (sequitur parum post) non verearis vsque ad mortem iustificari.*
Þat is: 'In tyme of sekenes (þat is, goostly þorow synne) shew þi
conuersacion þorow true shrift of þi mouþe, and be þou not
ashamed til to þe deeþ for to be iustefied, whiche is done by
200 true confession.'

Also, þei ben viciously doumbe þat, for þe greet synnis þat
þei / ben in, lusten not to open her mouþis to deuout preyouris f. 85ʳ
and honest spekyng, for þe deuel þat is wiþin hem stoppiþ her
mouþis and makiþ hem doumb fro þese two. But to speke
205 ribaudrie and bacbite, þe deuel is redy inow to open her
mouþis; and þe cause is for þer may no þing come oute at þe
broching of a vessel but suche as is wiþinne. And þerfore Crist
seiþe in þe gospel: *Ex habundancia cordis os loquitur.* Þat is: 'Of
þe plente of þe hert þe mouþe spekiþ.' And so, þorow a mannys
210 speking may men conceyue whether þat God be wiþin him by
grace or þe deuel þorow synne. For of suche moun be seide þe
wordis þat weren seide to Petre: *Loquela tua manifestum te facit.*
Þat is: 'Þi speche makiþ þee open.' And of doumbnes fro good
speche may be seide þe wordis of Dauid in þe Ps[auter], seying
215 þus: *Obmutui et silui a bonis.* Þat is: 'I haue ben doumbe and
ben stille fro good þingis.'

Ȝit þer is þe þrid maner of doumbnes, into whiche many
prestis fallen oft tyme—þat is: doumbnes of preching of þe
worde of God and of charitable vndernymmynge of her
220 breþeris synnis. For þere as God haþe ȝouen hem mouþis, [he]
haþe boden ʻhemʼ first in þe Olde Lawe to open hem to þis
werke, seying by þe prophete Ysay: *Exalta in fortitudine vocem
tuam, qui euangelizas Jerusalem.* Þat is: 'Enhaunce in strengþe
þi voyce, þou þat prechist to Jerusalem.' And in anoþer place
225 he seiþe, by þe same prophete: *Clama, ne cesses, quasi / tuba* f. 85
exalta vocem tuam. Þat is: 'Crie and cese þou not, as a trumpe
enhaunce þi voyce.' And Crist biddiþ hem also in þe New
Lawe: *Ite, predicate euangelium omni creature.* Þat is: 'Goþe,
and prechiþ þe euangelie to euery creature.'

230 Aȝeins þis, þe deuel haþe stoppid her mouþis þorow dyuerse
synnis into whiche he haþe led hem. Summe ben vnkunnynge
þerto, and þo ben lettid wiþ þe deuel of pride for to lerne. And

---

221 open] hopen.

summe han kunnyng to preche, and þ[o] ben lettid wiþ þe
feend of slouþe and negligence. And summe þe feend of
235 couetise implieþ so wiþ seculer nedis and worldly occupacions
þat to preche haue þei no wille, and so ben doumbe þerfro.

And alle suche he blamiþ, and clepiþ hem 'doumbe houndis
þat moun not berke', *Canes muti non valentes latrare.* Also, her
owne synnis letten hem to vndernym her breþeren of her
240 synnis, lest þei wolden sey aʒeyn to hem: *Medice, cura teipsum,*
'Leche, heel þiself', and also (*Mt.*7.[5]): *Ypocrita, primo ei[i]ce*
trabem de oculo tuo. Þat is: 'Ypocrite, first drawe oute þe beem
of þin owne yʒe.' But, allas! alle suche prestis shullen se þe
tyme þat when þei shullen seye wiþ greet sorow: *Ve mihi quia*
245 *tacui.* Þat is: 'Allas, or wo, to me! for I haue ben stille.'

Þe þrid myscheue þat men ben brouʒt to, in whom þe deuel
is þorow synne, is deefnes. And þat is in þre maners: oon is for
to here þe worde of God; anoþer for to here pleyntis of
myscheuys of hem þat ben oppressid and wrongfully disesid
250 for socoure / and mayntenaunce; and þe iij is for to here þe crie   f. 86ʳ
of pore nedy men after her bodile sustenaunce.

In þe first maner, men ben deef for to here þe worde of God.
For þe deuel þorow synne haþe so st[o]ppid her goostly eeris
þat ʻþeiʼ han leuer here romaunsis, gestis, or ydel talis, and
255 lengur þei wole susteyne wiþoute mete or drinke to here suche
vaniteis þen for to here þe blessid worde of God. And alle
suche deef men stonden in a perilous caas, for of euery suche
man his preyour is cursid, and þerfore seiþe þe Wyse Man
(*Prouer.*[28.9]): *Qui declinat aurem suam ne audiat legem Dei,*
260 *oratio eius execrabilis erit.* Þat is: 'He þat turniþ awey his eere
þat he here not þe lawe of God, his preyoure is cursid.'

Þe secound deefnes is of men þat ben greet men in lordship,
or men of lawe, to whos state it longiþ to here benig[n]ly þe
pleyntis of hem þat ben wrongfully disesid or oppressid by
265 false tyrauntrie and wolen not here hem, but turne þe deef eere,
but if þei bring hem presauntis, or ʒyue hem grete ʒiftis, or at
þe leest wey to behete hem at a certeyn day. And oft, ʒit þouʒ
þei so do, and þe strenger party wole ʒyue hem more, þei wolen
raþer here hem and deme for her partie, and so oft peruerte
270 riʒtwis dome. For þe Wyse Man seiþe: *Exenia et dona excecant*
oculos iudicium. Þat is: 'Presauntis and ʒiftis blenden þe yʒen of
iugis.' And suche ben cursid of God in his lawe, þere he seiþe

233 þo] þi.   235 seculer nedis] nedis seculer (*m. for r.*).
246 (*mar: spiritualiter surdus*).
253 stoppid] steppid.   259 28] 18.

þus (*Deut.*27.[25]): *Maledictus qui accipit | munera vt percu`ti´at*   f. 86ᵛ
animam sanguinis innocentis. Þat is: 'Cursid be he þat takiþ
275 ȝi[f]tis þat he smyte þe soule of innocent blood.' And also, alle
suche moune be sore afeerd of þe sentense of God þat he seiþe
by þe prophete in þis wyse: *Ignis deuorabit tabernacula eorum*
qui libenter accipiunt munera. Þat is: 'Fire shal brenne þe
tabernaclis of hem þat gladly taken ȝiftis'—þat is, for to
280 peruerte þe riȝtwis dome of God.

Þe iij deefnes is of riche men þat han greet superfluite of þese
worldly goodis and wolen not here þe crie of pore, nedy men
þat han greet defaute of mete, and drinke, and cloþe, to releue
hem of her myscheef wiþ suche as God haþe sent hem; but
285 gladly wolen here þe melodie of mynstrellis, þe flatering
heroudis þat blowen her name aboute, and so suche þei wolen
ȝyue of her golde wiþ a glad chere, and vnneþe a peny to þe
pore in a greet parte of a ȝere. And alle suche deef men stonden
in a perilous caas, for þe Wyse Man seiþe by suche a dredful
290 worde (*Prouer.*21.[13]): *Qui obturat aurem suam ad clamorem*
pauperis, et ipse clamabit et non exaudietur. Þat is: 'He þat
stoppiþ his eere fro þe crie of a pore man, he shal crie to God
and he shal not be herde.'

And þus, in þis maner as it it sumwhat shewid here tofore, þe
295 deuel, when he regnyþ in a man þorow synne, makiþ him boþe
blynde, doumbe, and deef.

I seide at þe biginnyng þat þe secound parte of þis gospel
makiþ mencion how perilous it is, aftur þat a man haþe put
oute þe feend of his soule þorow leuing of his synne, / to turne   f. 87ʳ
300 aȝeyn after to his synne, as proueþ pleynly þe wordis of þe text,
whiche seien þat after þat a man haþe so done þe last þingis of
suche a man ben made worse þen þe first. Suche a man, falling
aȝeyn to his synne, is a watrie place to þe feend, in whiche he
delitiþ for to dwelle, for as water flowiþ in his lustis and is
305 made vnstable by synne. Of suche seiþe þe prophete Jeremy
(*Tr.*1.[8]): *Peccatum peccauit Ierusalem, propterea instabilis*
facta est. Þat is: 'Jerusalem haþe synned, þerfore it is made
vnstable.' But a stable man and a stedfast whiche, after þat he
haþe forsaken his synne turneþ not to his synne aȝeyn, is a drie
310 plase by whiche þe deuel wandriþ seching rest and fyndiþ not.
And in suche on, for his stablenes, he fyndiþ no plase to abide
in.

---

275 ȝiftis] ȝiȝtis;   smyte] (s *added in word-space following* he).
297 (*mar: 2 principale*).   304–5 for...synne] (*n.*).

Many resonable bodily ensaumplis a man my3t shewe, if he
had tyme, to meue a man to hate þis synne of falling a3eyn, and
315 for to shew by reson hou perilous it is. But summe of hem a
man may touche.

If it were so þat a childe trespasid to his fader, and after his
fader for3aue him vpon a condicion þat `he´ trespasid so no
more, if after þe childe toke none hede þerfore, but falle into þe
320 same trespas, þen þis secound trespas were more greuous to þe
fader and myche more worþi to be punisshed þen þe first. Ri3t
so it is of oure gostly fader God, and of his goostly children.

Also, if a man be onys woundid and helid, and afterward in
þe same place be woundid, þen þe secound wounding is worse
325 þen þe first and more hard to be helid, for þe olde feblenes and
þe new hirting ben more greuous þen þe olde by þe selfe.

Also, a man / þat is onys poysound and by medicynis castiþ it   f. 87ᵛ
oute and is delyuerid þerof, if he d`r´onke after þe same
venoum þat he caste oute, he is wors poysond þen he wes first.
330 For after þe first casting oute, þe venoum is more fouler and
violent for to sle þen it wes tofore.

Also, suche turnyng a3eyn to synne doþe many harmys to
man. First, it makiþ him foule in þe si3t of God, for when he
doþe so he haþe boþe his olde synne and new and, wiþ þat,
335 rotiþ and stinkiþ in synne. And þat seiþe God openly by þe
prophete Jeremy (2 chapitre [36]), seying þus: *Quam vilis facta
es nimis, iterans vias tuas.* Þat is: 'Hou greetly foule arte þou
made, goyng a3eyn þi weies', by putting synne to synne. And of
her gostly roting spekiþ Dauid in þis wyse: *Putruerunt et
340 corrupte sunt cicatrices mee.* Þat is: 'Myn olde borsten oute
woundis han rotid and ben corrupt from þe face of my folie.'

Also, þis s[yn]ne causeþ a hardines and a maner of impossi-
bilite to rise a3eyn to grace, for þe postle seiþe (*Heb*.6.[4–6]):
Impossibile est eos qui semel sunt illuminati, et cetera. Þat is: 'It is
345 impossible hem þat ben onys li3tned and han tastid heuenly
3iftis by sorow and penaunce doing, and after fallen a3eyn to þe
same synne, eft to be renued to penaunce,' for no doute it is ful
harde and impossible to þe comyn cours of man, but not to
God, for to him alle þingis ben possible.

350 Anoþer myscheue also in þis synne is for þis synne, by
custom and malice, hardiþ a mannys hert, as it did King
Pharao, þat forþou3t hym for a tyme and after fel a3eyn to /
synne til his hert wes hardid, whiche after brou3t him to his   f. 88ʳ

317 (*mar: Exemplum*).
344 *Impossibile*] Inpossibile.
342 synne] signe.

deeþ, boþe bodile and gostle. So it fariþ by suche men þat
355 fallen alwey aȝein fro synne to synne, til þei falle so depe þat
þe`i´ kunnen no more arise, and þen dispisen Goddis mercy. Of
þis spekiþ þe Wise Man, þere he seiþe þus: *Homo, cum in
profundum peccatorum venerit, contempnit.* Þat is: 'A man, when
he comiþ into depnes of synne, he despisiþ.' And, in figure of
360 þis synne, þe wijf of Loth, [who] turned `and loked´ aȝeyn
aȝeins þe bidding of God, wes turned into an ymage of salt.
Also, þis synne vnabliþ a man to þe kingdom of heuen,
wherfore it is seide of Crist in þe gospel: *Nemo autem mittens
manum suam ad aratrum et respiciens retro aptus est regno Dei.*
365 Þat is: 'No man putting his honde to þe plowe and loking
bacward is able to þe kingdom of God', whiche is þus myche to
meen: no man conuerted fro synne whiche after puttiþ his
werkis to þe lawe of God and after fallen aȝeyn to olde synne, is
able to þe kingdom of God.

370   And þus, by many resons it is proued hou perilous it is after
synne is forsaken to turne aȝeyn þerto, whiche is þe mater of þe
secound parte of þis gospel, as I seide at þe bygynning. Also I
seide at þe bigynning þat þe þrid parte of þis gospel makiþ
mynde hou profitable it is to here þe worde of God, and kepe it,
375 and worche þer after. For he þat so doþe is blessid of God,
whos blessing is more worþe and bringiþ more pardoun, þat is:
more forȝyuenes of synnis, to synful soulis, and more profitiþ
þen alle þe bullis of alle synful prelatis here / in erþe, fro þe   f. 88ᵛ
hiest to þe lowest, for he is verrey pastoure and bisshop of alle
380 oure soulis, þat ȝaue frely his hert blode for sauacion of his
shepe. More pardoun it bringiþ in, for he þat is blessid of God
for þis cause haþe, as Crist seiþe in Jonys gospel, 'þe lijf þat
euer shal laste', and shal not come into þe dome, but shal passe
fro deeþ to lijf. And þis may no prelate graunte of his owne
385 autorite, be he neuer so greet, but oonly God himself þat seide
þese same wordis.

     Þis blessing bringiþ in more profite, for `by´ it `swich´ a man
is blessid in his worldly goodis, and in vertuis of his soule, and
euerlasting joyis of heuen.

390   First, in his temporal goodis, as God rehersiþ to his prophete
Moyses, in þe 28 chapitre of Deuter[onomie.5]. Herto acordiþ
also þe first book of Scripture seying þus: *Benedixit Dominus
Ysaac* and *locupletatus est.* Þat is: 'God blessid to Ysaac' and
'he wes made riche.'

---

372 (*mar: 3 principale*).

395   Also, he is blessid in soule in encresing of vertuis, for Dauid
seiþe: *Beatus homo quem tu erudieris, Domine, et de lege tua*
docueris eum. Þat is: 'Blessid is þat man whom þou enformest,
Lorde, and of þi lawe techist him.' For of alle suche also seiþe
þe same prophete: *Ibunt de virtute in virtutem, donec videbitur*
400   *Deus deorum in Syon.* Þat is: 'Þei shullen go fro vertu to vertu,
til þei se God of goddis in Syon'—þat is, in þe blisse of heuen,
into whiche blis alle suche shullen be clepid at þe Day of Dome
'þe blessid children of þe Fader', and þere þei shullen welde for
euer þe blessing of her Fader in ioyes wiþouten noumbre in þat
405   blessid place. Of whiche blessing spekiþ Crist in þe gospel
(*Luc.*14.[15]) / þere he seiþe þus: *Beatus qui manducabit panem*   f. 89ʳ
in regno Dei. Þat is: 'Blessid is he þat so haþe herde and kept þe
worde of God here in erþe, whiche is goostly etyng þerof,
þorow þe whiche he shal ete afterward breed in þe kyngdom of
410   God'—þat is, be fully fed wiþ þe glorious siȝt of þe Trinite in
þe blis of heuen.

Now God, for his eendles mercy, ȝyue vs grace so clenly to
put oute þe feend of oure soulis þat we moun after vertuously
boþe se and here and speke suche þing and none oþer þing but
415   as we may plese God wiþ, and neuer after turne aȝeyn to oure
synne, but here and kepe so þe worde of God, boþe in herte
and in dede, þat we moun euer haue his blessing, boþe here and
in heuen. Amen.

14
FOURTH SUNDAY
IN LENT

Abijt Jesus trans mare Galilee (*Jo.*6.[1]). The gospel of þis day
telliþ of a bodile myracle þat Crist did in deserte, feding a greet
noumbre of peple wiþ litel substaunce of mete, and it multiplied so in his hondis þat alle weren þerof fulfillid, and ȝit þere
5 laft ouer more quantite of releef þen wes þe first substaunce or
it were departid.

In þis dede, we ben tauȝt to `ȝyue´ large to nedy men after þe
quantite of goodis þat God haþe sent vs, setting a ful trist in
God þat, if we ȝyue it wilfully and prinsepaly for his loue, he
10 wole multiplie it in oure hondis so þat we shullen haue
sufficiently of lijflode and not feile to oure lyues eend. And for
to strengthe wiþ þis hope may also be brouȝt to þe story, in þe
þrid Boke of Kyngis, of þe wydue `of´ Sarapte: houȝ she fed
Helie in a dere / ȝere, and hir mete feilid neuer til plente came   f. 89
15 aȝeyn. And also, in þe þe fourþe Boke of Helie þe prophete:
hou he fed an hundrid hungri men wiþ þritti louis, and alle
haden inow, and greet releef was left.

Þis bodilie feest þat God made is figure of goostly feest þat
alle prelatis and prestis, whiche ben goostly leders of Cristis
20 peple, shulden make to hem wiþ goostly mete of þe worde of
God here in desert of þis worlde and, haue þei more, haue þei
lasse, wilfully to departe þerof, tristening holly in þe multiplying of God.

But þis gospel seiþe in þe byginnyng þat tofore `þat´ Crist
25 made þis feest he wente ouer þe see of Galile, þat wes clepid
Tyberiadis. Þis, me þinkiþ, may bitoken þat þo þat shulden be
feders of Cristis peple goostly shulden ouerpas þe see of þis
worlde, þat is: fully forsaken, as vnleful, desire of hauing of
temperal goodis of þis worlde. And for þis cause, Crist clepid
30 alle his disciplis fro þis worlde tofore he assigned hem to þis

---

1 *Abijt*] (*text indented for four lines; rubricated A written into the space*).
25 (*mar: mare*).

office. And þerfore he seide `to´ hem: *Nisi quis renunciauerit omnibus que possidet, non potest meus esse discipulus.* Þat is: 'But if a man renounce alle þo þingis þat he weldiþ, he may not be my disciple.'

35　Þis wrecchid worlde and his goodis may wel be likened to þe see, for þe vnstablenes of ebbing and flowing of hem, as þe see doþe. And Galile, also, for Galile is as myche to sey as 'a / whele'. So, in þis worlde, þe whele of Fortune settiþ men now　f. 90ʳ in hyȝe`r´ state `and´ nowe in lower, as it turniþ aboute. And

40　Tyberiadis also it may be clepid. Tyberiadis is to seie *visio*, þat is: 'siȝt', in whiche is siȝt of myche vanite to drawe mannys hert to vnleful lustis, whiche euery true preest shulde ouerpas, wiþdrawing his herte fro hem, and fully sett his goostly siȝt on Goddis goodis þat may not feile.

45　And so, suche a prelate or a curate in cuntre, forsaking þis wrecchid worlde for Goddis sake, lyuing a pore lijf after his Mayster, Crist, and fully ȝyuing to spiritual occupacion in preying, and studying, and preching Goddis lawe, is able to heel many men of her goostly sekenes of synnis þorow þe good

50　ensaumple of his vertuous lijf. And so, greet multitude of prestis dwelling fer aboute, in whos soule is left ony sparcle of grace, seing þe good and profite þat suche a man doþe, shulde be meued to sue in þe same trace.

But ȝit, as þe gospel seiþe, after þat Crist had passid þe see,
55　tofore þat he fed þe peple, he went into an hil. Þis may bitoken þat þouȝ a prelate or a prest forsakiþ þese wordly goodis, and lyueþ a pore lijf, and þenkiþ to fede goostly Goddis peple wiþ þe worde of God, ȝit he most fully purpos him to make ensaumple of his preching of Crist and his apostlis, whiche ben

60　clepid 'hillis' in many placis of Scripture. And þerfore seide God to Moyses, his prophete: *Fac secundum exemplar quod tibi in monte monstratum est*, 'Do after þe ensaumple þat is shewid to þe in þe hil.' Or ellis þus shulde euery prechoure first styȝe into þe hil in þis maner: loking prinspaly after no rewarde for

65　his preching here in erþe, but in þe hil of / God, þat is: þe hiȝe　f. 90ᵛ blis of heuen.

Þe sitting of Jesus in þe hil may betoken þe stable wille of alle prechouris in þis purpos, or ellis rest of contemplacion, whiche þat þei shulden haue among in Hooly Scripture and

---

31 to] (*int.*).
(*Foot of* f.89v. *catchword*: whele).
55 (*mar: mons*).

37 (*mar: galilea*);
40 (*mar: tyberiadis*).
67 (*mar: sessio christi*).

70 Cristis lijf and in þe siȝt of þe ioyes of heuen, þorow whiche þei
shulden drawe wit as Jon did oute of Cristis brest.

Þat it wes nyȝe Pasche Day, þe feest of þe Jewis, `it´ may
bitoken feiþ þat is nyȝ þe Day of Dome, in whiche day alle
feiþful knowlechers of Crist wiþ hert and mouþe shulde come
75 to þis feest. Prestis shulden þe raþer forsake þis worlde and sue
Crist in his lyuing, and knowleche to þe peple boþe him and his
lawe, and so bring himself and þe peple to þe feest.

Þat Crist lifted vp his yȝen and sawe þat greet multitude
came to hym may bytoken þe diligent yȝen of rewarde þat
80 euery prelate and curat shulde haue on his peple, seying hou
greet multitude peple is bitaken to hym of God into goostly
cure, to answere for hem alle at þe greet acount, and þat þei
may not be susteynid goostly in þe desert of þis worlde
wiþouten food of Goddis worde, cast vpon hem þen pitous yȝe
85 of mercy, wilnyng to fulfille it in dede wiþ suche as God haþe
sent hym.

But allas! men may seye, by many of hem, þe wordis þat ben
seide in þe gospel of Cristis apostlis þat slepten in þe tyme þat
Crist made his preyouris: *Oculi eorum erant grauati.* Þat is: 'Þe
90 yȝen liddis' of many prelatis and curatis now adayes 'ben
greued' and hol[den] / doun þorow her foule muck and worldly   f. 91ʳ
occupacion, so þat. for foule slumbur and slepe and lustis, þei
listen not onys to lift vp her goostly yȝen to þis werke. Þerfore,
me þinkiþ, Crist may wel seye to hem þe wordis þat he seide to
95 Petre: *Symon, dormis? Non potuisti vna hora vigilare mecum?*
Symon is as myche for to sey as 'obedience': in þe taking of þyn
ordre to wake vp my folke and ȝyue hem mete in tyme, 'myȝtist
þou not oon houre wake wiþ me?'—þat is, þe litel tyme of þi
lijf, whiche is lasse in comparison to euerlasting lijf þen is an
100 houre to al þe hool day, and for þe traueile of þat litel tyme þou
shuldest haue ben rewardid wiþ euerlasting blisse.

Ferþermore, in þe gospel, þere as Crist askid of Philip
wherwiþ þei shulden bye breed to fede wiþ al þat peple, here
may men lerne in what state euer þei be, be þei neuer so witty
105 or kunnynge of science, to aske oþerwhile counsel of oþer þat
ben in lower degre and of lasse wit and of symple letture, for
perauenture it may be so þat þei ben of hyȝer charite. And
charite, as Poule seiþe, 'bildiþ in grace þere often tyme
kunnyng blowiþ into pride'—*Scientia inflat, caritas edificat.*

---

72 (*mar: pascha*).   78 (*mar: oculi*).
91 holden] den *om.* (*n.*).

110   Also Seint Poule seiþe in anoþer plase þat oþerwhile vnderstonding of Scripture is ȝouen to oon of þe sitters in þe
auditorie þat is not alwey openid to him þat is prechoure. For
oft þo þat ben in hyȝe statis and in greet degre of scolis ben oft
ful presumptuous and proude of her kunnyng, þerfore God
115   wiþdrawiþ fro hem gostli vnderstonding and ȝyueþ it to meke
men þat ben of litel letture, seying Seint Jame of suche in þis
wise: *Superbis resistit; humilibus | dat gratiam.* Þat is: 'To f. 91ᵛ
proude he wiþstondeþ; to meke he ȝyueþ grace.' But ȝee
shullen vnderstonde þat not for þis cause Crist askid counsel of
120 Phelip, for as þe gospel seiþe afterward, he wist wel himself
afterwarde what he wolde do; but þis he seide for to tempt him
or asaye him of his sad byleue. Riȝt so, þouȝ men wisten in
many a case what were for to do, ȝit it were good for to comoun
þerof lowly wiþ her breþeren, to asay wheþer þei hadden verrey
125 knowleching of þe truþe and, if þei hadden not, þen do as Crist
did here: teche hem þe truþe, boþe in worde and in dede.

    Þe answere of Philip þat he ȝaue in þis mater, seying in þis
maner, as þe gospel telliþ after, þat þe louys of two hundrid
penis wolden not suffice to hem þat euery man myȝt take a litel
130 to susteyne wiþ her kynde, may wel betoken dredful and
vnfeiþful mennys counsel when men asken hem counsel to
preche to Goddis peple. Suche seyne þat who shulde be a
prechoure of þe peple, he must haue perfite kunnynge of
gramer and of logik, of philosofie and dyuinite to know wiþ þe
135 Scripture, and also he must haue perfite kunnyng of canoun
and of decreis. And of þe perfeccion of þese two lawis may be
vnderstonden by two hundrid peneworþe of breed, for an
hundrid is a perfite noumbur, as clerkis knowen wel, and wiþ /
al þis þei seyen a man is vnsufficient inowe for to be a f. 92ʳ
140 prechoure.

    And þei aleggen many colourid groundis. First, of Jeremy
(he wes clepid to þat office), he wes ful sore adred, and seide:
'A! A! A! Lorde God, I can not speke, for I am a childe.' And
Marke, for drede, kit of his þombe to vnable him to presthod.
145 But þe grettist ensaumple of hem alle hem þinkiþ is of oure
Lorde Jesus Crist, þat wes þe wisdom of þe Fader, as Seint
Poule seiþe, and ȝitt he abode til he were þritty ȝere of age to
ȝyue ensaumple to be dred of þis office, þouȝ þei haue perfite
kunnyng of many maner sciencis.
150 And þus þei drawen men aback wiþ her ferdful tresouns þat
vnneþe in a cuntre is one feiþful prechoure. Þerfore, me þinkiþ,
God may now pleyne him as a greet hosbond when it is nye
heruest and haþe myche ripe corne and fewe werk men, þerto

seyng Luke (10.[2]): *Messis quidem multa, operarii autem pauci.*
155 Þat is: 'Þere is myche ripe corn, forsoþe fewe werkmen.'
But many men þat ben so sore aferde for to preche to þe
peple ben not afeerd but bolde inow to take of þe peple boþe
tyþe and offringis, and many priue deuocions, but to do her
due dett aȝeyn þei drede not but litel. Suche ben like to false
160 seruantis þat wolen take her ful hire, but to slow her maystris
seruice haue þei no conscience, for þei seyen þei ben vnable to
suche a werke. But he þat is vnable to þe werke is vnable to þe
hire. For Seint Poule seiþe: *Qui non laborat, non manducet.* Þat
is: 'He þat / wole not traueile, is not worþi his mete', and   f. 92ᵛ
165 myche more þen not his hire. But it semeþ þat suche dreden
litel Cristis wordis þat he seiþe in þe gospel by alle suche:
Inutilem seruum proicite in tenebras exteriores, vbi erit fletus et
stridor dentium. Þat is: 'Þe vnprofitable seruaunt þrowiþ fer
into vttermore derknes, where shal be weping of yȝen and
170 gnasting of teeþ.'
Þat Andrew as þe gospel ferþermore seide: 'Þer is a childe
here þat haþe fyue barly louys and two fisshis; but what ben
þese among so many?' may bitoken vnfeiþful counselouris þat
sumwhat ȝit gone nere þe truþe, suche þat seyen þat þo þat
175 lyuen innocently as a childe, and þerto ben wel groundid in her
kunnyng of þe Olde Lawe, þat is bitokenid as doctouris seyne
by þese fyue barly louis. And also þe Newe Lawe may bitoken
þe two fisshis, for al holly þe Newe Lawe stondiþ in ij
braunchis of loue; and riȝt as a fisshe þat is swete mete
180 temperiþ þe bitternes of barly breed, so doþe þe Newe Lawe of
loue and mercy þe Olde Lawe of dreed and veniaunce. Suche
þat stonde in þat caas moun preche to her propur parishyns þat
ben not perfite and perceyuing (as þe pore comyn peple) but,
for to be a comoun prechoure, þei ben to lewid wiþ al þis. But
185 riȝt as Andrew had rewarde to þe quantite of mete and not to
þe myȝt of God þat manyfold can multiplie, riȝt so fariþ by
suche men þat oonly rewarden mannys kunnyng and setten not
hem in tristi hope of help of him in whom is al. Þat is seide by
Dauid, þe prophete, to counfort prechouris in þis wyse:
190 *Dominus dabit verbum euangelizan/tibus virtute multa.* Þat is: 'Þe   f. 9
Lorde shal ȝyue worde to prechouris in myche vertu.'
Firþermore, þe gospel telliþ þat þe peple wes made to sitt. In
þis sitting is vnderstonden þe necessarie disposicion of þe peple
þat shullen here þe worde of God effectuᵉlly to her profite, as
195 in þe toþer sitting of þe hil þe disposicion of prechouris. Þis

---

161 vnable] (*Followed by* to able *deleted*).

sitting bitokeneþ quiete and rest, boþe in body and in soule, fro
al maner worldly bysines and curis of þis wre`c´chid lijf; and
also fer fro fleishly lustis in tyme of hering of Goddis worde,
whiche   is   bytokened   by   þis   hey   vpon   whiche
200 þe peple shulde sitt. For þese two, if þei growen in mennys
hertis, as Crist seiþe, oppressen doun þe worde of God in
mannys soule fro goostly frute: *A solicitudinibus et voluptatibus
vite euntes suffocantur, et non referunt fructum.* Þat is: 'Þorow
bisines and lustis of þis lijf, þe worde of God is stranglid and
205 bringiþ forþe no frute.'
     And for þis cause also þe comoun peple drawen on Sondayes
and oþer holy dayes into a comoun chirche for to here þe worde
of God, whiche is comounly fer fett fro her propur dwelling
placis.
210   In þis quiete Magdaleyn sate at þe feet of Jesus Crist when
she herde þe worde of God, as þe gospel makiþ mynde, whil
Martha, hir sister, wente aboute dyuerse curis of þis lijf.
Þerfore it wes seide of Magdaleyn, by þe mouþe of Jesus Crist:
'Marie haþe chosen þe better party, whiche shal neuer be taken
215 fro hir.'
     Þat Jesus toke þe fewe louys and made þankingis to his
Fader, and after departed hem al aboute to þe peple þat wes
`isett, whiche wes´ fyue þousande in noumbur as þis / gospel f. 93ᵛ
makiþ mynde, may betoken þat euery prechoure shulde boldly
220 trist in Goddis help, and take wilfully of þat litel kunnyng þat
he haþe of Goddis worde, and make þankingis to þe Fader `fro´
whom comeþ al maner of good, mekely knowleching to him his
owne vnsufficiente: þat he haþe not of himself so myche as a
litel þouȝt, but al mannys sufficience is of God, as Poule seiþe
225 ([2] *ad Cor.*3.[5]). And after, prey hym, of his grace (þat
multiplied so largely þat litel mete þat it wes sufficient to fede
so greet noumbur of peple) þat he wole vouchesafe also to
multiplie so litel kunnyng þat [it] may be sufficient to fede wiþ
gostly Goddis peple. And when he haþe done þis deuoure,
230 boldly þen bygynne to preche, be þe peple neuer so greet, in
trist of help of hym þat bade to his apostlis for to go in al þe
worlde for þis werke, and drede not for no litel kunnyng, for he
wolde alwe`i´ be wiþ hem: *Ecce ego vobiscum sum vsque ad
consummationem seculi* [and] *Dabo vobis os et sapientiam.* Þat is:
235 'Lo! I am wiþ ȝou into þe eend of þe worlde' and 'I shal ȝyue
ȝou mouþe and wisdome to perfourme perfitly ȝoure werke.'

221 fro] (*mar*; *text has* of *deleted*).
225 2] 1.

And also in anoþer plase he seiþe, to counfort alle suche: *Non enim vos estis qui loquimini, sed spiritus Patris vestri qui loquitur in vobis.* Þat is: 'It ben not ȝee þat speken, [but] þe
240 spirit of ȝoure Fader þat spekiþ in ȝou.' And þen þe worþi worde of God shal profite to þe peple, be þei neuer so greet in noumbre, þat þei shullen be fed while þei wandren in þis wey, þat þei feile not in her jorne.

Þese fyue þousand of peple þat weren fed in Cristis / feest   f. 94ʳ
245 may wel bitoken þat oonly þo þat perfitly gouernen her fyue wittis in keping of þe Ten Comaundementis to þe profite of her soule ben able to be fed and fulfillid wiþ goostly mete of Goddis wordis. And alle suche moun be vnderstonden by þe noumbre of fyue þousand. For fyue, when it is doublid, it
250 encresiþ to ten; and ten, tentyme multiplied, is encresid to an hundrid, whiche þat is a perfite noumbre, as þese clerkis knowen wel; and ten, an hundrid siþis multiplied, makiþ þe noumbre of a þousande.

Þis grete releef of smal mete broken þat wes borne vp after
255 þis feest of þe apostlis of Crist, after þat alle men weren fulfillid, bitokeniþ þat hiȝe sotelteis of Holy Writ whe`che´ þe comoun peple may not take is reserued to þe doctouris and greet clerkis of hyȝe witt. And þus it semeþ wel herby þat men shulden preche to þe comoun peple graciously comoun mater
260 suche as þei may wel p[er]ceyue, and among greet cle[r]kis sotilteis of hier witt.

Þat þese men, after þat þei sawen þis greet myracle þat Jesus did wiþ litel mete in feding of so greet a peple, þei seiden þat 'þis is þe verre prophete þat is to come into þe worlde.' Þus
265 shulden men do noweadaies: when þei seen and heren þat many men wiþ her litel kunnyng prechen more bisile and turne þe peple fro her vicis for to lyue vertuously þen many oþer grete clerkis þat ben lettrid hilie, hauen greet joy / þerof, and arrett it   f. 94ᵛ
al to Jesus Crist, whiche is þe verre prophete þat shal come into
270 þe worlde at þe dredful Day of Dome for to deme al mankynde, and not to rett it to þe fende þe vertu of Goddis gracious worching, as false frowarde shrewis done, þat han ȝitt þe oolde enuy of Jewis þat turneden in Jesus Crist þe vertu of þe Holy Goost to þe worching of þe deuel þat þei clepiden 'Belzebub'.

275   Whoso wil preche on þis day, he may if him like procede forþe on þe gospel in þe maner þat is seide tofore. Or ellis, if

---

260–61 clerkis sotilteis] (*Erasure of about a line and a half between these two words*).

him like not so, he may take a theme of þe same gospel to procede in þat wey as in þis maner, whoso likiþ, þus.

15

AN ALTERNATIVE
TO SERMON 14

Cum gratias egisset, distribuit (*Jo*.6.[11]). 'Þe helpe and þe grace', *et cetera*.

    Oure Maister and oure Lorde, Jesus Crist, of whom alle cristen men shulden take ensaumple, and specialy prestis 5 whiche shulden be his next folowers, in euery feest þat he made boþe bodile and gostle, at þe bygynning tofore þat he departed of his mete he made þankingis to his Fader, as we fynden boþe in þe feest þat he made þis day of bodile mete, and also in þe feest þat he made on Short Þursday of goostly mete (þat wes, of 10 þe blessid sacrament of his bodi), and afterwarde ȝaue forþe of boþe to þe peple.

    And þis blessid Mayster seiþe to vs alle: *Exemplum dedi vobis, vt quemadmodum ego feci, ita faciatis et vos.* Þat is: 'I haue ȝouen to ȝou ensaumple, þat riȝt as I haue done, so do ȝee.' 15 Þerfore, me / þinkiþ alle cristen men, and specialy prestis,   f. 95ʳ tofore euery refeccion or mele þat þei shulden make, þei shulden seie gracis or make sum maner of þankingis to þe Fader of heuen.

    Wherfore I nowe at þis tyme, þouȝ I vnworþi be, am 20 ordeynid to fede al þis feire peple goostly wiþ þe precious mete of þe worde of God. And þerfore I owe as a disciple of Crist to folow my Maister in þis, þat is: to make þankingis tofore to þe Fader of heuen. And not oonly me þinkiþ þis longiþ to me, but also to ȝou alle whiche loken here today to be fed of þis goostly 25 feest.

    Lift we vp oure hertis þen togedir, and make we þankingis to oure Fader of heuen for alle þe grete goodnessis þat he haþe done to vs, his vnkynd children, fro þe bigynning of þe worlde into þis day! And prey we him herafter of his co[n]tynuaunce, 30 and specialy at þis tyme þat he wole vouchesafe of his grace þat

---

1 *Cum*] (*Text indented for three lines; rubricated C written into the space*).

he wole multiplie so þat litel goostly mete þat I haue in þe scrip
of my soule, whiche I purpose wiþ his help to make to ȝou a
goostly feest, þat we moun alle, þorow þe taking þerof, be
fulfillid of grace; so þat ȝee may, þorow þe strengþe of þat mete,
35 go wiþ Hely þe prophete to þe Mount of Oreb (þat is, to þe blis
of heuen, whiche shulde be þe eend of al oure journe) and
herwiþ haueþ recomendid to ȝoure preyouris alle þe statis, *et
cetera. Cum gratias egisset, et cetera, vbi prius*; 'Þe help and þe
grace', *et cetera.*
40   Cristen freendis, now we han made þankingis to þe Fader as
I seide tofore, now it is tyme to me, þat shulde be oon of
Goddis pan/teris, to sett forþe a boord to his peple. Fyue louis f. 95ᵛ
I purpo[s]e at þis tyme to sett forþ here for to departe to ȝou,
whiche I haue taken out of þis Lordis goostly pantere—þat is,
45 Holy Scripture. Þe first is þe lofe of þe worde of God. Þe
secound is þe lofe of penaunce. Þe þrid is þe lofe of holy
sustenaunce. Þe fourþe is þe lofe of þe worþi sacrament of
Cristis body. Þe fifþe is þe lofe of þe blessid ioy in heuen.
        Þe first is þe lofe of breed of þe worde of God. Of þis breed
50 spekiþ Crist in þe gospel, þere he seiþe: *Non in solo pane viuit
homo, sed in omni verbo quod procedit de ore Dei* (*Mt.*4.[4]). Þat
is: 'Not in oonly breed lyueþ man, but in euery worde þat goþe
oute of þe mouþe of God.'
        Of þe worþines of þis breed, and of þe profitis þat comen of
55 þe worþi eting of þis breed, and of þe perel þat is to hem þat
dispisen þis breed, is tretid in þe next gospel suyng.
        Þe cheef panteris of God, to whom longen prinspaly þe
setting foorþe and departing of þis breed, ben alle prestis and
alle þo þat han taken vpon hem þe office of presthod, to whiche
60 prelatis he bitoke þe office when, as M[atheu] telliþ in þe tenþe
chapitre ([6–7]), he clepid his twelue apostlis and seide to hem:
*Ite ad oues que perierunt domus Israel. Euntes autem predicate,
dicentes quia appropinquabit regnum celorum.* Þat is: 'Goþe to þe
shepe þat han perishid / of þe hous of Israel. And goþe and f. 96ʳ
65 prechiþ, seying þat þe kingdome of heuen shal nyȝe.' And herto
acordiþ Luk (9 chapitre [1–2]): þat Jesus 'clepid togedir his
apostlis and ȝaue hem vertu and power vpon alle feendis, and
for to hele sekenessis, and sent hem to preche þe worde of
God.' And to alle prestis he bitoke þis office when, as Luk telliþ
70 in þe X chapitre, he ordeyned oþer seuente and two disciplis,
and sent hem tofore him to þe same office (in whiche chapitre is
tretid and tolde to hem þe office and þe ordre of a prechoure)

43 purpose] purpofe.   45 (*mar: De 5 panibus*).   49 (*mar: 1 principale*).

and in two degreis: þat is, apostlis and disciplis ben figurid
bisshopis and prestis, as þe decree seiþe.

75 But, alas! I drede me lest many prelatis, curatis and prestis,
whiche shulden not oonly be as lordis pantreris to meyne, but
more tenderly as modris to children departe of þis breed, faren
to hem nowadayes as stepmodris to her children: þat is, if suche
children aske breed of hem, þei shul none haue; and if
80 þei taken it hemsilf, þei shullen be beten.

So, if þe peple nowadayes aske of her prelatis or curatis þis
breed (þat is, preching of þe worde of God), þei moun liȝtly
haue a short answere and neuer fare þe better. And if þei taken
it hemself (þat is, rede it or comoun þerof togidre), þei shullen
85 be beten wiþ somonyng, cursyng, and pursuyng, and prison-
yng. Þerfore it semeþ þat in suche placis is verified þe
prophecie of Amos, þat seiþe in þis wise: *Ecce dies venient, dicit
Dominus, et mittam fame[m] in terram; non famem panis, neque
sitim aque, sed audiendi verbum Domini.* Þat is: "'Lo! þe dayes
90 shullen come," seiþe þe Lorde, "and I shal sende hungur into
þe erþe; not / hungur of breed, ne þirst of watur, but of hering   f. 96
of þe worde of God".' For suche hungur it semiþ þer is, greet
pestilence in many places, and so myche peple goostly deed in
synne. For suche slauȝter alle trwe prestis of God shulden
95 mourne and sorow wiþ Jeremy, seying þus: *Quis dabit capiti
meo aquam, et oculis meis fontem lacrimarum, vt lugeam inter-
fectos populi mei.* Þat is: 'Who shal ȝyue water to myn heed, and
a wel of teeris to myn iȝen, þat I may mourne þe slauȝter of my
peple?'

100 Sum man myȝt sey: 'What is þis worde of God þat þou
spekist of and callist "þis loof", siþen þer ben in Goddis lawe
wordis wiþouten noumbre?' To þis may be answerid þat þis
worde is þe worde of loue, in whiche is comprehendid al
Goddis lawe, as Seint Poule seiþe: *Plenitudo legis est dilectio.*
105 Þat is: 'Þe fulnes of þe lawe is loue', and þerfore Cristis New
Lawe is clepid 'þe lawe of loue'.

Þis loof of breed most be departid in two. Þat is, into þe loue
of God and of ȝoure euencristen; for in þese two, as Crist seiþe,
hangiþ al þe lawe and prophesies. And ȝitt, ferþermore, if
110 tendir children shulden ete herof, þese ij parties mosten be
departid in ten mossels. Þat is, þe loue of God into þre, and þe
loue of þi breþeren into seuen; and þat makiþ ten, whiche ben
þe Ten Comaundementis of God. And þese mossels euery

88 *famem*] famen.

prelate shulde departe or breke to his children, of þis lofe of
115 Goddis worde, whiche is þe first lofe þat shulde be departid.

And here men may trete and declare þe Ten
Comaundementis, lenger or shorter, as þei seen it `is´ spedful. /

And alle þat eten of þis breed effectuelly, of Holy Scripture f. 97ʳ
shullen be fulfillid, for al þing þat is necessarie to þe gouer-
120 naunce of her soulis þei mowen taste and fynde þerinne. For
þei may fynde þerinne what good vertu doþe in plesaunce of
God and [profite] of mannys soule; and what harme synne doþe
in displesaunce of God and hyndryng of mannys soule. And
whoso tastiþ and feliþ þat, and on þe toþer side fyndiþ in his
125 conscience þat he haþe done many synnis, þen shal he falle into
a greet sorow for his synne, for Salamon seiþe: *Qui addit
scientiam, addit et dolorem.* Þat is: 'He þat addiþ kunnyng or
knowing, addiþ sorow' and so doþe greet penaunce in hope of
remission, whiche is þe secound lofe of breed þat I spake of at
130 þe bygynning.

Of þis lofe of penaunce spekiþ Dauid in þe P[sauter], seying
þus: *Fuerunt mihi lacrime mee panes die ac nocte.* Þat is: 'My
teeris werne to me louys [day and ny3t].' And, in anoþer place
he seiþe: *Cibabis nos pane lacrimarum.* Þat is: 'Þou shalt fede vs
135 wiþ breed of teeris.'

Þis breed of penaunce, to him þat etiþ it wilfully and gladly,
doþe many goodis, but prinspaly þre. First, it getiþ of God
for3yuenes of synnis, as witnesiþ Petre in þe Dedis of Apostlis,
seying: *Penitemini, et conuertimini vt dele`a´ntur peccata vestra.*
140 Þat is: 'Doþe penaunce, and beeþ conuertid, þat 3oure synnis
be done awey.' Also, by penaunce a soule is recounsilid to his
heuenly spouse, hou foule þat euer he haþe broken spousehed
wiþ, as he seiþe by þe / prophete Jeremy: *Tu autem fornicata es* f. 97ᵛ
cum amatoribus multis; tamen, reuertere et ego suscipiam te. Þat
145 is: 'Þou, forsoþe, hast done fornicasion wiþ many louers;
neþeles, turne a3eyn and I shal receyue þee.' Þe þrid is þat by
penaunce is geten þe kyngdome of heuen, witnesing Crist
himself and Jon Baptist, seying þus (*Mt.*3.[2] and 4.[17]):
Penitentiam agite; appropinquabit enim regnum celorum. Þat is:
150 'Doþe penaunce; þe kingdome of heuen shal ny3e.

Þe pantreris whiche God haþe ordeyned to 3yue aboute or
departe þis lofe of penaunce ben prestis whiche he put in þis
office when he seide þus: *Quecumque ligaueritis super terram
erunt ligata et in celis, et cetera* (*Mt.*18.[18]). Þat is: 'Whateuer

---

122 profite] (*n.*).
133 day and ny3t] ny3t and day.

131 (*mar: 2 principale*).
143 *fornicata*] fornicatata.

155 þingis 3ee bynden vpon erþe shullen be bounden in heuenys;
and whateuer þingis 3ee vnbynden vpon erþe shullen be
vnbounden in heuenys.' And also he seiþe in anoþer place:
Quorum remiseritis peccata, remittuntur et eis (Jo.20.[23]). Þat is:
'Whos synnis 3ee for3yuen, þei shullen be for3yuen to hem; and
160 whos synnis 3ee wiþholden, þei shullen be wiþholden.'

Þe keyis of þe pantre he bitoke hem when he seide to Petre,
in figure of alle prestis: *Tibi dabo claues regni celorem*
(*Mt*.16.[19]). 'Þo þee I shal 3yue þe keyis of þe kingdome of
heuenys.' Þese keyes, as þe Mayster of Sentence seiþe, ben
165 power and kunnyng. And þese ben so necessarie togedir þat þe
tone wole not vnlouke wiþoute þe toþer. But, for many prestis
taken þe keyis of power / and for3eten þe key of kunnyng,   f. 98ᵛ
þerfore oft when þei wenen to loke þei vnloken, and when þei
wenen to vnloke þei loken, as witnesiþ God by his prophete:
170 *Interficiunt animas que non moriuntur, et viuificant animas que
non viuunt* (*Eze*.13.[19]). 'Þei sleen soulis þat dien not, and þei
quykenen soulis þat lyuen not.' But þei þat han boþe keyes
moun sikerly open þe dore, and sett forþe, and departe truly to
þe peple of þis lofe of penaunce.

175   First, if men shulden ete wel of þis breed, it most be broken
into þre parties—þat is, it most be declarid by þe prestis þat
whoso doþe verrey penaunce, he most haue þre þingis: þat is,
contricion, confession, and satisfaccion. And eche of þese partis
most be broken into þre, so þat þis loof of penaunce most be
180 broken into nyne mossels.

Of þe first mossel (þat is, contricion) spekiþ Dauid, þe
prophete, þere he seiþe þus: *Cor contritum et humiliatum, et
cetera*. Þat is: 'A contrite herte and a meke, God, þou shalt not
despise.' And þis mossel most be broken into þre parties, as þe
185 doctour Lincolne seiþe, in his dictis. Þe first is hate of synne, as
þe prophete seiþe: *Qui diligitis Dominium, odite malum*. Þat is:
'3ee þat louen þe Lorde, hatiþ yuel.' And in anoþer plase he
seiþe: *Propterea odiui omnem viam iniquitatis*. Þat is: 'Þerfore I
haue hatid al þe weie of wickidnes.' Þe secound is contynuel
190 sorow for synne. Of þis also spekiþ þe prophete þus: *Dolor meus
in conspectu meo* / *semper*. Þat is: 'My sorow is euer in my si3t.' f. 9
And Austyn (*De Vera Penitentia*) seiþe: 'Where þat sorow

---

167 (*Foot of* f.97v. *catchwords*: and for3eten).
177 (*mar*: De vera penitencia).
179 so...penaunce] (*This phrase is repeated, but with the spelling* lofe *in the
second occurrence, and* of penaunce *erased but still visible in the first*).
181 (*mar*: I).   189 (*mar*: ij).

eendiþ, feiliþ penaunce.' Þe þrid parte of contricion is ful
purpos neuer to turne aʒeyn to synne. Þis moued Crist in þe
195 gospel (*Jo.*5.[14]), when he seide þus to þe seke man þat he
helid: *Ecce, iam sanus factus es; iam noli peccare, ne deterius tibi
aliquid contingat.* Þat is: 'Lo! now þou arte made hool; nowe
wole þou no more synne, lest ony þing falle worse to þee.'
　　Þe secound parte of þe loof of penaunce is confession, of
200 whiche spekiþ James, þe apostle (*Jac.*5.[16]): *Confitemini alter-
utrum peccata vestra.* Þat is: 'Knoulechiþ eche to oþer ʒoure
synnis.' And þis parte most be broken into þre mossels, for
confession most haue þe`se´ þre condicions:
　　First, it most be hasty, wiþoute delaying. Not þat a man
205 drawe along his confession til he be nyʒe his deeþ, as many men
done, but while he is on lyue and in good hele, `swich´ tyme as
he haþe synned. Þerfore seiþe þe Wyse Man: *Non demoreris in
errore impiorum; ante mortem confitere, et sequitur viuus et sanus
confiteberis.* Þat is: 'Dwelle þou not in errour of wickid men;
210 knouleche þou tofore þi deeþ, and it sueþ hool and lyuing þou
shalt knouleche.'
　　Þe secound condicion of shrift: þat is, þat it be hool wiþouten
departing. Not a gobet to oon and a parcel to an oþer, or for to
knouleche summe of þi synnys and leue summe behynd, for
215 God wole not departe his forʒyuenes. And þerfore it seiþe in
Jonys gospel: *Totum hominem fecit sanum.* Þat is: 'Al þe man he
made hool.'
　　Þe þrid condicion of confession is þat it shulde be nakid
wiþouten ony excusing, as / Dauid did, when he had synnid in f. 99ʳ
220 noumbring of þe peple and God punshid his peple, he seide:
*Ego sum qui peccavi, ego qui malum feci. Iste grex quid commer-
uit?* Þat is: 'I am þat haue synned, I þat haue done yuel. Þis
folke, what haþe it deseruid?' And, for þis meke accusing of
hymself in excusing of oþer, he gate forʒyuenes and plesid
225 God. But Adam and Eue, Anany and Saphire, for þei ex-
cusiden her synne, þerfore þei gaten no forʒyuenes, but
veniaunce and peyne. Þerfore seiþe Seint Ambrose (vpon þe
Ps[alme] *Beati immaculati*): *Qui se accusat, etsi sit peccator,
iustus esse incipit.* Þat is: 'He þat accusiþ himself, and þouʒ he
230 be a synner, he beginniþ to be riʒtwis.'
　　Þe þrid parte of þis loof of penaunce is satisfaccion, for
Thomas Alquin seiþ (*Verit*[*atis*] *Theo*[*logice*]): *Sicut in bellis*

193 (*mar*: iiij).　　　　203 (*mar: Confessio*).　　　204 (*mar*: I).
206 hele] (*Followed by* as *erased*);　　　swich] (*mar; no caret mark*).
212 (*mar*: ij).　　　　　　　　　　　　　218 (*mar*: iiij).

*restituta [amicitia], statim non remittit[ur] dampnum debitum
illati; ita post remissionem culpe in contricione, remanet debitum,*
235 *pene satisfaccionis.* Þat is: 'As in batels when frendship is
restorid, anone þe dett of þe harme þat is done is not forȝouen;
so, after remission of synne in contricion, leueþ dett of
satisfaccion peyne.'

And þis parte (of satisfaccion) ȝit most be broken into þre
240 partes: þat is, into preyer, fasting, and almesdede. Riȝt as a man
haþe soule, body, and goodis of fortune, and riȝt as wiþ þese he
haþe trespasid, so wiþ þese he must make satisfaccion. As
anentis þe soule, he most make satisfaccion wiþ preyoure;
anentis þe body, wiþ vertuous fasting; anentis þe goodis of
245 fortune, wiþ almisdede.

Of preyoure: sum is in hert; sum in mouþe; sum in dede. Of
þe first seiþe Poule to þe Corinth[ijs] / (xiiij chapitre [15]):   f. 99
Orabo spiritu et orabo mente. Þat is: 'I shal prey in spirit and I
shal prey in mynde.' Of þe secound seiþe James (*Jac.*5.[16]):
250 *Orate pro invicem, vt saluemini.* Þat is: 'Preyeþ eche for oþer,
þat ȝee be sauid.' Of þe þrid seiþ Crist in þe gospel (*Luc.*1[8.1]):
Quoniam oportet semper orare et non deficere. Þat is: 'For it
bihoueþ euer to pr[e]ie and neuer to feyle.'

Whoso wole lengur dilate þis mater of preyoure, loke he
255 more þerof in þe sermoun of Ephiphanie.

Þe secound parte of satisfaccion is fasting, and þat is boþe
fruteous and vnfruituous. Fructuous in þre maners. Oon is of
þe mouþe, þat is: abstinence fro metis, of whiche spekiþ Crist
in þe gospel, seying þus: *Cum ieiunatis, nolite fieri sicut ypocrite
260 tristes.* Þat is: 'When ȝee fasten, be ȝee not made as ypocritis
sorouful.' Þe ij is of þe hert, þat is: absteyning from vnordinate
lustis to synnis. Þerfore seiþe Crisostom (*O[m]e[lia]* 5): *Corporis quidem ieiunium est abstinere a cibis; anime autem ieiunium
est abstinere ab omni re mala.* Þat is: 'Fasting of body is for to
265 absteyne fro metis; but fasting of soule is to absteyne fro al
wickid þing.' Þe þrid fasting is of werke, þat is: absteyning fro
wickid werkis, of whiche Seint Poule spekiþ: *Ab omni specie
mala abstinete vos.* Þat is: 'Fro al maner yuel spice absteyne
ȝou.'

270 Vnfructuous fasting is in þre maners. Oon is of coueitous
men, for to fille þe purs; anoþer is of men þat lyuen after

---

251 8.1] 4.   256 (*mar: 2 pars satisfaccionis*).
257 (*mar: 3 ieiunium fructuosum*).   261 (*mar: ij*).
270 (*mar: ieiunium infructuosum; preceded by part of numeral trimmed away
at edge of page, probably 3*).

phisik, oonly for helþe of body; þe iij is of ypocritis, oonly for
to be seen.

Þe þrid parte of satisfaccion is almesdede. Whoso doþe
275 wilfully and discretly after þe boundis of Goddis lawe, brekiþ
wel / and departiþ þe þrid loof of breed, of whiche I spake of at   f. 100ʳ
þe bigyning—þat is, of temperal goodis for bodile sustenaunce.
In þis maner wyse Seint Austyn vnderstondiþ 'breed' þat we
asken of God in oure *Pater Noster* —þat is, al þing þat we
280 neden of oure sustenaunce to body, as mete, and drinke, and
hiling, and ouer þis al þat nediþ to sustenaunce of oure soulis.

Þis breed, if it be broken wysely and departid euenly, doþe
many goodis, but among alle oþer þese þre first: it clensiþ [a]
mannys synnis; and it delyueriþ a man fro deeþ þat he haþe
285 deseruid for synnis; and it makiþ a man to fynde euerlasting
lijf. Þis proueþ wel Tobie in his Boke, where he seiþe þus:
*Elemosina a morte liberat, et ipsa est que purgat peccata, et facit
inuenire vitam eternam.*

Þe pantreris of þis lofe ben prestis, for as Jon (*Jo.*[21.15–17])
290 makiþ mynde in his gospel, Crist bade Petre þries for his loue
fede his shepe. Seint Gregorius and oþer doctouris vnderstonden by þis þries feding: first, wiþ his temperal goodis
whiche þei han vnder her gouernaunce of tiþis and offringis,
taking þerof oonly to hem a streite lyuing, as Poule writiþ to
295 Thi[moþe]: *Habentes alimenta et quibus tegamur, hijs contenti
simus;* 'We hauing foodis and hiling, wiþ þese be we payde.' Þe
secound feding is wiþ good ensaumple of her lyuing. Þe þrid is
wiþ newe techyng of Goddis worde.

And not oonly prestis han panteris to breke and sett forþe of
300 þis breed, but also euery oþer man þat haþe plente of þis loof of
temperal goodis. For alle suche men God haþe made his
pantreris, and generally seide to hem þese wordis by Ysay, þe
prophete: *Frange esurienti panem tuum.* Þat is: 'Breke to / nedy   f. 100ᵛ
þi breed'—þat is, of worldly goodis.

305 But, for þat many men oft tyme breken þis breed (þat is,
ʒyuen almesdedis) and litel þanke han þei þerfore of þe cheef
Lorde, þerfore it were to wite what circumstauncis ben due
þerto to þat eend þat it myʒt plese þe Lorde and haue mede for
his seruice. Seuen circumstauncis I fynde groundid in Scrip-
310 ture, whiche ben necessarie to riʒt almesdede. First is: what
shal be ʒouun. Crist telliþ in þe gospel of Luke, and seiþe þus:
Quod superest, date elemosinam. Þat is: 'Ouerplus ouer þi nedful

---

274 (*mar: 3 principale*).   283 a] *erased.*   289 *Jo*] Jo vltimo.
308–9 (*mar: 7 circumstancie elemosine*).   310 (*mar: I*).

lyuing, 3yue to almes.' Þe secound is: to whom shulde almes be
3ouen. Crist telliþ in þe same gospel, and seiþe prinspaly to
315 þese: *Voca pauperes, debiles, claudos, cecos.* Þat `is´: 'Clepe pore,
feble, pore crokid, and pore blynde.' Þe þrid is: hou myche.
Herto answeriþ Tobie in his Boke, and seiþe þus: *Si multum
tibi fuerit, habundanter tribue; si exiguum fuerit, etiam exiguum
libenter impertir[i] stude.* Þat is: 'If þou haue myche, 3yue
320 plenteuously þerof; and if þou haue litel, 3yue a litel þerof
gladly.' Þe fourþe is: whan it shal be 3ouun. Anone, wiþoute
tariyng, seying þus: *Cor inopis ne afflixeris, et ne protrahas dare.*
Þat is: 'Ne disese þou not þe hert of þe nedy man, and draw
þou not on long for to 3yue to him þat is in anguysshe.' Þe fifþe
325 is: why men shullen 3yue. For þe loue of Crist. For Crist seiþe
in þe gospel of M[atheu]: *Quamdiu fecistis vni ex hijs minimis
fratribus meis, mihi fecistis.* Þat is: 'As long as 3ee han done to
oon of þese leest my breþeren, 3ee han done to me.' Þe sixt is:
hou it shulde be done. Þe Wy/se Man answeriþ in his Boke,   f. 10
330 and seiþe priuely it shulde be done, seying þus: *Conclude
elemosinam in s`i´nu pauperis, et hec pro te orabit ab omni malo.*
Þat is: 'Close þe almys in þe bosum of þe pore men, and it shal
prey for þee fro al yuel.' Þe seuent is: of what maner goodis
almys shulde be 3ouen. Herto answeren þe wordis of Zache in
335 þe gospel of Luke, of mannys owne goodis and not wrongly
geten, seying þus: *Dimidium bonorum meorum do pauperibus.* Þat
is: 'Þe half of my goodis I 3yue to pore men.'

   And Seint Gregorius seiþe, and is writen in þe Comoun
Lawe þus: *Elemosina illa redemptoris nostri oculis placet que non
340 ex illicitis et iniquitate congeritur, sed de rebus concessis et bene
adquisitis impenditur.* Þat is: 'Þat almes plesiþ to þe y3en of oure
Lorde whiche is not hepid togider of vnleful þingis and
wickidnes, but þat þat is 3ouen of þingis grauntid and wel
gotun.' And þus, whosoeuer dispendiþ his temperal goodis in
345 almes dedis wiþ þe vij circumstauncis þat ben here rehersid, his
is a good panter `to´ God, and brekiþ wel and departiþ þis þrid
lofe of breed after þe Lordis wille, þat is: þe lofe of bodile
sustenaunce.

   And whoso etiþ wel, and departiþ of alle þese þre louys of
350 breed þat ben rehersid tofore (þat is, first of þe worde of God,
and after of þe loof of breed of penaunce, and also of þe þrid,
þat is almesdede), he þen haþe wel proued himself and so is

---

313 (*mar*: ij).   316 (*mar*: iiij).   319 *impertiri*] impertire.
321 (*mar*: iiij).   324 (*mar*: v).   328 (*mar*: vj).
331 *sinu*] synu (*with* y *deleted and int*. i).   333 (*mar*: vij).

able for to ete of þe fourþe lofe of breed—þat is, þe worshipful
sacrament of Cristis bodi, of whiche breed spekiþ himself in þe
355 gospel / of Jon, seying þus: *Panis quem ego dabo vobis caro mea* f. 101ᵛ
est pro mundi vita. Þat is: 'Þe breed whiche I shal ȝyue to ȝou is
my fle`i´she for þe lijf of þe worlde.'

Þe corne of þis breed wes sowen in þe Virgyn Marie by þe
worde of God when she seide to þe aungel: 'Lo! þe handmayde
360 of God'; is sprungen vp in `h´is birþe; and wax in vertuis, and
age, and wisdom; and frutid by vertuous werkis til he wes ripe
to his passioun. And þen wes þis blessid corne repid vp of þe
erþe by his enmyes; and after bounden as a sheep fast to a piler;
and aftur þrosshen wiþ scourgis; and wynwed wiþ wynde of
365 disclaundring wordis of her mouþe, so þat al þe chaf of
vnfeiþful men wente awey fro him and he left al oone as þe
clene corne.

After, he wes sente to þe mylle (þat is, on þe cros) and þere,
bitwix two harde mylle stonys (of heþen men and of þe Jewis),
370 he wes grounden `in´ þe crosse into þe tyme þat þe clennest
floure of his blode came oute.

And þen he wes sente into þe ouen of þe sepulcre; and þe
þrid day wes þis breed drawen forþe and wiþ charite baken;
and wiþ his glorifiyng alle his coruptible humeris sopen vp, and
375 now it `is´ to counfort boþe aungels and men.

Þe panteris þat God haþe ordeynid of þis breed, for to ȝyue
aboute þerof to his peple, ben prestis oonly. In þis office he
bitoke hem on Sheer Þursday, after þe sopere, and after þat he
had made þis worþi sacrament, seying to hem in þis wyse: *Hoc*
380 *quotiescumque feceritis, in mei memoriam faciatis.* / Þat is: 'Þese f. 102ʳ
þingis, as oft as ȝee done, do ȝee hem into mynde of my
passion.' And whensoeuer þat a prest, in Este`r´ne Day or in
oþer tyme, ministriþ þis blessid sacrament to hem þat receyuen
it worþily, þen he departiþ þe fourþe breed þat I spake of at þe
385 byginnyng (þat is, þis worshipful breed of heuen, Cristis body)
in sacrament.

And whoso likiþ to trete lenger of þis mater, loke in þe
sermoun of Corpus Þirsday.

And whoso etiþ worþily `in þis worlde´ of þese foure louys
390 þat ben rehersid tofore, and feiþfully departiþ of hem in þe
maner as I haue seide (þat is, first þe lofe of þe worde of God
deuoutly hering, bisili keping, and feiþfully worching; and
after þe breed of penaunce for his synnis; and siþen þe breed of
almesdede doyng), and in þis maner able him and so receyue þe

353 (*mar: 4 principale*).   380 *quotiescumque*] quotienscumque.

395 fourþe breed (þat is, þis worþi sacrament of Cristis body), þen
shal he worþi be, as Crist seiþe in þe gospel of Jon, to lyue
wiþouten eend in þe ioy of heuen: *Qui manducat hunc panem
viuet in eternum.* Þat is: 'He þat etiþ þis breed shal lyue
wiþouten eend,'—whiche is þe fifþe loof of breed þat I spake of
400 at þe bygynning.

Of þis breed spekiþ þe gospel, seying (*Luc.*14.[15]): *Beatus
qui manducabit panem in regno Dei.* Þat is: 'Blessid is he þat shal
ete breed in þe kingdome of God'—þat is, blessid is he þat shal
see and fully weelde þe siȝt of þe blessid face of þe Trinite, and
405 all[e] oþer ioyes þat ben / in heuen.   f. 102

Þe panter of þis breed is none erþely man, but þe blessid
Lorde haþe reseruid þat office to himself, of þe gospel of Luke,
seying þus: *Precynget se, et faciet illos discumbere, et transiens
ministrabit illis.* Þat is: 'He shal girde hymself, and make hem
410 sitt to mete, and he passing shal ministre to hem'—þat is, þe
glorious siȝt of his godhed and manhed togider, whiche shal be
ful feding to alle þat ben in heuen, witnesing þe prophete
Dauid in þe P[sauter]: *Satiabor cum apparuerit gloria tua.* Þat
is: 'I shal be fulfillid when þi blisse shal apere.'

415 Whoso wole se more of þis mater, he may fynde in þe
sermoun of Deed Men þat bigynniþ: *Memorare nouissima tua.*

Now, for his greet goodnes, graunt vs þat grace þat, whil we
ben wandring here in þis worlde, to worche so wisely þat we
moun after ete of þis blessid breed in þe blisse of heuen. Amen.
420 Amen.

---

399 (*mar*: 5 *principale*).   401 gospel] gosspel.

FIFTH SUNDAY
IN LENT

Qvis ex vobis arguet me de peccato? (*Jo.*[8.46]). In þese wordis of
oure Lorde Jesus Crist, whiche he seide to þe comoun peple of
Jewis and to þe princis of her prestis as þe gospel of þis day
makiþ mynde, and in her answeris, we moun prinspaly lerne
5 foure þingis. First is þat euery prechoure of þe worde of God
shulde be clene of ony greet and notable synne, and þen houȝ
perilous it is not to ȝyue credence to þe true wordis of suche a
prechoure whos lijf is not reprouable. Þe secound is þis: þat
aȝeyns false wordis and wordis of sclaundre men shulden
10 excuse hemsilf mekely wiþ / perfite pacience and afterwarde   f. 103ʳ
cleerly declare þe contrary truþe. Þe þrid is þis: þat malicious
hertis and froward willis ben neuer correctid wiþ meke excusacion and true declaracion, ne wiþ charitable doctryne, but
raþer contynuen and encresen in her malice, falsely reporting
15 þe wordis of her techers or vndernymmers, pynnyng at her
wordis and putting on hem lesyngis. Þe iiij: þat is when suche
malicious men moun wiþ no colourable wordis bring aboute
her purpos to perfourme her yuel wille, þei sparen for no
shame to berste oute openly into malicious dede.
20   The first is groundid of þe first wordis of Crist in þis gospel,
þere he seiþe: 'Whiche of ȝou shal vndernym me of synne?'—
ȝyuing leue boþe to þe comoun peple and also to þe prelatis, if
þei myȝten fynde ony open synne in him worþi repreef, to
vndernym hym þerof. Who is þen, eiþer curat or prelate, so
25 proude þat wole not of his sogettis charitably be vndernymmed
of his defautis, hering þese meke wordis of oure Lorde Jesus
Crist?
    And þus it semiþ by þese wordis þat þe lijf of euery
prechoure of þe worde of God shulde be vnreprouable. Herto
30 acordiþ Seint Poule, ȝyuing a rule of prestis and prechouris to

---

1 *Qvis*] (*Text indented for four lines; rubricated Q written into the space*);
8.46] 6.   20 (*mar: 1 principale*).   25 proude] prooude.

Tite and Thimothie, his disciplis, þat stoden in þat degre,
seying þus: *Oportet episcopum sine crimine esse* (*ad Tit.*[1.7]).
Þat is: 'It bihoueþ a bisshop to lyue wiþout greet notable
synne.' And, in anoþer place: *Oportet episcopum irreprehens-*
35 *ibilem esse* ([1] *ad Thi.*3.[2]). Þat is: 'It bihouiþ a bisshope to be
vnre/preuable.' And þe cause is þis: for myche more meuiþ þe   f. 103ᵛ
peple þe open ensaumplis of perfite and vertuous lijf of þe
prechour þen nakid wordis only. And þerfore seiþe Seynt
Poule: *Non enim audeo aliquid eorum loqui que per me non efficit*
40 *Cristus.* Þat is: 'I dar not speke ony of þo þingis whiche Crist
worchiþ not by me.'

     And for þis same cause also Crist clepid his apostlis 'salt of
þe erþe', by whiche is bitokened ensaumple of good lijf. And
after he clepid hem 'liȝt of þe worlde', by which is bitokenid þe
45 true preching of her mouþe, meuing hem by þat first þei
shulden lyue wel, and after preche truly.

     Anoþer cause is þat þe peple to whom þe prechour shewiþ þe
worde of God haue no cause to sey to hym in repreef: *Medice,*
cura teipsum. Þat is: 'Leche, hele þiself.' And þerfore
50 Seint Poule seiþe: *Castigo corpus meum et in seruitutem redigo,*
ne forte cum alijs predicauero, ipse reprobus efficiar. Þat is: 'I
chastise my body and bring it into seruage, lest when þat I shal
preche to oþer men, I be made reprouable.'

     Wherfore, on þe toþer side, me þinkiþ þen þat alle þo þat
55 prechen þe worde of God and shewen open ensaumple of yuel
lijf moun be sore aferde of Goddis dredful wordis seide to alle
suche by þe mouþe of Dauid þe prophete: *Peccatori autem dixit*
Deus: Quare tu enarras iustitias meas, et assumis testamentum
meum per os tuum? et cetera. 'God seiþe to suche a synful man:
60 "Why shewist þou out my riȝtwisnessis, and takist my testament bi þi mouþe? Þou, forsoþe, hast hatid disciplinys, and
hast þrowen after byhinde my wordis. If þou se a þefe, þou
rennyst wiþ him, and wiþ spousebrekers þou putti[st] þi
porcion. Þi mouþe wes / ful plenteuous in malice, and þi tunge   f. 1c
65 coueitid trecheries. Sitting, þou spakist aȝeyn þi broþer, and
aȝeins þe son of þi moder þou puttist sˋcˊlaunder. Þese þingis
þou didest, and I helde my pees. Þou hopedist wickidly þat I
shal be like to þee, but it is not so, for I shal vndernym þe, and
set aȝeyns þi face".'

---

31 Tite and Thimothie] Thimothie and Tite.
32 *ad Tit.* 1.7] thi. 3.   35 *ad Thi.* 3.2] Tit' 2.
38–41 (*mar: Contra predicantes et non facientes*).
63 puttist] putting.

70 But euery suche prechour whos lijf is wiþout repreef, as I
seide tofore, and þerwiþ prechiþ no þing ellis but Goddis lawe
or þat þat may be groundid þerinne and whiche is true (as
Dauid seiþe in þe P[sauter]: *Lex tua veritas*. Þat is: 'Þi lawe is
truþe'), and prinspaly þe euangelie whiche is souereyn truþe
75 for þere is no falshede ne wrong worde þerinne (as witnesiþ þe
Wyse Man speking in þe persone of God, seying þus: *Iusti sunt
omnes sermones mei, et non est in eis aliquid prauum neque
peruersum*. Þat is: 'Alle my wordis ben riȝtwis, and þer is in
hem no shrewid þing ne wrong þing'), he may resonable aske of
80 þe peple to whom he prechiþ, lyuing in vicis: 'If I seye truþe to
ȝou, why bileue ȝee not to me?' For euery man þat lyuiþ in
synful lijf bileuiþ not to þe truþe of Goddis worde, for it is not
al oon to bileue Goddis worde and to bileue to Goddis worde.
'To byleue Goddis worde' is to byleue þat Goddis worde is
85 true, and so bileuiþ þe deuel, as James seiþe: *Demones credunt*.
Þat is: 'Feendis bileuen.' But 'for to bileue to þe worde of God'
is for to bileue þat þe worde of God is true in euery parte, and
also vertuous to lyue þerafter. And in þis maner is no man
perfitly in byleue but he þat is oute of dedly synne, and þis
90 bileue is gendrid b[y] vertuous hering of þe worde / of God.   f. 104ᵛ
    And alle suche ben a Goddis halfe, or membris of God, as
Crist witnesiþ wel here in þis gospel, seying: 'Whoso is a
Goddis half heriþ þe worde of God.' But Crist after shewiþ
cause why þat synful men han no wille to here vertuously þe
95 worde of God, and suyngly to bileue þerto, for þei ben not a
Goddis halfe.
    But here we mosten vnderstonde þat þere is fructiful hering
of þe worde of God, and also vnfructiful.
    Fructiful hering is when a man heriþ it wiþ bodile eeris, and
100 vnderstondiþ it wiþ goostly eeris, and worchiþ þerafter wiþ his
dedis. And for to do þus, two þingis shulden prinspaly meue
euery man. Oon is þe worþines and goodnes of þe worde of
God. Anoþer is þe manyfolde profitis þat it bringiþ to his
fructiful herer. The worþines and dignite of þe worde of God is
105 prouid by Seint Austyn, whiche makiþ comparison bitwix þe
worde of God and þe body of Crist, wher he seiþ þus (*i'. q. d.
Inter`r´ [og]o*): 'I aske to ȝou, breþeren or sustren, seiþ to me
what semiþ to ȝou to be more, þe body of Crist, or þe worde of
Crist? If ȝee wolen answere truly, þus ȝee shullen seie þat þe

---

90 by] be.
97–99 (*mar: Nota quod est fructuosa audienda verbi dei et infructuosa*).
107 *Interrogo*] (mar. r(2), og *om.*).

110 worde of God is not lesse þen þe body of Crist.' And after he
seiþe in þe same place þat 'we shulden kepe it as bisile and wiþ
as greet reuerence as we wolden þe body of Crist.'

And not oonly as Seint Austin seiþe it is euen wiþ þe body of
Crist, but as Seint Jon seiþ in his gospel, it is þe secound
115 persone in þe godhed þat toke fleische in þe mayden, seying
þus: *Verbum caro factum est.* Þat is: 'Þe worde is made fleishe.'

Also, þe worþines and þe vertu of þe worde of God may be
shewid herby, for it passiþ in worþines golde whiche is most
precious of alle me/tels, and it haþe mo vertuis þen ony   f. 105ʳ
120 precious ston; and þerfore seiþe Dauid þe prophete, þat knew
perfitly þe difference bitwix hem, in þis maner: *Dilexi mandata
tua super aurum et top[az]ion.* Þat is: 'I haue loued þi
comaundementis, whiche ben þi word, aboue golde and precious ston.'

125 The hiȝe vertuis of þe worde of God ben wiþouten noumbre,
but neþeles a man may telle whiche ben rehersid in þe glose of
Poulis pistlis vpon þis worde (ij' *ad Thimotheum* 2.[9]): *Verbum
Dei non est alligatum.* Þat is: 'Þe worde of God is not bounden')
where he rehersiþ vii vertuis of þe word of God.
130 Þe first is þat it liȝtniþ mannys soule and ȝyueþ him goostly
vnderstonding, as þe prophete Dauid seiþe in þe P[sauter]:
*Declaratio sermonum tuorum illuminat et intel[lectum] dat
paruulis.* Þat is: 'Þe declaring of þi wordis liȝtneþ and ȝyueþ
vnderstonding to meke men.'

135 Þe secound: it gladiþ mannys hert, as þe prophete Jere[my]
seiþe: *Factum est verbum tuum in gaudium et in leticia[m] cordis
mei, quoniam inuocatum est nomen tuum super me* (*Jere.*[15.16]).
Þat is: 'Þi worde is made into ioy and gladnes of myn herte, for
þi name is iclepid vpon me.'

140 Þe þrid vertu is þat it al tobrekiþ mannys harde herte by
drede and sorow, as þe prophete Jere[my] seiþe: *Numquid non
verba mea sunt quasi ignis, dicit Dominus, et quasi malleus
conterens petras* (*Jere.*23.[29]). Þat is: '"Wheþer þat my wordis
ben `not´ as fire," seiþe þe Lorde, "and as an hamer breking
145 togider stonys."'

Þe fourt vertu is þis: þat it makiþ mannys harde herte to
melte by loue into teeris, as Dauid þe prophete seiþe in þe
P[sauter]: *Emittet verbum suum et lique/faciet ea, flauit spiritus*   f. 1c

122 *topazion*] toposion.   129–31 (*mar: Nota 7 virtutes verbi dei* I).
135 (*mar:* ij).   137 15.16] 16.
140 (*mar:* iij).   146 (*mar:* ⟨iiij⟩. *red, rubbed*).

eius et fluent aque. Þat is: 'He shal sende oute his worde by his
150 true prechoure, and he shal melte hem by loue, and his spirit
blew (þat is, þe Hooly Goost wrouȝte in hem deuocion), and
watris shul flow (þat is, greet plente of teeris).'

Þe fifþe vertu is þat it heleþ al maner goostly sijknes of
mennys soulis. Þat proueþ þe Wyse Man in Holy Scripture
155 þere he seiþe þus: *Non herba neque malagma sanauit eos, sed tuus
sermo, Domine, qui sanat omnia* (*Sap.*[16.12]). 'Neiþer herbe ne
playster helid hem, but þi worde, Lorde, þat heliþ alle þingis.'
Also, Dauid in þe P[sauter] seiþe: *Misit verbum suum et sanauit
eos.* Þat is: 'He sen[t]e his worde and helid hem.'

160 Þe sixt is þat it areisiþ deed men, for it reisiþ sinful men out
of deeþ of deedly synne into goostly lijf of vertuis, witnesing
Crist himself in þe gospel of Jon þere he seiþe þus: *Venit hora,
et nunc est, quando mortui audient vocem Filij Dei, et qui auderint
viuent.* Þat is: 'Þe houre comeþ, and now is, when deed men
165 shullen here þe voyce of þe Son of God, and þei þat heren it
shullen lyue.'

Þe seuent vertu is þis: þat it delyueriþ a man from euerlasting deeþ. Also, as Crist seiþe in þe gospel of þis day: *Si quis
sermonem meum seruabit, mortem non gustabit in eternum*
170 (*Jo.*[viij.51]). Þat is: 'Whosoeuer shal kepe my worde, shal not
taste deeþ wiþouten eend.'

And þus, as it is sumwhat shewid, þe dignite and vertu of þe
worde of God shulden meue men to here it riȝtfully. Þe ij þing
þat shulde meue men to here it riȝtfully, as it is seide tofore, is
175 þe manyfolde profitis þat it bringiþ to suche hereris.

First, it gendriþ bileue in man, as þe apostle / seiþe to   f. 106ʳ
Romayns: *Fides autem ex auditu, auditus autem per verbum
Cristi.* Þat is: 'Bileue comiþ of þe worde of Crist.' And
'wiþouten bileue may no man plese God,' as þe apostle seiþ to
180 þe Hebr[ues]. Þen wiþout feiþful hering of þe worde of God
may no man plese God.

Þe secound profite of hering of þe worde of God is þat it
makiþ a man to dwelle stable and stedfast vpon þe ground of
his bileue, as witnesiþ Crist in þe gospel of M[atheu] (vij
185 [24–5]): *Omnis qui audit verba mea et facit ea, assimilabitur viro
sapienti qui edificauit domum suam supra petram; descendit
pluuia, venerunt flumina, flauerunt venti, et irruerunt in domum
illam, et non cecidit quia fundata erat supra petram.* Þat is:

153 (*mar*: v).   156 16.12] 13.   159 sente] sende.
160 (*mar*: vj).   167 (*mar*: vij).   170 viij.51] vj.
176 (*mar*: I).   182 (*mar*: ij).

'Euery man þat heriþ my wordis shal be made like to a wyse
190 man þat bildiþ his hous stedfast vpon a ston'—þat is, vpon
Crist, whiche bitokeniþ þe ston. 'And reyn descendid'—of false
preching. 'And flodis comen'—of sharp persecucion. 'And
wyndis blewen'—of venemous diffamacion. 'And fellen vpon
þe hous'—þat is, aȝeyns his conuersacion þat fruytfully her`iþ´
195 þe worde of God. 'And it fel not'—fro þe stedfastnes of his
bileue. And whi? Certis, 'for it wes bilde vpon a stedfast
ston'—whiche is þe lijf of Crist.

Þe þrid profite þat þe worde of God bryngiþ to his eeris is þat
[it] makiþ hem blessid of þe mouþe of God. Þis wittnesiþ
200 Crist himself in þe gospel of Lu[ke]: *Beati qui audiunt verbum
Dei, et custodiunt illud.* Þat is: 'Blessid be þei þat heren þe
worde of God, and kepen it.' And, as it is shewid in þe sermoun
of þe last Sonday, þis blessing is more worþe þen alle þe synful
prelatis blessing here in erþe.

205 Þe fourþe profite is þis: þat it makiþ his fruytful herer
commendid of God aboue hem þat done þe bodile dedis of
mercy. For riȝt as þe soule is more / perfite þen þe body, so þe   f. 106ᵛ
foode of þe soule is more worþi þen þe foode of þe body; and
siþen fedyng of þe soule is made by hering of þe worde of God,
210 þerfore fruytful herers of þe worde of God ben þe more
commendid. And in þis maner Magdaleyn sitting at þe fote of
Crist and deuoutly heryng his worde wes more commendid of
hym þen Martha, hir suster, þat wes occupied aboute her
bodile foode, seying of hir in þis wyse: *Maria optima partem
215 elegit, que non auferetur ab ea* (*Luc.*10.[42]). Þat is: 'Marie haþe
chosen þe better partie, whiche shal neuer be taken awey fro
hir.'

Þe fifþe profite þat it doþe is þis: þat it ministriþ to a man
greet hope þat he is þe childe of God and a membre of God
220 ordeynid to blis by þe wordis of God þat he seiþe in þis same
gospel: *Qui est ex Deo, verba Dei audit.* Þat is: 'He þat is of
Goddis parte, her`i´þ þe worde of God.'

Þe sixt profite is þis: þat it getiþ or purchasiþ to his herers
euerlasting lijf in blis. Þis witnesiþ Crist in þe gospel of Jon,
225 seying þus: *Qui verbum meum audit, et credit* [*ei qui*] *misit me,
habet vitam eternam.* Þat is: 'He þat heriþ my worde, and
byleuiþ to him þat sent me, haþe þe lijf þat euer shal laste.'

Þere is also, as I seide, vnfruytful hering of þe worde of God.
Þat is, when a man heriþ it wiþ þe eeris of his body and

198 (*mar*: iij).   200 Luke] luc'.   205 (*mar*: iiij).   218 (*mar*: v).
225 *et qui*] quem.   228–30 (*mar*: *De infructuosa audiencia verbi dei*).

230 takiþ no tent þerto wiþ þe eeris of his hert. Or ellis when he
heriþ wiþ eeris of body, and vnderstondiþ it wiþ his herte, and
lyueþ contrary þerto in his werkis. Aȝeyns þis maner of hering
spekiþ Seynt Jame in his pistil, seying: *Estote factores | verbi, et*   f. 107ʳ
non auditores tantum, fallentes vosmetipsos, et cetera. Þat is:
235 'Beiþ doers of þe worde of God, and not oonly hereris,
deceyuing ȝoureself.' Of þis vnfruytful hering of þe worde of
God men shulden be sore afeerd, for many perilis þat comen
þerof, and prinspaly for v:

First, for he þat heriþ not vertuously þe worde of God is
240 cursid of þe mouþe of God, as Jeremy þe prophete witnesiþ,
speking in þe persone of Crist: *Maledictus homo qui non audierit*
verba pacti huius quod precepi patribus vestris. Þat is: 'Cursid is
þat man þat heriþ not þe wordis of þis couenaunt þat I
comaundid to ȝoure fadris.'

245 Þe secound perel is þis: for þe preyour of euery suche
negligent herer is cursid, as witnesiþ þe Wyse Man in his
prouerbis (*Prouer.*28.[9]): *Qui auertit aurem suam ne audiat*
legem, oratio eius erit execrabilis. Þat is: 'He þat turneþ awey his
eer þat he here not þe lawe of God, his preyer shal be cursid.'

250 Þe þrid peril is þis: for dispite of hering of þe worde of God
is greet signe of damnacion, witnesing Crist in þ`is´ same
gospel, seying: *Propterea non auditis, quia ex Deo non estis.* Þat
is: 'Þerfore ȝee heren not, for ȝee ben not a Goddis half.'

Þe fourþe perel is þis: þat suche dispisers of þe worde of God
255 shullen be more bitterly dampned þen Sodomitis, for it is more
perel to distrie goostly seed of þe worde of God by whiche
Crist shulde be engendrid in mennys soulis þen for to distrie
bodile seed by whiche mannys body shulde oonly be engendrid. Þat witnesiþ Crist himself in þe gospel of M[atheu]
260 X [15]): *Amen dico vobis, tole|rabilius erit terre Sodomorum et*   f. 107ᵛ
Gomorreorum in Die Iudicij quam illi ciuitati, et cetera. Þat is:
'Forsoþe, I sey to ȝou, more sufferable it shal be to þe londe of
Sodom and Gommor in þe Day of Dome þen to þe cite þat
despisiþ þe worde of God.'

265 Þe fifþe perel is þis, as Seint Austyn seiþe in þe chapitre
Interrogo þat is aleggid tofore: þat 'not lesse gylty is he þat

---

233 (*Foot of* f.106v. *catchwords:* verbi et non).
236–8 (*mar:* 5 *pericula contra infructuose audientes verbum dei*).
240 witnesiþ] witneseþiþ.   245 (*mar:* ij).
250 (*mar:* iij).   251 þis] þe (e *deleted; mar.* is).
254 (*mar:* iiij).   260 *tolerabilius*] tollerabilius.
265 (*mar:* v).

negligently heriþ þe worde of God þen he þat þorow negligence
suffriþ þe body of Crist falle into þe erþe.'

    I seide also at þe bygynning þat þe secound parte of þis
270 gospel techiþ vs þat aȝeyns false wordis of sclaundris men
shulden excuse hemself mekely wiþ perfite pacience, and
afterward cleerly declare þe contrarie truþe. Þus did oure
Lorde Jesus Crist, when þe Jewis puttiden vpon him false
repreef to her entent, and wordis of disclaunder, seying þus:
275 'Þou art a Samaritan and hast a feend.' Ful mekely he answerid
to boþe, grauntyng þe ton to true vnderstonding, and denyed þe
toþer by expressid wordis.

    He grauntid þat he wes a Samaritan in þat þat he wes stille
and denyed it not. Not to her entent (þat he wes of Samarie and
280 contrarie to her lawe), but for he wes goostle þat Samaritan þat
þe gospel of Luke spekiþ of in X chapitre [33–5], whiche helde
in oyle and wyne into þe woundis of þe man þat came doun
from Jerusalem into Jerico. Samaritan is as myche for to seie as
'a keper', and þerfore Crist most nede graunt þat he is a keper,
285 for he is keper of al mankynde.

    He is oure keper in oure moder wombe. He is oure keper in
oure birþe. He is oure keper in oure tender age, tofore we
kunnen in ony maner help oureself. He is afterwarde oure
keper / in oure age fro oure enemyes, and prinspaly fro oure   f. 108
290 goostly enemyes, þat þei haue not so myche power vpon vs as
her wille were. Into þis eend he haþe ordeyned euery man an
aungel to be his leutenaunt in þis goostly keping, as Crisostom
seiþ in his Omelie.

    He wole also be oure keper at þe last houre of oure lijf, if we
295 serue him truly and trist to him feiþfully when we han moste
nede to him, for þen we shullen be most weyke and oure
enemyes most strong and moste bisi, for he wote wel if he may
not gete vs þen al his traueile is in veyne. And þus God is alwey
oure keper, boþe of body and soule, of al maner of yuel. And
300 þerfore to þis entent þe prophete Dauid seiþe: *Dominus custodit*
te ab omni malo; custodiat animam tuam Dominus. Þat is: 'God,
þe Lorde, kepiþ þee fro al yuel as anentis þi body, and kepe he
þi soule fro alle goostly perelis.' And also he seiþ of þis keper
þus: *Dominus custodiat introitum tuum et exitum tuum, ex hoc*
305 *nunc et usque in seculum.* Þat is: 'Þe Lorde kepe þi entre and þi
going out, from now to wiþout eend.'

269 (*mar: 2 principale*).
282–4 (*mar: Quomodo christus est Samaritanus Nota*).

After þis stille graunting þat he wes a Samaritan, he denyed
expressely to þe toþer ful myldely neþeles, seying: 'I haue no
feend'. For þis wes impossible, þat þei two þat ben so direct
310 con[t]rarious in her werkis shulden acorde togi`d´er, for Seint
Poule seiþe: *Que conuentio Christi ad Belial? Que societas luc[i]*
ad tenebras? Þat is: 'What acorde is of Crist to Belial? What
acorde is bitwene li3t and derkenes?'—a[s] who seiþe 'none'.
Lo! in þis meke answere of oure Lorde Jesus Crist we aw3t to
315 be ashamed of oure [wraþe], þat when we ben a litel sterid to
3yue hem a3eyn a wel worse worde þen we receyued of hem,
and afterwarde do to hem þe yuel þat we may, taking no hede /
of oure blessid Lorde þat took so greet wrong, wraþid him not f. 108ᵛ
þerwiþ, ne 3aue no wickid worde a3ein. For þou3 he wolde haue
320 answerid to þe same persones þat seiden to him þese wordis:
'3ee han feendis' or 'Þe deuel is wiþin 3ow' (for wel he my3t
haue seide þus, for but if þei hadden be fulfillid wiþ þe feend
þei my3t not so shrewidly haue seide by þat Lorde), but he
wolde not after þis wrong þat he toke sey þe truþe þat he my3t,
325 lest men my3t haue supposid þat he had do so more to venge
his iniurie þen for þe loue of truþe. In whiche dede of Crist `is´
vnderstonden þat in þat tyme þat we taken dispitis falsly of
oure nei3boris, we holde oure pees of yuelis whiche we knowen
of hem, an aunter lest þat þat shulde be medicyn of iust
330 correccion we turne into armure of oure `owne´ wickidnes.

Here also men may lerne þat if þe enemyes of God and of his
lawe put vpon true prechouris of þe euangelie dyuerse reprouable þingis, of whiche summe ben true to a good vnderstonding
and summe ben false and vnworshiping to God, þei may holde
335 her pees to þe first but alwey deny3e þe secound. As if a man
seide to suche on: 'Þou arte false, and þi teching, boþe!' He
may wel graunt þe first by a priue stilnes, or ellis expresly if
him like, for Dauid seiþe in þe P[sauter]: *Omnis homo mendax.*
Þat is: 'Euery man is a lyer', for euery man crokiþ fro þe first
340 truþe, whiche is a preued patron þat alle we shulden sue. But
þat þe euangelie is false whiche þat he techiþ, euer he shulde
deny, for þat is a blasphemye in God.

But after þat Crist had þus mekely answerid as it is seide
bifore, he mekely declarid his answere by þe / wordis þat suen, f. 109ʳ
345 seying: 'I honoure or worship my Fader.' For Crist, in alle his
myraclis worching, he preferrid þe honoure of God tofore þe
honour of his manhod, whiche is not possible of ony deceyuer

309–10 (*mar: Quomodo christus negauit se habere demone[m]*).
311 *luci*] lucis.   313 as] al.

þat worchiþ by þe feend. But þe Jewes vnhonoureden Crist
when þei put vpon hym þat in Belȝebub, prince of feendis, he
350 þrew feendis out of wood men, as þouȝ þe feend and he haden
ben sworne breþeren. Ne þei myȝt not sey þat for veynglorie he
did suche þingis, for þei þat sechen worshipis of þe worlde,
examine þei þe werkis of Crist and deme þei if þei sow[n]en
into þe worship of þe worlde as þe Jewes seiden. Or ellis it may
355 be expouned þus: þat Crist for þis tyme sechiþ not his owne
glorie, but God þe Fader sechiþ his worship after his passion,
and demeþ synners in him, punysshing hem.

   I seide also þat þe þrid parte of þe gospel techiþ vs þat
malicious hertis and froward willis ben not correctid neiþer wiþ
360 meke excusasion, true declaracion, ne charitable doctryne, but
raþer contynuen and encresen in her malice, falsly reporting þe
wordis of her techers, pynching at her wordis, and put[ting] on
hem lesyngis.

   In þis maner þe Jewes diden to oure Lord Jesus Crist. For
365 after þat he had mekely excusid him þat he had no feend and
cleerly declarid it, as it is seide tofore, ȝit ferþermore after þat
he ȝaue hem charitable doctrine, wilnyng ful hiȝly þe pro[f]ite
of her soulis, and seide in þis wise as þe gospel telliþ: 'For soþe,
I sey to ȝou, whoso kepiþ my worde / shal not taste deeþ   f. 10
370 wiþouten eend.' And not wiþstonding al þis excusacion, declaracion, and charitable doctrine, þei werne not correctid
þerby, but raþer continued and encresid in her malice, seying
þus: 'Now we knowen wel þat þou hast a feend;' and after þat
falsely reporting his wordis menyng of 'bodile deeþ' þere Crist
375 mente of 'deeþ wiþout eend;' and pynchid at his wordis also ful
frowardly, þat he souȝt veynglorie by menyng of his wordis, for
he made him more þen Abraham, her fader, whiche wes deed
and ȝit he kept ful wel þe worde of God; and after þat þei
puttiden lesyngis in his wordis in þat þat he seide of Abraham,
380 her fader: 'Forsoþe, I sey to ȝou, tofore þat Abraham shulde be
made, I am', siþen Abraham wes deed long or he wes borne,
not taking hede of þe euerlastyngnes of his godheed of whiche
Crist spake whiche receyuiþ no chaunging of kynde, ne passing
of tyme.

385   And here men moun touche hou þat wyckid men of froward
hert ben not amendid but raþer more apeired wiþ preching of
þe worde of God.

353 sownen] n om.   358 (mar: 3 principale).
362 putting] ting om. (n.).
367 profite] prophite.

For þe doctor Crisostom seiþe: 'Riȝt as a piler in an hous, if
it stonde vpriȝt after þat it takiþ birþen vpon it, þe more it is
390 made stedfast; and if it be a litel crokid and taken birþen vpon
it, it is not þerby made stedfast, but raþer it goþe asyde. Riȝt
so, mannus hert, if it be riȝt and it here þe worde of God or
ensaumple of a good man, is more conformed to good lijf; [but
if it be crokid and it se or here ensaumple of a good man,] not
395 oonly he is [not] conformed, but more stirid to enuy and more
peruertid.

'Also, þe sunne / shynyng on dyuerse materis, dyuersly f. 110ʳ
worchiþ; as, if it shyne vpon wexe and vpon cley, þe wexe it
meltiþ, þe cley it hardiþ, and þis is not longe vpon þe sunne,
400 but vpon þe dyuerse disposicion of þe materis vpon whom it
worchiþ. Riȝt so, worchiþ þe worde of God vpon good and
yuel.'

And in þis maner, as þe eend of þe gospel telliþ, when þe
Jewes sawen þat þei myȝten not wiþ no colourable wordis bring
405 aboute her malicious purpos, þen þei weren not ashamed to
berst out into mali[c]ious dede, taking vp stonys for to haue
stonid hym as a blasfeme`r´. And here men may se þat wraþe
and enuy moun not worche riȝtwisly. Þerfore seiþe Seint Jame:
Ira viri iustitiam Dei non operatur. Þat is: 'Þe wraþe of man
410 worchiþ not þe riȝtwisnes of God.' For riȝtwisnes of lawe in
demyng of blasfemye asken first accusing tofore þe iuge,
deposing of witnes, and þe sentence of þe domesman, and al þis
þei feylid. And also, [if] a man were commit by þe lawe, he
shulde be stonyd wiþout þe cite, as it is writen in Leuit[icus]
415 24.[23]; but þei wolden haue stonid him wiþinne þe temple,
whiche wes in al maner vnleful. For as þe story telliþ, in þe
fourþe Book of Kingis, þat Ioiada þe Bisshop made Athalia þe
Quene to be drawen out of þe boundis of þe temple tofore þat
she shulde be slayne, but þe cursid enuy of þe Jewis myȝten not
420 abyde al þis proces of lawe.

When Jesus saw þe malice of hem, he hid hymself and wente
out of þe temple. Þis Crist did for two causis. Oon wes for his
tyme wes not comen for to suffre passion, whiche he knew by
his godhed / tofore þe worlde wes made. Anoþer cause [wes] to f. 110ᵛ
425 teche vs by his dede for to fle þe malice of oure wrongful
pursuers and also of malicious and wickid wordis when we
kunnen se no goostly pro[f]ete comyng of oure abiding. And
herto acordiþ Seynt Poule, seying in þis wise: *Date locum ire.*
Þat is: 'Ȝyueþ plase to wraþe.'

427 profete] prophete.

430 Þis hidyng of God may also bitoken þat God hydiþ hym,
wiþdrawing grace nowhere in þis worlde from alle þo þat
dispis`en´ þe worde of God, and goþe oute of þe temple of her
soule; and also, at þe Day of Dome, shal hide him fro alle
suche, wiþdrawing fro hem þe glorious and blisful siȝt of his
435 godheed, seying by his prophete (*Jere*.18.[17]): *Dorsum et non
faciem ostendam eis in die perdicionis eorum*. Þat is: 'Þe bac and
not þe face I shal shewe to hem in þe day of her lesing.' In
anoþer place he seiþe þus: *Auertam faciem meam ab eis*. Þat is:
'I shal turne awey my face fro hem.'

432 dispisen] (*mar*. en).

SERMON
OF DEAD MEN

Memorare nouissima tua ([*Ecci.*7:36]).

The helpe and þe grace of oure Lord⟨e⟩ Jesus ⟨Cri⟩st, þat for
þe lijf of mankynde sprad abrode h⟨i⟩s body on þe crosse and
suffrid peynful de⟨þ⟩e þeron to pay ful ⟨raun⟩so⟨n⟩ and so to
5 make ful red⟨em⟩pcion of þe sy⟨nnes⟩ of ⟨man⟩kynde, be wiþ
vs here in al our⟨e⟩ ⟨lyuing⟩, þat is: in al oure woful pilgrimage, þat we mowen go riȝtfully in vertuis wiþouten ony erryng
in vicis, so þat at þe laste, at oure deeþ day, we may come to þe
ende of oure blessid pilgrimage de⟨siri⟩d, þat is: to þe blis of
10 heuen. Amen. /

Cristen breþeren, for þre causis groundid in Holy Scripture   f. 1ᵛ
me þinkiþ men mowen lefully come togider at þe exequies, or
byriyngis, or myndis, of deed men:

Oon is for to comforte her breþeren whiche ben made sory or
15 heuy by deeþ of her frendis þat ben late passid from hem oute
of þis worlde. And in þis maner wise oure Lord Jesus Crist
coumfortid boþe in worde and dede ij deuoute wymmen, Mare
and Martha, of her deed broþer Lazar, as we reden in þe gospel
of John (þe xj chapitur), when þei maden to hym her
20 compleynte þat her broþer wes deed in his absence. In worde,
when he seide to Martha: 'Þi broþer shal rise'—as who sey 'Be
þou not discoumfortid for þi broþeris deeþ, for he shal rise and
lyue!' And in dede also he coumfortid hem, when he clepid him
oute of his graue and fully restorid him to lijf aȝeyne. Also,
25 Luke makiþ mynde, Crist, seing a wydow wepynge for þe deeþ
of hir oonly son whiche wes borne oute at þe ȝate of þe cite

---

3 lijf] loue M;   on] vpon M.
4 to(2)] *om.* M.   5 mankynde] al mankynde M.
7 riȝtfully] riȝtli M.   14 (*mar*: .1.).
16 maner wise oure] manere of wise we reden in þe gospel of John þe eleuenþe
chapitre oure M.   18-19 Lazar...when] laȝar whanne M.
21,22 rise] arise M.   23 also he] also after he M.
24 Also] Also as M.   25 (*mar*: luc').

towarde his graue, benyngly coumfortid hir wiþ mylde wordis,
seying: 'Wepe þou not.' And anone aftur wiþ his dede, when he
reisid hym fro deeþ to lyue and bitoke him to his moder.

30   And þus shulde euery Cristen man, beyng a quike membre
of hooly chirche, seing his broþer in heuynes eiþer in disese for
þe deeþ of her frendis or for ony oþer cause, by þe ensaumple
of oure Lorde Jesus Crist, / coumfort hem at þe leest wiþ   f. 2ʳ
goodly wordis, and also wiþ charitable dedis if it lyue in his
35   power, hauynge in mynde þe wordis of þe Wise Man
(*Ecci.*[7.38]): *Non desis plorantibus in consolatione.* Þat is: 'Ne
feyle þou to coumfort hem þat wepen or ben sory.'

Þe secound cause for þe whiche men mowen lefully come to
þe biriyng of dede men is for to biholde in þat myrrour and
40   take ensaumple þat riȝt as þei ben passid hennys, so shul þei.
And þat myrrour eiþer biholding shulde be to a man a grete
bridel eiþer refreynyng, to kepe [him] fro synne. And þerfore
seiþ Seint Bernarde: 'I beholde in þe grauis of deed men, and I
se no þing ellis þere but wormys, stenche, and askis. Suche as I
45   am, suche weren þei; and suche as þei bene, suche shal I be.'
Also, Salamon seiþ in his prouerbis, in persone of hym þat is
deed to him þat lyueþ: 'Haue mynde on my dome, whiche God
haþe ȝeuen vpon me, of deeþ, for so shal be þine. Myn wes
ȝisturday; þine perauenture shal be tomorow.'

50   Þe þrid cause for whiche men mowen lefully be gederid
togedir at buryingis of deed men is to preie for hem þat ben
deed, þat God of his eendles mercy vouchsafe [þe sonnere to   M.f.
relese hem of her p]eynys, whiche [þei haue deseruid for her
syn]nis, and bringe hem t[o his blisse þat he haþ b]ouȝt hem to.
55   For þe P[hilosofre seiþe: 'Stronger is] vertu onyd and knitt[id
togider þen disseuerid'—fo]r better mowen / many men bere or   f. 2ᵛ
heue a þing togedir þen yche of hem by hymselfe. Riȝt so,
when many men ben gederid togider to prey, and fastnyd wiþ
one wille and one herte in loue and charite, þe raþer þei shullen
60   be herde of God for what þing þat þei preien.

Þus weren þe holy apostlis gederid togidre in preier aftur þe
ascencion of oure Lorde Jesus Crist, as Luke makiþ mynde in

33 leest] laste M.   36 Ecci] *om.* M;   (*mar:* Eccⁱ 7).
37 feyle þou] faile þou not M.   38 (*mar:* .ij.).
42 him] hem R.   43 (*mar:* .B'.).
47 lyueþ Haue] lyueþ *Memor esto iudicij mei sic enim erit & tuum . mei heri &
tui hodie þat is haue* M;   on] of M;   (*mar:* .*Prouer.*).
50 (*mar:* .iiij.).   52–6 (R *damaged*).   53 of] for M.
55 (*mar: Philosophus*).   61 Þus] þus M.

þe Dedis of þe Apostlis: *Erant omnes vnanimiter perseuerantes in oratione. Erat autem eis cor vnum et anima vna* (*Act*' [1.4; 4:32]).

65 Þat is: 'Þei werne togider alle wiþ one wille lasting in preyer,' and þerfore her preyer wes herde of God for whateuer þing þei preide fore.

In þis maner also Seint Petir coumfortiþ vs for to prey, and seiþe [*Omnes vnanimes in oratione estote* (1) *Pe*.3.[8]). Þat is:

70 'Beþe togider in preier alle of oon wille.' And þus, for to prey is a good cause for to come togider fore, þerfore seiþe Hooly Scripture (2 *Mach*.12.[46]): *Sancta ergo et salubris est cogitacio pro defunctis exorare etc.* Þat is: 'Hooly and heleful is þe þouȝt for to prey for hem þat ben deed, þat þei may be vnbounden of

75 her synnis' [þat is, of þe peynes þat þei haue deseruid for her synnis]. And þis is þe þrid cause, leful and goode, as I haue shewid ȝow.

Þus þen, for þese þre causis þat I haue touchid, or for summe of hem, and specialy for þ[e laste], I hope ⟨ȝe b⟩en   M.f. 51ʳ

80 gederid here togidre [þis day]—þat is, [to preie deuoutli] for þe soule of oure [deed frende for whom] ȝe ben [þus] gederid, which[e is late passid fro vs. And no]t oonly for þe dee[d, but also for þe quike—þa]t is, for al holi chirc[he, boþe restinge in purgator]i and / fiȝting in erþe.   f. 3ʳ

85 Liȝfte vp ȝoure hertis þen, wiþ one herte and one soule knyttid so fast wiþ þe bondis of charite þat alle þe feendis of helle shullen neuer mow disseuer hem, seying wiþ þe holy apostle Poule: *Quis n`o´s separabit a caritate Christi?* Þat [is]: 'If we be þus knyttid, who shal departe vs fro þe loue of Crist?'—

90 as who sey 'No man!' And þe preier of suche is alwey able to be herde, for to suche seiþe Crist in þe gospel of [Mark]: *Amen dico vobis, quecumque orantes, etc.* Þat is: 'Whatsoeuer ȝe asken preying, bileuiþ, for `ȝe shullen take´, it shal be done to ȝow.' Þen if ȝe ben þus knyt wiþ þis blessid bonde, I prey [ȝow] at þe

63 (*mar*: Act' .1.).
cor vnum] *vnum cor* M;
68 In þis maner] (*n*.).
69–70 (*mar*: .Pe.3.).
73 *exorare*] *exorare vt a peccatis solvantur* M.
75–6 synnis...synnis] synnis & R.
80 þis day] *om*. R.
84 and] and and R.
is] *om*. R.
92 *orantes*] *orantes petitis credite quia accipietis et fiet vobis* M;
93 take] take & M.

64 *oratione*] *oratione* act' 5 M;
Act' 1.4] *om*. M, Act' 2 R.
69 *Omnes*...1] *om*. R.
72 (*mar*: Mach'.12.).
79–84 (R *damaged*).
81 þus] *om*. R.
88 (*mar*: *Apostolus*);
91 Mark] John M, Ion R.
(*mar*: Joh').
94 ȝow] *om*. R.

95 bygynnyng, as ȝe ben wonte by comyn custom, to prey for al þe
state[s] of holy chirche.

First, for ʽhemʼ þat ben in grace [and] lyuen vertuously, þat
God encrese hem and continue hem for his eendles goodnes,
for ʽhe þat continueþ into þe eende, he shal be safe.ʼ And for þo
100 þat ben in dedly synne and lyuen viciously, þat God of his
endles mercy ȝiue hem grace of verray contricion and space of
satisfacioun, and to lyue and ende in perfite cha⟨rite and⟩ in þe
riȝt bileue of holy chirche.

[Preieþ also, I biseche ȝou,] for me, vnworþi ser[uaunt þow I M.f.5
105 be, þat God of his grete curtesie þis tyme sende me grace so to
open or declare to ȝou his worde, and ȝou so deuoutli to here it,
bere it in ȝoure mynde, and perfitly worche it in dede, þat it
may prinsepaly be to] / his worship and pleasaunce, and aftur f. 3ᵛ
saluacion to vs boþe, hauyng in mynde þe counsel of Seynt
110 Poule þere he seiþ þus: *Oratione instate, vigilantes in ea cum
gratiarum actione, orantes simul et pro nobis, vt Deus aperiat
nobis hostium sermonis ad loquendum misterium Christi, et sequitur vt manifestem illud ita vt oportet me loqui.* Þat is: ʽBeþe
bisi in preyer, waking in it wiþ doyng of þankingis, and preying
115 togider for me þat God open to me þe dore of his worde (þat is,
trew vnderstonding) to speke þe priuite of Crist, þat I make it
open so as it bihouyþ me to spekeʼ—þat is, neiþer to flater,
neiþer for coueitise neiþer for veynglorie, but oonly for þe loue
of God and profite of his peple.

120 For þis techiþ Seynt Poule þat a true precher shulde do,
seying ʽofʼ himself in ensaumple of alle true prechouris in þis
maner: *Non enim aliquando fuimus in sermone adulacionis, sicut
scitis, etc.* Þat is: ʽWe were not at ony tyme in þe worde of
flatering, as ȝe knowen; neyþer in occasion of coueitise, God is
125 witnes; neiþer seching veyneglory or worship of men, neiþer of
ȝow, neiþer of oþer.ʼ

Þat I may [per]⟨fourme þis⟩ [worshipful office] in þe ma[ner M.f.
as Seint Poule techiþ] vs [in þis tixt, I preie ȝou for charite
prey]iþ for [me. And not oonly for me, but for alle þ]o

97 hem] (*mar.*) R, þo M;   and] *om.* R.   100 dedly] *om.* M.
102–8 (R *damaged*).   109 boþe] *om.* M.   110 (*mar:* ⟨*A*⟩*postolus*).
114 preyer] preieres M.   118 (*mar:* Nor for couetise).
120 þis] þus M.   121 himself] him *om.* M.
123 scitis etc] scitis neque in occasione auaricie Deus testis est neque querentes
ab hominibus gloriam neque a vobis neque ab alijs M;
Þat is: We] we ne M;   worde] world M.
125 veyneglory] veyne *om.* M.   127–32 (R *damaged*).

130 þat [God wole be preied for, boþe quike and] deed: [*Pater
Noster, et Aue, etc. Memorare*] ⟨*nouissima*⟩ *tua* ⟨*etc*⟩. [Þe helpe
and þe grace þat we bisou3te] by/fore be wiþ vs now and euer. f. 4ʳ
Amen.

Cristen breþer[en] and frendis, God almy3ty, þe Fader of
135 heuen, is an erþe tilier, as witnesiþ his owne son in þe gospel of
John, worching alwey and tilying þe feiþe of þe euangelie in
Cristen mennus soulis; in whose teme alle Cristen men shulden
draw as oxen, vnder þe softe and li3t 3ocke of loue; of whiche
teme þo þat han taken þe office of presthod shulden be þe
140 dryuers, wiþ þe crie of her mouþis wiþoute cesying of true
preching of þe word of God, as Ysay þe prophete seiþe: *Clama
ne cesses*, also wiþ biting [of] sharpe sentensis, as wiþ a pricke in
a gode, shulde stire bysily þe peple to drawe ri3tlye wiþoute
balkis of synne in þis blessid tilþe. Of whiche dryuers I oon, al
145 þow I be vnworþi, am set here at þis tyme to dryue þis worþi
teme, and of alle þe sentensis þat I can fynde in Scripture
moste sharply pricking to moue 3ow to drawe spedily and euen,
I haue put in my goode now at þis tyme, seying þe wordis þat I
toke to my teme: *Memorare nouissima tua, etc.* Þat is: 'Haue
150 mynde on þi laste þingis, etc.'

Hooly Scripture in many placis diffusely spekiþ of many
þingis whiche men shulden haue in her mynde, but for we
mowen not now in þis shorte tyme speke of hem alle, þerfore I
þenke, wiþ þe leue of God, to speke of þat þat is moste
155 pertinent and moste conuenient for / þis tyme: þat is, to 'haue f. 4ᵛ
in mynde [þi] laste þingis', as oure teme seiþe.

Breþeren, 3e shullen vnderstonde þat þere ben foure laste
þingis whiche shulden prinsepaly euer be holden in mannys
mynde: þe first laste þing is mannys bodily deeþ; þe secounde is
160 þe Day of Dome; þe þrid is þe peynes of helle; þe fourþe is þe
joyes of heuen.

The first last þing is mannys bodily deeþ, for þat is þe last
eende of his temporal lijf, of whiche spekiþ Holy Scripture (2
Re. 14.[14]): *Omnes morimur, et quasi aque dilabimur in terram,*
165 *que non reuertuntur.* Þat is: 'Alle we dyen, and as watir we

---

131 *nouissima tua etc*] *etc vide prius* M.   134 breþeren] en *om.* R.
136 tilying] techinge M.   137,139 teme] tyme M (*n.*).
140 þe] *om.* M.   142 of] and R;   (*mar*: .Ysaie.).
149 *tua etc*] *om.* M.   150 þi] þe M;   (*mar*: t⟨hema?⟩ *cf.* 975).
151 many(1)] diuerse M.   155 to] forto M.   156 þi] þᵗ R, þe M.
157 (*mar*: *Nota* . 4 . *fines*).   162 (*mar*: 1 *principale*).
164 dilabimur] desolabimur M;   (*mar*: R̈e.14).   165 Þat is] *om.* M.

shullen slide into þe erþe, þe whiche turnen nouȝt aȝeyn; and if
we turnen nouȝt aȝeyn, þen shal þat be þe laste eend here.' Þis
last þing, þat is: oure deeþe, we shulden euer haue in mynde,
and specialy for þre causis: þe first cause is for it is vncerteyne;
170   þe secounde for it is peynful; þe þrid for it is dredful.

First, for it is vncerteyne, as Seint Bernarde seiþe: *Nichil
certius morte, et nichil incertius hora mortis.* Þat is: 'No þing is
more certeyn þen deeþ, and no þing vncerteyner þen þe houre
of deeþ.'

175   If it were so þat a man had a precious juel which, if it were
wel kepte, he myȝt be auaunsid foreuer, and if it were stolen
awey, he myȝte be losten foreuer; and if suche a man had noon
oþer house to kepe it inne but a feble on wiþ teerid wallis; and
if so were þat a þefe had aspied it, and sent to hym þat he wolde
180   stele it, but þerof set no certeyn day ne houre, / a grete fole   f. 5ʳ
were he þat were in suche a case þat ne he wolde euer be
waking, and neyþer slumur ne slepe, but alwey lye in awaite for
þe comyng of þis þefe. Riȝt in þe same wise shulde euery
Cristen man fare, for euery man haþe a soule whiche is a ful
185   precious juel. Þe preciosite þerof may be knowen by þe price
þat wes ȝeuen þerfore, for þe wisist marchaunte þat euer wes
ȝaue þerfore his precious lijf, whiche wes more worþe þen al
heuen and erþe. And þis juel man haþe in a ful britel house or
vessel of his erþely body, as Seynt Poule seyþe: *Habemus
190   thesaurum in vasis fictilibus.* Þat is: 'We han tresouris in vessels
of erþe.' Þis juel, if it be wel kepte, a man may be a⟨uaun⟩sid
into þe blis of heuen; and if it be loste, he shal be vndone and
lefte into perpetual peyne of helle.

Þe deeþ þat comiþ sodeynly as a þefe haþe sente to euery
195   man worde þat he wole come, for euery man is þerof certeyn;
but he haþe not sette þe day ne þe houre in whiche he wole
stele þis precious juel oute of þis feble house. Þerfore, me
þinkiþ it were grete nede to worche aftur þe wise counsel of

---

166 þe(1)] *om.* M.

170 þe secounde] þe secounde is M.
(*mar:* .B'.).
vncerteyner] more vncerteyn M.
179 if so were] if it were so M.
183 þis] þat M.
(*mar: Apostolus*).
192 into] in M.
195 certeyn] in certeyn M.
in] in þe M.

169 cause] *om.* M.
171 (*mar:* ⟨*Pri?*⟩*ma causa*);
173 and] but M;
175 (*mar: Exemplum*).
181 he(2)] *om.* M.
190 *vasis fictilibus*] vs fictile M;
191 auaunsid] wel auaunced M.
193 lefte] lost M.
196 þe(2)] *om.* M;
198 it] him M.

oure Lorde Jesus Crist, where he counseliþ þus: *Vigilate, etc.*
200 *Illud autem scitote, quoniam si sciret, etc.* Þat is: 'Wakiþ,' seiþ
Crist—þat is: alwey beeþ in vertuous lijf, oute of dedly synne,
'for þis,' he seiþe, 'knowe ȝe wel: þat if þe housholder wist what
houre þe þefe wolde come, forsoþe he wolde wake and not
suffur his house to be vndurmynid.' And siþen þat no man /
205 wote redily w`h´en þis þefe wole come (þat is: deeþ), for þe   f. 5ᵛ
Wise Man seiþe: *Nescit homo finem suum,* 'No man knowiþ his
eende,' wheþer it shal be in ȝouþe, mydel age, or eelde, þen me
þinke it were grete wisdom euermore bisily to lye in awayte for
sodeyne comynge of þis þeef, þat is: for to eschewe synne and
210 lyue vertuously, and euer haue deeþ in mynde.

But alas! it semyþ by her dedis þat þere ben many men in þis
worlde ful recheles and taken litel hede to kepe þis juel and
awayte þis þefe, but alwey slepen and slumbren in synne into
þe tyme þat þis þefe come and robbe hem of þis juel and of alle
215 her oþer goodis. And þese ben suche men þat euermore
contynuely lyuen in hyȝe and orrible cursid pride, aftir her
fader Lucifer, in ouer costious apparayle, boþe of hemself and
of her housholde, like to þe riche man þat wes biried in helle,
and in cursid extorcions and wrongis to her neiȝboris biside
220 hem, wiþ vsure, symonye, and false purchasis, to mayntene wiþ
her lustis and likingis in slouþe, glotony and leccherie, and þer
wil þei make none eende al þe while þei mowen lyue þus.

Þese ben like to fisshis whiche, as clerkis þat treten of kyndis
seyne, þat þei han a kyndly desire myche for to slepe, and when
225 þei slepen þei houen in þe watir stille as þow þei weren deed,
no þing mouyng but oonly þe tayle. And þis aspien wel crafty
fisshers, and comen vpon hem at þat tyme, and taken hem wiþ
her gynnis. Riȝt so faren suche / men þat deliten hem in lustis   f. 6ʳ
and likingis of þis lijf, as a man þat is on slepe, and no þing
230 mouyng in vertuis but oonly þe tayle. Þat is, if men speke to

---

199–200 *Vigilate...sciret etc*] *Vigilate et sequitur illud augmentum scitote quoniam
si sciret paterfamilias qua hora fur venturus esset vigilaret vtique et non sineret
perfodi domum suam ideo et vos parati quia nescitis diem neque horam* M;
(*mar: Scriptura*).   200–201 Þat...Crist] Þat is seiþ Crist wakeþ M.
202 þis] þus M.   204 siþen þat] seþen it is so þat M.
206 (*mar: Sap'*).   209 þis] þe M.
213 into] vnto M.   216 hyȝe...pride] cursed lyif & orrible pride M.
217 in...apparayle] ouer costious in aparail M.   219 and(1)] *om.* M.
221–2 and þer wil þei] & of þese wole M.   223 Þese] þei M.
226 crafty] *om.* M.   228 Riȝt] & riȝt M.
230 mouyng] moueþ M.

him and counsel him to leue his synne, he seiþe he hopiþ to
haue repentaunce at his eend, and he shal be saue. But ofte it
fariþ by hem as þe Wise Man seiþe: *Sicut pisces capiuntur hamo,
et sicut aues capiuntur laqueo, sic capiuntur homines in tempore*
235 *malo.* Þat is: 'Riȝt as fisshes ben taken wiþ þe hoke, and briddis
wiþ þe snare, so ben suche men taken in yuel tyme'—þat is, in
dedly synne, for whiche synne þei shullen be dampnyd. Of
whiche men spekiþ also þe holy man, Job, þere he seiþe þus:
Ducunt in bonis dies suos, et in puncto ad inferna descendunt. Þat
240 is: 'Þei leden in lustis and in likingis her dayes, and in a poynte
þei fallen doune to helle.' For ofte tyme suche men setten to
hemsilf a terme of longe lijf, and when hem beste lusten to
lyue, in þe myddil of her dayes or bifore, sodenly þei ben taken
wiþ deeþ or þei ben war. Of suche spekiþ Dauid in þe Sauter,
245 and seiþe: *Viri sanguinum et dolosi non dimidiabunt dies suos.* Þat
is: 'Men of blood (þat is, synful men) and trecherous (þat is,
whiche done trecheries to God, and to her breþeren, and to her
owne soule) shullen vnneþe lyue halfe þe dayes whiche þei
shulden if þei had plesid God in vertuous lijf.' Of suche me
250 þinkiþ may / wel be seide þe wordis of Ysay þe prophete,   f. 6ᵛ
seying þus: *Non posuisti hec super cor tuum, neque recordata es
nouissimorum tuorum.* Þat is to sey: 'Þou hast not put þese
þingis vpon þi herte, neiþer hast had mynde on þi laste þingis.'
And þus, as I haue shewid, vncerteynte of deeþ is þe first
255 cause, as I seide, why men shulden haue myche her deeþ in
mynde.

Þe secounde cause I seide is for deeþ is so peynful. And þat
semyþ wel, and may be preued by ensaumple of Crist, and by
autorite, and bi reson. Oure Lorde Jesus Crist, boþe God and
260 man, whiche knew al þing by his godhed bifore it were done, a
litel tofore he wente to his passion, seying by his godhed hou
peynful þat deeþ wes whiche he shulde in a while aftur suffur
in his body, seide to ⟨h⟩is Fader or disciplis þese wordis:
Tristis est anima mea vsque ad mortem. Þat is: 'Sory or heuy is

---

232 he shal] þenne he shal M.   233 seiþe] seiþ eccⁱ 9 M;
(*mar:* Eccᵉˢ .9.).   234 *capiuntur(2)*] comprehenduntur M.
237 dampnyd] (*n.*).   238 (*mar:* Job);   spekiþ also] also spekeþ M.
243 bifore] tofore M.   244 (*mar: Nota. Later hand, red*).
245 (*mar:* .P'.).   247 her(1)] his M.   251 (*mar:* Ysay).
252 to sey] *om.* M.   254 vncerteynte] þe vncerteyne M.
257 (*mar: ij causa*);   (*mar: dethe ys peyneful. Later hand*).
260 whiche...bifore] whiche bi his godhede knew al þing tofore M.
261 tofore] bifore M.   263 Fader or disciplis] fader M.   264 (*mar: Christus*).

265 my lijf to þe deeþ.' Siþen þen þe lijf of oure Lorde Jesus wes so
peynful, þat died so wilfully and oonly for loue, hou peynful
þen shal oure deeþ be þat dyen aȝene oure wille and also for
synne!

Þat deeþ also is peyneful is preued by autorite of Seynt
270 Austyn, þere he seiþe þus: 'Deeþ is so yuel and so greuous þat
þe peyne may not be tolde ne be fled by ony reson.' Þerfore þe
Wise Man, seing deeþ so peynful, seide þus: *O mors, quam
amara est memoria tua.* Þat is: 'O deeþ, how bittur is þe mynde
of þe.' It is bittur to him þat heriþ it, and more bittur to hym
275 þat seeþ it, but moste bittur to hym / þat feliþ it. For þowȝ an   f. 7ʳ
hool man be in a house, and a man þat bigynnyþ to dye be
bisidis in anoþer, and a walle bitwix hem boþe, ȝit neþelese and
þe hool here þe noyse of þe sijȝhing, grynting, and gronyng of
hym þat drawiþ to þe deeþ, it is ful peynful for to here. But
280 myche more peynful is it to him if he go into þe house þere þe
seek liþe, and seeþ þe wannes and palenes of his visage, þe
staring of his yen, þe mouȝyng of his chere, and froþþing of his
mouþe, þe bolnyng of his breste, and betyng of his armys, and
many oþer signes þat he makiþ tofore his deeþ. But ȝit it is
285 most peynful to hym þat it feliþ, and þat may wel be schewid
by reson, me þinkiþ:

If it myȝt be so þat a tre whiche haþe many rotis were
plauntid inne at þi mouþe into þi body, and þe prinsepal rote
set in þi herte, and in euery lyme of þi body sette oon of þe
290 rotis, if it so were þen þat þis tre by gret violence shulde be
pullid oute at þi mouþe at onys, reson techiþ þat þis shulde be a
passyng peyne. Riȝt so fariþ it at mannys deeþ: þe lijf shal be
pullid oute sodeynly al at onys oute of his body, whiche
prinspaly is rotid in his herte, and also in alle his oþer parties,
295 þen mote þis nedis be a passyng grete peyne. And þus by þis
reson it semiþ þat deeþ is a ful grete peyne whiche, as I seide, is
þe secounde cause whi we shulden haue deeþ myche in mynde.

Þe þrid cause is, as I seide, for deeþ is so dredful. And þat
for þre / causis prinsepaly: þe first is for þe dredful siȝt of   f. 7ᵛ
300 fendis, whiche euery man shal se in þat houre; þe secounde is

265 to] toward M.   270 (*mar*: Austyn).   272 (*mar*: Sap').
273 *tua...deeþ*] *tua* O deþ M.   276 a(2)] anoþer M.
281 palenes] þe palenesse M.   282 froþþing] þe froþing M.
286 me þinkeþ] as me þinkeþ M.   287 haþe] hadde M;
(*mar*: *Exemplum*).   295 mote þis nedis] mut nedes þis M.
297 haue deeþ myche in mynde] haue here deþ in oure mynde M.
298 (*mar*: iij *causa*);   as] *om.* M.

for þe grete batayle þat shal be bytwene man and þe fende in
þat houre; þe þrid is for no man wote in certeyne where he shal
bycome aftre þat houre.

The first is, [as I seide], for þe dredful siȝt of fendis þat
305 shullen apere to a man in þat houre. Þat þei shullen so apere
semiþ wel, for in þe lijf of Seynt Martyn it is writen how þe
fende aperid to þat holy seynt at his dying, whiche hooly
chirche clepiþ *gemma sacerdotum*—þat is: þe precious ston of all
prestis. If þen he aperid to so hooly a man, hou myche more to
310 lower men! Also, as summe doctouris seyne, he aperid at þe
passion of Crist vpon þe crosse, to aspie if he myȝt ony þing
cacche holde in hym of synne. And þis wolde seme soþe by þe
wordis of oure Lorde Jesus Crist, þere he seiþe þus: *Venit enim
princeps mundi huius, etc*, 'Forsoþe, þe prince of þe worlde is
315 comen, and in me he haþe no þing'—þat is, of synne.

Þis apering of þe fend at þat tyme shal be to man ful dredful,
for þer is a doctour þat seiþe: *Sola visio demonum exsuperat
omne genus tormentorum*. Þat is: 'Oonly þe siȝt of fendis
ouerpassiþ al kynde of tormentis.' Þerfore Dauid þe prophete,
320 seing in spirit tofore þis grete drede þat he shulde haue in þat
siȝt, preying to þe Fader of heuen, seide þese wordis: *A timore
inimici eripe animam meam*. Þat is: not only fro þe power, but
'fro þe drede of þe enemy, Lorde delyuer / my soule.' And þus f. 8ʳ
þe dredful siȝt of fendis þat man shal haue in þe houre of his
325 deeþ is þe first cause whi deeþ is to drede.

Þe secound cause [is as] I seyde: for þe grete batayle þat shal
be bitwix man and þe feende in þat houre.

If it were so þat þere were set a day of batel wiþinne þe listis
bitwene þe and a grete champion, whiche were myȝty, sotil,
330 and slye, and had ouercomen many men in þat same batel, and
þat day were vnknowen to alle men but onely to þe kynge, and
þe kyng wolde not telle it vnto þe; and if þe batel were set vpon
þis condicion: þat if it were so þat þou were ouercomen, þou
shuldist be put into perpetual prison wiþouten ony remedi, and
335 if þou ouercome hym, þou shuldest be crowned kyng of a
glorious rewme, a grete fole were þou in þis case but if þou

304 as I seide] M, sey R;   (*mar*: .1.).   310 þe] *om*. M.
314 *huius etc*] *huius & in me non habet quicquam* M;   (*mar: Christus*).
316 to man] *om*. M.   317 (*mar: doctor*).
319 kynde] þe kynde M;   Dauid] *om*. M.   322 Þat] domine þat M.
323 (*Foot of f.7v. catchwords*: my soule).   326 is as] *om*. R.
328 (*mar: Exemplum*);   þe] *om*. M.
332 vnto] to M;   if] *om*. M.   336 if] *om*. M.

woldist euer drede þis day, when it wolde come, and make þe
redy to þis batayle, come when it shulde, in armoure and in al
þing þat longiþ to þis fiȝt, and aspie þe sotelteis of þin enemy,
340 in whiche he wolde deceyue þe. Þus it fariþ by euery man þat
lyuiþ here in þis worlde: þe day is set of oure deeþ, oonly
knowen vnto [God, in whiche] we shullen fiȝt wiþ þe s[otel   M.f. 56ʳ
fende, we mowen] it not astarte. Of þat b[atayle is writen þus
in] Gen. (3 chapitur [15]) where God s[eide to þe serpent:
345 'Þou] shalt aspye to his hele.' [In þe hele—þat is, þe laste] parte
of a man—is vnde[rstonde þe ende of his] / lijf, to þe whiche þe   f. 8ᵛ
deuel moste aspieþ, and þat tyme moste sharply fiȝtiþ, for he
wote wel if he lose him þen, he shal neuer aftur recouer hym.
And in þat batayle he haþe ouercomen many a man hertofore;
350 and whoso haþe grace to ouercome hym, he shal be crowned in
heuen wiþ þe crowne of lijf; and if he be ouercomen wiþ þe
feend, he shal be þrowen into helle, þere to wone foreuer.

Þen siþen þis batayle is so perilous, and þe day also
vnknowen, it were good [we] had it in mynde euer an aunter
355 when it comyþ, and arme vs ful surely for þis myȝty enemy,
and aspie and lerne his sotelteis by whiche he worchiþ moste.
The sikerist armour þat we may haue is of suche a knyȝt þat
haþ fouȝten wiþ him in his batayle, whiche armour wes so sure
þat he myȝt nowhere hirt him. Þis worshipful knyȝt is oure
360 Lorde Jesus Crist, boþe God and man, of whose armour spekiþ
þe apostle Poule, þere he seiþe þus: *Induite vos armatura Dei,*
etc. (*Eph.* 6.[11]). Þat is: 'Cloþe ȝou wiþ þe armour of God.'

The first parcel of þis armour is for to girde þe leendis in
truþe—[þat is, to restr]eyne wiþ abstinense, as wiþ a [girdel,   M.f. 56ᵛ
365 alle þe bodily] lymes wiþouteforþe [and alle þe power of þe]
soule wiþinneforþe [from alle maner of vicis]. Þe secound is þe
habur[ioun of riȝtwisnes—þat] is, to ȝyue to euery creatu[re þat
þat longiþ to him]. First to God, worship, / loue, and drede; to   f. 9ʳ
þi souereynis, boþe spiritual and temporal, subieccion and
370 obediens; to þin owne soule, holynes and keping of þe
comaundementis of God; to þi breþer[en], boþe frendis and
enemyes, loue and charite; to þi sogettis, teching and chastising; to þi pore breþeren, releuyng wiþ þi goodis. Þe þrid is þat

342 vnto] to M.   342–6 (R *damaged*).   351 wiþ(2)] to M.
352 into] to M.   353 þis batayle is] þese bata.les be M.
354 we] he R;   in mynde euer] euere in mynde M.
357 we] he M.   360 boþe] *om.* M;   whose] þe whiche M.
362 *Eph*] ad Eph M.   363 (*mar: Armatura dei*).   364–8 (R *damaged*).
371 breþeren] breþer R.   373 (*mar: .iij.*).

alle þe affeccions of þi soule (þat is: þi goostly fete) be set
375 prinsepaly to preche truly þe gospel of Crist, if þou be a prest,
and if þou be none, þat þi loue be set to rule prinsepaly þi lijf
aftur þe holy gospel. Þe fourþe is þat þou take þe sheelde of
true byleue, of whiche þre corneris shulde be peyntid wiþ þe
Fader and Sone and þe Holy Gooste, and wiþinne alle oþer
380 articlis of byleue, and fast enerued wiþ senous of charite. Þe
fifte is þe helme or basnet of hope—þat is, þat a man, þorow þe
mercy of God and þorow his owne meritis, haue tristi hope to
be saued. Þe sixte is þe swerde of þe worde of God, of whiche
þe feend is sore aferde, for wiþ þat he wes ouercomen in alle his
385 þre batels þat he toke aȝeyn oure Lord Jesus Crist. Þerfore take
[it] in þi honde and suffur him [neuer] come w[iþinne þe]   M.f.
poynte, for al his des[ire wole be for to come wiþ]inne þis
swerde—þat is, [wiþ sotel argumentis and] sly to deceyue þe
sy[mple soule to misvnder]stonde þe worde of G[od, and so to
390 bringe him in]to dispeyre, and þen he h[aþ þe victorie.

Þe] / first argument þat he wil make is þis: 'Þou hast done   f. 9ᵛ
many grete and orible synnis wiþouten noumbre, fro þe tyme
þat þou kouþist synne into þis day, and now þou hast no space
to do satisfaccion for hem alle. For þis is þe last houre, and
395 God is riȝtwis and wole not þat ony synne be vnponyshid;
wherfore by Goddis riȝtwisnes þou most nedis be dampnid!'

Here be war of þis sotil feend, and suffur him nouȝt wiþ þis
sleiȝt to come wiþinne þi swerdis poynte. Strecche oute þi
swerde in þis maner, and put it boldely into his face: 'Cursid
400 fend! I bileue fully þat God is riȝtwis, as þou seist. But his
mercy passiþ hye aboue, and he seiþe by his prophete þat he
wil not þe deeþ of a synful man, but more þat he be conuertid
and lyue. And also he seiþe, in anoþer plase, þat ʿinˊ whateuer
houre a synful man repentiþ him and makiþ sorow for his
405 synne, he shal be safe. And þis shewid wel in dede þe merciful
Lorde in coumforte of alle synful men, hanging on þe crosse, to
þe þefe þat henge bisidis hym, þat in þe last houre of his deeþ,
seing his grete sorow þorow meke taking [of h]is peyne, þat   M.f
⟨he⟩ grauntid him not oonly þat [he askede him], but
410 [wiþo]uten ony oþer peyne to be [wiþ him þat day in blisse.

---

375 Crist] god M.
378 þe] om. M.
386–91 (R damaged).
391 (mar: Primum argumentum).
399 (mar: responsio).
404 a] þat a M.

377 gospel] gospe M;
381 (mar: .v.).

(mar: .iiij.).

383 (mar: .vi.).
388 þe] a M.
392 þe] om. M.
400 is...seist] as þou seist is riȝtwes M.
408–15 (R damaged).

And I w]ote wel þat he is curtey[s ʒet þis day, and euer wole] be
wiþouten eend, and so [I hope to his mercy for] alle my synnis
if I ha[ue sorow.' And þus kepe him a]t þe poynte, and he shal
[neuer do þe harm.

415 T]he secound argument þat / he wole make is þis: 'I wes f. 10ʳ
dampnid, as þou wotis wil, for one synne al oonly; and þou hast
done synnis vnnoumbrable as greuous or more greuous þen
euer wes þat. Þen if God wolde dampne me, þat did but oonly
one [synne], and saue þe, þat hast done so many, he most nedis
420 be vnriʒtwis, whiche he may not be. Wherfore, `of´ Goddis
riʒtwisnes þou most nedis be dampnid!'

   ʒit holde hym oute at þe poynte, and answere him in þis
wise: 'Cursid feend! Þe synne þat þou didest, þou didest it of
þin owne malice, and þe synne þat I did, I did it at þe stiring of
425 þee, enuyous feend, þat lyist in wayte nyʒt and day vpon me,
for grete enuy þat þou hast þat I shulde restore þe place þat þou
fel fro; and also at þe stiring of my fleishe, fro whiche I may not
fle away; and at þe stiring of þe worlde, þat is euere before myn
yʒen. And for þis cause, þe blessid and merciful Lord, aʒen
430 whom I offendid, toke my kynde to saue me, and neuer þi
kynde to saue þee. And þus I hope of his mercy to be sauid, for
alle my synnis, þereas þou, cursid fende, shalt be dampnid for
þat one.'

   The þrid reson þat he wil make is þis: 'I wes þe hyist aungel
435 in heuen, and knew þere þe priu[eteis] of God. And þere I
knew tofore who shul[lde be damp]nid [and who shulde be
sauid, and among oþer I knew þat þou shuldest be dampned],
and þat þat is tofore ordeyned of [God may] not be chaungid,
wherfore þou mo[st nedis] be dampned!'

440 ʒit take God to þin helpe and [stonde] stifly in þis batel, and
holde hym at þe sw[erdis poynte], / and þou shalt not feyle to f. 10ᵛ
haue þe better. Sey to him in þis maner: 'False feend! Þis haþe
euer be þi custom, wiþ lesyngis to bigile man; for, as Crist
witnesiþ of þe, þou arte a lyer and fader of lesyngis. For wiþ þi
445 lesyngis þou deceyuedist oure auncestouris in paradise, and
wiþ þi lesyngis þou woldist haue deceyued oure Lorde Jesus
Crist. Þerfore I wonder not, þow wiþ þi lesyngis þou woldist
deceyue me. False feend! Þere þou lyist, where þou seist þat

---

416 wotis wil] wost wel M.   419 synne] om. R.   422 (mar: Responsio).
423 þou didest it] is M.   424 malice] malice wiþouten ani oþere stirynge M;
I did it] was M.   425 wayte] awaite M.   429 yʒen And] om. M.
430 þi] þe M.   434 (mar: ⟨?⟩ argument⟨um⟩).   435–41 (R damaged).
436–7 and...dampned] om. R.   440 stifly] stif M.

þou knew in heuen who shulde be dampnyd, and who shulde
450 be saued; for þou knewist not þere þyn owne dampnacion, and
if þou knew not þin owne dampnacion, myche more þou knew
not myne. And so, for alle þi cursid lesyngis, I hope to þe
mercy of God þat þou shalt neuer bringe me in dispeire, as þou
woldist.' And þus, if þou ouercome him in þese þre, þorow
455 vertu of þe Trinite, he shal turne his backe and fle, and neuer
eft tempt þee, and þus þou shalt haue þe glorious victory of þis
dredful batel.

And þis perilous batayle whiche man shal haue at his deeþ is
þe secound cause, as I seide, whi þat deeþ is dredful. [Þe þrid M.f.
460 cause whi þat deeþ is dredful] is for no man wote in certeyn
where he shal bycome after þat he [is] deed.

If it were so þat þou shuldist be exilid ou[te of þe] rewme in
whiche þou were borne and fed [aftur a certe]yn day, and þis
day were in no mannys kno[wyng bu]t oonly in þe kyngis wille;
465 and also if þou [knew no]t after þou were exilid into what londe
þou [shuldist] go, wheþer þere as þou shuldist be bilouyd, / or f. 1▸
þere as þou shuldist be hatid, and in þis case þou woldist stonde
in grete drede and, but if þou were a verrey fole, euermore
ordeyne for þi goyng. In þis same case is euery man
470 in þis worlde. Alle we shullen be exilid oute of þis worlde in
whiche we han ben borne and fed after þe day of oure deeþ,
whiche is oonly knowen to God, and þat day is fully sette,
whiche we may by no wey passe. And wheþer we shullen to
heuen or helle, in whiche we shullen be louid or hatid, it is
475 vnknowen to ony man here, but is reseruid til afturwarde. Þis
witnesiþ wel þe Wise Man in his boke, þere he seiþ þus: *Sunt
iusti atque sapientes, et opera eorum in manu Dei; et tamen nescit,
etc.* Þat is: 'Þer ben riȝtwis and wise men, and her werkis ben in
þe hondis of God; and neþeles, a man wote not wheþer he be
480 worþi loue or hate, but alle þingis ben kepte vncerteyne into
tyme to comynge aftur.' And siþ it stondiþ wiþ vs þus
perilously, me þinkiþ we han cause to drede oure deeþ.

Þus þen, for þese þre causis þat I haue shewid ȝow (þat deeþ
is so vncerteyn, so peynful, and so dredful), I counsel, as I

453 in] into M.   457–8 batel...batayle] bataile & perelous M.
459–60 Þe...dredful] *om.* R.   461–66 (R *damaged*).   462 so] *om.* M.
467 be hatid] be bihated M;   (f.11r. *upper mar: dies iudicij*).
472 whiche] þe whiche M.   474 helle] to helle M;
be louid] be biloued M (*cf.* 467).   475 til] to M.
476 (*mar:* Sap').   477 *sapientes*] *multi sapientes* M;
tamen nescit etc] *Nescit homo vtrum amore an odio dignus sit sed omnia
reseruantur incerta in futurum* M.   478 men] manie men M.

485 seide at þe byginnyng in oure teme, haue mynde on þis laste
þing—þat is, on þi deeþ, whiche is þe first þat I spake of.

The secound last þing whiche I spake of at þe bygynnyng,
þat a man shulde haue in mynde, is þe day of þe general
iugement of God, whiche shal be at þe last day of þis worlde.
490 Of whiche / last day spekiþ Crist in þe gospel (*Jo*.6): *Ego* f. 11ᵛ
resuscitabo eum in nouissimo die. Þat is: 'I shal arayse hym in þe
last day.' And Martha also, in þe gospel of Jon, seiþe: *Scio quia*
resurget in resurreccione in nouissima die. 'I wote wel `þat´ he
shal arise in rising in þe last day.'

495 Þis last day shulde euer be had in mynde, and specialy for
þre causis: oon is for þe grete accounte þat shal be made þat
day; þe secound is for þe dredful apering of þe iuge, and of
oþere þat shullen apere þat day; þe þrid is for þe dredful
sentense þat þe iuge shal ȝyue vpon hem þat shullen be
500 dampned in þat day.

First, I sey, for þe grete acounte þat shal be ȝyuen þat day.
And wel may it be seyde 'grete', for þre þingis:

First, for þe lorde is grete þat shal here þese acountis. For as
Jon seiþe in þe Apocalipis: *Rex regum, etc.* Þat is: 'He is kynge
505 of alle kyngis, and lorde of alle lordis.' He is so grete, as Dauid
seiþe, þat 'of his greetnes is none eende.' He is so myȝty þat
noþing may aȝeynstonde his wille, as Holy Writ witnessiþ: *In*
ditione tua cuncta sunt posita, etc. Þat is: 'In þi comaundementis
alle þingis ben put, and þere is no þing may aȝenstonde þi
510 wille.' He is [so] wise þat no þing may be hid fro hym:
Sapientie eius non est numerus. 'Of his wisdom is no noumbur.'
He is so riche hym nediþ no þing: *Dominus vniuersorum tu es.*
'Of alle þingis þou arte lorde.' He is so riȝtwis þat no þing at
þat day shal boo`w´ hym fro his purpos, for Dauid seiþe:
515 *Justitia eius manet in seculum seculi.* 'His / riȝtwisnes dwelliþ f. 12ʳ
wiþouten eend.'

It shal also be grete for þe grete noumbre of peple þat shal
acounte in þat day, for no man shal be þere absen[t] þat euer
wes or euer shal be. For as Seynt Poule seiþe: *Omnes nos*

---

487 (*mar: Secundum principale*).   490 (*mar:* Jo.6.).
492 seiþe] seiþ jo. 11 M;   (*mar:* Jo.12).   493 he] I M.
498 apere] apere þere M.   501 (*mar: Prima causa*).
504 *regum etc* Þat is] *regum & dominus dominantium* M;   (*mar:* Apoc').
507 aȝeynstonde] wiþstonde M;   witnessiþ] witnesseþ hit M.
508 *tua*] *tua domine* M;
posita...is] *posita et non est qui possit resistere voluntati tue* M.
509 aȝeynstonde] wᵗstonde M.   510 so] also R, M.   511 (*mar:* dd).
518 absent] absence R.   519 (*mar:* Ro'.14).

520 *manifestari oportet, etc.* Þat is: 'Alle we moten nedis be shewid
opunly to þe sete of dome of our Lorde [Jesus] Crist, þat euery
man telle forþe þe propur werkis of his body as he wrouȝt hem,
wheþer þei ben good or yuel.'

In þat day, to alle astatis þe domesman shal sey þese wordis:
525 *Redde raccionem villicacionis tue, etc.* Þat is: 'Ȝeelde acounte of
þi baylye.' First, prelatis and prestis, for þei weren hyest heedis
of Cristis chirche, shullen ȝeelde acounte of her baylie. First,
hou þei camen into her prelacye or ordre: wheþer by symony or
true title of God, wheþer by þe dore as a true heerde, or by þe
530 rofe as a false þefe; wheþer þei haue led her lijf aftur þe rule of
Goddis lawe, in good ensaumple to her sugettis; wheþer þei
han dispendid þe goodis of her chirchis, of whiche þei weren
ordeyned of God procuratouris for pore men and not lordis,
vpon suche pore nedy men whiche God haþe lymytid in his
535 gospel; wheþer also þei han bisile, trule, and freli, prechid
Goddis lawe to þe peple, wiþoute feynyng, faging, flatering, or
favoure of plesaunce of þe peple, or profijt of þe purse.

Temporal / lordis also shullen þere ȝeelde her acountis.   f. 12
First, hou þei han lyued in her owne personys in vertuous
540 ensaumple to oþer; hou also þei han gouernyd her wyues and
her children, her meyne and her housholde, and her pore
tenauntis; hou þei han stonden by þe gospel, and true prechouris þerof; hou þei han chastisid false prechouris and
antecristis disciplis þat disceyuen þe peple in her bileue and in
545 her temporal goodis; hou þei han holpen wydouse and faderles
children in her riȝt, þat no man wrongfully oppressid hem
aȝeyn þe lawe of God.

Þe comoune peple also shullen acounte þere, boþe marchauntis, artificeris, and laboreris of þe erþe. First, hou þei han
550 kepte þe comaundementis of God; her fyue wittes wel dispendid; and fulfillid þe dedis of mercy; and lyued in loue and
charite to God and her breþeren, wiþoute falshed or disseyte
ony of hem to oþer; and vertuously tauȝt her children vp fro
her ȝouþe.

520 *oportet etc*] *oportet ante tribunal domini nostri christi vt referat vnus
quisque propria corporis prout gessum siue bonum siue malum* M.
521 Jesus] *om.* R.   525 *etc*] *om.* M;   (*mar:* luc').   526 (*mar: Nota*).
529 as a true heerde] *om.* (*but a space here in MS.*) M.
530 false] *om.* M.   532 of...weren] as þei were M.
538 þere ȝeelde] ȝelde þere M.   540 wyues] wyif M.
548 also] *om.* M;   þere] þere firste M.   549 First] *om.* M.

555 If alle þese þre parties han gouerned hem in þis wise, þei
shullen haue heuen to here mede, as God haþ bihiȝt: *Qui bona*
egerunt, etc. But if it be so þen þat prelatis and prestis holden
not þis rule þat I haue rehersid, as Goddis lawe techiþ, but ben
more prouder þen ony temporal men in costious aray for her
560 owne bodies; and in grete aray in hallis and in chaumbris boþe;
and sitten shynyngly at mete, as it were a duke, wiþ rial
cupbordis arayid of siluer and of golde; and euery page in her
hous / serued in siluer; and at euery drauȝt þat þei drinken,   f. 13ʳ
men knelen as to a god; and fynden many wast[i] squyers of þe
565 goodis of þe chirche, þat done ful litel goode but bringen forþ a
disshe; and many fat horse in stable, and gay gilte sadlis, and
myche oþer nyce aparayle þat longiþ not to her astate;
   If þei ben also wraþeful men and enuyous boþe—and
specialy to þo men þat vndernymmen hem of her synne, and
570 tellen hem her office þat longiþ to her astate, and prechen truly
to her sogettis as þei shulden do—and if þei in her [wraþþe]
curse suche men, and in her foule enuy [falsely] disclaundren
hem, and pursuen hem, and prisonen hem, and perauntur to þe
deþ;
575 If þei ben also coueitouse men to gidre worldly goodis to
hepe hem togidre and helpe ful litel þe pore, but to bye hem
beneficis and prouenders and oþer hye astatis, and make grete
her kyn wiþ þe goodis of þe chirche, þorow purchase or
mariage or summe grete office;
580 If þei ȝiuen [hem] to glotony to fede fat her fleishe wiþ
costious metis and delicious drinkis of diuerse wynis, whatsoeuer þei coste, sittyng as longe at mete as þow þei were
kyngis, wiþ myrþis of mynstralsie and many oþer iapis, and þe
sely pore men abiden at þe ȝate to be fed wiþ her trenchouris
585 þat comen from her borde;
   And if þei lyuen in slouþe, in longe lying in bedde, and aftir
momole her matyns and her mynde þeron ful litel, and aftir
occupie þe / day in ydel talis telling, or of tretis of þe rewme, or   f. 13ᵛ

---

556 (*mar: Scriptura*).   557 *etc*] *ibunt in vitam eternam* M;
prelatis and prestis] & preestis & prelatis M;   (*mar*: 1).   559 ony] *om.* M.
561 mete] þe mete M.   562 of(2)] *om.* M.
564 knelen] knelinge adoun M;   wasti] waste R.   565 þe] *om.* M.
566 and(1)] *om.* M.   568 If] ȝet M.   569 specialy] principali M.
571 wraþþe] *om.* R.   572 foule] ful M;   falsely] cursidly R.
575 If] ȝet M.   576 hepe] helpe M;   helpe...pore] helpe þe pore ful litel M.
580 If] ȝet M;   hem] *om.* R.   581 costious] deliciouse M.
583 of] *om.* M.   586 if] ȝet M.   588 þe(1)] al þe M.

typingis of be3onde, or talinge of her temporalities, or tifeling
590 wiþ ladies, and touche l`i´tel of Goddis lawe for þei mowne not
tent þerto;

If þei lyuen þen in leccherie, priue or aperte, þorow her ydel
lijf, and her lusty fare of hye wynis and hote spicis, and nyce
daliaunce, and spenden þus her tyme in þe seuen dedly synnis,
595 harde veniaunce wole come to suche at þe day of her acountis,
for mys spending of her hye degre, and her yuel ensaumple.
And of suche spekiþ þe Wise Man þere he seiþ þus: *Iudicium
durissimum, etc.* Þat is: 'Harde dome shal be to prelatis þat
lyuen in þis maner.'

600 If lordis also, and kny3tis, spenden her goodis in costy aray
passing her astate, and þerfore waxen extorcioneris on þe pore
peple, and maytenen þe enemyis of Cristis holy gospel, and
haten true prechouris þat wolen telle hem þe soþe, and suffren
her children and her meyne to despise God wiþ proude
605 boostyng and lyes, and al torende him wiþ oþis, alle suche
my3ty men at þe grete acounte my3tily shullen be peyned, as
witnessiþ Holy Writ: *Potentes potenter, etc.* þat is: 'My3tily
my3ti men shullen suffur tormentis.'

If ony of þe comyn peple (þat is, þe þrid degre) haue not
610 loued God in her lijf, ne kepte his hooly heestis, but wastid her
wittis aboute worldly goodis, and not spende hem vpon / pore,   f. 1
but þere as [wes no nede, and] lyued oute of charite to her ny3e
nei3boris, and mayntenyd her children to dispise her elders, for
whiche God sendiþ pestilence to make hem short lyued, suche
615 vnprofitable seruantis at þe day of acounte shullen be þrowen
into þe fire, as Crist hymselfe seiþe: 'Þe vnprofitable seruauntis
þrowiþ fer into vtturmore derkenes, þere as shal be weping of
y3en and gnasting of teeþ.'

The þrid cause whi þis acounte may be seyde grete is þis: for
620 in þat day alle men shullen reken of alle þing þat euer þei diden
in her lyue, in þou3t, worde, and ded.

Þat men shullen reken of her þou3tis seiþe þe Wise Man
(*Sap.* 1.[9]): *In cogitacionibus impij erit interrogatio.* Þat is: 'In
þe þou3tis of þe wickid man shal be asking.' Þat men shullen
625 reken of her wordis seiþe Crist hymself in þe gospel (*Mt.*

589 tifeling] triflinge M.   592 If] 3et M;   her] *om.* M.
597 Man] man Sap' 6º M.   598 *etc] hijs qui fiet* M;   (*mar:* Sap' .6.).
600 (*mar:* 2).   601 on] vpon M.   605 and lyes] *om.* M.
607 Writ] writt Sap'.6. M;   *etc] tormenta pacientur* M;   (*mar:* Sap' .6.).
607–8 My3tily...men] Mi3ti men mi3tili M.   609 (*mar:* 3).
612 wes...and] no nede wes R;   ny3e] *om.* M.   616 into] into þe M.
619 acounte] doom M.   624 men] manie M.

12.[36]): *De omne verbo otioso, etc.* 'Euery idel word (of whiche comyþ no fruyt) whiche men [speken], þei shullen acount at þe day of dome.' And þat men shullen answere of her dedis spekiþ Seint Poule þere he seiþ þus [(2. *Cor.* 5.[10]): *Omnes nos*
630 *manifestari, etc.*] 'Alle we moten be made open tofore þe trone of oure Lorde Jesus Crist, þat euery man telle forþe þe propre dedis of his body, as he haþ done hem, wheþer good or yuel.'

Siþen þen, as þese autoriteis preue, no þing shal `be´ vnrekenyd in þat day, and no þing may be hid fro þe iuge, for
635 alle þingis ben nakid and open to þe yen / of God, þen me þinke f. 14ᵛ it were nedful þat alle men dredden gretely þat day [and had `it´ gretely in mynde to make redy her bookes aȝen þat grete day].

The secound cause why þat last day shulde be had in mynde is for þe ferful siȝt of hem þat shullen apere in þat day. For as
640 þe doctor Januensis rehersiþ vpon þe gospellis: þat aboue men in þat day shal apere þe iuge þat is offendid, shewing hymself ful wraþful to hem þat shullen be dampned.

Vnderneþe shal be þe blake hydous pit of helle, open and redy to swolowe hem þat shullen be dampned. On þe riȝt side,
645 alle a mannys synnis, redy to accuse him. On þe lift side, feendis wiþouten noumbre, redy to drawe him to his peyne. Byhinde shal alle þe worlde be set on fire. Bifore, strong aungels putting hem bacwarde to helle. Wiþinne forþe, a mannys owne conscience biting ful bitturly, and holy seyntis
650 approuyng þe sentence of þe domesman, and alle wickid men openly knowing þe synnis of hem þat shullen be dampned.

Alas! when þe wrecchid synful man is þus biset on euery side, whider shal he fle? Vpwarde he may not, for þere is þe domesman, and oute of his mouþe goþe a swerde two eggid, as
655 Seint Jon seiþe in þe Apocalips, for ferdfulnes of whos face þei shullen sey to grete hillis and smale: 'Falliþ doune vpon vs, and hiliþ vs!' Neyþer to `þe´ riȝt side may he fle, for as Seynt Ber[nard] seiþe: 'Þere shullen be his synnis redy togider, speking and seying, "Þou hast / done vs. We ben þi werkis, and f. 15ʳ
660 we shullen not leue þee, but we shullen go wiþe þee to þe dome".' Neyþer to þe lift side, for þere shullen be feendis accusing, for as Seint Austin seiþe: 'Þen þe feendis shal be redy, rehersing what we han done, and in what day and in what plase we han synnid, and al þat euer we shulden haue done.' Ne

---

626 *etc*] þat is of M. 627 speken] *om.* R. 629–30 2 Cor...*etc*] *om.* R;
(*mar*: Cor'.14.). 636–7 and...day] *om.* R. 638 (*mar*: .ij. *causa*).
640 (*mar*: Januens). 647 on] a M. 648 hem] him M.
649 holy] alle holi M. 650 approuyng] axinge M.
652 þe] *om.* M. 654 of his] whos M. 655 (*mar*: Apoc').
657 hiliþ] hideþ M; as] *om.* M; (*mar*: .B'.).

665 he may not hide himself wiþinne himselfe, for þere is þe worme
of conscience remorsing, as Ysay seiþe (vlt' chapitur [24]):
'The worme of hem shal not dye.' Neiþer he may fle aȝeyne
into þe worlde, for þere is fire brennyng, settyng on fire al þat is
lafte, as Dauid seiþe in þe Sauter: 'Fire shal go bifore hym.'
670 Þen is þere no plase lefte suche synful wrecchis to fle to, but
oonly falle doune into þe foule fournes of þe fire of helle.

The þrid cause why þat þe last dredful day shulde be had in
mynde is for þe dredful sentense of iugement þat þe iustise shal
ȝyue þat day to hem þat shullen be dampnyd. For alle þe peynis
675 þat God sendiþ to a man in þis worlde is but as a curtesie and
esy chastising, as þe fader chastisiþ his tender childe wiþ a fewe
russhis or wiþ a litel ȝerde. Þe peynes of purgatory ben as a
staf, wiþ whiche a man betiþ hys son when he comyþ to
[grettere] age. But for in þese two chastisingis is [coumfort and
680 hope of] mercy, þerfore seiþ Dauid: '⟨Virga tua⟩, etc. 'Þi
ȝerde,' he seiþe, 'and þi staf, þei han coumfortid me.' But þe
dredful sentense of God, þe riȝt/ful iuge, in þat day shal be as   f. 15
an yren scourge, as Dauid seiþe: Reges eos in virga ferrea. 'Þou
shalt gouerne hem in an yren ȝerde, and as þe vessel of a potter
685 þou shalt al toberst hem togider, whiche may neuer be repeyrid
aȝeyn.' Of þis scourge, Crist spekiþ hymself in þe gospel of
Matheu, where he seiþe þus: Discedite a me, etc. 'Departiþ awey
fro me, `ȝe cursid´, into þe fire þat euer shal laste, whiche is
arayed tofore to þe deuel and his aungels.'
690 In whiche yren scourge shal be seuen knottis, þat whoso is
beten wiþ hem shal be wounden wiþouten ony heling. Þe first
knotte of þis scourge `is´ a bittir puttyng oute, whiche is notid
in þis worde 'departiþ'. Þe secound knot is departing fro God,
whiche is notid in þis worde 'fro me'. Þe þrid knot is þe cu`r´se
695 of God, whiche is notid in þis worde 'ȝe cursid'. Þe fourþe knot
is þe closing inne wiþ bitter peyne, whiche is notid in þis worde
'into þe fire'. Þe fifþe knot is dispeire of delyueraunce, whiche
is notid in þis worde 'euerlasting'. Þe sixt knot is þe araying
tofore of peyne þat is assignid, whiche is notid in þis worde

666 vlt' chapitur] vlt' vermis eorum non extinguetur M.
668 into] to M;   on] a M.   669 lafte] lyf;   (mar: dd).
671 falle] to falle M.   672 þe] om. M.   678 wiþ] om. M.
679 grettere] grete R;   coumfort...of] hope & R.   680 (mar: dd);
etc] & baculus tuus ipsa me consolata sunt þi ȝerde & þi staf he seiþ M.
683 an] om. M;   (mar: dd);   ferrea] ferrea etc M.
684 an] om. M;   þe vessel of a] a vessel of M.   685 al toberst] alto breke M.
687 Discedite...etc] om. M.   688 ȝe cursid] (mar.).   689 his] to his M.
690 (mar: Nota de vij nodis flagelli nostri dei).
695 þe fourþe] þe fourþe þe fourþe M.   696 wiþ] a M.

700 'whiche is arayed tofore'. Þe seuent knot is euerlasting felouship of feendis, whiche is notid in þis worde 'wiþ þe deuel and
his aungelis'. *Hic* Thomas, *De Veritate Theo[logie]*, *libro* 1, *ca.*
18.

⟨Wiþ⟩ þese seuen knottis of þis dred/ful sentense, alle þo   f. 16ʳ
705 shullen be beeton wiþinne þat day þat lyueden and endeden in
þe seuen deedly synnys, for þei ben peynis iustly acordant wiþ
hem.

Þe first knot is aȝeyn proude men, for God shal sey þat day
to hem: 'For as myche as ȝe weren proude and rebel, and
710 dispisid me and my lawe and þe trewe techers þerof (for whoso
dispisiþ hem, despisiþ me; *qui vos spernit, me spernit*), [þerfore]
I shal iustly put ȝow awey fro me and fro glorie, smyting ȝow
wiþ þe first knot of my scourge, seying "Go awey!"'

Þe secound knot is aȝeyns enuyous men. 'For as myche as ȝe
715 han longe rotid enuy in ȝoure hertis, þorow þe whiche [ȝou]
cursiden and waried ȝoure breþeren and wolden haue on hem
no mercy, þerfore I shal iustly punysshe ȝou wiþ þe peyne
acordaunt to ȝoure trespas, smyting ȝou wiþ þe secounde
knot—þat is, wiþ my curse.'

720 Þe þrid knot is aȝeyns wraþful men. 'For as myche as ȝe, for
[a] litel trespas, brenneden hote in ȝoure hertis wiþ þe fire of
wraþe aȝeyn ȝoure breþeren, þorow whiche ȝe chidden,
sclaundreden, þratten, and fouȝten and slowen hem, þerfore I
shal iustly punysshe ȝou wiþ peyne acordant to ȝoure trespas,
725 smyting ȝow wiþ þe þrid knot of my scourge, þrowing ȝow into
þe fire of helle.'

Þe fourþe knot is aȝeyne slowful men. 'For as myche as ȝe
contynuid alwey in ȝoure synnis and list neuer to rise / to   f. 16ᵛ
penaunce, but if ȝe myȝt euer haue lyued, euer ȝe wolden haue
730 lyued in synnis, þerfore I shal ponysshe ȝou wiþ peyne
acordant to ȝoure trespas, smyting ȝow wiþ þe fourþe knot—
þat `is´, wiþ euerlasting peyne.'

Þe fifþe knot is aȝeyns glotorous men. 'For as myche as ȝe
weren euer redy to ete and drinke, erly and late, as wel on nyȝt
735 as on day, as an vnresonable beest, þerfore I shal punysshe ȝou
wiþ peyne acordant to ȝoure trespas, smyting ȝow wiþ þe fifþe

---

702 *Hic...ca.*18] *om.* M.   706 wiþ] for M.
708 (*mar*: .1.).   709 (*mar*: *quia tu scientiam*).
710 þerof] þerof *Quia tu scientiam repulisti ego repellam te* M.
711 þerfore] *om.* M.   714 (*mar*: .ij.).   720 (*mar*: .iij.).
721 a] *om.* R.   722 whiche] þe whiche M.   727 (*mar*: .iiij.).
730 synnis] synne M.   733 (*mar*: .v.).

knot of my scourge—þat is, wiþ peyne þat is redy arayed
tofore.'

Þe sixt knot is aȝeyns leccherous men. 'For as myche as ȝe
740 leften clennes of my chastite, and chesid to ⟨ȝow⟩ þe foule filþe
of leccherie, boþe in þouȝt, worde, and dede, and þe vnclene
cumpany niȝt and day of suche persoones þat loueden it,
þerfore I shal punysshe ȝow wiþ peyne acordant to ȝoure
trespas, smyting ȝow wiþ þe sixt knot of my scourge, putting
745 ȝou to þe foule felouship of þe deuel.'

Þe seuent knot is to beete wiþ coueitous men. 'For as myche
as ȝe gederid togider grete hepis of golde and siluer, and þouȝt
þat ȝe hadden neuer ynow, and when I nedid in my membris ȝe
wolden not breke þat grete cumpany to parte wiþ me þerof,
750 þerfore I shal punnysshe ȝow wiþ peyne acordant to ȝoure
trespas, smyting ȝou wiþ þe seuenþe knot of my scourge,
put/ting ȝou into þe vnnoumbrable hepe of `þe´ deuelis   f. 17ʳ
aungelis.'

Þese seuen wordis þat I haue rehersid of þis hidous iugement
755 beren also ful answeris to alle þo þat shullen be dampned in alle
maner of preyers þat þei myȝt make to þe iustice in þat day:

For þow þei wolden prey þus: 'Now Lorde, siþen þorow oure
deser`uyng´, as we seen wel, iustly we shullen be
dampned, lete vs haue oure peyne—if it be þi wille—in þi siȝt,
760 þat þe coumfortable siȝt of þee may make vs bere oure peyne
`þe´ more esely,' herto may þe iustice answere by þe first worde
of his sentence, seying: Discedite a me. Þat is: 'Þat shal not be,
but goþe oute of my siȝt, neuer to se me more.'

When þei sene þat þis preyer may not be grauntid hem, þow
765 þei wolden prey ferþermore in þis maner: 'Now Lorde, siþen it
is so þat we shullen be dampned and go oute of þi siȝt and
neuer se þe more, gracious Lorde—if it be þi wille—ȝiue vs þi
blessing or we go, þat we may fare þe better in what plase þat
we comen,' herto may þe iustise answere by þe secound worde
770 of his sentense, seying: Maledicti. Þat is: 'Goþe oute of my siȝt,
neuer to se me more, wiþ my curse acursid.'

---

739 (mar: .vj.).   740 ȝow...filþe] ȝou filþe of þe foule synne M.
746 (mar: .vij.).   748 þat] om. M.
752 þe...þe] þe fyir vn⟨?⟩erable help of M;   þe(2)] (mar.);
(foot of f.16v. catchwords: ting ȝou).   755 beren] beþ M.
756 of] om. M.   762 Þat(2)] it M.   770 Goþe] goþ awey M.

When þei seen ȝit þat þis wole not be grauntid, þow þei
wolden prey forþermore in þis maner: 'Now Lorde, siþen it `is´
so þat we dampned wrecchis shullen go out of þi siȝt and neuer
775 se þe more, and we shullen also go wiþ þi curse, good Lorde—
if it be / þi wille—graunte vs þat we may be þere as we shullen   f. 17ᵛ
haue none oþer peyne, siþen þis is peyne grete ynow, to lese þi
siȝt, and haue þi curse,' herto may þe iustise answere by þe þrid
worde of his sentence, seying: *In ignem.* Þat is: 'Nay, I wole not
780 so; but goþe oute of my siȝt, neuer to se me more, and wiþ my
curse, into [þe] fire.'

When þei seen ȝit þat her bone is not grauntid, if þei wolden
be har`dy´ and aske ȝit ferþermore in þis maner: 'Now Lorde,
siþen it is so þat we woful dampned wrecchis shullen go oute of
785 þi siȝt, and wiþ þi curse, into þe fire, merciful Lorde, if we dar
aske þe—if it be þi wille—þow we shullen be þere an hundrid
ȝere, or a þousand ȝere, or a þousand þousand ȝere, ȝyue vs
[grace at þe laste] þat oure peyne may haue an eend, so þat we
may come oute and come to þi blisse,' herto may þe iustise
790 answere and sey by þe fourþe worde of his sentense, þat is: [*In*]
eternum. Þat is: 'So shal it not be; but goþe oute of my siȝt,
neuer to se me more, wiþ my curse, into þe fire þat euer shal
laste.'

ȝit þow þei wolden aske ferþermore: 'Now Lorde, siþen it is
795 so þen þat we shullen go oute of þi siȝt, wiþ þi curse, into þe
fire þat neuer shal haue eend, piteous Lorde, graunte vs—if it
be þi wille—siþen þe peyne aftur we come þerto shal endure so
longe, þat we may haue space or tarying tofore, an hundrid
ȝere or whatso þe likiþ, in þe whiche we may be re/fresshid   f. 18ʳ
800 tofore þat þis peyne be arayed to vs,' herto may þe hiȝe iustise
answere by þe fifþe worde of his sentense, seying: *Qui prepar-
atus est.* Þat is: 'Nay, ȝe shullen not fare so wel; but goþe oute
of my siȝt, cursid, into þe fire þat euer shal last, whiche is redile
arayed tofore, wiþouten ony tarying.'

805 ȝit þow þei wolden not be [answerid] herby, but ȝit aske
ferþermore: 'Now Lorde, siþen it is so þat we shullen go oute
of þi siȝt, wiþ þi curse, into þe fire þat euer shal last, whiche is

775 also go] go also M.   778 answere] *om.* M.   780 neuer] & neuere M.
781 into] to M;   þe] *om.* R.   786 be(1)] were M.
787 or a þousand þousand ȝere] *om.* M.   788 grace...laste] *om.* R.
790 and sey] *om.* M;   *In*] *om.* R.   791 So] nay so M.
794 Now] *om.* M.   798 an] of an M.   800 hiȝe] *om.* M.
801 fifþe] sixte M.   801-2 *Qui...est*] *Discedite a me* M.
803 redile] redi M.   804 tarying] araying M.

arayid, blessid Lorde—if it be þi wille— graunte vs felouship of
summe good creaturis, whos coumfort in oure grete peynys
810 may sumwhat alegge oure disese,' herto may þe iustise answere
by þe sixt and seuent wordis of his sentence, seying: *Discedite,
etc; cum diabolo et angelus eius.* Þat is: 'Nay, 3e ben not worþi
þerto; but þe felouship þat 3e shullen haue shal be þe deuel and
his aungelis, whiche shullen euerlastingly torment 3ow in
815 helle.'

Siþen þen, as Crist seiþe þat may not lye, þe sentense þat is
rehersid bifore shal be 3yuen þat day vpon hem þat endiden
here in dedly synne, in whiche shal be no refresshyng ne
coumforte, ne none hope, and þat day is vnknowen to alle men
820 but to God alone, me þinkiþ þen, as I seyde bifore, it were good
wisdome to alle men to haue þis last day in mynde euermore.
And þerfore I sey, as I seyde afore: 'Haue mynde on
þe laste þingis.' /

The þrid last þing þat men shulden ofte haue in mynde, of f. 18ᵛ
825 whiche I spake at þe bygynyng, is þe euerlasting peyne of helle,
of whiche last þing spekiþ Crist in þe gospel (*Luc*'.14.[9]), þere
he seiþe þus: *Tunc incipient cum rubore nouissimum locum tenere.*
Þat is: Þen at þat day of dome, men þat shullen be dampned
shullen byginne wiþ shame to take þe last place.' And þe Wise
830 Man seiþe in his prouerbis (*Prouer*.[15.24]): *Semita vite super
eruditem, vt declinet de inferno nouissimo.* Þat is: 'Þe paþþe of lijf
vpon him þat is lerned, þat he bowe awey fro þe last helle.' In
þis hydous plase shullen be peynis wiþouten noumbur to
ponysshe wiþ þe enemyes of God; but among alle, men mowen
835 by grounde of Scripture reherse summe to make men raþer for
drede of hem wiþdrawe hem fro synne and 3yue hem to vertuis.
Ten grete peynis I fynde þat shullen be þere, whiche I purpose
by þe leue of God to reherce in þis place:

Þe first is þe hydous prisoun in whiche alle dampned men
840 shullen be closid togidur, as a fagete bounden togedir wiþouten

810 disese] gret disese M.
814 euerlastingly] haue euerlastingly M.
821-2 in mynde euermore] euere in mynde M.
822-3 afore...þingis] afore *Memorare nouissima* haue in mynde þe laste þingis
M.   824 (*mar: Tercium principale*).
830 prouerbis...*Semita*] prouerb' *Semita* M.
831 *nouissimo*] *nouissimo prouer* iijº M.
835 raþer] þe raþer M.
837 (*mar: Nota de .X. pen⟨i⟩s inferni*).
840 a fagete] a knycche oþer a faget M.

812 *etc*] *a me etc* M.
818 ne] no M.

828 þat day] þe day M.

836 vertuis] vertue M.
839 alle] we M.

ony lousyng, to brenne in þe fire of helle, of whiche spekiþ þe
prophete Ysay, seying: *Congregabuntur in congregacione, etc.* þat
is: 'Þei shullen be gederid togedir in þe congregacion of a
knyche, into þe lake, and þere þe`i´ shullen be shit in prison.'

845   In þis woful prison, first shal be grete / fire þat neuer may be   f. 19ʳ
quenchid, to brenne wiþ þese fagetis of synful soulis, of whiche
fire spekiþ Crist in þe gospel and seiþe: (*Mt.*13.[42.50]):
Mittent eos in caminum ignis. Þat is: Þei shullen sende hem into
þe chymnay of fire.' And, in anoþer plase: *Ignis eorum non*
850   *extinguitur.* 'Þe fire of hem shal not be quenchid.' For, as
doctouris seyne, þow al þe se ran þorow it, it myȝt not quenche
it, neiþer abate. Þe hete of þis fire of helle passiþ as myche þe
hete of þe fire of þis worlde as þis fire passiþ þe hete of a fire
peyntid on a wal. Þis fire, as Ysid' seiþe, shyniþ not to hem to
855   her coumforte, þat þei myȝt se wherof þei shulden ioy, but to
ekyng of [here peyne and] `her´ sorowis, þat þei [myȝt] se
wherof þei shullen sorow.

Of þis goþe oute an hydous smoke, whiche makiþ hem wepe
euer wiþouten eend, of whiche smoke spekiþ Ysay þe prophete,
860   seying þus: *Ascendit fumus eius in generacionem, etc.* Þat is:
'Smoke from it shal stie from generacion [to generacion], and it
shal be discoumforted into þe worlde of worldis.'

Þe þrid peyne in þis prison shal be grete colde, as [of] forst or
snow, of whiche spekiþ þe prophete Baruc, and seiþe þus: *Ecce*
865   *proiecta sunt in calore solis, etc.* 'Loo! þei ben þrowen fer awey
in þe hete of þe sunne and forst of þe nyȝt, and þei been deed in
worst sorowis.' Þis colde is so grete þat al þe fire of þe worlde
myȝt not quenche it, neiþer a litel refreishe it. Þis colde
ma/kiþ hem make a grete noyse, wiþ chakeling of her teeþ   f. 19ᵛ
870   togider. Oute of þis fire into þis colde, and oute of þis colde into
þis fire aȝeyn þei shullen be possid wiþ foule feendis, hider and

---

841 of helle] *om.* M.   842 (*mar:* ⟨ysaye?⟩);
congregacione etc] *congregacione vnius fascis in lacum & claudentur ibi in
carcere* M.   845 (*mar:* .ij. *pena*).   847 Mt.13.] *om.* M.
848 (*mar:* .Mt.).   849 plase] place he seiþ M.
850 Þe fire] þat is þe fyir M;   (*mar:* spalr = *spiritualiter*?).
851 (*mar:* Augustus).   854 seiþe] telleþ M.
856 here...and] her R.   859 euer] eueremore M.
860 eius...etc] *eius a generacione in generacionem & desolabitur in secula
seculorum etc.* M;   (*mar:* .ysaye.).   861 to generacion] *om.* R.
862 þe] *om.* M.   863 forst] of forst M.   864 (*mar:* .Baruc.).
865 solis etc] *solis et gelu noctis et mortui sunt in doloribus pessimis* M.
869 make] to make M.

þider wiþoute cesyng, of whiche spekiþ Job in his boke
([24.19]): *Ab aquis niuium in calorem nimium transibunt.* Þat is:
'Þei shullen go from watris of snow to grettist hete.' Of þis
875 weping of yen and chakeling of teeþ whiche shullen be causid
of þis hete and of [þis] colde spekiþ Crist in þe gospel, þer he
seiþe þus: *Ibi erit fletus et stridor dentium.* Þat is: 'Þere shal be
weping and gnasting of teeþ.'

Þe fourþe peyne shal be þe worme of her conscience þat shal
880 euermore bite hem more bitterly þen ony cancre or rust fretiþ
[tre or] yrun, euer grucching `in hem´silf why þei myspendiden
þe grace þat God sende hem, why aȝen her owne knowing þei
left þe good and token þe yuel. And þis worme of grucching
shal neuer dyȝe, of whiche spekiþ Crist in þe gospel, seying:
885 *Vermis eorum, etc.* Þat is: 'Þe worme of hem shal neuer dyȝe.'

Þe fifþe peyne of þis prisoun shal be so grete derkenessis þat
þe`i´ mowen be felid, of whiche spekiþ Holy Scripture
(*Exo*.10), where God sende suche derkenes[sis] to þe peple of
Egipt for her synnis, whiche werne figures of þe peynes of
890 helle. And of þese derkenessis spekiþ Crist in þe gospel, where
he seiþe þus: *Inutilem seruum proicite, etc.* Þat is: 'Þe vnprofitable / seruaunt þrowiþ oute into vttermore derkenessis.' In   f. 20ʳ
þese derkenessis shullen dampyned men crie nyȝt and day ful
hydously, as þe seruice of holy chirche telliþ, seying þus: *Ve!*
895 *Ve! Ve! quante sunt tenebre!* Þat is: 'Wo! Wo! Wo! (or Allas!
Allas! [Allas!]) hou grete ben þese derkenessis!'

Þe sixt peyne of þis prison shal be contynuel, orrible and
foule stynke þat þei shullen haue, boþe of her owne cursid
cariouns þat shal euer stynke of þe synnes þat þei haue done,
900 and also of þe fire þat shal brenne hem þere, of brymston and of
piche, as Jon seiþe in þe Apocalipse. And Ysay, in his boke,
spekiþ of þese two stynkis in dyuerse placis. For þe first, he
seiþe þus: *Descenderunt ad fundamenta laci qui cadauer put-
ridum.* Þat is; 'Þei han descendit to þe fundamentis of þe lake as
905 rotid cariouns.' And for þe secound, seiþe þus: *Erit pro suaui
odore fetor.* Þat is: 'Þere shal be for swete sauoure stynke.'

872 (*mar:* Job).   873 24] 20 R, xx M;   *in] ad* M;   Þat] etc þat M.
876 þis(2)] *om.* R.   879 her] her owne M;   (*mar:* iiij *pena*).
881 tre or] *om.* R;   why þei] whiche M.   883 of] *om.* M.
885 *etc] non extinguetur* M.   886 (*mar:* v *pena*).
888 *Exo*.10] exod þe X chapitre M;   (*mar:* Exo.).   890 þese] þis M.
891 *etc] in tenebras exteriores* M.   892 into] into þe M.   896 Allas(2)] *om.* R.
897 (*mar:* vj *pena*).   899 þat(1)] þei M;   synnes] foule synnes M.
900 hem] *om.* M.   903 (*mar:* .ysay.).   905 seiþe] he seiþ M.

Þe seuent peyne of þis prison shal be drede and quaking whiche shal be þere, boþe for þe [ferdful] siȝt and þe hydous noyse of feendis, and drede of her dyuerse peynis in þo
910 derkenessis, and horroure or hydousnes, of whiche spekiþ Dauid in þe Sauter, seying: *Timor et tremor venerunt super me, etc.* Þat is: 'Drede and quakyng ben comen vpon me, and derkenessis han hiled me togider.' Of whiche hydousnes / spekiþ Job in his boke, þere he seiþe þus: *Vbi vmbra mortis, etc.* f. 20ᵛ
915 Þat is: 'Where is shadow of deþe and non ordur, but euerlasting horroure and hydousnes dwelliþ þerinne.'

Þe eiȝt peyne of þat prisoun shal be discorde and discoumforte of felouship, for þere shal be none oþer felouship but feendis and dampned men. Of feendis shul þei no coumfort
920 haue, for þei shullen be bisy and [glad] euerlastingly to turment hem; ne none of hem shal haue coumfort of oþer, for þe fader shal hate þe sone, and þe sone þe fader, and wary and curse yche oþer. And þerfore seiþe Jeremye þe prophete: *Non est consoletur eam ex omnibus caris eius.* 'Þere is none þat shal
925 coumfort oþer of alle hir dere derlingis.' But riȝt as in heuen þe mo þer comen þider, þe more is þe blis encresid of hem þat ben þere, riȝt so þe co[n]trarie: þe mo þer comen to helle, þe more is encresid her peyne to yche of hem alle.

Þe nynþe peyne of þis prisoun is [þe] grettist of alle: þat is,
930 wanting of þe siȝt of God in blisse. For riȝt as in heuen þe most ioy þat seyntis and aungels haue is þe glorious siȝt of God in his trone, riȝt so þe most peyne þat dampnyd men shullen haue in helle shal be wanting of þat siȝt. For, as doctouris seyne, if it myȝt be possible þat men in þe peyne[s] of helle myȝten see þe
935 siȝt of / God in his blisse, alle þe peynys in helle shulden not f. 21ʳ greue hem for [joy of þat siȝt]. And seyntis hadden leuer to chese, if it were possible to be put in her choyse, raþer to be in helle peynys and haue þat siȝt, þen in þe ioyes of heuen and wante þat siȝt. Of þe wanting of þat siȝt to dampned men

907 quaking] quaking & horrour & hidousnesse M;
(*mar:* vij *pena*).   908 þere] for M;   ferdful] ferdfulnes R;
þe(2)] *om.* M.   910 derkenessis...hydousnes] derknesses M.
911 seying] seyinge þus M.   912 etc] &*contexerunt me tenebre* M.
914 (*mar:* .Job.).   916 horroure and hydousnes] horrour M.
917 (*mar:* viij *pena*).   920 glad] *om.* R, glad & bisie M.
923 (*mar:* Jeremy).   928 her peyne to] þe peyne in M.
929 þe(2)] *om.* R;   (*mar:* ix *pena*).
930 blisse] his blisse M.   934 peynes] peyne R.
936 joy of þat siȝt] þe siȝt of þat joy R.

940 spekiþ þe prophete Ysay (26.[10]), þere he seiþe þus: *In terra*
sanctorum iniqua gessit, etc. Þat is: 'In þe londe of hooly men he
haþe wrouȝt wickid þingis, and he shal not se þe glory of þe
Lorde.' And, in anoþer place: *Tollatur impius ne videat gloria*
Dei. Þat is: 'Be þe wickid man taken away, þat he se not þe
945 glorye of God.'

Þe last peyne of þis prisoun is dispeire of remedy, for alle þe
freris preyers of þe foure ordris, ne letters of fraternite, ne þe
Popis pardoun, may no man bye oute of þat woful plase. Þat
preueþ Job, þere he seiþe þus: *In inferno nulla est redempcio, etc.*
950 Þat is: 'In helle is noon aȝeynbying.' And Jeremy þe prophete
seiþe also in þis maner: *Quare factus est dolor meus perpetuus, et*
plaga mea desperabilis? Þat is: '"Why," seiþe þe dampnyd man,
"is my sorow eendles, and my wounde dispeyrable for to be
helid?"' Also, it may be preued by reson þat þere is dispeyre of
955 remedy. For if þere were ony hope of remedy, þen were þere
ioy, for euery hope is a maner of ioy; and þat is impossible, for
þere / [is] alle maner of peyne and wanting of al maner of ioy.   f. 21ᵛ

Siþen þen [þe] peynis þat I haue rehersid by grounde of
Holy Scripture ben so grete, ȝe! and gretter þen ony tunge may
960 telle or herte may þenke, me þinke þen to beholde þis peyne,
whiche shal be þe last rewarde for synne in þe last day, shulde
euery man, and specialy men in her myddil age when lust and
likyng of corage stiriþ hem most awey fro þe seruise of God,
make a jornay in her þouȝt to þe ȝatis of helle, to se hou
965 hydously synne is vengid in þat plase. Of whiche iornay may be
seide þe wordis of Scripture þat [sueþ]: 'I seide "in þe myddi[l]
of my dayes, I shal go to þe ȝatis of helle".' And if he byholde
hem verily wiþ abyding mynde, and if he haue ony sparcle of
grace, it shal myche wiþdrawe hym fro lust and liking of synne
970 þat lastiþ but as a moment, aȝeyn euerlasting peynis þat ben
ordeynid þerfore, and ȝyue hem to vertues þat leden to
euerlasting lijf. And if þou þus hast mynde, as I haue rehersid,
on þi last deeþ day, and on þe day of dome, and on þe peynis of
helle, þen doist þou as I counselid in þe bygynnyng in my
975 teme, seying þese wordis: *Memorare, etc.*

940 þe...26] ysa þe prophet M;   (*mar*: .ysay.).
941 *etc*] *non videbit gloriam domini* M. 945 God] þe lord M. 946 (*mar*: x *pena*).
947 fraternite] fraternitees M.   948 bye] aȝen bye M.   949 preueþ] fermeþ M.
951 (*mar*: Jeremy).   958 þe] *om*. R.
961 last...in] laste reward synne to M.   966 sueþ] seiþe R;
myddil] myddis R.   972 lijf] blisse M.
975 teme] theeme M;   *etc*] *nouissima* M;   (*mar*: *thema*).

Þe fourþe last þing þat I spake of in þe bygynnyng, and whiche euer man shulde haue in mynde, is þe joy of heuen, for þat shal be þe last rewarde to hem þat lyueden in / þis worlde f. 22ʳ vertuously, and eendiden in charite. Of whiche last þing spekiþ

980 þe Wise Man in his boke, þere he seiþe þus: *Timenti Deum bene erit in nouissimo.* Þat is: 'To hym þat drediþ God, it shal be wil in þe last tyme.' And Job also seiþe in þis maner: *In nouissimo die de terra, etc.* Þat is: 'In þe last day I shal arise of þe erþe, and eft I shal be cloþid wiþ my skyn, and in my fleishe I shal se

985 God, my sauioure, whiche shal be þe grettist joy in þe blisse of heuen.'

Þat þis joy also shal be þe last rewarde to Goddis true seruauntis, preueþ wel þe parable of oure Lorde Jesus Crist, of þe [vyneȝerde, where it telliþ þat þe lorde of þis] vyneȝerde (þat

990 is, God þe Fader) biddiþ to his procuratour (þat is, to his Son), to whom he haþe ȝyuen al þe dome at þe euentyde of þe day (þat is, at þe eende of þis worlde), to calle þe werkemen of his vyneȝerde (þat is, þe true seruauntis of þe chirche) and ȝeelde hem her mede (þat is, þe peny whiche is þe eendles blis of

995 heuen). Þis blisse stondiþ prinsepaly in foure þingis:

First, in þe delitable siȝt and beyng of þat feire and m`e´ry cite þat men shullen be in heuen. Þe secound is in þe ioy þat þei shullen haue in hemsilf, boþe in body and in soule. Þe þrid is in [þe] blessid and worshipful cumpany þat þei shullen haue þere.

1000 Þe fourþe is in þe glorious siȝt of God, boþe of his godhed and of his manhed, whiche þei shullen haue þere.

First, I sey, in þe / delitable siȝt and being of þat feyre and f. 22ᵛ mery cite of heuen. Of þat cite spekiþ Seynt Austyn and seyþe: *Vera pax ibi erit, nihil aduersitas nec a seipso nec ab alio pacietur.*

1005 Þat is: 'Verrey pees shal be þere, where neyþer man shal suffre aduersite oþer of himself or of ony oþer.' Byholde we þen þe

976 in] at M;   (*mar*: 4 *principale*).
977 euer man shulde] man shulde euere M.
978 lyueden] haue lyued M.   980 (*mar*: Sap').
981 *erit*] *sit illi* M;   wil] wel M.   982 (*mar*: .Job.).
983 *etc*] *surrecturus sum & rursum circumdabor pelle mea pellem* [sic] *mea & in carne mea videbo deum saluatorum meum* M.
989–90 vyneȝerde þat is] vyneȝard where it telleþ þat þe lord of þis vyneȝard þat is M.   994 hem] hem eueriche M.
995 (*mar*: *Nota de iiij gaudijs celum*).   996 feire and] *om.* M.
998 in(3)] *om.* M.   999 þe] *om.* R.   1001 whiche] þe whiche M.
1002 þe] *om.* M;   siȝt] *om.* M: (*mar*: *Primum gaudium*).
1003 and seyþe] *om.* M.   1004 *ibi erit*] *ibi est vbi* M;   (*mar*: Austyn).

worþines of þat blessid cite in as myche as it is possible vs to biholde, for to comprehende it in mannys wit verily as it is, no wit of man sufficiþ þerto.

1010   What may be blessider þen þis cite, where shal be no drede of pouerte, ne of sikenes, ne no feblenes, ne drede of þe deuel, ne none aspies of feendis, ne no drede of helle? Þere shal neiþer deeþ be of body, ne of soule, but vndeedlynes, euerlasting pees, and continuel gladnes. Þere shal be real shynyng of liȝt; not þis 1015 þat is now, but so myche clerer hou myche it is blessider. For þat cite, as Seynt Jon seiþe in þe Apocalipse, shal not nede þe liȝt of þe sunne, but almyȝty God shal liȝten it, and his launterne is þe lombe.

Þere shal be no nyȝt, ne derkenessis, ne rennyng togidre of 1020 cloudis, no sharpnes of colde, or brennyng hete; but suche temporaunse shal be þere of þingis, which neyþer yȝe haþe seen, neiþer ere herde: neiþer it haþe stiȝed into mannus herte, but oonly of hem þat ben founden worþi to weelde hem, whos namys / ben writen in þe boke of lijf, and han wasshen her f. 23ʳ 1025 stolys in þe blode of þe lombe, and ben tofore þe fete of God and seruen hym day and nyȝt.

Þere shal be no age, ne mysese of age, whil al men shullen come togidur þere into a perfite man of þe age of Crist.

Þe excellence and worþines of þe goodis of þe cite ouerpassen 1030 alle þe goodis of þis worlde, specialy in fyue þingis:

First, in gretnes, for Seynt Petur seyþe: *Credentes exultabitis, etc.* þat is: 'Ȝe þat bileuen, ȝe shullen ioy wiþ gladnes þat may not be tolde.' And Dauid seiþe: 'How grete is þe multitude of þi swetnes, Lorde, whiche þou shalt hyde to hem þat louen 1035 þee.'

Þe secound, þei ben many, for Seynt Poule seiþe: *Oculus non vidit, etc.* 'Yȝe haþe not seen, neiþer ere herde, neiþer stiȝed into mannys herte, whiche þou hast arayed to hem þat louen þe.' Also, Seynt Austin seiþe: *Cogita quicquid vis, et quicquid* 1040 *potes, omnem cogitacionem excedit omne desiderium, superat illa*

1007 is] *om.* M.
1007–8 vs...comprehende it] forto biholde or to comprehende hit M.
1011 ne of] no M;   ne drede] no drede M.
1012–3 neiþer deeþ be] be neiþer deþ M.   1014 real] rial M.
1016 (*mar:* Apoc').   1019 ne(2)] no M.   1020 no] ne M.
1022 ere] eere haþ M.   1031 (*mar:* .Pe.2).   1032 *etc] leticia inenarrabili* M.
1034 shalt hyde] hast hid M.   1036 (*mar:* Apostolus).
1037 *etc] nec auris audiuit nec in cor hominis ascendit* þat is M.
1038 hem] men M.

felicitas. Þat is: 'Þenke whateuer þou wil, and whateuer þou maiste, and þat blessidnes [ouerpasseþ] al þou3t, and ouer-comeþ al desire.'

Þe þrid, þei ben euerlasting, for Ysay seiþ: *Leticia sempiterna* 1045 *super capita eorum.* Þat is: 'Euerlasting gladnes vpon þe heedis of hem.'

Þe fourþe, þei shullen be restful, of whiche spekiþ Seynt Poule, seying in þis wise: *Pax Dei, que exsuperat omnem sensum.* Þat is, 'Þe pees / of God, þat ouerpassiþ alle mannys [wit], kepe f. 23ᵛ 1050 3oure hertis and 3oure vndurstonding.'

Þe fifþe, þei shullen be siker, for of hem may be seide þese wordis of Holy Scripture whiche God seide to his peple of Israel by `þe´ londe of biheest, whiche wes figure of þe blis of heuen: *Dormietis et non erit qui exterreat, etc.* Þat is: '3ee shullen 1055 slepe and no man shal fere 3ow, and I shal take awey yuel beestis fro 3ou, and swerde shal not passe by 3oure cuntreis.'

Of þis cite seiþe Seint Bernarde: *O ciuitas celestis, mansio secura, patria totum continens quod delectat.* Þat is: 'O þou heuenly cite, a siker dwelling, a cuntre conteynyng al þing þat 1060 delitiþ.' And þerfore Dauid seiþe of þis cite: *Gloriosa dicta sunt de te, ciuitas Dei.* Þat is: 'Glorious þingis ben seyde of þee, þou cite of God.' Towarde þis cite we ow3ten to hy3e vs fast, for of þis worshipful cite we ben not straungers and comelingis, but we ben burgeysis and cytesyns, and þe homely meyne of þe 1065 kyng of þis cite, and his eyris, and euen eris wiþ his son, Jesus Crist, if we kepen his comaundementis and lyue and eend in charite.

The secound þing þat þis joy prinsepaly stondiþ inne is in ioy þat men shullen haue in hemsilf, boþe in body and eke [in] 1070 soule.

First, men shullen be endowid in her bodies wiþ foure maner of ioyes: þat is, wiþ clerte, agilite, sotilte, and immort-alite.

1042 ouerpasseþ] ouercomyþ R (*n.*).   1044 þei] þat þei M.
1048 *sensum*] *sensum custodiat corpora vestra & intelligencias vestras* M.
1049 wit] *om.* R.   1053 figure] figured M;
(*mar: figura*).   1054 *erit*] *sit* M;
etc] *auferam malas bestias a vobis & gladius non transibit terminos vestros*
&*c* M.   1057 (*mar:* .B'.).
1058 þou] þat M.   1060 (*mar:* dd).
1065 eyris...wiþ] eyres wiþ M.   1068 (*mar:* ij *gaudium*).
1069 in] & R.   1071 (*mar: De dotacione corporis*).

First wiþ / clerte, for þen mennys bodies shullen shyne as f. 24ʳ
1075 clere as þe sunne, as Crist witnessiþ: *Fulgebunt iusti sicut sol,*
etc. And þe sunne þen shal be seuen syþis briȝter þen it is now,
as þe prophete witnessiþ. Þen mennys bodyes shullen be seuen
siþis briȝter þen is þe sunne now.

Þe secound is agilite, þat is: swifnes. Þat is, as Seynt Austyn
1080 seiþe: 'Wheresoeuer þe soule wole, anon þer shal be þe body.'
Of þis dowery spekiþ þe Wise Man in þe Boke of Wisdom and
seiþe: *Tanquam scintille in arundineto, etc.* Þat is: 'Þei shul run
whider þei wil, as swiftly as sperkis in a redy plase.'

Þe þrid is sotilte. Þat is, mennys bodies shul be so sotil þat
1085 þei mai perse whatso þei wil, and no þing shal let hem to go
w`h´ere þei wil.

Þe fourþe is immortalite, þat is: vndeedlynes, þat þei mowe
neuer aftur dye no more, of whiche spekiþ Jon in þe Apocalipse
and seyþe: *Mors vltra non erit.* Þat is: 'Deeþ shal be no more to
1090 hem.'

Þe joy þat men shullen haue in her soulis in þat place shal
stonde in þre þingis: þat is, clere biholding, loue, and euerlasting weelding.

First in clere byholding, for þere as 'we seen him nowe as it
1095 were in a derke myrrour, we shullen se hym þen face to face'
riȝt as he is, as witnessiþ Seynt Poule to þe Corinthyes.

Þe secound dowery or ioy of þe soule is loue, for þen
mannys loue shal be so clere þat it shal / be sette in God oonly, f. 24ᵛ
whiche is best good, wiþouten ony contrarious affeccion.

1100 Þe þrid is siker welding euerlastingly of þat ioy of whiche
spekiþ Crist to his disciplis, saying: *Et gaudium vestrum nemo*
tollet, etc. Þat is: 'Ȝoure joy no man shal take awey fro ȝow.'

Þe þrid þing þis ioy prinsepaly stondiþ inne is in þe
worshipful, blessid, and coumfortable cumpany þat shal be in
1105 þat place. Þat is, first, of þe feloushipe, myrþe, and melody of

---

1075 witnessiþ] witnesseþ himself seyinge M.
1076 *etc*] *in regno Patris mei* M;   þen shal] shal þanne M.
1078 is þe sunne] þe sonne is M.   1079 swifnes] swiftnesse M.
1080 (*mar*: .Austyn.).   1081 dowery] dower M.
1082 (*mar*: Sap');   *etc*] *discurret* M.
1083 sperkis...plase] sparcles in areodi place M.
1086 where] whereso M.   1089 (*mar*: Apoc').
1092 (*mar*: *De dotacione anime*).   1096 Poule] Poule writynge M;
(*mar*: *Apostolus*).   1097 dowery] dower M.
1100 þat...whiche] þat ioye of þat whiche M.
1102 *etc*] *a vobis* M.   1103 (*mar*: iij *gaudium*).

aungels and archaungels of þe nyne ordris, into whiche cumpany of ordris men shullen be receyuid hyer or lower, after þei haue deseruid in eerþe. Also, þei shullen þere haue cumpany of olde and worshipful patriarkis, prophetis, apostlis, martirs, 1110 confessouris, and virgyns, in whiche cumpany is euerlasting loue and charite.

Þe wille of oon is þe wille of anoþer. Þe mo þat þei ben, þe more is her blis. Þere no man is hirte, ne no man is wroþe. No man is enuyous of oþer mannys good. Þere no couetise of good 1115 brennyþ mannys herte, for þei han more ioy þan þei kan desire, for loue is her lawe and lediþ hem euerychone. Þ[ere] is no willing aftur worship, ne desire after degre, but yche man holdiþ him apayed of þe state þat he is inne.

Þere is oon pees, oon acorde, and euerlasting gladnes. Þei 1120 shullen `comownen´ her cunnyng togider, and her Maister wiþ hem alle. / Þei shullen dwelle togider wiþoute dyn or daunger f. 25ʳ any of oþer, but plesaunce and perfite pees shal be among þat peple. Þere shal be ȝouþe wiþouten ony age. Þere shal be feyrnes wiþouten ony spot of filþe. Þere shal be helþe wiþouten 1125 ony sikenes. Þere shal be riches wiþouten ony pouerte. Þere shal be kunnyng wiþouten ony ignoraunce. Þere shal be rest wiþouten ony werines. Þere shal be fulnes wiþ`outen´ ony wanting. Þere shal be worship wiþouten ony vileny. Þere shal be largenes wiþouten ony þristing. And shortly, al þat may be 1130 good shal be among þat cumpany.

Þe fourþe good þing in whiche prinsepaly þat blisse shal stonde inne shal be þe glorious siȝt of þe Trinite, boþe in his godhed and in his manhed, of whiche spekiþ Crist in þe gospel of Jon, seying þus: *Hec est vita eterna vt cognoscant, etc.* Þat is: 1135 'Þis is þe lijf þat euer shal last, þat þei know þee, verrey God in Trinite, and whom þou sendist, Jesus Crist.' Þis siȝt of God in his godhed and manhed togider þe aungels desiren euer to biholde þerin, as þe apostil Peter witnessiþ in his pistil.

1108 þere haue] haue þere M.
1113 blis] blisse for loue is her lawe & ledeþ hem euerichone M (*cf.* 1116);
wroþe No] wroþ ne no M.   1114 Þere no] þere is no M.
1115–6 desire...euerychone] desire M (*cf.* 1113).
1120 comownen] (*mar. different hand*; comyn *deleted in text*) R, comene M.
1126 ony] *om.* M.   1127 wiþouten] (*mar:* outen).
1131 (*mar:* iiij *gaudium*).
1134 *etc*] *te verum deum & tri' & quem misisti Iesum Christum* M.

Þis is þe 'boke of lijf' þat Jon spekiþ of in þe Apocalipse. Þis
1140 boke makiþ man þat lokiþ [þerinne] so kunnyng of þe first day
þat he knowiþ al clergy and kunnyng of craftis, and al wit haþe
at his wille of what he wole desire. Alle myraclis and
meruey/lis, þe most þat euer God made, whiche were wonder-   f. 25ᵛ
ful to her wit while þei wandrid her, shal be to hem liȝt ynow
1145 þat loken on þis book. Þe lewidest knaue of þe kychyn here shal
be þere clerke, and take dignite of degre in dyuinite at þe first
lesson þat he lokiþ in þis boke, when alle deynous doctouris
shullen drawe þere abacke, þat now letten suche lewid men to
lerne here Lordis lawe. For what persoone þat plesiþ God most
1150 perfitly in þis worlde—be he clerke, knyȝt, or knaue—when he
þider comyþ, shal be most made of and next þe mageste.

Þis boke shal neuer be claspid vp, ne closid in no cloyster,
but as opun to one as to anoþer, for þat is oure Lordis ordre.
Þis boke is so briȝt and so breme to hem alle þat he nediþ neuer
1155 oþer liȝt of launterne ne of laumpe, as large as þe plase is, to
loke in her lesson. Þe louely loking on her lesson shal like hem
so wel þat þei shal euer wake and neuer winke, wiþouten ony
werines, and euer fast wiþouten feding of ony worldly fode, for
þe feire siȝt of his face shal fully feest hem alle.
1160   Now blessid is þat blessid place and alle þe peple þerein, and
blessid is þat briȝt body þat bryngiþ hem al þat witt.

Lorde, for þe blode þat þou bleddist to bye man wiþ so dere,
ȝyue vs grace to haue in mynde þese foure last þingis, þat we
mo`w´ se wiþ þi seyntis þe siȝt of þi face. Amen. Amen.

1139 (*mar*: Apoc').   1140 þerinne] inne R.
1141–2 al(2)...wille] haþ al witt at his wille M.
1143 merueylis] mereiles M.   1144 be to hem] to hem be M.
1145 (*mar*: Nota).   1146 clerke] a clerk M.   1147 in þis] on þis M.
1152 no] *om.* M.   1155 oþer] non oþer M.   1158 feding] any feedyng M.

NOTES TO THE TEXT

IN THESE NOTES, *Cf.* indicates a source which, while not precisely quoted in the Text, is closely paraphrased, with or without interpolation(s). Sources introduced by 'See' are to be regarded as possibly significant, but less certainly so than those introduced by *Cf.*

Abbreviations

Apology	*An Apology for Lollard Doctrines*, ed. J.H. Todd. Camden Society (London, 1842).
AV	The Authorised (1611) Version of the Bible.
Catena	The *Catena Aurea* of Aquinas.
Compendium	Compendium *Theologicae Veritatis*, sometimes attributed to Aquinas during the Middle Ages. Other attributions include Albertus Magnus (see the Venice edition, 1588) and Bonaventura (*Opera*, Rome 1596). The second of these two has been used in compiling the Notes to this text.
E.E.T.S.	Early English Text Society, Original Series (o.s.), or Extra Series (e.s.).
Glossa	*Glossa Ordinaria*, including the *Postilla* of Lyra (6 vols. Antwerp, 1617).
Gratian	*Corpus Iuris Canonici: Decretum Magistri Gratiani*, ed. E. Friedberg (2 vols. Leipzig, 1879–81). Notes indicate volume and column numbers.
Legenda	*Legenda Aurea*, Jacob de Voragine (2nd edn. Leipzig, 1850).
MS A	British Library MS Additional 41321.
MS B	Bodley MS 143: A Wycliffite Commentary on Luke's gospel.

MS M	John Rylands Library MS English 412.
MS R	Bodleian Library MS Rawlinson C. 751.
MED	*Middle English Dictionary* (Ann Arbor, 1954–).
Mustanoja	*A Middle English Syntax*, Tauno F. Mustanoja (Helsinki, 1960).
O.F.	Old French.
OED	*The Oxford English Dictionary.*
Op. Imp.	The collection of homilies known as the *Opus Imperfectum in Matthaeum* (*P.G.* 56, col. 601–946) was attributed to Chrysostom throughout the Middle Ages. Erasmus subsequently put forward the view, still held, that these homilies were written by an Arian bishop, in Latin, but that the author knew Greek (see *P.G.* 56, col.601–2). Modern scholars think that they were written in the first quarter of the fifth century, in the region corresponding to present-day Yugoslavia.*
P.G.	*Patrologiae Cursus Completus, Series Graeca*, ed. J.P. Migne (161 vols. Paris, 1857–66). Notes indicate volume and column number.
P.L.	*Patrologiae Cursus Completus, Series Latina*, ed. J.P. Migne (221 vols. Paris, 1844–64). Notes indicate volume and column number.
Rosarium	The Middle English translation of the *Rosarium Theologie*: Cambridge, Gonville and Caius College MS 354/581. A Selection, edited by Christina von Nolcken, Middle English Texts 10 (Heidelberg, 1979).
SEWW	*Selections from English Wycliffite Writings*, ed. Anne Hudson (Cambridge, 1978).

---

* I am indebted to Fr. Joop van Banning, s.j., formerly of Campion Hall, Oxford, for this information, and for guidance in locating relevant texts.

Trefnant	*Registrum Johannis Trefnant*, ed. W.W. Capes, The Canterbury and York Society, xx (London, 1916).
V	The Vulgate.
WEV	The Wycliffe Bible (Early Version). See *WLV* below.
WLV	The Wycliffe Bible (Later Version), ed. J. Forshall and F. Madden (4 vols. Oxford, 1850). Parallel texts of *WEV* and *WLV*.
Wyclif's *Sermones*	*Wyclif's Latin Works*, ed. J. Loserth. The Wyclif Society Series (*Sermones*: 4 vols. London, 1886–89).

SERMON 1. *First Sunday in Advent, Matthew 21:1–9*

1/26–33 **proude men...**] *Cf.* Sermon 2/417–30, Sermon 11A/229–46, and DM/557–67.

1/64–6 **Jerome**, *Commentaria in Evangelium Matthaei, Liber IV, caput* xxiii (on Matthew 24:14; *P.L.* 26, col.177, §194).

1/86 **Jerusalem... þe syth of pees**] Also in Sermon 7/37.

1/148 **his vyne**] *Cf.* lines 317–18 and 323–5 of this sermon, and see Sermon 8 *passim*, where images of the vine and vineyard are extensively developed. See also DM/987–94.

1/148 **wordli**] The high incidence of this form of 'worldly' in Middle English manuscripts (*i.e.* with the **l** omitted before the **d**) has given rise to the generally held view that this reflects usage, as distinct from a tendency to scribal error. Analysis of the seventeen sermon texts edited here, however, gives pause for thought. The noun forms **world** and **worlde** occur 128 times, with one occurrence of **wolrld**, one occurrence of **wordl**, and only one occurrence without the **l**. In the case of the adjective 'worldly', on the other hand, there is a conspicuous degree of variability. The forms **worldeli** and **worldely** occur 14 times, while **wordeli** and **worldli** occur 19 times, with one occurrence each of **worli** and **woreli**. The DM text has no occurrences of either noun or adjective with the **l** omitted. One possible inference from this evidence is that the consonant cluster **rldl** was particularly conducive to scribal error. Another is that the language of the writer did indeed include two adjectival forms, *i.e.* with and without **l**.

1/205 **han al aboute bounden**] *L. circumplexi sunt*; but *cf.* *WEV* 'wounden aboute'; *WLV* 'biclippid'; *AV* 'robbed.

1/209 **feet... affeccions**] This image occurs again in Sermon 2/368–9, Sermon 3/199–200, Sermon 12/235, and DM/374. For an illuminating discussion of this topic, see Vincent Gillespie, 'Mystic's Foot: Rolle and Affectivity' in *The Medieval Mystical Tradition in England*, ed. M. Glascoe (University of Exeter, 1982), pp.199–230. *Cf.* also Sermon 2/200–1 Note.

1/280–2 **Gregorius**] *Gregory, Regulae Pastoralis Liber, Pars Secunda, caput iv* (*P.L.* 77, col.31, §17). Also in Sermon 2/154–8, 242–3.

1/282–5 *Ibid*: *i.e.* not '**in anoþer place**].

1/290–96 This wax/clay image occurs again in Sermon 16/397–402, where it follows the *Op. Imp.* text that it here precedes (see next Note). Source not traced.

1/297–307 **Crisostom**] Also in Sermon 16/388–96. *Cf. Op. Imp. Homilia* XXXVIII (*P.G.* 56, col.842).

1/345–6 **Maudelyn... mynde**] See Sermon 8/137–8, and Sermon 10/416–26, Note.

1/404 **extorcions and**] MS. extorcōns: *i.e.* the suspension sign indicates the noun form, expanded throughout this edition as **-ion**.

1/453 **likynge hors**] 'as horses in fit condition (for)'; *OED* '**Liking**' *ppl. a.* (1).2.

SERMON 2. *Second Sunday in Advent. Luke 21:25–33*

2/154–8 and 242–3 **Gregorius**] See Sermon 1/280–2, Notes.

2/200–1 **þeues taken wiþ þe feet**] For the literal connotations of this somewhat cryptic phrase, *cf.* the punishment of the law-breaker in *Piers Plowman* B, IV.85–6. See also Proverbs 3:26 (*WLV* 'For the Lord schal be at thi side; and he schal kepe thi foot, that thou be not takun'), the context of which (Proverbs 3:1) corresponds to the theme here. The sense seems to be that all who obstruct or violate God's law will bring about their own downfall and, like thieves (see 175ff), will be forcibly constrained. See also Sermon 12/219–24, 234–8, and 239–41, and Sermon 1/209, Note.

2/249   **folewyng**] The MS has **folewynge sueynge**. Perhaps we have here an interesting glimpse into the process of translation and the problems of lexical choice. The Latin *sequentes* has been rendered into two words, as is *complens* below (line 252, **fulfullen** and **perfoorme**).

2/297   **þe laste Sundai bifore**] See Sermon 1/280–85.

2/297–300   **Crisostom** *Op. Imp. Homilia* XLIV (*P.G.* 56, col.881).

2/301–10   **Austeyn**] Primary source not traced, but this passage occurs in the *Rosarium* (headword 'Prechour', f.102v.) with the same puzzling attribution to a Prologue by Augustine. Christina von Nolcken points out (see *Rosarium* edition, p.121) that this passage also occurs in Cambridge Trinity College MS B. 14. 50 (f.19r), a manuscript containing Wycliffite texts, and in the *Apology* (p.32/14–19). The text from lines 303–10 also corresponds very closely to the Latin attributed to Swynderby, in Trefnant, p.258.

2/337   **and if God**] Conjectural emendation. Although the context suggests only a very brief omission, signatures at the foot of f.14r (v.2) and f.15r (v.4) suggest that an entire page is missing. See discussion of the manuscript in the Introduction, p.xi above.

2/368–9   **feet... affeccions**] See Sermon 1/209, Note.

2/417–30   **hir pride**] *Cf.* Sermon 1/26–33 Expansion 11A/229–46, and DM/557–67.

2/433–4   **Jeremy 6:13**] The Latin gives the first part of the verse; the English the second.

2/448   Other references to **popes** occur in this sermon, lines 394 and 651, and in Sermon 4/235. The words **þe Pope** occur in Sermon 4/229 and Sermon 12/90.

2/461–9   **Crisostom**] *Cf. Op. Imp. Homilia* XXIV (*P.G.* 56, col.818).

2/510–11   **pressure of puttynge down**] *L. pressura*; *WEV* (*WLV*) 'ouerleying (-leiyng)'; *AV* 'distress'.

2/596–9, 602–4 **þe glose seiþ, allegeþ**] No precise source(s) identified, but *cf.* MS B f.293(a) (b).

2/602 **hym**] Antecedent probably **a man**, line 599 above. See Glossary **al(l)egge**.

2/606–7 **Anima...iusti**] Not in *V*. Augustine attributes this phrase to the Scriptures, without location, in his *Ennaratio in Psalmum* XLVI (*P.L.* 36, col.529–30, §10). He uses it again in *Sermo* CC (*P.L.* 38, col.1029, §1), this time with the location *Sapientia* VII. See Etienne Catta, 'Sedes Sapientiae', *Maria, Etudes sur la Sainte Vierge*, ed. Hubert du Manoir, s.j., tom.vi, Paris 1961, pp.689–866, where it is suggested (pp.697–8) that the form 'anima justi sedes sapientiae' may have been known to Augustine from a Latin version following the Septuagint Greek of Proverbs 12:23. Gregory ascribes the phrase to Solomon, in *Homiliarum in Evangelia, Liber* II, *Homilia* XXXVIII (on Matthew 22:1–13; *P.L.* 76, col.1282D), and cites it again, but without ascription, in *Moralium, Liber* XXIX *in Job* xxxviii (*P.L.* 76, col.508B). The phrase is also found in Bernard, *Sermo 5 pro Dominica in Kal. Nov.* in Is.6.3; *Opera*, v, Romae, 1968, p.321, (cf. *P.L.* 183, col.355), and *Sermo 1 in Purificatione S. Mariae*; *Opera*, iv, Romae, 1966, p.337, (cf, *P.L.* 183, col.367–8).

2/630–6 **Crisostom**] Cf. *Op. Imp. Homilia* XLIX (*P.G.* 56, col.919).

2/639–42 **chalenge... hie corneris**] The translation of this biblical passage is very literal at the end, with *V. angulos excelsos* rendered **hie corneris**. Cf. *WEV* (*WLV*) 'heeȝe (hiȝe) corner(i)s'. This suggests that although **dai of chalenge** ('day of malicious accusation') makes good sense, its probable *L.* source was *dies calumniae* rather than the usual *dies calamitatis*. Cf. *WLV* 'ne(e)dynesse' and *MED* 'Chalenge' *n.*

2/663–4 **þe sermoun of Dede Men... memorare nouissima**] *i.e.* the last text in this edition, pp.207–40, referred to editorally throughout as the Sermon of Dead Men, or DM. Another internal cross-reference to it occurs in Sermon 15/416.

2/686–90 **Crisostom**] *Op. Imp. Homilia* XLIX (*P.G.* 56, col.920).

2/696–8 **Crisostom**] *Op. Imp. Homilia* XLVI (*P.G.* 56, col.892 and *cf.* col.894).

2/703–5 **Crisostom**] *Cf. Ibid.* col.894.

SERMON 3. *Third Sunday in Advent, Matthew 11 :2–10*

3/8–9 **for... here**] The syntax here coincides precisely with the *WLV* rendering of *propter Herodiadem uxorem Philippi fratris sui quia duxerat eam.* The sense is 'at the instigation of Herodias, wife of Herod's brother Philip, who had married her'.

3/36 **ar þei die fro hem**] i.e. 'before they die and leave them.' *Cf.* Sermon 1/276 **departe fro hem.**

3/39 **þe lawe of God**] The emendation here is supported by the context (*cf.* 3/36 and 3/255) and by usage throughout the entire text where references to '**Goddis la(u)we(s)**' can be found 43 times. The genitive as here occurs at 12/245, 13/261, 13/368, 16/249 and DM/547. For this construction with **axe** see *OED* '**Ask**' *v.* II.2.c and *MED* 1b.

3/49–51 **Þe cause... Aduent**] See Sermon 1/134–7.

3/72–8 **Crisostom**] *Cf. Op. Imp. Homilia* XXVII (*P.G.* 56, col.772).

3/121–8 **Bede, Gregorius**] *Cf. Bede, In Marci Evangelium Expositio, Liber* IV (on Mark 16:17–18; *Corpus Christianorum Ser. Lat.* 120, p.645). Gregory, *Homiliarum in Evangelia, Liber* II, *Homilia* XXIX (on Mark 16:14–20; *P.L.* 76, col.1215B). See next Note.

3/129–45 **Austyn**] Augustine, *Sermo* LXXXVIII, *caput* iii; *alias De Verbis Domini* 18 (on Matthew 20:30–34; *P.L.* 38, col.540). The *Rosarium* has this same question (headword 'Miracle', f.78r.) with the location *De Verbis Domini, Sermone* 18; it is preceded there by the Bede/Gregory quotation as above, lines 123–8.

3/136–7 **þe soule... þe helþe of þe bodi**] *Cf.* Sermon 16/207–11.

3/146–55 **Ysidor**] Isidor, *Sententiarum, Liber* I, *caput* xxiv, *De Sanctorum Miraculis* (*P.L.* 83, col.591B, to 592A). The *Rosarium* includes this quotation (headword 'Miracle', f.78v.) and gives the location as *De Summo Bono*. There, as here, the English translation is clumsy and defective. The Latin source gives the following sense: 'in the church nowadays, to live well is more [*sc.* valued] than to manifest signs. The reason why the church does not now perform miracles, as it did under the apostles, is that then it was necessary to make the world believe through miracles, whereas now belief should shine forth through good works. Then, they put their trust in external signs to strengthen inner faith; now, whoever possesses the faith and looks for miracles seeks vainglory in order to be praised [*i.e.* for self-aggrandizement].'

3/156–8 Perhaps a paraphrase of Gregory, *op. cit.*, above Note 121–8 (*P.L.* 76, col.1216A).

3/199–200 **feet... affeccions**] See Sermon 1/209, Note.

3/218–26 **Ambrose**] Cf. *De Dignitate Sacerdotali, caput* v, (*P.L.* col.577A); Gratian, *Causa* I, *quaestio* I, *caput* xiv (I, col.361). And cf. *Expositio Evangelii Secundum Lucam, Liber* IV (on Luke 4:27; *P.L.* 15, col.1628B); Gratian *Causa* I, *quaestio* I, *caput* xvi (I, col.362).

3/249–52 **Prouer**] Two Scriptural sources seem to have been conflated here: Proverbs 21:13 and 28:9.

3/255–7 **Gregorius**] No precise source traced, but for Gregory on God's severity towards sinners, *cf. Liber Regulae Pastoralis* III, 20 (*P.L.* 77, col.85D); and on Proverbs 28:9 (see lines 249–52 above), *cf. Moralium* X.15 and *Moralium* XVI.21 (*P.L.* 75, col.936C and col.1133C). Further discourse on those whose prayers were abhorrent to God occurs in *Moralium* XXXIII.22 (*P.L.* 76, col.700D–701C). Some interesting correspondences can be seen between the text here (252–7) and a passage in one of the tracts in *SEWW*, 16/122–6, p.86.

3/304 **sclaundred**] Most occurrences of this word in this text correspond to the Modern English sense ('slandered'). But the sense is far from clear here, as the discussion to line 329 confirms. The *V* reading (Matthew 11:6) is *scandalizatus*; *AV* has 'offended'; *WEV* and *WLV* shed no light: each has 'sclaundrid'. The *Rosarium* (headword 'Sklaundre', f.115v.) discusses the word at length.

3/320ff. **Crisostom**] Source not traced.

3/326 **Crisostom**] Source not traced.

3/343, 345 **3e**] The MS has puzzling inconsistencies in the pronoun here. *V/WEV/WLV* readings of Matthew 11:7–8 have the second person pronoun, as emended in this text; but here (and at line 461) the MS has **he**. At line 461, however, an interlinear **y** above the **e** suggests uncertainty (on the part of a corrector?).

3/408, 411   **miri... mirþ**] An example of word play? Late Middle English **miri** is recorded as a spelling for both 'miry' and 'merry'. Given the metaphoric sense of this extended discourse in which the concrete properties of the reed are likened to certain moral defects of man, the sermon-writer may intend the sense of the noun **mirþ** (411), ostensibly formed from **miri** ('merry'), to be coloured by the proximity of **miri** ('miry') at 408. The **mirþ** ('delight') enjoyed through the manifestations of lechery listed at 412–3 is thus likened to the defiling and entrapping mud (**so fals a grounde**, 455) of a mire or swamp, at both 411 and 456. On other possible word play in these sermons, see also Sermon 8/377, 378, Note, and DM/134–150, Note.

3/418   **bastarde siouns**] L. *spuria vitulamina*; *WEV* 'auoutrie plantingis'; *WLV* 'plauntyngis of auoutrie'. See *OED* '**Bastard**' B, *adj.* 3b.

3/445–9   **Crisostom**] *Cf. Op. Imp. Homilia* XLV (*P.G.* 56, col.885).

3/485   **to comyng**] *i.e.* 'to come'. *Cf.* DM/481, where this form occurs again, and see Mustanoja, p.513, for discussion of Middle English infinitives ending in **-ing**.

3/496–7   **houȝ... Aduente**] See Sermon 1/126–32.

3/517   **God... prophete**] No Scriptural source traced. The sense (to line 519) is not clear, but *cf.* 2 Corinthians 11:13–14.

SERMON 4.   *Fourth Sunday in Advent, John 1:19–28*

4/84–90   **Austyn**] *Cf.* Augustine, *Liber De Conflictu Vitiorum et Virtutum, caput* xix (*P.L.* 40, col.1101); Gratian, *Causa* XXII, *quaestio* II, *caput* xiii (I, col.871).

4/103–5   **Austyn... Maister of Stories**] Augustine, *Contra Mendacium, Liber* I, *caput* xii (*P.L.* 40, col.537). The Master of Stories is Peter Comestor.

4/110-17 **Austyn**] Augustine, *De Verbis Apostoli, Sermo* CLXXXI, *caput* iv (*P.L.* 38, col.981); Gratian, *Causa* XXII, *quaesto* II, *caput* ix (I, col.870).

4/118-20 **þe same doctoure**] Augustine, *Super Iohannem, Tractatus* XLIII, *caput* xv (*P.L.* 35, col.1712); Gratian, *Causa* XXII, *quaestio* II, *caput* xi (I, col.870).

4/135-8 **in Comun Lawe**] *i.e.* Canon Law. Augustine, *De Mendacio, caput* xxi* (*P.L.* 40, col.516); Gratian, *Causa* XXII, *quaestio* II, *caput* viii (I, col.870). *N.B. Gratian gives the location as *caput* xiv.

4/139-43 **þe same doctoure**] Augustine, *Enchiridion, sive de Fide, Spe et Charitate, Liber* I, *caput* xviii* (*P.L.* 40, col.240); Gratian, *Causa* XXII, *quaestio* II, *caput* xii (I, col.871). *N.B. Both the *Rosarium* (*loc. cit.* Note 156-7 below) and this MS give the location as chapter 10.

4/143-51 Source not traced. The topic of lying is discussed in *Enchiridion, caput* xviii and xxii (*P.L.* 40, col.240 and 243), and in *De Doctrina Christiana, Liber I, caput xxxvi (P.L. 34, col.34). Cf.* the next Note.

4/156-7 **Austyn**] Augustine, *De Doctrina Christiana, Liber* I, *caput* xxxvi (*P.L.* 34, col.34). The *Rosarium* (headword 'Mendacium', ff. 74v–75v.) cites this work and, as in this MS, gives the location as chapter 41. The passage quoted in the *Rosarium* is not the one used here; it is however, from the same chapter: *i.e.* 36.

4/161-72 **Austyn**] Augustine, *De Mendacio, caput* v (*P.L.* 40, col.491–2). Augustine's commentary is, for the most part, omitted. The writer has simply given Augustine's selection of Scriptural texts.

4/206-9 **Gregorius**] *Cf.* Gregory, *Homiliarum in Evangelia, Liber* I, *Homilia* VII (on John 1:19–28; *P.L.* 76, col.1100B–C).

4/244 **þe foure doctoures**] Ambrose, Augustine, Jerome and Gregory.

4/291 **clergie...can**] The word **science** (= 'knowledge') occurs in several apparently tautological collocations: e.g. here **clergie** = 'knowledge' and **can** = 'know'. *Cf.* Sermon 9/60 **science of knowynge**; Sermon 14/105 **kunnynge of** science; and Sermon 14/109, where *L. scientia* (1 Corinthians 8:1) is translated **kunnyng**.

4/296–9 **þat was...in þe gospel**] *Cf.* MS B ff.9r(b)–9v(a) and 15r(a).

SERMON 5.   *Christmas Day, Luke 2:1–14.*

5/48–9, 58   **profession... know(e)lechynge**] Both *WEV* and *WLV* render the *L. profiterentur* by means of this doublet. *Cf. AV* 'to be taxed'.

5/67–71   **Michie 5:2**] The text quoted here is Matthew 2:6, which cites the prophecy of Micah.

5/111–20   **þe Lawe**] *i.e.* Canon Law. Ambrose, *Expositio Evangelii Secundum Lucam, Liber* IV (on Luke 5:4; *P.L.* 15, col.1634B); Gratian, *Causa* XI, *quaestio* I, *caput* xxviii (I, col.634).

5/128–32   **Also, þe aungel...**] The syntax is very awkward and elliptical here. The angel of Matthew 1:20 is cited as further **autorite aȝenst hem...matrymonie** (lines 123–5). The antecedent of **he** (lines 129 and 130) is **Joseph**: *cf.* Matthew 1:19 and 24.

5/138–55   **þe Mayster of Sentence**] *i.e.* Peter Lombard: See *Sententiarum, Liber* IV, *Dist.* xxviii and xxix (*P.L.* 192, col.1107B–C). *Cf.* Augustine, *De Nuptiis et Concupiscentia, Liber* I, *caput* xi (*P.L.* 44, col.420–1); and *De Genesi Ad Litteram, Liber* XI, *caput* vii (*P.L.* 34, col.397). Sources not traced for all of this passage.

5/168   **fantasie**] *Cf.* Sermon 6/74–7, Note.

5/217–8   **Anastase, wiþ creuen hoondes**] The *Legenda* contains two readings for December 25th: VI, *De Nativitate domini nostri Jesu Christi*, and VII, *De Sancta Anastasia*. The first of these includes the story of the midwife Salome, who doubted the virginity of Mary, and whose hands, which withered suddenly when she touched Mary, healed as suddenly when she touched the Christ child. This episode is dramatised in the *Ludus Coventriae* 'Birth of Christ' (E.E.T.S. e.s. 120, pp.143–4). I have been unable to find any account of the life of St Anastasia which corresponds to this passage. The reading **creuen** is an emendation. The scribe has written an initial **t** very clearly. This may be a miscopying of **creuen** (deriving from *O.F.* **crever** 'to split open, crack').

5/233-7   **as doctouris seyn... wederis**] See *Legenda* VI, *De Nativitate domino nostro Jesu Christi*; also Peter Comestor, *Historia Scholastica, In Evangelia, caput* v, *De Nativitate Salvatoris* (*P.L.* 198, col.1539-40).

5/238-41   **an oxe...dispensis**] See *Legenda* (*ibid.*). Lyra source not traced.

5/332-3   **to his knowlechynge**] *i.e.* 'to recognise as worthy', 'to single out for special notice'.

5/453   **wyckede**] Omission of preposition? *WEV* 'to vnpitous'; *WLV* 'to wickid'.

SERMON 6.   *Circumcision (New Year's Day), Luke 2:21*

6/20   **xii**] The MS reading is **xvij**, but the text at lines 21-2 (and 23-6) comprises first a quotation from, then a paraphase of, Genesis 12:1 (and 12:7). Lines 29-31, however, quote (then paraphrase) Genesis 17:10-11 (and 17:23).

6/59-69   **þe Maister of þe Sentence**] *i.e.* Peter Lombard. See *Sententiarum, Liber* IV, *Dist.* I (*P.L.* 192, col.840) and *Dist.* III (*P.L.* 192, col.846).

6/74-7   **Manicheijs...Valentyne**] The teachings of Mani (born A.D. *c.* 216) and of Valentinus (an influential Gnostic of the second century A.D.) were branded as heretical by the medieval Christian church. The discussion here refers to the tenet of these teachings that denies the human, physical nature of Christ. See Augustine, *De Haeresibus, Liber* I, §XLVI, *Manichaei* (*P.L.* 42, col.37-8); and §XI, *Valentiniani* (*Ibid.* col.27-8). See also John Capgrave's *Life of St Augustine*, ed. J.J. Monroe, (E.E.T.S. o.s. 140, 1910, p.9/26-31), which attributes to the Manicheans the view that Christ 'had not very flesch and blood as oþir men haue, but rather a fantastical body mad of þe eyr...' See also MS B f.20r(a)(b) '...to shewe þe treuþe of flesche aȝenus manncheus & hem þat seyen þᵗ Crist cam forþ apperyngly. þat is semide man & was not...& þat he brouȝte not þe body fro heuen as ualentyne seide.'

6/309-10   **þis matere...more herof**] There is no such matter in the Lenten group in R: i.e. Sermons 12-16.

SERMON 7.   *Epiphany (Twelfth Day), Matthew 2:1–12*

N.B. Unlike the other sermons in this collection, this one gives no Scriptural locations.

7/37   **Jerusalem... siȝt of þees**] Also in Sermon 1/86.

7/152–5   **þe womman of Chanan**] Matthew 15:21–8: the text for Sermon 12 (the Second Sunday in Lent).

7/156   **in charite**] See DM/102, Note.

7/159–64   **Crisostom**] *Cf. Op. Imp. Homilia* XIII (*P.G.* 56, col.708–9).

7/176   *memorare nouissima*] See Sermon 2/663–4 and Note; also Sermon 15/416 and 15/1–2, Note.

7/203–4   **as Seint Poule seiþ**] Perhaps a gloss on Galatians 3:29 and 4:7.

SERMON 8.   *Septuagesima Sunday, Matthew 20:1–16*

This parable is cited in DM/987–94. The image of the vineyard is also touched upon in Sermon 1/148, 314–18, 323–25.

8/22–7   **Gregorius**] Gregory formulates five ages (corresponding to the hours of the parable), not seven as here. *Cf. Homiliarum in Evangelia, Liber* I, *Homilia* XIX (on Matthew 20:1–16; *P.L.* 76, col.1154C).

8/30–35   **Crisostom**] *Op. Imp. Homilia* XXXIV (*P.G.* 56, col.818).

8/66–94   **Crisostom**] *Ibid.* (col.818–19). MSS A and R have exactly the same inconsistencies in the text. Both have **vertu** at lines 77 and 83, where Migne has *vitem* (i.e. 'vine'), as at lines 73, 80, 85, 87 and 94. And see line 92, where neither A nor R translates *nec congaudes* (here conjecturally supplied by analogy with lines 69–70), although both include the correlative phrase of the source: *sed congaudes meliori.*

8/89   **bedenfastynge**] See Glossary. The **beden-** component here probably derives from the *p. pl.* of **beden** or **bidden**, two verbs which coincide at several points in form (**be-** and **bo-**) and sense ('ordered', 'commanded'). The *OED* ['**Bid**' *v.*] includes the two forms found in MSS A and R, The *MED* ['**Boden**' *v.* (1) 2 (b)] gives a definition and a supporting citation which correspond well to the context here (note particularly **after... apostele**), but this does not account for the **be-** form in MS A.

8/139   **Gregorius**] *Cf.* Gregory, *Homiliarum in Evangelia, Liber* II, *Homilia* XXXIV (on Luke 15:1–10; *P.L.* 76, col.1248B–C).

8/159–63   **Gregorius**] See Gregory, *Ibid. Liber* I, *Homilia* XIX (on Matthew 20:1–16; *P.L.* 76, col.1156B–C). See also Wyclif's *Sermones* I (*Sermo* XV), p.103/14–15.

8/169   **ryue**] Despite the clear reading **ryne** in MS A, both form and sense seem to favour the MS R reading. *Cf.* line 352, where a similar difficulty has arisen, and the MS A reading **rynede** has been emended to **rife**, as in MS R.

8/181   **it is lefful... likeþ**] 'A man is entitled to do as he pleases with what belongs to him.'

8/226ff.   **what þou art...**] See Bernard, *Meditationes de Cognitione Humanae Conditionis, caput* iii (*P.L.* 184, esp. col.490). *Cf.* DM/43–5.

8/257–64   **Crisostom**] *Cf. Op. Imp. Homilia* XIX (*P.G.* 56, col.740).

8/269–82   This passage is a complex development of the imagery expounded at 31–5, where the vineyard of the parable is interpreted as 'righteousness', and the vine as the virtues that comprise this quality. The syntax at 279–80 is confusing. The sense is perhaps 'to show them [*i.e.* the evil-doers] the way to the vine of virtuous deeds, which they [*i.e.* the prelates and priests] have nurtured in their parishioners by means of personal example'.

8/377, 378   **þe synguler wilde best**] This phrase corresponds precisely to the *L. singularis ferus* (Psalm 79:14; see also 293 above), but there is a possible element of word play in the way the adjective is being used here. *Cf. OED* 'Sanglier' *sb.* (from *O.F.*: 'a wild boar'), and the extended imagery of the **boor of þe wode** from lines 338 and 375–6. Another example of word play in this sermon may perhaps lie in the use of **slowis, sleuþe**, and **slowe**, lines 357, 358, and 362. See also Sermon 3/408, 411, Note, and DM/134–50, Note.

8/391–3 **Gregorius**] Gregory, *In Septem Psalmos Poenitentiales*, *Expositio III* (on Psalm 37; *P.L.* 79, col.569c).

SERMON 9. *Sexagesima Sunday, Luke 8:5–15*

9/20 **weyue fro**] MS R has **weyne forþe**. MS A is ambiguous: *i.e.* **u** and **n** are often indistinguishable. The editorial choice made here is based on *OED* '**Waive**' *v.*[1] 4(= 3b). See Glossary.

9/25–6 **Jerom**] Source not traced, but see *Glossa*, V, col.798: marginal gloss on Luke 8:8.

9/42–62 **Crisostom**] *Cf. Op. Imp. Homilia* XXXI (*P.G.* 56, col.796–7). The phrase **to excuse excusacions** (49–50) renders *V. ad excusandas excusationes*. *WEV* has 'to ben excusid excusaciouns'; *WLV* has 'to excuse excusingis'. *AV* has nothing corresponding to this, the sense of which seems to be 'seek exculpation on the grounds of extenuating or mitigating circumstances'.

9/60, 62 **deserue, deseruest**] But *cf.* R reading: **discerne, discernyst**. *Op. Imp.* (see preceding Note), *loc cit.*, col.797, lines 28 and 30–1 has *merebaris*; the manuscripts have *merebaris* and *merearis*. The variant readings in R may have arisen from an exemplar with (a) a **di-** or **disc-** form of **deserue** (see *WEV* and *WLV*, Hebrews 13:16 for the former, and *OED* citations for the latter) and (b) an ambiguous medial **u/n**.

9/63–70 **Crisostom**] *Op. Imp. Homilia* XLIV (*P.G.* 56, col.881).

9/91–2 **Jerom**] *Cf.* Jerome, *Epistola* CXXV, *Ad Rusticum Monachum*, XI (*P.L.* 22, col.1078).

9/96 **God**] Emended by analogy with 9/92, supported by R reading.

9/139–48 **Gregorius**] *Cf.* Gregory, *Homiliarum in Evangelia*, *Liber* I, *Homilia* XV (on Luke 8:4–15; *P.L.* 76, col.1131C–D).

9/149–52 *Cf. Ibid.* (col.1133A).

9/216 *Groosthed*] Grosseteste: *c.* 1175–1253; Bishop of Lincoln, 1235–53.

9/217–59 **Pauper et inops...**] See Oxford Laud Misc. MS 402,ff. 135r, 135v, 137r, 138r, 138v. Other manuscripts containing the Grosseteste sermon from which passages have been translated and paraphrased here have been listed by S. Harrison Thomson in *The Writings of Robert Grosseteste* (Cambridge, 1940); see pp.164, 166 (1), also 215. And see Sermons 10/133–62, 11A/41–2, 15/184–5 and Notes. The thematic connection with Romans 6 at line 226 seems tenuous, but the sermon writer may have had in mind a gloss as yet unidentified. *Cf.* Lyra on the final sentence of Romans 6:21, *Glossa* VII, col.86.

9/265   **Jerom... wille of hauynge**] Source not traced, but see *Glossa* V, col.323–4; interlinear gloss on Matthew 19:27.

9/288–9   **What... bifore**] See Sermon 8/215–42.

9/313–4   **rennest a wegge**] 'The plough-fote is a lyttell pece of wodde, with a croked ende set before in a morteys in the plough-beame, sette faste with wedges, to dryue vppe and downe'. John Fitzherbert, *The Boke of Husbandry*, 1534, cited *OED* '**Wedge**' *sb.* 1.

9/315–9   **Austeyn**] See Augustine, *Liber de Vera et Falsa Poenitentia*, *caput* x.25 (*P.L.* 40, col.1122).

9/327–8   **Austeyn**] See Augustine, *Ibid.*

9/365   **to litel men**] *L. parvulis*. *WEV* and *WLV* render this variously as 'litil men'; 'litle'; 'pore'; and 'litle/smale children'.

9/378–95   On the notion of three degrees of the fruit of charity (matrimony, widowhood and virginity), *cf. Piers Plowman* (Skeat's edition), B.XVI, 67–72 and C.XIX, 84–100.

SERMON 10.   *Quinquagesima Sunday, Luke 18:31–43*

10/32   **scourgynge**] The R reading is consistent with the context. *Cf.* lines 35–9 and 58–80.

10/132   **þe doctur Lyncoln**] Grosseteste. See Sermon 9/216, Note.

10/133–62   **Qui Christi sunt...**] See Oxford Magdalen College MS 202, ff. 152v–153r, an exposition by Grosseteste of Galatians 5:24. For other manuscripts containing this, see S. Harrison Thomson (*op. cit.*, Sermon 9/217–59, Note): pp.164 (17), and 173 (17).

10/178 **clerete, agilite, sutilte, and immortalite**] See DM/1071–90 for an extended discussion of the four dowers or attributes of the resurrected body, and see Note, DM/1072–3.

10/186 **'Lord... beo'**] Not in *V*, or in all versions of *WEV*, or in *AV*; it is, however, in *WLV*, and in the *Apology*, pp.56–7.

10/187–91 **Crisostom**] *Cf.* Chrysostom, *Homilia in Matthaeum* LIV/LV (*P.G.* 57, col.536).

10/248–58 **Crisostom**] *Op. Imp. Homilia* XLIII (*P.G.* 56, col.878–9).

10/259–61 **Crisostom**] *Cf. Op. Imp. Homilia* II (*P.G.* 56, col.638).

10/311 *Marginalia* (H3): *foot of* f.85r: De votis f⟨acti⟩s ⟨yma⟩ginibus et cetera (*part of the margin is cut away*).

10/319 **worschipeþ more**] Emended to R reading on the assumption that the antecedent of 'þat' is 'þei' (preceding line). *Cf. SEWW*, 16/91–6, p.85, and 16/167–70, p.87. *Cf.* also Glossary **lo(o)ueþ**.

10/357–63 **Crisostom**] *Cf. Op. Imp. Homilia* XLIV (*P.G.* 56, col.884–5).

10/371–4 **Austeyn**] *Cf.* Augustine, *Sermones de Scripturis*, LVI (*P.L.* 38, col.381).

10/372–6 *Marginalia* (H3): *Nota sign, followed by*: quod aliquo modo quilibet est mendicus.

10/382 **menynge**] A medial **n** seems likely here, in view of the MS R reading: **bymenyng**. (See *OED* '**Bemean**' *v.*[2], and *MED* '**Bimene**' *v.*, and '**Menen**' *v.*(1) 3(f), and '**Mening(e)**' *ger,* (1) 1). This scribe does not always distinguish **n** and **u**, however (*cf.* Sermon 9/20, Note), and a reading **meuynge** is not incompatible with the context. *Cf.* Sermon 3/134, and Sermon 4/290. See *OED* '**Moving**' *vbl. sb.* 3, and '**Motion**' *sb.* 9, and *MED* '**Meving(e)**' *ger.* 3(b) 'action'.

10/406 **3e**] Emended reading based on *V intrabitis*, and *WEV/WLV*.

10/414–26 **Dauid... lyue**] *Cf.* Augustine, *Liber de Conflictu Vitiorum et Virtutem, caput* xv (*P.L.* 40, col.1098–9); cited in *Glossa* IV, col.1324: marginal gloss on Ezekiel 33:11.

10/454–5 **mouþe... herte**] Reading emended here, despite the agreement between the two manuscripts, because the sense is not otherwise compatible with the context (*cf.* especially lines 477–80). See further discussion of this, Introduction, p.lvi above.

SERMON 11. *First Sunday in Lent, Matthew 4:1–11*

11/209   **þe þridde heuen**] See 2 Corinthians 12:2.

11/245–6   **haue studie of reste**] *L. opera detis ut quieti sitis; WEV* '3yue werk, *or bisynesse*, that 3e be quyet'; *WLV* 'taken kepe, that 3e be quyet']; *AV* 'study to be quiet'.

11/263–9   **Crisostom**] *Op. Imp. Homilia V (P.G.* 56, col.667). N.B. The argument from **And þerfore** (269–70) to **deceyued wiþ** (273) is essentially derived from the same source.

11/283–4   **Gregorius**] Source not traced. But *cf.* Wyclif's *Sermones* I (*Sermo* XXIII), p.158 ...*omnia opera humanitatis Christi sint exemplaria a fidelibus exequenda.*

11/316–35   **Crisostom**] *Op. Imp. Homilia* V (*P.G.* 56, col.671).

11/320   **he**] *i.e.* **þe goode angele** (line 318).

11A.   *An Optional Expansion of Sermon 11*

11A/40   **Seneca**] *Cf. Ad. Lucilium Epistulae Morales,* 83 (Loeb edition, Vol.II, p.270). See the next Note.

11A/41–2   **Lyncoln... herte**] From *Dictum* 147 by Grosseteste (see Sermon 9/216, Note), incorporating a quotation from Hosea 4:11. See Bodley MS 798, f.120r(a). Other manuscripts containing *Dicta* by Grosseteste are listed by S. Harrison Thomson (*op. cit.,* Sermon 9/217–59, Note). *Cf.* also Sermon 15/184–5 and Note. This quotation and the one from Seneca that precedes it occur, just as here, in the *Rosarium* (headword: '*Ebrietas*') f.31v.

11A/229–46   **prelates þat ben nowadaies...**] *Cf.* Sermon 1/26–33, Sermon 2/417–30, and DM/557–67.

11A/395–8   **þei... plee**] The pronouns and possessive adjectives here are somewhat confusing and ambiguous. The sense is that **pore tenauntis** and **semple nei3heboris** (393) are glad, in order to be left in peace, to pay the fines imposed on them by **kny3tes and squyers** (392). Such poor and simple men know that they might just as well give up their land without a fight if the rich knights and squires lay claim to it, because they are powerless to withstand such oppressors.

11A/435 **putt into**] *L. posita in*; *WEV*/*WLV* 'kept in to'; *AV* 'laid up for'.

11A/524 **et cetera**] Presumably the intention is to echo the theme that runs like a refrain through lines 518, 519 and 523: **is vnable to be fulfillid**.

11A/543 **woute**] Not in the *OED*. Perhaps **wourte**, which is recorded in the *OED* as a form of '**Wort**'; *OED* citations ('**Wortworm**') includes *WLV* 'worte-worm', Joel 1:4.

SERMON 12. *Second Sunday in Lent, Matthew 15:21–8*

12/51 **O tortuose serpens**] The *Breviarium ad usum insignis ecclesiae Sarum*, ed. F. Proctor and C. Wordsworth, fasc. I, p.715 (Cambridge, 1882) has a hymn for the night prayer of Compline in Passiontide, beginning *Cultor Dei, memento*, the fifth stanza of which opens with the words quoted here. The English (51–2) is a translation of the entire stanza. The hymn is included in the Cathemerinon by Prudentius, a Spanish lawyer (348–*c*.410).

12/100 **rauysshing**] *L. rugiens*; *WEV*/*WLV* 'roryng(e)'; *AV* 'roaring'.

12/215–6 **Seint Steuen**] See *Legenda* (VIII, *De Sancto Stephano*) p.53.

12/235 **fote... affeccion of þi soule**] See Sermon 1/209, Note.

12/295 **soule**] This reading constitutes a gloss on *V filia* (*WEV*/*WLV* 'dou3ter'; *AV* 'daughter'), to which the sermon text corresponds at lines 320, 334, and 520. But *cf*. the interpretation of Matthew 15:22 at lines 358–63, and *Glossa* V, col.266F.

12/347 **male**] Refers to Matthew 15:22 (*male... vexatur*); see line 295 above: **traueilid yuel**.

12/414–5, 423   **preyden for...**] The paraphrase here, and the commentary deriving from it (415–20), conflict puzzlingly with the *V* reading: *Dimitte eam: quia clamat post nos*, to which both *WEV* and *WLV* correspond.

12/456   **homely...feiþe**] *i.e.* 'those within the fold of the church'; *cf. WEV* 'houshold meyne of the feith'; *WLV* 'hom-liche of the feith'; *AV* 'the houshold of faith'. *MED*, '**homli**' *adj.* 2(a), glosses this phrase as 'belonging to the community of Christians'.

12/471–4   **Crisostom**] *Op. Imp. Homilia* XV (*P.G.* 56, col.716). N.B. line 472: **marchaunte** and **lijf** indicate a source text with *mercator* and *vit(a)e*; *P.G.*, however, has *mediatrix* and *viae*. The source text may also have had a reading other than *P.G. ante faciem orationis*, which could explain an implied distinction between **þe preyoure** and **preyer** (473): *i.e.* 'one who prays' and 'the act of praying'.

12/509–11   **In...saaf**] *Cf.* DM/403–5, and Sermon 10/423–6 (see 10/414–26, Note).

SERMON 13.   *Third Sunday in Lent, Luke 11:14–28*

N.B. Many Scriptural locations are given in this sermon; but, unlike the other sermons in this collection, it contains no attributions to specific authorities, although there are indications at two points that material from such sources has been used: see lines 57–8 and 127.

13/57–8   **diuerse... acorden**] *Cf. Glossa* V, col.797: marginal and interlinear glosses on Luke 8:2.

13/304   The correlative element of a simile seems to have been lost here. Given the number of omissions in R clearly attributable to 'eye-skip' between two occurrences of the same word (12/158–60, DM/436–7, DM/459–60, DM/989; see Introduction, pp. above), the 'shape' of the missing pasage is likely to have been '**as water flowiþ** [*in something and does something*, **so such a man flowiþ**] **in his lustis...** etc', with **flowiþ** used concretely the first time and figuratively the second, giving the sense 'abounds'—see *MED* **flouen** *v.* 3(c).

SERMON 14. *Fourth Sunday in Lent, John 6:1–14*
(*Cf.* SERMON 15)

14/16 **þritti louis**] *V. viginti panes hordeacos*; *WEV* 'and ten
barly loouys'; *WLV* 'ten looues of barli'; *WEV/WLV margin*:
'summe bokis han *and xx looues of barly*, but this word *and*, is
not in Ebreu...' The attribution here is 'Lire'. *Cf. Glossa* II,
col.885–6; *AV* 'twenty loaves of barley'.

14/91 **holden**] Conjectural emendation based on the occurrence of **doun** at the start of f.91v: *i.e.* the phonemic resemblance could explain the omission of **-den** at the end of
f.91r.

14/144 **Marke...þombe**] *Cf. Legenda* (LIX, *De Sancto
Marco Evangelista*) p.265: '...*propter nimiam humiliatatem pol-
licem sibi amputasse dicitur...*'

14/245–6 **fyue wittis**] *Cf.* DM/550, and *Sir Gawain and the
Green Knight* II, 640.

14/260–1 **clerkis sotilteis**] The MS has an erasure between
these two words. Ultra-violet light reveals the following reading (with dots beneath the characters): **pᵗ beṉ lettrid hyȝly
haṉ greͤ/te ⟨ioye?⟩ þerof & arett it al to ihū crist**. The same
words occur at lines 268–9; but note the variant forms **hilie**
and **greet** and (less certain) **joy**.

SERMON 15. *Fourth Sunday in Lent, John 6:11*

(An alternative to Sermon 14: see the end of that sermon, lines
275–8). This sermon is discussed by Christina von Nolcken in
'Some Alphabetical Compendia and How Preachers Used
Them in Fourteenth-Century England', *Viator* 12 (1981),
pp.271–88. And see Note 15/358–75.

15/1–2 **Þe helpe and þe grace**] It seems likely, from the
way in which this phrase is used here, and again at lines 38–9
(*i.e.* incomplete and not a translation of the Latin that precedes
it), that it is a formulaic introduction commonly used in
vernacular prayers. This hypothesis is supported by the prayer
at the opening of the Sermon of Dead Men (the concluding
text in this edition, referred to in Sermon 15/416 and in
Sermon 2/663–4). Dr. A.I. Doyle has pointed out another

example, the opening of Mirk's *Festial* in Durham Cosin MS V.III.5:

> 'The helpe and the grace of almighty god . thurgh
> the blissyng of his blissid modir Marie . be with us
> at oure begynyng...'

15/35–6 **Hely... Oreb**] *i.e. AV*: Elijah...Horeb; 1 Kings 19:7–8.

15/37 **haueþ... statis**] 'to bring it about that you pray to God for all the estates of society' (*i.e.* the priests, the knights, and the common people, see also DM/95–6); and see *OED* '**Recommand**' *v.* 1, c and '**Recommend**' *v.* 1, (b).

15/54–6 **...þis breed...þe next gospel...**] Refers to John 6:32–58, especially verses 35 and 48: *Ego sum panis vitae.*

15/61 **his twelue apostlis**] There are erasures on either side of the word **twelue**. Ultra-violet light reveals the following readings: **his** (**eleuen** *erased*) (**disciplis** *erased*) **twelue** (**disciplis** *erased*) **apostlis**. The erased words have expunctuation dots beneath each character. See Introduction, p.xxv, Note 2.

15/70–1 **ordeyned... hem**] This is not at all a clear translation of *V: designavit...et alios septuaginta duos. Cf. WLV*: 'ordeynede also othir seuenti and tweyn, and sente hem bi tweyn and tweyn' (*V: misit illos binos*), which coincides with the rendering in MS B, f.93r(a).

15/73–4 **apostlis...decree seiþe**] See Gratian, *Distinctio* XXI, *caput* i (I, col.67), and *Distinctio* LXVIII, *caput* v and vi (I, cols.255–6, and *Distinctio* XCIII, *caput* xxv (I, col.329).

15/116–17 There is a treatise on the Ten Commandments in the same manuscript as this sermon, *i.e.* MS R, ff.120r–143r, followed by a shorter work entitled 'Þe charge of þe heestis', ff.143r–146r, and preceded by a Prologue, ff.119v–120r.

15/122 **profite**] The antonyms **plesaunce** and **displesaunce** conflict with the MS reading **hyndring...hyndryng**. Unless a manuscript with another reading is found, we can only speculate about the missing noun by scrutinising the rest of the text. The concept of 'profit' fits the context well. The collocation 'profit... soul' occurs eleven times: Sermon 1/75; Sermon 7/130, 131–2, 135; Sermon 9/29; Sermon 10/515; Sermon 13/377, 387–8; Sermon 14/246–7; Sermon 16/207, 367–8.

15/164–5 **þe Mayster of Sentence**] *i.e.* Peter Lombard. *Cf. Sententiarum, Liber* IV, *Dist.* 18 (*P.L.* 192, col.1101A). *Cf.* The *Rosarium* (headword 'Absolucion', f.iv.).

15/184–5 **þe doctour Lincolne**] Grosseteste (see Sermon 9/216, Note). *Cf. Dictum* 106* (Bodley MS 798, f.88r.a.) which begins *Cor contritum* and uses the image of a three-part pestle, by means of which the heart may be 'ground into' rejection of sin. Although the three-fold relationship to sin in the *Dictum* (*timore pene... horrore feditatis... rubore et verecundia peccati*) does not coincide precisely with that given here, there are some significant correspondences: *cf.* lines 193–4, 198 **ful purpos neuer to turne aȝeyn to synne.. lest ony þing falle worse to þee** (*i.e.* fear of punishment); and line 185 **hate** (*i.e.* disgust); and lines 189–90 **contynuel sorow** (*i.e.* shame). *See S. Harrison Thomson (*op. cit.*, Sermon 9/217–59, Note) pp.227 (106), 189 (65), and list of manuscripts, p.215.

15/192–3 **Austyn**] See Augustine, *De Vera et Falsa Poenitentia, caput* ii, 4 (*P.L.* 40, col.1114).

15/223 **what...deseruid?**] *i.e.* 'What have they done to deserve this?'

15/225 **Anany and Saphire**] *i.e. AV*: Ananias... Sapphira; Acts 5:1–10.

15/227–30 **Ambrose**] *Expositio in Psalmum* CXVIII (*P.L.* 15, col.1244C).

15/232–8 **Alquin...peyne**] See the *Compendium* (*Liber* VI, *caput* xxiv, *De Satisfactione*) p.829. A confused English rendering of the text at 15/235–8 occurs in the *Rosarium*. See the next Note.

15/237–8 **dett of satisfaccion peyne**] This translation is gramatically consistent with the Latin at line 235, but neither yields any clear sense. A defective source text seems likely. The reading in the *Compendium* (see the preceding Note) is: *debitum poenae satisfactoriae*. The Latin *Rosarium* has *debitum pene satisfactorie*, which is rendered, in the English *Rosarium* (headword 'Satisfaccion', f.115v.), 'dette of peyne satisfactorie'. The most probable sense seems to be 'the debt of atoning punishment'.

15/255 **þe sermoun of Ephiphanie**] See Sermon 7/126–69.

15/262–6 **Crisostom**] *Op. Imp. Homilia* V (*P.G.* 56, col.669).

15/278–9 **Austyn...breed...Pater   Noster**]   *Cf.*   Sermon 10/371–4 and Note.

15/291ff. **Gregorius and oþer doctouris**] *Cf. Glossa* V, cols.1325–6 (*Moraliter*).

15/338–44 **Gregorius...Comoun Lawe**] Gregory, *Epistolarum Liber* IX, *Epistola* CVI (*P.L.* 77, col.1030A) ...Canon Law: Gratian, *Causa* XIV, *quaestio* V, caput vii (I, col.739).

15/358–75 Christian von Nolcken has pointed out that the text here corresponds precisely to a passage in the collection of Wycliffite Latin sermons in Oxford Laud Misc. MS 200, ff.93v–94r. (See 'An Unremarked Group of Wycliffite Sermons in Latin', *Modern Philology*, Vol.83, 1986, pp.233–49; See especially p.246). Dr. von Nolcken has found other manuscripts containing these sermons; one of which (Bodleian 803) also contains a Latin text of the *Rosarium*. The full significance of these coincidences should emerge from her continuing work on this material.

15/416 **sermoun of Deed Men...**] *i.e.* the last text in this edition, pp.207–40, referred to editorially throughout as the Sermon of Dead Men, or DM. Another internal cross-reference to it occurs in Sermon 2/663–4.

SERMON 16.   *Fifth Sunday in Lent, John 8 :46–59*

16/105–112, 265–8 **Austyn**] Augustine, *Sermones Supposititii, Sermo* CCC, 2 (*P.L.* 39, col.2319). Gratian, *Causa* I, *quaestio* I, *caput* xciv (I, col.391–2).

16/207–11 **þe soule...þe foode of þe body**] *Cf.* Sermon 3/136–7

16/291–3 *Crisostom*] *Cf. Op. Imp. Homilia* XVIII (*P.G.* 56, col.733).

16/362 **putting**] Emendation supported by the same collocation occurring at line 16 above.

16/388–96 **Crisostom**] (*Cf.* also Sermon 1/297–302) *Op. Imp. Homilia* XXXVIII (*P.G.* 56, col.842). The conjectural reading at lines 393–4 is a rendering of the omitted correlative subordinate clause: *si autem fuerit perversum cor, videns opera alicujus viri justi, aut audiens.*

16/397–402   See the same wax/clay image in Sermon 1/290–6 where it precedes the *Op. Imp.* text that it here follows (see Note 16/388–96). Source not traced.

DM   *The Sermon of Dead Men, Ecclesiasticus 7:36*

The title given to this text is taken from references to it in Sermon 2/663–4 and Sermon 15/416.

DM/2–10   **The helpe... Amen**] See Sermon 15/1–2, Note.

DM/43–5   **Bernarde**] *Meditationes de Cognitione Humanae Conditionis, caput* ii (*P.L.* 184, col.487D). *Cf.* Sermon 8/226ff. and Note.

DM/54   **bouȝt hem to**] *i.e.* (*fig.*) 'puchased for them' (?) See *OED* 'To' *prep.* 30.

DM/55–6   **þe Philosofre**] *i.e.* Aristotle. If we read **þen** as 'rather than' (*OED* 'Than' 3a), this aphoristic utterance comes close to two Latin versions attributed to Aristotle in the Middle Ages:

1)   *Omnis virtus unita fortior est se ipsa dispersa.* See *Les Auctoritates Aristotelis: un florilège médiéval; étude historique et édition critique.* Ed. J. Hamesse (*Philosophes Médiévaux* XVII, Louvain/Paris 1974), p.232 (13).

2)   *Omnis virtus unita plus est infinita quam virtus multiplicata.* See *Le Liber de Causis* XVI.138 (*Tiijdschrift voor Filosofie*, Louvain 1966).

The ultimate source of the continuation (56–7) may well be Aristotle, *Physica*, vii.5. See the translation by R.P. Hardie and R.K. Gaye, *The Works of Aristotle* II (Oxford, 1930), 250a, 16–19.

DM/68   **In þis maner**] The punctuation in MS M clearly places this phrase at the end of the preceding sentence, following with a capital initial on **Also**. MS R equally clearly punctuates so as to start a new sentence as transcribed here.

DM/95–6   **al þe states**] *Cf.* Sermon 15/37 and Note.

DM/102   **in charite**] *i.e.* 'in a state of loving God and one's fellow-men'. See also DM/979 and 1066–7, Sermon 7/156 and 159, and Sermon 8/282.

DM/123–4   **in... flatering**] *i.e.* 'given to flattering utterances'.

DM/134–50   The extended metaphor of this passage relies on word play deriving from two senses of **teme** ('team' and 'theme', see Glossary), and on a correspondence between the concrete and figurative senses of **tilier** ('tiller'). It should be noted, however, that the nature of the variant readings in MS M is such that both word play and metaphor are lost, leaving a passage of considerably less imaginative eloquence and somewhat blurred sense. *Cf.* 136: **tilying** R but **techinge** M; also 137 and 139, where R has **teme**, but M has **tyme**. At 146, 149 and 156, R and M both have **te(e)me**, but in all three instances the word is used in juxtaposition with **tyme**, which may account for the unsatisfactory M readings at 137 and 139.

DM/171–4   **Bernarde**] *Cf. Meditationes de Cognitione Humanae Conditionis, caput* iii (*P.L.* 184, col.491C), and *Epistola* CV (*P.L.* 182, col.240C–D).

DM/237   **dampnyd**] Followed in MS R by 'Of suche men me þinkiþ may wel be seide þe wordis of Ysay þe prophete seying þus Non... tuorum' (as at lines 250–2). This repetition does not occur in M. MS R has 'Ysaie' in the margin at this point.

DM/270–1   **Austyn**] Source not traced.

DM/306–7   **þe lijf of Seynt Martyn**] See *Legenda* (CLXVI *De Sancto Martino episcopo*) pp.747–8.

DM/317–9   **a doctour**] Precise source not traced, but *cf. De Triplici Habitaculo** (*Incerti Auctoris*), *Liber* 1, *caput* i (*P.L.* 40, col.992): *Cruciat... diaboli.* *This work is also cited in Note DM/1039–43.

DM/354–5   **euer an aunter (when it comyþ)**] *i.e.* 'in a sustained state of fear and uncertainty (about when it will take place)'.

DM/374   **affeccions... fete**] See Sermon 1/209, Note.

DM/380   **enerued**] The context precludes the sense recorded in the *MED* ('weakened, enervated') and suggests a verb formed from the prefix en- (*OED* 'en-' *prefix*[1], 1.b) and the noun **nerve** ('the sinews of an animal used in the construction of a shield or bow' *MED*). The imagery of **fast... charite** thus gives the sense 'firmly reinforced by means of the strengthen-

ing properties of charity'. *Cf.* a similar image in Sermon
12/322–3.

DM/401–5 **he seiþe by his prophete...safe**] *Cf.* Sermon
12/509–11, also Sermon 10/423–6 and Sermon 10/414–26,
Note.

DM/480–1 **but...comynge**] This corresponds to the *WLV*
rendering of Ecclesiastes 9:1–2. *N.B.* **into** = 'until', **to
comynge** = 'to come'. For discussion of Middle English
infinitives ending in -**ing**, see Mustanoja, p.513.

DM/550 **fyue wittes**] *Cf.* Sermon 14/245–6 and Note.

DM/557 **prelatis and prestis...**] *Cf.* Sermon 1/26–33, Sermon 2/417–30, and Sermon 11A/229–46.

DM/557–96 A single syntactic construction is extended across
this entire passage, through the sequence of suspended con-
ditional clauses introducing the Seven Deadly Sins (557 Pride;
568 Wrath and Envy; 575 Avarice; 580 Gluttony; 586 Sloth;
592 Lechery), culminating in the main clause at 595–6
(**harde... ensaumple**).

DM/640–54 **Januensis**] *i.e.* Jacobus de Voragine. See *Sermones Quadragesimales* (Brescia 1483), *Sermo* XI on the text
Cum venerit filius hominis in maiestate sua (Mat. xxv); and
Legenda (I. *De Adventu Domini*), p.11. The elements listed here
(640–54) coincide with those in the *Compendium* (*Liber* VII,
caput xvii, *De Iudicio Extremo*), pp.838–9.

DM/658–61 **Bernard**] *Meditationes Cognitione Humanae Conditionis*, *caput* ii (*P.L.* 184, col.488C).

DM/662–4 **Austyn**] Precise source not traced, but for a dis-
cussion relevant to the implications of this passage, see J.
Rivière, 'Role du démon au jugement particulier chez les
Pères,' *Revue des Sciences religieuses* (4), 1924, pp.43–64.

DM/702 **Hic Thomas**] See the *Compendium* (*Liber* I, *caput*
xviii, *De Aeternitate Dei*), pp.739–40.

DM/850–1 **as doctouris seyne**] No sources traced.

DM/854–5 **Ysid**] A paraphrase of Isidor, *Sententiarum*, *Liber*
I, *caput* xxviii, *De gehenna* (*P.L.* 83, col.597B).

DM/854–957 *The Pains of Hell. Cf.* some interesting correspondences in the *Compendium* (*Liber* VII, *caput* xxi and xxii, *De Poenis Inferni* and *De Diuersitate Poenarum*), pp.840–1.

DM/895–6 **Ve!... derkenessis!**] From the Office for the Dead (*Dirige*, Lesson IX). See *The Prymer or Lay Folks' Prayer Book*, edited by H. Littlehales from Cambridge MS Dd. 11. 82, (E.E.T.S. o.s. 105, London, 1895), p.70/5–7. See also 'The Prymer in English' edited by W. Maskell from what is now British Library (BL) Additional MS 17010, in *Monumenta Ritualia Ecclesiae Anglicanae*, Vol.III (Oxford, 1882), pp.151–2. Maskell believed that this passage, and its immediate context in the Primers, was an addition found in only two manuscripts and therefore 'remarkable'. In fact, it is also in BL Add. 39574, f.50v; BL Add. 27592, f.35v; Bodleian MSS Digby 102, f.127v; Douce 246, ff.76v–77r and Douce 275, ff.60r–v; and Cambridge MS St John's College G.24, f.72r. None of these instances includes the Latin phrase, but *cf.* Matthew 6:23. [I am indebted to Peter Meredith for suggesting the line of enquiry that led to the information set out here. G.C.]

DM/933ff. **as doctouris seyne**] No sources traced.

DM/988–95 **parable... vyne3erde**] See Sermon 8 *passim* where this parable and the imagery of the vine and the vineyard are extensively developed. It also occurs, briefly, in Sermon 1/148, 317–8, and 323–5.

DM/1003–6 **Austyn**] Augustine, *De Civitate Dei*, *Liber* 22, *caput* xxx (*P.L.* 41, col.801).

DM/1015 **so myche...hou myche**] Correlatives of comparison (*cf. L: tanto...quanto*). The sense here is that, in contrast to the quality of light experienced in this life, the degree of brightness in heaven is greater to an extent that corresponds to its superior, beatific nature.

DM/1038 **whiche**] *WLV*: 'what thingis'.

DM/1039–43 **Austin**] Precise source not traced, but *cf. De Triplici Habitaculo** (*Incerti Auctoris*), *Liber* 1, *caput* i (*P.L.* 40, col.991–2): *Bona... cogitari potest.* *This work is also cited in Note DM/317–19.

DM/1042 **ouerpasseþ**] M seems more likely than R, which translates both *excedit* and *superat* by **ouercomyþ (-eþ)**. Some uncertainty remains because both manuscripts have **ouerpas-siþ (-eþ)** for *exsuperat* at DM/1049; but A and R agree at 12/122, where *superatus est* is translated **ouercomen**. Further support for the emendation is found in the similarity of collocation at 1042/1049 (**al þou3t/alle... wit**).

DM/1057–60 **Bernarde**] *Meditationes Cognitione Humanae Conditionis, caput* iv (*P.L.* 184, col.492D).

DM/1072–3 **clerte, agilite, sotilte, and immortalite**] The four dowers or attributes of the resurrected body, discussed here in some detail (1074–90),are mentioned briefly in Sermon 10/176–80. And *cf.* the *Compendium* (*Liber* VII, *caput* xxvii and xxviii, *De Dotibus Corporis in Generali* and *De Dotibus Corporis in Speciali*), pp.842–3.

DM/1079–80 **Austyn**] Augustine, *De Civitate Dei, Liber* 22, *caput* xxx (*P.L.* 41, col.801).

DM/1091–1130 *The Joys of Heaven.* Cf. some interesting correspondences in the *Compendium* (*Liber* VII, *caput* xxxi, *Enumeratio Caelestium Gaudiorum*), p.844.

DM/1120–1 **comownen...alle**] *i.e.* 'they will pool their resources of skill and knowledge, and their Master will share his with all of them.'

DM/1126–9 **rest...þristing**] Unlike the preceding polarities (1123–6 **3ouþe...ignoraunce**), the pairs of abstractions here are not mutually defining contraries. Glossing the passage has therefore been somewhat conjectural.

DM/1151 **most made of**] *i.e.* 'esteemed most highly' or 'accorded the greatest possible respect.'

SCRIPTURAL INDEX I: sermon by sermon

SCRIPTURAL INDEX II: alphabetical

IN MOST cases the locations listed in these indices correspond precisely or very closely to the Scriptural readings within the text. Where the location is a probable but not certain source of an allusion or paraphrase, the entry is introduced by *See.* Where the location has some significant relationship to the Scriptural reference in the text, without corresponding to it precisely, the entry is introduced by *Cf.* The square brackets on some entries in Index I indicate that the location reference is given in the manuscript text, though it should be noted that all *verse* references are editorial additions. In Index I, full line references are given for all Scriptural readings, allusions and paraphrases; in Index II, only single line numbers are given, indicating the points where such Scriptural correspondences are introduced into the text. Throughout, names are in English (AV) forms, except for those that occur only in (V), which are given in Latin, and **Samuel**, **Kings** and **Chronicles**, where both (AV) and (V) forms are included for ease of reference. All entries relating to the **Psalms** in Index I give (V) and (AV) locations; in Index II, only (V) locations are given.

SCRIPTURAL INDEX I (sermon by sermon)

Sermon 1
The first Sunday in Advent: Matthew 21:1–9

1/1	[Matthew 21:1]
1/11	*See*: John 1:18
1/16–18	[John 16:28]
1/35–6	Psalm 19:8–9 (V); 20:7–8 (AV)
1/40–42	Zechariah 9:9
1/48–50	[John 14:23]
1/51–5	[Revelations 3:20]
1/58	*As* 2/6–7
1/61–3	İsaiah 3:14]
1/79–85	Matthew 21:1–3
1/90	Ephesians 2:14
1/91–2	Psalm 15:8 (V); 16:8 (AV)
1/95	John 1:12
1/101–3	Psalm 144:18 (V); 145:18 (AV)
1/104–6	*See* Ezekiel 18:27; 33:12

Sermon 3
The third Sunday in Advent: Matthew 11:2–10

Sermon 4

The fourth Sunday in Advent: John 1:19–28

11A:
An Optional Expansion of Sermon 11.

11A/333-6	[Job 20:6-7]
11A/338-40	[Proverbs 11:2]
11A/341-2	[Proverbs 13:10]
11A/348-9	[*Ecclesiasticus* 10:7]
11A/352-4	[James 4:6]
11A/364-5	Psalm 72:18 (V); *cf*: 73:18 (AV)
11A/382-3	*See*: 1 Timothy 6:10
11A/386-7	Jeremiah 8:10
11A/421-3	[*Ecclesiasticus* 21:5]
11A/425-8	[Proverbs 28:22]
11A/430-2	*See*: [Genesis 13:7]
11A/434-6	[Luke 12:19]
11A/440-3	*Ecclesiasticus* 47:20-1
11A/448-50	[Isaiah 5:8]
11A/451-2	Habakkuk 2:6
11A/453-5	[Isaiah 33:1]
11A/455-7	[Luke 6:24]
11A/458-9	Jude 1:11
11A/460-1	[*Ecclesiasticus* 10:9]
11A/482-4	Habakkuk 2:5
11A/517-18	[*Ecclesiasticus* 14:9]
11A/518-20	*Ecclesiasticus* 5:9
11A/521-3	[Proverbs 30:15]
11A/532-3	Luke 16:9
11A/536-7	[Ezekiel 7:19]
11A/541-2	Psalm 61:11 (V); 62:10 (AV)
11A/565-8	[1 Timothy 6:7]
11A/571-3	[Luke 12:15]
11A/572-5	*See*: Matthew 6:20
11A/578-9	Matthew 25:40
11A/584-5	[Matthew 25:34]

Sermon 12
The second Sunday in Lent: Matthew 15:21-8

12/1-2	[Matthew 15:21]
12/14-16	Psalm 18:7 (V); 19:6 (AV)
12/25-8	[Luke 11:21-2]
12/32-3	*See*: Matthew 12:28-9
12/33-4	*See*: Revelations 20:3
12/58	*Sapientia* 2:24
12/70-1	*Not Psalms*: Deuteronomy 32:23
12/81-2	Psalm 105:29 (V); 106:29 (AV)
12/88-9	*Ecclesiastes* 1:15
12/93-5	Jeremiah 9:1
12/98-101	[1 Peter 5:8-9]
12/104-7	[Ephesians 6:16]
12/120-3	1 *Regum* 2:4 (V); 1 Samuel 2:4 (AV)
12/136-7	*See*: Romans 2:7; James 5:7, 8, 11; Luke 21:19
12/147-54	Psalm 49:19-21 (V); 50:19-21 (AV)
12/164-5	Psalm 21:17 (V); 22:16 (AV)
12/166-7	Isaiah 53:7
12/167-9	1 Peter 2:23
12/172-3	*See*: *Ecclesiasticus* 10:9

14/88–91	*See*: Matthew 26:39–44
14/95–8	Mark 14:37
14/102–3	*See*: John 6:5
14/108–9	1 Corinthians 8:1
14/110–12	[?]
14/117–18	James 4:6
14/127–30	*See*: John 6:7
14/143	Jeremiah 1:6
14/154–6	[Luke 10:2]
14/163–4	*Cf*: 2 Thessalonians 3:10
14/167–70	Matthew 25:30
14/171–3	John 6:9
14/190–1	Psalm 67:12 (V); *cf*: 68:11 (AV)
14/192	*See*: John 6:10
14/202–5	Luke 8:14
14/210–15	*See*: Luke 10:39–42
14/216–18	*See*: John 6:11
14/224–5	[2 Corinthians 3:5]
14/233–6	Matthew 28:20; Luke 21:15
14/237–40	Matthew 10:20
14/264	John 6:14
14/271–5	*See*: Matthew 12:24; Mark 3:22; Luke 11:15

Sermon 15
(an alternative to Sermon 14)
The fourth Sunday in Lent: John 6:1–14

15/1	[John 6:11]
15/12–14	John 13:15
15/35	*See*: 3 *Regum* 19:7–8 (V); 1 Kings (AV)
15/50–3	[Matthew 4:4]
15/62–5	[Matthew 10:6–7]
15/66–9	[Luke 9:1–2]
15/69–72	*See*: Luke 10:1–11
15/87–92	Amos 8:11
15/95–9	*Cf*: Jeremiah 9:1
15/104–5	Romans 13:10
15/126–8	*Ecclesiastes* 1:18
15/132–3	Psalm 41:4 (V); 42:3 (AV)
15/134–5	Psalm 79:6 (V); 80:5 (AV)
15/139–41	Acts 3:19
15/143–6	Jeremiah 3:1
15/149–50	[Matthew 3:2; 4:17]
15/153–7	[Matthew 18:18]
15/158–60	[John 20:23]
15/162–4	[Matthew 16:19]
15/170–2	[Ezekiel 13:19]
15/182–4	Psalm 50:19 (V); 51:17 (AV)
15/186–7	Psalm 96:10 (V); 97:10 (AV)
15/188–9	Psalm 118:104 (V); 119:104 (AV)
15/190–1	Psalm 37:18 (V); 38:17 (AV)
15/196–8	[John 5:14]
15/200–2	[James 5:16]
15/207–11	*Ecclesiasticus* 17:26

16/168–71   [John 8:51]
16/177–8   Romans 10:17
16/179   Hebrews 11:6
16/185–90   Luke 11:28
16/214–7   [Luke 10:42]
16/225–7   John 5:24
16/233–6   James 1:22
16/241–4   Jeremiah 11:3
16/247–9   [Proverbs 28:9]
16/260–4   [Matthew 10:15]
16/275   John 8:48
16/280–3   *See*: [Luke 10:33–5]
16/300–3   Psalm 120:7 (V); 121:7 (AV)
16/304–6   Psalm 120:8 (V); 121:8 (AV)
16/308–9   John 8:49
16/311–13   2 Corinthians 6:15, 14
16/338–9   Psalm 115:11 (V); 116:11 (AV)
16/345   John 8:49
16/348–50   *See*: Luke 11:15
16/365   *See*: John 8:49
16/368–70   John 8:51; *and* 16/385
16/373–8   *See*: John 8:52–3
16/403–7   *See*: John 8:59
16/409–10   James 1:20
16/413–14   *See*: [Leviticus 24:23]
16/416–19   *See*: 4 *Regum* 11:15 (V); 2 Kings (AV)
16/421–2   *See*: John 8:59
16/428–9   Romans 12:19
16/435–7   [Jeremiah 18:17]
16/438–9   Ezekiel 7:22

Sermon of Dead Men (DM)
DM/1   [*Ecclesiasticus* 7:36]
DM/19–24   [John 11:23; 43–4]
DM/25–9   Luke 7:12–15
DM/36–7   [*Ecclesiasticus* 7:38]
DM/46–9   *Cf*: Ecclesiasticus 38:23–4
DM/63–5   Acts 1:14; 4:32
DM/69–70   [*Cf*: 1 Peter 3:8]
DM/72–5   [2 Maccabees 12:46]
DM/88–9   Romans 8:35
DM/91–3   *Cf*: Mark 11:23–5 *and* John 15:7
DM/99   Matthew 10:2
DM/110–17   Colossians 4:2–4
DM/122–6   1 Thessalonians 2:5–6
DM/141–2   Isaiah 58:1
DM/149–50   *As* DM/1
DM/164–7   [2 *Regum* 14:14 (V); 2 Samuel (AV)]
DM/189–91   2 Corinthians 4:7
DM/199–204   Matthew 24:42–3
DM/206–7   *Ecclesiastes* 9:12
DM/233–6   *Ecclesiastes* 9:12
DM/239–41   Job 21:13

SCRIPTURAL INDEX II (alphabetical)

GLOSSARY

This Glossary is designed to make the text accessible to readers unfamiliar with Middle English, as well as to specialists. It includes words no longer in use in Modern English, and obsolete senses of surviving words. Where words occur in the text with both modern and obsolete senses, only the latter are included here. Obsolete but recognisable forms are ignored where the sense is that familiar to modern readers.

The headwords include all forms found in the text, with the following exceptions:
1. **i/y** variants, where only the **i** form is given, unless (infrequently) the **y** form is conspicuously predominant;
2. **u/w** variants, where some **w** forms have been omitted;
3. verb inflections, where regular.

Orthographical variants are included in the Glossary; wherever possible, they are incorporated into one headword—e.g. **abro(o)d(e)**. Letters in brackets in such entries are not taken into account in the alphabetical sequence of the Glossary. At least one location reference is given for each form cited, usually formed by *etc* where applicable. Where there are no more than three occurrences of a given word, however, each location reference is included.

In the alphabetical arrangement of the entries, **3** follows **g**; vocalic **i** and **y** are not distinguished; **þ** follows **t**; and **vn-** precedes vocalic **v-**, which is followed by consonantal **v-**.

VERBS. Where there is no infinitive in the text, the grammatical form cited has been determined by either frequency or the need to include a specific occurrence. In general, references are given for inflexions different from that of the headword only where there is also a difference of sense. In such instances, the precise form is not given unless it is markedly unlike that of the headword.

The sign ~ is used for the headword, in any of its forms, occurring in phrases.

Other procedures

1. *see* cross-refers to a form of the headword to be found elsewhere in the Glossary;
2. *see n*: directs the reader to Notes to the Text;
3. MS A: or MS R: or MS M: draws the reader's attention to an interesting reading in the non-base text (also recorded in the Apparatus).

Isolated problems have from time to time dictated departures from the procedures set out here. Where this happens, the commonsense of the reader is assumed.

abay *see* **at**.

able(n) *v.* *refl.* make (themselves/himself) worthy 2/56 *etc*; *pr. 3 sg.* 3/282, 9/357.

able, abil *adj.* worthy 1/368 *etc*; fit 9/401; ~ **to** fit for 5/253 *etc*.

abobbid *see* **bobbid**.

aboue *adv.* to a greater extent 9/160.

aboute *adv.* on every side (?) 11A/394; *and see* **be(e)**.

abro(o)d(e) *adv.* far apart 6/229; **sprad** ~ spread out 11A/527; distributed 11A/530; stretched out DM/3; *see also* **departe**.

abuye *v.* pay for 11A/297.

acceptynge (of persones) *n.* partiality 1/58 *etc*.

acorda(u)nt *adj.* appropriate 11A/506, DM/706 *etc*.

acordynge (to) *adv.* conforming to 7/7.

acorde *n.* affinity 16/312, 313.

acorde *v.* agree 1/185 *etc*; assent 1/444; correspond 2/40; be in harmony 13/94 *etc*; ~ **to** is in agreement 5/440.

acount(e)(e) *n.* reckoning 1/316, DM/496 *etc*; *pl.* 4/311, DM/503 *etc*. [**-ee** *form not in OED or MED*].

acount(e) *v.* answer for their actions DM/518, 548; be accountable for DM/627.

adrad, adred *ppl. adj.* greatly afraid

3/44, 14/142 *etc*.

aduersarie *adj.* inimical 3/322.

afert *adj.* afraid 4/215.

affec(c)io(u)n(s) *n.* emotions 1/209 (*see n.*) 3/213, 355 *etc*; loving attachment 2/504; attribute 10/311; emotional disposition 12/235; **contrarious** ~ inner conflict DM/1099.

after *prep.* in accordance with 1/340 *etc*; as 1/59 *etc*.

agilite *n.* agility (*one of the four properties of Christ's body and of the dowry of resurrected man*): the ability to move anywhere, at any speed 10/178, DM/1072, 1079; *see also* **clerete** and **sutitle**.

agoo *pp.* vanished 11A/91.

aȝen(s), aȝein(s), aȝeyne, aȝenst *adv. prep. conj.* facing 1/82 *etc*; in contrast with 1/391, 12/517 *etc*; again 2/86 *etc*; in anticipation of 2/595 *etc*; before 12/154; against 12/157; in the sight of 3/308 *etc*; contrary to 6/74 *etc*.

aȝeynbying *n.* redemption DM/950.

aȝeynstonde *v.* resist DM/507, 509.

al *adv. or adj.* (*as intensifier*) 1/211 *etc*; ~ **oute** entirely 12/68; ~ **oon(e)** quite isolated 15/366; exactly the same 16/83; ~ **oonly** alone DM/416.

aleidest *see* **al(l)egge** *v.*[1]

al(l)egge (for) *v.*[1] cite 3/160 *etc*; *pr. 2
sg* quote (with reference to)
11/203 *and see* n: 2/602; ~ **for
him** offers in support of his
argument 6/60; ~ **hem**
quoted to them 4/212; cite as
testimony on their own behalf
4/241; **aleidest (to)** *pa. t. 2 sg.*
presented as evidence against
11/195.

al(l)egge *v.*[2] alleviate DM/810.

aloneli *adv.* merely 4/255.

alþerleest *adv.* (at) the very least
8/114.

amendes *n.* compensation 11A/415.

amende *v.* rectify 9/312 *etc*; (*refl.*)
make amends 1/427 *etc*.

amerciamentes *n.* discretionary
(*i.e. at the mercy of the in-
flicter*) fines, penalties
11A/394.

amydde *prep.* just as he is about to
(act on this) 9/185.

and *conj.* if 1/300 *etc*.

anectid *pp.* summoned for interrog-
ation (?) [*MS A* areyned]
12/153.

anent(is), anens, anend *prep.* in
respect of 2/696, 13/79 *etc*; in
the sight of 3/305; with 2/653,
4/205.

angris *n.* tribulations 11A/555.

any þyng *adv.* to any extent 7/45.

ano(o)n(e) *adv.* immediately 1/85; ~
as as soon as 9/131 *etc*.

apai(e)d(e), apayid *pp.* satisfied
2/546, 9/21, 11/250, 11A/274
etc.

ap(p)arayle *n.* trappings 2/252,
DM/217, 567 *etc*.

aparaylit, apareilid *pp.* furnished
2/420; equipped 11A/239.

apeire *v. trans. and (intrans.)*
impair(ed) 10/92; *pr. 3 sg.*
10/85, *pa. t.* 10/114, 12/537;
made worse 16/386.

aperte *adj.* unconcealed DM/592.

apostata(s) *n.* renegade(s) 11A/195,
202.

ap(p)reued *pp.* authorised 4/233; ap-
proved 11/183.

aproprid (to) *ppl. adj.*, the rightful
possession of 11A/146.

apte *adj.* suitable 11A/506, 508.

ar *adv.* before 3/36 *etc*.

arai(e) *n.* attire 1/34 *etc*.

araie, raie *v.* prepare 2/153, 9/343
etc; *pp.* attired 9/125 *etc*.

araier *n.* one who prepares 12/472.

arere, rere *v.* bring forth 4/95; raise
up 11A/321, 361 *etc*; prompt
11A/362.

arett(e), rett *v.* give credit for 3/107,
14/268; impute 14/271; *pp.*
reckoned responsibility for
12/321, 519.

armure, armuris *n.* armour 2/68,
16/330.

artificeres *n.* craftsmen 11A/410,
DM/549.

as (tyme as) *adv. conj.* as soon as
1/98 *etc*.

as (who seiþ) *adv. phrase*, as if to say
emphatically (*reinforcing an inference believed to be incon-
trovertible*) 2/481 *etc*.

asay(e) *v.* find out 12/44; test 14/122,
124.

asaie *n.* a putting to the test 11/176.

askis *n.* ashes DM/44.

asoylyng(e) *n.* absolution 4/25,
6/118.

assoiled *pp.* absolved 6/120.

aspie *v.* observe covertly DM/311 *etc*;
~ **to** lie in wait for DM/345; *pr.
3 sg.* watches out for DM/347;
pp. caught sight of DM/311.

aspies *n.* snares DM/1012.

asta(a)t, esta(a)t(e) *n.* rank 2/419
etc; social position 2/550 6/214
etc; calling 3/488 *etc*; circumstances 5/246, 318 *etc*; condition 11A/82, 316; *pl.* pro-
fessional positions 2/251 *etc*;
mannes ~ 5/87, 8/191.

astarte *v.* avoid DM/343.

at abay (vpon him) *adv. phrase* surrounding him, barking (*i.e. as
with a hunted animal*) 12/160.

atones *adv.* at once 2/236 *etc*.

atourne, (lettris of) *n.* documents
authorising someone to represent a litigant in court 12/333.

auaunsid *ppl. adj.* put in a more advantageous position DM/176; elevated DM/191.

auditorie *n.* the assembled hearers 1/379 *etc.*

auncetrie *n.* ancestry 11A/267.

auncetres *n.* ancestors 11A/260, 262.

(an) aunter (lest) *conj. phrase* for fear 16/329; *and see n:* DM/354–5

auoutrie *n.* adultery 3/412.

axeþ, -iþ *pr. 3 sg.* calls for 3/463, 488, 8/278; necessitates 11A/270; *pa. t.* 5/196.

bagge *n.* (*fig.*) truth [*cf. Fr. vider le sac* 'to spill the beans'] 9/327; *pl.* bags 9/275; a type of full, trailing sleeve 11A/292.

bailie *n.* stewardship 4/311.

bailifes *n.* stewards 8/98.

balkis *n.* ridges overlooked during ploughing 9/303, DM/144.

balkiþ *pr. 3 sg.* (*fig.*) neglects 9/306.

baptem, baptim *n.* baptism 3/378 *etc.*

basnet *n.* 'A hemispherical helmet, without a visor, worn under the fighting helmet' (*MED* **bacinet**) DM/381.

bastard(e) *adj.* (*fig.*) spurious *see n:* 3/418; unusually large 11A/244.

be(e), beo, ben *v.* be 1/27, 309, 327, 2/478; **am** *pr. 1 sg.* 3/80; **art(e)** *pr. 2 sg.* 1/385, 12/171; **is** *pr. 3 sg.* 1/2; **be(e)n** *pr. pl.* 1/157, 363; **buþ** *pr. 1 pl.* 5/283, 472; **arn(e)** *pr. 3 pl.* 3/409, 12/87; **be(e), beo** *subj. sg.* 1/76, 2/17, 1/300; **be, beiþ** *imper. pl.* 3/287, 16/235; **was, wes** *pa. t. sg.* 1/10, 12/15; **were(n), werne** *pa. t. pl.* 1/240, 262, 15/133; **be(e), beo** *pp.* 1/175, 6/155, 1/262; ~ **aboute** *pr. 3 pl.* are concerned to 2/197 *etc*; **were** *pa. t. subj. 3 sg.* 1/31.

bedenfastynge (dai) *n.* one of the fast days prescribed by the church *see n:* 8/89.

beere *n.* bier 11A/355, 358.

beestli, beestliche *adj.* brutish 3/398; lacking spirituality and reason 5/289.

begger *adj.* mendicant 4/226.

(of) beʒonde *prep. as n.* from abroad DM/589.

behete *v.* promise 13/267.

benygnite *n.* goodwill 2/505.

benignly, benyngly *adv.* indulgently 13/263; compassionately DM/27.

bere vp *v.* support 1/298 *etc.*

berne *n.* barn 9/402, 11A/497.

better *adj. as n.* upper hand DM/442.

bi *prep.* about 5/20.

biclippyngis *n.* embraces 6/230.

biclippynge *pr. ppl.* embracing 5/410.

bidde *v.* urge 8/113 *etc*; pray 9/181; command 11/123 *etc.*

biden *pr. 1 pl.* expect, await 3/4 *etc.*

bieþ aʒen *pr. 3 pl.* redeem 8/134; **bou(ʒ)te** *pa. t. 3 sg.* redeemed 2/677, 10/441; **bouʒtist** *pa. t. 2 sg.* 8/117.

bigeten *adj.* begotten 5/61.

bigrucche *v.* begrudge 8/180.

bihe(e)ste *n.* promise 2/685, 7/13 *etc.*

bihiʒt(e) *see* **bihoteþ.**

biholding *n.* image DM/41; vision DM/1092.

bihoteþ *pr. 3 pl.* swear pledges 10/307; **bihote, bihiʒt(e)** *pp.* promised 7/14, 3/77, 4/106 *etc.*

bile *n.* bill, beak 11A/118, 121.

bile(e)ue *n.* faith 1/306, 2/676 *etc.*

bileeuede *pa. t.* trustingly expected 6/43.

bileue *pr. 3 sg.* is left abandoned 11A/561.

bynde *v.* to with-hold absolution from one unfit to receive it (*because of the nature of the sin committed, an inadequate state of repentance, or absence of true confession*) 9/317.

byndyng (of) *n.* the with-holding of absolution (by) 6/118.

birdoun, birþen *n.* load 1/302, 12/346 *etc*; responsibility 6/90.

biriels *n.* graves 11A/545.

birþen *see* **birdoun.**

bisidis *prep.* alongside 1/404 *etc*; **go** ~ **þe weie** pass by 8/291 *etc.*

bisie *v. (refl.)* occupy, exert 1/323 *etc.*

bisines(se) *n.* diligence 10/510, 12/530.

biþenke (þe) *v. imper. (refl.) sg.* call to mind 7/176 *etc; pl.* let them reflect 4/291; *(not refl.) sg.* consider 12/174; *pa. t. subj. 3 pl.* **biþouȝte (hem)** if they were to reflect 2/276.

bitore *n.* bittern 11A/118, 13/175.

blended *pp.* made blind 3/170 *etc.*

bobbid *ppl. adj. (fig.)* unseeing, therefore deluded 10/303; *cf.* **pleyen abobbid** play blind-man's buff 10/303.

boche *n.* running sore 2/263.

bolle *n.* tankard 11A/123 *etc.*

bolnyng *n.* swelling DM/283.

bone *n.* prayer DM/782.

bookes *n.* account books DM/637.

bo(o)rd(e) *n.* table 12/529, 15/42, DM/585.

boote *n.* boat 9/263.

boriouned *see* **burione.**

borsten oute *pp.* broken out 2/265; putrified 13/340.

boteries *n. pl.* store rooms 5/269.

bouȝt- *see* **bieþ aȝen.**

boun *pa. t.* bound 3/8; *pp.* **bounden forþe** shut away 12/33.

boundes, boundis *n.* (the conditions of) confinement 3/2, 6; re-straints 15/275; confines 16/418.

boute *see* **bieþ aȝen.**

bowe (to) *v.* comply (with) 2/628; *pr. 3 sg.* gives way 1/303, 7/80; *pa. t. 2 sg.* **boudest** didst incline 11A/443 *pp.* persuaded to be lenient 2/657; *imper. sg.* swerve 1/244; *imper. sg. (pl.)* incline 9/49, (3/239); ~ **hire knees** kneel 8/14–15.

bowes *n.* branches 1/389, 441.

breke *v. imper. sg.* distribute 15/303.

breme *adj.* gleaming DM/1154.

brenne *v.* burn 8/405 *etc.*

brerdes *n.* top [*MS R* **brinkis**] 11A/494.

broching *n.* piercing 13/207.

burgeysis *n.* burgesses DM/1064.

burione *v.* begin to grow 2/227; boriouneþ *pr. 3 sg.* 2/688; **buriouned** *pp.* 2/686.

bustis, bustus *adj.* uncultivated 5/289; fierce 6/225.

but if *conj.* unless 1/124 *etc.*

caas *n.* circumstances 4/159 *etc.*

can, kunne(n), kunneþ *aux. vb. sg/pl. (with infin.)* am/is/are able (to) 2/243, 10/366, 11/299, 13/356 *etc; pa. t. 2 sg.* **kouþist** DM/393 *as independent vb. trans.* **kunne** know 2/325, 4/12; *intrans.* 4/291, 292.

cunnyng, kunnyng(e) *n.* skill(s) 1/142, 13/233, DM/1120 *etc; and see* **kunnyng** *adj.*

canoun *n.* canonical writings 13/106; Canon Law 14/135.

careyne *n.* corpse 3/140, 141.

catel *n.* possessions 7/117 *etc.*

causes *n.* conditions 11/239.

ceelis *n.* seals 8/334.

censures *n.* condemnatory judg-ments 8/278.

certefied *pp.* assured 4/91.

certeyn *n.* truth 2/8; **a ~ of rent** a fixed of money 10/269.

certeyn *adj.* triumphant 11/213.

certis *adv.* indeed 16/196.

chakelinge *n.* chattering (of teeth) DM/869, 875.

chalenge *n.* accusation 2/545; *and see n:* 2/639–42.

chapmen *n.* merchants 4/128.

chare *n.* chariot 4/55; *pl.* 1/36.

charge *n.* load, weight 1/300; re-sponsibility 1/307; duty 2/157; penalty 6/91.

chargeus *adj.* oppressive 11A/99.

chargid *pp.* burdened 9/250.

cha(u)mbre(s) *n.* private room(s) 2/420, 11A/68 *etc.*

chaunteris *n.* choristers 3/433.

chauntries *n.* endowments for the maintenance of one or several priests to sing daily masses for the souls of benefactors 2/92.

checker *n.* (the) Exchequer 2/439.

cheke (bones) *n.* jaws 11A/139.

chepe *subj. sg.* asks the price of 4/73.

chepyng *n.* market (place) 8/42.
chere *n.* behaviour 9/131 *etc*; **mou3yng of his** ~ his facial contortions DM/282.
chees *pa. t. 3 sg.* chose 3/293 *etc.*
cheualrie *n.* knights 8/249.
chyilde *v.* give birth to a child 5/61; *pr. ppl.* 5/410.
chyif *adj.* most important 5/48.
chyncherie *n.* miserliness 9/194.
chiterynge *n.* twittering 10/262.
circumcide *v.* circumcise 6/28 *etc.*
cisouris *n.* assizers (*i.e. jurymen of the lay courts*) 8/316.
clene *adj.* pure 5/401 *etc*; unadulterated 15/367; innocent 16/6; *comp.* **clannere** 11A/465; *superl.* **clannest** 1/12.
clene, clenly *adv.* entirely 2/208, 13/412 *etc.*
clepe *v.* call 5/180 *etc*; appeal 5/274 summon 8/198 *etc*; *pp.* **(i)cleped** 5/51, 16/139 *etc*; named 5/10 *etc.*
clere *adj.* bright 7/119; distinct 2/128; unimpaired DM/1094 pure DM/1098.
clere *adv.* brightly DM/1075.
clerete, cleerte *n.* radiance 5/204, 2/359 *etc.*
cleernesse *n.* radiance 5/307.
clergy *n.* learning DM/1141; *and see n*: 4/291.
close *v. imper.* place securely 15/332; *pp.* made inaccessible 5/273.
clo(o)þ *n.* garment 8/157, 10/50.
cnaue *see* **knaue.**
cockel *n.* a species of weed commonly found growing among grain 2/704.
co(o)lo(u)r *n.* apparent (*with strong connotation of* 'false') claim 11A/396; **under** ~ by deception 7/70, 11/107.
colouren *pr. 3 pl.* disguise in order to render plausible 1/170.
colourid, colourable *adj.* plausible 14/141, 16/17, 404.
comelingis *n.* foreign travellers DM/1063.
comenaunt *n.* an agreement, pact 13/139.

commitacions *n.* dealings and transactions (?) 5/237.
comoun *v.* discuss 14/123, 15/84; **comynede,** *pa. t.* associated 11A/215; **comowen togider** share harmoniously DM/1120; *see n*: DM/1120–21.
comprehendeþ *pres. 3 sg.* encompasses 5/3; *pp.* contained 15/103.
comun(es) *n.* the common people 3/482; ~ **of þe pepul** the community of ordinary people 9/75.
conceyue *v.* understand 4/320, 13/210; apprehend 11/306.
conferme *v.* reinforce 3/116 *etc.*
conforme *v.* be in accordance 3/109 *etc.*
confortable *adj.* edifying 2/625; reassuring 5/370, 11/6. [*The expansion of this word, and the verb forms, is uncertain; the medial* **n** *could be* **m** *in each case.*]
confusio(u)n *n.* ruin, shame 7/75 12/436; **for** ~ **of þe soun** because of the tumultuous commotion (?) 2/511.
congregacion *n.* a cluster or gathering; *see n*: DM/843.
coniectide *pa. t.* contrived 12/149.
contrarie *v.* conflict wioth 5/466; *pa. t.* 4/46.
contrari(o)us *adj.* mutually opposed 1/184, 16/310; antagonistic 3/244; ~ **to** in conflict with 4/59, 68.
contynance *n.* (?) outward appearance 7/71.
conuersacion *n.* way of living 2/221 *etc*; spiritual dwelling-place 3/511.
corage *n.* inner drives DM/963.
cordynge *adj.* appropriate 6/58.
corn *n.* grain 11A/497.
corneris *n.* (?) *see n*: 2/639–42.
cor(r)upcion(s) *n.* contagion(s) 2/261, 10/333; decay 7/175.
coruptible *adj.* subject to decay 15/374.
costeris *n.* hangings at the sides of a bed 5/252.

cost(e)li, costi *adj.* extravagant 3/431, 5/257, 11A/232 *etc.*

costious *adj. sense as preceding* 5/253 *etc.*

costlew *adj. sense as preceding* 2/422.

costiousli *adv.* extravagently 3/471.

couenable *adj.* suitable 3/361.

coupleþ *pr. 2 pl.* join 11A/450; *pp.* 9/391; ~ **togedere** copulated 5/131.

couplynge *n.* copulation 5/124 *etc.*

cours *n.* direction 2/532, 539; narrative 3/109; procedure 6/3; practice 13/348.

couert(e) *n.* shelter, cover 12/201 *etc.*

cracche *n.* manger 5/189, 313.

crachi *adj.* rubbed sore 11A/553.

creuen *adj.* withered (?) *see n:* 5/217.

criar, crier(e) *n.* one who proclaims 1/281, 4/186, 190.

cri(e) *n.* shouting 1/389; voice raised in urgent entreaty 2/573 *etc.*

crie *v.* clamour 10/69 *etc*; entreat out loud 10/205 *etc.*

cr(i)ying(e) *vbl. n.* proclaiming 2/158, 9/27; clamouring 12/273.

cryous *adj.* loudly lamenting 10/387.

crokeþ *pr. 3 sg.* curls 11A/370; deviates 16/339.

crokid, croked(e) *adj.* lame 3/100, 197 *etc*; devious 1/302 *etc.*

cultur *n.* coulter 9/292.

cumbrid *pp.* overwhelmed 1/216, 2/457.

cunnyng *see* **can.**

cuntre(e), (contree) *n.* region (2/535), 5/79 *etc*; countryside 8/316, 14/45.

cure *n.* spiritual charge 5/354; office 8/325; care 7/24 *etc.*

curious(e) *adj.* intricate 3/431; painstakingly chosen 7/148.

curteis *adj.* gracious 10/199, DM/411.

curtesie *n.* an act of kindness DM/675.

curtel *n.* tunic 11A/289.

custummabli *adv.* usually 8/43.

dampnabli *adv.* in a manner deserving condemnation 2/305.

daunger *n.* arrogance DM/1121.

debate *n. and v.* quarrel 5/450, 11A/52.

declare *v.* explain, interpret 4/285 *etc*; proclaim 16/11 *etc*; *pr. ppl.* making manifest 5/433.

declaracion *n.* elucidation 6/124; explanation 16/13, 360, 370–71.

declaring(e) *n.* expounding 4/49, 16/133.

decreis *n.* decretals 14/136.

dedignacion *n.* disdain [*MS A* **dedeyn**] 12/400.

de(e)dly *adj.* mortal 2/75, 4/282 *etc.*

defau(3)te *n.* lack 2/133 *etc*; defect 2/313 *etc*; offence 2/330 *etc*; **for** ~ **þat... mai not come** by preventing... from (coming) 2/240.

defoule *v.* trample on 11/201 *etc*; disfigure 3/225 *etc*; *pp.* defiled 10/414.

defoulynge *n.* crushing down 2/563.

degneþ *pr. 3 sg.* condescends 3/135.

del(e) *n.* part 11A/283; **a** ~ the smallest amount 12/218.

delectacion *n.* enjoyment 12/63.

delfeli *adv.* wretchedly 8/237.

delicis, delitis *n.* a state of self-gratification 8/74, 10/292.

delueþ *pr. 3 sg.* digs 11A/547; **doluen** *pp.* buried 8/237.

deme *v.* judge 1/58 *etc*; impose a penalty 16/357.

demyng(e) *n.* judgment 10/234 *etc*; suspicion 16/411.

denteuous *adj.* rare 5/258.

denieþ *pr. 3 sg.* renounces 4/144; *pp.* 10/416; *pp. refl.* practised self-abnegation 10/129; **denyinge** *pr. p.* rejecting 2/507.

denyinge *n.* refusal 1/351.

departe *v.* separate 2/232 *etc*; share 5/250 *etc*; apportion 10/274 *etc*; ~ **abrode,** ~ **al aboute** distribute 12/28, 14/217.

departing(e) *n.* division 9/321, 15/58 *etc*; separation DM/693.

dere (3ere) *adj. (n.)* time of scarcity 14/14.

dere *adv.* dearly 10/441.

derk *adj.* difficult to understand 9/64.

derlingis *n.* devout men, those beloved of God 2/625 *etc.*

desese *see* **disese.**

despite *n.* contempt, insult 11A/13, 183.

destenyes *n.* astrological prognostications 10/259.

deue *n.* deaf 3/235.

deuer, deuoure *n.* task 9/187, 202, 14/229.

deuoutli *adv.* reverently DM/106.

deuys *see* **poynt.**

deuoure *see* **deuer.**

deynous *adj.* arrogant DM/1147.

deynteis *n.* delicacies (*i.e. food*) 12/528.

diches *n.* pits, ditches 11A/130.

dictis *n.* sayings 15/185.

(for) difference (of) *n.* to distinguish them from 3/518.

diffusely *adv.* at length (*perhaps with connotation of that which is difficult to understand*) DM/151.

di(n)gnite(e) *n.* social rank 4/23 *etc*; elevated spiritual and moral office 3/484; excellence 16/104 *etc*; *see n*: DM/1146; *pl.* honours 2/441.

diȝt *pp.* adorned 5/252; prepared 9/202.

dyn *n.* clamour, rowdiness DM/1121.

directli *adv.* entirely 1/184.

dischargid *pp.* rid of the burden 9/250.

disciplinis *n.* chastisements 1/434 *etc.*

discla(u)ndre *v.* slander 11A/59 *etc*; *pp.* offended 9/119.

discre(y)uynge *n.* census 5/33, 51.

discreue *v.* register 5/52.

discunfite *v.* discourage 11/215.

discunforte *n.* adversity 11A/247.

disese *n.* suffering 1/195; **in ~ in** a state of suffering 12/417, 423.

disesed *pa. t.* illtreated 2/518, 13/249, 264.

disgysid *ppl. adj.* dressed in an ostentatiously modish or eccentric style 2/425 *etc.*

dispendid *pp.* used DM/550-51; **~ vpon** distributed among DM/532.

dispensis *n.* expenses 5/241.

dispeyre *n.* absence of hope DM/954.

dispeyrable *adj.* beyond hope DM/953.

displeasaunce *n.* vexation 15/123.

disposicion *n.* ordering of things 11/320.

disseuerid *pa. t.* divided DM/56.

dissimyleþ *pr. 3 sg.* disregards 7/103.

distorb(e)lid *pp.* alarmed 7/51, 55.

do(o) (on cros) *imper.* crucify 1/398 *pr. 2 sg.* **~ awey** puttest an end to 3/492; **(be) to done** (is) needful 5/454.

dockedist *pa. t. sg.* cut away a part 11/196.

doctrine *n.* precepts 2/216 *etc*; a lesson 4/65; **~ of** instruction in 1/362.

doluen *see* **delueþ.**

do(o)m(e) *n.* judgment 1/63, 8/27 *etc.*

domesman, -men *n.* judge(s) 11A/181 *etc.*

doseris *n.* tapestries 5/252.

doublenesse *n.* duplicity 4/160.

doutful *adj.* expressing uncertainty 3/70.

dowues *n.* doves 2/453.

draw(e) *v.* become involved (in) 2/438; withdraw 12/201; pull 9/344, DM/138; derive 14/71; *refl.* go 5/47; **drowȝ** *pa. t. refl.* went 5/228; **drowe(n)** *pa. t.* induced to make their way 7/62; **~ oute** drained 11A/490; **~ on longe, ~ alonge** delay, 15/205, 323-4; **~ alonge** drag in their wake 12/192; **~ aback** discourage 14/150; hesitate DM/1148; **~ to** approach DM/279.

(to) drede *v.* to be feared DM/325.

dredful *adj.* terrifying 2/8 *etc.*

drenchen, drynchen, -eþ *pr. 3 pl.* plunge 11/252; (*sg.*)/*pl.* (drowns) 11A/67; totally submerge(s) 2/534, 554.

dresse *v.* direct (*physically*) 2/368 (*the mind, emotions*) 10/145; make ready 4/186 *etc*; *pa. t. sg.* addressed 12/432.

drynchen *see* **drenchen**.

dritte *n.* excrement 8/227.

droos *n.* dross 9/230.

dropesi *adj.* afflicted with dropsy 11A/485.

drow3, drowe(n) *see* **draw(e)**.

dueli(che) *adv.* as is right (*custom, time, manner*) 1/127, 9/202.

duellen *pr. 3 pl.* are preoccupied with 11A/131; **duellynge** *pr. p.* dwelling 11/317.

duke *n.* ruler 5/71.

duwe *adj.* incumbent as a duty 4/307.

dwellynge *adj.* for residing permanently 5/284.

eche *v.* lengthen 11A/31; extend 12/403; *pa. 3 sg.* enlarged 5/12.

echeuwid *see* **enchewe**.

eelde *n.* maturity 8/48.

eerdon *adj.* previously committed 1/428.

effectuel, -al *adj.* efficacious 1/114 *etc.*

eft(e) *adv.* again 5/413; afterwards 11/248, 13/347.

eggid *pp.* harrowed 9/207.

eggynge *n.* harrowing 9/347.

eie *n.* egg 11A/186.

eke *adv. and conj.* also 1/433 *etc.*

eleccion *n.* choice 8/328.

emperise *n.* empress 5/255.

emperrie *n.* empire 5/12 *etc.*

enbatelynge *n.* battlement 1/168.

enchesoun *n.* cause 5/64.

enchewe, e(s)cheu(w)- *v.* shun 3/337, 4/116 *etc*; *pp.* 4/119, 9/390.

endid *pp.* died 4/312; completed 10/4.

enerued *pp. see n:* DM/380.

enformed *pp.* instructed 3/35; *pr. 2 sg.* 13/397.

engreggid *pp.* made worse 2/122 *etc.*

enhaunce *imper.* raise 13/223, 227; *pp.* exalted (*in status or power*) 6/221 *etc.*

enioyned(e) *pa. t. sg.* imposed 1/276; *pp.* entrusted 4/308, 10/296.

en(n)orneþ *pr. 3 pl.* adorn 1/363, 364.

enpeired *pp.* weakened (*morally*) 1/269.

enspire *v.* impart insight 7/187 *etc.*

entent(e) *n.* intention 2/529 *etc*; **takeþ, 3eue** ~ pay attention 3/238, 441; **to her** ~ for their own purposes 16/274; for their reasons 16/279.

entre(e) *n.* coming 6/68, 16/305; the right to enter 6/133.

eþer *see* **oþer**.

e(e)rie *v.* plough 9/290, 11A/412 *etc.*

e(e)rynge *n.* ploughing 8/208, 9/290, 291.

ernest *n.* an instalment 6/142, 266.

errynge *n.* going astray DM/7.

escheu- *see* **enchewe**.

esi *adj.* but little 5/336; moderate DM/676.

eskis *n.* ashes 12/173.

esta(a)t(e) *see* **asta(a)t**.

estimacions *n.* the opinions of others 4/19.

even(e) *adj. and adv.* upright 1/300; balanced rightly 1/305; straight 3/209; equal 7/204 *etc*; evenly 10/294; directly (?) 7/30; ~ **cristen** fellow Christian, neighbour 15/108.

eueriche *pron.* every one 13/96; each one 7/98.

euerichon *pron.* every single one 2/341.

except *pp.* exempted 5/96, 99.

excercitacion *n.* exertion 11/86.

excusable *adj.* deserving of (or entitled to claim)) leniency 1/66.

exequies *n.* funerals or memorial services DM/12.

experyment *n.* a putting to the test 11/176.

fagete, (-is) *n.* bundle(s) of firewood DM/840, 846.

faging *n.* insincere cajoling DM/536.

faile, feile *v.* fail to come about 2/14 *etc*; *pr. 3 sg.* misses 2/85; cease to exist 2/704 *etc*; falter 9/120 *etc.*

fayn *adj.* eager 9/192; willing
11A/395.
fayn, feyn *adv.* gladly 11A/512,
12/135.
faitouris *n.* imposters 10/283.
falle *n.* strike down 12/67; happens
2/687, 8/43; belongs 11A/143.
fals(h)ede *n.* dishonesty 8/211,
11A/410; deception 16/75.
fame *n.* reputation 10/84 *etc.*
fantasie *n.* delusion 5/168, *see n:*
6/74–7; **fantesies** irrational
beliefs 10/263.
fantastik *adj.* unreal *see n:* 6/74–7.
fardel *n.* bundle 1/24.
fare(n) *v.* happen 2/372 *etc;* behave
3/454 *etc;* exist 2/135 *etc;* do
15/83 *etc;* is/are 2/373, 235 *etc;*
go (elsewhere) 10/283 *etc;* ~
amys go wrong 11/157.
feile *see* **faile.**
fey *n.* faith 6/42.
feyn *see* **fayn.**
feyned *adj.* pretended 1/169 *etc;* false
2/183 *etc.*
feyneþ *pr. 3 pl.* put on 9/131.
feynyng(e) *n.* pretence 3/363,
DM/536.
feyntise *n.* holding back 8/210.
feire *n.* market-place 11A/176.
feyrnes *n.* loveliness DM/1124.
felawis *n.* companions 10/346 *etc.*
felawship, felauship, feloschipe *n.*
community 11A/310 *etc.*
felid *pp.* felt (as a physical sensation)
DM/887.
fend(e), fynde the Devil 5/398,
8/288 *etc; quasi-adj.* cruel,
wicked 7/12.
ferdful *adj.* alarming 14/150.
fere *v.* frighten DM/1055; *pp.* filled
with fear 2/666.
ferþer *adj.* front 1/197.
feruent *adj.* turbulent 2/561; ardent
9/28.
fesned *pp.* put down firmly 3/127.
festened *pp.* fixed 2/478.
(fer) fett *adj.* + *pp.* at a distance
14/208.
figure *n.* tangible manifestation
2/451 *etc;* allegorical repres-
entation 11/22, 14/18, 15/162;

prefiguration 12/274.
figurid *pp.* represented 9/375; pre-
figured 15/73.
filþe *n.* depravity DM/740; **spot of** ~
defiling blemish DM/1124.
fynde *see* **fend(e).**
fyndingis *n.* innovations 2/96; inven-
tions 3/477; 'gimmicks' 12/79,
83.
fyne *v.* to pay fines 11A/395.
fire, firi *adj.* fiery 4/55, 12/61 *etc.*
first, þrist *n.* thirst 5/195, 11A/491,
12/386.
fleynge *adj.* fleeting 11A/166.
folled *adj.* misguided (?) 3/363.
foole *n.* foal 1/349.
foormed, fourmed *pp.* informed
(*i.e. made sound, stable*) 7/41,
12/7.
for *prep.* instead of DM/906.
forbode(n), -oun *pp.* forbidden 3/48
etc.
fordoþ *pr. 3 sg.* destroys 11A/152.
forþinking *n.* repentance 12/268.
forþou3t *pa. t. (refl.)* repented of
12/313; was regretful 13/352.
fouchesa(a)f *see* **vouchesafe.**
foule *adv.* in foul manner 9/306,
15/142.
frelte *n.* weakness (*physical or moral*)
1/97, 189.
frelnesse *n.* frailty 1/216.
fretiþ *pr. 3 sg.* devours DM/880.
froward *adj.* malevolent 2/505; per-
verse 3/243 *etc.*
fruteous, fructuous, fructiful *adj.*
(*lit. and fig.*) fruitful 15/257,
16/97 *etc.*
frute *v.* to bear fruit 9/196 *etc;* **frutid**
pp. cultivated 15/361.
fulfille, fulfulle *v.* carry out 1/305
etc; satisfy the appetite of
11A/508 *etc;* expend 12/71; *pp.*
satisfied 11A/519 *etc;* completed 5/165, 10/4; **be** ~ **of**
have carried out 1/137 *etc.*
fulle *v.* fulfil 1/340.
fulnes *n.* fulfilment 15/105; abun-
dance DM/1127.
fume *n.* smoke 7/160.
fundamentis *n.* the bottom DM/904.

gadereþ *pr. 3 sg.* stores up 8/391 *etc*;
pp. piled up 11A/526, 528.

gallid *adj.* chafed 11A/553.

gat(e)(n) *pa. t.* earned 10/415,
15/224, 226; conceived 11A/74.

gate *n.* pace (?) *or* path (?) 1/192.

gedere *see* **gadereþ**.

geett *n.* goats 11A/380; *also* **getis**
goats' 11A/372.

gestis *n.* heroic adventure stories
13/254.

geten *pa. t.* conceived 3/409.

gyle *n.* cheating 2/434.

gyn(nis) *n.* snare(s) 12/227, 258,
DM/228.

gladen *pr. 3 pl.* rejoice 1/164 *etc*;
gladeþ *imper. pl.* 11/332.

gladli *adv.* usually 3/385; willingly
13/279.

glose *n.* an explanatory commentary
2/596 *etc*.

gloser *n.* flatterer 12/243; *pl.* 12/224.

glosynge *n.* insincere praise 7/40.

glotorous *adj.* gluttonous DM/733.

gloterie *n.* gluttony 2/266, 10/508.

gna(a)styng(e) *n.* gnashing 2/287 *etc*.

gobet *n.* lump 8/103; morsel 15/213.

god *adj.* good 1/249; *as n.* wothwile
deed. 11A/66.

go(o)de *n.* goad DM/143, 148.

goodwille *n.* generous, charitable
feeling towards others 8/94 *etc*.

go(o)stle, **go(o)stli** *adj.* (*adv.*)
spiritual(ly) 1/112, 3/520,
12/418 *etc*; (1/76, 2/57, 16/280
etc.).

goteris *n.* gutters 6/227.

grace *n.* luck 9/336.

graciousli *adv.* by God's grace (*i.e.
as the means by which God's
beneficence is transmitted*)
7/188; with goodwill 14/259.

graunte *n.* the granting 12/5.

gredynge *n.* the raucous cawing
10/261.

greyn *v.* to produce grain 9/210.

greiþe *v.* prepare 9/400.

gresis *n.* stairway 11/185.

greued *pp.* weighed down 11A/11;
made heavy 14/91; ~ **vpon**
loaded onto 12/347.

grynting *n.* grunting DM/278.

grisbatynge *n.* grinding 8/235.

grobbyng *n.* digging 8/207.

grucchen *n.* grumble 8/174 *etc*.

grunnynge *n.* grimacing 8/235.

gult *adj.* gilded 1/30, 2/423, 11A/244.

gurd *pp.* (*lit:* **girt**) restrained 6/167.

ȝede(n) *pa. t. 3 sg. (pl.)* went 5/44;
~ **into** withdrew to 12/2.

ȝelde *v.* pay back (bad sense)
11A/350; *imper.* 4/310, 8/120;
pl. 5/93; *v.* (*refl.*) ~ **hym** give
away 1/299; *pr. 3 pl.* 12/115.

ȝemen *n.* yeoman 11A/225, 235, 275.

ȝenge, **ȝonge** *see* **ȝiynge**.

ȝerde *n.* chastising rod 1/195 *etc*;
yard (*measurement*) 4/73; penis
6/18, 29, 273.

ȝeue, **ȝyue** *v.* give 1/449 *etc*; (*refl.*)
devote (oneself) 1/310 *etc*; *pp.*
ȝouen having strong inclinations 3/467, 10/196; ~
aboute distribute 15/151,
376-7.

ȝiynge *adj.* young 3/125; *also* **ȝenge**,
ȝonge.

ȝit *adv.* (*intensifier*) even DM/805.

haburioun *n.* a coat of mail DM/367.

halden *see* **ho(o)lde**.

halewes *n.* saints 6/139, 140.

halewen *pr. 3 pl.* treat with rever-
ence 6/123.

half(e) *n.* side 10/111, 12/212 *etc*.

halles *n.* entertaining or assembly
rooms (*in public buildings or
private residences; in contrast
with* **cha(u)mbre(s)** *smaller
domestic rooms, including bed-
rooms*) 2/420 *etc*.

halte *adj.* crippled 3/198.

halteþ *pr. 3 sg.* limps 3/198, 202; ~
into wavers between 3/205-6.

haltynge *n.* wavering 3/206, 209.

hang *v.* base 13/66; *pr. 3 sg.* authority
rests 2/475, 9/182; *pl.* confi-
dently rely, depend 4/125.

hap and hele *n. phrase* fortune and
well-being 9/182.

happili *adv.* by chance 9/213.

hard *adj.* apathetic (?) 3/118; **of** ~
nolle stiff-necked 3/246.

hard(e) *adv.* firmly 9/213; **of** ~
hardly ever 2/689.

hardely *adv.* emphatically 4/102.

hardi *adj.* unvanquishable 2/610; strong 11/2; foolhardy 8/349.

harlot *n.* fellow (*pejorative*) 10/67, 13/21.

harlotrie *n.* scurrility 13/110.

he(e)d *n.* person in charge 4/260, 8/326.

heed *adj.* mortal 13/70.

he(e)ld(e) *pr. 3 pl.* pour 2/214; *pa. t sg.* 16/281; ∼ **to hem** pour water on them 3/126.

heerde *n.* shepherd DM/529.

heeste(s) *n.* commandment(s) 1/311, 3/522.

hele *n.* health 15/206.

heleful *adj.* conducive to salvation 1/225.

hepid (togider) *pp.* accumulated 15/342.

herboru *n.* shelter 5/234.

heres *n.* ears 2/574.

heroudis *n.* heralds 13/286.

heued(es) *n.* head(s) 10/288 *etc.*

heuenli *adj.* celestial *see n:* 6/74–7.

heuy *adj.* dejected DM/15, DM/264.

heuynes *n.* a state of grief DM/31; ∼ **of herte** misery 9/241.

hyde (to) *v.* keep hidden (for), (*i.e. concealed from all others*) DM/1034.

hidownesse *n.* extreme terror 2/597.

hied *pp.* raised 11A/466; **hiȝeþ** *pr. 3 sg.* (*refl.*) assumes superiority 12/378.

hyȝe *v.* hasten DM/1062; **hieþ** *pr. 3 sg.* 11A/426.

hiȝe *adj.* ∼ **wyttede** clever 5/288.

hiȝe, hie, hili(e) *adv.* highly 5/337 *etc.*

hiȝeþ *see* **hied.**

hiȝte *pp.* promised 6/240.

hild(e) *see* **ho(o)lde.**

hile *v.* conceal 10/71 *etc*; protect 11A/224 *etc.*

hil(l)ing *n.* clothing 15/281, 296; concealment 12/204.

hynes *n.* shepherds 5/356.

hoge *adj.* huge 13/178.

ho(o)l *adj.* healthy 10/213, 15/217, DM/276, 278; uninjured 6/187 *etc.*

hold *n.* support 11A/376 [*MS(R)*:

golde].

holde *v.* keep 6/145; consider 6/215 *etc*; **ho(o)lde(n), helde** *pp.* 4/98, 182, 12/521; indebted 6/96; obligated 6/145; **hild** *pa. t. 3 sg.* held captive 3/8; **hilde(n)** *pa. t. 3 pl.* esteemed 3/78; regarded as 4/251; **holden out** *pp.* deprived 5/394; ∼ **doun** sealed *see n;* 14/91; **halden togedere** are firmly united 5/468.

holly *adv.* entirely 11A/551 *etc.*

homeli *adj.* domestic 10/121, DM/1064.

homely *n.* (?) *see n:* 12/456.

hoo *interj.* whoa! stop! 11A/523.

hoor *adj.* white 11A/416.

ho(o)pe *v.* believe 1/271; *pa. t. sg.* 1/124, 2/140; *pr. 3 sg.* expects DM/231; *pr. 1 sg.* DM/412 *etc.*

hosid *ppl. adj.* clad in leg-wear 11A/294.

ho(u)sbond(e) *n.* a peasant who owns his house and land 14/152; *pl.* 11A/412.

hosbandrie *n.* all the activities and expertise of farming 9/367.

hosterie *n.* inn 5/190 *etc.*

housis *see* **office.**

houen *pr. 3 pl.* float DM/225.

humeris *n.* humours (*i.e. bodily fluids believed to determine physical attributes and temperament*) 15/374

hure *n.* reward 8/6; payment 8/52, 125.

hure *v.* employ for wages 8/99 *etc.*

hurid *adj.* working for payment 5/355.

iangelyng *pr. p.* babbling 2/162.

iapynge *n.* jesting 3/362.

iapis *n.* stunts DM/583.

ydiotes *n.* ignorant men 4/237.

iȝe(n), ye(n), yȝe(n), ien *n.* eye(s) 3/138 *etc.*

ymage *n.* likeness 5/91 *etc*; effigy 10/308 *etc.*

immediat *adv.* directly 12/432.

implieþ *pr. 3 sg.* keeps busy 13/235.

inclepe *v.* call upon 1/37 *etc.*

indignacion *n.* anger 2/581, 8/153.

informacion *n.* means of instruction [*MS(R)*: **confirmacion**] 11/284.
inow3, inou3, inow(e) *adj. and adv.* enough 2/358 *etc.*
inpugned *pa. t.* called into question 3/321.
into *prep.* until *see n*: DM/480–81.
intruser *n.* usurper 7/12.
iorne, jo(u)rne(e) *n.* journey 1/361, 5/86; day's labour 8/52; 'pilgrimage' through life 14/243, 15/36.
ipreued *see* **preued.**
iridelid *pp.* pierced with holes 11A/292.
ironne *see* **renne.**
issu *n.* orifice 8/230.
itiled *see* **tiled.**
iustified *pp.* absolved 13/199.
iuy *n.* ivy 11A/367, 371.

kepe *v.* look after 8/286 *etc*; support 11A/371; *subj.* protect 16/305.
kerue *v.* cut up 9/294; *pr. 3 pl.* out into 9/292.
keuere *v.* recover 8/318; *pr. 3 sg.* **kyuereþ** protects 12/207.
kikede *pa. t.* was rebellious 11A/19.
kynd(e) *n.* nature (*sometimes human*), innate properties, character 1/15 *etc*; kin 5/76; *pl.* the properties of natural phenomena DM/223.
kynde *adj.* proper 5/285.
kyndeli *adj.* natural 2/532 *etc*; beneficient 6/249.
kyuereþ *see* **keuere.**
knaue(s) *n. pl.* servants 2/651; *sg. as adj.* male 6/273.
knyche *n.* bundle DM/844.
knouleche, knoweleche, kneleche *v.* make known, acknowledge, confess 13/180 *etc*; *imper.* 15/210.
knowelechynge *n.* declaration (?); *see n*: 5/48–9, 58; **(to his) knowlechynge** (as his) close acquaintances 5/332–3.
knowing *n.* knowledge 15/128, DM/464.
kouþist *see* **can.**
kunne(n), kunneþ *see* **can.**

kunnyng(e) *n. see* **cunnyng.**
kunnyng *adj.* knowledgeable DM/1140.

large *adj.* generous 1/429, 6/237, 11A/573.
large *adv.* generously 14/7.
largeli *adv.* extensively 1/377 *etc*; copiously 6/227; abundantly 14/226.
largenes *n.* 'the virtue whose opposite is covetousness' (*MED*) DM/1129.
laste *subj.* persevere 10/489.
leche *n.* doctor 13/241, 16/49.
leendis *n.* loins DM/363.
lees *n.* leash 12/182.
le(e)se *v.* lose 4/168, 9/230 *etc.*
leesing(e) *n.* losing 9/146.
leeste *n.* the very minimum (*both quantity and value*) 11A/557.
lef(f)ul *adj.* permissible 2/323, 4/101; lawful 3/10 *etc*; *see n*: 8/181; right DM/76.
lefully *adv.* rightfully DM/12, 38, 50.
leie *v.* put 8/219 *etc*; *pa. t. 3 sg.* **leyde (to)** set before 11/254.
leiser *n.* leisure 9/166.
lepers (ouer londe) *n.* vagrants 10/304.
lepre *n.* leprosy 3/221 *etc*; leper 3/224.
lerid *adj. as n.* educated 11A/388.
lesewe *n.* pasture 11A/414.
lesing(e) *n.* lying 3/321, 13/23 *etc*; lie 4/104 *etc.*
lette *n.* hindrance 2/101 *etc.*
lette *v.* obstruct 10/435 *etc.*
lettyngis *n.* interferences 10/444.
lett(e)re, letture *n.* the literal sense 1/38 *etc*; learning 5/336; document 1/132; *pl.* lettris, ~ **of atourne** written authorisation 1/133, 12/333.
lett(e)rid, litterid *ppl. adj.* educated 5/337, 6/6 *etc.*
leþi *adj.* weak 1/197.
leude *see* **lewid(e).**
leue *v.*[1] give up 1/85 *etc*; *pr. 3 sg.* remains 10/160, 15/237; *subj.* 10/174.
le(e)ue *v.*[2] believe 3/27, 95; *pr. p.* 9/81.

leuer(e) *adv.* rather 2/169, 9/230 *etc.*
leuetenaunt *n.* deputy 16/292.
lew(i)d(e) *adj.* worthless 2/89, 10/264; uneducated 2/323, 11A/388, **leude** 10/263; crude 6/127; ignorant 5/221, 14/184.
libbeþ *pr. 3 pl.* earn a livelihood 10/304.
licour *n.* juice 8/408.
lyif *adj.* living 3/372.
lif(e)lode(s) *also* **liȝf-, liyf-, lijf-** *n.* income 10/415, 11A/261, 272, 288; necessities of life 11A/106, 14/11.
liggynge *n.* prostrating oneself on the ground (?), sleeping on a hard surface (?) 8/220.
ligge *pr. 3 pl.* lie 9/310.
liȝt, liȝþ *pr. 3 sg.* lies 2/136, 7/164.
liȝt(e)neþ *pr. 3 sg.* enlightens 2/360, 16/130, 133.
liȝtenynge *n.* illumination 10/239.
liȝtliere *adv.* more easily 1/215.
like *v.* please 8/409, 430, DM/1156; *pr. 3 sg. (impers.)* 11A/136; *subj.* 14/275.
liking(e)(is) *n.* enjoyment(s) 1/146, 9/150, 12/64 *etc*; **likynge hors** *see n:* 1/453.
lymytid *pp.* specified DM/534.
lystes *see* **lust(e)** *n.*
lyuerei *n.* **a distinctive suit of clothes** (*probably*) [*MS R:* leuersun] 11A/299.
lodli *adj.* loathsome 11A/200.
longe *v.* be characteristic 3/499 *etc*; *pr. 3 sg.* is proper 1/226 *etc*; is incumbent 8/273 *etc*; is necessary DM/339; *pr. 3 pl.* are appropriate 12/406 *etc.*
longe (on) (vpon) *adj.* attributable (to) 1/288, 292, 16/399.
lo(o)ueþ *pr. 3 pl.* worship and obey 1/423, 10/319.
losengeris *n.* flatterers 11A/181.
loueli *adj.* humble 6/230; unpretentious DM/1156.
louli, lowly *adv.* humbly 11A/216, 14/124.
lousyng *n.* loosening DM/841.
lowed *pp.* (*refl.*) humbled (himself)

3/284.
lust(e) *n.* pleasure 2/271, 3/173 *etc*; appetite 6/55, 10/158 *etc*; craving 2/549 *etc*; *pl.* **lystes** 2/666.
luste(n) *pr. 3 pl.* want 13/202; (*impers.*) it pleases 11/95.
lustly *adv.* self-indulgently 3/299.

madschipe *n.* madness 11A/43.
magnifie *v.* glorify 10/511.
maidenhood *n.* virginity 5/158, 9/389.
mayn(e), -ie *see* **meyne**.
maytene *see* **meynte(y)ne**.
malice *n.* wickedness 1/157 *etc.*
manerli *adj.* fair and decent 5/108.
mansleer *n.* murderer 10/414, 11A/109.
marchaunde *v.* trade 2/440.
marchaundie *n.* commerce 4/83.
markeþ *n.* market-place 8/60.
marreþ *pr. 3 sg.* hinders 9/185.
(in þis) mater(e) *n.* (on this) subject 1/270, 6/70 *etc.*; ~ **to,** ~ **of** grounds for 5/406, 6/160; **take** ~ **of euele** make something bad 8/180.
maugre (ne) *prep.* nor even in the face of 3/13.
maumetrie *n.* idolatry 8/298, 10/329.
maundement *n.* commandment 8/300.
mawmetis *n.* images 11/291.
me(e)de *n.* payment 8/121 *etc*; reward 9/236.
meyne(e), mayne(e), -ie *n.* household 3/34, 338, 5/57, 8/13, 10/122, 512 *etc.*
meyntene, maynte(y)ne *v.* preserve 8/372 *etc*; support 2/527, 5/465, 11A/111 *etc*; *pr. 3 pl.* reinforce DM/602; *pa.t.* encouraged DM/613.
meyntenouris *n.* those who impede the course of justice by aiding and abetting wrongdoers 8/316.
meke *v.* humble 12/487, 492; *pp.* **mekid** 8/327, 12/378.
melody *n.* spiritual harmony DM/1105.

membre, -is *n.* part(s) of the body 6/164 *etc*; one of the body of believers 12/322 *etc*; constituent parts 1/138; *pl. (fig.)* **in his pore** ~ towards his poverty-stricken fellow-men 12/462.

mene *n.* means (of attaining) 3/289.

mene *adj.* of low rank 11A/266.

mene *v.* signify 11/231; *pr. 3 sg.* intends 4/77; implies 6/112; intends the sense 5/101; *subj. sg.* infer 5/174.

menynge *n.* intended sense 4/62 *etc*; *see n:* 10/382.

mesche(e)f, mischef, myscheue *n.* misfortune 3/289, 9/163, *pl.* 13/249 *etc*; harmful circumstance(s) 2/(71), 103 *etc*.

mesel *n.* leper 6/205, 10/107; *pl.* 3/216.

meselrie *n.* leprosy 3/216.

mesure, musure *n.* moderation 10/510, 12/527 *etc*; **out of** ~, **ouer** ~ *adv.* immoderately 5/249, 11A/105; beyond all bounds 6/156.

mete *n.* meals 2/426 *etc*; food 3/465 *etc*.

meue *v.* persuade 3/134 *etc*.

meuynge *n.* prompting 4/290.

mi3te(n) *see* **mow(e).**

myiste *n.* mist, fog 2/640.

mynde, muynde *n.* reminder 7/171 *etc*; memory 8/38 *etc*; awareness 9/31, 185; **make** ~ commemorates 1/5; records 1/346; recounts 5/175 *etc*; **haue** ~ reflect DM/47, 150; *pl.* **myndis** commemorative services for the dead DM/13.

miri *adj.* swampy *see n:* 3/408; **mury** 8/345.

mirþ(e) *n.* delight 3/411, 455.

misbile(e)ue *n.* erroneous belief 3/351, 10/265 *etc*; superstition 10/243.

mysese *n.* affliction 3/289; infirmity DM/1027.

mysproude *adj.* arrogant 13/21.

mysrulid *pp.* neglected 9/186.

moldwarpe *n.* mole (*i.e. the animal*) 11A/543.

momole *v.* mumble DM/587; *pa.t.* **momelid** 3/254.

moori *adj.* marshy 3/408.

moost *adv.* in particular 3/38, 4/305.

morewetide *n.* the early morning 8/4.

mossel(s) *n.* piece(s) 15/111, 181 *etc*; *pl.* **morsellis** 11A/97.

mo(o)st(e)(n), mote(n) *pr. sg./pl.* **mut** *pr.sg.* must 1/444, 2/336, 3/468, 10/130, 12/29, 272, DM/630 *etc*; ~ **nede(s)** *sg./pl.* must inevitably 16/284, DM/520 *etc*; (*impers.*) DM/295.

mote *n.* a speck of dust 10/365.

mote(n) *v. see* **mo(o)st(e)(n).**

mou3yng *n.* grimacing DM/282.

mouþ *n.* moth 11A/574.

mow(e) *v.* have power 7/106, DM/87; **not** ~ be unable (to) 10/179, 11/7; may, can *pr. subj. 3 sg.* 3/304 *etc*; *pr. subj. 1 pl.* DM/1164; *pr. subj. 3 pl.* DM/1087; **mowen** *pr. subj. 1/3 pl.* 15/120, DM/7, 12; **moowe** *pr. subj. 3 pl.* 3/17; **moun, mowen** *pr. 1 pl.* 1/75, DM/343; *pr. 3 pl.* 1/184; **mowne** *pr. 1/3 pl.* 12/202, 421, DM/590; **mi3te(n), my3t(t)(e)** might, could *pa.t. 3 sg.* 5/401; *pa.subj. 3 sg.* 1/234, 2/173, 12/119; *pa.subj. 3 pl.* 1/309, 351, 2/517, 10/468, 16/323; **my3tist** *pa.subj. 2 sg.* 14/97.

mury, myri, mery *adj.* joyful 11/101; blissful DM/996, 1003; **makeþ þe** ~ be happy 11/99.

musure *see* **mesure.**

mut *see* **mo(o)st(e)(n).**

name *n.* reputation (*i.e. good name*) 10/86 *etc*.

nameli *adv.* especially 11A/357.

nei3he, ny3e-, neih- *v.* ~ **ni3, ny** draw(n) near 1/79, 2/672, 6/195, 11A/468, 15/65 *etc*.

neldul *n. as adj.* needle 9/257.

nemeneþ *pr. 3 sg.* specifies 10/331; *pp.* mentioned by name 1/339; assigned 6/112, 115.

nese *n.* nose 8/231.

(be) neuer(e) (so) *adv. phrase* no matter how (*i.e. indicating unlimited extent*) 8/237–8 *etc.*

next *adj.* most intimate 5/267, 10/76, 11A/211; placed nearest to DM/1151.

nygardes *n.* misers 11/38.

ni3(h), ni3li, ny3(e) *adv.* near 2/460 *etc*; close by 1/102; almost 3/23; recently 4/5; nearly 14/72, 73 *etc.*

nyce *adj.* extravagant 12/78, DM/567, dissolute DM/593.

niseli *adv.* extravagantly 2/425, 3/472, 11A/236.

nobel *n.* a coin (*first minted by Edward III*) 7/118.

nolle, (nollis) *n.* the top or back of the head 3/246, (12/194).

(for the) nones *adv. phrase* expressly for the occasion 1/33.

norische *v.* sustain 2/515, 520; *pr. 3 sg.* thrives; *pr. 3 pl.* give rise to 5/449; nourish 11A/531; *pp.* fostered 3/421, 467.

not *pron.* nothing 12/254.

no þyng(e) *n. and adv.* nothing 2/481, 3/29–30 *etc*; not at all 1/237 *etc.*

noumbrid *pp.* counted (*as in a public census*) 5/28, 229.

noumbrynge *n.* counting 5/31, 33.

noyce, noyse *n.* noise 13/177, 2/535 *etc.*

noyus *adj.* injurious 11/252.

obiect(is) *n.* objection(s) 1/286, 270.

obeien *pr. 3 pl.* are subservient to 11/277.

(in) occasion (of) *n.* motivated by DM/124.

office (housis of) *n.* outhouses, or parts of a house, used for domestic services 11A/234.

onyd *pp.* united DM/55.

onehede *n.* unity 5/388.

oo *adj.* one 1/165 *etc.*

oore *n.* brass 11A/442.

ooste *n.* army 2/624.

open(e) *pr. 3 sg.* make accessible 9/58; *pp.* 9/365; *pa. t.* explained 9/22.

open(e) *adj.* exposed 2/187 *etc*; blatant 3/12 *etc*; accessible 3/143 *etc*; public 4/190; responsive 6/257; without concealment 12/293; **makiþ þee ~** discloses (what you really are) 13/213; **made ~** made to appear publicly DM/630; *cf.* **shewid opunly** DM/520–21.

openynge *n.* publicly stating 6/117; explanation 9/71; exposing by removing obstructions 8/215, 216.

ordeyne *v.* make due preparations DM/469; *pp.* placed 1/92, DM/533; decreed 2/598 *etc.*

oþer, eþer *conj.* or 1/126 *etc.*

ouercastiþ *pr. 3 sg.* casts down 11A/177.

ouercomeris *n.* those who have triumphed 8/16.

ouergild *ppl. adj.* gilded 11A/244.

ouergo *v.* over-run 8/244 *etc.*

ouerlede *imper.* get the better of 12/142; *pr. 3 pl.* oppress 11A/393; *pr. ppl.* tyrannizing 2/569.

ouerledynge *n.* oppression 2/571.

ouerpas *v.* pass beyond 14/27; transcend 14/42; *pr. 3 sg.* exceeds DM/319, DM/1042 surpass(es) DM/1049, *pr. 3 pl.* 8/136.

ouerplus *n.* excess 15/312.

ouerplus *adj.* left over 11A/104.

ournementis *n.* adornments 3/432.

outweis *adv.* 'inside-out' 8/228.

ouwer *adv.* anywhere 11A/237.

owe *pr. 1 sg.* ought 3/67, 15/21; *pr. 3 sg.* 12/323.

palfrai *n.* palfrey 11A/239.

palice *n.* palace 7/58.

panter(e), pantre *n.* one in charge of the bread in a large establishment 15/44 *etc.*

panteries *n.* bread-rooms (*possibly where other foods were kept as well as bread*) 5/269.

parcel *n.* part 9/322 *etc.*

parfite *see* **perfite**.

parfourme *see* **perfo(o)rme**.

parishyns, parishenys *n.* parishioners 12/448, 14/182.

parte *v.* share DM/749.

partener *n.* companion 8/390, 12/434; *pl.* participants 10/271.

partie(s) *n.* parts 3/299 *etc*; division(s) of society DM/555; side (in a dispute) 13/268.

pasche *n.* Passover 14/72.

pas *n.* pace 1/191; *pl.* steps 3/209, 210.

passe *v.* to rise above 2/550; avert DM/473; ~ **by** pass through, be anywhere in DM/1056; *pr. ppl.* exceeding what is appropriate to DM/601.

passyng *adj.* extreme DM/292, 295.

passyngli *adv.* 11A/548.

patron *n.* founder 4/252; master 4/254 *etc*; 'one who holds the right of presentation to an ecclesiastical benefice' (*OED*) 8/330.

peyne *n.* punishment *see n*: 15/237–8; the sufferings of hell DM/646 *etc.*

peyned *pp.* afflicted with painful punishment DM/606.

peirynge *n.* damaging 9/285.

pelers *n.* pillars 2/603.

pelure *n.* fur 2/422 *etc.*

peraunture, peraunter *adv.* perhaps 4/74, DM/49, 573 *etc.*

perceyue *v.* understand 14/260; *pa t.* became aware of 10/87.

perceyuing *adj.* having insight and understanding 14/183.

pere *n. as adj.* equal 11A/198.

perfite, parfite *adj.* accomplished 3/29, 30, 11A/410, 14/183; word-perfect 9/183.

perfo(o)rme, perfourme, parfourme *v.* carry out 2/254 *etc*; do 9/154 *etc.*

persche *v.* be cut off 6/274.

perse *v.* penetrate DM/1085.

persons *n.* parsons 11A/243, 403.

personage *n.* the benefice of a parson 8/325.

perteynen *pr. 3 pl.* pertain 2/254; *pa. t.* 5/400; *subj. sg.* 9/65.

peruertid *pp.* led astray 16/396.

pese *n.* pea 8/390, 11A/296.

pesible *adj.* peaceful 5/446.

phisik(e) *n.* medical science 11/37; **after** ~ for medical (*i.e. therapeutic*) reasons 15/271.

pies *n.* magpies 10/262.

pilen *pr. 3 pl.* plunder 2/554 *etc.*

pynchid *pa. t.* cavilled 16/375.

pyneþ *pr. 3 pl.* distress 11A/555; *pp.* afflicted with pain 11A/562; **pynnyng** *pr. ppl.* complaining 16/15.

piste(e)l, pistil(e), -ole *n.* epistle 1/319, 178, 2/245, 3/271, 6/128 *etc.*

pitee *n.* piety 11/87.

piteouse, pitous *adj.* compassionate 11/87, 14/84; pious 7/148.

piteousli *adv.* devoutly 10/24.

playn *adj.* clear 4/2; flat 9/86.

playne, pleyne (him) *v. (refl.)* complain 14/152; lament 8/415; *pr. 3 sg.* 12/189.

playster *n.* plaster (*i.e. for application to a wound*) 16/157.

plede *v.* prosecute 11A/403.

plee *n.* legal action 11A/398.

pleyne *see* **playne.**

pleynli, -ourly *adv.* fully 3/341, 12/397; cleary 6/20, 13/300.

pleyntis *n.* complaints 13/248, 264.

plesaunce *n.* giving pleasure 15/121; cordial joy DM/1122; **to his** ~ pleasing to him DM/108; **fauoure of** ~ **of** currying favour with DM/537.

poynt(e) -is *n.* **in** ~ (*position in time*) just about (to) 2/601; ~ **of pride** self-aggrandizing particulars 2/429; grounds for arrogance 8/233; ~ **deuys** to perfection 9/367; **at all** ~ in every detail 11A/239; **in a** ~ all of a sudden, in an instant DM/240.

possid *pp.* tossed DM/871.

postyn *n.* a gathering of purulent matter 11A/538.

preciosite *n.* great value DM/185.

prepucie *n.* foreskin 6/84.

presentacion *n.* the action of recommending a clergyman for a benefice and presenting him to the bishop 8/328.

preued, prou- *pp.* shown by experience 5/156, 9/201, 13/370, **ipreued** scrutinised closely 8/233.

preued *adj.* tested 9/200; trustworthy 16/340.

preyoure *n.* (?) *see n:* 12/471–4.

prikid *pp.* spurred on 1/217.

prikynge *n.* goading, or spurring 1/191, 193.

principal *n.* the most important part 1/275, *cf.* 3/116.

priue *adj.* concealed from anyone else 5/62, DM/592 *etc*; private 7/89 *etc*; furtive 12/181.

priueite(s), priuetees, priuite(is) *n.* mysteries 5/336, DM/116, DM/435 *etc*; innermost thoughts 9/298; **Book of** ~ the Apocalypse 10/289.

priueli *adv.* secretly 7/68; discreetly 10/93; not publicly 15/330.

proces(se) *n.* procedure (in law) 16/420: course (of events) 5/40 *etc*; narrative 6/262 *etc*; **bi** ~ in the course (of time) 2/260, 11/89.

procurat(o)ur *n.* overseer 8/119, 124; *pl.* 1/324.

profescioun, profession *n. see n:* 5/48–9, 58; **make** ~ to acknowledge and fulfil an obligation 5/45 *etc*.

prophite *n.* profit 7/140.

propre, propur *adj.* relating exclusively to (the person specified) 11/307, DM/522, 631; own 14/182, 208; **in** ~ as private property (*i.e. in contrast with* 'in common') 11A/406.

prouenders *n.* prebendaries DM/577.

publicacion *n.* promulgation 6/129.

punshid *pa. t.* punished 15/220.

purchas(e)(is) *n.* financial transaction(s) for private gain DM/220, 578.

purpos(e) *v.* (*refl.*) be determined 14/58; (*non. refl.*) *pr. 1 sg.* intend 1/77 *etc*.

purpur *n.* purple cloth 10/50.

pursue *v.* wreak vengeance 12/198; *pa. t.* 12/198; *pp.* persecuted 2/616 *etc*.

pursuer(i)s *n.* persecutors 2/700, 16/426.

pursuying *n.* persecution 15/85.

putt *n.* pit 11/304.

put(t)(e) *pp.* ~ **abak** rejected 6/83, 12/518; ~ **awei fro** deprived of 8/309; *pa. t.* ~ **in** incorporated DM/148, 509; *pp.* ~ **into** invested (?) *see n:* 11A/435; *inf.* ~ **oute** burst forth 8/313; ejected 13/6; *pp.* ~ **to** bestowed upon 6/110; *pa. t.* ~ **vpon** alleged against 16/273, 349; *pr. ppl.* ~ **on hem lesyngis** accusing them of telling lies 16/16, 362; *pa. t.* 16/379.

puttyng(e) *vbl. n.* ~ **bacwarde** thrusting back DM/648; ~ **doun** oppression *see n:* 2/510; ~ **oute** expulsion DM/692; ~ **to (into)** placing in DM/744–5, (752); ~ **too** addition 1/333.

quenche *v.* extinguish 12/106; *pp.* 11A/491.

quyk(e), -ik *adj.* live 7/160; living 3/141, 320.

quykenen *pr. 3 pl.* bring to life 15/172.

quyte *v.* repay 11A/283, 284; *pa. t sg.* **quytt** 8/177; *pa. t pl.* **quyteþ** 11A/111.

raie *see* **araie.**

raggis *n.* decorative fabric trimmings (*contemptuous*) 11A/294.

raþer *adv.* sooner 8/183 *etc*; *also* **raþlier** the more rapidly 8/240.

raueyne, rauayne *n.* robbery 11/241, 11A/374.

rauysshing *ppl. adj.* in search of prey (?) *see n:* 12/100.

real, rial(le) *adj.*[1] royal 5/15 *etc*; fit for a king 5/260 *etc*; magnificent 5/270 *etc*.

real *adj.*[2] real 2/450.

realli *adv.* in regal manner or style 2/608 *etc*.

rebel *adj.* disobedient DM/709.

recheles *adj.* negligent 5/356.

re(c)ken *see* **rikene.**

recomendid *pp. see n:* 15/37.

recounsilid *pp.* reconciled 15/141.

rede *pr. 1 sg.* advise 11/98.
redy *adj.* abounding with reeds DM/1083.
reem *see* rewme.
refeccion *n.* meal 15/16.
refreyned *pp.* restrained 6/167.
refreynyng *n.* restraint DM/42.
refreishe *v.* relieve DM/868.
refresshyng *n.* relief DM/818.
refute *n.* refuge 2/516, 12/157, 200; protection 2/519.
regard *see* reward.
reherce *v.* enumerate 2/93 *etc*; *pr. 3 sg.* recounts 4/103 *etc*; *pp.* rehercid, rehersid 3/165, 10/36; *pr. ppl.* quoting 3/121.
reken *see* rikene.
releef *n.* remains (of food) 14/5 *etc*.
remission *n.* pardon 11A/531 *etc*.
remorsing *pr. p.* inducing remorse DM/666.
remuyng *n.* removal 12/409.
renne *v.* spread 5/347 *etc*; ironne *pp.* run 2/83.
rente(s) *n.* income(s) 2/537, 10/269.
renued (to) *pp.* restored (by) 13/347.
reodes, rud(e)(s) *n.* reed(s) 3/344, 406, 459, 10/52 *etc*.
rere *see* arere.
reste *n.* repose 6/68; relaxed and untroubled state of mind 7/56; (?) *see n*: 11/246.
rett *see* arette.
reward(e), regard *n.* regard 7/38, 12/341, 185; in regard of in relation to 2/464.
rewme(s), reumes, reem *n.* realm(s) 2/438, 5/27, 37, 11A/265 *etc*.
rial(le) *see* real.
(i)ridelid *pa. t.* pierced with holes 11A/292.
riȝt, rite *n.* rite 6/125; practice 6/18.
riȝtli *adv.* properly 1/444; directly 7/78, 200.
riȝsynge aȝen *n.* resurrection 10/190.
rikene, re(c)ken *v.* give an account 9/161, DM/620, 622, 625; *pr. 3 pl.* regard as being of any concern 11A/72.
ripe *n.* harvest 2/705.
ripe *v.* dig 11A/413; *imper.* rip 9/203.

ripe (to) *adj.* ready (for) 15/361.
rite *see* riȝt.
rith *adv.* right 1/154.
ryue *adj.* amply endowed (?) *see n*: 8/169.
ryuen *ppl. adj.* ornamentally slashed (*i.e. fabric*) 11A/293.
rode (tree) *n. as adj.* the cross on which Christ died 7/206.
roket *n.* a loose garment such as a smock (*can be a linen surplice worn by a bishop or abbot*) 11A/293.
ro(o)ted *pp.* fixed firmly 1/214, 9/133 *etc*.
roten *v.* rot 11A/529; rotid *pp.* decayed DM/905.
rud(e)(s) *see* reodes.
rude *adj.* imperfect 4/262; plain 4/270.
ruþe *n.* compassion 1/222.

sabot *n.* Sabbath 10/111.
sacringe *n.* 'the consecration of the eucharistic elements in the service of the mass' (*OED*) 4/25.
sad(d)e *adj.* steadfast 2/473, 12/298 *etc*.
sadde *v.* confirm 2/680; *pp.* strengthened in faith 7/73.
sadnesse *n.* gravity 11/91.
sai *see* seyinge.
salue *v.* greet courteously 12/186.
satisfaccio(u)n *n.* the performance of the acts required of a sinner as the third and final part of the sacrament of penance 1/427, 11/44 *etc*; amends 12/314; *see n*: 15/237–8.
sauereþ *pr. 3 sg.* smells 7/160, 163; *pr. ppl.* 8/235.
sauour, sauur *n.* odour 8/346, 365.
scarlet *n.* [*probably*] an expensive scarlet fabric used for ceremonial costumes, worn by high-ranking persons 11A/241.
schal, s(c)hul *aux. verb.* shall, will *pr. 1 sg.* 1/54, 11/182, 12/71; *pr. 3 sg.* 1/85, 2/294, 12/27; *pr. 1 pl.* 1/36, 50, 12/407; s(c)halt *pr. 2 sg.* 2/233, 12/153; s(c)hulle(n) *pr. 1 pl.* 3/52, 11A/576, 12/7, DM/237; *pr. 2*

pl. 1/82, 13/10, DM/93; *pr. 3 pl.*
1/88, 2/2, 12/186, DM/87;
shulleþ *pr. 2 pl.* 2/312;
s(c)hulde(n), scholde(n)
should, ought to *pa. t. 1 sg.*
DM/426; *pa. t. 3 sg.* 1/23,
9/152, 12/56; *pa. t. 1 pl.*
DM/297; *pa. t. 3 pl.* 1/28,
10/73, 11A/406, 12/21; **shuldest, -ist** *pa. t. 2 sg.* 12/172,
14/101; **scholde** *pa. t. 3 sg.* is
said to 2/223; **schuldest** *pa. t.
2 sg.* were to 7/94; **schulde** *pr.
subj. sg.* is to 1/245; *pr. subj. pl.*
are to 1/135.
sc(h)ape *subj. sg.* may escape 11/265,
267.
schar *n.* 'the iron blade in a plough
which cuts the ground at the
bottom of the furrow; a
ploughshare' (*OED*) 9/292.
s(c)harp(e) *adj.* strict 1/194 *etc*;
harsh 3/332 *etc*; severe 3/464
etc; violent 10/66 *etc*.
scharpnesse *n.* severe austerity 4/43.
schides *n.* pieces of wood 11A/512.
s(c)hynyng(e)li *adv.* in glittering
brilliance 2/426, DM/561; re-
splendently 11A/438.
schire *n.* district 2/568.
schilfulli, ski- *adv.* reasonably (*i.e.*
*because based on sound reason-
ing*) 1/330 *etc*.
scired *pp.* endowed with insight (and
thus cleansed) 10/429.
schrewe, shrewis *n.* wicked
person(s) 8/335, 14/272.
schrew(i)de, shrewid *adj.* wicked
1/289, 8/363, 13/183 *etc*.
science *n.* knowledge 4/291 *etc*; *see
n*: 4/291.
(be) sclaundered (in) *v.* shall not
take offence at (?) *see n*: 3/304.
sclaundris *adj.* guilty of uttering
slander 16/270.
scleeþ, scleiþ *pr. 3 sg.* slays 2/558,
4/90, 166; **scleen** *pr. 3 pl.*
3/323; *pp.* **sclawe, sclayne**
3/17, 18.
scole *n.* a university, or faculty
thereof 11A/383 *etc*.
scrip *n.* a bag, '*esp.* one carried by a
pilgrim, a shepherd, or a

beggar' (*OED*) 15/31.
scweerd *n.* sword 5/464 [*not in
OED*].
seek *adj. as noun* the sick man
DM/281.
seel *see* **ceelis.**
seelde, selden *adv.* seldom 1/264,
2/689, 4/230.
se(e)li *adj.* innocent 4/77; simple
8/264, DM/584; humble
11A/225.
seyinge *pr. ppl.* seeing 2/597; **sai** *pa.
t sg.* saw 10/344; **siʒe** *pa. t. pl.*
10/513; **seie, seyin** *pp.* seen
4/253, 6/24, 7/106, 11/322.
semynge *ppl. adj.* to all appearances
(*i.e. deceptively so*) 2/710,
11/179; *as n.* **to mennes ~** in
the sight of men 11A/179.
semyþ (wel) *impers.* is most apt
DM/258, 306.
senevi (corn of) *n.* (grain of) mus-
tard 11A/497.
sengulerli *see* **singule(e)r.**
senowis, senous *n.* sinews 12/323;
see n: DM/380.
sentence, -se *n.* argument 1/338,
13/276 *etc*; pronouncement
1/387 *etc*; didactic utterance
4/109 *etc*.
(bring into) seruage subdue 16/52.
set(t) *v.* put (things) right 12/154
(16/69); **~ by** have any respect
for 12/142; **~ to** *pr. 3 sg.*
spreads out (as a trap) 12/222;
pr. 3 pl. **~ to hemsilf** take it
for granted that they will have
DM/241-2 *pa. t. 3 sg.* **~
aboute** (?) made an effort
3/24; *pp.* **riʒt ~** resolved firmly 1/304.
seþþe(n), siþ(en), syþ(þ)(e) *conj. adv.
prep.* since 1/74, 262, 2/488,
3/284, 12/37, DM/481 *etc*; then
7/191 *etc*.
shapid (to) *pp.* devised (for) 12/352.
sharply *adv.* severely 12/153; closely
12/180.
Sheer *adj.* Maundy 15/378.
shewist (out) *pr. 2 sg.* dost expound
16/60.
Short *adj.* Maundy 15/9.
sibbi *n.* close relative 11A/72.

siȝe v.[1] strain out 10/362.

siȝe v.[2] see **seyinge**.

sikir, -er adj. safe 2/599 etc; certain 11A/277; superl. DM/357.

symonient adj. practising simony 2/180, 3/231.

symonientis n. those who practice simony 12/437.

singule(e)r adj. solitary 2/87; exclusive 2/496; isolated from the herd (?) 8/293; see n: 8/377, 378.

senguleri adv. singly 5/428.

siouns n. shoots see n: 3/418.

syth n. vision 1/86.

siþ(en), syþ(þ)e see **seþþe(n)**.

siþis n. times 14/252 etc.

skilfulli see **schilfulli**.

slakiþ see **sleke**.

slaundri adj. offensive 8/354.

sleiȝt(is), sleiþe n. cunning 11/172; deceitful tricks 12/50, 118, DM/398.

sleke v. extinguish 11A/512; **slakiþ** pr. 3 sg. satisfies 12/386.

sleuful, slouful adj. slothful 5/344, 355, 8/372, DM/727 etc.

sleuþe, slouþe n. sloth 7/49, 11/52, 12/284 etc.

slide v. flow away DM/166.

slouful see **sleuful**.

slouþe see **sleuþe**.

slowe adj. slothful 8/362.

slowis n. sloughs 8/357.

slowen pa. t. pl. killed DM/723.

slumur v. doze DM/182.

smallere adj. made up of finer particles 9/208, 346; of minor or lesser rank 11A/392.

smartli adv. energetically 9/95.

sogettis n. parishioners 16/25, DM/372, 571.

solempne adj. of great dignity and importance 4/11; **make ~** perform with ceremonious formality 6/138 etc.

somer hors n. a pack- (sumpter-) horse 11A/549.

sondes n. those things which God has provided 2/546.

sondid [emended reading] pp. provided (?) 2/547.

sopen pp. soaked 15/374.

sore adj. severe 8/220; sorrowing 12/92.

sore adv. (intensifier) to a great extent 1/27 etc; severely 1/393 etc; **sorre** compar. even more deeply 3/37.

sotil, sotilte see **sutel** and **sutilte**.

soþe n. truth 4/10; **for ~** adv. truly 2/193.

soþeli adv. indeed 10/190.

soþsawes n. truthful utterances 4/130.

sounen (to), sownen (into) pr. 3 pl. incline towards 13/111, 16/353–4.

souereyn(e) adj. supreme 9/399, 16/74; superl. greatest 1/257.

souereyne (in schrift) n. confessor 10/297.

space n. time (in which to do) DM/(101), 393; an interval DM/798.

spare v. hold back 1/148 etc; be lenient 2/655; hoard 9/195, 11/39.

spede v. meet with success 12/457; pr. 3 sg. it is profitable 1/378; pp. **sped** successful 3/84.

spedful adj. profitable 15/117.

spice n. appearance 2/506, 15/268; kind 9/376 etc.

spot see **filþe**.

spotil n. spittle 10/104.

spousebreche, -breking n. adultery 8/424 etc.

spousebreker(s) n. adulterer(s) 10/414, 495, 16/63.

(broken) spousehed (lit: destroyed matrimony) pp. committed adultery 15/142.

spoyle v. rob 2/530; pr. 3 pl. 2/182.

sprad see **abro(o)d(e)**.

staat, state n. condition 4/199 etc; standing 4/17 etc; **stonden in ~** to occupy the position 3/298; pl. estates 15/37 (see n.), DM/96.

stablenes(se) n. steadfastness 3/354; firmness 13/311.

stabelte n. stability 2/709.

stagis n. levels 8/12.

stanchid pp. satisfied 11A/492.

statis see **staat**.

stede, **stide**, **stude** *n*. (*lit*: place); **in** ~ instead 5/260, 261 *etc*; **stonden in no** ~ serves no purpose 7/165; **in his** ~in his place (*i.e. as if equal*) 4/302.
stentist *pr. 2 sg*. stoppest 9/314.
steren *pr. 3 pl*. arouse, provoke 12/80 *etc*.
stide *see* **stede**.
stie, **stiȝe** *v*. ascend 7/74, 9/126, 10/9, 14/63 *etc*.
stif(fe) *adj*. rigid 8/246, 252.
stifly *adv*. steadfastly 2/527, 3/330; resolutely 11/309; *compar*. more firmly 1/301, 306.
stille *adj*. motionless *or* silent 2/309 *etc*.
stille, **stilly** *adv*. silently 11A/121, 12/180, 13/174.
stiþie *n*. anvil.
stire *v*. arouse from inaction DM/143; *pr. 3 pl*. excite the feelings DM/963.
stiring *n*. prompting DM/424 *etc*.
stockynge *n*. digging up 9/287.
stolys *n*. garments DM/1025.
stonden (by) *pp*. adhered to DM/542.
strawyde, **strawiden** *pa. t*. scattered on the ground 1/381, 382.
streiȝt(e) oute *pp*. extended 10/160; [*MS R* **streyned**] spread 11/265.
streyned *pp*. bound 6/225.
streite *adj*. strict 2/582, 15/294.
streytenesse *n*. restricted space 5/227.
streytli, **streiteli** *adv*. forcibly 6/225, 12/154; strictly 10/260; tightly 11A/446.
stryif, **striues** *n*. discord 5/450; quarrels 11A/130, 342.
stude *see* **stede**.
studie *n*. *see n*: 11/245–6.
studien (to) (in) *pr. 3 pl*. devote effort (to) 11/276 *etc*.
stupre *n*. rape 3/413.
subsidies *n*. pecuniary aid exacted by persons in power 11A/219.
suchon *n*. such a person 1/445 *etc*.
sue *v*. follow 1/445 *etc*.
sufferable *adj*. endurable 16/262.
sufficience *n*. substenance 12/253, 14/224.
sufficient(e) *adj*. adequate 6/152, 154.
suget *adv*. in a state of subjection 6/87.
suggestion *n*. prompting 11/287, 12/59; **fals** ~ deliberately misleading statement 10/286.
sumpne *v*. summon (*i.e. before a court, to answer a charge*) 11A/401.
somonyng *n*. being summoned to appear at court 15/85.
superflu *n*. that which is superfluous 11A/102.
(have) suspecte *pr. 1 sg*. regard with suspicion 11/305–6.
(of) sute *n*. (in) matching livery 11A/275.
sutel, **sotel**, **-il** *adj*. subtle 2/32, DM/342 *etc*; cleverly contrived 4/65, 8/323, 11/8 *etc*; skilfully executed 4/263; not easily understood 4/271.
sutilte, **sotilte** *n*. one of the four properties of Christ's body and the dowry of resurrected man: tenuity, penetrability 10/178, DM/1072, 1084; *pl*. abtrusive matters 14/256, 261; ingenious contrivances 3/436, DM/339, 356.
swellynge *adj*. puffed up with arrogance 2/505.
swyngynge vp *ppl. n*. vigorous raising (*with connotation of* 'swigging') 11A/132.
swot *n*. sweat 2/557, 6/172.

takyng (of) *n*. submission to DM/408.
tal(l)iagis *n*. levies, rates 11A/219, 390.
talinge (of temporalities) *n*. counting their temporal possessions DM/589.
talwe *n*. fat 8/103.
tauȝt *pp*. guided, directed DM/553.
teerid *adj*. made of mud DM/178.
telisteris *n*. fortune-tellers 10/245.
teme *n*.[1] team of animals harnessed together DM/137, 139, 146.
teme *n*.[2] theme DM/149 *etc*.
temporalities *see* **talinge**.

tempreþ *pr. 3 sg.* controls 9/320 *etc*; *pp.* adjusted 9/314.

tendeþ pr. 3 sg. kindles 2/290.

tendynge *n.* paying attention 3/236.

tent(e) *n.* attention 9/384.

terren *pr. 3 pl.* provoke by exasperating 3/473; *pp.* 3/475.

testament *n.* God's law as transmitted to man (?) 16/60.

tifeling *n.* frittering time DM/589.

tiȝe v. go 11A/414.

tiled *pp.* cultivated 8/94; worked on 9/204; *pr. ppl.* **tilying** DM/136.

tilier *n.* tiller DM/135.

tilþe *n.* tillage DM/144.

tyndes *n.* prongs 9/347, 352.

tipet *n.* a trailing strip of fabric attached to the hood or sleeve 11A/294.

title *n.* authorisation DM/529.

tiþe *v.* exact tithe (*i.e. one tenth of goods or earnings*) 11A/412.

tyþynge(s) *n.* news 5/6 *etc.*

tobrekiþ *pr. 3 sg.* (*with intensifier* **al**) bursts open, shatters 16/140; *pp.* entirely broken down, worn out 11A/550.

togeder(e), **(-is)**, **-edir**, **id(e)r(e)** *adv.* together 1/156, 2/261, 393, 440, 603, 3/225, 12/183, 15/342 *etc.*

token(e)(s) *n.* sign(s) 2/2, 34, 468 *etc*; evidence 2/264 *etc.*

token *pa. t. pl.* took 4/266 *etc*; underwent 6/65; ~ **of** got from 6/55.

(þe) ton(e), **toon** (... **þe toþer**) *pron.* the one (... the other) 3/181 *etc.*

tort *n.* turd 11A/330; *pl.* **toordis** 13/109.

topazion *n.* topaz 7/110.

torende *v.* (*with intensifier* **al**) tear to pieces DM/605; *pr. 3 pl.* **torendiþ** 9/146.

tosquatte *v.* (*with intensifier* **al**) entirely crush 11/150.

toþer, **-ur** *see* **ton(e)**.

touche (of) *v.* mention 1/329 *etc*; *pr. 3 sg.* **towchiþ** touches 9/132; *subj.* 11A/335; *pp.* 8/425.

trace *n.* path 14/53.

translatid *pp.* transported 1/180, 4/55; transformed 2/385.

trauaile, **-e(i)le** *n.* exertion 1/322, 8/149 *etc*; toil 2/670 *etc*; hardship 6/252 *etc.*

traue(i)le, **trauaile** *v.* work hard 6/174, 8/132; *pa. t pl.* 8/141; *pr. 3 pl.* harass 11A/219 *etc*; *pp.* tormented 12/358.

tree, **treo** *n.* wood 1/395, 6/226, 10/309.

trenchouris *n.* platters DM/584.

tresouns *n.* betrayals (*i.e. of the trust reposing in their office*) 14/150.

trespace(s), **trespas** *n.* transgression(s) 1/117, 8/320, 13/320 *etc.*

treo *see* **tree**.

tretablenesse *n.* docility 3/189.

trete *v.* discourse 6/309 *etc.*

tretis *n.* treaties DM/588.

trist(e) *n.* trust 10/324, 11A/471 *etc.*

tristi *adj.* trusting 1/118 *etc.*

trist *v.* trust 14/220 *etc*; *pr. ppl.* **tristening** having trust 14/22.

tristili *adv.* with trust 1/271.

troweþ *pr. 3 sg.* believes 11A/170.

truauntis *n.* those who behave maliciously 5/108.

trumpe *n.* trumpet 2/641, 13/226.

tunne *n.* cask 11A/489.

turnen (aȝeyn) *pr. 3 pl.* change back DM/166, 167.

þilke *dem. adj.* this very 6/110.

þyng *see* **any þyng** *and* **no þyng**.

þon(g)ke *n.* good will 11A/576, 578.

(doþ) þonkynges *imper. pl.* express gratitude (in prayer) 11/332–3.

þo(o) *pron.* those 1/135, 383 *etc.*

þo(w) *conj.* although 10/481, 12/482, DM/757 *etc.*

þraldom *n.* captivity 11/24, 25.

(his) þralles *n.* those who owe (him) homage 10/48.

þratten *pa. t. pl.* threatened DM/723.

þretynge *adj.* threatening 11A/87, 394.

þrist *see* **first**.

þristing *n.* (*fig.*) craving, or rapaciousness (?) DM/1129; *see n:* DM/1126–9.

þrosshen *pp.* thrashed 15/364.

vnable *see* **able**.

vnbynde *v.* absolve 1/234 *etc.*
vnclannes(se) *n.* moral impurity 3/171, 188.
vncontynent *adj.* lacking self-restraint 2/505.
vncoupliþ *pr. 3 sg.* unleashes 12/129, 134.
vndedli *adj.* immortal 11A/149.
vnde(e)delynesse *n.* immortality 10/179, DM/1013.
vnfructiful, -uit-, -ut- *see* **fruteous.**
vnhoneste *n.* indecency 13/110.
vnhonoureden *pa. t.* dishonoured 16/348.
vnkynd(e) *adj.* ungrateful 2/503, 15/28.
vnkyndeli *adj.* unnatural 2/533.
vnkunnynge *n.* ignorance 2/305, 8/111, 10/264.
vnkunnynge *adj.* ignorant 13/231.
vnlef(f)ul *adj.* unlawful 9/379 *etc*; not spiritually permissible 14/28, 42.
vnlo(u)ke *v.* unlock 15/166, 169.
vnmiȝti *adj.* weak 8/70, 224.
vnneþe *adv.* hardly 4/237 *etc.*
vnpertynent *adj.* irrelevant 11A/505.
vnresonable *adj.* lacking good sense 3/57, DM/735; irrational 8/341.
vnsaciable *adj.* insatiable 11A/479.
vnsoteli *adv.* unpleasantly 8/236.
vnstab(e)l(e), vnstabul *adj.* fickle 1/399 *etc*; vacillating 3/351 *etc*; changeable 10/211 *etc.*
vnsufficient *adj.* not adequate 14/139.
vnsufficiente *n.* limitations 14/223.
vnwar *adj.* off guard 11A/360.
vndurmynid *pp.* destroyed by burrowing underneath DM/204.
vndernym, vndirnam *v.* rebuke 10/432, 12/152 *etc.*
vndernymmers *n.* admonishers 16/15.
vndirstondiþ (vpon) *pr. 3 sg.* responds with compassion (to) 10/399.
vnite *n.* harmony 5/471.
vpwaxen *pr. 3 pl.* grow 9/206.
vsen *pr. 3 pl.* customarily carry out 6/4 *etc*; *subj.* 11/89; *pp.* pract-

ised 1/237 *etc.*
vtaues *n.* the eighth day of a festival 6/137 *etc.*
vtte(r)mer(e), -more, -mure *adj.* outermost 2/286, 4/316, 6/18, 29, 14/169.

vanite(i)(s) *n.* folly 14/41; *pl.* futile occupations 13/256; frivolities 2/170.
veyn *adj.* worthless 3/424.
veyn(e)glorie *n.* self-glorification 3/154, 11/56 *etc.*
velayns *adj.* depraved 13/115.
venia(u)nce *n.* vengeance 2/450, 582, 3/473, 10/483.
venioure *n.* avenger 4/84.
verray, verr(e)(y), -ie *adj.* 1/335, 3/512, 5/169, 6/300, 14/264, DM/101 *etc.*
ver(r)ili *adv.* really and truly 1/131 *etc.*
vertu *n.* power 2/507 *etc*; strength 11/27 *etc*; moral excellence 3/289 *etc*; *pl.* **mouyng in** ~ generating effective energy (?) DM/230.
vertues *adj.* virtuous 3/410, 5/202, 7/188.
viker *n.* representative 4/229.
vileny *n.* degradation 11A/378, DM/1128.
vyner *n.* vineyard 8/243.
voide *v.* get rid of 4/28; (*refl.*) remove himself 3/24; *pa. t.* avoided 4/35.
voide *adj.* empty 3/420 *etc*; lacking 8/325, 408.
voment *n.* vomit 12/489.
vouchesafe, fouchesa(a)f *v.* condescend 6/100, 7/90; grant 14/227; bestow 15/30.

wagged *pp.* made to move restlessly 3/344.
wayle *see* **weyle.**
wake *v.* be vigilant 2/13 *etc*; *imper.* 6/180, DM/200; *pr. ppl.* DM/114.
wakeris *n.* those who watch over 5/353.

wante *v.* be lacking 8/242; *pr. 3 pl.* lack 2/164 *etc*; *impers.* **hem ~** they lack 5/451–2.

wanting *n.* lack 2/121 *etc*; deprivation DM/1128.

wantunnesse *n.* recklessness 8/273.

war *adj.* aware 7/123 *etc*; wary 9/286 *etc.*

warly *adv.* apprehensively 12/239.

wardid *adj.* fortified 2/641.

wary *v.* utter imprecations DM/922; *pa. t pl.* DM/716.

wast *n.* extravagance 2/424.

wasti (of) *adj.* guilty of squandering DM/564.

waxe, wexe *v.* 2/495, 11/90 *etc*; *pr. 3 sg.* increases 2/375 *etc*; *pa. t sg.* grew stronger 9/280.

web *n.* cataract 10/334, 342.

wegg(e) *n.* wedge 9/314, 320; *see n:* 9/313–4.

weyle, wayle *v.* cry out in lamentation 2/629, 12/95 *etc.*

weileaweie *interj.* alas! 8/426.

weyue (fro) *v.* forsake *see n:* 9/20.

we(e)lde *v.* experience 15/404, DM/1023; possess 9/235; *pr. 3 sg.* 14/33; *imper.* take possession 6/305.

we(e)lding *n.* possession DM/1093, 1100.

wem *n.* blemish 5/214.

wendeþ *pr. 3 pl.* go 10/473.

wene *v.* suppose 2/691; *pr. 3 sg.* suppose mistakenly 11A/38; *pr. 3 pl.* 1/400 *etc*; *pa. t. 2 sg.* **wendest** 12/151; *pr. 3 pl.* expect 9/310.

werkis *n.* deeds DM/478, 522.

wex(e) *see* **wax(e)**.

whar *see* **wher(e)**.

what ... (what) (and) *conj.* both ... and 5/15, 6/201–2.

wher(e), whar *conj.* whether 3/462, 4/96, 100, 11/64.

wherto, wharto *adv.* why 1/261, 4/239 *etc.*

whicchis *n.* coffers 11A/493.

whitiþ *pr. 3 sg.* pays back 13/186.

whose *pron.* whosoever 8/358.

whulynge *pr. p.* howling plaintively 10/262.

wiȝtes *n.* weights 6/235.

wil *pr. 3 sg.* wishes (*perhaps implying intention*) DM/402.

wil *adv.* well DM/416.

wilful *adj.* deliberate 1/329, 336, 11A/40; willing 2/390 *etc.*

wilfulli *adv.* willingly 1/22 *etc.*

w(h)ile *adv.* it being so that 6/86, 12/401.

wilne *v.* desire, want 4/159 *etc.*

wynde *v.* travel along 4/332; (*refl.*) envelop 3/509.

winke *v.* close the eyes DM/1157.

wynnynge *n.* gain 4/126.

wynwed *pp.* winnowed 15/364.

wische[1] *pa. t.* washed 11A/216.

wischeþ[2] **(after)** *pr. 3 sg.* longs (for) 11A/63.

wyte *v.* know 4/14; *pr. 1/3 sg.* **wot(e)** 2/9, 16/297, DM/493 *etc*; *pr. 2 sg.* **wost, wotis** 7/177, DM/416; *pa. t. 3 sg.* **wist(e)** 1/23, 14/120 *etc*; *pa. t. 3 pl.* **wisten** 14/122; *subj. sg.* **wist** DM/202; **it were to wite** one should know 15/307; *imper.* be assured 1/174.

wit, wytte *n.* sense 2/161 *etc*; mind 2/276; good judgement 5/15 *etc*; understanding 14/71, DM/1008; intellect 14/106.

witty *adj.* clever 14/104.

witterli *adv.* undoubtedly 10/289.

wiþout(t)(e) *adv.* outside 16/414; **~ forþ** outwardly 1/155, 3/421 *etc.*

wo *pron.* who 2/480; *but cf.* **woo**.

wod(e), wood *adj.* mad 2/270, 11A/43, 16/350 *etc.*

wodnesse *n.* madness 11A/40, 41.

woke(s) *n.* week(s) 1/14, 402.

wolward(e) *adj.* **~ goynge, ~ werynge** wearing wool next to the skin 8/220, 9/348–9.

wone *v.* dwell 4/338, 11/305, DM/352.

wond *pp.* accustomed 11A/264.

woo *interj.* woe 3/46 *etc.*

woos, whos *pron.* whosoever 3/180, 8/327 *etc.*

worche *v.* to carry out DM/107; **to ~ aftur** to act in accordance with DM/198.

worde *n.* *see n:* DM/123–4.

worship(e) *n.* honour DM/108; esteem DM/368; respect DM/1128; ~ **of** renown amongst DM/125, 1117.

wost, wot(e), wotis *see* **wyte.**

woute *n.* wortworm (*i.e. a cabbage caterpillar*)? *see n*: 11A/543.

writtes *n.* writings 10/246, 250.

wriþen *pp.* entwined 6/198.

wrongwisly *adv.* wrongfully 2/518.

wrot *n.* snout 8/354.

wrotid (vp) *pp.* dug up (with the snout) 8/292.

wrouȝte *pa. t. sg.* accomplished 5/39, 212; brought about 16/151; *pp.* created 8/427; **wrowten** worked 8/64.

3 5282 00127 9069